ANNALS OF THE NEW YORK ACADEMY OF SCIENCES

VOLUME 158, ART. 1 PAGES 1–438

May 16, 1969

Editorial Director
PETER D. ALBERTSON

Editor-in-Chief
MARC KRAUSS

Associate Editor
MILDRED MONGÉ

ELECTRONIC ASPECTS OF BIOCHEMISTRY*

Consulting Editor
PHILIP FEIGELSON

Conference Cochairmen
BERNARD PULLMAN AND PHILIP FEIGELSON

CONTENTS

Opening Remarks: Quantum-Mechanical Calculations of Biological Structures and Mechanisms. *By* BERNARD PULLMAN 1

Electronic Structure of Iron in Porphyrin Complexes. *By* MASAO KOTANI 20

Hückel and Extended Hückel Calculations on Bonding in Phosphate Diesters. *By* ROBERT L. COLLIN 50

The Electronic Structure of Purines and Pyrimidines. *By* ALBERTE PULLMAN 65

Some Aspects of the Hydrogen Bond in Molecular Biology. *By* PER-OLOV LÖWDIN .. 86

The Double Minimum of the Adenine-Thymine Hydrogen Bond. *By* R. G. SHULMAN 96

Free Radicals from Biological Purines and Pyrimidines. *By* WALTER GORDY 100

Polarography of Biological Purines and Pyrimidines. *By* PHILIP J. ELVING 124

Ionization Potentials of Biological Molecules. *By* ERNST D. BERGMANN 140

Charge-Transfer Complexes in Biological Systems. *By* SIDNEY SHIFRIN 148

Semiconduction in Proteins and Lipids—Its Possible Biological Import. *By* BARNETT ROSENBERG AND ELLIOT POSTOW 161

Semiconduction in Nucleic Acid and Its Components. *By* M. E. BURNEL, D. D. ELEY, AND V. SUBRAMANYAN 191

DNA-Polylysine Interaction as Studied by Polarization of Fluorescence. *By* JAY EVETT AND IRVIN ISENBERG 210

The Electrostatic Free Energy of Macromolecular Systems. *By* A. I. MCMULLEN ... 223

Charge Fluctuation Forces in Biological Systems. *By* HERBERT JEHLE 240

Contribution of Nuclear Magnetic Resonance to the Study of the Structure and Electronic Aspects of Nucleic Acids. *By* P. O. P. TS'O, M. P. SCHWEIZER, AND D. P. HOLLIS 256

* This series of papers is the result of a conference entitled Electronic Aspects of Biochemistry, held by The New York Academy of Sciences on December 11, 12, and 13, 1967.

The Theory of Hypochromism of Biopolymers: Calculated Spectra for DNA. *By* HOWARD DEVOE 298

Solvent Effects on Cis-Trans Azobenzene Isomerization: A Detailed Application of a Theory of Solvent Effects on Molecular Associations. *By* TIMUR HALICIOĞLU AND OKATAY SINANOĞLU 308

Electronic Aspects of Catalysis of the Oxygenases. *By* OSAMU HAYAISHI 318

Electron-Nuclear and Electron-Electron Spin Interactions in the Study of Enzyme Structure and Function. *By* HELMUT BEINERT AND WILLIAM H. ORME-JOHNSON . 336

Measurements of Subnanosecond Fluorescence Lifetimes with a Cross-Correlation Phase Fluorometer. *By* RICHARD D. SPENCER AND GREGORIO WEBER 361

Approaches to the Mode of Action of Carboxypeptidase. *By* BERT L. VALLEE 377

Tyrosine Fluorescence in Proteins. *By* HAROLD EDELHOCH, ROBERT L. PERLMAN, AND MEIR WILCHEK 391

Electronic Structures and Spectra of Flavins: An Improved Pariser-Parr-Pople MO and Semiempirical Unrestricted Hartree-Fock Computations. *By* PILL-SOON SONG ... 410

A Proposed Mechanism for Subunit Interaction in Hemoglobin. *By* J. PEISACH 424

OPENING REMARKS: QUANTUM-MECHANICAL CALCULATIONS OF BIOLOGICAL STRUCTURES AND MECHANISMS*

Bernard Pullman
Institut de Biologie Physico-Chimique
Paris, France

It is an honor and a pleasure for me to open the International Conference on the Electronic Aspects of Biochemistry. Although one of the youngest, it is also one of the most dynamic branches of modern biochemistry. The fact that The New York Academy of Sciences has selected this subject for one of the meetings held in celebration of the sesquicentennial year of its founding underlines both the maturity and the actuality of this field of research. The first general symposium on this subject, sponsored by NATO, was held in Ravello, Italy, about four years ago in September, 1963. I do not doubt that a comparison of the results of our present meeting with the proceedings of the Ravello symposium will certainly show the important progress achieved during these last few years.

The electronic aspects of biochemistry are being explored both by a series of modern experimental techniques such as the nuclear magnetic resonance or the electron-spin resonance, and by theoretical methods based on quantum mechanics, so that the new and—to some people—still somewhat puzzling designation of "quantum biochemistry" recently entered the scientific vocabulary. Scientists more qualified than myself will describe the utilization of a variety of experimental techniques for the elucidation of the submolecular, electronic aspects of biochemistry. In these introductory remarks I should like to make only a few general comments on the quantum-mechanical aspects of these investigations.

The purpose of quantum biochemistry is to apply the general ideas and methods of wave-mechanics to the study of the electronic structure of biological molecules in relation to their behavior as substrates of life, i.e., to their involvement in the biochemical and biophysical processes characteristic of the living matter. A similar penetration of quantum-mechanical ideas and methods has already been accomplished some time ago in organic and physical organic chemistry, and has resulted in an extraordinary enrichment of these disciplines. The enrichment concerned in particular the deeper understanding in the appropriate terms of the nature of the electronic factors responsible for the structural and dynamic properties of organic compounds. It resulted in new concepts, daring suggestions and predictions all of which stimulated the remarkable blooming of that discipline.

It may therefore seem strange, at first sight at least, that the similar penetration of these powerful and obviously fruitful ideas and techniques into biochemistry has been delayed for so long and, in fact, only started in a systematic and quantitative way about ten years ago.

The explanation of this puzzle probably lies in the mutual ignorance of biochemistry by quantum chemists and of quantum chemistry by biochemists. In my opinion, the fault in this respect lies more on the side of the quantum chemists than of the biochemists.

Of course, the relative complexity of the biological molecules and processes,

* This work was supported by grant GM 12289 of the United States Public Health Service (National Institute of General Medical Sciences).

together with the indisputable weakness of the methods of quantum chemistry (all of them essentially approximation methods) might have hindered somewhat the development of research in this field. I do not, however, think that this is the real reason because the very basic constituents of biochemistry, its building blocks, are generally organic molecules of a medium degree of complexity, in fact of dimension and even category (e.g., conjugated heterocycles) quite similar to the molecules with which the quantum chemists have been particularly fond of dealing for many years, and about which they have accumulated—in spite of the limitations of the available methods—a wealth of useful and impressive results. Whatever the difficulties of switching over from these building blocks to actual biological structures and mechanisms, I still think that the ignorance of quantum chemists of the nature of these building blocks is responsible, to a large extent, for the late beginnings of quantum biochemistry.

On the other hand, it seems possible to distinguish quite clearly the reasons which produced an accelerated beginning of quantum-mechanical calculations on biological molecules in the middle of the 1950's. In the first place, it is the transformation of biology itself into a molecular science, the realization and the solemn proclamation that the fundamental phenomena of life are embodied in the properties of a number of fundamental molecules or macromolecules and in their interplay, which necessarily enhanced the need for the elucidation of the electronic characteristics of these compounds because of the known role of the electronic factors in molecular behavior. More specifically it is, in fact, the determination of the molecular structure of the nucleic acids and of the central role played in their biological properties by purines and pyrimidines, i.e., by compounds very similar to those that quantum chemists have been studying for a long time, which pointed to the possibility and the necessity of applying the ideas and methods of quantum chemistry to problems of biochemistry. I must add immediately that, although it was realized from the beginning, at least in our laboratory, that the biological problems were—if only because of the polymeric nature of their principal agents—much more complicated than those usually encountered in quantum chemistry, it was nevertheless felt that great interest was connected with the elucidation of the electronic structure of the monomeres. The more so since the possibility was early considered that such knowledge might lead to the deduction of a certain number at least of the properties of the polymers, say, by an appropriate introduction of their mutual interactions. Very recent developments on the nature of the intermolecular interactions governing the overall structure and the stability of the nucleic acids have fully substantiated this viewpoint.

The second factor that prompted the development of quantum calculations in biochemistry is the simultaneous appearance and propagation of electronic computors, which greatly simplified the material difficulties of the calculations and widely increased their possibilities.

Finally, one may also quote among these factors the simultaneous development of refined quantum-mechanical methods, particularly for the study of the conjugated molecules to which a large number of biomolecules belong, and also the appearance of methods of calculation appropriate for saturated molecules. These are essentially methods based on the self-consistent field molecular orbital approach, in its different approximations and variants. Truly speaking, this factor was not really among the decisive ones which prompted the development of quantum biochemistry. Initially, for obvious reasons, it was the simplest approximation of the molecular orbital method, in particular the

Hückel approximation, very carefully parametrized, that was used essentially for the study of the electronic structure of biological molecules. The field of application was so large and so virgin that this approximation has provided an enormous amount of useful and significant results which moreover, retain, to a very large extent, their complete significance today. More recently, and this is quite natural too, of course, the more refined approximations of the molecular orbital method, in particular the different versions of the Pariser-Parr-Pople SCF approximation, with or without configurational interaction—and still more recently, techniques taking into account all valence electrons—have been utilized, so that today the majority of the older calculations, at least for the more important biomolecules, have been reevaluated in the more refined approximations. Thus, although this factor of technical refinement has not played a dominant role in the first period of development of quantum biochemistry, its importance may be clearly felt today, particularly in the increase of the quantitative precision which it is bound to bring about, and through the extension of the possible limits of applicability of the method to, say, spectroscopic problems, which can hardly be dealt with properly by the simple approximations. The problem is not, however, as straightforward as it may seem to be. More, of course, is being asked and should be asked of the more refined methods than of the simple ones. Thus, while it is generally acknowledged that the simple methods—namely the Hückel method frequently referred to as semiempirical—are particularly well suited for the comparative study of the electronic structure of molecules—in other words, for the classification on a relative scale of compounds of molecular regions or their constituent atoms with respect to the electronic properties under investigation, the refined methods are assumed to yield, in principle, more reliable absolute values of a number of indices of electronic structure and should, therefore, be suitable for a more direct comparison of theoretical and experimental results. In practice, although the whole scheme of the refined procedures is, of course, more satisfactory than that of the semiempirical methods, it must be realized that they suffer, particularly in calculations concerning heteromolecules (and almost all biomolecules are heteromolecules), from many of the drawbacks of the semiempirical methods. Generally, they do introduce in one way or another some semiempirical parameters into their scheme, particularly in connection with the different integrals related to heteroatoms. As a consequence of this situation, unless the calculations are carried out very carefully, the absolute values of the quantities which they evaluate may be appreciably in error. I am sorry to say that, because of the lack of such care, a number of published, so-called refined calculations e.g., on purines and pyrimidines are, in my opinion, less significant than the simpler calculations on the same compounds. On the other hand, when both types of calculations are carefully parametrized they yield strikingly similar results as far as comparable indices are concerned, although the field of application of the refined calculations is, generally broader, extending in particular to problems of excited states.

In connection with this situation, I must therefore stress that a constant and as complete as possible confrontation of theoretical and experimental results is one of the essentials for this type of work. Strange as it may seem, this is unfortunately not done by all workers in this field. It even happens, and I have recently come across a preprint of an extensive work of this type, that the authors make a very large effort in comparing among themselves the results of many calculations carried out by different methods and approximations, without caring for the comparison of the results with the experiment.

Such an omission deprives their work of what could have been its fundamental significance.

Having thus indicated the caution which must be exercised in properly utilizing the quantum-mechanical methods in biochemistry, we may now ask ourselves what are the principal advantages of this approach. It seems to me that aside from its obvious merit of interpreting the observed experimental facts in terms of the appropriate fundamental physical entities which correspond to these facts, the application of quantum-mechanical methods to the study of the electronic structure of biomolecules or to the investigation of biophysical and biochemical problems presents three complementary advantages.

The first advantage is the general, universal character of the method, its unlimited applicability. Thus, the usual experimental methods of physics and chemistry are intended to study essentially one (sometimes more, but never too many) specific molecular property. Each such method can, therefore, give only a partial view of the molecular reality. The situation is quite different in the quantum-mechanical studies: in these procedures a single calculation, the solution of the wave equation, leads to a multiplicity of results which, in principle (i.e., if we were really able to solve rigorously the extensive equations), yields the complete information about all the structural properties of the atomic or molecular system under investigation. In fact, even if—as is the case in practice—we can only solve approximately somewhat reduced equations, the amount of information, although approximate and partial, still generally covers a wide variety of aspects of the problem studied.

It may reasonably be supposed then that, because of the complexity of biochemical systems and problems, such a multivalent approach may be particularly useful in these sciences.

The second advantage of the quantum-mechanical approach to biochemistry and biophysics resides in the possibility that it offers to precede experimentation in a number of fields in which this experimentation seems to be particularly difficult to carry out. Thus, the calculations frequently allow us to determine the values (more or less exact values, of course, following the degree of refinement of the calculations) of a series of physicochemical characteristics of molecular systems that seem at present to be beyond the possibilities of experimental determination, or which are very difficult to measure at present. Among these characteristics are: dipole moments, ionization potentials, electron affinities, resonance energies, etc., all of which are fundamental quantities for the understanding of the physicochemical properties of molecules. The calculation of these quantities frequently permits us to discover and predict new correlations between structure and behavior—sometimes even completely new aspects of biochemical problems.

There are, of course, limits to what one may expect the theoreticians to be able to predict. Thus, somebody once reproached the quantum theoreticians for not having discovered the Krebs cycle. I think that the only possible answer to this reproach is that there are many more experimentalists who did not discover the Krebs cycle than there are theoreticians.

Since this question of predictions is sometimes a hot one, it may be worthwhile to consider that, when speaking about predictions, we have also to consider the capacity or incapacity of the method and the capacity or incapacity of those who utilize the method. If a given method can be utilized without any new modification for explaining a new, observed fact this is then equivalent—in my opinion at least—to a prediction. It is the scientist, not the methods, who was not able to make the prediction because, say, of his lack of imagination. It is he who did not know how to use it—how to apply it to a new, challenging situation; but the theoretical result was there, inherent and latent. Any method can be used to make predictions, if one just has enough imagination in order to visualize what to predict. The difference between a good and a bad method is, of course, that the first will lead to a correct prediction and the second to an incorrect one. But if any theoretician complains that he can't make predictions altogether, it is his fault, not that of the method used.

Finally, although it is probably the ground state chemistry (and thus the ground state quantum chemistry) that is essentially involved in most biological phenomena, some biochemical processes—particularly those which involve radiation effects, excited states, or electron and energy migrations—can only be properly formulated and dealt with through the use of the concepts of quantum mechanics. Their understanding is, therefore, entirely dependent upon the application of these concepts to biochemistry.

Present Status of the Calculations

The quantum-mechanical calculations which have so far been performed in the field of biochemistry may be considered from a double viewpoint. In the first place, they may be classified with respect to the different groups of biomolecules to which they refer. Secondly, they may be classified in connection with the general biochemical problems with which they have dealt. The two classifications overlap, of course, general problems sometimes being related to a specific group of molecules and sometimes involving compounds belonging to different series. The bibliography attached to this paper presents a double classification which sums up the essential quantum-mechanical calculations which have been performed so far in connection with both the electronic properties of the principal groups of biomolecules and with a number of general problems of biochemistry with which they have dealt. The list is, of course, not exhaustive.

Another possible classification concerns the quality of the method employed in the calculations, essentially whether it is a Hückel-type or a SCF-type approximation. It is understood, however, that the mere lable of "refined" procedure does not guarantee a higher quality in the results.

Examination of the bibliography suggests a few general remarks concerning the present status of the calculations and some trends predictable for their development, in the near future, at least. By far the greatest number of calculations has been devoted to the purine and pyrimidine bases and base-pairs of the nucleic acids. This concerns not only the calculations quoted under these headings in the bibliography but also the majority of those quoted under such headings as "hydrogen bonding," "intermolecular forces," "semiconductivity," "mechanisms of mutagenesis," etc. This is, of course, quite natural in view of the fundamental importance of these molecules in modern molecular biology, although it must be observed that a number of the published calculations represent duplications, sometimes even imitations, of previous works—in a somewhat different approximation, of course, but without any broadening of the subject. Calculations on these molecules have been carried out, until now, by a large variety of methods and, as a result of these concentrated efforts, we have today a large amount of reliable data about a number of aspects of the electronic structure of these type of compounds. It may be useful to stress that for a number of years a number of these indices, e.g. dipole moments, ionization potentials, electron affinities, spin densities in free radicals originating from the bases, etc., have been known only theoretically. In recent years, however, these molecular properties have been studied experimentally, and we have the pleasure of having here among us some of the most succesful investigators in these fields. The agreement between theory and experiment, remarkable in some respects, needs to be refined in other, more delicate ones, such as the characteristics of the triplet states. I hope that these different aspects of the problem will come out in the discussion.

Calculations in regard to other types of fundamental biomolecules are much less abundant. It is relatively surprising to observe how few quantum-mechanical calculations have been performed, for example, for the porphyrins and their derivatives in view of the elucidation of their biological properties, although important work in this field has, of course, been done by Professor Kotani and his coworkers. Some groups of molecules such as pteridines, quinones, carotenoids or retinenes seem to have been investigated, from the biochemical point of view, only in our laboratory. The same seems to be true about the coenzymes, with the exception of the oxidation-reduction coenzymes, which have attracted somewhat more attention, and which are the only ones to have been investigated both in the Hückel and in the more refined approximations.

In the field of problems, I would like to stress the great and successful development, during the last few years, of calculations on intermolecular interactions, especially those of the Van der Waals-London type in which hydrogen bonding seems to represent a particular case. Although carried out essentially for the purine-pyrimidine type of interactions, these studies made a useful contribution to the understanding of the factors responsibles for the structure and stability of the nucleic acids and related macromolecules, a topic of very fundamental importance in molecular biology. In view of what seemed to be *a priori,* a very approximate character of the procedure employed in the calculations, the results represent an appreciable success.

During recent years, a great deal of discussion has concerned the possible role of charge-transfer complexes in biological structures and mechanisms. Owing to more thorough recent investigations of this problem, both theoretical and experimental, it appears today that the role of charge transfers in biology has probably been overestimated, particularly in relation to the involvement of purines and pyrimidines in such phenomena. Also, it is to the merit of recent calculations that they indicate the important role of the Van der Waals-London interactions in the so-called charge transfer complexes.

Although some aspects of the problems connected with semiconductivity, radio- and photobiology have been analyzed quantum mechanically in a number of laboratories, the theoretical contributions are of restricted validity and scope. This is a field in which much more should, and probably is, being done today.

Problems of mutagenesis have attracted wide theoretical interest, and have been approached from different theoretical viewpoints. Because of the precise physicochemical definition of the mutagenic process (a perturbation of the order of the base-pairs in DNA), this is one of the few biological problems susceptible of a direct connection with the results of quantum-mechanical calculations. Two major lines of approach may be distinguished in this field: one uses the more classical concepts of, say, tautomeric shifts, ionization equilibria, chemical interactions, etc., studying them, in the light of quantum-mechanical calculations, whereas the second, advocated in particular by Löwdin, appeals to more sophisticated concepts such as proton tunneling. Although the applicability of the first mode of approach is straightforward and generally has proved successful, the significance of the second mode of approach is more difficult to ascertain, which makes it more challenging and interesting.

Regarding the problem of carcinogenesis, a comment must be made about some of the references which are not listed in our bibliography. In recent years, a number of publications have appeared proposing all kinds of quantum-mechanical explanations of chemical carcinogenesis, frequently in terms of some imaginary charge or energy transfers. I have not included these references in my list because it can be easily shown that, quite generally, these propositions are superficial and without any firm basis, if not totally incorrect. The so-called correlations on which they are based are due to the choice of a few selected compounds and vanish when examined seriously. Some of these propositions really touch upon science fiction. Those interested may find an analysis of these theories in some of the references quoted.

Surprisingly, the development of quantum-mechanical calculations in biochemistry has had a strong, widespread and stimulating effect on the development of similar calculations in the field of pharmacology. I feel particularly gratified about this result because I advocated this development in my closing talk at the Ravello symposium. Truly, the achievements obtained till now are very restricted and limited to a few type of drugs, but the extreme difficulty of this type of research must also be stressed. Those who undertake it deserve, therefore, our deep appreciation.

As can be judged from this rapid review of the past, the elucidation of the electronic aspects of biochemistry, although a relatively very young branch of science, has already achieved some substantial results. If judged by the constantly increasing number of publications, it is going to progress rapidly. If judged by the most recent developments, it is, technically, going to climb to constantly higher levels. What seems to be absolutely essential for its real success is that it broadens still the scope of its applications. To some extent too many people involved in quantum-mechanical studies of biochemistry are, in my opinion, concentrating on the very same substances and problems. Or to put it more appropriately, not enough of them are studying other (new) substances and problems. It is, of course, simpler and easier to recalculate in a somewhat different approximation what others have already done, to correct or refine existing calculations and theories. It is, moreover, a useful type of work and, because approximations are what they are, should be done. But it isn't enough. More efforts should be made towards the still greater broadening of the scope and limits of quantum biochemistry. Entire fields of investigation lie untouched. I am waiting impatiently for somebody courageous enough to apply quantum-mechanics, say, to steroids and the mechanism of hormone action. So many people are interested in the relation of structure to activity in carcinogens. What about the same problems in estrogens? It is by showing the usefulness of the quantum-mechanical concepts and calculations in the most diversified fields of biochemistry that we can best put into evidence their general and fundamental importance.

Appendix: List of Representative References

General References

Pullman, B. & A. Pullman. 1963. Quantum Biochemistry. Interscience Publishers. New York, N. Y.

Horizons in Biochemistry. 1962. M. Kasha & B. Pullman, Eds. Academic Press, New York, N. Y.

Electronic Aspects of Biochemistry. 1964. B. Pullman, Ed. Academic Press, New York, N. Y.

Molecular Biophysics. 1965. M. Weissbluth & B. Pullman, Eds. Academic Press, New York, N. Y.

Szent-Györgi, A. 1960. Introduction to a Submolecular Biology. Academic Press, New York, N. Y.

Quantum Aspects of Polypeptides and Polynucleotides. 1963. M. Weissbluth, Ed. Biopolymers Symposia No. 1.

The Structure and Properties of Biomolecules and Biological Systems. 1964. J. Duchesne, Ed., Interscience Publishers. New York, N. Y.

Pullman, A. & B. Pullman. 1955. Cancérisation par les Substances Chimiques et Structure Moléculaire. Masson. Paris, France.

Purines and Pyrimidines

Pullman, A., B. Pullman & G. Berthier. 1956. Recherches sur la structure électronique des composés actifs en chimiothérapie du cancer. Compt. Rend. Acad. Sci. (Paris) **243:** 380–382.

Pullman, A. & B. Pullman. 1958. Recherches sur la structure électronique des constituants cellulaires fondamentaux et des composés actifs en chimiothérapie anticancéreuse. II. Les bases puriques fondamentales. Bull. Soc. Chim.: 766–772.

Pullman, B. & T. Nakajima. 1958. Recherches sur la structure électronique des constituants cellulaires fondamentaux et des composés actifs en chimiothérapie anticancéreuse. IV. La force basique des purines et des pyrimidines. Bull. Soc. Chim.: 1502–1506.

Pullman, A. & B. Pullman. 1959. Recherches sur la structure électronique des constituants cellulaires fondamentaux et des composés actifs en chimiothérapie anticancéreuse. VI. Les pyrimidines naturelles fondamentales. Bull. Soc. Chim.: 594–597.

Nakajima, T. & B. Pullman. 1959. Recherches sur la structure électronique des constituants cellulaires fondamentaux et des composes actifs en chimiothérapie anticancéreuse. VII. La force acide des purines et des pyrimidines. Bull. Soc. Chim.: 663–668.

Veillard, A. & B. Pullman. 1961. Calcul par la méthode du champ moléculaire self-consistant de la structure électronique des bases puriques et pyrimidiques fondamentales. Compt. Rend. Acad. Sci. (Paris) **253:** 2277–2279.

Veillard, A. & B. Pullman. 1963. Etude par la méthode du champ moléculaire self-consistant de la structure électronique des bases puriques et pyrimidiques d'intérêt biochimique. J. Theoret. Biol. **4:** 37–51.

Fernandez-Alonso, J. I. 1964. Electronic structures in quantum biochemistry. *In* The Structure and Properties of Biomolecules and Biological Systems. J. Duchesne, Ed.: 3–83. Interscience Publishers. New York, N. Y.

Bradley, D. F., S. Lifson & B. Honig. 1964. Theory of the optical and other properties of biopolymers: Applicability and elimination of the first-neighbor and dipole-dipole approximations. *In* Electronic Aspects of Biochemistry. B. Pullman, Ed.: 77–91. Academic Press. New York, N. Y.

Nesbet, R. K. 1964. Interaction of paired bases in polynucleotides. Biopolymers Sympos. **1:** 129–139.

Berthod, H. & A. Pullman. 1965. Sur le calcul des caractéristiques du squelette σ des molécules conjuguées. J. Chim. Phys.: 942–946.

Nagata, C., A. Imamura, Y. Tagashima & M. Kodama. 1965. Semi-empirical self-consistent field molecular orbital calculation of the electronic structure of the base components of nucleic acids. Bull. Chem. Soc. Jap. **38:** 1638–1645.

Berthod, H., C. Giessner-Prettre & A. Pullman. 1966. Theoretical study of the electronic properties of the purine and pyrimidine components of the nucleic acids. I. A semi-empirical self-consistent field calculation. Theoret. Chim. Acta **5:** 53–68.

LADIK, J. & K. APPEL. 1966. Pariser-Parr-Pople calculations on different DNA constituents. Theoret. Chim. Acta **4:** 132–144.

KWIATKOWSKI, S. 1966. SCF MO CI calculations on purine and cytosine. Acta Phys. Polon. **29:** 573–575.

TANAKA, M. & S. NAGAKURA. 1966. Electronic structure and spectra of adenine and thymine. Theoret. Chim. Acta **6:** 320–332.

BERTHOD, H., C. GIESSNER-PRETTRE & A. PULLMAN. 1967. Theoretical study of the electronic properties of biological purines and pyrimidines. II. The effect of configuration mixing. Internat. J. Quantum Chem. **1:** 123–137.

DENIS, A. & A. PULLMAN. 1967. Theoretical study of the electronic properties of biological purines and pyrimidines. III. The representation of the methyl group and the structure of thymine. Theoret. Chim. Acta **7:** 110–116.

BERTHOD, H., C. GIESSNER-PRETTRE & A. PULLMAN. 1967. Sur les rôles respectifs des électrons σ et π dans les propriétés des dérivés halogenes des molecules conjuguées. Application à l'étude de l'uracile et du fluouracile. Theoret. Chim. Acta **8:** 212–222.

IMAMURA, A., H. FUJITA & C. NAGATA. 1967. The electronic structure of peptide and the base components of nucleic acids in the triplet state. Bull. Chem. Soc. Jap. **40:** 21–27.

KUPRIEVICH, V. A. 1967. SCF-CI and SCF open-shell studies of the base components of the nucleic acids. Internat. J. Quantum Chem. **1:** 516–575.

DUPUY-MAMELLE, N. & B. PULLMAN. 1967. Recherches théoriques sur la structure électronique des purines et pyrimidines biologiques. IV. Les pyrimidines saturées sur la liaison 5–6. J. Chim. Phys. **64:** (No. 4): 708–712.

Purine-Pyrimidine Base Pairs

PULLMAN, B. & A. PULLMAN. 1959. The electronic structure of the purine-pyrimidine pairs of DNA. Biochim. Biophys. Acta **36:** 343–350.

DEVOE, H. & I. TINOCO, JR. 1962. The stability of helical polynucleotides: Base contributions. J. Molec. Biol. **4:** 500–517.

PULLMAN, A. 1963. Sur l'intéraction de deux systemes conjugués à travers une liaison hydrogene. Compt. Rend. Acad. Sci. (Paris) **256:** 5435–5438.

LADIK, J. 1964. Some new results in the quantum-mechanical calculation of DNA. *In* Electronic Aspects of Biochemistry. B. Pullman, Ed.: 203–219. Academic Press. New York, N. Y.

LÖWDIN, P. O. 1964. Some aspects of DNA replication; Incorporation errors and proton transfer. *In* Electronic Aspects of Biochemistry. B. Pullman, Ed.: 167–201. Academic Press. New York, N. Y.

REIN, R. & F. E. HARRIS. 1964. Studies of hydrogen-bonded systems. I. The electronic structure and the double well potential of the N-H..N hydrogen bond of the guanine-cytosine base pair. J. Chem. Phys. **41:** 3393–3401.

BRADLEY, D. F., S. LIFSON & B. HONIG. 1964. Theory of the optical and other properties of biopolymers: Applicability and elimination of the first-neighbor and dipole-dipole approximations. *In* Electronic Aspects of Biochemistry. B. Pullman, Ed.: 77–91. Academic Press. New York, N. Y.

REIN, R. & F. E. HARRIS. 1965. Studies of hydrogen-bonded systems. II tunneling and tautomeric equilibria in the N.H...N hydrogen bond of the guanine-cytosine base pair. J. Chem. Phys. **42:** 2177–2180.

LÖWDIN, P. O. 1965. Quantum genetics and the aperiodic solid. Some aspects of the biological problems of heredity, mutations, aging and tumors in view of the quantum theory of the DNA molecule. Advan. Quantum Chem. **2:** 213–360.

REIN, R. & F. E. HARRIS. 1965. Studies of hydrogen-bonded systems. III potential-energy surface, tunneling and tautomeric equilibria in the N-H...N and O...H-N bonds of the guanine-cytosine base pair. J. Chem. Phys. **43:** 4415–4421.

NASH, H. A. & D. F. BRADLEY. 1965. Interactions between tri-nucleotides: the electrostatic contribution and its possible relation to the mechanism of translation of the genetic code. Biopolymers **3:** 261–273.

KRUGLYAK, YU A., V. I. DANILOV & O. V. SHRAMKO. 1965. Schemes of pairing of the bases of nucleic acids. Biofizika **10:** 399–403.

SHRAMKO, O. V., V. I. DANILOV & YU A. KRUGLYAK. 1965. Molecular Biophysics: π-electron structure of rare pairs of bases of DNA and the mechanism of spontaneous mutations associated with tautomery of the bases. Biofizika **10:** 561–566.

PULLMAN, B. 1965. Aspects of the electronic structure of the nucleic acids and their constituents. *In* Molecular Biophysics. B. Pullman & M. Weissbluth, Eds.: 117–189. Academic Press. New York, N. Y.

PULLMAN, B., P. CLAVERIE & J. CAILLET. 1966. Van der Waals London interactions and the configuration of hydrogen bonded purine and pyrimidine pairs. Proc. Nat. Acad. Sci. U.S.A. **55:** 904–912.

PULLMAN, B., P. CLAVERIE & J. CAILLET. 1966. On the exclusivity of hydrogen-bonded pairing between the Watson-Crick complementary bases. J. Molec. Biol. **22:** 373–375.

PULLMAN, B., P. CLAVERIE & J. CAILLET. 1966. Sur le rôle des forces de Van der Waals-London dans les interactions entre les bases puriques et pyrimidiques. Compt. Rend. Acad. Sci. (Paris) **263:** 2006–2009.

NASH, H. A. & D. F. BRADLEY. 1966. Calculation of the lowest energy configurations of nucleotide base pairs on the basis of an electrostatic model. J. Chem. Phys. **45:** 1380–1386.

POLAK, M. & R. REIN. 1966. On the hydrogen bonding scheme between purines and pyrimidines. J. Theoret. Biol. **11:** 490–494.

IMAMURA, A., H. FUJITA & C. NAGATA. 1967. Semi-empirical self-consistent field molecular orbital calculation of the electronic structure of the base pairs of deoxyribonucleic acid. Bull. Chem. Soc. Jap. **40:** 522–526.

Purine and Pyrimidine Analogs

PULLMAN, B. & A. PULLMAN. 1958. Recherches sur la structure électronique des constituants cellulaires fondamentaux et des composés actifs en chimiothérapie anticancéreuse. III. Les antimétabolites des bases puriques. Bull. Soc. Chim.: 973–979.

PULLMAN, A. & B. PULLMAN. 1958. Structure électronique des pyrimidines entrant dans la constitution des acides nucléiques et des antimétabolites apparentés intervenant en chimiothérapie anticancéreuse. Compt. Rend. Acad. Sci. (Paris) **246:** 611–614.

MAUTNER, H. G. & G. BERGSON. 1963. Some remarks on position conditioned differences of the ultraviolet spectra and chemical reactivities of disubstituted pyrimidines and purines. Acta Chem. Scand. **17:** 1694–1704.

FERNANDEZ-ALONZO, J. I. 1964. Electronic structures in quantum biochemistry. *In* the Structure and Properties of Biomolecules and Biological Systems. J. Duchesne, Ed.: 3–83. Interscience Publishers. New York, N. Y.

PITHOVA, P., A. PISKALA, J. PITHA & F. SORM. 1965. Nucleic acid components and their analogues LVIII. 5-Azacytidine and related compounds; study of structure tautomerism and possibilities of pairing with purine derivatives. Coll. Czech. Chem. Comm. **30:** 1626–1634.

BERTHOD, H. & A. PULLMAN. 1966. Elements pour l'étude de la structure électronique des composés soufrés. Compt. Rend. Acad. Sci. (Paris) **262:** 76–79.

PULLMAN, B. & N. DUPUY. 1966. Quelques caractéristiques électroniques des pyrimidines biologiques saturées sur la liaison 5–6. Compt. Rend. Acad. Sci. (Paris) **262:** 2773–2775.

PITHA, J., P. FIEDLER & J. GUT. 1966. Nucleic acids components and their analogues. LXXXII. The fine structure of 6-azaisocytosine and its derivatives. Coll. Czech. Chem. Comm. **31:** 1864–1871.

α-Amino Acids, Peptides and Proteins

EVANS, M. G. & I. GERGELY. 1949. A discussion of the possibility of bands of energy levels in proteins. Electronic interaction in nonbonded systems. Biochim. Biophys. Acta **3:** 188–197.

SUARD, M., G. BERTHIER & B. PULLMAN. 1961. Sur les états électroniques des protéines. Biochim. Biophys. Acta **52:** 254–265.

ITOH, R. 1961. Band structure and its relation to transport phenomena in protein. Ann. Rept. Res. Group Biophys. **1:** 11–14.

SUARD, M. 1962. Sur les états électroniques des protéines. Introduction de l'intéraction de configurations. Biochim. Biophys. Acta **59:** 227.

SUARD, M. 1962. Sur les états électroniques des protéines. Participation de l'atome d'hydrogene des liaisons hydrogene à la conjugaison entre chaînes polypeptidiques. Biochim. Biophys. Acta **64:** 400–402.

DEL RE, G., B. PULLMAN & T. YONEZAWA. 1963. Electronic structure of the

α-amino acids of proteins. I. Charge distributions and proton chemical shifts. Biochim. Biophys. Acta **75:** 153–182.

YOMOSA, S. 1963. The exciton in proteins. J. Phys. Soc. (Japan) **18:** 1494.

PULLMAN, A. 1964. Electron delocalization through hydrogen bonds in proteins. Biopolymers Sympos. **1:** 29–33.

YONEZAWA, T., G. DEL RE & B. PULLMAN. 1964. Electronic structure of the α-amino acids of proteins. II. Dissociation constants. Bull. Chem. Soc. Jap. **37** (7): 986–989.

YOMOSA, S. 1964. π-electronic structure of peptide group and hydrogen-bonded polypeptides. Biopolymers Sympos. **1:** 1–33.

PULLMAN, A. 1965. Hydrogen bonding and energy bands in proteins. *In* Modern Quantum Chemistry. Istamboul Lectures. O. Sinanoğlu, Ed.: **III.:** 283–312. Academic Press. New York, N. Y.

SUARD, M. 1965. Etude théorique de la délocalisation électronique dans les systemes polypeptidiques. I. Etude d'un nombre fini d'unités. J. Chim. Phys. **62:** 79–88.

SUARD, M. 1965. Etude théorique de la délocalisation électronique dans les systemes polypeptidiques. II. Etude d'une chaîne infinie. Discussion. J. Chim. Phys. **62:** 89–98.

IMAMURA, A., M. KODAMA, Y. TAGASHIRA & C. NAGATA. 1966. The semiempirical SCF treatment of σ-π system. I. Peptide molecule. J. Theoret. Biol. **10:** 356–369.

KAYA, K. & S. NAGAKINA. 1967. Vacuum ultraviolet absorption spectra of simple amides. Theoret. Chim. Acta **7:** 117–123.

BASCH, H., M. B. ROBIN & N. A. KUEBLER. 1967. Electronic states of the amide group. J. Chem. Phys. **47:** 1201–1210.

Pteridines

PULLMAN, B. 1958. Structure électronique des éléments intervenant dans l'étude de l'activité antitumorale des antimétabolites de l'acide folique. Compt. Rend. Acad. Sci. (Paris) **246:** 3292–3295.

FERNANDEZ-ALONZO, J. I. 1964. Electronic structures in quantum biochemistry. *In* The Structure and Properties of Biomolecules and Biological Systems. J. Duchesne, Ed.: 3–83. Interscience Publishers. New York, N. Y.

BOPST, A. 1967. Essai d'interprétation des propriétés chimiques des ptérines au moyen de calcul d'orbitales moléculaires. Helv. Chim. Acta **50:** 1480–1491.

Porphyrins and Metal Porphyrins

PULLMAN, B., C. SPANJAARD & G. BERTHIER. 1960. Features of the electronic structure of the iron-porphyrin complexes with special reference to the oxido-reductive properties of cytochromes. Proc. Nat. Acad. Sci. U.S.A. **46** (8): 1011–1020.

OHNO, K., Y. TANABE & F. SASAKI. 1963. Simple molecular orbital calculations on the electronic structure of iron-porphyrin complexes. Theoret. Chim. Acta **1:** 378–392.

KOTANI, M. 1963. On the electronic state of iron in hemoglobins with a short introduction to problems of quantum biophysics. Rev. Mod. Phys. **35:** 717–720.

KOTANI, M. 1964. Electronic structure and magnetic properties of hemoproteins, particularly of hemoglobins. *In* The Structure and Properties of Biomolecules and Biological Systems. J. Duchesne, Ed.: 159–181. Interscience Publishers. New York, N. Y.

DAY, P., G. SCREGG & R. J. P. WILLIAMS. 1964. Low energy excited states of metal complexes. Biopolymers Sympos. **1:** 271–282.

GRIFFITH, J. S. 1964. Magnetic properties of hemoglobin and myoglobin derivatives. Biopolymers Sympos. **1:** 35–46.

VEILLARD, A. & B. PULLMAN. 1965. Complements sur la structure électronique des ferroporphyrines biologiques. J. Theoret. Biol. **8:** 317–326.

ZERNER, M. & M. GOUTERMAN. 1966. Porphyrins: III. Extended Hückel calculations on transition metal complexes. Theoret. Chim. Acta **4:** 44–63.

Bile Pigments

PULLMAN, B. & A. M. PERAULT. 1959. On the metabolic breakdown of hemoglobin and the electronic structure of the bile pigments. Proc. Nat. Acad. Sci. U.S.A. **45:** 1476–1480.

Carotenoids and Retinenes

BERTHOD, H. & A. PULLMAN. 1960. Aspects de la structure électronique du rétinène et de ses isomères d'intérêt biologique. Compt. Rend. Acad. Sci. (Paris) **251:** 808–810.

PULLMAN, A. & B. PULLMAN. 1961. The cis-trans isomerization of conjugated polyenes and the occurence of a hindered cis-isomer of retinene in the rhodopsin system. Proc. Nat. Acad. Sci. U.S.A. **47** (1): 7–14.

SUZUKI, H., N. TAKIZAWA & Y. TANIKAWA. 1966. Theory of optical absorption spectra of trans-carotenoids. Mem. School Sci. & Eng. (Waseda Univ.) **30:** 141–156.

GALINDO, I. G. 1966. A charge transfer process in the visual pigments. Dissertation. Univ. Chicago. Chicago, Ill.

Energy-Rich Phosphates

GRABE, B. 1958. Electron distribution in some high energy phosphates and transfer of energy from catabolism to anabolism. Biochim. Biophys. Acta **30:** 560–569.

GRABE, B. 1959. A quantum mechanical calculation of the electron distribution in carboxyl-phosphate and some related molecules. Arkiv for fysik. **15:** 207–224.

PULLMAN, B. & A. PULLMAN. 1960. Electronic structure of energy rich phosphates. Rad. Res. (Suppl.) **2:** 160–181.

FUKUI, K., K. MOROKUMA & C. NAGATA. 1960. A molecular orbital treatment of phosphate bonds of biochemical interest. I. Simple LCAO MO treatment. Bull. Chem. Soc. Jap. **33:** 1214–1219.

FUKUI, K., A. IMAMURA & C. NAGATA. 1963. A molecular orbital treatment of phosphate bonds of biochemical interest. II. Metal chelates of adenosine triphosphate. Bull. Chem. Soc. Jap. **36:** 1450–1453.

COLLIN, R. L. 1966. The electronic structure of phosphate esters. J. Amer. Chem. Soc. **88:** 3281–3287.

Oxidation-Reduction Coenzymes

PULLMAN, B. & A. PULLMAN. 1959. The electronic structure of the respiratory coenzymes. Proc. Nat. Ac. Sci. U.S.A. **45:** (2): 136–144.

KARREMAN, G. 1961. Contributions to quantum biology. I. Mobile electronic characteristics of riboflavin radicals. Bull. Math. Biophys. **23:** 55–68.

KARREMAN, G. 1962. Electronic aspects of quantum biology. Ann. N.Y. Acad. Sci. **96:** 1029–1055.

PULLMAN, A. 1963. Relations entre le potentiel d'oxydo-réduction des systemes réversibles et les indices caractéristiques de leur structure électronique. Tetrahedron **19:** (Suppl. 2): 441–453.

MALRIEU, J. P. & B. PULLMAN. 1964. Configuration spatiale et propriétés électroniques du noyau d'isoalloxazine. Theoret. Chim. Acta **2:** 302–314.

GRABE, B. 1964. Quantum mechanical calculations on the isoalloxazine part of flavin. Biopolymers Sympos. **1:** 283–291.

FOX, J. L., K. NISHIMOTO & L. S. FORSTER. 1965. Self-consistent field calculations of isoalloxazine. Biochim. Biophys. Acta **109:** 626–628.

KOZIOL, J. 1966. Studies on flavins in organic solvents. I. Spectral characteristics of riboflavin, riboflavin tetrabutyrate and lumichrome. Photochem. Photobiol. **5:** 41–54.

FOX, J. L., S. P. LA BERGE, K. NISHIMOTO & L. S. FORSTER. 1967. Electronic structures of lumazines and isoalloxazines. Biochim. Biophys. Acta **136:** 544–550.

KURTIN, W. E., M. A. LAFINO & P. S. SONG. 1967. A study of photochemistry of flavins in pyridine and with a donor. Photochem. Photobiol. **6:** 247–259.

SONG, P. E. & W. E. KURTIN. 1967. On triplet states of flavins. J. Amer. Chem. Soc. **89:** 4248–4249.

Folic Acid Coenzymes

PERAULT, A. M. & B. PULLMAN. 1960. Electronic structure and biochemical function of folic acid coenzymes. Biochim Biophys. Acta **44:** 251–262.

PERAULT, A. M. & B. PULLMAN. 1961. Structure électronique et mode d'action des antimétabolites de l'acide folique. Biochim. Biophys. Acta **52:** 266–280.

COLLIN, R. & B. PULLMAN. 1964. On the mechanism of folic acid reductase inhibition. Biochim. Biophys. Acta **89:** 232–241.

NEELY, W. B. 1967. Molecular orbital calculations on folic acid and folic acid analogs. Molec. Pharmacol. **3:** 108.

Pyridoxal Phosphate

PERAULT, A. M., B. PULLMAN & C. VALDEMORO. 1961. Electronic aspects of the reactions of pyridoxal phosphate enzymes. Biochim. Biophys. Acta **46:** 555–575.

PULLMAN, B. 1963. A quantum-mechanical investigation of pyridoxal dependent reactions. *In* Proceedings of the Symposium on Chemical and Biological Aspects of Pyridoxal Catalysis. Rome: 63–121. Pergamon Press. London, England.

Thiamine Pyrophosphate

PULLMAN, B. & C. SPANJAARD. 1961. Electronic aspects of the mechanism of thiamine catalyzed reactions. Biochim. Biophys. Acta **46:** 576–587.

COLLIN, R. & B. PULLMAN. 1964. Some electronic aspects of the mechanism of thiamine action. Arch. Biochem. Biophys. **108:** 535–541.

Vitamin B_{12}

VEILLARD, A. & B. PULLMAN. 1965. Aspects de la structure électronique de la vitamine B_{12} et de ses analogues. J. Theoret. Biol. **8:** 307–316.

DAY, P. 1967. A theory of the optical properties of vitamin B_{12} and its derivatives. Theoret. Chim. Acta **7:** 328–341.

Hydrogen Bonding

PULLMAN, B. & A. PULLMAN. 1959. The electronic structure of the purine-pyrimidine pairs of DNA. Biochim. Biophys. Acta **36:** 343–350.

PULLMAN, A. 1963. Sur l'interaction de deux systemes conjugués à travers une liaison hydrogene. Compt. Rend. Acad. Sci. (Paris) **256:** 5435–5438.

LÖWDIN, P. O. 1964. Some aspects on DNA replication; incorporation errors and proton transfer. *In* Electronic Aspects of Biochemistry. B. Pullman, Ed.: 167–201. Academic Press. New York, N. Y.

LÖWDIN, P. O. 1964. Some aspects on quantum biology. Biopolymers Sympos. **1:** 293–311.

REIN, R. & F. E. HARRIS. 1964. Studies of hydrogen-bonded systems. I. The electronic structure and the double well potential of the N–H . . .N hydrogen bond of the guanine-cytosine base pair. J. Chem. Phys. **41:** 3393–3401.

LÖWDIN, P. O. 1965. Quantum genetics and the aperiodic solid. Some aspects of the biological problems of heredity, mutations, aging and tumors in view of the quantum theory of the DNA molecule. Advan. Quantum Chem. **2:** 213–360.

REIN, R. & F. E. HARRIS. 1965. Studies of hydrogen bonded systems. II Tunneling and tautomeric equilibria in the N.H...N hydrogen bond of the guanine-cytosine base pair. J. Chem. Phys. **42:** 2177–2180.

REIN, R. & F. E. HARRIS. 1965. Studies of hydrogen bonded systems III. Potential-energy surface tunneling and tautomeric equilibria in the N-H . . . N and O . . . H-N bonds of the guanine-cytosine base pair. J. Chem. Phys. **43:** 4415–4421.

NASH, H. A. & D. F. BRADLEY. 1965. Interactions between trinucleotides: the electrostatic contribution and its possible relation to the mechanism of translation of the genetic code. Biopolymers **3:** 261–273.

REIN, R. & F. E. HARRIS. 1966. Studies of hydrogen-bonded systems. IV radiation induced tunneling and tautomeric equilibria in the guanine-cytosine base pair. J. Chem. Phys. **45:** 1797.

PULLMAN, B., P. CLAVERIE & J. CAILLET. 1966. Van der Waals-London interactions and the configuration of hydrogen-bonded purine and pyrimidine pairs. Proc. Nat. Acad. Sci. U. S. A. **55:** 904–912.

PULLMAN, B., P. CLAVERIE & J. CAILLET. 1966. On the exclusivity of hydrogen-bonded pairing between the Watson-Crick complementary bases. J. Molec. Biol. **22:** 373–375.

PULLMAN, B., P. CLAVERIE & J. CAILLET. 1966. Sur le rôle des forces de Van der

Waals-London dans les interactions entre les bases puriques et pyrimidiques. Compt. Rend. Acad. Sci. (Paris) **263:** 2006–2009.

NASH, H. A. & D. F. BRADLEY. 1966. Calculation of the lowest energy configurations of nucleotide base pairs on the basis of an electrostatic model. J. Chem. Phys. **45:** 1380–1386.

LUNELL, S. & G. SPERBER. 1967. Study of the hydrogen bonding in the adenine-thymine, adenine-cytosine and guanine-thymine base pairs. J. Chem. Phys. **46:** 2119–2124.

Intermolecular Forces

DEVOE, H. & I. TINOCO, JR. 1962. The stability of helical polynucleotides: base contributions. J. Molec. Biol. **4:** 500–517.

SALEM, L. 1962. Attractive forces between macromolecular chains of biological importance. Nature **193:** 476–477.

SALEM, L. 1962. The role of long-range forces in the cohesion of lipoproteins. Canad. J. Biochem. Physiol. **40:** 1287–1298.

BRADLEY, D. F., S. LIFSON & B. HONIG. 1964. Theory of the optical and other properties of biopolymers: Applicability and elimination of the first neighbor and dipole-dipole approximations. *In* Electronic Aspects of Biochemistry. B. Pullman, Ed.: 77–91. Academic Press. New York, N. Y.

SINANOĞLU, O. & S. ABDULNUR. 1964. Hydrophobic stacking of bases and the solvent denaturation of DNA. Photochem. Photobio. **3:** 333–342.

JEHLE, H., W. C. PARKE & A. SALYERS. 1964. Intermolecular charge fluctuation interactions in molecular biology. *In* Electronic Aspects of Biochemistry. B. Pullman, Ed.: 313–333. Academic Press. New York, N. Y.

JEHLE, H., W. C. PARKE, R. M. SHIVEN & D. K. AEIN. 1964. Biological significance of charge fluctuation forces (London-Van der Waals) between sterically complementary and sterically similiar molecules. Biopolymers Sympos. **1:** 209–233.

PULLMAN, B., P. CLAVERIE & J. CAILLET. 1965. Intermolecular forces in association of purines with polybenzenoid hydrocarbons. Science **147:** 1305–1307.

NASH, H. A. & D. F. BRADLEY. 1965. Interactions between trinucleotides: the electrostatic contribution and its possible relation to the mechanism of translation of the genetic code. Biopolymers **3:** 261–273.

SINANOĞLU, O. & S. ABDULNUR. 1965. Effect of water and other solvents on the structure of biopolymers. Fed. Proc. **24:** S12–S23.

GERSCH, N. F. & D. O. JORDAN. 1965. Interaction of DNA with aminoacridines. J. Molec. Biol. **13:** 138–156.

JEHLE, H., W. C. PARKE & A. SALYERS. 1965. Charge fluctuation interactions and molecular biophysics. Biophysics **9:** 433–447.

PULLMAN, B. P. CLAVERIE & J. CAILLET. 1966. Van der Waals-London interactions and the configuration of hydrogen-bonded purine and pyrimidine pairs. Proc. Nat. Acad. Sci. U. S. A. **55:** 904–912.

PULLMAN, B., P. CLAVERIE & J. CAILLET. 1966. Van der Waals-London interactions between stacked purines and pyrimidines. J. Theoret. Biol. **12:** 419–434.

PULLMAN, B., P. CLAVERIE & J. CAILLET. 1966. On the exclusivty of hydrogen-bonded pairing between the Watson-Crick complementary bases. J. Molec. Biol. **22:** 373–375.

PULLMAN, B., P. CLAVERIE & J. CAILLET. 1966. Sur le rôle des forces de Van der Waals-London dans les interactions entre les bases puriques et pyrimidiques. Compt. Rend. Acad. Sci. (Paris) **263:** 2006–2009.

NASH, H. A. & D. F. BRADLEY. 1966. Calculation of the lowest energy configurations of nucleotide base pairs of the basis of an electrostatic model. J. Chem. Phys. **45:** 1380–1386.

PULLMAN, B., P. CLAVERIE & J. CAILLET. 1967. Interaction energies in hydrogen-bonded purine pyrimidine triplets. Proc. Nat. Acad. Sci. U. S. A. **57:** 1663–1669.

PULLMAN, B. & J. CAILLET. 1967. Van der Waals-London interaction energies in hydrogen bonding between purine and pyrimidine base analogues. I. Interactions involving 2, 6-diaminopurine. Theoret. Chim. Acta **8:** 223–227.

Electron Donor and Acceptor Properties, Charge Transfer

PULLMAN, B. & A. PULLMAN. 1958. Electron donor and acceptor properties of biologically important purines, pyrimidines, pteridines, flavins and aromatic amino acids. Proc. Nat. Acad. Sci. U. S. A. **44:** 1197–1202.

PULLMAN, B. & A. PULLMAN. 1960. Some electronic aspects of biochemistry Rev. Mod. Phys. **32:** 428–436.

SZENT-GYÖRGYI, A. 1960. Introduction to a submolecular biology. Academic Press. New York, N. Y.

KARREMAN, G. 1961. Studies in quantum biology. II. The mobile electron characteristics of tryptophan in relation to those of FMN^-, FMNH and $FMNH_2$. Bull. Math. Biophys. **23:** 135–140.

KARREMAN, G. 1962. Electronic aspects of quantum biology. Ann. N. Y. Acad. Sci. **96:** 1029–1055.

KARREMAN, G. 1962. Electronic features of some psychopharmacological compounds. *In* Data Acquisition and Processing in Biology and Medicine: 51–59. Pergamon Press. London, England.

BRILLOUIN, L. 1962. Giant molecules and semiconductors. *In* Horizons in Biochemistry. M. Kasha & B. Pullman, Eds.: 295–318. Academic Press. New York, N. Y.

PULLMAN, B. 1964. Les complexes de transfert de charge en biochimie. Sixth Internat. Cong. Biochem. **10:** 737–738. New York, N. Y.

ROSSI, M. & A. PULLMAN. 1964. The ionization potentials of the π and lone pair electrons of biochemical purines and pyrimidines. Biochim. Biophys. Acta **88:** 211–212.

PULLMAN, B. 1964. On the complexes of actinomycin with purines and deoxyribonucleic acid. Biochim. Biophys. Acta **88:** 440–441.

MANTIONE, M. J. & B. PULLMAN. 1966. Sur les caractéristiques des complexes par transfert de charge impliquant les bases puriques et pyrimidiques d'intérêt biologique. Compt. Rend. Acad. Sci. (Paris) **262:** 1492–1494.

PULLMAN, A. & B. PULLMAN. 1966. Charge transfer complexes in biochemistry. *In* Quantum Theory of Atoms. Molecules and the Solid State. P. O. Löwdin, Ed.: 345–359. Academic Press. New York, N. Y.

BULLOCK, F. J. 1967. Charge transfer in biology. *In* Comprehensive Biochemistry. M. Florkin & E. H. Stotz, Eds. **22:** 81–147. Elsevier. Amsterdam, Holland.

YOMOSA, S. 1967. Charge-transfer molecular compounds in biological systems. Progr. Theoret. Phys. (Suppl.) **40:** 249–263.

Free Radicals in Biology

PULLMAN, B. & A. PULLMAN. 1959. The electronic structure of the respiratory coenzymes. Proc. Nat. Acad. Sci. U. S.A. **45:** 136–144.

GUZZO, A. V. & G. TOLLIN. 1963. Electron paramagnetic resonance studies of riboflavin and its derivatives. I. The isoalloxazine semiquinones in acid. Arch Biochim. Biophys. **103:** 231–244.

PULLMAN, A. 1964. Etudes théoriques de radicaux libres d'intérêt biologique. J. Chim. Phys. **61:** 1666–1680.

MALRIEU, J. P. & B. PULLMAN. 1964. Sur les propriétés électroniques de la phénothiazine et de son radical. Theoret. Chim Acta **2:** 293–302.

PULLMAN, B. & M. J. MANTIONE. 1965. Sur les densités de spin dans les radicaux libres provenant de bases puriques et pyrimidiques par fixation d'un atome d'hydrogene. Compt. Rend. Acad. Sci. (Paris) **260:** 5643–5645.

PULLMAN, B. & M. J. MANTIONE. 1965. Recherches complémentaires sur la structure électronique des radicaux libres dérivés de bases puriques et pyrimidiques par fixation d'un atome d'hydrogene. Compt. Rend. Acad. Sci. (Paris) **261:** 5679–5681.

HERAK, J. N. & W. GORDY. 1965. Free radicals formed by hydrogen atom bombardment of the nucleic acid bases. Proc. Nat. Acad. Sci. U. S. A. **54:** 1287–1292

HERAK, J. N. & W. GORDY. 1966. Interaction of hydrogen atoms and hydroxyl radicals with 5-halogen uracils. Proc. Nat. Acad. Sci. U. S. A. **56:** 1354–1360.

Semiconductivity

EVANS, M. G. & I. GERGELY. 1949. A discussion of the possibility of bands of energy levels in proteins. Electronic interaction in nonbonded systems. Biochim. Biophys. Acta **3:** 188–197.

SUARD, M., G. BERTHIER & B. PULLMAN. 1961. Sur les états électroniques des protéines. Biochim. Biophys. Acta **52:** 254–265.

PULLMAN, A. & B. PULLMAN. 1961. The band structure of melanins. Biochim. Biophys. Acta **54:** 384–385.

ELEY, D. D. 1962. Semiconductivity in biological molecules. *In* Horizons in Biochemistry. M. Kasha & B. Pullman, Eds.: 341–380. Academic Press. New York, N. Y.

PULLMAN, B. 1963. Les bandes d'énergie et la structure électronique de la polyglycine. Compt. Rend. Acad. Sci. (Paris) **257:** 2488–2491.

LADIK, J. 1964. Some new results in the quantum-mechanical calculation of DNA. *In* Electronic Aspects of Biochemistry. B. Pullman, Ed.: 203–219. Academic Press. New York, N. Y.

HOFFMAN, T. A. & J. LADIK. 1964. Quantum mechanical considerations on some properties of DNA. *In* the Structure and Properties of Biomolecules and Biological Systems. J. Duchesne, Ed.: 84–158. Interscience Publishers. New York, N. Y.

ELEY, D. D. & R. B. LESLIE. 1964. Electrical conduction in soild proteins. *In* Electronic Aspects of Biochemistry. B. Pullman, Ed.: 105–117. Academic Press. New York, N. Y.

PULLMAN, B. 1965. Aspects of the electronic structure of the nuclei acids and their constituents. *In* Molecular Biophysics. B. Pullman & M. Weissbluth, Eds.: 117–189. Academic Press. New York, N. Y.

Mechanisms of Photobiology

PULLMAN, A. & B. PULLMAN. 1961. The cis-trans isomerization of conjugated polyenes and the occurence of a hindered cis-isomer of retinene in the rhopsin system. Proc. Nat. Acad. Sci. (47) **1:** 7–14.

PULLMAN, A. & B. PULLMAN. 1963. On the mechanism of ultraviolet induced mutations. Biochim. Biophys. Acta **75:** 269–271.

MANTIONE, M. J. & B. PULLMAN. 1964. Sur le méchanisme de la photodimérisation de la thymine. Biochim. Biophys. Acta **91:** 387–398.

PULLMAN, B. & M. J. MANTIONE. 1965. Electron distribution in the triplet state and photodimerization of thiothymine. Biochim. Biophys. Acta **95:** 668.

NAGATA, C., A. IMAMURA, Y. TAGASHIRA & M. KOPAMA. 1965. Quantum-mechanical study on the photodimerization of aromatic molecules. J. Theoret. Biol. **9:** 357–365.

IMAMURA, A., H. FUJITA & C. NAGATA. 1967. The electronic structure of peptide and the base components of nucleic acids in the triplet state. Bull. Chem. Soc. Jap. **40:** 21–27.

DANILOV, V. I. 1967. Research note on the mechanism of photodimerization of pyrimidine bases. Photochem. Photobiol. **6:** 233–235.

Radiation Effects and the Mechanism of Radio Resistance

PULLMAN, B. & A. PULLMAN. 1960. Structural aspects of radiation effects on nucleic acids and related substances. *In* Comparative Effects of Radiation. M. Burton, J. S. Kirby-Smith & J. L. Magee, Eds.: 105–123. John Wiley & Sons. New York, N. Y.

PULLMAN, B. 1961. Aspects structuraux des effets des radiations sur les substances d'intérêt biologique. Mem. Acad. Roy. Belg. (33) **3:** 174–190.

DUCHESNE, J. & A. VAN DE VORST. 1965. Origine de la radioresistance des acides nucléiques en phase solide. Bull. Classe Sci. Acad. Roy Belg. **51:** 778–809.

VAN DE VORST, A., M. RICHER & K. V. RAJALAKSHMI. 1966. Radiorésistance et délocalisation des électrons π. Bull. Classe Sci. Acad. Roy. Belg. **52:** 276–295.

LACROIX, M., J. DEPIREUX N A. VAN DE VORST. 1967. On the nature of free radicals induced by X-rays in puric bases. Proc. Nat. Acad. Sci. U.S.A. **58:** 399–401.

Mechanisms of Mutagenesis

PULLMAN, B. & A. PULLMAN. 1962. La tautomérie des bases puriques et pyrimidiques et la théorie des mutations. Biochem. Biophys. Acta **64:** 403–405.

PULLMAN, A. & B. PULLMAN. 1963. On the mechanism of ultraviolet-induced mutations. Biochim. Biophys. Acta **75:** 269–271.

NAGATA, C., A. IMAMURA, H. SALTO & K. FUKUI. 1963. Changes of π-electron distribution of dexyribonucleic acid after alkylation and their possible relation to the biological effect. GANN. **54:** 109–117.

PULLMAN, A. 1964. The influence of heteroatoms and substituents on the tautomeric equilibria in biochemical purines and pyrimidines. 1. Azapurines and azapyrimidines. Biochim. Biophys. Acta **87:** 365–369.

LÖWDIN, P. O. 1964. Some aspects on DNA replication. Incorporation errors and proton transfer. *In* Electronic Aspects of Biochemistry. B. Pullman, Ed.: 167–201. Academic Press. New York, N. Y.

REIN, R. & F. E. HARRIS. 1964. Studies of hydrogen-bonded systems I. The electronic structure and the double well potential of the N-H . . . N hydrogen bond of the guanine-cytosine base-pair. J. Chem. Phys. **14:** 3393–3401.

REIN, R. & F. E. HARRIS. 1965. Studies of hydrogen-bonded systems II. Tunneling and tautomeric equilibria in the N-H . . . N hydrogen bond of the guanine-cytosine base-pair. J. Chem. Phys. **42:** 2177–2180.

REIN, R. & F. E. HARRIS. 1965. Studies of hydrogen bonded systems III. Potential-energy surface, tunneling and tautomeric equilibria in the N-H . . . N and O . . . H-N bonds of the guanine-cytosine base pair. J. Chem. Phys. **43:** 4415–4421.

LÖWDIN, P. O. 1965. Quantum genetics and the aperiodic solid. Some aspects of the biological problems of heredity, mutations, aging and tumors in view of the quantum theory of the DNA molecule. Advan. Quantum Chem. **2:** 213–360.

Mechanisms of Carcinogenesis

PULLMAN, A. 1945. Sur une relation entre les repartitions des charges électroniques et le pouvoir cancérigene d'une certaine classe d'hydrocarbures. Compt. Rend. Acad. Sci. **221:** 140–142.

PULLMAN, A. & B. PULLMAN. 1955. Cancérisation par les Substances Chimiques et Structure Moléculaire Masson, Ed. Paris, France.

PULLMAN, A. & B. PULLMAN. 1955. Electronic structure and carcinogenic activity of aromatic molecules. New developments. Advan. Cancer Res. **3:** 117–169.

PULLMAN, A. 1964. The theory of chemical carcinogenesis and the problem of hydrocarbon protein interactions. Biopolymers Sympos. **1:** 47–65.

PULLMAN, B. 1964. Aspects of the electronic structure of the nucleic acids in relation to the theories of mutagenesis and carcinogenesis. Biopolymers Sympos. **1:** 141–159.

PULLMAN, B. 1964. Electronic aspects of the interactions between the carcinogens and possible cellular sites of their activity. J. Cell. Comp. Physiol. (Suppl. 1) **64:** 91–110.

PULLMAN, B., P. CLAVERIE & J. CAILLET. 1965. Intermolecular forces in association of purines with polybenzenoid hydrocarbons. Science **147:** 1305–1307.

Biochemical Evolution and the Origin of Life

PULLMAN, B. & A. PULLMAN. 1962. Electronic delocalization and biochemical evolution. Nature **196:** 1137–1142.

PULLMAN, B. & A. PULLMAN. 1964. π molecular orbitals and the processes of life. *In* Molecular Orbitals in Chemistry Physics and Biology. P. O. Löwdin & B. Pullman, Eds.: 547–571. Academic Press. New York, N. Y.

Optical Properties of Biopolymers

TINOCO, I. 1960. Hypochromism in polynucleotides. J. Amer. Chem. Soc. **82:** 4785–4790.

RHODES, W. 1961. Hypochromism and other spectral properties of helical polynucleotides. J. Amer. Chem. Soc. **83:** 3609–3617.

RHODES, W. 1962. Symmetry of helical polymers. Electronic states of double-stranded polynucleotides. J. Chem. Phys. **37:** 2433–2439.

DEVOE, H. & I. TINOCO. 1962. The hypochromism of helical polynucleotides. J. Molec. Biol. **4:** 518–527.

BRADLEY, D. F., S. LIFSON & B. HONIG. 1964. Theory of optical and other properties of biopolymers: Applicability and elimination of the first-neighbor and dipole-dipole approximations. *In* Electronic Aspects of Biochemistry. B. Pullman, Ed.: 77–91. Academic Press. New York, N. Y.

TINOCO, I. 1965. Absorption and rotation of polarized light by polymers. *In* Molecular Biophysics. B. Pullman & M. Weissbluth, Eds.: 269–291. Academic Press. New York, N. Y.

ROSENHECK, K. & B. SOMMER. 1967. Theory of the far-ultraviolet spectrum of polypeptides in the β consomation. J. Chem. Phys. **46B**: 532–536.
BUSH, C. A. & I. TINOCO JR. 1967. Calculation of the optical rotarory dispersion of dinucleoside phosphates. J. Molec. Biol. **23:** 601–614.

Miscellaneous Enzymatic Reactions

PULLMAN, A. & B. PULLMAN. 1959. Elements of a general theory of enzymatic hydrolysis. Proc. Nat. Acad. Sci. U.S.A. **45:** 1572–1582.
PERAULT, A. M., C. VALDEMORO & B. PULLMAN. 1961. Electronic aspects of the mechanism of action of xanthine oxidase. J. Theoret. Biol. **2:** 180–189.
PERAULT, A. M. & B. PULLMAN. 1963. Electronic aspects of enzymic acetyl transfer reactions. Biochim. Biophys. Acta **66:** 86–92.
PERAULT, A. M. & B. PULLMAN. 1963. Aspects électroniques des transferts enzymatiques des groupes méthyles. Biochim. Biophys. Acta **75:** 1–11.
SONG, P. S. & T. A. MOORE. 1967. Molecular-orbital studies of the mechanism of xanthine oxidase-catalysed oxidation of purines, especially 2-chloropurine. Internat. J. Quantum Chem. **1:** 699–719.

Electronic Aspects of Pharmacology

KARREMAN, G., I. ISENBERG & A. SZENT-GYÖRGYI. 1959. On the mechanism of action of chlorpromazine. Science **130:** 1191–1192.
PULLMAN, B. & C. VALDEMORO. 1960. Electronic structure and activity of organophosphorus inhibitors of esterases. Biochim. Biophys. Acta **43:** 548–550.
FUKUI, K., C. NAGATA & A. AMAMURA. 1960. Electronic structure and nicotine like stimulant activity in choline phenyl esters. Science **132:** 87–89.
FUKUI, K., K. HOROKUMA, C. NAGATA & A. IMAMURA. 1961. Electronic structure and biochemical activities in diethyl phenyl phosphates. Bull. Chem. Soc. Jap. **34:** 1224–1227.
KARREMAN, G. 1962. Electronic features of some psychopharmacological compounds. *In* Data Acquisition and Processing in Biology and Medicine.: 51–59. Pergamon Press. London, England.
BAN, T. 1962. Newer approach to the electronic structure of cholinesterase inhibitors. Japan J. Pharmacol. **12:** 72–78.
COCORDANO, M. & J. RICARD. 1963. Biologie moléculaire de la croissance. I. Structure électronique et mécanismes d'action de dérivés chlorés de l'acide phénoxyacétique. Physiol. Veg. **1:** 129–138.
PULLMAN, B. 1964. Electronic aspects of pharmacology. *In* Electronic Aspects of Biochemistry. B. Pullman, Ed.: 559–578. Academic Press. New York, N. Y.
MALRIEU, J. P. & B. PULLMAN. 1964. Sur les propriétés électroniques de la phénothiazine et de son radical. Theoret. Chim. Acta **2:** 293–301.
GREEN, J. P. & J. P. MALRIEU. 1965. Quantum chemical studies of charge-transfer complexes of indoles. Proc. Nat. Acad. Sci. U.S.A. **54:** 659–664.
NEELY, W. B. 1965. The use of molecular orbital calculations as an aid to correlate the structure and activity of cholinesterase inhibitors. Molec. Pharmacol. **1:** 137–144.
AGIN, D., L. HERSCH & D. HOLTZMAN. 1965. The action of anesthetics on excitable membranes: A quantum chemical analysis. Proc. Nat. Acad. Sci. U.S.A. **54:** 952–958.
SNYDER, S. & C. R. MERRIL. 1965. A relationship between the hallucinogenic activity of drugs and their electronic configuration. Proc. Nat. Acad. Sci. U.S.A. **54:** 258–266.
SNYDER, S., C. R. MERRIL & D. F. BRADLEY. 1966. Inhibition of histamine methyl transferase by serotonin and chlorpromazine derivatives: Electronic aspects. Biochim. Biophys. Acta **118:** 316–324.
YEARGERS, E. & L. AUGENSTEN. 1966. Molecular orbital calculations on photosensitizing psoralen derivatives. Nature **212:** 251–253.
COCORDANO, M., J. RICARD & A. JULG. 1966. Relations between the electronic structure and auxinic activity of chlorinated benzoic acids. J. Theoret. Biol. **12:** 291–296.
MALRIEU, J. P. 1967. Quantum chemistry and pharmacology: Application to phenothiazines and other neuroactive compounds. *In* Molecular Basis of Some Aspects of Mental Activity. O. Walaas, Ed.: 83–93. Academic Press. London, England.

GREEN, J. P. 1967. The application of quantum mechanics to pharmacology: some substances active in the nervous system. *In* Molecular Basis of Some Aspects of Mental Activity. O. Walaas, Ed.: 95–111. Academic Press. London, England.

MUTSCHLER, E. 1967. Elektronenverteilung und dissoziationskonstanten bei pharmakologish wirksamenarecaidin derivation. Arzt. Forsch **17:** 833–837.

MUTSCHLER, E., O. WASSERMANN & H. WOOG. 1967. Über struktur wiskungs. Beziehungen beicyclishen acetylcholin. Analogen der aminophenol. Reihe Arzt. Forsch. **17:** 837–841.

GIORDANO, W., J. R. HAMANN, J. J. HARKINS & J. J. KAUFMAN. 1967. Quantum mechanical calculation of stability in 2-formyl N-Methyl pyridinium (cation) oxime (2-PAM$^+$) conformers. Molec. Pharmacol. **3:** 307–317.

MUTSCHLER, E., H. SCHERF, P. VOSS & O. WASSERMAN. 1967. Uber beziehungen zwischen der electronen verteilung in monoguanyl-hydrazonen und ihrer pharmakologischen wirkung. Arch. Pharmak. u. exp. Path. **256:** 367–382.

KIER, L. B. 1967. Molecular orbital calculation of preferred conformations of acetylcholine, muscarine and muscarone. Molec. Pharmacol. **3:** 487–494.

ELECTRONIC STRUCTURE OF IRON IN PORPHYRIN COMPLEXES*

Masao Kotani
Osaka University
Osaka, Japan

INTRODUCTION

In the present paper I should like to discuss the electronic structure of the iron atom in heme, which is the well-known prosthetic group of hemoproteins. Since heme is a molecule consisting of a porphyrin and an Fe atom, the problem of the electronic structure of the Fe atom in heme is a part of the problem of the electronic structure of hemes. Many experimental results, however, particularly those of magnetic measurements, can be explained and discussed from the atomic viewpoint, in which the Fe atom or ion is considered to be subjected to electrostatic and other influences due to surrounding atoms such as the pyrrole and imidazole nitrogens. We can use ligand field theory, which has proved very effective in theoretical interpretations of energy levels and other electronic properties of coordination compounds of metallic ions.

The heme found in Hb and Mb has the structure shown in FIGURE 1; the porphyrin of this heme is called protoporphyrin, and has two vinyl groups and two propionic acid groups, as well as methyl groups, attached to peripheral carbon atoms. Pi electrons of vinyl groups are conjugated with those of the main porphyrin ring. If we disregard these "tails," the porphyrin and the heme possess tetragonal symmetry. The porphyrin is essentially planar, but there are evidences from x-ray analysis of hemes and myoglobin that the Fe atom is sometimes located above the porphyrin plane by as much as 1/2 Å. The geometry of hemin chloride, separated from protein, has been measured in detail by König[1] by the x-ray diffraction method, and the result is shown in FIGURE 2. This shows that the Fe atom is actually out of the porphyrin plane, and the symmetry of the molecule viewed from the Fe atom is approximately C_{4v}. In the following, a Cartesian coordinate system is introduced, with its origin at Fe nucleus, z axis perpendicular to the porphyrin plane, and x, y axes parallel to lines connecting pyrrole nitrogens, which are located diagonally opposite. These four pyrrole nitrogen atoms constitute the four ligands of the Fe atom under consideration.

In the case of the native hemes in which we are interested, the Fe atom is further coordinated by another nitrogen atom of the imidazole of histidine. This nitrogen atom is the fifth ligand, and is situated approximately on the negative z axis. The plane of the imidazole ring is roughly perpendicular to the porphyrin plane, and the tetragonal symmetry is reduced, if we take the imidazole into account. Furthermore, at the sixth coordination point on the positive z axis, different kinds of small molecules and atomic ions can be coordinated, at least in myoglobin and hemoglobin. The reversible attachment of oxygen molecule at the sixth position is important in the physiological function of these molecules.

Now, hemes can include the reduced and oxydized forms. The Fe atom exists in ferrous states in the reduced form and in ferric states in the oxidized form. The following abreviations are used for hemoglobins and myoglobins: $Hb(Fe^{2+})X$, for the hemoglobin whose hemes are in reduced form, $Hb(Fe^{3+})X$ for the oxidized form, and similar designations for myoglobins. Here X denotes the ligand which

* The research in our laboratory, presented in this paper, has been supported by grants-in-aid from the Ministry of Education.

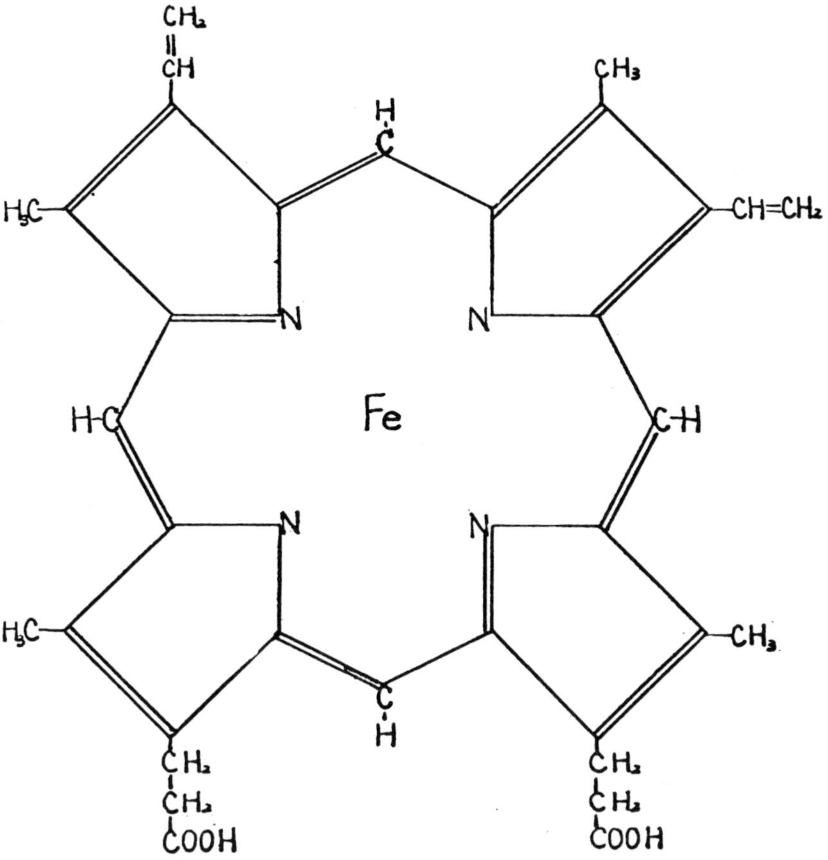

FIGURE 1. Fe-protoporphyrin (protoheme).

attaches to the heme at the sixth coordination position. For lack of this ligand in deoxymyoglobin, deoxyhemoglobin and deoxymyoglobin are denoted by deoxy-Hb(Fe^{2+}) and deoxy-Mb(Fe^{2+}) respectively. Ferri-Hb and ferro-Hb show different optical spectra, as shown in FIGURE 3; ferri-Hb and ferri-Mb show EPR signals, although no EPR signals have been observed on ferro-Hb, ferro-Mb. Hemoglobin and myoglobin exhibit their physiological activities—reversible oxygenation—in reduced ferrous form, but in the case of cytochromes both reduced and oxidized forms participate in their biological activities.

Ferrous and ferric ions have six and five electrons in 3d orbitals. Since there are five independent d orbitals, and ten electrons can be accommodated in these orbitals, the d shell is incomplete in ferrous and ferric ions. In most cases, this situation produces, as one of its consequences nonvanishing magnetic moments for the normal electronic states of these ions, arising from unpaired spins and partly from partially quenched orbital angular momenta of electrons. It is well-known that, as early as the 1930's, Pauling and Coryell succeeded in measuring the paramagnetic

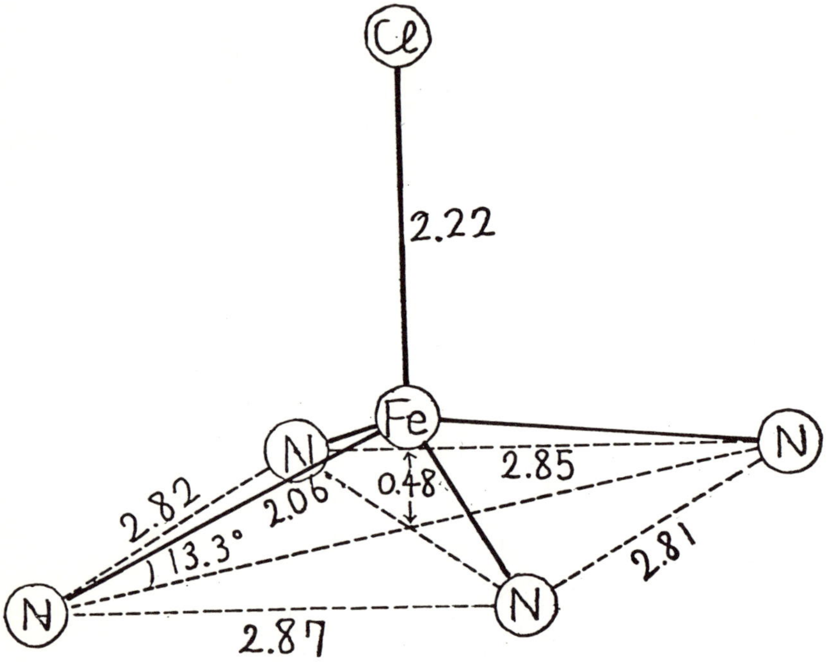

FIGURE 2. Schematic representation of the position of iron ions in chlorohemin. (By D. F. Koenig.[1])

susceptibility of some derivatives of hemoglobin and myoglobin at room temperature, and they assigned the magnitude of total spin S for these compounds.[2,3] According to Langevin-Curie's theory of paramagnetism, the paramagnetic part of the susceptibility is given by the simple formula

$$\chi = N \frac{\mu^2}{3kT} \tag{1}$$

where N is the number of magnetic ions in the amount of the substance concerned, k is the Boltzmann constant, T, the absolute temperature, and μ the magnetic dipole moment. In quantum theory, the natural unit for the magnetic moment is the Bohr magneton defined by

$$\beta = \frac{eh}{4\pi mc},$$

and

$$\frac{\mu}{\beta} = n \tag{2}$$

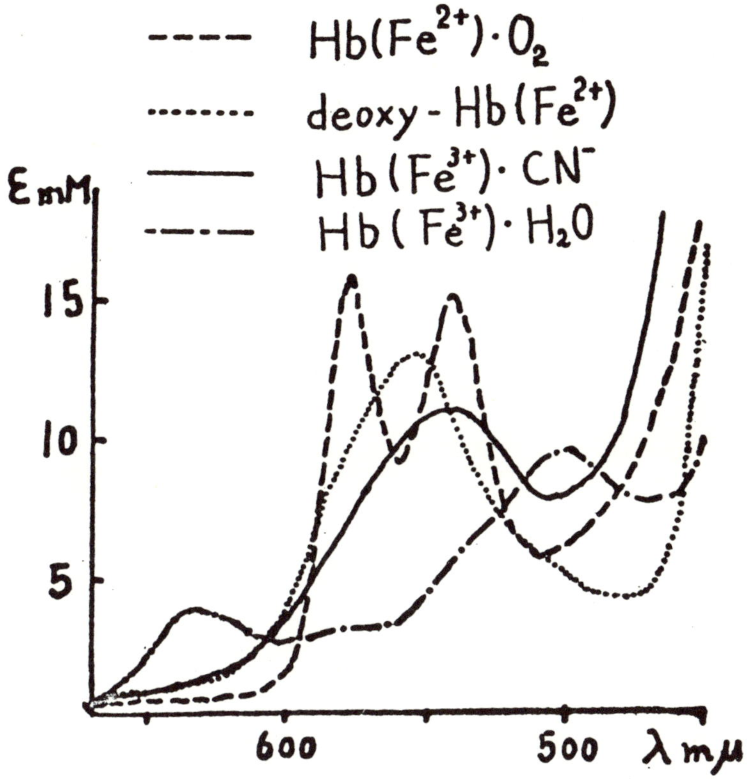

FIGURE 3. Visible optical spectra of ferri- and ferro-Hb's.

is known as Bohr magneton number. Thus, we have

$$\chi = N \frac{\beta^2 n^2}{3kT}. \tag{3}$$

If the magnetic moment is due to free spin, quantum mechanics gives

$$n = 2\sqrt{S(S+1)}, \tag{4}$$

where S, the spin quantum number, is the maximum possible value of z component of spin angular momentum, measured in units of $h/2\pi$. Since each electron contributes 1/2 to S,

$$S = \frac{f}{2},$$

where f denotes the number of electrons with parallel spins. The possible maximum value of S for ferric ion is 5/2, whereas the maximum S for ferrous ion is 2, because 6 electrons in the d shell must have one pair of antiparallel spins, giving $f_{max} = 4$.

According to the Pauling-Coryell measurements, $Hb(Fe^{3+})F^-$ gives n = 5.9, while $Hb(Fe^{3+})CN^-$ gives n = 2.5.[3] The former fits nicely to (4) with S = 5/2, which is the maximum possible S for ferric ions. The latter falls between "spin-only" n values for 1.73 for S = 1/2 and 2.84 for S = 1, but S = 1 is not possible for a system of an odd number of electrons. Moreover, we may expect some contribution from orbital magnetic moment in this case (as discussed in studies of low-spin ferric states). Thus, S = 1/2 is the reasonable assignment for $Hb(Fe^{3+})CN^-$. It is evident then that there are two kinds of hemoglobin derivatives: those with high-spin S = 5/2 and those with low-spin S = 1/2. In the case of derivatives of ferrous hemoglobin, Pauling and Coryell again found high-spin and low-spin compounds. Native hemoglobin which is not attached by oxygen (deoxy-$Hb(Fe^{2+})$) has S = 2, whereas oxygenated hemoglobin ($Hb(Fe^{2+})O_2$) is diamagnetic (S = 0). $Hb(Fe^{2+})CO$ belongs to this diamagnetic group.

Summarizing these results, we can say that there are four main cases for hemes as far as electronic state is concerned. They are shown in the following Table:

TABLE 1

	Oxydized (ferri-hemoproteins)	Reduced (ferro-hemoproteins)
High-spin	S = 5/2 Ex. $Mb(Fe^{3+})F^-$	S = 2 Ex. deoxy-$Mb(Fe^{2+})$
Low-spin	S = 1/2 Ex. $Mb(Fe^{3+})CN^-$	S = 0 (diamagnetic) Ex. $Hb(Fe^{2+})O_2$ $Hb(Fe^{2+})CO$

High-spin and low-spin species show different characteristics, not only in magnetic properties but also in optical spectra. FIGURE 4 shows the absorption spectra of $Mb(Fe^{3+})F^-$ and $Mb(Fe^{3+})CN^-$.

Characteristic Feature of Electronic Structure of Fe in Hemes

The distinction between high-spin and low-spin cases is not as clear-cut as described above. It is well-known that some derivatives of Mb and Hb, particularly their hydroxides, give effective Bohr magneton numbers that are intermediate between high-spin and low-spin values. Their optical spectra are also intermediate between spectra characteristic of high-spin and low-spin species, as shown in FIGURE 4. This situation was analyzed by George, Beetlestone and Griffith,[4] who concluded that hydroxides of Mb and Hb at room temperature are actually mixtures of high-spin and low-spin molecules in thermal equilibrium. Recently, more conclusive evidence has been obtained by Iizuka, using susceptibility measurements over the temperature range between room temperature and 70 °K.[5] FIGURE 5 shows the magnetic susceptibilities of $Hb(Fe^{3+})OCN^-$ as function of $1/T$. In the case of $Hb(Fe^{3+})OCN^-$, the slope of the curve at lower temperatures corresponds to the low-spin case; but at higher temperatures it becomes steeper, suggesting that the hemes are mainly in the high-spin state. The entire curve may be analyzed as the thermal equilibrium between high-spin and low-spin states. On the other hand, $Mb(Fe^{3+})H_2O$ is in the high-spin state at lower temperatures, and the low-spin state becomes excited as the temperature approaches 0 °C. The thermal mixing of high- and low-spin states was further ascertained by the temperature dependence of the optical spectrum at low temperature. FIGURE 6 shows the changes in the optical spectrum of $Hb(Fe^{3+})OCN^-$ between liquid N_2 temperature and 200 °K.

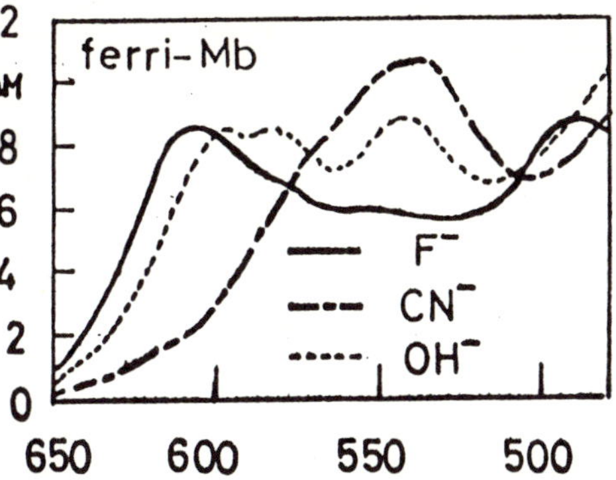

FIGURE 4. Optical absorption spectra of typical high-spin ($Mb(Fe^{3+})F^-$), typical low-spin ($Mb(Fe^{3+})CN^-$) and intermediate-spin ($Mb(Fe^{3+})OH^-$) compounds. (By George, Bettlestone and Griffith.[4])

The spectrum has isosbestic points at about 463 mμ, 522 mμ and 580 mμ. When the temperature increases from the liquid N_2 temperature, the characteristic absorption of low-spin states at about 540 mμ decreases and that of the high-spin state around 500 mμ increases. In these substances and several other derivatives of Mb and Hb, the low-spin and high-spin states are separated by energies of the order of thermal energy, i.e., a thousand cm^{-1} or less.

In the case of reduced hemoproteins such as ferro-Mb, ferro-Hb and their derivatives, direct evidence for thermal coexistence of high-spin and low-spin (diamagnetic) states has not yet been obtained. However, the fact that deoxy-$Mb(Fe^{2+})$ and deoxy-$Hb(Fe^{2+})$, which normally have high spin, can easily be converted to low spin by attaching O_2 or CO with small binding energies suggests strongly that the low-spin states of deoxy-$Mb(Fe^{2+})$ and deoxy-$Hb(Fe^{2+})$ are not very high.

Summing up these experimental results, we reach the conclusion that in hemes of hemoproteins, particularly of Mb and Hb, the high-spin and low-spin states are separated by very small energy intervals, in comparison with ordinary atomic excitation energies which are of the order of several electron volts. This is our basic assumption, and we will proceed to examine the meaning of this assumption in the light of ligand field theory.

In applying the ligand field theory, the symmetry of the ligand field around the Fe ion is of primary importance. Since the Fe ion in a heme is nearly coordinated by six electronegative atoms, four nitrogens of porphyrin, a nitrogen of im do :ole and the sixth ligand such as N, O and F, cubic symmetry O_h may be assumed as the first rough approximation. Tetragonal symmetry C_{4v} is the next approximation, and the interpretation of some experimental results makes it necessary to take into account the rhombic part of the ligand field.

There are five independent d orbitals which have a common energy in the free ion. In a cubic ligand field, this common energy is split into two: dϵ and dγ; dϵ and dγ comprise three orbitals and two orbitals, respectively. The explicit forms of wave functions for these orbitals are as follows (provided that distortion due to the ligand field is negligible):

$$d\gamma : d_{x^2-y^2} = \frac{1}{2} CR(r)(x^2 - y^2), \qquad d_{z^2} = \frac{1}{\sqrt{12}} CR(r)(2z^2 - x^2 - y^2),$$

$$d\epsilon : d_{yz} = CR(r)yz, \qquad d_{zx} = CR(r)zx, \qquad d_{xy} = CR(r)xy$$

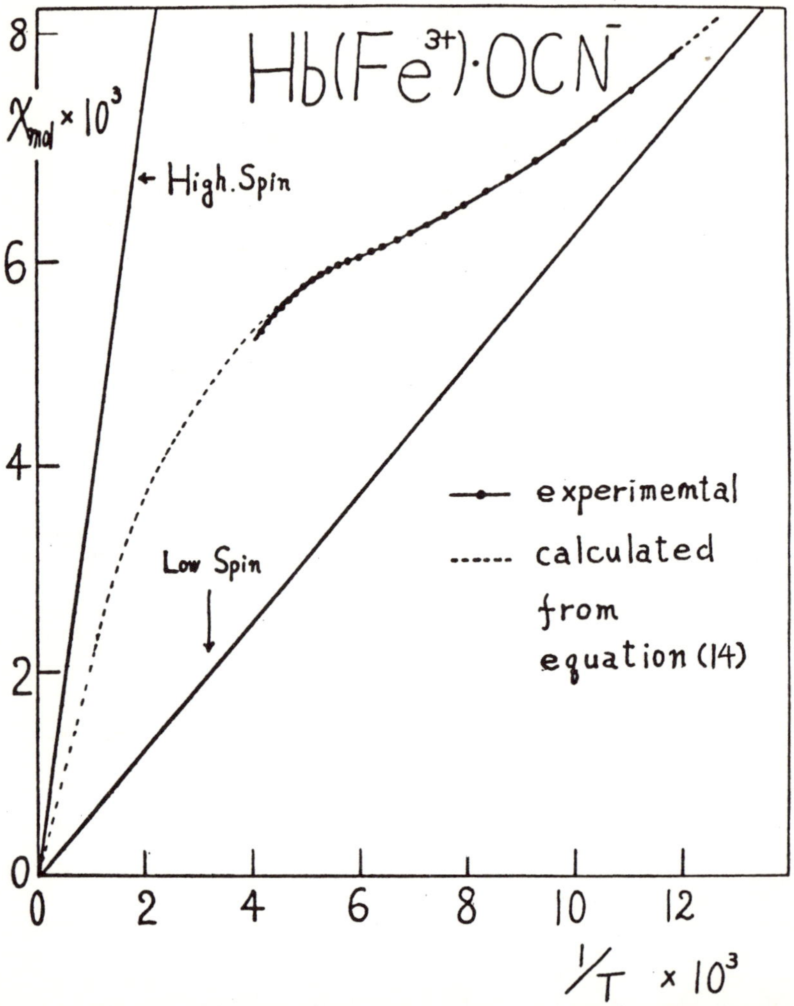

FIGURE 5. Temperature dependence of the magnetic susceptibility of Hb(Fe^{3+})OCN^-. Transition from low-spin state to high-spin state actually occurs in this temperature region. Broken line is the result calculated by use of Equation ( ) when $\epsilon = 249$ cm^{-1} and $\gamma = 0.328$. (For the meaning of ϵ and γ, see text.)

These orbitals constitute an orthonormal set, if R(r) is normalized by

$$\int_0^\infty R(r)^2 r^6 \, dr = 1 \quad \text{and} \quad C = \sqrt{\frac{15}{4\pi}}.$$

In octahedral coordination, $d\gamma$ is higher than $d\epsilon$, and this separation in energy will be denoted by Δ.

In a ferric ion, there are five electrons in d orbitals when each orbital has one electron, and the electron configuration is $(d\epsilon)^3(d\gamma)^2$, the state of the total sys-

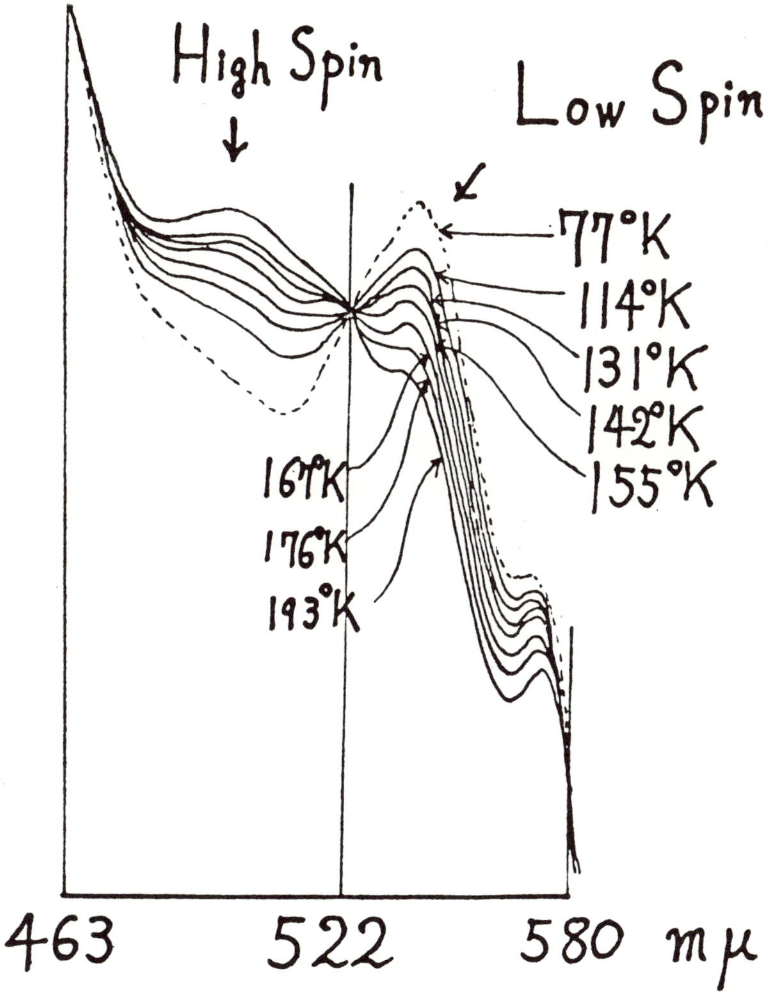

FIGURE 6. Temperature dependence of optical absorption spectra of Hb(Fe^{3+})OCN^- between 77° K and 200° K.

tem is spin sextet, orbitally nondegenerate and totally symmetric. This is denoted by $^6A_{1g}$. Thus, the high-spin state is

$$(d\epsilon)^3(d\gamma)^2\ {}^6A_{1g}.$$

On the other hand, the lowest low-spin is obtained by putting all electrons in $d\epsilon$. Since there are five electrons, two orbitals of $d\epsilon$ must accommodate pairs of electrons with antiparallel spins, and one orbital accepts a single electron with unpaired spin. Since three choices of this orbital are possible, this spin-doublet state is orbitally triply degenerate. The notation for this state is

$$(d\epsilon)^5\ {}^2T_{2g}.$$

As far as orbital energy is concerned, ${}^6A_{1g}$ is higher than ${}^2T_{2g}$ by 2Δ. However, repulsive Coulomb interaction between electrons is less effective in high-spin states than in low-spin states because the Pauli principle reduces the probability of close approach of two electrons with parallel spins. Actually, in the case of free ferric ion in which Δ vanishes, the ground state is ${}^6S$, which corresponds to ${}^6A_{1g}$, and the lowest doublet state, ${}^2I$, from which ${}^2T_{2g}$ is generated, is higher than ${}^6S$ by about 4.8 eV. Accordingly, when Δ is small the high-spin state must be lower than the low-spin state; but when Δ becomes large enough to overcompensate the difference of interelectronic Coulomb energy, the low-spin state becomes the ground state. Therefore, at some critical value of Δ, which we denote by Δ_c, the crossing of high-spin and low-spin states must occur. Our basic assumption then is that, in heme iron, Δ is very near to Δ_c.

A relatively low excited state, which is important in our theoretical discussion, is the lowest state with the intermediate spin $S = 3/2$. This state is obtained by promoting one electron from $d\epsilon$ to $d\gamma$ from ${}^2T_{2g}$, and is represented by

$$(d\epsilon)^4(d\gamma)\ {}^4T_{1g}.$$

In regard to orbital energy as well as interelectronic repulsive energy, this state is intermediate between ${}^6A_{1g}$ and ${}^2T_{2g}$. From this simple argument, we may expect relative positions of ${}^6A_{1g}$, ${}^2T_{2g}$, ${}^4T_{1g}$ as shown qualitatively in FIGURE 7. It may be noted that the excitation energy of ${}^4T_{1g}$ from the ground state is least at $\Delta = \Delta_c$. Therefore, in the case of Fe in hemes, a relatively low excited state with the intermediate spin is expected, although this state has not been observed experimentally so far. A rough estimate of the excitation energy is 6,000 cm^{-1} or about 3/4 eV.

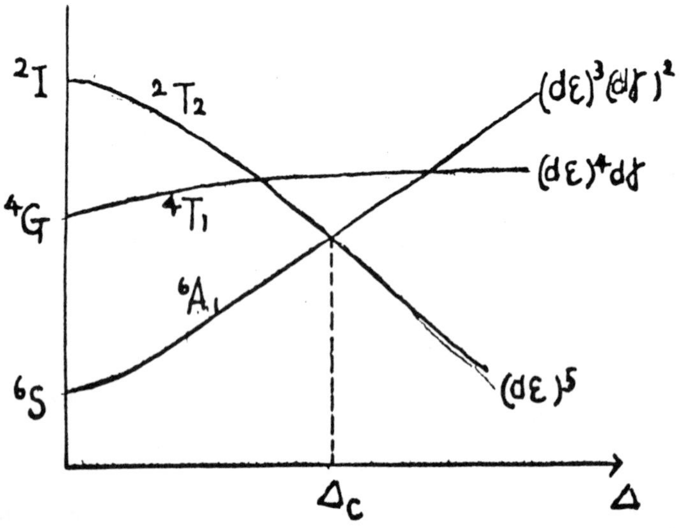

FIGURE 7. Schematic diagram of the low-lying energy states of F^{3+} ion $[(3d)^5]$ in cubic field.

Employing the perturbation method, quantum mechanical calculation of these and higher energy levels of d^n configuration in the cubic field was carried out by Tanabe and Sugano.[6,7] FIGURE 8 reproduces their diagram for the case of five d^5 electrons. In this diagram, the normal state is taken as zero of energy through all values of Δ, so that all energy levels have sharp bends at $\Delta = \Delta_c$. A similar situation applies in the case of ferrous ions in hemes. High-spin, low-spin and intermediate-spin states are:

$$(d\epsilon)^4(d\gamma)^2 \ {}^5T_{1g}$$

$$(d\epsilon)^6 \ {}^1A_{1g}$$

$$(d\epsilon)^5(d\gamma) \ {}^3T_{2g} \quad \text{and} \quad {}^3T_{1g}.$$

Here again, crossing of low-spin and high-spin takes place at $\Delta = \Delta_c'$, and the excitation energies to intermediate-spin states are smallest at this point (see FIGURE 9).

In this way, our basic assumption leads to the conclusion that Fe ions in hemes have many low excited states crowded together. Taking high-spin and low-spin states only, ferric and ferrous ions have 12 and 16 independent states, respectively, and these numbers increase to 24 and 34 if we include states of intermediate spin. In many cases, low- and high-spin states coexist at room temperature, and intermediate-spin states strongly affect the character of low- and high-spin states because of their low excitation energies. This means that Fe ions in hemes possess uniquely

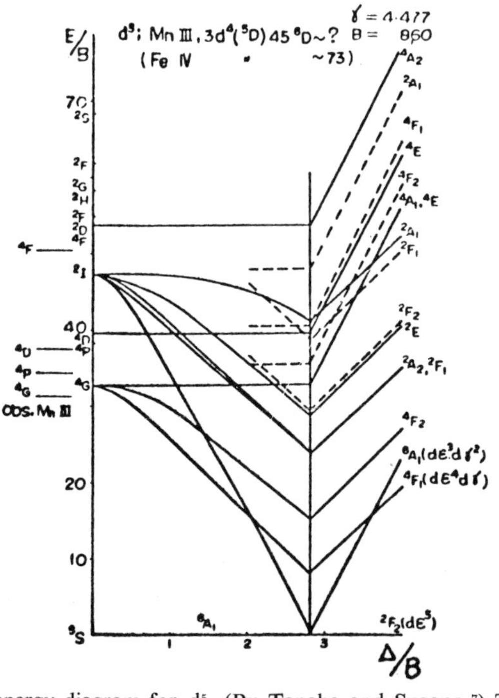

FIGURE 8. The energy diagram for d^5. (By Tanabe and Sugano.[7]) The notations F_2 and F_1 are identical to T_1 and T_2 used in this paper.

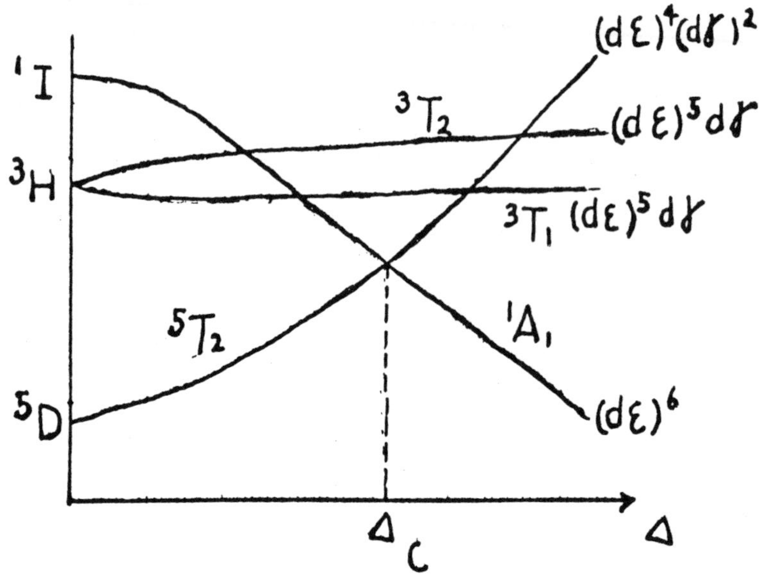

FIGURE 9. Schematic diagram of the low-lying energy states of Fe^{2+} ion $[(3d)^6]$.

flexible and adaptable electronic properties. This situation is seldom encountered in inorganic Fe complexes, and perhaps we may be allowed to say that this unique feature is characteristic of biological iron.

ELECTRON PARAMAGNETIC RESONANCE (EPR) STUDIES (HIGH-SPIN CASE)

Gibson, Ingram and their collaborators have shown in their classical work on EPR studies on $Mb(Fe^{3+})H_2O$ and $Hb(Fe^{3+})H_2O$ single crystals that hemes in these substances show highly anisotropic EPR signals.[8] In terms of g value defined by

$$h\nu = g\beta H,$$

where ν is the frequency of microwave, β is the Bohr magneton, H is the intensity of the magnetic field at which absorption occurs, $g \doteqdot 6.0$ when the magnetic field is parallel to the heme plane, whereas $g \doteqdot 2.0$ when it is perpendicular to this plane. From the variation of g-values with the direction of applied magnetic field relative to the crystallographic axes, they have succeeded in determining orientations of heme planes in the crystals. In the case of Mb there are two different orientations; in the case of Hb there are four (as shown in FIGURE 10). The results show that the spin sextet ${}^6A_1$ is split into three doublets already in zero field, and the signal comes from the lowest doublet corresponding to $S_z = \pm 1/2$. It is easy to show that, on applying the magnetic field, this doublet is split in such a way that $g = 2S + 1$ when the field is parallel to the heme plane. This gives $2S + 1 = 6$ or $S = 5/2$. I believe that this is the most conclusive evidence for this particular value of S.

From theoretical ground, the zero-field splitting of spin sextet can be expressed by a quadratic spin Hamiltonian, of which the most general formula is

$$D\{S_z^2 - 1/3S(S+1)\} + E(S_x^2 - S_y^2) \qquad (5)$$

This formula contains two parameters, D and E. Identifying z-direction with the

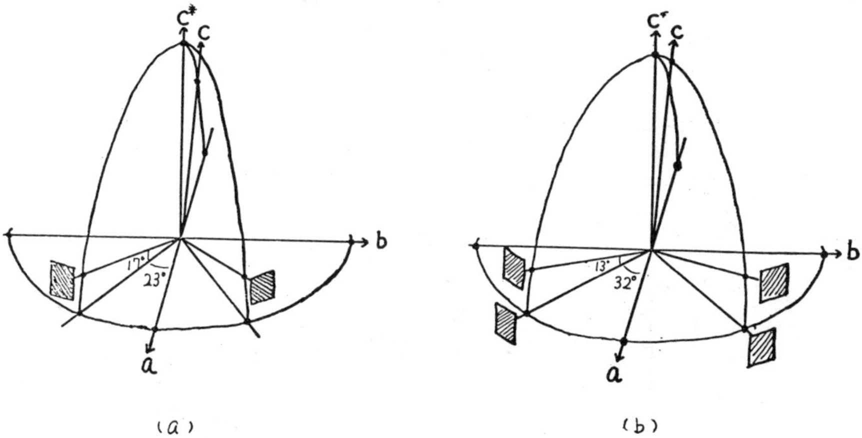

FIGURE 10. Orientations of hemes in the unit cell of the crystal for $Mb(Fe^{3+})H_2O$ (sperm-whale type A) (a) and $Hb(Fe^{3+})H_2O$ (horse) (b).

normal to the heme plane, E measures the anisotropy within the heme plane. According to Gibson and Ingram, E is very small in comparison with D. If E is zero, three doublets are represented by $S_z = +1/2$, $S_z = +3/2$ and $S_z = +5/2$, and the energy intervals are 2D ($S_z = +1/2$ to $+3/2$) and 4D ($+3/2$ to $+5/2$). EPR measurements have given the lower limit to D as $D \gtrsim 5\ cm^{-1}$, but have been unable to determine its absolute magnitude.

The presence of small, but nonvanishing E has been confirmed by Morimoto on single crystals of $Mb(Fe^{3+})H_2O$ and $Mb(Fe^{3+})F^-$. If E is taken into account, the g-value is not constant when the magnetic field is rotated in the heme plane, but varies according to the formula

$$g = 6 - 24\frac{E}{D}\cos 2\varphi,$$

where φ is the azimuth of the magnetic field measured from the x-direction. This sinusoidal variation is actually observed as shown in FIGURE 11, and E/D is determined as follows:

$$\frac{E}{D} = \begin{cases} 0.002_5 & \text{for}\quad Mb(Fe^{3+})H_2O \\ 0.003_8 & \text{for}\quad Mb(Fe^{3+})F^-. \end{cases}$$

Recently, larger values of E/D have been found for M-type abnormal human hemoglobins. Hayashi and collaborators have observed the splitting of the signal at $g = 6.0$ on Hb M_{Boston}, Hb $M_{Saskatoon}$ and Hb $M_{Hyde\ Park}$ in patients' blood, as

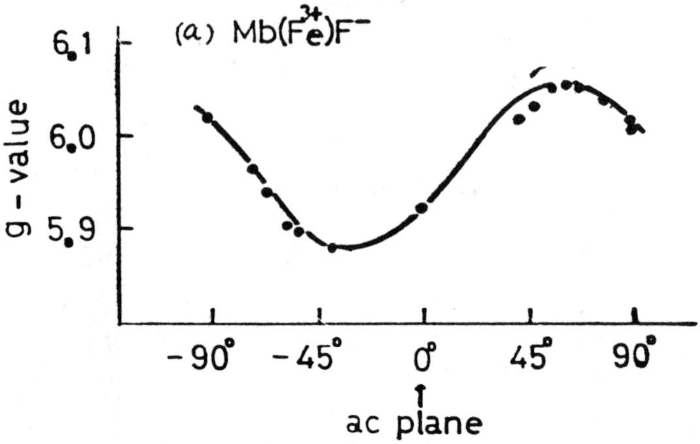

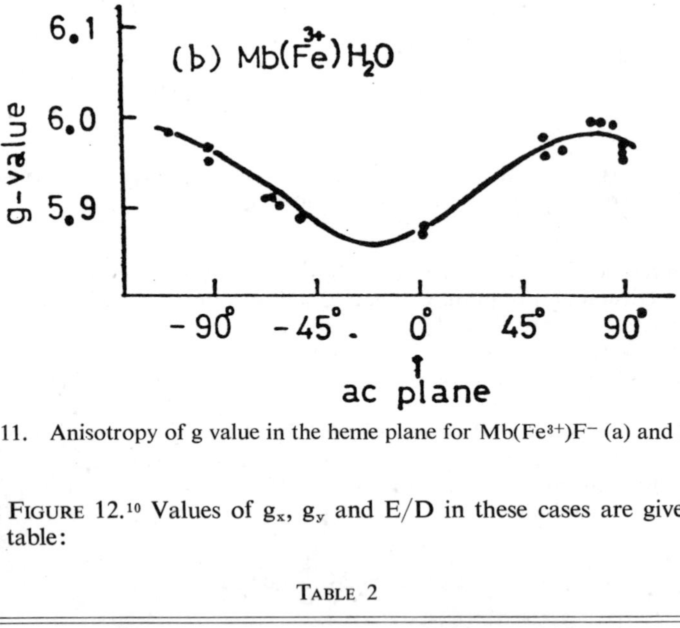

FIGURE 11. Anisotropy of g value in the heme plane for $Mb(Fe^{3+})F^-$ (a) and $Mb(Fe^{3+})H_2O$ (b).

shown in FIGURE 12.[10] Values of g_x, g_y and E/D in these cases are given in the following table:

TABLE 2

	g_x	g_y	E/D
Hb M_{Boston}	6.30	5.71	0.012
Hb $M_{Saskatoon}$	6.6_5	5.3_5	0.027
Hb $M_{Hyde\ Park}$	6.31	5.68	0.015
Hb M_{Iwate}	6.2	5.8	0.008

PARAMAGNETIC SUSCEPTIBILITY AND ITS ANISOTROPY (FERRIC HIGH-SPIN CASE)

The value of parameter D in the spin-Hamiltonian that could not be obtained from EPR measurements can be determined from the analysis of temperature de-

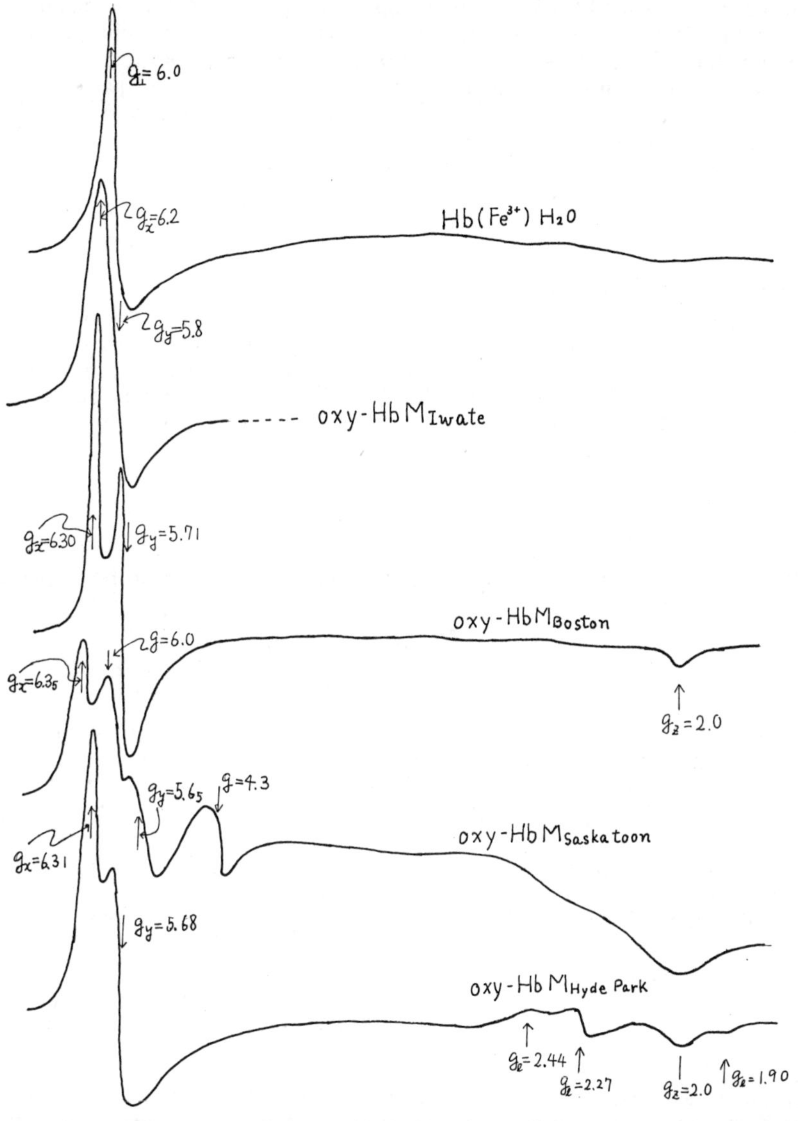

FIGURE 12. EPR spectra of the patient's blood containing M-type abnormal Hb's EPR spectrum for normal acid ferrihemoglobin ($Hb(Fe^{3+})H_2O$) is added for the sake of comparison. Main signals for all these Hb's are indicated by g_x, g_y and g_z. But a few kinds of signals other than these are seen in the spectra of oxy-$HbM_{Saskatoon}$ and oxy-$HbM_{Hyde\ Park}$. Temperature: liquid nitrogen. Microwave frequency: 9200 Mc/s.

pendence of paramagnetic susceptibility and its anisotropy. For this purpose the measurements should cover the temperature range in which the thermal energy kT is comparable with excitation energies, 2D and 6D, of higher doublets within the sextet state $^6A_1$. In our laboratory, these measurements have been carried out over temperatures ranging from room temperature to liquid helium temperature.

In the case of assembly of noninteracting, randomly oriented, rigid magnets with magnetic moment $\mu = n\beta$, the paramagnetic part of the susceptibility is given by Equation 3. In crystals of hemoproteins, however, hemes are not randomly oriented, they have not only intrinsic magnetic moments but also induced parts, and these moments are different for different substates of the sextet. Hence, simple Curie's law (Equation 3) does not hold. Nevertheless, it is convenient to express the paramagnetic part of the susceptibility in a form similar to Equation 3:

$$\chi_{para} = N\frac{\beta^2 n_{eff}^{\ 2}}{3kT}. \tag{6}$$

In this case n_{eff} is temperature-dependent.

Quantum-mechanical theory of paramagnetic susceptibility is well established[11], so that only the results that concern us will be given here, without derivation. First, consider a fictitious crystal in which all the hemes are oriented parallel to each other. If spin-Hamiltonian $DS_z^{\ 2}$ is assumed for ferric ions, where z is the direction of the normals to the heme planes, this crystal is magnetically uniaxial; its susceptibility in z direction is given by Equation 6[12] with

$$n_{eff\,\parallel}^{\ \ 2} = \frac{3}{1 + e^{-2x} + e^{-6x}}(1 + 9e^{-2x} + 25e^{-6x}) \tag{7}$$

while its susceptibility in directions perpendicular to z (parallel to heme planes) is given by the same formula[12] with

$$n_{eff\,\perp}^{\ \ 2} = \frac{3}{1 + e^{-2x} + e^{-6x}}\left(9 + \frac{8}{x} - \frac{11}{2x}e^{-2x} - \frac{5}{2x}e^{-6x}\right) \tag{8}$$

In Equations 7 and 8, x is $= D/kT$. Suffices $\parallel$ and $\perp$ of n_{eff} denote parallel and perpendicular to z, i.e., to heme normals, and not to heme planes.

Mean Susceptibility

For isotropic samples of hemoproteins, such as a condensed solution in which orientations of hemes are random, only the mean susceptibility is measurable. The corresponding effective Bohr magneton number $n_{eff\,av}$ is given by

$$\begin{aligned} n_{eff\,av}^{\ \ 2} &= \tfrac{1}{3}\,n_{eff\,\parallel}^{\ \ 2} + \tfrac{2}{3}\,n_{eff\,\perp}^{\ \ 2} \\ &= \frac{1}{1 + e^{-2x} + e^{-6x}}\left\{19 + \frac{16}{x} + \left(9 - \frac{11}{x}\right)e^{-2x} + \left(25 - \frac{5}{x}\right)e^{-6x}\right\} \end{aligned} \tag{9}$$

$n_{eff\,\parallel}$, $n_{eff\,\perp}$ and $n_{eff\,av}$ are illustrated as functions of x in FIGURE 13. At high temperatures all n_{eff}'s converge to $\sqrt{35}$, which is the standard spin-only value $2\sqrt{S(S + 1)}$ for $S = 5/2$. In the low-temperature limit, only the lowest doublet, $S_z = \pm 1/2$, comes into play. This doublet is magnetically anisotropic, and gives $n_\parallel = \sqrt{3}$ and $n_\perp = 3\sqrt{3}$, with $n_{av} = \sqrt{19}$.

Such temperature dependence of n_{av} has been observed by Tasaki and Otsuka,[13] who measured the susceptibilities of various hemoprotein samples in paste form down to the liquid helium temperature. Results obtained by them for ferri-Mb are easy to interpret. FIGURE 14 shows the temperature dependence of observed $n_{eff\,av}$ for sample of sperm-whale Mb. They tried to fit the observed curve by the theoretical formula (Equation 9) by adjusting the value of parameter D. Best fit was ob-

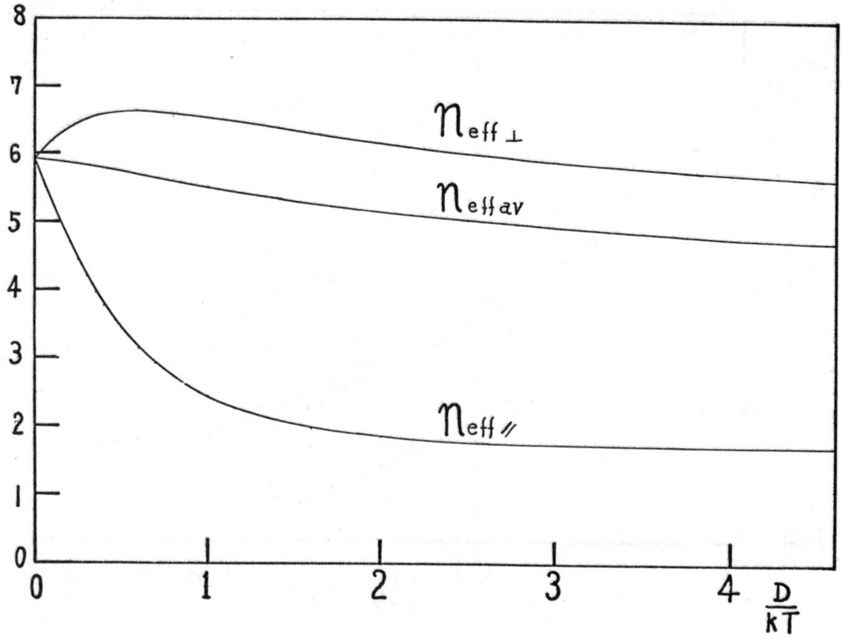

FIGURE 13. Effective Bohr magneton number calculated from spin Hamiltonian $H_s = DS_z^2 + 2\beta\, HS$.

tained by taking $D = 10\ cm^{-1}$; the theoretical function for this choice of D is shown in the Figure by a broken curve.

Hemoproteins other than $Mb(Fe^{3+})H_2O$ seem to give $n_{eff\ av}$ curves which deviate more or less from theoretical curve corresponding to Equation 9 for the high-spin case. The most important reason for this deviation may be coexistence of high-spin and low-spin molecules. For instance, $Hb(Fe^{3+})H_2O$ gives lower values of $n_{eff\ av}$ than those given in Equation 9. This suggests the coexistence of high spin and low spin in $Hb(Fe^{3+})H_2O$. Thermal mixing of high spin and low spin will be discussed in more detail elsewhere.

Anisotropy of Paramagnetism in Single Crystals

As shown in the preceding section, hemes manifest strong paramagnetic anisotropy. This anisotropy may be characterized by

$$\Delta(n_{eff}^2) \equiv n_{eff\perp}^2 - n_{eff\parallel}^2 \tag{10}$$

$$= \frac{3}{1 + e^{-2x} + e^{-6x}} \left\{ 8\left(1 + \frac{1}{x}\right) - \left(\frac{11}{2x} + 9\right)e^{-2x} - 5\left(\frac{1}{2x} + 5\right)e^{-6x} \right\}$$

This anisotropy can be observed by measuring the torque exerted on single crystal samples in a magnetic field.

Consider a single crystal sample of hemoprotein suspended in a horizontal uniform magnetic field, H, in such a way that the sample can rotate around the vertical axis. Then the susceptibility of the crystal in the horizontal plane depends on the

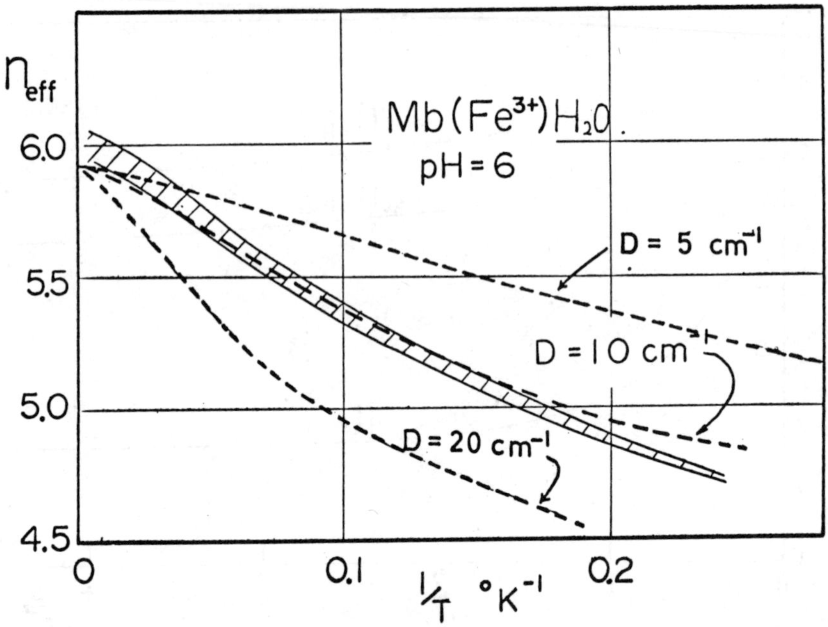

FIGURE 14. Temperature dependence of the effective Bohr magneton number calculated from the experimentally obtained magnetic susceptibility of $Mb(Fe^{3+})H_2O$. The shaded area shows its error limits. The broken line shows the theoretical curves for D = 5, 10 and 20 cm^{-1}.

azimuth of the applied magnetic field H. If the azimuth φ is measured from one of the directions of principal axes, in the plane, the angular dependence of the suseptibility is given by

$$\chi = \tfrac{1}{3}(2\chi_\perp + \chi_\parallel) + (\chi_\perp - \chi_\parallel)C\cos 2\varphi,$$

where $\chi_\perp$ and $\chi_\parallel$ are susceptibilities of a fictitious sample containing all hemes in parallel orientation, in the directions perpendicular and parallel to heme normals, respectively, and C is a constant which depends on orientations of hemes in the actual crystal.

Now the crystal will be exerted by a torque if χ depends on φ. Since the magnetic energy is $-1/2\chi H^2$, the torque L is given by

$$L = -\frac{1}{\partial\varphi}\left(-\frac{1}{2}\chi H^2\right)$$

$$= C(\chi_\perp - \chi_\parallel)\sin 2\varphi H^2$$

Expressing $\chi_\perp$ and $\chi_\parallel$ in terms of n_{eff}'s, we have

$$L = N\frac{\beta^2}{3kT}C\,\Delta(n_{eff}{}^2)\sin 2\varphi\cdot H^2$$

It is interesting to note that products of NC and $\Delta(n_{eff}{}^2)$ can be determined from torque measurement, in which the latter factor is expected to vary according to the theoretical formula Equation 10. The factor NC yields information about the distribution of directions of heme normals. Dependence of C on the choice of axis of suspension will increase the amount of information of the latter nature.

Since C is expected to be independent of temperature, we can check the theoretically predicted temperature dependence of $\Delta(n_{eff}^2)$ even without complete knowledge about C, and thereby determine the value of D. FIGURE 15 shows the theoretical curves of $\Delta(n_{eff}^2)$ and the experimentally obtained data at the temperatures obtained by controlling the vapor pressure of liquid nitrogen, liquid hydrogen and liquid helium. To plot the data, the following values of D are used that fit the data to theoretical curve best.

$$\begin{aligned} D &= 10.5\ \mathrm{cm}^{-1} && \text{for}\quad Mb(Fe^{3+})H_2O \\ &= 6.5\ \mathrm{cm}^{-1} && \text{for}\quad Mb(Fe^{3+})F^- \\ &= 11.2\ \mathrm{cm}^{-1} && \text{for}\quad Hb(Fe^{3+})H_2O \\ &= 6.0\ \mathrm{cm}^{-1} && \text{for}\quad Hb(Fe^{3+})F^- \end{aligned}$$

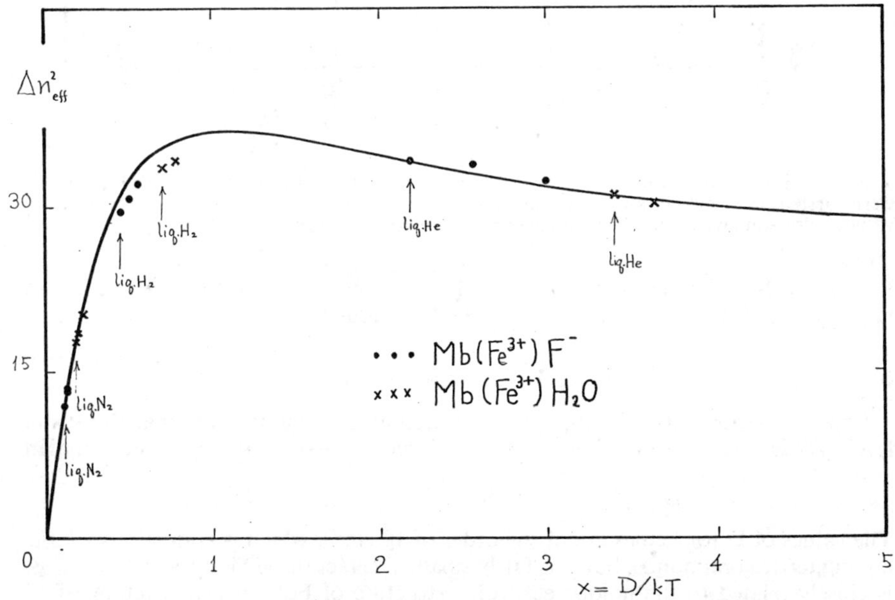

FIGURE 15a. Comparison between the theoretical curves (Δn_{eff}^2 vs D/kT) and experimentally obtained values for $Mb(Fe^{3+})H_2O$ and $Mb(Fe^{3+})F^-$. Measurements were carried on type A myoglobin single crystals in the ab plane. D was determined from temperature dependence of Δn_{eff}^2 (see text). Using this D, the data were plotted in the figure. Since experimental values were somewhat larger, they were reduced by a certain factor common to all the values for the same sample in order to see temperature dependence only.

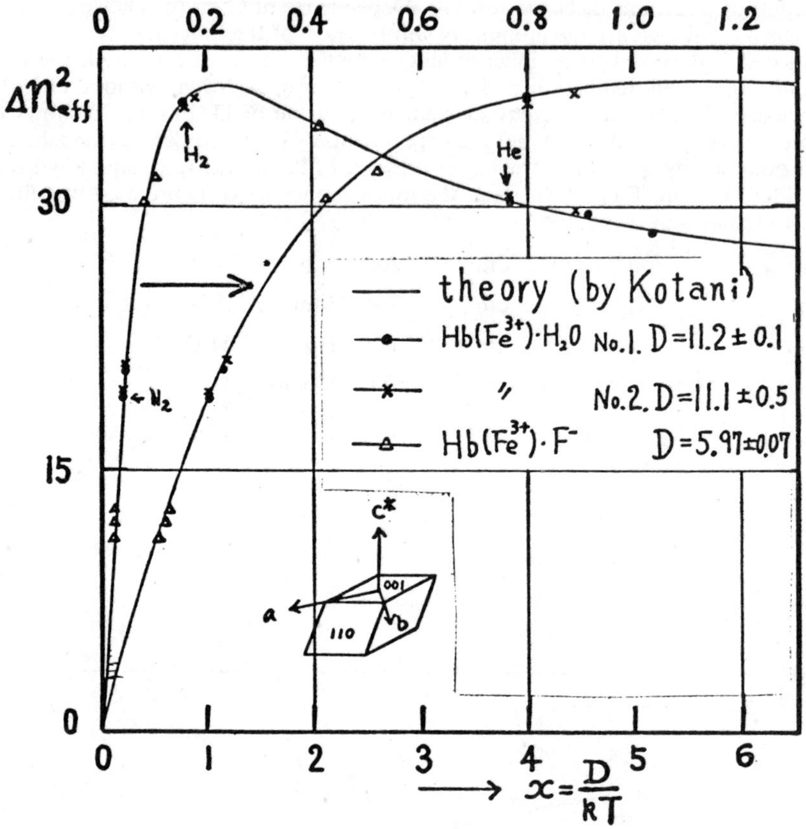

FIGURE 15b. The same figure as (a) for $Hb(Fe^{3+})H_2O$ and $Hb(Fe^{3+})F^-$. Measurements were carried on horse hemoglobin single crystals in the ab plane. In this case, experimental values were somewhat smaller; they were multiplied by a common factor.

Results for $Mb(Fe^{3+})H_2O$ and $Mb(Fe^{3+})F^-$ are consistent with those derived from mean susceptibility measurements described previously.

Theoretical Interpretation of D and E

Experimental results described in the preceding sections indicate that the sextet level $^6A_1$ is the split into three doublets as represented by the spin-Hamiltonian

$$D\{S_z^2 - \tfrac{1}{3}S(S+1)\} + E(S_x^2 - S_y^2),$$

The values of D for hemes are of the order of 10 cm^{-1}, which is anomalously large among ferric compounds, but E is fairly small. The fact that D is anomalously large is closely related to the unique electronic structure of Fe^{3+} in hemes (emphasized in the section above on the electronic structure of Fe in hemes).

It seems reasonable to assume that the local symmetry at the Fe ion is lower than cubic, and the deviation of the ligand field from cubic gives rise to the splitting of $^6A_1$. However, the ground state is orbitally totally symmetric, and the spin cannot "feel" the ligand field directly. Spin-orbit interaction $a\,\Sigma 1_i \cdot s_i$ relates spin to orbitals, but matrix elements of this interaction vanish within the sextet $^6A_1$.

It can be shown, however, that spin-orbit interaction combines the ground state $^6A_{1g}$ with quartet states $^4T_{1g}$. It was found (in the section on Fe in hemes) that there is one $^4T_{1g}$ state whose excitation energy is very low. Then $^6A_{1g}$ mixes somewhat with $^4T_{1g}$ through spin-orbit interaction. As long as the symmetry is cubic, this mixing yields only a common shift of all six substates of $^6A_{1g}$. But if the symmetry is lowered to tetragonal, $^4T_{1g}$ itself is split into two levels, $^4A_2$ and ^4E, and then the shift may be different for different substates. This produces splitting of $^6A_{1g}$, as represented by $DS_z{}^2$. This consideration leads to the following formula for D:

$$D = k^2 \frac{a^2}{5} \left\{ \frac{1}{E(^4A_2) - E(^6A_1)} - \frac{1}{E(^4E) - E(^6A_1)} \right\}, \qquad \textbf{(11)}$$

where a is the coefficient of spin-orbit interaction and k is a numerical constant that depends on configuration interaction. In good approximation, k can be taken as unity. In Equation 11, we see that the low excitation energy of $^4T_{1g}$ is closely related to the large value of D.

According to Equation 11, the sign of D depends on the relative positions of $^4A_2$ and ^4E; D is positive if $^4A_2$ is lower. Now, $^4T_{1g}$ had four electrons in $d\epsilon$ shell, of which three have plus spins and one has a minus spin. In $^4A_2$, this electron with a minus spin occupies d_{xy} orbital, whereas in ^4E this occupies d_{xz} or d_{yz} orbitals. Hence $D > 0$ requires that the energy of orbital d_{xy} be lower than that of d_{xz} or d_{yz}. This conclusion is useful for our discussion of ferric low-spin EPR measurements.

More detailed theoretical analysis based on ligand field theory has been made by Otsuka,[14] taking higher excited states into account. FIGURE 16, reproduced from his paper, gives the contour map of D in the ZY plane, where 3/2Z is the separation of orbital energies of d_{xz}, d_{yz} and d_{xy}, and 2Y is the separation of orbital energies of $d_{x^2-y^2}$ and d_{z^2}. Racah parameters, which are measures of interelectronic Coulomb interaction, were chosen as $B = 820\ cm^{-1}$, $C/B = 4.7$, and spin-orbit interaction coefficient a was assumed to be $=400\ cm^{-1}$. The distance between the center of gravity of $d\gamma$ orbitals and that of $d\epsilon$ was taken fized at Δ_c. If the symmetry of the ligand field is further reduced to rhombic, ^4E is split into two sublevels ^4E_x and ^4E_y, in which electron with minus spin is accommodated in d_{xz} and d_{yz}, respectively. This situation gives nonvanishing E:

$$E = k^2 \frac{a^2}{10} \left\{ \frac{1}{E(^4E_x) - E(^6A_1)} - \frac{1}{E(^4E_y) - E(^6A_1)} \right\}$$

The smallness of E indicates that d_{xz} and d_{yz} have almost the same energy in hemes in high-spin state.

STUDIES OF LOW-SPIN FERRIC STATES

Ferric hemes in number of hemoprotein derivatives give EPR signals characteristic of low-spin states. Imidazol derivatives and azides are examples. They give three widely separated principal g values. For instance, $Mb(Fe^{3+})N_3^-$[15] gives

$$g_{x'} = 1.73, \qquad g_{y'} = 2.22, \qquad g_z = 2.80$$

where the z axis is in the direction of heme normal, x′, y′ are two orthogonal directions in the heme plane.

In low-spin state $S = \frac{1}{2}$, five electrons are accommodated in three $d\epsilon$ orbitals, so that we have three configurations $d_{xz}{}^2d_{yz}{}^2d_{xy}$, $d_{xz}{}^2d_{yz}d_{xy}{}^2$ and $d_{xz}d_{yz}{}^2d_{xy}{}^2$. These

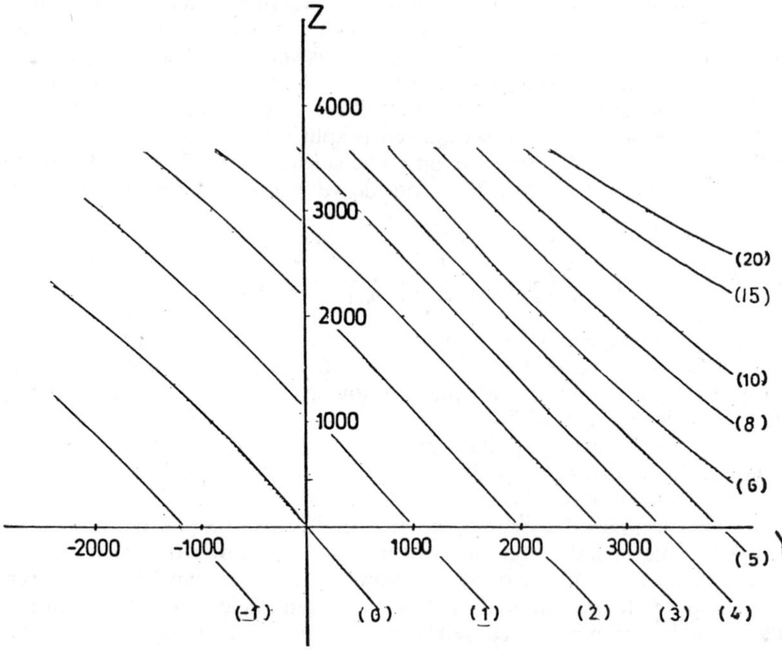

FIGURE 16. The value of D for various Y and Z when Δ is equal to 28.35B. (For the definition of Y, Z, B and Δ, see text.) The values of D are indicated in parentheses in cm^{-1}, where B and a are taken as 820 cm^{-1}, and 400 cm^{-1}, respectively.

configurations give a single level $^2T_{2g}$ under cubic symmetry. In the field of rhombic and lower symmetries these three configurations have different energies, so that we have three low-lying doublet states. However, if the ground state corresponds exactly to one of the above three configurations, say $d_{xz}d_{yz}{}^2d_{xy}{}^2$, its magnetic moment must come from the spin of the electron in d_{xz}, and g should be nearly isotropic and $\doteqdot 2.0$. Experiments show, however, that the principal g values are very much different from 2.0 as given above. This is due to the mixing of three configurations caused by spin-orbit interaction; this mixing allows orbital magnetic moment residual in $d\epsilon$ to make some contribution to the magnetic moment of the lowest doublet.

If the orbital energies ϵ_{xz}, ϵ_{yz}, ϵ_{xy} and the coefficient a of spin-orbit interaction were known, the mixing mentioned above could be calculated and principal g values of the lowest doublet could be obtained. By using the reverse procedure, orbital energies can be derived from observed principal g values.[12,16] The results obtained for $Mb(Fe^{3+})N_3^-$ are as follows:

$$\epsilon_{yz} - \epsilon_{xy} = 5.94a, \qquad \epsilon_{xz} - \epsilon_{xy} = 3.54a$$

This shows that among the three $d\epsilon$ orbitals d_{xy} lies lowest. This is in agreement with results obtained from ferric high-spin state; a is $\doteqdot 435$ cm^{-1} in free ion, but in complexes a may be smaller. Taking a = 350 cm^{-1}, d_{yz} and d_{xz} are located above d_{xy} by about 2000 cm^{-1} and 1200 cm^{-1}. The separations of three doublet states are of this order of magnitude, which is very small in comparison with ordinary excitation energy in atoms, although it is higher than thermal energy kT at room temperature.

It is remarkable that the separation between d_{yz} and d_{xz} is not much smaller than the separation between d_{xz} and d_{xy} in $Mb(Fe^{3+})N_3^-$. This corresponds to the large difference of g_x and g_y, and indicates a strong rhombicity of the heme iron. In the high-spin case, however, E is very much smaller than D, and the symmetry is almost tetragonal. This lowering of symmetry in $Mb(Fe^{3+})N_3^-$ seems to arise from two causes. The first is the direct electrostatic influence of N_3^- ion on d orbitals. From x-ray analysis[17] N_3^- has been shown to be attached to heme in oblique orientation, and its electrostatic interactions with d_{xz} and d_{yz} are very different. The second cause is the Jahn-Teller effect. In a symmetric heme with tetragonal symmetry, two doublets $d_{xz}d_{yz}^2d_{xy}^2$ and $d_{xz}^2d_{yz}d_{xy}^2$ should have the same energy. Now, by introducing rhombicity, e.g., by distorting the square formed by four pyrrole nitrogens into a rhombus, d_{xz} and d_{yz} get separated and the energy one of the doublets will decrease. Too large a distortion will be resisted by vibrational energy of porphyrin, but the system will be stabilized by a certain amount of spontaneous distortion. This is the basic idea of the Jahn-Teller effect. The first cause is specific to the sixth ligand, but the second one is not. Since many Mb and Hb derivatives with low spin—including hydrooxides—show EPR signals similar to azides, the second cause (Jahn-Teller effect) seems to be important. Detailed calculation for the case of the azide has been made by Mizuhashi and Kamimura.[18]

Thermal Equilibrium Between High-Spin and Low-Spin States

In some hemoprotein derivatives the high-spin and low-spin states coexist in thermal equilibrium at room temperatures, and give intermediate values of effective Bohr magneton number. Recently, Iizuka found that this phenomenon is fairly common in many ferri-Mb and ferri-Hb derivatives[5] by extending measurements of the mean susceptibility to lower temperatures down to 77° K. Some of the results are shown in Figure 17.

If the high-spin state is above the low-spin state by an energy ϵ, and the statistical weights of these states are w_h and w_l, then the probabilities of finding a heme in low-spin state and in high-spin state are

$$\alpha = \frac{w_l}{w_l + w_h e^{-\epsilon/kT}} \quad \text{and} \quad 1 - \alpha = \frac{w_h e^{-\epsilon/kT}}{w_l + w_h e^{-\epsilon/kT}} \tag{12}$$

respectively. Here, we have ignored the splitting of the high-spin sextet because this splitting is not so important in the temperature range above 77° K. Sister doublets born from $^2T_{2g}$ are also ignored because they are considered too high to be significant, even at room temperature.

α can be evaluated from observed susceptibility or effective Bohr magneton number n_{eff}. If the values of n_{eff} in low-spin state and in high-spin state are denoted by $n_{eff,l}$ and $n_{eff,h}$, respectively, n_{eff} for the hemoprotein is given by

$$n_{eff}^2 = \alpha n_{eff,l}^2 + (1 - \alpha) n_{eff,h}^2 \tag{13}$$

In the temperature range concerned, $n_{eff,l}^2$ and $n_{eff,h}^2$ are nearly 5 and 35, respectively, in good approximation. Thus, α can be determined by the formula

$$n_{eff}^2 = 35 - 30\alpha$$

as function of temperature.

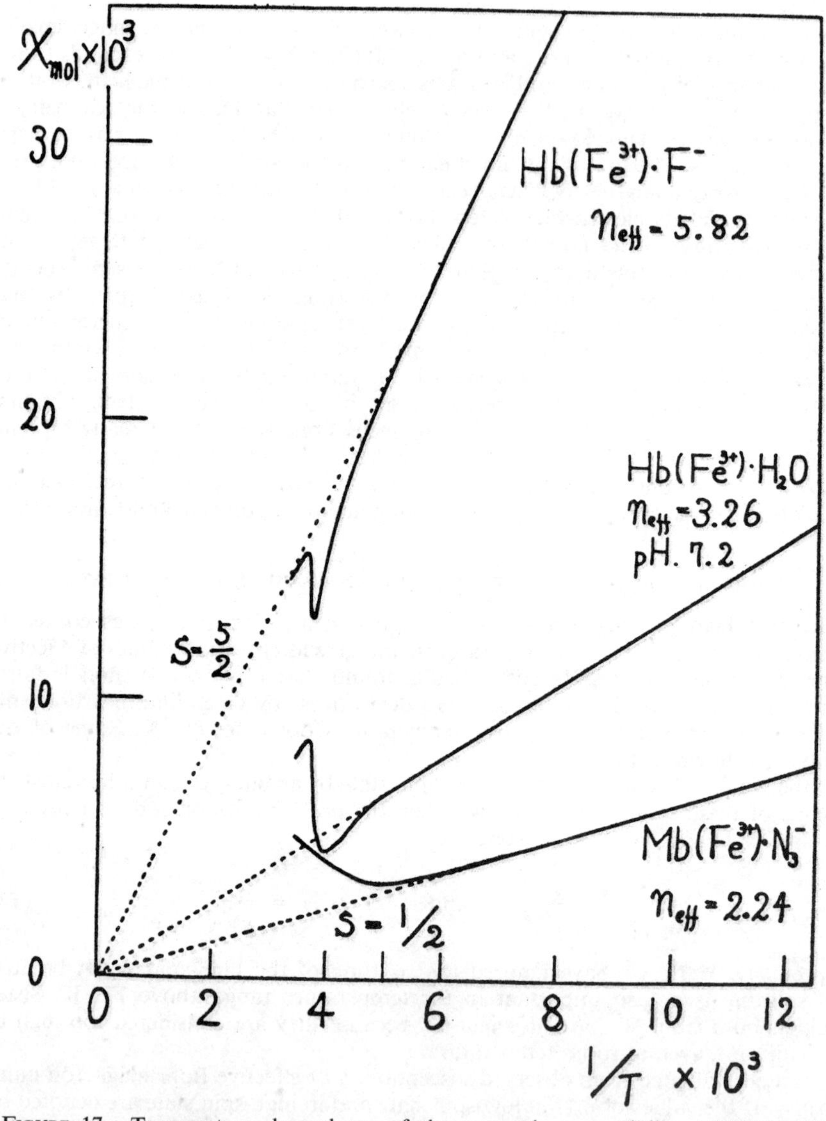

FIGURE 17. Temperature dependence of the magnetic susceptibility of $Hb(Fe^{3+})F^-$, $Hb(Fe^{3+})H_2O$ and $Mb(Fe^{3+})N_3^-$. Susceptibilities of these derivatives all show the deviation from the proportionality to inverse temperature. Hb derivatives also show the marked change in susceptibility at ice point.

In regard to the statistical weights, $w_l = 2$ and $w_h = 6$ if spin weight only is counted. Taking into account possible changes of weights due to other degrees of freedom, such as vibration and internal rotation, we write

$$\frac{w_h}{w_l} = 3\gamma$$

Then we have

$$\frac{\alpha}{1-\alpha} = \frac{1}{3\gamma} e^{\epsilon/kT} \tag{14}$$

FIGURE 18 shows the plot of $\log \alpha/(1-\alpha)$ vs $1/T$ for $Hb(Fe^{3+})OCN^-$, $Hb(Fe^{3+})F^-$ and $Mb(Fe^{3+})N_3^-$. Observed points for each substance fall fairly well on a straight

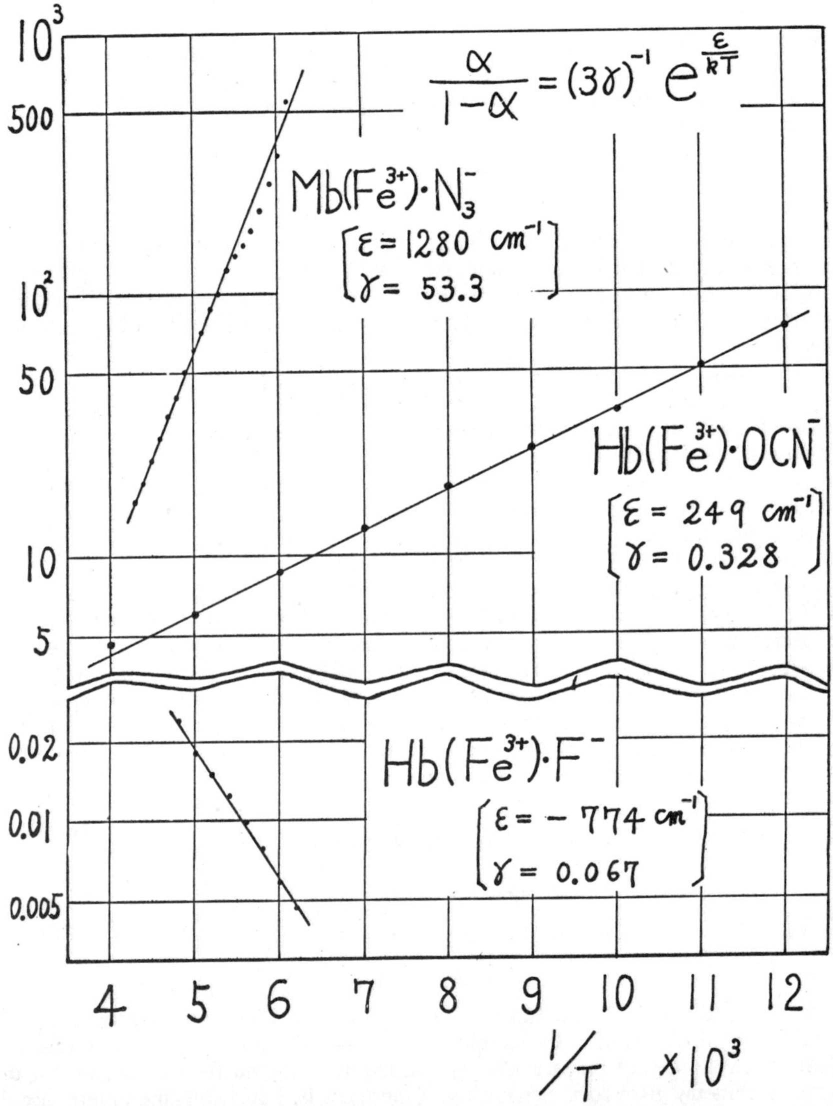

FIGURE 18. Analysis of the thermal equilibrium between high-spin and low-spin states. α denotes the proportion of the low-spin state, whereas $(1-\alpha)$ denotes that of high-spin state.

line. From the slope and the position of the straight line ϵ and γ can be determined. The results are given in the following Table:

TABLE 3

	ϵ	γ
$Hb(Fe^{3+})OCN^-$	$+249\ cm^{-1}$	0.328
$Mb(Fe^{3+})N_3^-$	$+1280\ cm^{-1}$	53.3
$Hb(Fe^{3+})F^-$	$-774\ cm^{-1}$	0.067

In $Hb(Fe^{3+})OCN^-$ and $Mb(Fe^{3+})N_3^-$ the low-spin state is the ground state, but in ferri-Hb·F^- the low-spin state lies higher than the high-spin state. Using these data, we can reproduce the temperature dependence of the susceptibility by the following equation:

$$\chi = \frac{N\beta^2}{3kT}\cdot 5\,\frac{e^x + 21\gamma}{e^x + 3\gamma} \qquad \left(x = \frac{\epsilon}{kT}\right) \qquad \textbf{(15)}$$

which can be derived from Equations 6, 13 and 14, and assuming $n_{eff}^2 = 35$ for high-spin state and 5 for low-spin state. Abnormal values of magnetic susceptibilities for some hemoprotiens at room temperature that have been measured by many workers since Pauling can be interpreted by a certain combination of values of ϵ and γ.

In most cases, especially in Hb derivatives, a sudden change of susceptibility is observed at the ice point 0° C. In the case of $Hb(Fe^{3+})F^-$, for instance, n_{eff} decreases with the increase of temperature below 0° C due to the mixing of low-spin state; but when the temperature increases through 0° C there occurs a sudden jump of n_{eff}, which rises to its low temperature value 5.92 again. The temperature dependence of visible spectra of these derivatives including the changes at ice point for Hb derivatives is consistent with the magnetic susceptibility data as described in the section on electronic structure of Fe in hemes.

It is surprising that the values of γ obtained are very much different from unity. For $Mb(Fe^{3+})N_3^-$, γ is greater than 1, whereas in $Hb(Fe^{3+})F^-$ it is less than 1. These unexpected values of γ seem to suggest that the high-spin state and the low-spin state are different not only in electronic structure of Fe ion, but also in the molecular structure in various parts of the protein. In order to clarify this point, dependence of γ on physical and chemical conditions of the protein has to be investigated; this may throw some light on the clarification of the mechanism—how the protein moiety can control the activity of the heme.

STUDIES OF HIGH-SPIN FERROUS CASE

Theoretical Consideration

In a field of cubic symmetry the ground state of a ferrous iron Fe^{2+} is

$$(d\epsilon)^4(d\gamma)^2\ {}^5T_{1g}$$

$5 \times 3 = 15$ independent eigenfunctions belong to this state. Spin-orbit interaction splits this into three levels with energies $-3/4a$, $-1/4a$ and $1/2a$. These levels are triplet, quintet and sept respectively. Introduction of ligand field of tetragonal or rhombic symmetry gives further splitting of these levels. Level splitting in tetragonal field was calculated by Otsuka,[14] and his result is illustrated in FIGURE 19. Some of

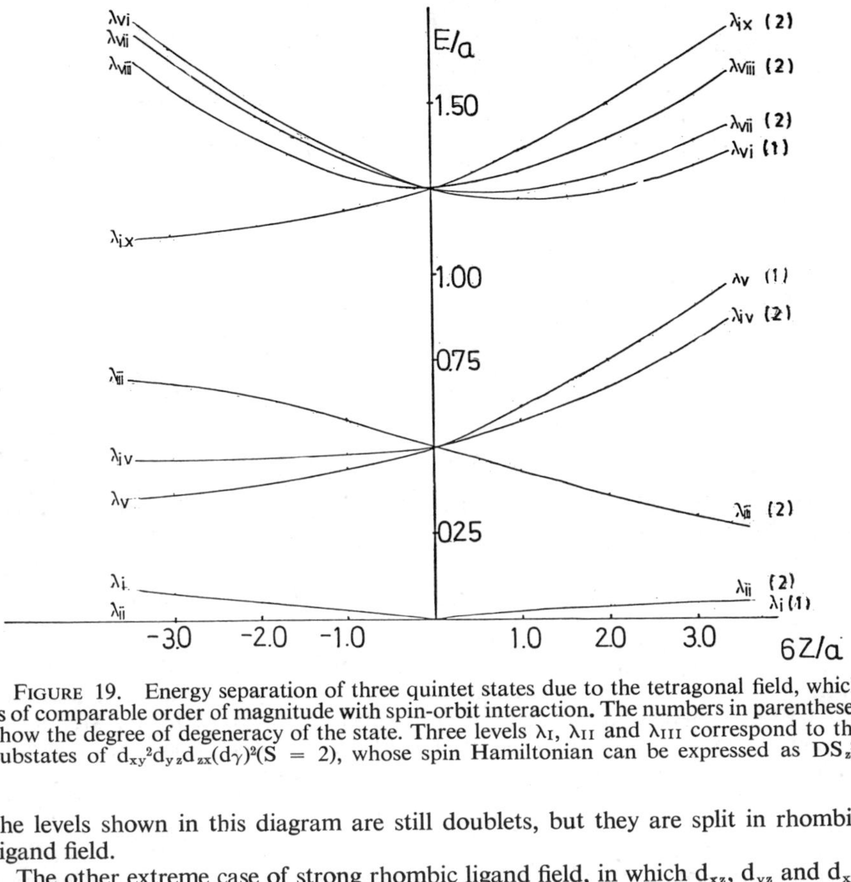

FIGURE 19. Energy separation of three quintet states due to the tetragonal field, which is of comparable order of magnitude with spin-orbit interaction. The numbers in parentheses show the degree of degeneracy of the state. Three levels λ_{I}, λ_{II} and λ_{III} correspond to the substates of $d_{xy}^2 d_{yz} d_{zx} (d\gamma)^2 (S = 2)$, whose spin Hamiltonian can be expressed as DS_z^2.

the levels shown in this diagram are still doublets, but they are split in rhombic ligand field.

The other extreme case of strong rhombic ligand field, in which d_{xz}, d_{yz} and d_{xy} are separated by energies much larger than spin-orbit interaction a, can be described in simple terms. If a is neglected, we have three spin quintets corresponding to the following configurations:

A $\quad d_{yz}^2\, d_{xz}\, d_{xy}\, (d\gamma)^2$

B $\quad d_{yz}\, d_{xz}^2\, d_{xy}\, (d\gamma)^2$

C $\quad d_{yz}\, d_{xz}\, d_{xy}^2\, (d\gamma)^2$

Introduction of spin-orbit interaction gives some mixing of these configurations, and each quintet is spit into five sublevels. In good approximation, the splitting of each quintet is represented by a quadratic spin-Hamiltonian. Spin-Hamiltonian for the quintet A is given by

$$D' S_x^2 + E'(S_y^2 - S_z^2),$$

where

$$D' = \frac{a^2}{32}\left(\frac{1}{\epsilon_{xz} - \epsilon_{yz}} + \frac{1}{\epsilon_{xy} - \epsilon_{yz}}\right)$$

$$E' = \frac{a^2}{32}\left(\frac{1}{\epsilon_{xz} - \epsilon_{yz}} - \frac{1}{\epsilon_{xy} - \epsilon_{yz}}\right)$$

Spin-Hamiltonians for states B and C can be obtained from these formulas by cyclic permutations of x, y, z.

An interesting situation arises when one of the dϵ orbitals is very high. For instance, if $\epsilon_{xy} \gg \epsilon_{xz} > \epsilon_{yz}$, we have $D' \doteqdot E' > 0$, so that the spin-Hamiltonian for A reduces to

$$D'(S_x^2 + S_y^2 - S_z^2) = \text{const.} - 2D'S_z^2 \qquad (16)$$

and the spin-Hamiltonian for B is

$$\text{const} + 2D'S_z^2$$

In this limiting case, spin-Hamiltonians become uniaxial and quintets are split into three levels—even in the rhombic field.

The general case in which the energy differences between dϵ orbitals are comparable with spin-orbit energy is complicated, and energy levels are obtained by solving secular equations of high orders. Readers are referred to Otsuka's paper[14] for further details.

Paramagnetic Anisotropy of Deoxy-Hb(Fe^{2+}) Crystal

Experimental data are not so numerous for ferrous states as for ferric states, although the former are more important for deoxy-Mb(Fe^{2+}) and deoxy-Hb(Fe^{2+}) from the viewpoint of their physiological activities. EPR has not been successful for ferrous hemes, which have an even number of electrons. In our laboratory, paramagnetic anisotropy of single crystals of deoxy-Hb(Fe^{2+}) has been measured at low temperatures, and this result will be briefly presented here.

Torque exerted on a suspended single crystal of deoxy-Hb(Fe^{2+}) by a horizontal magnetic field was measured, as described in the section on anisotrophy of paramagnetism in single crystals. The results are shown in FIGURE 20. It was noted that $\Delta(n_{eff}^2)$ increased monotonously as temperature was lowered from liquid nitrogen temperature to liquid helium temperature. If we may assume DS_z^2 for the spin-Hamiltonian, $\Delta(n_{eff}^2)$ takes the form:

$$\Delta(n_{eff}^2)/8 = \frac{\frac{9}{x} - \left(3 + \frac{7}{x}\right)e^{-x} - \left(12 + \frac{2}{x}\right)e^{-4x}}{1 + 2e^{-x} + 2e^{-4x}} \qquad (17)$$

where $x = D/kT$. If D is positive, $\Delta(n_{eff}^2)$ should have a maximum at an intermediate temperature, and observed points of $\Delta(n_{eff}^2)$ cannot be closely fitted by any choice of D. The observed points seem to be fitted by taking a negative value $-18\ cm^{-1}$ for D (for $D < 0$, Equation 17 is < 0, so that the absolute value of Equation 17 is to be taken for $\Delta(n_{eff}^2)$).

A plausible explanation for negative D is to assume that this D corresponds to $-2D'$ of Equation 16. If this interpretation is correct, the order in energy of dϵ orbitals is such that d_{xy} is sufficiently high, and the interval between d_{xz} and d_{yz} is larger than a. Both possibilities $\epsilon_{xz} \gtrless \epsilon_{yz}$ are allowed. It is to be noted, however, that other possibilities exist to have a uniaxial spin-Hamiltonian DS_i^2 with negative D, if i may be one of x, y and z. The necessary condition is that one of the dϵ orbitals be located very high. If this high dϵ orbital is d_{yz} or d_{xz}, then i is x or y. In these

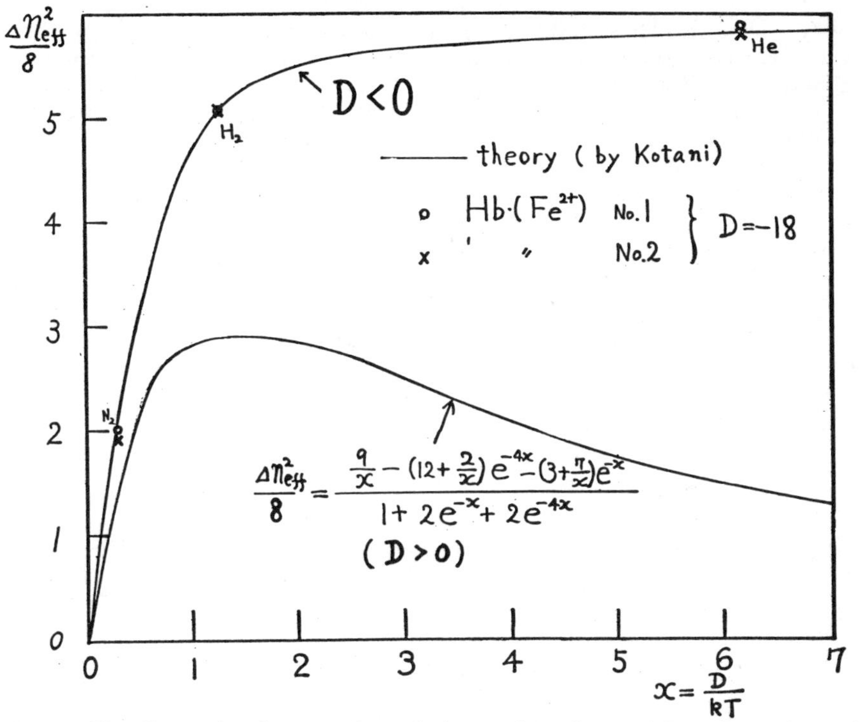

FIGURE 20. Comparison between theoretical curve (Δn_{eff}^2 vs D/kT) and experimental value for deoxy-Hb(Fe^{2+}). Since orientation of hemes in this crystal is not yet known, the absolute value of Δn_{eff}^2 cannot be determined by this experiment. Therefore, experimental data are multiplied by a common factor to observe temperature dependence. When D = -18 cm^{-1}, the experimental data agree excellently with the theoretical curve.

cases, the lowest quintet is always characterized by a uniaxial spin-Hamiltonian with negative D. In order to find out whether i corresponds to z or x, y, the absolute values of the torque must be examined carefully, utilizing information available concerning the orientations of hemes in the crystals.

THE HEME-HEME INTERACTION OBSERVED IN THE EPR SPECTRUM OF HB $M_{\text{HYDE PARK}}$

As described in the section on theoretical interpretation of D and E. M-type abnormal Hb's have characteristic EPR spectra (see FIGURE 12). These abnormal Hb's have a feature in common: two proximal or distal histidines of the α- or β-subunits of Hb are replaced by tyrosine, and the iron atoms of the abnormal subunits are in ferric state even in erythrocyte. Therefore, EPR absorption can be observed at liquid nitrogen temperature using the untreated blood of the patient. In the patient's blood, iron ions in normal Hb's and normal subunits of abnormal Hb's are in ferrous state and do not contribute to EPR absorption. Only the ferric ions in the abnormal subunits of abnormal Hb's show EPR signals.

Recently Hayashi and collaborators observed that the EPR spectrum of Hb $M_{\text{Hyde Park}}$ is affected by deoxygenation.[10] In this abnormal Hb, the proximal histidines (the fifth coordination position of the heme iron) of β-subunits are replaced by tyrosine, and the iron atoms in β subunits are in ferric state as other

M-type abnormal Hb's. FIGURE 21 shows EPR spectra of oxygenated (equilibrated with air), deoxygenated and reoxygenated blood containing the component of this abnormal Hb. The spectrum of deoxygenated blood differs markedly from that of oxygenated blood, although the spectrum of reoxygenated blood is in good agreement with that of oxygenated blood. This result shows that the removal of oxygen molecules from the hemes of normal α subunits affects the EPR spectrum of ferric ions in abnormal β subunits. This phenomenon, then, can be considered one of the expressions of the heme-heme interaction. Concretely, the conformational change also occurs in Hb $M_{\text{Hyde Park}}$ by deoxygenation of α subunits as it occurs in normal Hb by deoxygenation, and it affects the electronic state of the ferric ions in β subunits.

The spectrum of deoxygenated Hb $M_{\text{Hyde Park}}$ is composed of signals of more than

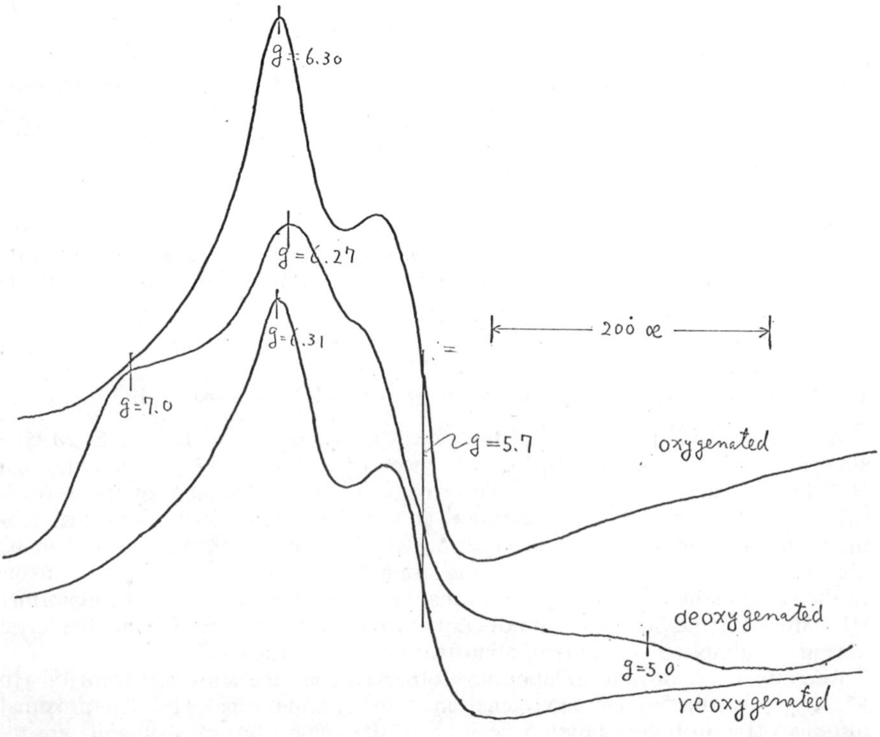

FIGURE 21. EPR spectra of oxygenated, deoxygenated and reoxygenated patient's blood containing Hb $M_{\text{Hyde Park}}$. Temperature: liquid nitrogen. Frequency: 9200Mc/s.

two components. Inhomogeneity of the spectrum may probably be due to the inhomogeneity in the states of molecules of Hb $M_{Hyde\ Park}$. If so, this unusual molecule having a half of its hemes in ferric high-spin state and the other half in ferrous high-spin state may be considered to be in the intermediate state in the course of oxygenation since, from x-ray analysis, conformation of $Hb(Fe^{3+})H_2O$ is identical with that of the $Hb(Fe^{2+})O_2$ but different from that of deoxy-$Hb(Fe^{2+})$. The new component appears by deoxygenation having g values of 7, 5 and 2. These g values corresponds to E/D of 0.04. Further studies, especially the studies on the single crystal of this Hb, are necessary to determine what occurs in heme and in the neighborhood of heme.

References

1. Koenig, D. F. 1965. Acta Crystallogr. **18:** 663.
2. Coryell, C. D., F. Stitt & L. Pauling. 1937. J. Amer. Chem. Soc. **59:** 633.
3. Taylor, D. S. & C. D. Coryell. 1961. J. Amer. Chem. Soc. **60:** 1177.
4. George, P., J. Beetlestone & J. S. Griffith. 1961. Haematin Enzymes. J. E. Falk, R. Lemberg & R. K. Morton, Eds.: 105. Pergamon Press. Oxford, England.
5. Iizuka, T. 1969. To be published.
6. Tanabe, Y. & S. Sugano. 1954. J. Physiol. Soc. Jap. **9:** 753.
7. Tanabe, Y. & S. Sugano. 1954. J. Physiol. Soc. Jap. **9:** 766.
8. Bennett, J. E., J. F. Gibson & D. J. E. Ingram. 1957. Proc. Roy. Soc. A **240:** 67.
9. Kotani, M. & H. Morimoto. 1967. Magnetic Resonance in Biological Systems. A. Ehrenberg, B. G. Malmström and T. Vänngård, Eds.: 135. Pergamon Press. Oxford, England.
10. Hayashi, A., T. Suzuki, A. Shimizu, H. Morimoto & H. Watari. 1967. Biochim. Biophys. Acta **147:** 407.
11. Van Vleck, J. H. 1932. The Theory of Electric and Magnetic Susceptibilities. Oxford University Press. New York, N. Y.
12. Kotani, M. 1961. Prog. Theoret. Phys. (Suppl.) **17:** 4.
13. Tasaki, A. & J. Otsuka. 1967. Biochim.. Biophys. Acta **140:** 284.
14. Otsuka, J. 1968. J. Phys. Soc. Jap. **24:** 885.
15. Gibson, J. F., D. J. E. Ingram & D. Schonland. 1958. Discuss. Faraday Soc. **26:** 72.
16. Griffith, J. S. 1957. Nature **180:** 29.
17. Stryer, L., J. C. Kendrew & H. C. Watson. 1964. J. Molec. Biol. **8:** 96.
18. Mizuhashi, S. & H. Kamimura. Personal communication.

HÜCKEL AND EXTENDED HÜCKEL CALCULATIONS ON BONDING IN PHOSPHATE DIESTERS*

Robert L. Collin
Department of Radiation Biology and Biophysics
University of Rochester
School of Medicine and Dentistry
Rochester, N. Y.

Introduction

Phosphates and polyphosphates are so widely distributed in biology and participate in such a wide variety of biological transformations that a knowledge of their electronic structure is of utmost importance for an understanding of biological systems on a molecular level. We are now at a stage of quantum mechanical sophistication with regard to molecular problems where an elucidation of the behavior of the electrons in these molecules can be started.

A Hückel type, π-bonding molecular orbital theory has been proposed to study the bonding in phosphate and polyphosphate esters.[1] It rests on a number of assumptions, and some of these assumptions will be examined by more detailed calculations that will attempt to include both σ- and π-interactions.

The Phosphorus-Oxygen Bond

In phosphates and polyphosphates, phosphorus is surrounded in a roughly tetrahedral arrangement by four oxygen atoms (the arrangement is exactly tetrahedral in PO_4^{-3}). This suggests that hybrid orbitals of sp^3 type can be formed on phosphorus, as is the case with tetrahedral carbon. Indeed, the 3s and 3p orbitals on phosphorus are energetically available for this and, of the five electrons beyond the filled second shell, four can be used, as in carbon, to form four covalent bonds.

There have been a number of discussions in regard to why this cannot be the entire bonding picture, and these have been summarized in the review by Hudson.[2] The evidence from crystallographic studies on 2-aminoethyl phosphoric acid[3] and 2-aminoethyl phosphonic acid[4] is particularly striking. Schematic drawings of these two compounds are shown in FIGURE 1 with some pertinent bond distances and angles. These distances are not unique but are typical for the molecules of their class which have been studied. The errors in bond distances are probably around 0.01Å. The geometry of the phosphorus is similar in both cases, except that the esterified oxygen in the phosphoric acid is replaced by a carbon in the phosphonic acid.

The phosphorus-oxygen and phosphorus-carbon bond distances are of particular interest. The phosphorus-carbon bond would be expected to be close to an ordinary single covalent bond. This distance of 1.81Å plus the covalent radius of carbon (half the carbon-carbon distance, or 0.76Å) can be used to calculate the covalent radius of phosphorus. This is $1.81 - 0.76 = 1.05$Å. The covalent radius of the esterified oxygen in the phosphoric acid can be calculated from the oxygen-carbon distance and the carbon covalent radius. It is $1.43 - 0.76 = 0.67$Å. Both these radii are in good agreement with

* This paper is based on work performed in part under United States Public Health Service Training Grant No. 1 T1 DE 175-01 and in part under contract with the U. S. Atomic Energy Commission at the University of Rochester Atomic Energy Project, and has been assigned Report No. UR-49-869.

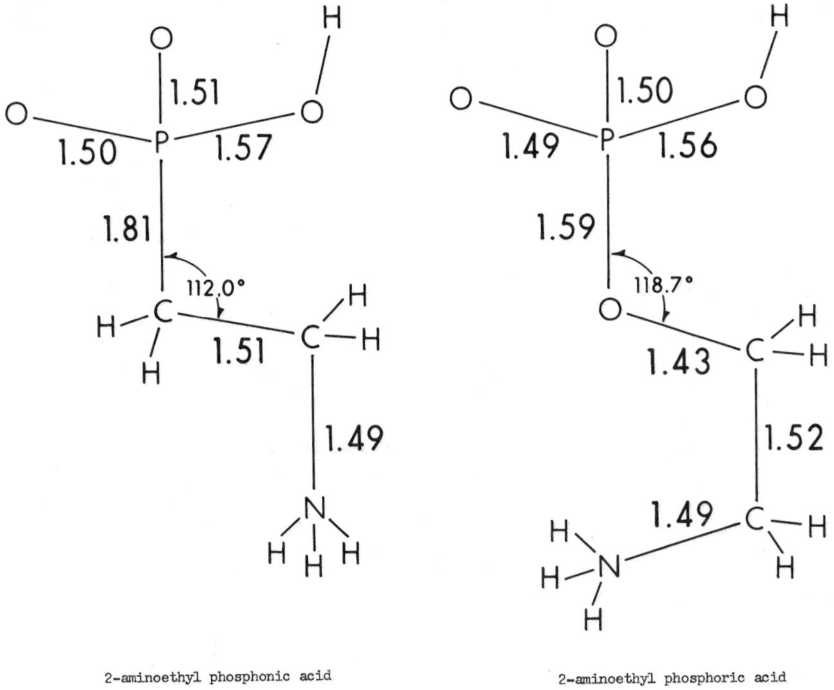

FIGURE 1. Some bond distances and angles in 2-aminoethyl phosphonic acid and 2-aminoethyl phosphoric acid.

those found in other compounds in which pure single covalent bonds are suspected. The radii of phosphorus and oxygen can be used to calculate the expected phosphorus-oxygen single bond distance, and this is 0.67 + 1.05 = 1.72Å—longer than the 1.59Å that is observed for the ester bond, and much longer than the other phosphorus-oxygen distances. The discrepancy can be reduced a little by applying the Schomaker-Stevenson correction[5] for the electronegativity difference of phosphorus and oxygen, but only by 0.03Å. We are forced either to assume that the Schomaker-Stevenson correction varies with atomic number in some irregular fashion or that the phosphorus-oxygen bonds in 2-aminoethyl phosphoric acid contain some extra type of bonding not present in the phosphorus-carbon bond: i.e., some extra bonding occurs above that from the overlap of sp^3 hybrids on phosphorus with appropriate hybrid orbitals on oxygen.

The bond angles in these two compounds also suggest that extra bonding does occur. The angle $\widehat{COP}$ is close to 120°, what one would expect for trigonal sp^2 bonding about oxygen. If sp^2-hybridization does occur on the ester oxygen, then there is a p orbital perpendicular to the COP plane which could participate in π-bonding with phosphorus. This hybridization is illustrated in FIGURE 2. And, indeed, there are low-lying orbitals on phosphorus available for such bonding. The 3d orbitals on phosphorus can form both σ- and π-type bonds with a 2p orbital on an esterified oxygen. Similarly, there are p orbitals available on the non-ester oxygens that could overlap with the 3d orbitals on phosphorus.

Calculations show that, particularly when phosphorus is surrounded by

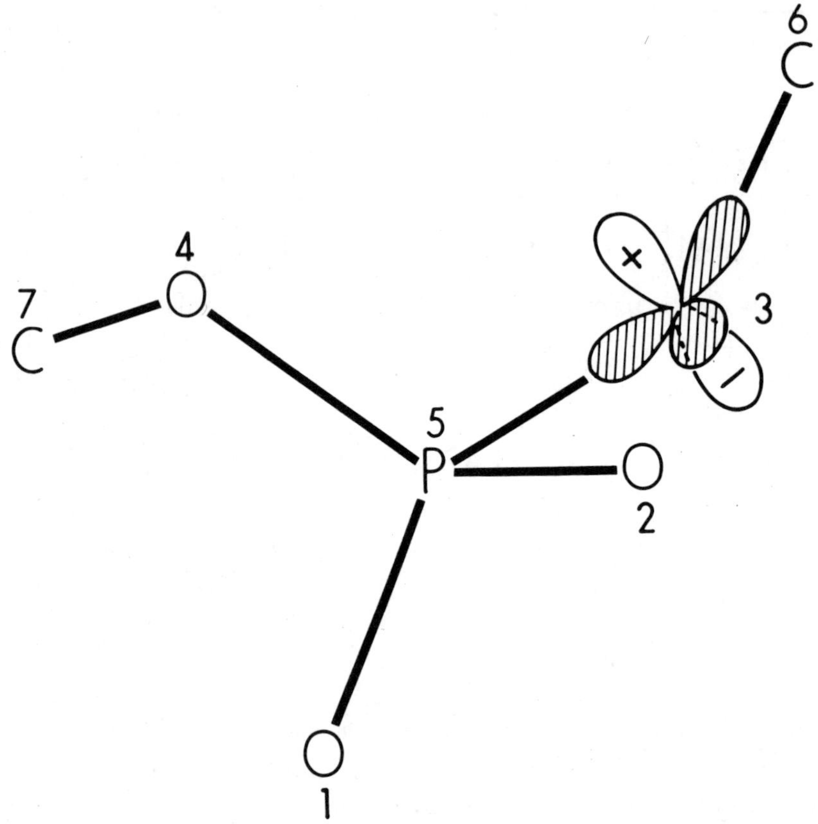

FIGURE 2. The sp^2 hybrid orbitals (shaded) on an esterified oxygen, and the 2p orbital perpendicular to the POC plane. The numbering identifies the various atoms and is used elsewhere.

electronegative ligands, the overlap integrals of the 2p-3d type can be of sufficient magnitude to give bonding.[6] Hartree-Fock self-consistent field calculations on the hypothetical molecules PO and PO^- show that the 3d orbitals contribute to the bonding between phosphorus and oxygen.[7] It is, therefore, reasonable to attribute this extra bonding in phosphates to overlap between 3d orbitals on phosphorus and a 2p orbital on oxygen, and to assign the task of explaining the bond shortening and bond angles to the 3d-2p overlap. A note of caution must be added. The 4s and 4p orbitals on phosphorus could contribute to this bonding and there are suggestions from free atom calculations[8, 9] that the energy levels for these orbitals lie close to those for the 3d orbitals. A decision in regard to the importance of the 4s and 4p orbitals in phosphates must await more complete Hartree-Fock type calculations than have been carried out to date.

The general approach in this study will be to postulate that the 3d orbitals on phosphorus are the ones that are important for the extra bonding in phosphates. It will be shown that this leads to a reasonable description of the bonding.

Pi-Bonding Calculations

Cruickshank's suggestions[10] on the nature of bonding in phosphates were put on a quantitative basis in a simple Hückel calculation that treated only the π-type overlap between 2p orbitals on oxygen and 3d orbitals on phosphorus.[1] Appreciable extra bonding did occur—at least with the parameters used in that work—and the π-energy values for different conformations of the ester group suggested a potential barrier for rotation about the phosphorus-ester oxygen bonds in diesters and triesters. The stable conformation for the diester is illustrated in FIGURE 3, and was a structure with both ester groups rotated 90° about the P-O bond out of the (C)OPO(C) plane. There was also an increase in positive charge on the phosphorus atom as the conformation was changed from the stable to the unstable form. The position of the rotational barrier was in reasonable accord with crystal structure evidence and the charge on the phosphorus could be correlated with the chemical properties and ^{31}P nuclear magnetic resonance chemical shifts in cyclic and acyclic esters.

The calculated energy minimum for the diester places the ester groups closer to one oxygen than another, and the observed angles in crystals where the molecule is not distorted by intermolecular hydrogen bonds are always in a direction toward more nearly bisecting this $\widehat{OPO}$ angle. This suggested a competition between π-energy minimization and nonbonded repulsions, and a factor which attempts to represent the repulsion between the ester group and nonbonded oxygens was included in the

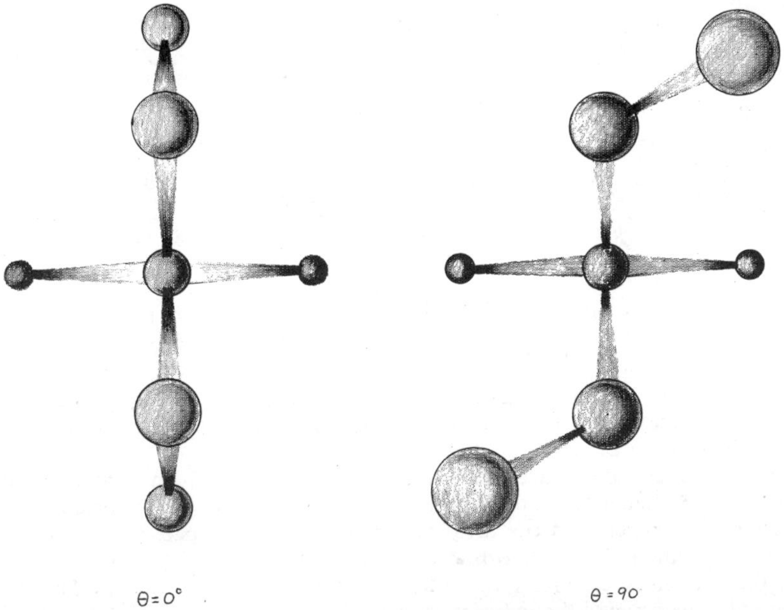

FIGURE 3. Two possible conformations of the diester phosphate anion. The phosphorus atom is bonded to four oxygen atoms. The two upper oxygen atoms are esterified, and the ester groups are represented by spheres. The angle θ describes the rotation of the ester group about the phosphorus-oxygen bond. The position where COPOC are in the same plane and the carbon atoms closer to phosphorus is taken as $\theta = 0°$.

calculation. This was done by modifying the Coulomb integrals on oxygen.[11] These repulsion terms added to the Coulomb integrals were assumed to be proportional to the inverse twelfth power of the internuclear distance, and the proportionality constant was determined by fitting values at distances of 1.4 to 10Å to those tabulated by Pariser[12] for two carbon atoms. The π-energy calculated with these modified Coulomb integrals for models representing acyclic and cyclic diesters are shown in FIGURE 4. The rotation angles, θ, about P-O(C) observed in barium diethyl phosphate,[13] methyl pinacol phosphate[14] and methyl ethylene[15] phosphate are indicated on the figure and all are in agreement with conformations which maximize the π-energy.

The rotation barrier can be viewed as arising from competition by the π-orbitals on the various oxygen atoms for overlap with the 3d orbitals on phosphorus, as was suggested for $(CH_3)_2NSO_2N(CH_3)_2$ by Jordan and collaborators.[16] The overlap integrals for the diester are listed in TABLE 1. In the 0° conformation the ϕ^p orbital overlaps with d_{xy} and d_{xz}, which are also strongly overlapped by ϕ and ϕ'. In the 90° conformation, part of the competition is shifted unchanged to d_{z^2}, but the rest is divided among $d_{x^2-y^2}$ and d_{yz}, which are not as strongly overlapped by ϕ and ϕ'. This decrease in competition effectively increases the π-bonding in the 90° conformation. If the molecule can be distorted into a form where the π-bonding is less, then the electron density on phosphorus will decrease and this, in turn, may lead to changes in chemical properties. This could be an important factor in enzyme and metal

TABLE 1

DIESTER PHOSPHATE 2p-3d OVERLAP INTEGRALS IN THE SIMPLE π-BONDING CALCULATION

	d_{z^2}	$d_{x^2-y^2}$	d_{xy}	d_{xz}	d_{yz}
			$\theta = 0°$		
ϕ *	0	0	.282	0	.157
ϕ'	−.282	.138	0	−.169	0
ϕ^p	0	0	.222	.174	0
			$\theta = 90°$		
	d_{z^2}	$d_{x^2-y^2}$	d_{xy}	d_{xz}	d_{yz}
ϕ	0	0	.282	0	.157
ϕ'	−.282	.138	0	−.169	0
ϕ^p	.222	.137	0	0	−.045

* ϕ and ϕ' are the π orbitals on the non-esterified oxygen, and ϕ^p is the 2p orbital on the esterified oxygen that is assumed to be available for overlap with the 3d orbitals on phosphorus.

ion catalysis of polyphosphate reactions. Here, conformation changes could be brought about by the interaction of the polyphosphate with the enzyme or by coordination to the metal.

The calculated effects are small and the results depend on a number of assumptions. Particularly important is the assumption of sp^2-hybridization on the esterified oxygen and the localization of an electron pair in one of the sp^2 orbitals, leaving only a 2p orbital available for bonding to phosphorus. Before the model is extended to more complex systems, it would appear appropriate to investigate the validity of these assumptions.

Extended Hückel Calculations

The ordinary Hückel molecular orbital method, which has been quite successful in providing insight into chemical and physical properties of conjugated molecules containing π-electrons, has been extended by Hoffman and Lipscomb[17, 18] to include both σ- and π-electrons and applied to many organic and inorganic molecules. The calculation, based on a method first used by Wolfsberg and Helmholtz,[19] treats each atom of the molecule as a core containing a nucleus with its surrounding inner shell electrons. The atomic orbitals that are expected to participate strongly in bonding are used to form a basis set for the linear combination of atomic orbital approximation to the wavefunction. The secular determinant is set up using this basis set and solved for the energy levels, and the total energy of the molecule is taken as the sum of the one-electron orbital energies.

A critical feature of the method lies in the choice of numerical values for the Coulomb and resonance integrals. The Coulomb integrals are usually taken to be the valence state ionization potentials for the various atomic orbitals in an isolated atom. The resonance integrals are taken to be proportional to the overlap integral and to some simple function of the Coulomb integrals of the two atomic orbitals involved. Of course, no assumptions about hybridization need be made, since the basis set can consist of orbitals of the type s, p_x, p_y, p_z on each atom. No distinction need be made between σ- and π-orbitals, and interactions between all orbitals in the basis set are included in the calculation. Since both the valence state ionization potentials and the overlap integrals vary with the charge on an atom, an attempt can be made to include a self-consistent charge feature in the calculation in order to calculate the input Coulomb and resonance integrals for the next cycle.

In the calculations to be described here, the 2s and 2p orbitals on carbon, fluorine and oxygen, and the 3s, 3p, and 3d orbitals on phosphorus have been used as basis functions. In some calculations, the 3d orbitals have been omitted to illustrate their effect better. The valence state ionization potentials and their dependence on charge have been calculated from atomic spectroscopic data by Cusachs,[20, 21] and these are used to evaluate the Coulomb integrals. Overlap integrals have been calculated by the usual formulas,[22-25] with appropriate corrections.[25]

The atomic orbitals are approximated by Slater functions, where the orbital exponent, ζ, is allowed to depend on the atomic charge according to $\zeta = \zeta_0 + 0.35/n\ Q$, where Q is the charge on the atom, n is the principal quantum number 1, 2 or 3, and ζ_0 is the Slater exponent calculated from Slater's rules.[26] For the 3d orbitals on phosphorus, a ζ_0 of 1.40 was used, a value suggested by Hartree-Fock calculations on the PO^- molecule.[7] The resonance integrals are given by the relation[27] $\beta_{ij} = -2.0 \times \sqrt{\alpha_i \times \alpha_j} \times S_{ij}$, where S_{ij} is the overlap integral between orbitals i and j, while α_i and α_j are the Coulomb integrals associated with orbitals i and j.

In the self-consistent charge calculations, the charges were found to fluctuate widely from cycle to cycle and a damping factor method[28] was used to obtain convergence.

The computer program also includes a population analysis scheme that is used to calculate orbital and overlap populations, atom populations and bond populations.[29] No symmetry is assumed in the calculations and the population, and energy level symmetry that does appear can be used as one check on the correctness of the calculations.

The calculations have been done on models for diester phosphate anions and, in order to study the hybridization on the ester oxygens in greater detail, the ester groups have been replaced by fluorine atoms which are isoelectronic with the methyl group.[16] This gives too concentrated a core charge,

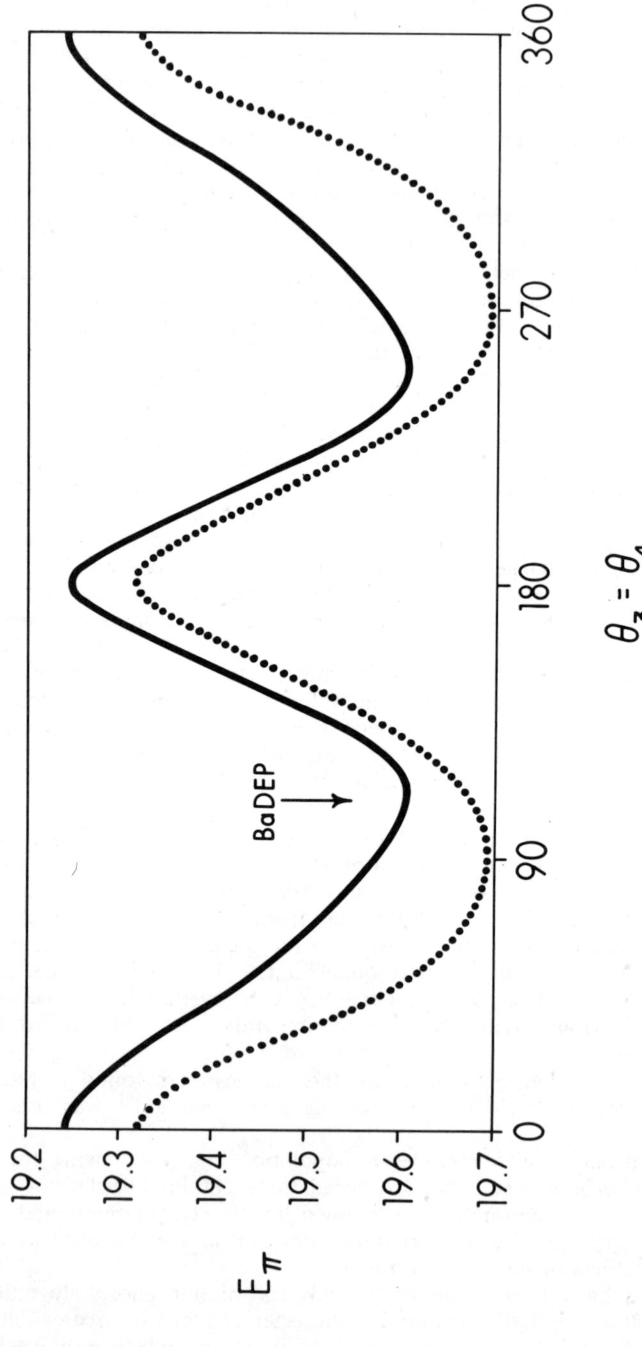

FIGURE 4. The barriers to rotation are phosphate esters calculated with the simple π-bonding theory. The dotted line is from a calculation with the unmodified Coulomb integrals, and the solid line is with the Coulomb integrals modified to include a term for nonbonded repulsions. a) The acyclic diester anion. The observed conformation of barium diethylphosphate[13] is indicated.

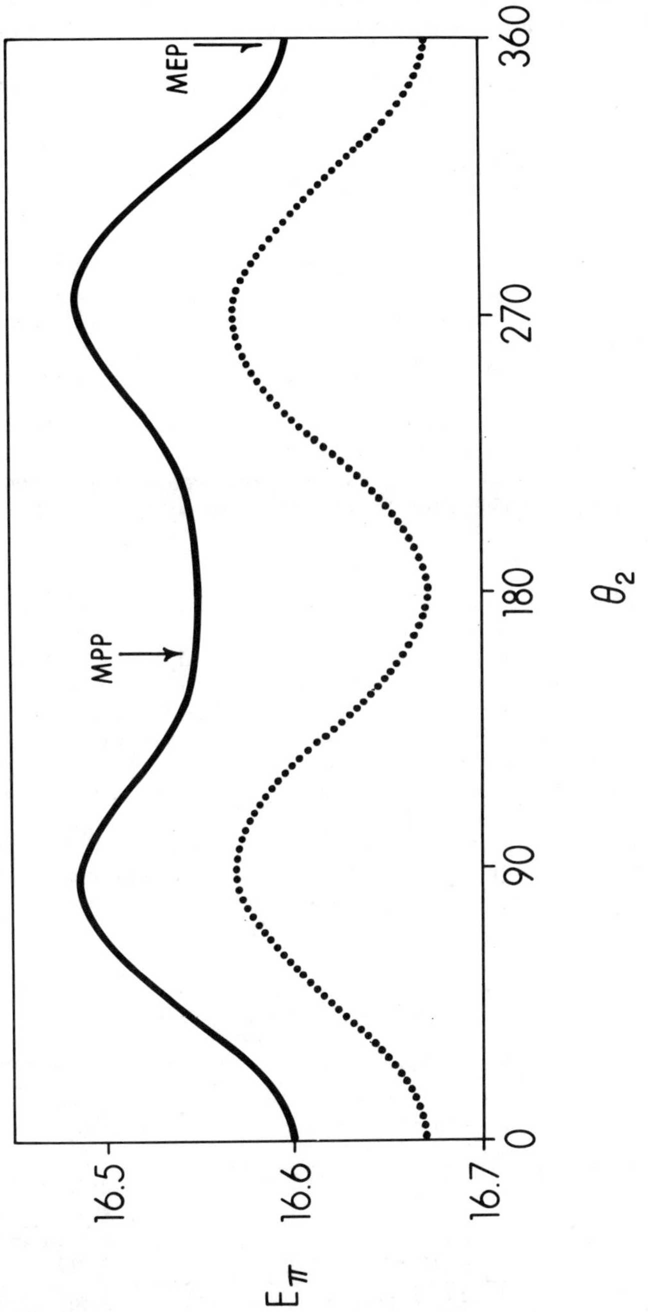

FIGURE 4b. The 5-cyclic triester. The calculated π-energy for various conformations of the extracyclic ester group is shown, and the rotational conformations of the methyl groups observed in methyl ethylene phosphate[15] and methyl pinacol phosphate[14] are indicated.

therefore, the effect of reducing this charge has been studied by replacing the fluorine with a carbon core: i.e., the valence state ionization potentials and the orbital exponents for carbon have been assigned to fluorine in some calculations.

The bond distances and angles of the model diester are taken close to those found in barium diethyl phosphate.[13] The dimensions are F-O = 1.440Å, P-O = 1.500Å, P-O(F) = 1.600Å, $\widehat{OPO}$ = 121.60°, $\widehat{(F)OPO(F)}$ = 103.50°, $\widehat{POF}$ = 120.00°. The planes OPO and (F)OPO(F) are assumed perpendicular—only 1° off from that observed in the crystal structure.

In studying different conformations of $F_2PO_4^-$, corresponding to rotation about the P-O(F) bond, the charges have been made self-consistent to within 0.02 electrons for only one conformation, and these have then been used to calculate Coulomb integrals and Slater parameters for the other conformations as well. Thus, the only varying parameter between conformations is that involving the geometrical dependence of the overlap integrals. Calculations have also been made omitting the 3d orbitals from the basis set but maintaining the other integrals. The self-consistent Coulomb integrals and orbital exponents derived from $F_2PO_4^-$ at $\theta = 0°$ are given in TABLE 2. For $C_2PO_4^-$, the Coulomb integral for the pseudocarbon atom was taken as −20.35 e.v. for 2s, and −10.65 e.v. for 2p. The orbital exponent was 1.625.

Discussion

A comparison of bond populations (the number of electrons that can be identified with a particular bond) with and without the inclusion of 3d orbitals on phosphorus is shown in TABLE 3. For both conformations, the increase in bond population in the P-O_1 and P-O_3 bonds on adding 3d orbitals is marked. Also, the bond population increase in the P-O_1 bond is over twice that in the P-O_3 bond. This is in accord with the postulated role of the 3d orbitals and can explain, in a qualitative sense at least, the phosphorus-oxygen bond lengths in phosphate esters. More extensive calculations are necessary before quantitative arguments can be made.

The total orbital energies listed in TABLE 4 show an appreciable barrier to rotation in the isoelectronic $F_2PO_4^-$ model for a dimethyl phosphate anion when 3d interactions are included. The energy minimum is close to 90°, and

TABLE 2

COULOMB INTEGRALS AND ORBITAL EXPONENTS DERIVED FROM SELF-CONSISTENT CHARGE CALCULATIONS ON $F_2PO_4^-$

		Coulomb Integrals (e.v.)	Orbital Exponents
P	3s	−22.665	1.640
	3p	−13.685	1.640
	3d	− 7.122	1.440
O	2s	−28.099	2.212
	2p	−11.550	2.212
O(F)	2s	−32.187	2.212
	2p	−15.638	2.212
F	2s	−37.716	2.566
	2p	−17.116	2.566

TABLE 3

SELECTED NET ATOM AND BOND POPULATIONS FOR TWO CONFORMATIONS OF $F_2PO^-_4$ AND $C_2PO^-_4$

	$F_2PO^-_4$					$C_2PO^-_4$			
	With 3d Orbitals		Without 3d Orbitals			With 3d Orbitals		Without 3d Orbitals	
Atom or bond*	$\theta = 0°$	$\theta = 90°$	$\theta = 0°$	$\theta = 90°$	Atom or bond	$\theta = 0°$	$\theta = 90°$	$\theta = 0°$	$\theta = 90°$
P	2.5329	2.6394	1.4673	1.4687	P	2.6100	2.6174	1.5141	1.5182
O_1	5.6993	5.5459	6.7887	6.7708	O_1	5.7718	5.7442	6.8078	6.8105
O_3	5.5452	5.5323	5.7776	5.7812	O_3	6.0809	6.0530	6.3504	6.3380
F_6	7.0623	7.1273	7.0534	7.0665	C_6	6.3455	6.4062	6.4213	6.4318
$P-O_1$	1.4345	1.4737	0.8069	0.8085	$P-O_1$	1.4230	1.4409	0.8117	0.8122
$P-O_3$	0.7780	0.8176	0.6036	0.6047	$P-O_3$	0.7933	0.8070	0.6117	0.6177
O_3-F_6	0.3591	0.3385	0.3414	0.3355	O_3-C_6	0.4239	0.4339	0.3939	0.3986
F_5-F_6	0.0000	0.0000	0.0000	0.0000	C_5-C_6	−0.0001	0.0002	0.0000	0.0001
F_6-O_1	−0.0004	−0.0020	−0.0003	−0.0010	C_6-O_1	−0.0070	−0.0202	−0.0052	−0.0137
F_6-O_4	0.0000	0.0000	0.0000	0.0000	C_6-O_4	0.0003	−0.0016	0.0004	−0.0015
F_6-P	−0.0771	−0.0956	−0.0412	−0.0408	C_6-P	−0.0623	−0.1058	−0.0782	−0.0871

* Atom numbering is according to FIGURE 2.

TABLE 4

TOTAL ORBITAL ENERGIES (kcal/mole)

	$F_2PO_4^-$		$C_2PO_4^-$	
θ	With 3d Orbitals	Without 3d Orbitals	With 3d Orbitals	Without 3d Orbitals
0°	−20915.9	−20697.5	−17778.1	−17555.1
90°	−20930.8	−20699.6	−17772.4	−17552.8
110°	−20927.5	−20699.3	−17767.3	−17555.0
130°	−20922.8	−20691.4	−17761.0	−17535.3
$E_{90} - E_0$	+14.9	+2.1	−5.7	−2.3

this is in rough agreement with the conformation in barium diethyl phosphate. That the rotational barrier is almost wholly the result of d-orbital participation is apparent when the calculations are made omitting the 3d orbital on phosphorus.

When the effective core charge on the ester group is decreased by replacing the fluorine Coulomb integral and orbital exponents with those of carbon, the barrier decreases and changes character. In a similar calculation on $F_2NSO_2NF_2$, the effect of decreasing the core charge of the fluorine was just the opposite—the barrier became greater.[16]

The explanation for the barrier is the same as that proposed with the simple π-bonding theory: i.e., in the stable conformation, both types of P-O bond are stronger because of decreased competition for overlap with 3d orbitals. The data in TABLE 5 show that the O(F) overlap population with d_{xz} and d_{xy} decreases as the molecule goes from the unstable to the stable form, whereas the overlap population with d_{z^2} and $d_{x^2-y^2}$ increases. The largest change in the

TABLE 5

ORBITAL OVERLAP POPULATIONS FOR THE 3d ORBITALS ON PHOSPHORUS WITH ORBITALS ON OXYGEN

	$F_2PO_4^-$					
	O(F)			O_1		
	0°	90°	Δ	0°	90°	Δ
d_{z^2}	0.0368	0.0917	+.0549	0.1150	0.1212	+.0065
d_{yz}	.0186	.0186	0	.0998	.1001	+.0003
$d_{x^2-y^2}$	.0106	.0513	+.0407	.0750	.0769	+.0019
d_{xz}	.0585	.0300	−.0285	.0995	.1087	+.0092
d_{xy}	.0594	.0294	−.0300	.1818	.1989	+.0171
Totals	.1839	.2210	+.0371	.5711	.6061	+.0350
	$C_2PO_4^-$					
	O(C)			O_1		
	0°	90°	Δ	0°	90°	Δ
d_{z^2}	0.0539	0.0953	+.0414	0.1247	0.1212	−.0035
d_{yz}	.0283	.0084	−.0199	.0932	.0994	+.0062
$d_{x^2-y^2}$	−.0063	.0540	+.0603	.0529	.0724	+.0195
d_{xz}	.0657	.0243	−.0414	.0954	.0954	0
d_{xy}	.0571	.0230	−.0341	.1834	.1852	+.0018
Totals	.1987	.2050	+.0063	.5496	.5736	+.0240

O_1 overlap population occurs with d_{xz} and d_{xy}, and this is an increase as the molecule goes from the unstable to the stable conformation.

The overlap integrals in TABLE 6 are more complicated to interpret than the ones in the π-bonding case, but the trend is the same. In the $\theta = 0°$ conformation, P_x corresponds to the direction of the pure 2p orbital and P_z lies close to the direction of the sp^2 hybrid. In the $\theta = 90°$ conformation, the roles are reversed. If the sp^2 hybrid is completely localized on oxygen, then this picture becomes equivalent to the simple π-bonding model. If, however, the lone pair in the sp^2-hybrid can become delocalized, it will contribute to the bonding in a sense opposite to that of the pure 2p orbital: i.e., a rotational conformation change that would increase the bonding of the 2p and 3d orbitals would decrease the bonding of the sp^2-hybrid and 3d orbitals. Such an effect would tend to smooth out any potential barrier, and a situation could be imagined where the effects of the two orbitals might nearly cancel each other. This appears to be what happens when the core charge on the fluorine is decreased to the value for carbon.

As the conformation of $C_2PO_4^-$ is changed from 0° to 90°, there is only a small change in the P-O_1 and P-O_3 bond population (TABLE 3) compared to the case with $F_2PO_4^-$. On a qualitative picture we would expect that the less electronegative carbon would not attract the bonding electrons from oxygen as strongly as would fluorine. Thus, the bonding electrons between oxygen and carbon would have more 2s character than those existing between oxygen and fluorine. The 2s orbitals used in a bond to carbon would not be available for bonding to the phosphorus 3d orbitals, and the bonds to these orbitals would take on more 2p character. Particularly, the orbital assumed to be an sp^2-hybrid in the simple π-bonding theory would become more p-like and more similar to the pure 2p orbital. Such a change would tend to smooth out the rotational barrier which is observed.

The fraction of 2p character in the orbitals available for overlap with the phosphorus 3d orbitals can be calculated from the orbital and overlap population matrix. These calculations are outlined in TABLE 7 in which some orbital and overlap populations around the ester oxygen are shown. The gross populations available for bonding to phosphorus 3d orbitals are the gross populations minus half the sum of the tabulated P-O(F) and O-F overlap populations. The fraction of 2p character in this quantity for $F_2PO_4^-$ is 0.735, and for $C_2PO_4^-$ it is 0.769. Clearly, the bonds to the 3d orbitals have more 2p character in $C_2PO_4^-$, and this should contribute to a lessening of the rotational barrier in the manner described above.

There are also changes in bond populations between various nonbonded atoms which may be important in this regard. A comparison of the lower sec-

TABLE 6

OVERLAP INTEGRALS BETWEEN PHOSPHORUS 3d AND OXYGEN IN $F_2PO_4^-$

	O_1 (Non-ester Oxygen)				O_3 (Ester Oxygen)			
	S	P_x	P_y	P_z	S	P_x	P_y	P_z
d_{z^2}	−.0647	−.0953	0	−.2138	.0322	0	−.1556	.1763
d_{yz}	0	0	−.1542	0	.3626	0	−.1552	−.0395
$d_{x^2-y^2}$	.2987	−.0194	0	.1651	−.2300	0	−.0110	.1639
d_{xz}	−.3339	.1759	0	.0914	0	.1726	0	0
d_{xy}	0	0	.2759	0	0	.2190	0	0

TABLE 7

ORBITAL AND OVERLAP POPULATIONS AROUND THE ESTER OXYGEN

	$F_2PO_4^-$			
	P-O(F) Overlap Population Exclusive of 3d	O-F Overlap Population	Gross Populations on Oxygen	Gross Population Available for P_{3d} Overlap
2s	0.3009	0.0608	1.6641	1.4833
2p	0.2932	0.2983	4.4172	4.1214
	$C_2PO_4^-$			
	P-O(C) Overlap Population exclusive of 3d	O-C Overlap Population	Gross Populations on Oxygen	Gross Population Available for P_{3d} Overlap
2s	0.2584	0.2448	1.5756	1.3240
2p	0.3536	0.2825	4.7275	4.4095

tion of TABLE 3 suggests that there are strong nonbonding repulsions between carbon and oxygen, as well as between carbon and phosphorus, that are more pronounced in $F_2PO_4^-$. The interaction with oxygen is of the type introduced into the simple π-bonding calculation by adjusting the Coulomb integrals. The increase in the negative overlap population in the phosphorus-fluorine or phosphorus-carbon bond on going from $\theta = 0°$ to $\theta = 90°$ can be attributed almost entirely to interactions involving 3d orbitals on phosphorus and orbitals on fluorine or carbon. The overlap integrals between 2p and 3d orbitals are almost doubled when fluorine is replaced by carbon, and this undoubtedly is the major factor which contributes to making this nonbonded repulsion more important in $C_2PO_4^-$.

It is now possible to discuss the opposite effects of change in core charge on fluorine in $F_2PO_4^-$ and $F_2NSO_2NF_2$. In both models, a decrease in core charge on fluorine gives more 2s character to the electrons in the fluorine-nitrogen and fluorine-oxygen bonds, and this increases the 2p character of the electrons available to bond to the phosphorus 3d orbitals. In $F_2NSO_2F_2$, there is only one lone pair orbital available, and an increase in its p character will accentuate its directional properties and lead to an increase in the potential barrier to rotation. In $F_2PO_4^-$ there are two orbitals available for bonding to the 3d orbitals of phosphorus. An increase in 2p character makes them more nearly alike and more nearly at right angles to each other, with a consequent decrease in the rotational barrier.

The large amount of s character for the O-C overlap population (46% from TABLE 7) indicates that a $\widehat{POC}$ angle of 120° would not be a stable bond angle in $C_2PO_4^-$. Calculations designed to test the stability of the $\widehat{POF}$ and $\widehat{POC}$ angles to distortion away from the assumed 120° suggest that 120° is close to a stable position for $\widehat{POF}$ but not for $\widehat{POC}$. The total orbital energies in electron volts for three values of $\widehat{POF}$ in $F_2PO_4^-(\theta = 90°)$ are -906.9238 (110°), -907.2761 (120°) and -907.3047 (130°). In $C_2PO_4^-$, the corresponding energies are -769.2122 (110°), -770.3696 (120°) and -771.1279 (130°). From this evidence and the observed

$\widehat{POC}$ angle of 117° in barium diethyl phosphate, one would conclude that fluorine, in this calculation, is a closer approximation to an aliphatic ester group than is the pseudocarbon atom.

Conclusion

The calculations with the extended Hückel method verify some of the assumptions regarding the noninteraction of the σ and π structures made in the simple π-bonding theory. The contribution of the 3d orbitals to the phosphorus-oxygen bonding is appreciable and, qualitatively at least, offers an explanation for the observed bond shortening in phosphate esters. This is independent of the assumed core charge on the ester group, within wide limits.

A potential energy barrier to rotation about the phosphorus-oxygen bond, brought on by the nature of the 3d-2p overlap, appears in the extended Hückel calculations as well as in the π-bonding theory.

The extended Hückel calculations focus attention on one place where the assumptions of the simple π-bonding theory may break down. This is the hybridization scheme on the ester oxygen. These calculations suggest that the hybridization is sensitive to the effective electronegativity of the ester group but, unfortunately, the nature of the calculation is so approximate that it can say nothing quantitative about the hybridization in, for instance, a diethyl phosphate anion. The experimental crystallographic bond angle evidence suggests that the hybridization is close to sp^2 in phosphate esters. Hybridization changes of this nature will certainly be pronounced in polyphosphates where the bridge angle $\widehat{POP}$ is often considerably greater than 120°, and in the strained cyclic phosphates where the angle $\widehat{POC}$ is less.

References

1. Collin, R. L. 1966. J. Amer. Chem. Soc. **88:** 3281.
2. Hudson, R. F. 1965. Structure and Mechanism in Organo-Phosphorus Chemistry. Academic Press. New York, N. Y.
3. Kraut, J. 1961. Acta Crystallogr. **14:** 1146.
4. Okaya, Y. 1966. Acta Crystallogr. **20:** 712.
5. Schomaker, V. & D. P. Stevenson. 1941. J. Amer. Chem. Soc. **63:** 37.
6. Craig, D. P. & C. Zauli. 1962. J. Chem. Phys. **37:** 609.
7. Boyd, D. B. & W. N. Lipscomb. 1967. J. Chem. Phys. **46:** 910.
8. Palmieri, P. & C. Zauli. 1967. J. Chem. Soc.: 813.
9. Cusachs, L. C. & J. R. Lin, Jr. 1967. J. Chem. Phys. **46:** 2919.
10. Cruickshank, D. W. J. 1961. J. Chem. Soc.: 5486.
11. Cambron-Brüderlein, H. & C. Sandorfy. 1966. Theor. Chim. Acta **4:** 224.
12. Pariser, R. 1956. J. Chem. Phys. **24:** 250.
13. Kyoguka, Y. & Y. Iitaka. 1966. Acta Crystallogr. **21:** 49.
14. Newton, M. G., J. R. Cox, Jr. & J. A. Bertrand. 1966. J. Amer. Chem. Soc. **88:** 1503.
15. Steitz, T. A. & W. N. Lipscomb. 1965. J. Amer. Chem. Soc. **87:** 2488.
16. Jordan, T., H. W. Smith, L. L. Lohr, Jr. & W. N. Lipscomb. 1963. J. Amer. Chem. Soc. **85:** 846
17. Hoffman, R. & W. N. Lipscomb. 1962. J. Chem. Phys. **36:** 2179, 3489.
18. Hoffman, R. 1963. J. Chem. Phys. **39:** 1397
19. Wolfsberg, M. & L. Helmholtz. 1952. J. Chem. Phys. **20:** 837.
20. Cusachs, L. C. & J. W. Reynolds. 1965. J. Chem. Phys. **43:** S160.
21. Cusachs, L. C., J. W. Reynolds & D. Barnard. 1966. J. Chem. Phys. **44:** 835.

22. MULLIKEN, R. S., C. A. RIECKE, D. ORLOFF & H. ORLOFF. 1949. J. Chem. Phys. **17:** 1248.
23. JAFFÉ, H. H. & G. O. DOAK. 1953. J. Chem. Phys. **21:** 196.
24. JAFFÉ, H. H. 1953. J. Chem. Phys. **21:** 258.
25. BISHOP, D. M., M. RANDIČ & J. R. MORTON. 1966. J. Chem. Phys. **45:** 1880.
26. SLATER, J. C. 1930. Phys. Rev. **36:** 57.
27. BALHAUSEN, C. J. & H. B. GRAY. 1962. Inorg. Chem. **1:** 111.
28. REIN, R., N. FUKUDA, H. WIN, G. A. CLARKE & F. E. HARRIS. 1966. J. Chem. Phys. **45:** 4743.
29. MULLIKEN, R. S. 1955. J. Chem. Phys. **23:** 1833, 1841, 2338, 2343.

THE ELECTRONIC STRUCTURE OF PURINES AND PYRIMIDINES*

Alberte Pullman
Institut de Biologie Physico-Chimique
Paris, France

Introduction

The electronic structure of the fundamental purines and pyrimidines of the nucleic acids was first investigated in the π-electron approximation using the simple Hückel procedure,[1–3] and a careful analysis of the results has allowed a general interpretation of a large body of experimental data concerning these compounds, as well as a number of predictions which have since been substantiated by subsequent experimentation.[4] The general picture of the π-electronic structure so obtained has been largely confirmed by early calculations using the Pariser-Parr-Pople method.[5†]

It was soon recognized, however, that the influence of the σ-framework was to be taken into account both implicitly in the parametrization of the self-consistent procedure[9] for π-electrons, and explicitly for the accurate evaluation of the dipole moments. A simple localized-bond approximation[10] was adapted to conjugated molecules[11, 12] and used to evaluate the σ-electron distribution in the nucleic bases. Meanwhile, a careful optimization of the Pariser-Parr-Pople set of integrals was performed on a series of reference compounds and used to calculate the π-electron structure which was to be associated with the σ-distribution.[7, 13] Although the σ and the π electrons were still treated separately, their mutual influence was implicitly taken into account by the fitting of the calculated properties (e.g. dipole moments, ionization potentials) on experimental data for the reference compounds. Moreover, the agreement with the known experimental data in a large number of molecules[7, 14] bore out the image of the overall electron distribution obtained in this fashion. Nevertheless, the simultaneous treatment of the σ and π electrons of these compounds was highly desirable in order to gain further insight into their actual electronic properties.

The recent development of new methods within the molecular orbital formalism together with the availability of high-speed computers today allows such simultaneous treatment of all valence electrons in large conjugated molecules.

Three of these procedures have recently been used in our laboratory for such all valence electrons computation of the main bases of the nucleic acids and this paper gives a general comparison of the results obtained.

Methods

The pioneer contribution in the field of computations, including all valence electrons in conjugated molecules, was made by Hoffmann.[15, 16] In Hoffmann's method, the molecular orbitals φ_i are built up as a linear combination of Slater atomic orbitals χ_μ:

* This work was supported by grant GM 12289-02 of the United States Public Health Service (National Institute of General Medical Sciences).

† The apparent disagreements arrived at by some authors in a similar calculation[6] have been shown to be due to misinterpretations.[7, 8]

$$\varphi_i = \sum_{\mu} c_{i\mu}\chi_{\mu} \tag{1}$$

the coefficients and the orbital energies being obtained by solving the set of secular equations:

$$\sum_{\nu} c_{i\nu}(H_{\mu\nu} - ES_{\mu\nu}) = 0 \qquad i = 1, 2, \cdots n \tag{2}$$

where H is an effective Hamiltonian.

The atomic basis set is made of one 1s orbital for each hydrogen atom (Slater exponent 1.0), one 2s and three 2p orbitals for each carbon and each heteroatom (with Slater orbital exponents). The diagonal matrix elements $H_{\mu\mu}$ are the atomic valence-state ionization potentials for each orbital, and the nondiagonal matrix elements $H_{\mu\nu}$ are approximated by the Wolfsberg-Helmholtz formula

$$H_{\mu\nu} = 0,5K(H_{\mu\mu} + H_{\nu\nu})S_{\mu\nu} \tag{3}$$

with K = 1,75.

This method is an extension of the well-known Hückel approximation for π electrons in the sense that the molecular orbitals are obtained as the eigenvalues of an effective Hamiltonian H that is not explicit, the matrix elements of H being treated as empirical input characteristic of the atoms involved. For this reason, the procedure is called the Extended Hückel Theory (EHT) although it differs from the Hückel set of hypotheses in that it includes overlap as well as all nondiagonal elements in the secular determinant. This procedure has met with considerable success in the last few years, particularly in problems concerned with molecular shape and conformations.[17–19] It has recently been used successfully in our laboratory[19] to predict the preferred conformations of the ribosides of guanine, adenine, cytosine and uracil. Calculations on the bases themselves have been performed at the same time by the extended Hückel scheme, and are used here as a basis of comparison with more elaborate procedures. The values used for the $H_{\mu\mu}$ elements are listed in TABLE 1.

Despite its remarkable achievements in conformational chemistry, the extended Hückel theory is obviously not entirely satisfactory from a theoretical point of view, and it has been the object of a number of criticisms—some of them constructive enough to give rise to improved procedures. The essential modifications proposed which seem worth retaining include:

1) the use of the best single Slater orbital exponents as determined by Clementi and Raimondi,[20] instead of the usual set of Slater exponents in the basis set;

2) the replacement of the Wolfsberg-Helmholtz formula by Cusachs' expression:[21, 22]

TABLE 1

VALUES OF $-H_{\mu\mu}$ IN THE EXTENDED HÜCKEL THEORY (EV)

atom	s	p
H	13.6	
C	21.4	11.4
N	26.0	13.4
O	35.3	17.76

$$H_{\mu\nu} = (2 - |S_{\mu\nu}|)\, S_{\mu\nu} \frac{H_{\mu\mu} + H_{\nu\nu}}{2} \tag{4}$$

so as to better satisfy the requirements of the Virial theorem:

3) the generalization of the old Wheland-Mann idea[23] (or ω-technique[24]) for making the diagonal matrix elements of the Hamiltonian depend on the net atomic charges and solving the equations by an iterative process.[25–28]

These various modifications have recently culminated in a number of Iterative Extended Hückel Theories (IEHT) advocated by different authors[28, 29] to yield results in more satisfactory agreement with experiment than the unmodified Hoffmann Technique, particularly in the field of properties deriving from the coefficients of the atomic orbitals, such as the dipole moments.

We have thus used an iterative extended Hückel scheme as a second trial for the computation of the nucleic bases. The equations are those of Hoffmann's theory with modifications 1) and 2) indicated above. Moreover, the diagonal matrix elements, H, have been made dependent on the orbital occupancy n and on the net atomic charge q through the relation:[27]

$$H_{\mu\mu} = A(n) + Bq \tag{5}$$

The numerical values used for A and B are the smoothed valence-state ionization potentials of Reference 27 (TABLE 2).

The two previous methods are both based on an effective Hamiltonian, and are thus similar in nature to the Hückel-Wheland π-electron theory. Other methods have been proposed[30–34] in recent years for treating all the valence electrons in the framework of a Hartree-Fock theory within the set of approximations known in the π-electron theory as the Pariser-Parr-Pople method. Among the different versions of these SCF methods, we have used the CNDO/2 procedure[35] mainly for its conceptual and practical simplicity.

According to this procedure, the molecular orbitals are obtained as a linear combination of atomic orbitals as in **(1)** by solving a set of secular equations similar to **(2)**, in which the usual Hartree-Fock Hamiltonian F is used instead of the effective Hückel Hamiltonian. As usual, the matrix elements of F are divided into a core matrix and an interaction matrix:

$$F_{\mu\nu} = I_{\mu\nu} + G_{\mu\nu}. \tag{6}$$

With the essential assumption of complete neglect of differential overlap, the interaction matrix reduces, as in the Pariser-Parr-Pople π-electron approximation, to:

TABLE 2

DIAGONAL PARAMETERS IN THE ITERATIVE EXTENDED HÜCKEL SCHEME (eV)

Atoms	$A_{(s)}$	$A_{(p)}$	B
H	13.8		14.3
C	21.2	11.4	11.9
NH	25.5	14.4	13.7
NH	27.4*	14.4	13.7
O	32	16.45	15.2

* 12.5 for p_2.

$$G_{\mu\mu} = 1/2 P_{\mu\mu}\gamma_{\mu\mu} + \sum_{\lambda \neq \mu} P_{\lambda\lambda}\gamma_{\mu\lambda}. \tag{7}$$

$$G_{\mu\nu} = -1/2 P_{\mu\nu}\gamma_{\mu\nu}, \tag{8}$$

where

$$P_{\mu\nu} = 2 \sum_{i} c_{i\mu} c_{i\nu} \tag{9}$$

is the familiar charge and bond order matrix.

The other fundamental features of CNDO/2 are: i) the replacement of all coulomb integrals $\gamma_{\mu\nu}$ for μ, ν on differents atoms A and B by an average taken as $\gamma_{2s_A 2s_B}$. ii) the expression of the core Hamiltonian as follows:

$$I_{\mu\mu} = U_{\mu\mu} - \sum_{B \neq A} V_{BA} \tag{10}$$

where $U_{\mu\mu}$ is the local core of the atom A bearing electron μ, and V_{BA} is the core potential of atom B. This may be written as:

$$I_{\mu\mu} = -1/2(I_{\mu} + A_{\mu}) + (Z_A - 1/2)\gamma_{AA} - \sum_{B \neq A} Z_B \gamma_{AB} \tag{11}$$

where Z_P is the number of electrons contributed to the system by atom P, I_μ, and A_μ is the valence-state ionization potential and electron affinity of orbital μ.

Finally, the nondiagonal elements are written:

$$I_{\mu_A \nu_B} = 1/2(\beta_A{}^0 + \beta_B{}^0)\, S_{\mu\nu} \tag{12}$$

in terms of quantities characteristics of the atoms carrying electrons μ and ν. The β^0-values have been empirically chosen[35] to fit *ab initio* calculations on small molecules. In practice, these are the only "fitted" quantities of the CNDO/2 method.

The basis orbitals used in CNDO/2 are Slater orbitals with the Slater exponents with, however, $\zeta = 1.2$ for hydrogen.

Computations of uracil, fluorouracil,[36] adenine, guanine, thymine and cytosine[37] have been performed in our laboratory by the CNDO/2 procedure, and the results concerning the nucleic bases will serve here as our third element of comparison. TABLE 3 summarizes the atomic input quantities used in our calculation: the β^0 values are those of Reference 35 with no modification.

The results obtained by the three previous procedures will be compared for the four fundamental bases—adenine, guanine, uracil and cytosine. All calculations have been performed for the geometries previously used in our

TABLE 3

ATOMIC PARAMETERS FOR CNDO/2 (EV)

Atom	1/2(I + A)		β°
	s	p	
H	7.176		−9
C	14.051	5.572	−21
N	19.316	7.275	−25
O	25.390	9.111	−31

Pariser-Parr π-computation.‡ In the discussion, we shall use the numbering of the atoms summarized on FIGURE 1 for the purine and pyrimidine skeletons, respectively.

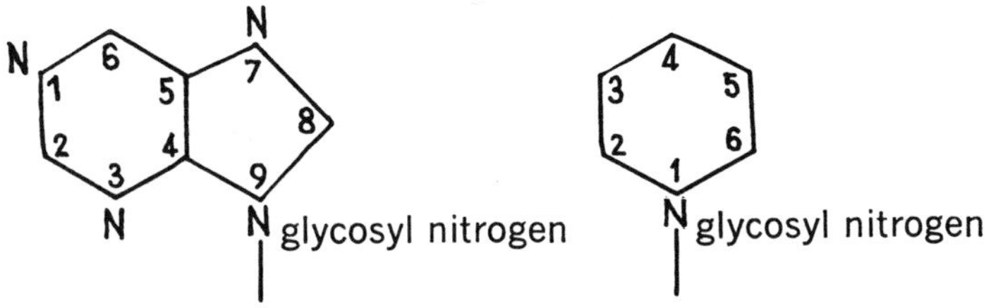

FIGURE 1. Numbering of the atoms on the puric and pyrimidic skeletons.

COMPARISON AND DISCUSSION OF THE RESULTS

Electron Distribution

The total net charges as well as the separate σ- and π-net charges are given in FIGURES 2, 3 and 4.

The analogous distributions corresponding to the simple σ-representation of Reference 12 are given for comparison in FIGURE 5 together with the self-consistent Pariser-Parr-Pople π-distribution. FIGURE 6 gives the total net charges obtained in the early calculations[12] using the simple σ-representation associated with an optimized Hückel π-electron calculation.

Since an examination of the voluminous data on the distribution of electronic charges would be lengthy, we shall limit our discussion here to the more outstanding features.

Total Net Charges and Dipole Moments

Although the general aspects of global electron distribution are necessarily similar in all methods (the oxygens carry a net negative charge, the nitrogens —whether pyrrolic, amino, or pyridine-like—are also negative), appreciable differences appear in the numerical values of the gross charges from one method to another, their relative ordering being sometimes parallel and sometimes different. Generally speaking, the net charges obtained by EHT are much larger (whether negative or positive) than those obtained by the other procedures.

Other features worth mentioning are that in all computations the more negative oxygen is always that of cytosine, the carbon atoms of the C_5C_6 bond of the pyrimidines are of opposite polarity, with C_5 negative, whereas all carbons are globally positive (with the exception of C_5 of the purines in CNDO). The overall image of the NH_2 group also shows a fair constancy.

‡ The adenine, guanine and uracil geometries are those of Spencer.[38] The geometry of cytosine is that of Barker and Marsh.[39]

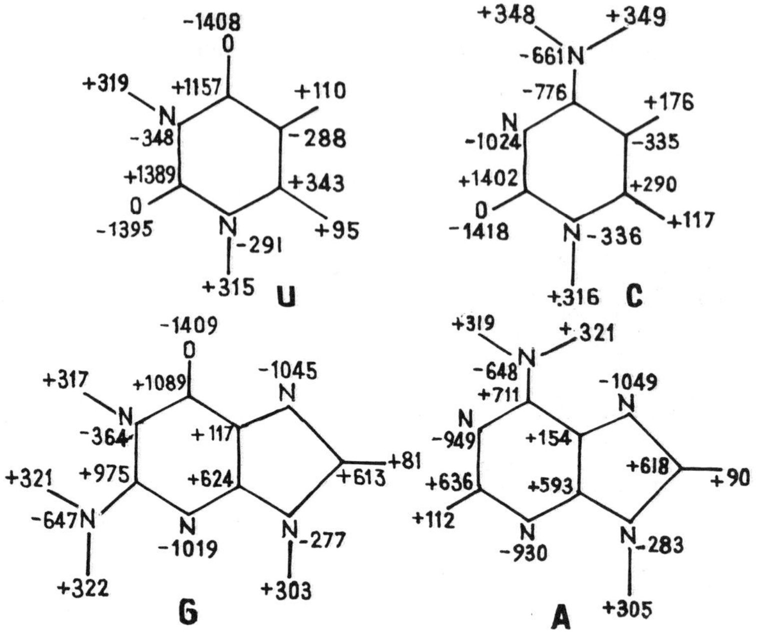

Fig: 2a

FIGURE 2. Net atomic charges in EHT. (10^{-3} electron units).
a) total net charges.

Without exploring further the detailed comparison of the total charges, it is particularly instructive to examine comparatively the values and the directions of the dipole moments predicted by the different procedures. The results are summarized in FIGURE 7 and TABLE 4.

It may be observed that the EHT method yields relatively large dipole moments, a predictable feature in view of the large values of the net charges already mentioned. The CNDO procedure gives moderate values of the di-

TABLE 4

TOTAL DIPOLE MOMENTS (DEBYE UNITS)[a]

	σ/π_1[b]		σ/π_2[c]		EHT*		IEHT[d]		CNDO[d]		Exptl. Value[f]
A	3.2	77	2.0	73	5.1	65	4.1	112	2.9	64	3.0
U	3.6	39	3.3	35	12.3	43	7.1	36	4.6	36	3.9
G	6.8	−36	7.2	−36	16.6	−14	13.6	−33	7.3	−27	—
C	7.2	97	7.1	110	16.5	109	12.9	121	7.6	102	—

[a] The first number is the moment, the second its angle $\theta°$, with the vertical axis (measured counterclockwise).

[b] π-moment obtained from the best Hückel parameters and added to the σ-moments evaluated as in Reference 12.

[c] π-moment obtained by the Pariser-Parr-Pople computations,[7] and added to the same σ-moment.

[d] Hybrid moments included.

[f] For 9-methyl-adenine and 1, 3-dimethyl uracile.[50]

* Hybrid moments not included.

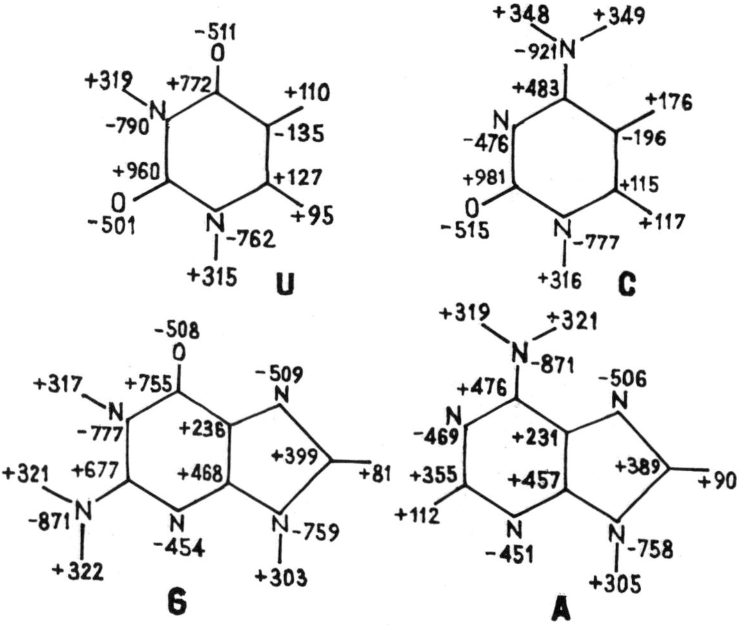

Fig: 2b

b) σ-net charges.

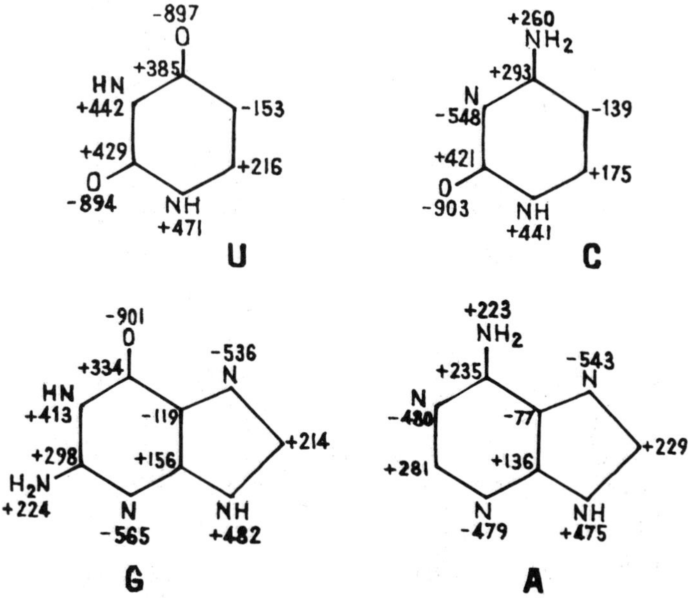

Fig: 2c

c) π-net charges.

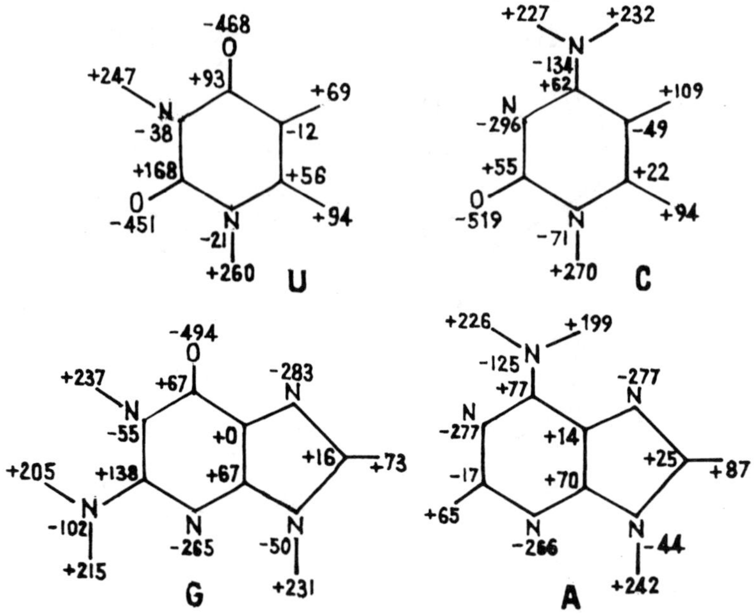

Fig: 3a

FIGURE 3. Net atomic charges in IEHT. (10^{-3} electron units).
a) total net charges.

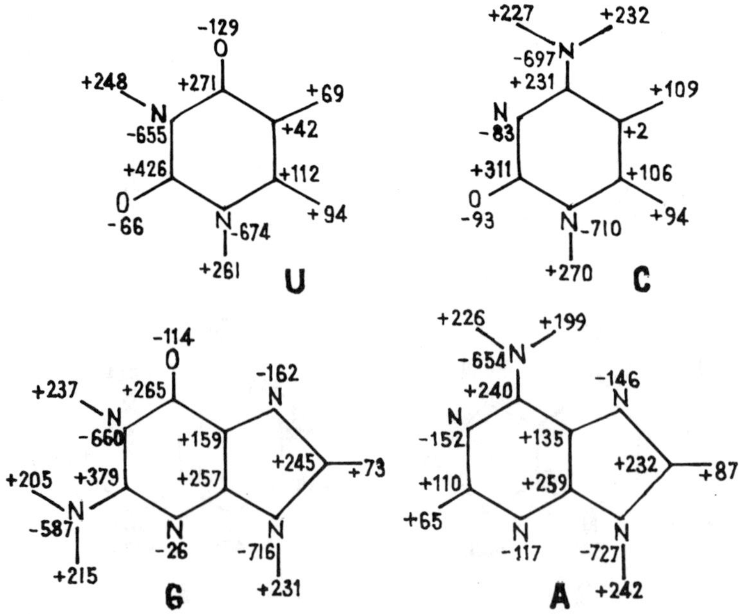

Fig: 3b

b) σ-net charges.

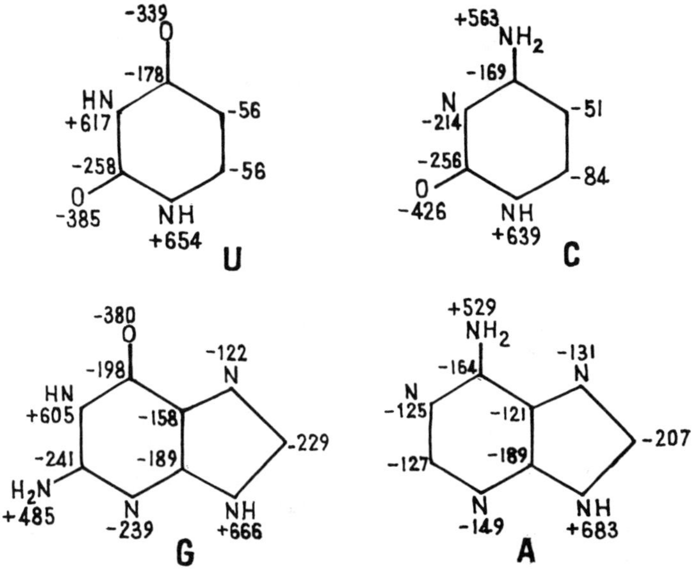

Fig: 3c

c) π-net charges.

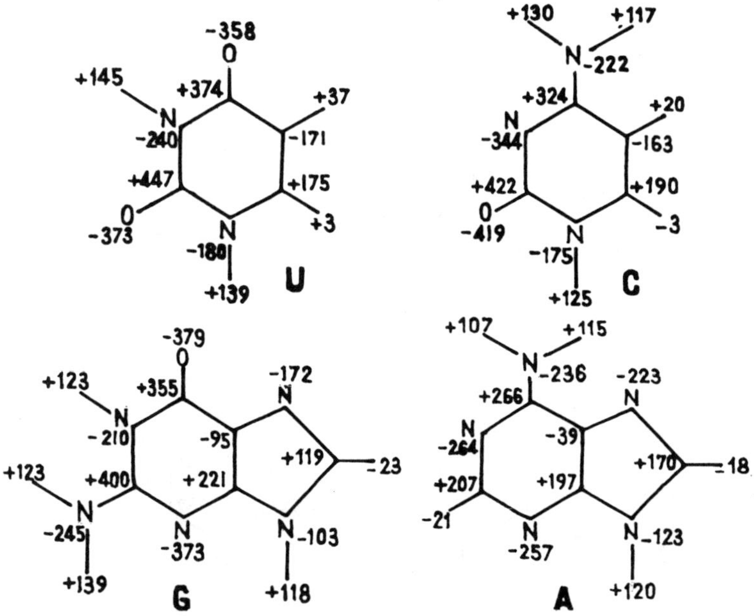

Fig: 4a

FIGURE 4. Net atomic charges in CNDO. (10^{-3} electron units).
a) total net charges.

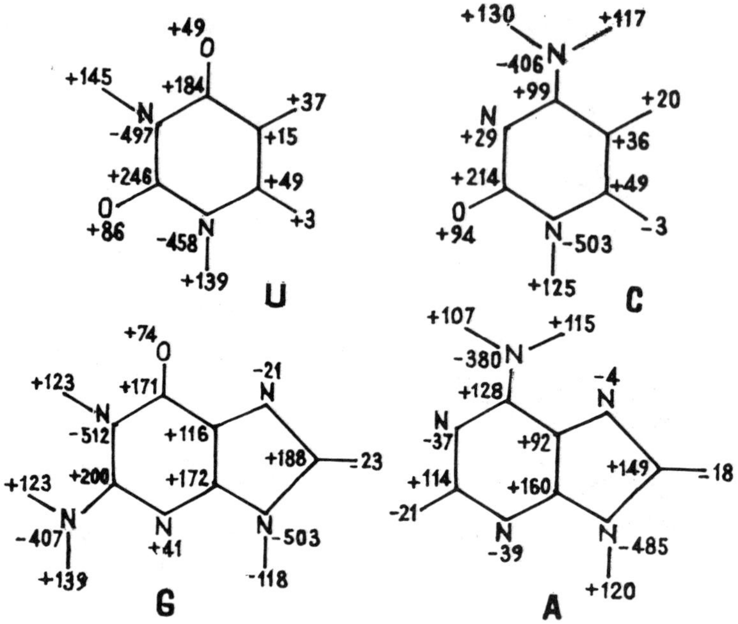

Fig: 4b

b) σ-net charges.

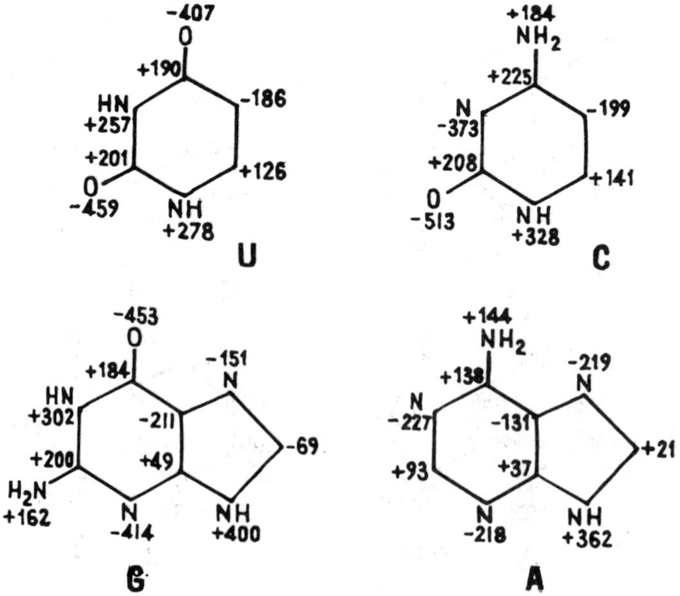

Fig: 4c

c) π-net charges.

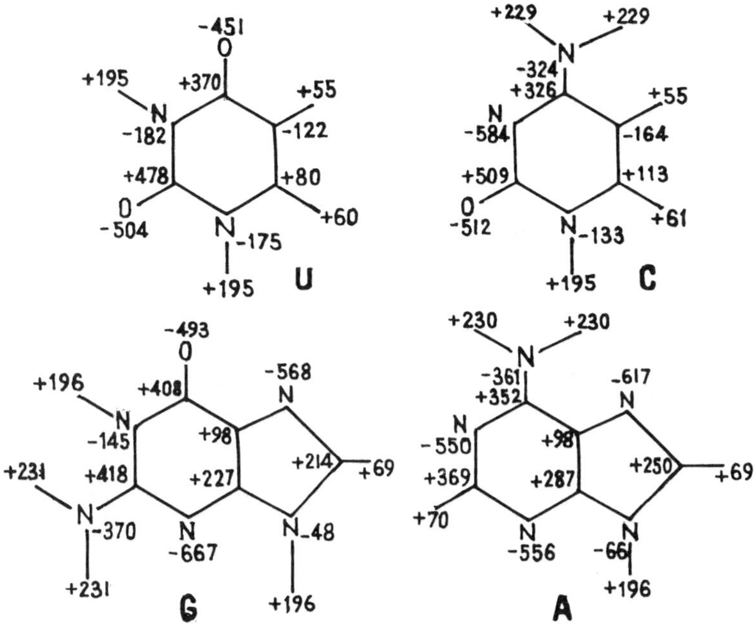

FIGURE 5. Separated σ and π calculations (10^{-3} electron units).
a) total net charges (σ BP + π PPP).

pole moments, very close to those obtained by combining the Berthod-Pullman σ-distribution[12] with either the Hückel or the Pariser-Parr-Pople π-distribution; the IEHT method yields intermediate values.

A remarkable feature is that all methods predict greater dipole moments for guanine and cytosine than for uracil which, in turn, should have a slightly greater moment than adenine, a trend already present in De Voe and Tinoco's early evaluation. (See Reference (f) in TABLE 4.) The comparison of the theoretical values with the experimental ones available only for simple derivatives of adenine and uracil indicates that the CNDO and the σ + π (Hückel or PPP) calculations are in very satisfactory agreement with experiment. It may, therefore, reasonably be expected that the values predicted for G and C in these last two procedures are the reliable ones. What is still more striking is the similarity in the directions of the moments predicted for the bases by all methods. Obviously, in spite of the quoted differences in charge distributions, the overall polarity of the molecules is well-reproduced by all procedures although somewhat exaggerated by some of them.

π-Net Charges

It is particularly interesting to compare the distribution of the π-charges obtained in all-valence electron calculations with the results of the usual previous π-electron computations.

The most striking feature in this respect is the very close analogy between the CNDO and the simple σ + PPP-π-results, this observation being valid

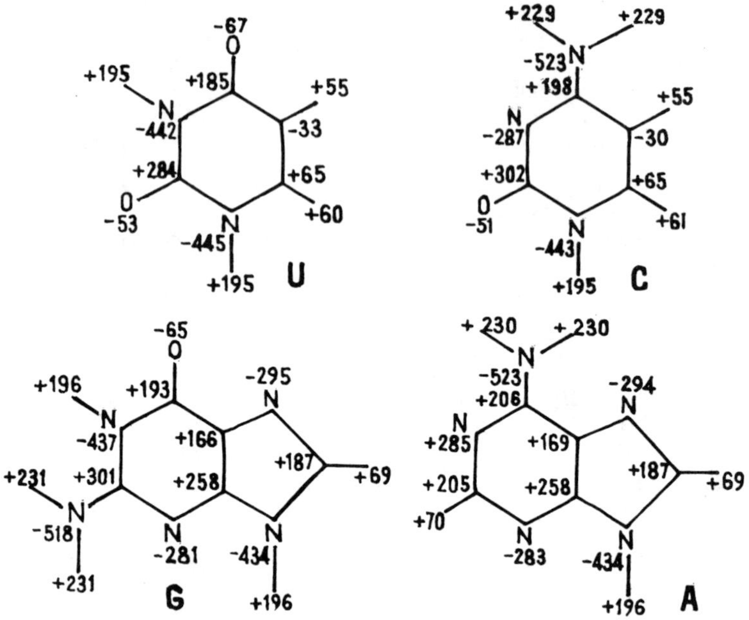

Fig: 5b

b) σ BP net charges.

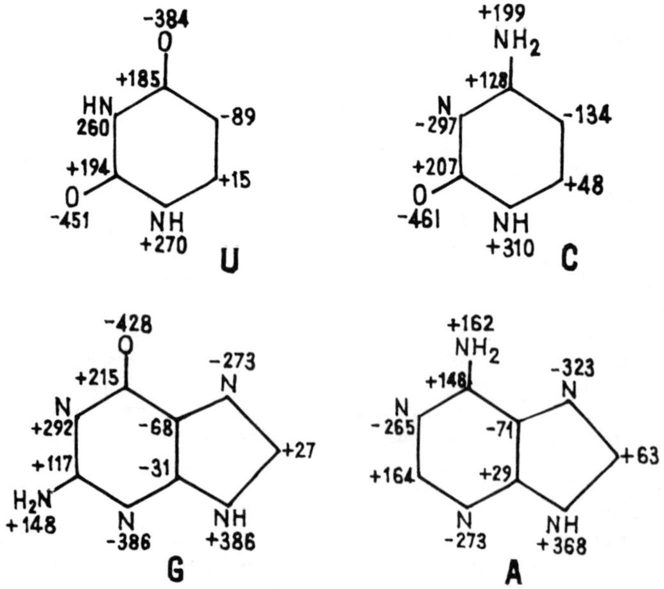

Fig: 5c

c) π PPP net charges.

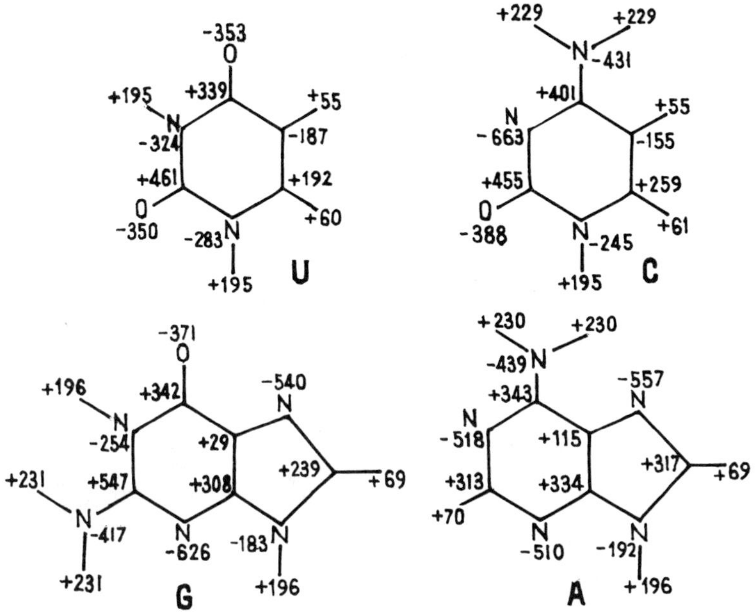

FIGURE 6. Total net charges (σ BP + best Hückel), (10^{-3} electron units).

both in regard to the overall qualitative aspects of the distribution and the order of magnitude of the charges at the different positions. On the other hand, the EHT and IEHT procedures obviously suffer from some imperfections: EHT, for instance, exaggerates the π-charge displacements in particular, leading to too high accumulation of π-electrons on the oxygens. IEHT, on the other hand, exaggerates particularly the delocalization of the π lone pairs of the NH and NH_2 groups yielding, as a consequence, too positive nitrogens and too negative carbons. This factor is controlled by the exaggeration of the σ-displacements towards the pyrrolic nitrogens which, in turn, through the ω-technique process brings about a strong repelling of the π-electrons on these centers.

Nevertheless, some constancy in the positioning of the most reactive centers and in their relative ordering is observed in a number of cases: thus, the most negative oxygen of all the bases is that of cytosine in all calculations. The order of decreasing positivity (increased delocalization of the π lone-pair) of the glycosidic nitrogen is always G > A > C > U, except in IEHT where A and G are inverted. Another important constancy is the π-polarity of the $C_5 - C_6$ bond in the pyrimidines, with C_5 negatively charged and C_6 positively charged (here again there is a different behavior pattern in IEHT, where both carbons bear an excess of π-electrons). Finally, the large negative charge of N_3 of guanine appears in all results, but the detailed ordering of the pyrimidic nitrogens with respect to their negative π-population varies from one calculation to another.

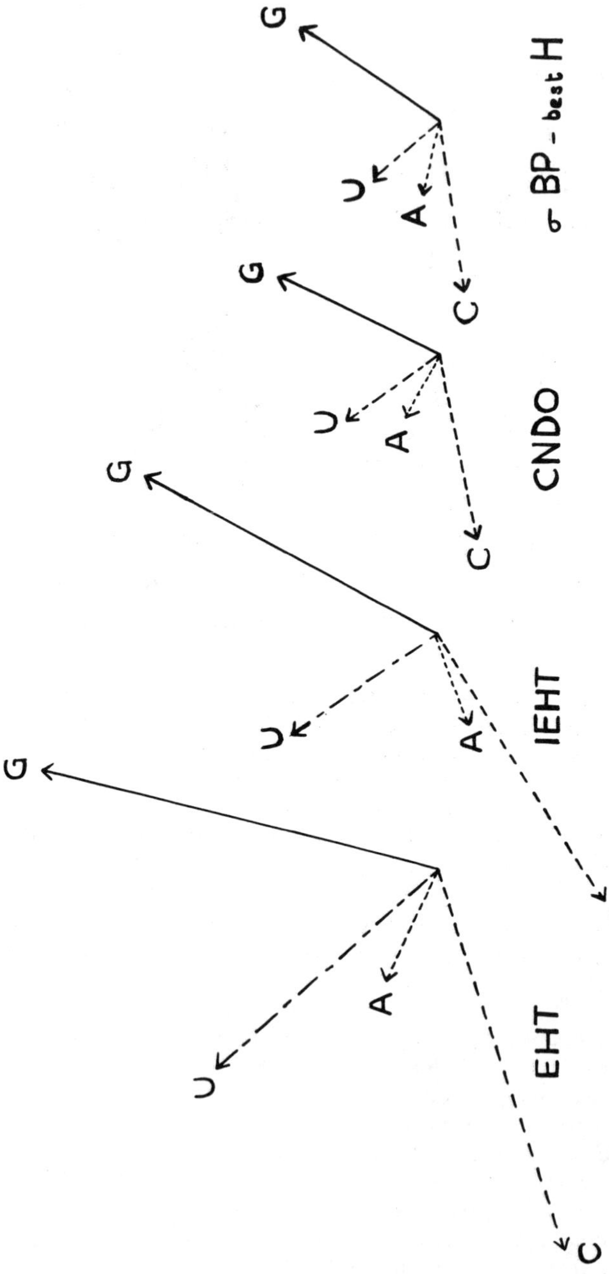

FIGURE 7. Comparison of dipole moments calculations in different approximations.

σ-Net Charges

The results concerning the σ-distributions unveil new aspects of the problem insofar as the only previously available data were due to a localized-bond approach.

At the present stage of the methods there exists, undisputably, a number of divergencies between their indications. Thus, although the general aspect of the σ-distribution is rather similar in EHT and in Del Re's method, the first procedure probably overestimates the displacements as already noted for the π-distribution. This is no doubt a result of the parametrization of EHT. The iterative procedure diminishes the difference somewhat but, as previously mentioned, it seems that the electron-attracting effect of nitrogen is exaggerated in NH and NH_2 groups. In CNDO, we observe the surprising fact that the pyridine-type nitrogens carry very small negative charges, or may even be positive. In the same fashion, the CNDO-oxygens are slightly positive, whereas they are slightly negative in the other representations; it may be remarked that, in any case, the σ-polarity of the oxygens is low. In regard to the hydrogen atoms, all procedures confirm an appreciable discharge for hydrogens bound to nitrogen (NH or NH_2) and, generally, a smaller discharge for hydrogen bound to carbon atoms. However, this last effect is smaller in CNDO and is sometimes even reversed, a feature which seems rather characteristic of the procedure[36, 37, 40, 41] and which requires further investigation.

In spite of the differences observed, there is an interesting outcome of all calculations that supports the fundamental hypothesis of the simple σ representation used earlier: the σ atomic charges are essentially determined by the nature of the atom and by its nearest neighbors and not by long-range interactions. This is true even in molecules containing strongly electronegative substituents like fluorine.[36]

Of course, we do not have enough experimental data which would enable us to decide between the different results. It must be realized that these all-valence electron methods are in the first stage of their development and are subject to appreciable refinement. A number of the preceding discrepancies undoubtedly spring from imperfect parametrization, the improvement of which is, therefore, one of the immediate necessities. Work is beeing carried out along these lines in our laboratory, and it may be hoped that it will smooth out the divergences.

Energies of the Molecular Orbitals

TABLES 5, 6 and 7, give the calculated energies of all the occupied molecular orbitals obtained by the three procedures. EHT and IEHT give a similar spread of 20 to 25 ev in energy levels, whereas the CNDO levels extend deeper—features which are characteristic of the procedures. There is no doubt that the numerical values of the orbital energies should not be taken as absolute in any of the methods.

The following observations can be made on the data:

1. In the three procedures, one observes a very large intermingling of the σ and π-levels, with no appearance of a superficial "π-shell" as was sometimes implicitly admitted in π-electron calculations. Although the details may differ, the interspersing of the σ-levels among the π-orbitals seems to be a constant feature in all calculations. The same mixing appears also in recent nonempiri-

TABLE 5

OCCUPIED ORBITALS (EHT) EV—UNLABELED ORBITALS ARE σ LEVELS

U	C	G	A
37.19	37.03	37.04	32.74
36.93	31.39	32.56	30.99
30.39	29.51	31.22	29.74
28.18	27.29	28.45	27.50
25.45	25.42	27.66	26.82
20.56	20.25	26.97	23.97
20.04	19.87	23.52	20.03
18.41	π 18.14	20.05	19.33
π 18.18	17.90	19.22	18.55
π 18.14	17.67	18.78	16.67
18.12	16.78	π 18.15	16.28
17.59	16.16	17.86	15.79
17.18	15.44	17.48	π 15.78
16.52	π 15.27	16.45	15.35
15.58	14.86	16.19	π 15.05
π 14.92	14.40	π 15.74	14.85
14.74	π 14.40	15.65	π 14.54
14.07	13.83	15.32	14.32
π 13.90	π 13.51	π 15.12	14.08
13.37	12.58	14.69	π 13.59
π 12.71	π 12.50	14.23	13.58
		π 14.10	π 13.35
		13.73	12.92
		π 13.52	12.08
		13.51	π 11.95
		π 13.39	
		12.38	
		π 11.84	

cal SCF calculations made in a Gaussian basis set on pyrrole,[42] pyridine[43] and pyrazine.[44] Such a constancy in the outcome of procedures, which are quite different in their principles, is probably a strong indication in favor of the picture obtained. It may be added that this mixing of σ- and π-levels occurs much less in the virtual orbitals in which the π-levels are often grouped below the σ-levels.

2. In both EHT and CNDO, the homo (highest occupied molecular orbital) is a π-orbital. In IEHT, it is a σ-orbital, the first π-level coming below. (In uracil, there are even two such σ-orbitals above the first π-level.) Before commenting on this IEHT σ-homo, let us look more carefully at the highest occupied π-level. The order of its increasing energy is (in absolute values):

$$G < A < C < U$$

in EHT and CNDO and

$$G < C < A < U$$

in IEHT. Thus, in all cases, insofar as the homo gives a measure of the electron-donor ability of a molecule, guanine appears as the best π-donor and uracil as the worst one among the four bases, in agreement with our previous Pariser-Parr-Pople π calculations.[7] It is very interesting in this connection that the recently measured values of the ionization potentials for the bases are[45] in the order:

TABLE 6

OCCUPIED ORBITALS (IEHT) eV—UNLABELED ORBITALS ARE σ LEVELS

U	C	G	A
33.09	31.35	32.36	31.56
29.53	28.56	30.60	29.33
27.96	26.76	28.73	26.97
25.98	23.87	25.77	24.94
23.63	22.89	25.13	23.67
20.03	18.94	24.84	22.07
19.14	18.28	21.54	18.85
17.70	16.92	19.12	18.49
16.56	16.23	18.67	17.98
16.33	15.63	18.24	16.81
π 16.29	π 15.25	17.02	15.99
π 14.53	14.28	16.50	π 15.86
14.29	13.72	π 16.10	15.34
13.85	π 13.68	15.54	π 14.28
π 13.70	13.11	15.40	14.20
12.19	π 12.99	π 14.74	14.13
11.46	11.17	14.68	13.59
π 11.31	10.86	π 14.14	π 13.44
π 11.08	π 10.54	13.71	13.01
9.89	π 10.39	12.87	π 12.15
9.43	9.07	π 12.46	11.84
		11.97	π 11.67
		π 11.73	11.07
		11.52	π 10.43
		π 10.93	10.26
		10.43	
		π 10.31	
		9.21	

$$A = C < T < U.$$

The measurements for guanine are, unfortunately, missing. However, a strong electron-donor ability of this compound seems indicated by its easy charge-transfer complexation with chloranil.[46]

Returning to the special results of IEHT regarding the σ-character of the homos, two remarks must be made: 1) It is not the first time that an all-electron calculation yields a σ homo in conjugated compounds. This happened in Gaussian-basis calculations[43] and in CNDO/2 calculations on pyridine[47] and ethylene.[41] The available experimental data both on the fundamental heterocycles[48] and on the purines and pyrimidines[45] do not seem, however, to favor a σ-first ionization potential. Thus, we are inclined to think that the treatment of all (or all-valence) electrons nowadays available shows a tendancy to overestimate the energy of σ-orbitals with respect to π-orbitals. This is a theoretical point which needs investigation. At any rate it shows the danger of limiting oneself to only one procedure. 2) By examining the IEHT orbital wave functions, one discovers that in all the carbonyl compounds (U, C, G) the σ-homo(s) are essentially made up of the oxygen p_x and p_y orbitals. Moreover, looking at the same compounds in the CNDO methods, one observes that here the σ-homo (that is the second homo) is also made up essentially of the p_x and p_y orbitals of the oxygens. This does not appear at all however in the EHT orbitals, in which the oxygenlike molecular orbitals are buried rather deep toward the middle of the energy range, and the second

TABLE 7

OCCUPIED ORBITALS (CNDO) eV—UNLABELED ORBITALS ARE σ LEVELS

U	C	G	A
52.87	52.36	55.49	55.33
45.09	44.91	51.27	50.39
43.64	41.69	48.23	44.13
40.22	38.85	42.73	38.86
36.88	36.61	39.50	37.34
32.25	31.66	38.98	33.94
27.41	27.75	32.08	30.41
π 26.38	25.74	30.57	29.94
26.36	π 25.53	28.50	27.73
25.71	25.45	27.82	π 27.07
21.39	20.96	π 27.60	25.64
π 20.07	20.01	26.48	22.62
19.83	π 19.91	π 22.82	π 21.15
19.12	18.40	22.46	20.51
π 18.65	17.91	21.61	19.82
17.72	π 17.20	20.60	18.07
16.42	15.56	π 19.66	π 17.89
13.83	13.68	19.55	17.31
π 13.18	π 13.21	17.38	15.76
12.90	11.81	16.75	15.11
π 11.88	π 10.78	15.65	π 14.14
		π 15.34	13.11
		15.08	π 12.57
		π 14.21	11.46
		π 13.11	π 10.08
		12.77	
		11.55	
		π 9.06	

homos are combinations of p_x and p_y orbitals of the different nitrogen atoms.

Let us recall that a semiempirical evaluation in the Pariser-Parr-Pople type of approximation of the π and lone-pair ionization potentials had led us to the prediction:[9]

$$I_\pi < I_n(0) < I_n(N)$$

in the nucleic bases. The last inequality would agree with the two iterative methods used here, and disagrees with EHT. To conclude this point in the discussion, let us mention that none of the three methods permits us to see pure lone-pairs on nitrogens in the sense that no σ-orbital appears as a pure or nearly pure one-nitrogen lone-pair, whereas oxygen in-plane (x or y) atomic orbitals appear nearly pure in the molecular orbitals.

Transition Energies

None of the three procedures outlined has been devised initially for the calculation of transition energies. It is, however, interesting to use the orbitals obtained for such calculations. Until now, only the CNDO/2 results have been exploited in this direction.[37] The energies obtained for the first singlet and triplet are given in TABLE 8.

It should be emphasized that no numerical agreement with experimental value was expected, since the theoretical values of the coulomb integrals $\gamma_{\mu\nu}$ are used in the calculation. As in a π-electron SCF treatment, these must

TABLE 8

CNDO FIRST SINGLET AND TRIPLET TRANSITIONS (EV)

	Singlet	Triplet
A	9.2	6.5
U	9.3	5.9
G	7.6	6.0
C	8.3	6.5

probably be reduced if good electronic transitions are to be obtained.

The qualitative features of the results show, however, two satisfactory trends: (1) the first singlet and triplet transitions are $\pi - \pi$ in nature. (2) G and C should absorb at longer wavelength than A and U, in agreement with the experimental results that were well accounted for in our previous Pariser-Parr-π calculations.[14] More computations are being performed in our laboratory concerning the excited states.

CONCLUSIONS

We believe we have shown that there are some differences in the results of the different procedures. This, no doubt, is bound to the parametrization of each method: thus, the high charge displacements and high dipole moments in EHT are most probably due to the choice of VOIPs for the diagonal elements, and the still too high dipole moments of IEHT show that the iteration process in the form adopted is not sufficient for correcting this defect.[49] As was mentioned briefly, the IEHT procedure, as utilized, certainly suffers from an inadequate parametrization of NH groups. None of these inconveniences appear in CNDO for reasons which shall be discussed elsewhere,[49] but this procedure itself does not seem reliable for predicting all properties.

On the other hand, the simultaneous treatment of all-valence electrons, with no hypothesis on the atom hybridization state, does not (with the obvious exception of the mixing of the σ- and π-energy levels) seriously upset the general image of these heterocycles which was obtained with the previous semi-empirical methods insofar as they were carefully and sensibly parametrized. Needless to say, however, the differences found should be further explored.

Furthermore, we hope we have shown that it is not yet possible to use any of the existing procedures for the accurate prediction of all molecular properties, and the label "all-valence electrons" calculation should not be taken as a guarantee that the results obtained by one singled-out method represent the molecular truth, as is well illustrated by the discussion on the highest filled orbitals or the energy-location of the oxygen lone-pairs. Even nonempirical SCF calculations[42–44] depend on the atomic basis and, until comparisons of different basis sets have been carried out, one must exercise caution in reaching conclusions.

ACKNOWLEDGMENT

Thanks are due to Dr. Jordan for kindly communicating some unpublished data.

REFERENCES

1. PULLMAN, A., B. PULLMAN & G. BERTHIER. 1956. Recherches sur la structure électronique des composés actifs en chimiothérapie du cancer. Compt. Rend. Acad. Sci. Paris. **243:** 380–382.

2. PULLMAN, A. & B. PULLMAN. 1958. Recherches sur la structure électronique des constituants cellulaires fondamentaux et des composés actifs en chimiothérapie anticancéreuse. II. Les bases puriques fondamentales. Bull. Soc. Chim.: 766–772.
3. PULLMAN, A. & B. PULLMAN. 1959. Recherches sur la structure électronique des constituants cellulaires fondamentaux et des composés actifs en chimiothérapie anticancéreuse. VI. Les pyrimidines naturelles fondamentales. Bull. Soc. Chim.: 594–597.
4. PULLMAN, B. & A. PULLMAN. 1963. Quantum Biochemistry. Interscience Publishers. New York, N. Y.
5. VEILLARD, A. & B. PULLMAN. 1963. Etude par le champ moléculaire self-consistant de la structure électronique des bases puriques et pyrimidiques d'intérêt biochimique. J. Theoret. Biol. **4:** 37–51.
6. NAGATA, C., A. IMAMURA, Y. TAGASHIMA & M. KODAMA. 1965. Semi-empirical self-consistent field molecular orbital calculation of the electronic structure of the base components of nucleic acids. Bull. Chem. Soc. Japan, **38:** 1638–1645.
7. BERTHOD, H., C. GIESSNER-PRETTRE & A. PULLMAN. 1966. Theoretical study of the electronic properties of the purine and pyrimidine components of the nucleic acids. I. A semi-empirical self-consistent field calculation. Theoret. Chim. Acta **5:** 53–68.
8. PULLMAN, A. & B. PULLMAN. 1967. Aspects of the electronic structure of the purine and pyrimidine bases of the nucleic acids and of their interactions. Advan. Quant. Chem. **44:** 267–325.
9. PULLMAN, A. & M. ROSSI. 1964. The ionization potentials of the π- and lone pair electrons of biochemical purines and pyrimidines. Biochim. Biophys. Acta **88:** 211–212.
10. DEL RE, G. 1958. A simple MO LCAO method for the calculation of charge distributions in saturated organic molecules. J. Chem. Soc.: 4031–4040.
11. BERTHOD, H. & A. PULLMAN. 1964. The role of the σ-framework in the properties of the biological purines and pyrimidines: dipole moments and tautomeric equilibria. Biopolymers **2:** 483–488.
12. BERTHOD, H. & A. PULLMAN. 1965. Sur le calcul des caractéristiques du squelette σ des molécules conjuguées. J. Chim. Phys. **55:** 942–946.
13. DENIS, A. & A. PULLMAN. 1967. Theoretical study of the electronic properties of biological purines and pyrimidines. III. The representation of the methyl group and the structure of thymine. Theoret. Chim. Acta **7:** 110–116.
14. BERTHOD, H., C. GIESSNER-PRETTRE & A. PULLMAN. 1967. Theoretical study of the electronic properties of biological purines and pyrimidines. II. The effect of configuration mixing. Int. J. Quant. Chem. **1:** 123–137.
15. HOFFMANN, R. 1963. An extended Hückel theory. I. Hydrocarbons. J. Chem. Phys. **39:** 1397–1412.
16. HOFFMANN, R. 1964. An extended Hückel theory. II. σ-orbitals in the azines. J. Chem. Phys. **40:** 2745.
17. HOFFMANN, R. 1964. Toward an understanding of non-classical carbonium ions. J. Amer. Chem. Soc. **86:** 1259–1261.
18. ALLEN, L. C. & J. D. RUSSEL. 1967. Extended Hückel theory and the shape of molecules. J. Chem. Phys. **46:** 1029–1037, and references therein.
19. JORDAN, F. & B. PULLMAN. 1968. Molecular orbital calculations on the preferred conformation of nucleosides. Theor. Chim. Acta **9:** 242–252 (and references therein).
20. CLEMENTI, E. & D. L. RAIMONDI. 1963. Atomic screening constants from SCF functions. J. Chem. Phys. **38:** 2686–2689.
21. CUSACHS, L. C. 1964. Semi-empirical molecular orbitals for general polyatomic molecules I. Rept. No. 50 Quantum Theory Proj., University of Florida: 36.
22. CUSACHS, L. C. 1965. Semi-empirical molecular orbitals for general polyatomic molecules. II. J. Chem. Phys. **43:** S157–S159.
23. WHELAND, G. W. & D. E. MANN. 1949. The dipole moments of fulvene and azulene. J. Chem. Phys. **17:** 264–268.
24. STREITWIESER, JR., A. 1960. A molecular orbital study of ionization potentials of organic compound utilizing the ω-technique. J. Amer. Chem. Soc. **82:** 4123–4135.
25. VISTE, A. & H. B. GRAY. 1964. The electronic structure of permanganate ion. Inorg. Chem. **3:** 1113–1123.

26. BERTHIER, G., P. MILLIE & A. VEILLARD. 1965. Recherches théoriques sur les complexes. I. J. Chim. Phys. **62:** 8–19.
27. CUSACHS, L. C. & J. W. REYNOLDS. 1965. Selection of molecular matrix elements from atomic data. I. J. Chem. Phys. **43:** S160–S164.
28. CARROLL, D. G., A. T. ARMSTRONG & S. P. MCGLYNN. 1966. Semi-empirical molecular orbital calculations. I. J. Chem. Phys. **44:** 1865.
29. REIN, R., N. FUKUDA, H. WIN & G. A. CLARKE. 1966. Iterative extended Hückel theory. J. Chem. Phys. **45:** 4743.
30. KLOPMAN, G. 1964. A semi-empirical treatment of molecular structures. J. Amer. Chem. Soc. **86:** 4550–4557.
31. POHL, H. A., R. REIN & K. APPELL. 1964. Simplified SCF method for σ-bonded systems. I. J. Chem. Phys. **41:** 3385–3392.
32. POPLE, J. A. & G. A. SEGAL. 1965. Approximate self-consistent molecular orbital theory. I. J. Chem. Phys. **43:** S129–S135.
33. DEWAR, M. J. S. & G. KLOPMAN. 1967. Ground states of σ-bonded molecules. I. J. Amer. Chem. Soc. **89:** 3089–3098.
34. POPLE, J. A. & G. A. SEGAL. 1966. Approximate self-consistent molecular orbital theory. III. J. Chem. Phys. **44:** 3289–3296.
35. POPLE, J. A. & G. A. SEGAL. 1965. Approximate self-consistent molecular orbital theory. II. J. Chem. Phys. **43:** S136–S149.
36. BERTHOD, H., C. GIESSNER-PRETTRE & A. PULLMAN. 1967. Sur les rôles respectifs des électrons σ et π dans les propriétés des dérivés halogenes des molécules conjuguées. Application à l'étude de l'uracile et du fluorouracile. Theor. Chim. Acta **8:** 212–222.
37. GIESSNER-PRETTRE, C. & A. PULLMAN. 1968. All valence electron calculations of the biological purines and pyrimidines. I. A CNDO calculation. Theor. Chim. Acta. **9:** 279–287.
38. SPENCER, M. 1959. The stereochemistry of deoxyribonucleic acid. I. Covalent bond lengths and angles. Acta. Crystallogr. **12:** 59–65.
39. BARKER, D. L. & R. E. MARSH. 1964. The crystal structure of cytosine. Acta Crystallogr. **17:** 1581–1587.
40. POPLE, J. A. & M. GORDON. 1967. Molecular orbital theory of the electronic structure of organic compounds. I. J. Amer. Chem. Soc. **89:** 4253–4261.
41. JORDAN, F. 1967. Molecular orbital calculations on strained molecules and ions. Ph.D. dissertation. University of Pennsylvania, Philadelphia, Pa.
42. CLEMENTI, E., H. CLEMENTI & D. R. DAVIS. 1967. Study of the electronic structure of molecules. III. J. Chem. Phys. **46:** 4725–4730.
43. CLEMENTI, E. 1967. Study of the electronic structure of molecules. IV. J. Chem. Phys. **46:** 4731–4736.
44. CLEMENTI, E. 1967. Study of the electronic structure of molecules. V. J. Chem. Phys. **46:** 4737–4742.
45. LIFSCHITZ, C., E. D. BERGMANN & B. PULLMAN. 1967. The ionization potentials of biological purines and pyrimidines. Tetrahedron Lett. **46:** 4583.
46. MACHMER, P. & J. DUCHESNE. 1965. Charge transfer between nucleic acid bases and chloranil. Nature **206:** 618–619.
47. GIESSNER-PRETTRE, C. & A. PULLMAN. Unpublished data and Reference 37.
48. EL SAYED, M. A., M. KASHA & Y. TANAKA. 1961. Ionization potentials of benzene, hexadenterobenzene and pyridine. J. Chem. Phys. **34:** 334–336.
49. PULLMAN, A. σ-electronics in confugated Heterocycles. *In* σ-Molecular Theory. O. Sinanoĝlu & Benjamin K. Wiley, Eds. In press.
50. DE VOE, H. & I. TINOCO, JR. 1962. The stability of helical polynucleotides: base contributions. J. Molec. Biol. **4:** 500–517.

SOME ASPECTS OF THE HYDROGEN BOND IN MOLECULAR BIOLOGY

Per-Olov Löwdin

Department of Quantum Chemistry, Uppsala University, Uppsala, Sweden, and Quantum Theory Project, Nuclear Sciences Building, University of Florida Gainesville, Fla.

In modern chemistry, a hydrogen bond is a proton shared between two electron lone pairs. These fundamental particles are all wave packets obeying the laws of quantum mechanics, and the theoretical properties of a hydrogen bond should therefore be studied accordingly. Each electron lone pair offers the proton an attraction represented by a potential well, and a proton in a hydrogen bond is usually situated in a double-well potential with two minima separated by a barrier. The proton may move between the two minima either above the barrier or through the barrier by means of the quantum-mechanical tunnel effect. Since the proton in its motion is surrounded by a cloud of negative electricity, the proton often serves also as an electron carrier.

In molecular biology, the hydrogen bonds are of particular importance in the proteins and in the nucleic acids. In the proteins, the hydrogen bonds stabilize the secondary structure of the molecule (according to Pauling): the α-helix consists of a linear chain of amino acids with the fundamental groups situated on a cylindrical surface, and these groups are small conjugated systems linked together by hydrogen bonds across the chain. If an extra electron is introduced at one end of the α-helix, the electron may slide on a conjugated system to a hydrogen bond, where the proton carries it over to the next conjugated system, etc., so that the electron may pass from one end to the other. Such processes may be of importance in the action of oxidation-reduction enzymes, and they are now studied quantum-mechanically as time-dependent transport phenomena.

In the Watson-Crick model of DNA, the genetic template consists essentially of a system of hydrogen bonds. If these bonds fit together in a base pair, one has complementarity between the bases, and tautomeric errors in the form of a misplaced proton may then lead to erroneous pairing and cause mutations. It is evident here that, in the replication process, the incorporation of single tautomeric errors is exceedingly rare due to the energy properties of the hydrogen bonds in the center of the replication area in the conventional replication model.

In addition, the properties of the hydrogen bonds are important in the stationary state of DNA. The genetic code, in the form of hydrogen bonds, consists of a definite pattern of protons and electron lone pairs. Since each proton may easily pass from one classical equilibrium position to another in the hydrogen bond by means of the above-mentioned tunnel effect, the genetic code could easily deteriorate with time. The potential energy surfaces for the mobile protons in a base pair of DNA are calculated by quantum-mechanical methods taking the polarizing effect of the protons into account. These surfaces are found to be highly asymmetric with respect to the minima, and the tunneling errors for the GC- and AT-pairs in equilibrium at $T = 310°$ K amount to 10^{-10} and 10^{-11}, respectively. These figures are in good agreement with the experimental biological data in regard to the spontaneous mutation rates per base pair and generation, which are estimated to be in the region between 10^{-8} and 10^{-12}.

The Hydrogen Bond

In classical chemistry, a hydrogen bond consists of a hydrogen atom shared between two electronegative atoms, namely F, O, N, etc. A hydrogen bond may occur inside a molecule as a stabilizing factor, or it may occur between different molecules in solution or in crystals; it is, for instance, of fundamental importance in understanding the properties of water and ice. The main features of the hydrogen bond in chemistry have been discussed extensively by Pauling,[1] Huggins,[2] and other authors.

The importance of the hydrogen bond in biochemistry was emphasized by Pauling[3] and coworkers in their crystallographic study of the structure of proteins, in which they found that the hydrogen bonds were essential in stabilizing the secondary structure of the α-helix. This was a discovery of great importance in biology. Through the work of Avery[4] and coworkers, and Chargaff[5] and collaborators it had further become clear that the genetic information in the chromosomes was contained in a giant molecule of deoxyribonucleic acid (DNA). Crystallographic studies of these molecules by Wilkins[6] and by Watson and Crick[7] had revealed that they were double helixes consisting of two sugar-phosphate strands held together by pairs of nitrogen bases. In the Watson-Crick model of DNA, the pairing of the nitrogen bases was specific depending on the possibilities for forming hydrogen bonds which were essential for the stability of the various base pairs and hence for the entire structure. This means that the genetic template consists essentially of hydrogen bonds. In biochemistry, these bonds are hence of great importance for the stability of both proteins and nucleic acids.

Hydrogen Bonds in Quantum Chemistry

In modern quantum chemistry, the fundamental properties of the hydrogen bond are even better understood with the aid of the concepts of hybridization introduced by Slater[8] and Pauling.[9] In this way, the importance of the connection between the properties of hydrogen bonds and the classical Lewis bases and acids has been stressed.

Of great importance in biochemistry are certain planar molecules with alternating single and double bonds, so-called conjugated systems. They are conveniently described by the molecular orbital method introduced by Mulliken.[10] In this picture, the single bonds correspond to localized σ-electrons having orbitals symmetric with respect to the molecular plane, whereas the classical double bonds correspond to mobile π-electrons having orbitals antisymmetric with respect to the plane. The π-electrons seem to be responsible for the aromatic properties of ring systems, and their behavior has been studied by Hückel[11] using the MO-LCAO-method in simplified form. The general features of the π-electron system may be summarized in the charge- and bond-order matrix introduced by Coulson and Longuet-Higgins.[12] During the last two decades, this approach has been used extensively by the Pullmans[13] in their broad study of conjugated systems.

We now focus our attention on the σ-electrons. As a simple example, we will consider the benzene molecule, C_6H_6, where each carbon atom has four valence electrons which occupy three σ-orbitals of sp^2-hybridization in the plane and one π-orbital of 2pz-type perpendicular to the plane. Each hydrogen atom has one valence electron which enters the single bond to the nearest carbon atom. According to Lewis, each covalent bond corresponds to an electron pair shared between the two atoms involved, and this picture has been interpreted quantum-mechanically by Heitler and London.[14]

The σ-skeleton of benzene has, therefore, the form schematically outlined in FIGURE 1, where H is a proton and two dots (:) represent an electron pair. If one makes the thought-experiment of dropping one proton into a carbon nucleus, one obtains a nitrogen nucleus and an electron lone pair sitting outside the ring in a sp^2-hybrid in a pyridine molecule:

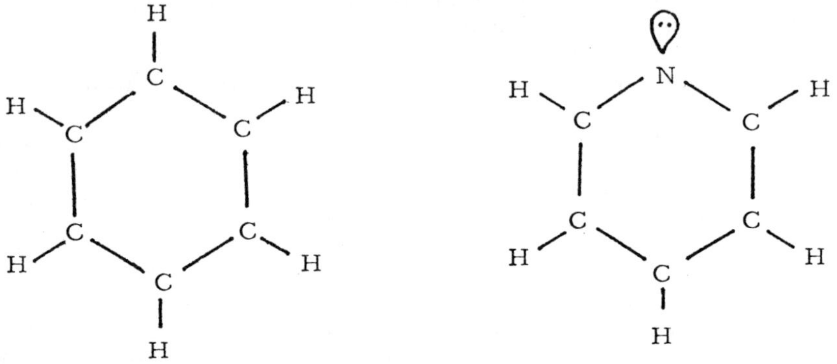

FIGURE 1. The σ-skeleton of the benzene and pyridine molecules.

The electron lone pair would like to get hold of another proton to form a pyridinium-ion $NC_5H_6^+$. Apparently, the electron lone pair is characteristic for a Lewis base, and one has the reaction

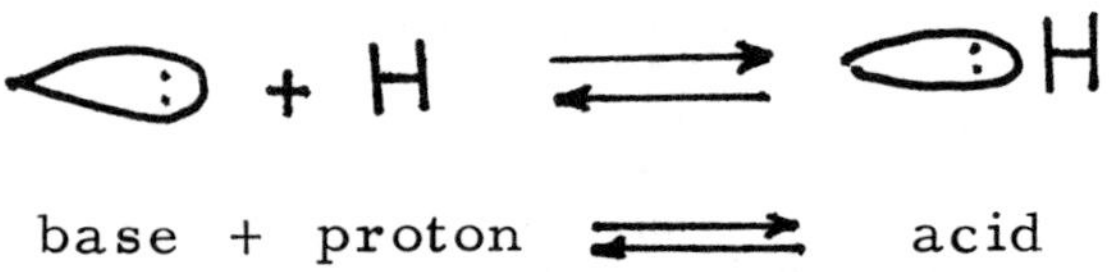

FIGURE 2. The characteristic reaction for a Lewis base and acid.

If two pyridine molecules attract one and the same proton, a link between the two molecules which may be described as a proton bond is obtained but, for classical reasons, it is still called a hydrogen bond:

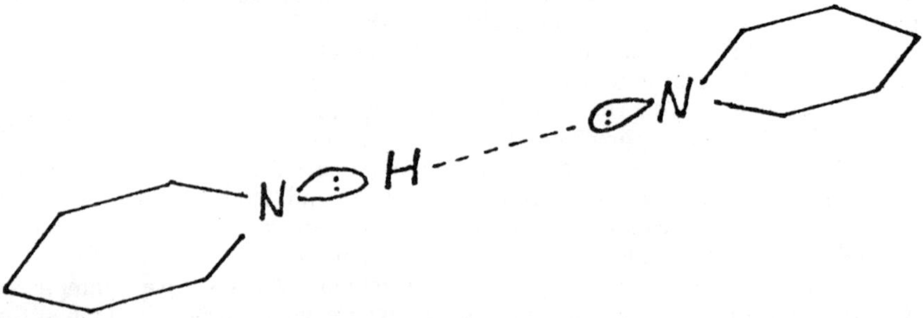

FIGURE 3. Two pyridine molecules attracting the same proton, leading to the formation of a hydrogen bond.

In modern quantum chemistry, *a hydrogen bond is a proton shared between two electron lone pairs.* Each lone pair offers the proton an attraction which may be described as a potential well with a definite minimum corresponding to a classical equilibrium position, and the proton in a hydrogen bond is thus usually situated in a double-well potential having two minima separated by a certain barrier (see FIGURE 4).

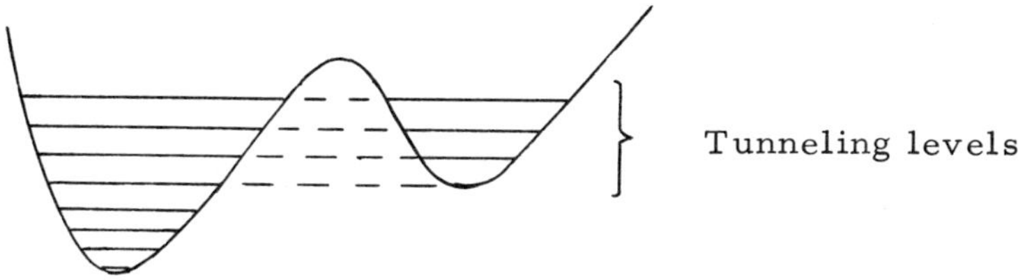

FIGURE 4. A proton in a hydrogen bond is usually situated in a double-well potential with two minima separated by a barrier.

The proton may pass from one equilibrium position to another above the barrier or through the barrier by means of the quantum-mechanical tunnel effect, but the transfer is dependent on the distribution over various energy levels and is, therefore, temperature-dependent.

The proton polarizes the electron lone pairs and the other electrons on each side of the hydrogen bond and, in order to calculate the potential of the proton, it is necessary to solve the electronic Schrödinger equation for a series of positions of the proton in its motion. In the Watson-Crick model of DNA, there are at least two mobile protons in the genetic code in each base pair, and the computational problems in calculating the potential energy surface for these two protons thus become rather formidable.

If the hydrogen bond is interpreted as a hydrogen atom shared between two electronegative atoms, the proton will carry with it a full electron when it shifts from one equilibrium position to another. In reality, the proton is surrounded by a certain cloud of negative electricity, and it serves as an electron carrier in the hydrogen bond; but for a neutral system, the electron transport from one side of the hydrogen bond to the other seems to be comparatively small. If the hydrogen bond is situated between two coplanar conjugated systems, it seems that the conjugating power of the proton would not be appreciable. On the other hand, if one adds an extra electron to one of the conjugated systems, the proton feels a new attraction and, under certain circumstances, it may then change equilibrium position, go over to the other side, pick up the extra electron and carry it over to the other side of the hydrogen bond. The hydrogen bond seems hence to have a great deal of flexibility, and we will now discuss some applications in biochemistry.

Properties of Hydrogen Bonds in Proteins

The proteins are linear molecules built up from amino acids of the type

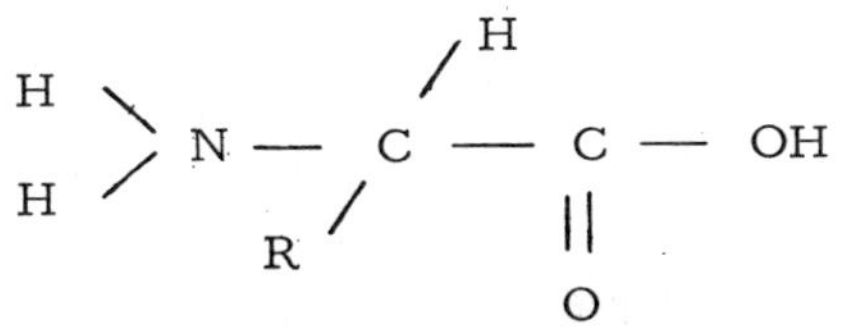

where R is a radical. It is remarkable that all the proteins in nature are built up essentially from 20 amino acids, i.e., 20 different forms of the radical R. Two amino acids may be joined by the peptide bond

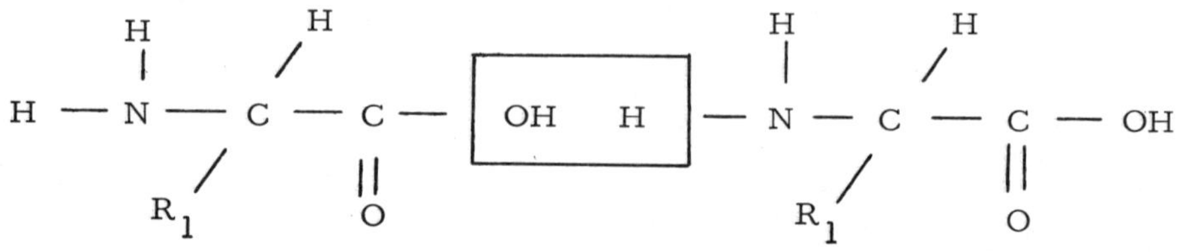

and the procedure leads to polypeptides with the structure:

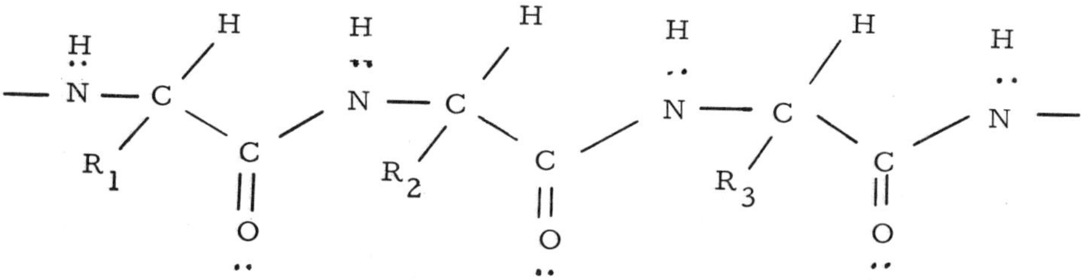

where we have indicated the existence of some important electron pairs: According to Pauling, two polypeptide chains (or two parts of the same chain) may stabilize each other by means of hydrogen bonding as indicated below:

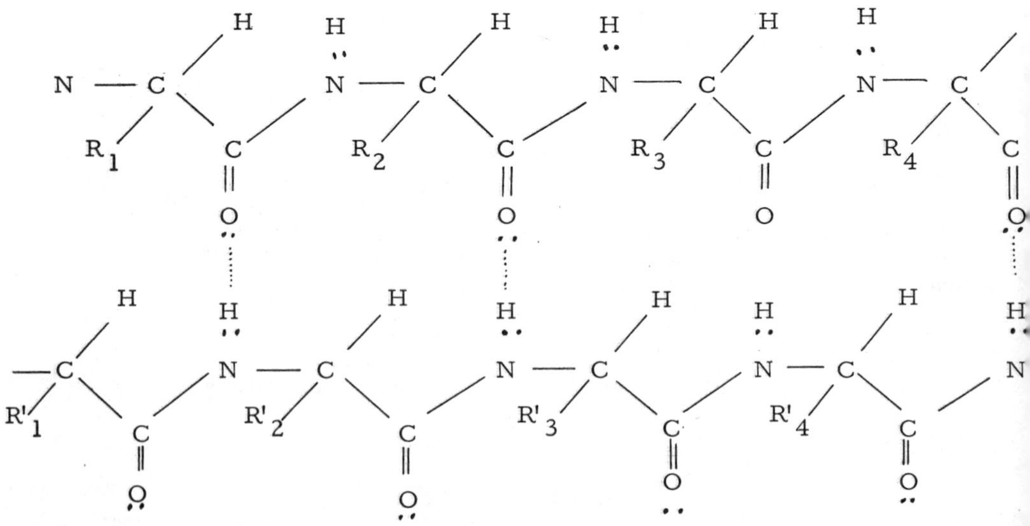

It should be observed that each group

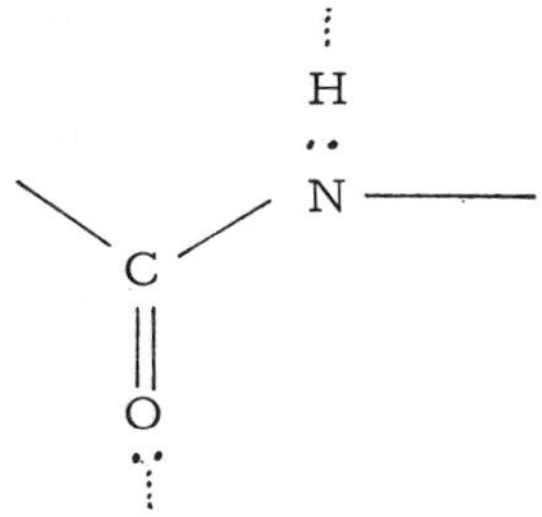

is a small planar conjugated system which is linked to similar systems in the neighboring chains by means of hydrogen bonds. For the sake of simplicity, we will consider the structure of the α-helix in some greater detail.

If the amino acid radicals are omitted and attention is focused essentially on the polypeptide chain, one finds that the α-helix contains a cylindrical structure consisting of a series of planar OCNH-groups joined by hydrogen bonds:

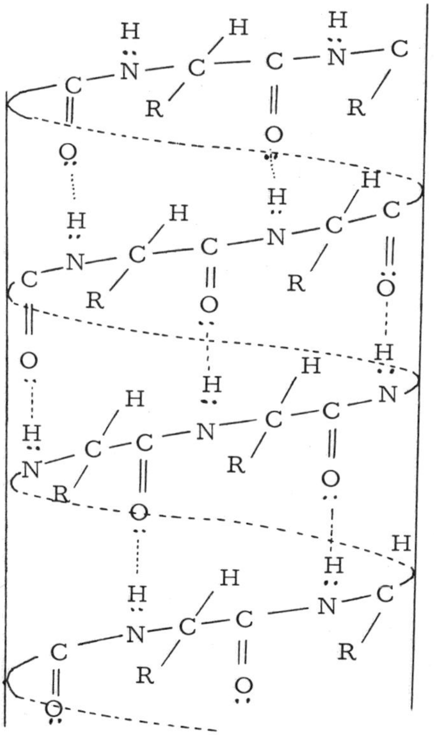

If it is assumed that the protons in the hydrogen bonds have a certain conjugating power, the α-helix contains a series of linked conjugated systems. It is well-known that, under ordinary circumstances, the proteins are rather poor semiconductors, since it takes a considerable amount of energy to get some free carriers. However, if one adds an extra electron at the top of the α-helix, the proton in a neighboring hydrogen bond feels an extra attraction and may flip from the N-position to the O-position in the bond. Since the molecule tries to preserve its gross electric neutrality, this leads to a cooperative phenomenon in which one proton jump induces another proton jump, etc. However, if the first proton picks up the electron and carries it over to the next NCO-group, the electron may slide on this conjugated system to the next hydrogen bond where the procedure is repeated. In this way, the extra electron sees a certain pathway where the protons are "ferries" between the small pieces of "highways" represented by the conjugated systems.

The question is whether this semiconductivity of the proteins with respect to extra electrons plays any essential role in the enzyme action, particularly with respect to oxidation-reduction processes. Perhaps the enzyme gets attached to the two molecules involved by means of two hydrogen bonds and then serves essentially as a bridge for an electron wave packet going from one component to the other. After serving as a bridge, the enzyme could become free again and move to the next pair of molecules, or it could stay and repeat its purpose indefinitely in an oxidation-reduction chain. This model,[15] suggested in 1963, agrees surprisingly well with modern ideas about catalysis,[16] and provides an interesting alternative to the more conventional descriptions of enzyme action.

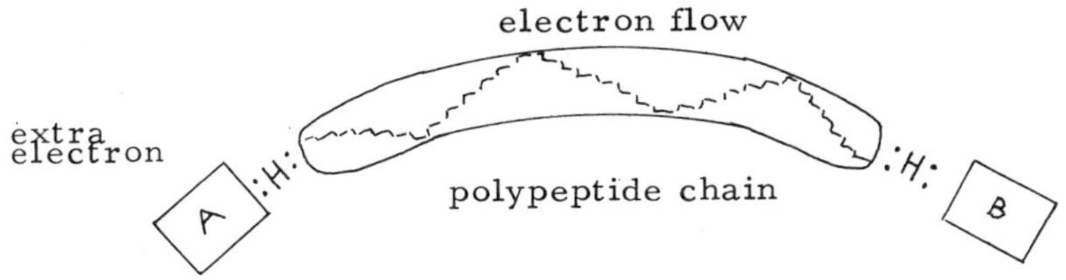

Properties of Hydrogen Bonds in DNA

In biology, the genetic information in the chromosomes is contained in the DNA molecule. According to Watson and Crick,[7] the molecule is a double helix consisting of two sugar-phosphate strands joined by pairs of nitrogen bases held together by hydrogen bonds. This means that, if the hydrogen bonds in the α-helix are essentially of longitudinal character parallel to the axis, the hydrogen bonds in DNA are of transverse character perpendicular to the axis.

The nitrogen bases adenine, guanine, thymine, and cytosine are often denoted by the symbols A, G, T, and C, and we note that the pairing is specific according to the rules A-T, T-A, G-C, and C-G, depending on the properties of the hydrogen bonds.

A study of the hydrogen bonds shows that each base is characterized by a genetic template, which consists of electron pairs and protons according to the following patterns:

$$\mathrm{A}\left\{\begin{matrix} :\mathrm{H} & & : \\ : & & \mathrm{H}: \end{matrix}\right\}\mathrm{T} \qquad \mathrm{G}\left\{\begin{matrix} : & & \mathrm{H}: \\ :\mathrm{H} & & : \end{matrix}\right\}\mathrm{C}$$

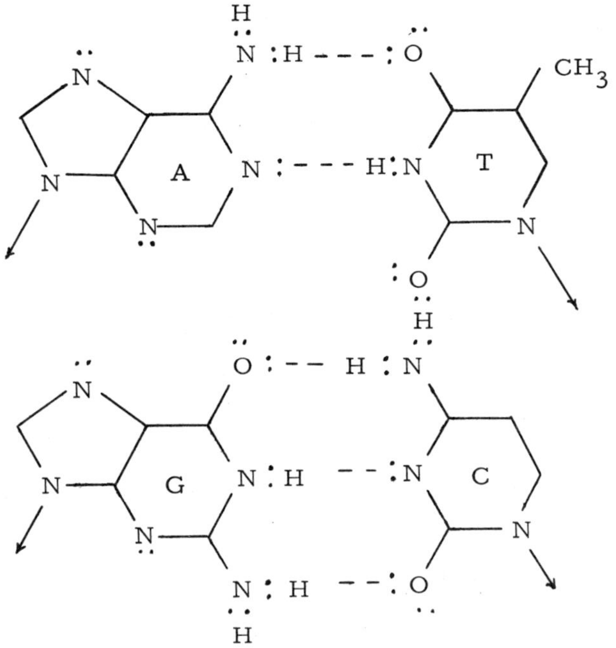

If a proton is misplaced, one obtains tautomeric forms of the type

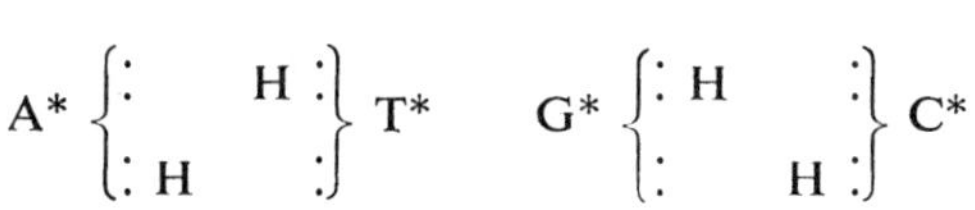

which have erroneous pairing schemes

$$A^* - C, \qquad T^* - G, \qquad G^* - T, \qquad C^* - A.$$

The genetic code is essentially given by the series of bases along one of the strands, say AGATCATTG . . . , whereas the other strand contains the complementary sequence TCTGTAAC. . . . It is interesting to note that the bacterium *Escherichia coli* has a chromosome consisting of a circular DNA molecule containing about 3 million base pairs, and that it would take a volume the size of the Encyclopaedia Britannica to print this code in terms of the letters A, G, T, and C.

At DNA-replication the two strands are separated from each other, and each strand, with its nitrogen bases serves as a template for forming a complementary strand of the nutrition material in the neighborhood. If there are tautomeric molecules in this material, they may be incorporated in the new DNA molecule according to erroneous pairing schemes, which may lead to a change in the genetic code, i.e., to a mutation.[7]

In biology, mutations are rare, and Freese has estimated that the spontaneous mutation rates per base pair and generation should be in the region between 10^{-8} and 10^{-12}. Experimental experience has indicated, however, that the tautomeric forms are not particularly rare and the equilibrium constants are of the order 10^{-3} to 10^{-4}. At first sight, these figures would indicate that incorporation errors are not at all rare, and that the chromosome of *E. coli* should contain roughly 10^2 to 10^3 errors per replication. That this is not the case may be explained by the simple fact that the addition of the mutation material occurs in a replication plane which contains two old bases and two new ones.[17] In such a case, the groups attached to the 6-positions form a characteristic parallelogram around the helix axis, and we note that they are either amino groups or keto oxygens.

If two normal bases are added, this parallelogram will contain two amino groups and two keto oxygens joined by hydrogen bonds:

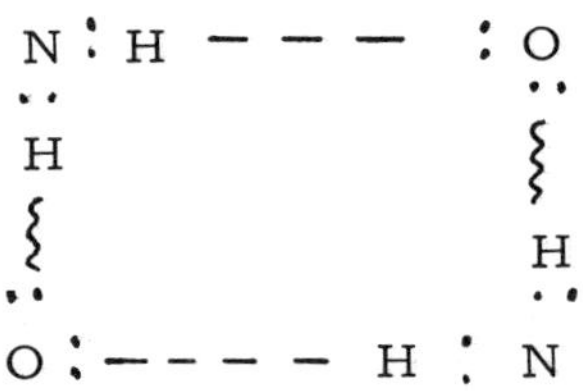

two of these hydrogen bonds will be broken in the next step when the daughter molecules separate. If, on the other hand, one tries to incorporate one normal base and one tautomeric form, the parallelogram is going to contain three modified amino groups or three modified keto oxygens:

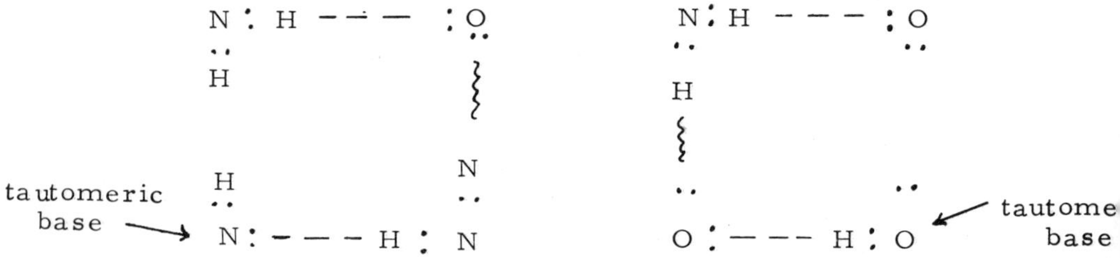

Since these forms have energies which are several electronvolts higher than the normal forms, the Boltzmann factor, $B = \exp(\Delta E/kT)$, indicates that it is highly improbable that they will occur at all. The mechanism does not prevent incorporation of double tautomeric errors, but the probability of this occurring seems to be much smaller.

Even in the stationary state of DNA, genetic errors may occur because of the fact that each proton has two classical equilibrium positions. If a proton moves along a hydrogen bond, e.g. by means of the tunnel effect, it is very likely that the other proton moves in the opposite direction to keep the gross electronic neutrality of the base pair. This means that double-proton tunneling leads to the transitions:

$$A - T \rightleftarrows A^* - T^*, \qquad G - C \rightleftarrows G^* - T^*$$

which may cause mutations at the next replication of the molecule.

In order to study the stability of the genetic code, it is necessary to calculate the energy potential surfaces for the mobile protons in the genetic code, taking into account their polarizing influence on the electronic clouds. The potential is considered essentially a function of the coordinates of two protons and, for a network of protonic positions, the electronic Schrödinger equation is solved in the MO-LCAO-SCF approximation. The calculations on the G-C pair were carried out in Uppsala by Rein and Harris,[18] who found that the G*-C* form had an energy that was 0.65 eV higher than the normal form and which, at T = 310° K, corresponds to a Boltzmann factor, $B = 10^{-10,5}$. Using the same method, Lunell and Sperber[19] investigated the A-T pair and found that the A*-T* form had an energy which was 0.7 eV higher than the normal form and which, at T = 310° K, corresponds to a Boltzmann factor of $B = 10^{-11,4}$. These figures are almost too good to be true, but it would certainly be very interesting if one could explain the spontaneous mutation rates in biology on the basis of the laws of physics and chemistry.

For a more complete discussion of these problems, the reader is referred to some recent surveys.[20] In conclusion, it should be observed that all the quantum-mechanical calculations of the properties of DNA carried out in Uppsala strongly support the Watson-Crick model.

References

1. Pauling, L. 1939. The Nature of the Chemical Bond. Cornell University Press. Ithaca, N. Y.
2. Huggins, M. L. 1962. Amer. Sci. **50:** 485.
3. Pauling, L., R. B. Corey & H. R. Branson. 1951. Proc. Nat. Acad. Sci. U.S.A. **37:** 205; Pauling, L. & R. B. Corey. 1951. Proc. Nat. Acad. Sci. U.S.A. **37:** 251.
4. Avery, O. T., C. M. MacLeod & M. McCarty. 1944. J. Exp. Med. **79:** 137.
5. Chargaff, E. 1950. Experientia **6:** 201. See also Chargaff, E. 1963. Essays on Nucleic Acid. W. D. McElroy & B. Glass, Eds. Johns Hopkins Press. Baltimore, Md.
6. Wilkins, M. H. F., A. R. Stokes & H. R. Wilson. 1953. Nature **171:** 738.
7. Watson, J. D. & F. H. C. Crick. 1953. Nature **171:** 737, 964; Crick, F. H. C. & J. D. Watson. 1954. Proc. Roy. Soc. (London) **A223:** 80.
8. Slater, J. C. 1931. Phys. Rev. **37:** 481.
9. Pauling, L. 1928, 1931. Proc. Nat. Acad. Sci. U.S.A. **14:** 359; J. Amer. Chem. Soc. **53:** 1367.
10. Mulliken, R. S. 1928. Phys. Rev. **32:** 186, and a long series of papers. For a survey, see Molecular Orbitals in Chemistry, Physics, and Biology. 1964. P. O. Löwdin & B. Pullman, Eds. Academic Press. New York, N. Y.
11. Hückel, E. 1930, 1931. Z. Physik **60:** 423; **70:** 204; **72:** 310.
12. Coulson, C. A. & H. C. Longuet-Higgins. 1947, 1948. Proc. Roy. Soc. (London) **A191:** 39; **192:** 16-1948. **193:** 447, 456; **195:** 188.
13. For a general survey, see Pullman, B. & A. Pullman. 1963. Quantum Biochemistry. John Wiley & Sons. New York, N. Y.
14. Heitler, W. & F. London. 1927. Z. Physik **44:** 455.
15. Löwdin, P. O. 1964. Biopolymers **1:** 293.
16. See for example Proc. Study Week on Intermolecular Forces. 1966. Pontifical Academy. Rome, Italy.
17. Löwdin, P. O. 1964. Electronic Aspects of Biochemistry. B. Pullman, Ed.: 167. Academic Press. New York, N. Y.
18. Rein, R. & F. Harris. 1964, 1965. J. Chem. Phys. **41:** 3393; Science **146:** 649; J. Chem. Phys. **42:** 2177; **43:** 4415.
19. Lunell, S. & G. Sperber. 1967. J. Chem. Phys. **46:** 2119.
20. Löwdin, P. O. 1965. Advances in Quantum Chemistry. P. O. Löwdin, Ed.: 213. Academic Press. New York, N. Y.; 1966. Proc. Study Week on Intermolecular Forces. Pontifical Academy. Rome, Italy.

THE DOUBLE MINIMUM OF THE ADENINE-THYMINE HYDROGEN BOND

R. G. Shulman
Bell Telephone Laboratories, Inc.
Murray Hill, N. J.

In the Watson-Crick DNA base-pairing scheme there are two hydrogen bonds between adenine and thymine, as shown in FIGURE 1. The possibility of a double minimum in the hydrogen bond potential function has been the subject of considerable speculation and even some approximate molecular orbital calculations, but its existence has not been established. Here, we would like to present a simple argument which, by utilizing published data, strongly suggests the existence of such a double minimum. Our reasoning concerns the hydrogen bond between N_3 of thymidine and N_1 of adenosine. Thymidine loses this proton at high pH in solution whereas when adenosine becomes protonated in solution, it gains a proton at its N_1 position.[1] The pK's for these reactions are 9.8 and 4.2, respectively. From these, one can calculate the standard free energy change for the reaction

$$T + A \rightleftarrows T^- + AH^+$$

and at 300° K this is

$$\Delta F° \approx 7600 \text{ cal/mole} \approx 2650 \text{ cm}^{-1}.$$

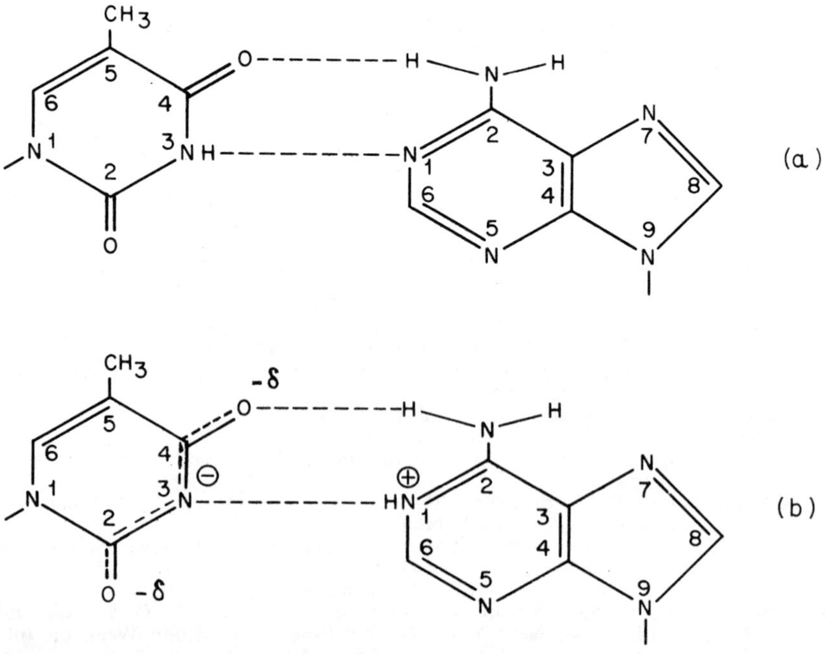

FIGURE 1. (a) The A-T base pair. (b) The electronic structure of the thymine anion as deduced from the carbonyl stretch.

In solution, we can certainly neglect the contributions of the entropy to this reaction and set $\triangle F = \triangle H$. Hence, the energy required to transfer a proton from T to A in solution is ~2650 cm^{-1}. The effect of going from free molecules in solution to the adenine-thymine hydrogen-bonded base pair can only be to lower this energy. From an electrostatic viewpoint, it would require less energy for thymine to retain the proton partially and for adenine to accept it only partially—as would be found in the hydrogen bond—than for the transfer to be complete, as it is in solutions. Furthermore, in the hydrogen bond there is the possibility of a proton flip-flop with a proton coming back to the thymine carbonyl from the amino group of adenine with, once again, the consequent lowering of this energy of proton transfer as compared to the single proton transfer of the isolated molecules. This flip-flop would be helped by the electronic structure of T^- which has been shown from infrared studies of the carbonyl stretch to be changed toward the enol form shown[2, 3] in FIGURE 1 (b). In this form, the negative charge on the oxygen would attract the amino proton. From the foregoing we conclude that 2650 cm^{-1} is an upper limit for the energy required to transfer the N_3 proton of thymidine across the hydrogen bond to the N_1 of adenosine. This upper limit of the relative energies of the proton is shown by the solid horizontal lines in FIGURES 2 (a) and (b). The question to be answered is whether the potential has the form shown in either FIGURE 2 (a) or (b).

The distinction between the two is made by comparing the NH stretch frequency of thymidine (or uridine), with or without the hydrogen bond, to adenine. Kyogoku and coworkers[4] have observed these spectra of nucleosidelike molecules isolated in nonaqueous solvents. The relevant aspect of their results is that, while the thymidine NH stretch frequency changes upon the formation of an adenine hydrogen bond, it does not change appreciably. Exact wavelengths for uracil are available, i.e., the free NH stretch at 3395 cm^{-1} is shifted to 3184 cm^{-1}. Approximately equal shifts are observed when uracil derivatives, including thymine, are hydrogen-bonded to 9-ethyladenine. The frequency of an harmonic oscillator is

$$\omega = \frac{h}{2\pi c}\sqrt{\frac{k}{\mu}}$$

where the potential is

$$V = 1/2k(\Delta\chi)^2$$

in which $\triangle\chi$ is the distance from equilibrium. Hence, a six percent change in the frequency corresponds to a twelve percent change in the potential energy. Thus, the changes in the potential function upon hydrogen bonding are small. For example, compare these results with those for triethylamine HCl.[5] In the latter, the NH stretch shifts by ~1000 cm^{-1} upon the formation of a hydrogen bond, indicating very severe changes of the potential function. From these considerations we conclude that, since the potential near the thymine is changed only slightly by the nearby low-lying level of protonated adenine, the potential function must be a double minimum as shown in FIGURE 2 (b).

One interesting consequence of these experimental results that is independent of the shape of the potential is that at 300° K and any pH between 4.2 and 9.8, the ratio of $[AH^+] + [T^-]$ to $[A] + [T]$ is $10^{-5.6} \approx 3 \times 10^{-6}$. Since this is considerably larger than the rate of spontaneous mutations, as quoted by Löwdin,[6] it is clear that a single transferred proton in this position

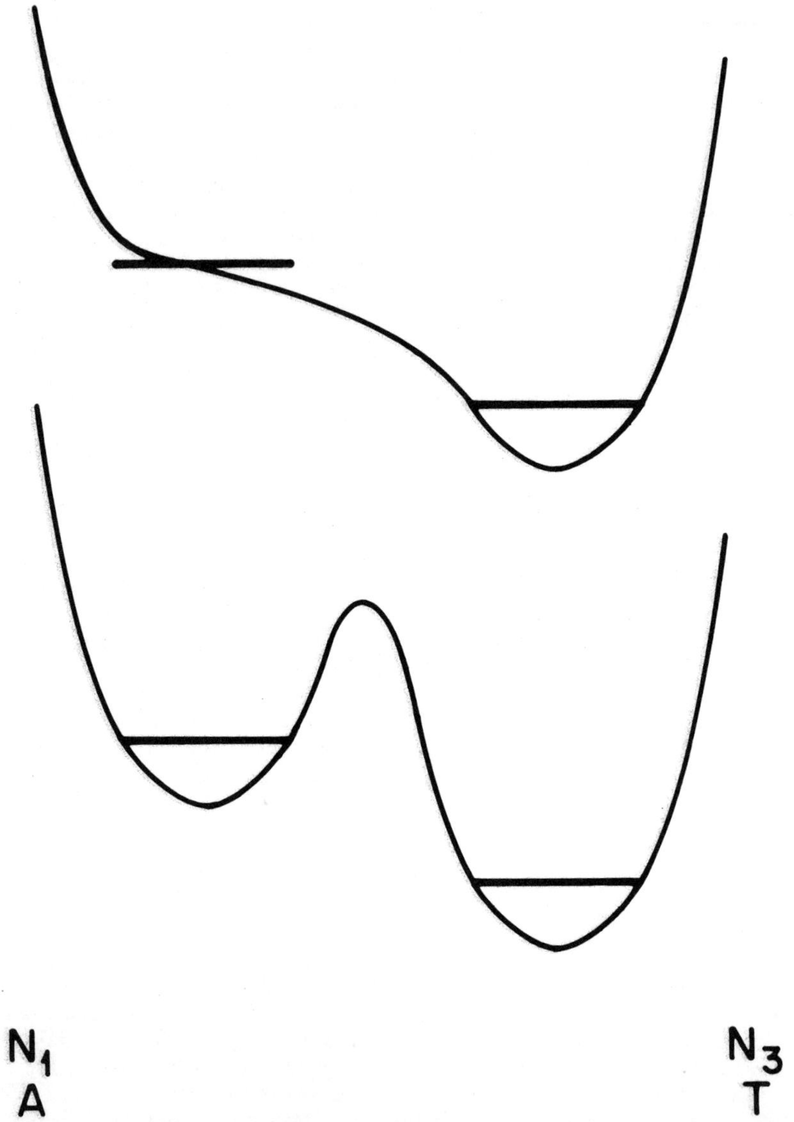

FIGURE 2. The relative energies of a proton at N_3 of thymine vs N_1 of adenine showing schematically (a) a single potential minimum (b) a double minimum.

of the A-T base pair must have a very small rate of mispairing bases when compared to the rate of proper pairing with the neutral adenine or thymine molecules.

Acknowledgment

I would like to thank A. A. Lamola for stimulating the ideas I have presented here.

References

1. COCHRAN, W. 1951. Acta Crystallogr. **4:** 81.
2. WIERZCHOWSKI, K. L., E. LITONSKA & D. SHUGAR. 1965. J. Amer. Chem. Soc. **87:** 4621.
3. MILES, H. T. Personal communication.
4. KYOGOKU, Y., R. C. LORD & A. RICH. 1967. Proc. Nat. Acad. Sci. **57:** 250; J. Amer. Chem. Soc. **89:** 496.
5. LORD, R. C. Personal communication.
6. LÖWDIN, P. This monograph.

FREE RADICALS FROM BIOLOGICAL PURINES AND PYRIMIDINES*

Walter Gordy

Department of Physics, Duke University
Durham, N. C.

The purine and pyrimidine rings are the alphabet of the genetic language, the code letters with which the life processes and living forms are described. Since the establishment of the Watson-Crick model for DNA, few bioscientists doubt this. Now, it is beginning to be strongly suspected that what man learns—if he remembers it very long—is also coded in these same molecular groups. I hope that you are recording this discussion in the purine and pyrimidine letters of your brain. If you record it only in amino acid letters, it won't last.

Ionizing radiations are known to produce mutagenic, carcinogenic, aging, and other effects on living things. It is reasonable to postulate that such effects could result from chemical changes induced directly or indirectly by the radiation in the information groups—the purine and pyrimidine rings of the nucleic acids. Several years ago we set out to find what, if any, information could be gained about these chemical alterations from the electron spin resonance (ESR) of possible free radical intermediaries of these radiation-induced alterations. This method does not detect the normal molecules in which all electrons are paired; it detects only the free radicals. Because microwave radiation used for observation of electron spin resonance readily penetrates organic solids or liquids, the ESR method can be used to examine free radicals trapped in almost any biochemical in almost any form.

In this exploration, the first question to be asked is whether the free radicals produced by ionizing radiation in the purines and pyrimidines are sufficiently long-lived for detection with ESR. This question was soon answered in the affirmative.[1, 2] All the purines and pyrimidines, including the nucleosides, nucleotides and the nucleic acid polymers, were found to give observable ESR signals after irradiation with suitable dosage of x-rays and γ-rays. What are the chemical forms and electronic structures of the observed free radicals? What are the specific mechanisms of their production? These questions are being answered today, but more slowly.

Scientists working in many laboratories other than ours have made ESR observations on irradiated purines and pyrimidines. These include: Muller and his collaborators working in Germany; the Ehrenbergs in Sweden; Shen, Blyumenfeld, Kalmanson, and Pasynskii in Russia; Van de Vorst, Duchesne and others in Belgium; Lacroix and Williams-Dorlet in France; Charlesby, Omerod and others in England; Pihl, Sanner and Henriksen in Norway; Schulman, Pershan and their collaborators at the Bell Telephone Laboratories; Heller and Cole at the Ford Laboratories; Myers and his collaborators at U.C.L.A. It is impossible to review here the many studies on the subject, but fortunately an excellent review by Müller[3] is now available. Schoffa's monograph[4] on the applications of spin resonance to the study of free radicals in biological systems, and Poole's book on experimental techniques[5] for elec-

* This study was sponsored by the Air Force Office of Scientific Research, Grant AF-AFOSR-66-0493A, and by the U. S. Army Research Office (Durham), Grant DA-ARO-D-31-124-G731.

tron spin resonance provide recent material on the subject. This paper will be concerned primarily with the work done in our laboratory at Duke University.

Early Work on Powdered Samples

In our original work[1, 2] with Howard Shields, characteristically different ESR patterns were observed for various purine and pyrimidine derivatives irradiated in the powder form. FIGURE 1 shows the spectra we obtained for thymidine, cytidine, desoxyguanosine, and desoxyadenosine. The base thymine gave a pattern like that of thymidine, but a much weaker one for the same x-ray dosage. No signals could be detected for the pure bases adenine and guanine, although for adenylic acid and guanylic acid signals similar to those of adenosine and guanosine were detected.

A comparison of results indicated that the complex pattern of thymidine and the triplet pattern of the purines came from radicals formed in the basic ring structures. The sugar constituents irradiated separately produced entirely different patterns. We demonstrated that the observed thymidine pattern agreed with a theoretical pattern (represented by bars in FIGURE 1) consisting of a triplet from two equally coupling protons of the order of 40 gauss, a quartet substructure arising from the CH_3 group with equivalent proton couplings of 23 gauss. Likewise, it was evident that the triplet splitting observed for the purine derivatives indicated an equal coupling by two protons of the order of 40 gauss. It was not apparent to us, however, how radicals having two protons with equivalent coupling of 40 gauss could be produced directly by the radiation in these compounds. Now we know, from evidence which I shall describe, that these radicals are not produced directly by irradiation but are, in fact, produced by migrating H atoms which add to the purine or pyrimidine rings. The source of the H atoms is not definitely known, but it is probable that they are released by the irradiation from the sugar groups in the nucleosides and the nucleotides, as is indicated by the greater difficulty in production of observable concentrations of the radicals by irradiation of the unsubstituted bases. The H atoms may be released in pairs with the formation of a double bond, so that no primary free radicals are formed. However, in adenosine single crystals (see later discussion), we have observed both a radical formed by an H addition on the ring and a radical on the sugar group formed by loss of an H atom. The source of the H atoms which give rise to the weak signals observed in thymine may be the CH_3 group, or possibly an impurity.

The cytidine pattern (FIGURE 1) is a triplet having components of equal intensity and spacing of about 10 gauss. This hyperfine structure evidently arises from coupling of the N^{14} nucleus which has spin $I = 1$. This structure was not resolved in the ESR of the irradiated cytosine, for which the radical is evidently different. Although Shields and Gordy[2] recognized this N^{14} coupling, they could not ascertain the nature of the radical nor learn which of the N^{14} nuclei of the cytidine led to the triplet splitting. Later results in our laboratory on single crystals of cytidine revealed the probable structure of the radical, which will be described in the discussion of pyrimidine single crystals which follows.

From quantitative measurements of the intensities of the ESR lines, Müller and Köhnlein[6] have derived values for the free radical yields for various

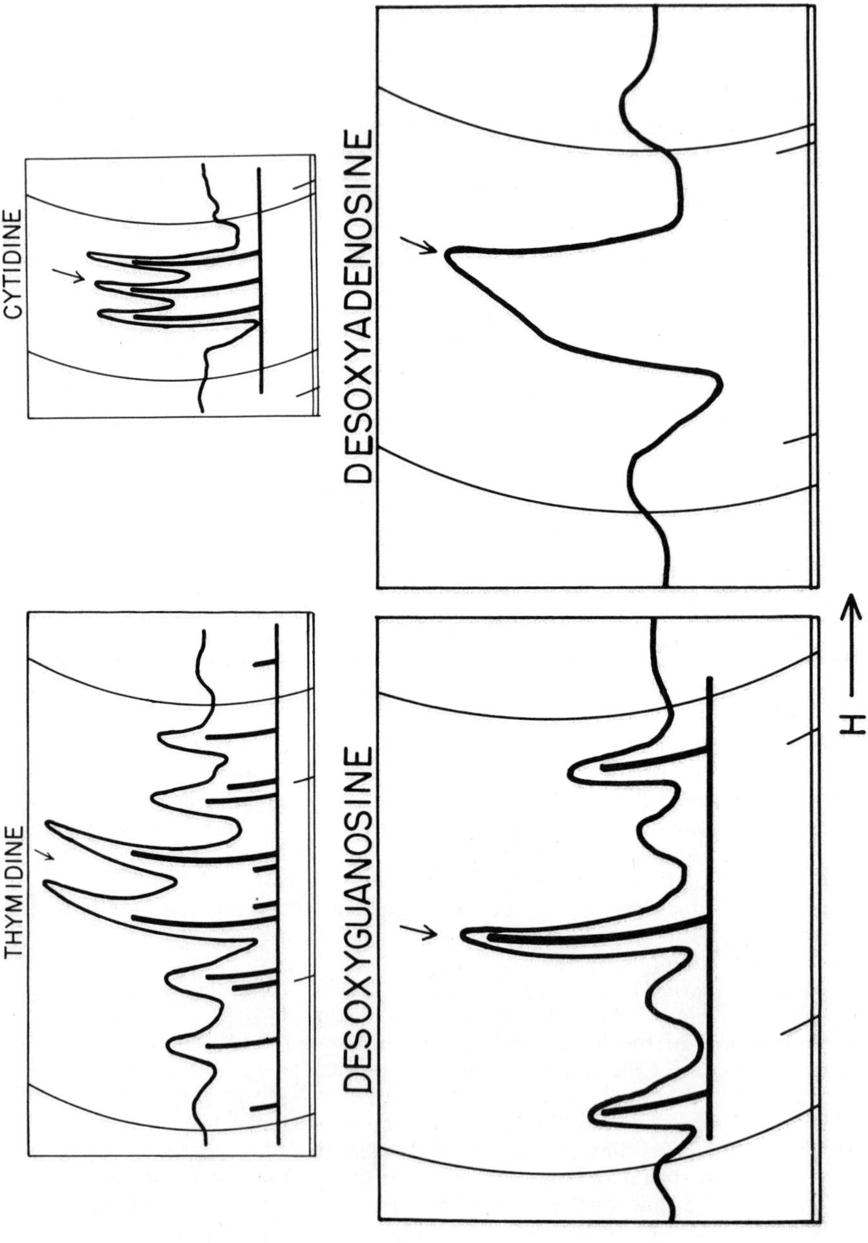

FIGURE. 1. ESR patterns of γ-irradiated pyrimidine and purine powders at room temperature. (From Reference 2)

dosages of radiation in the purine and pyrimidine bases as well as in the nucleosides and nucleotides.

H and D Bombardment

After single crystal[7] measurements in our laboratory and work by Pershan and collaborators on deuterium substitution[8] in the Bell Telephone Laboratories had shown that radicals observed in irradiated thymine or thymidine resulted from H addition on $C_{(6)}$ of the ring, Herak and the author[9] bombarded various purines and pyrimidines with gaseous H atoms at thermal velocities, to determine whether H addition radicals could be produced in this direct manner. We used ESR to detect any radicals which might be formed. In order to distinguish radicals formed by H addition from those which might be formed by H abstraction or from thermal dissociation by the bombarding particles, we also observed samples similarly bombarded with D atoms. These experiments were successful in demonstrating beyond any doubt that H-addition radicals are formed not only on thymine but also on the basic rings of all the purines and of the other pyrimidines, and that the atoms added were from the gaseous streams. Although we were unable in our earlier experiments to obtain signals for H addition on cytosine at room temperature, we later found such radicals[10] for cytosine bombarded at 77° K. Since these radicals disappeared as the cytosine was warmed to room temperature, the warming process evidently expelled the added H atoms. However, H-addition radicals were observed up to room temperature in desoxycytidylic acid.[11]

Independently, and almost simultaneously with us, Heller and Cole[12] reported radicals in thymine produced by H bombardment that were similar to the radicals produced previously by ionizing irradiation. They did not, at the same time, produce signals with D atoms. Holmes and coworkers[13] have reported detection of addition radicals at room temperature when various purines and pyrimidines were bombarded with H and D atoms. They used a special technique of depositing the samples on quartz wool in order to increase the surface area. Their results agree with ours, except that they were able to obtain signals from cytosine bombarded at room temperature. Though the cause of these differing results is not entirely clear, it must be related to quartz wool.

The H-addition radicals observed in the purine and pyrimidine bases are:

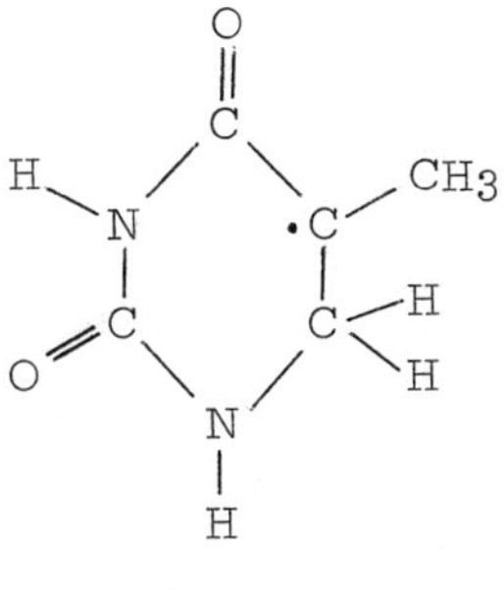

(I)

thymine + H

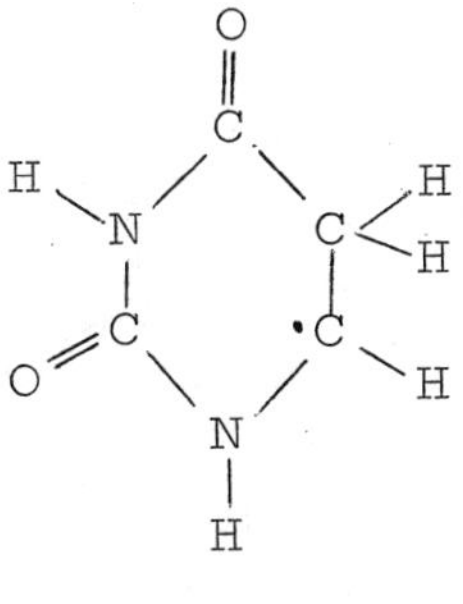

(II)

uracil + H

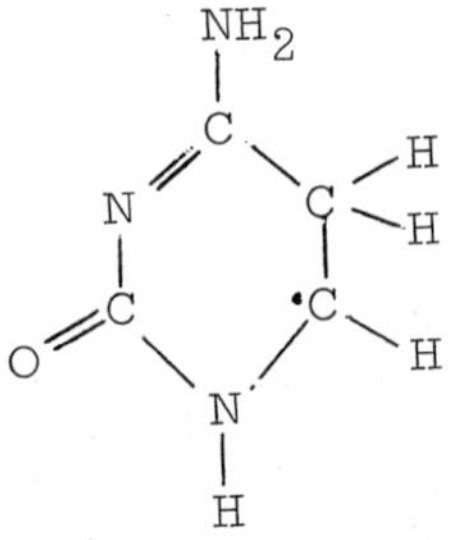

cytosine + H

(III)

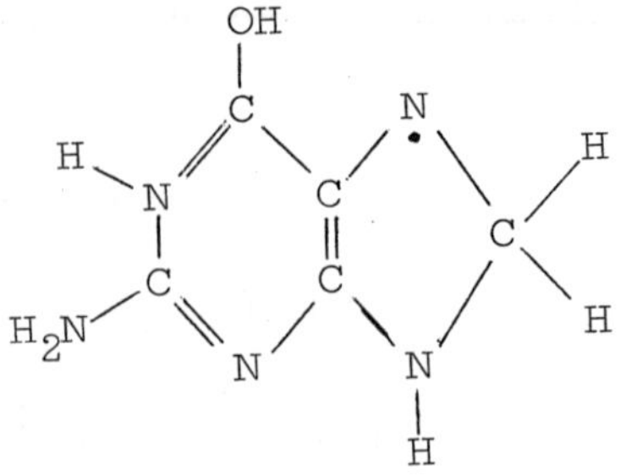

guanine + H

(IV)

either

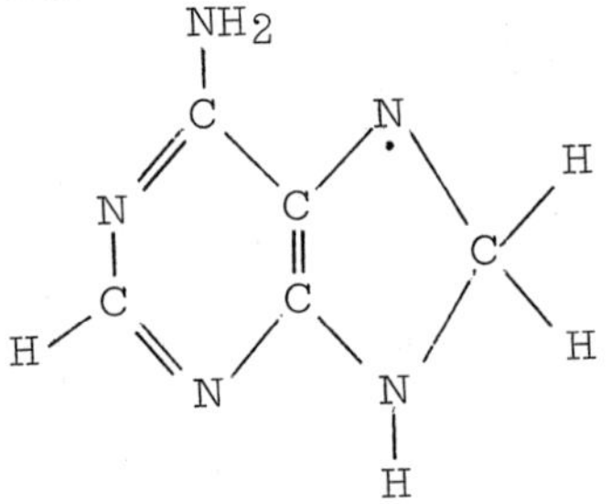

(V)

or

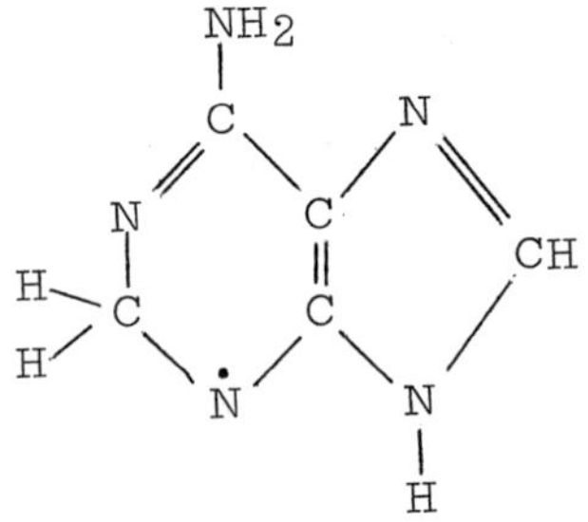

(VI)

adenine + H

FIGURE 2 shows the characteristic ESR patterns produced by H bombardment of the powdered samples of thymine, uracil, guanine, and adenine at room temperature. FIGURE 3 shows a comparison of cytosine and uracil when H-bombarded and observed at 77° K. Note the similarity between these two spectra and the differences between the pattern for uracil at 77° K and that at 300° K. The latter difference is due to the change in orientation of the CH_2 bonds relative to the molecular plane. At 300° K, the two CH bonds have equivalent orientations relative to the molecular plane.

TABLE 1 gives the proton coupling for the nucleic acid bases at 77° K and at 300° K. TABLE 2 gives the proton couplings observed for the corresponding H-addition radicals[11] in the nucleosides and the nucleotides produced by bombardment of these various compounds with H atoms. The values listed in TABLE 2 are for 77° K unless otherwise indicated.

OH Bombardment

In a similar way, we bombarded the nucleic acid bases with gaseous OH radicals[14] at thermal velocities. All the observations were carried out at room temperature. The OH radicals were made by the action of an electric discharge on H_2O_2 vapor. Direct OH-addition radicals were readily detected for uracil, but not for the other bases.

The observed pattern for uracil bombarded with OH atoms is shown in FIGURE 4. Note the differences between this pattern and that for H-bombarded uracil shown in FIGURE 2. The hyperfine pattern is what would be ex-

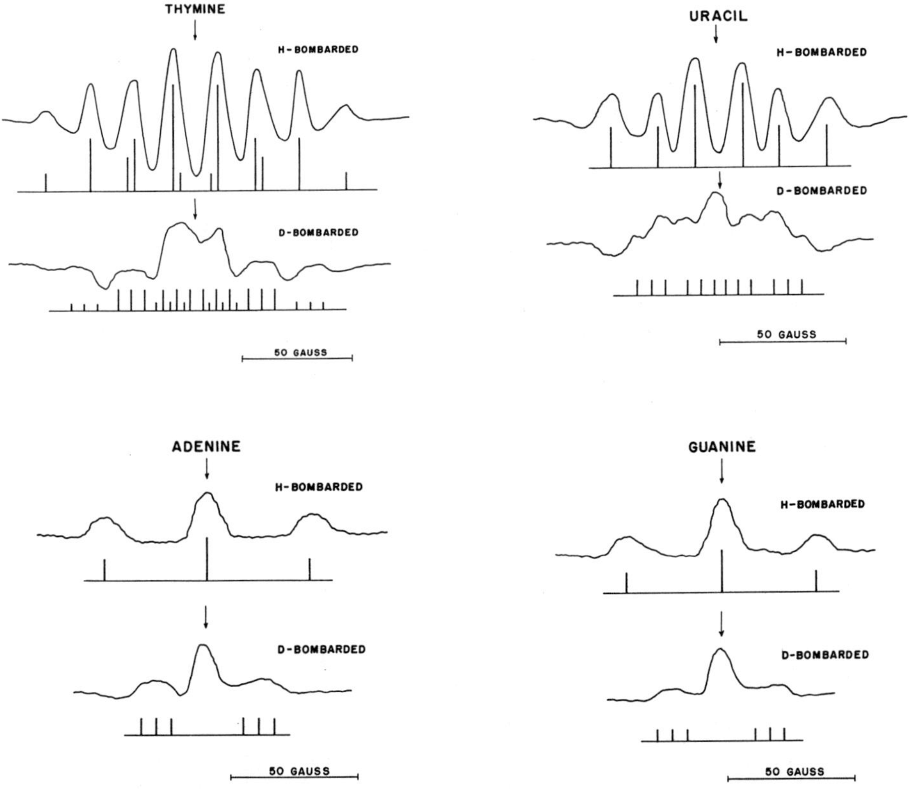

FIGURE 2. ESR patterns of pyrimidine and purine powders after bombardment with gaseous H or D atoms at room temperature. (From Reference 9.)

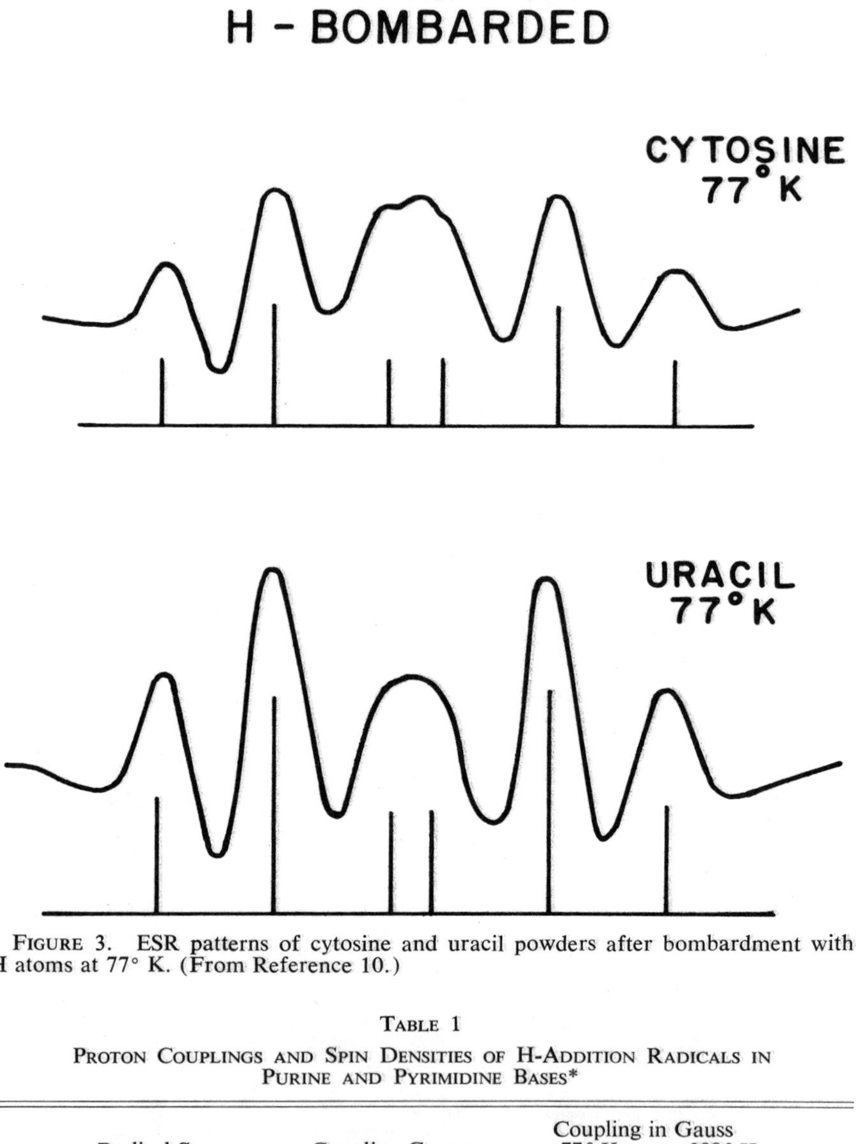

FIGURE 3. ESR patterns of cytosine and uracil powders after bombardment with H atoms at 77° K. (From Reference 10.)

TABLE 1

PROTON COUPLINGS AND SPIN DENSITIES OF H-ADDITION RADICALS IN PURINE AND PYRIMIDINE BASES*

Radical Source	Coupling Group	Coupling in Gauss 77° K	300° K
Thymine	$>C_{(6)}H_2$	34 42	38
	$-CH_3$	20.5	20.5
Uracil	$>C_{(5)}H_2$	19.5 46	33
	$>C_{(6)}H$	19.5	18.5
Cytosine	$>C_{(5)}H_2$	19.5 48	
	$>C_{(6)}H$	19.5	
Adenine	$>C_{(2)}H_2$		40
Guanine	$>C_{(8)}H_2$	38	38

* From Reference 10.

TABLE 2

PROTON COUPLINGS AND SPIN DENSITIES OF H-ADDITION RADICALS IN NUCLEOSIDES, NUCLEOTIDES AND RNA*

Compound	Coupling Group	Coupling in Gauss	Spin densities on C_α
Cytidine	$C_{(6)}H$	$a_1 = 20$	0.76[b]
	$C_{(5)}H_2$	$a_2 = 20$; $a_3 = 50$	
Cytidylic acid	$C_{(6)}H$	$a_1 = 19$	0.73[b]
	$C_{(5)}H_2$	$a_2 = 19$; $a_3 = 46.5$	
Deoxycytidine	$C_{(6)}H$	$a_1 = 20$	0.76[b]
	$C_{(5)}H_2$	$a_2 = 14$; $a_3 = 48.5$	
Deoxycytidylic acid	$C_{(6)}H$	$a_1 = 20$; $(a_1 = 21)$[a]	0.76[b](0.80)[a]
	$C_{(5)}H_2$	$a_2 = 13$; $a_3 = 50$ $(a_2 = 12.5$; $a_3 = 50)$[a]	
Thymidine	$-CH_3$	$a_1 = a_2 = a_3 = 20.5$	0.70[c]
	$C_{(6)}H_2$	$a_4 = a_5 = 39$	
Thymidine 5′-mono-phosphate	$-CH_3$	$a_1 = a_2 = a_3 = 20.5$	0.70[c]
	$C_{(6)}H_2$	$a_4 = a_5 = 38$	
Uridine	$C_{(6)}H$	$a_1 = 20$	0.76[b]
	$C_{(5)}H_2$	$a_2 = 20$; $a_3 = 46$	
Deoxyuridine	$C_{(6)}H$	$a_1 = 19.5$	0.74[b]
	$C_{(5)}H_2$	$a_2 = 19.5$; $a_3 = 46$	
Uridylic acid	$C_{(6)}H$	$a_1 = 20$	0.76[b]
	$C_{(5)}H_2$	$a_2 = 20$; $a_3 = 43$	
Guanosine	$C_{(8)}H_2$	$a_1 = a_2 = 37$	
Guanylic acid	$C_{(8)}H_2$	$a_1 = a_2 = 37$	
Deoxyguanosine	$C_{(8)}H_2$	$a_1 = a_2 = 37$	
Deoxyguanosine 5′-monophosphate	$C_{(8)}H_2$	$a_1 = a_2 = 37$	
RNA			
Pyrimidine	$C_{(6)}H$	$a_1 = 19.5$	0.75
	$C_{(5)}H_2$	$a_2 = 19.5$; $a_3 = 42$	
Purine	$C_{(8)}H_2$	$a_1 = a_2 = 38$[a]	

* From References 10, 11.
[a] At 300° K.
[b] Calculated with the equation $a\,\alpha = Q_\alpha \rho_\alpha$ with $Q_\alpha = 26.2$ gauss.
[c] Calculated from the equation $a\,\beta = \rho_\alpha Q_\beta \cos^2\theta$ with $Q_\beta = 58.5$ gauss.

pected for two equally coupling protons of 28 gauss. The coupling is isotropic and arises from hyperconjugation. The radical giving this pattern is evidently

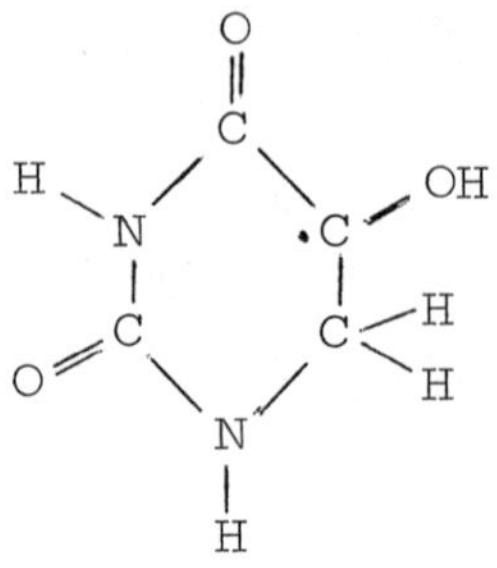

(VII)

uracil + OH

It could be formed by a direct OH addition on $C_{(5)}$ with a subsequent transfer of the H from $C_{(5)}$, to which it was originally bonded, to $C_{(6)}$. We also studied the interaction of OH radicals with 5-halogen uracils, as described below.

5-Halogen Uracils

When 5-I-uracil or 5-Br-uracil was bombarded with H atoms, the ESR signals obtained were like those for H-bombarded uracil itself. We concluded that the impinging H atoms replaced the bromine or the iodine to form uracil, which later captured an H atom to form the uracil radical. In contrast, 5-Cl-uracil formed the direct addition radical

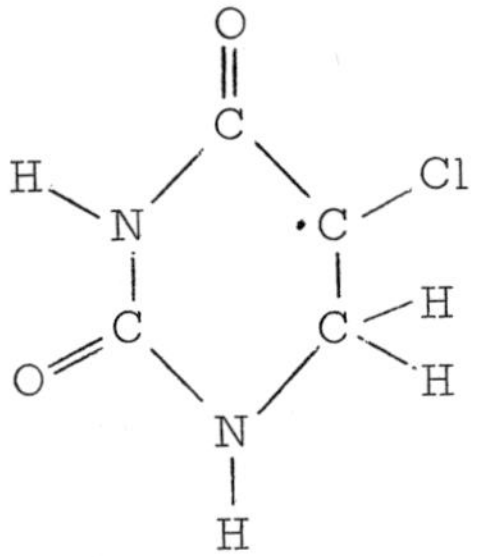

(VIII)

5-Cl-uracil + H

The conditions for this addition are critical. At lowered temperature, Cl replacement occurred.

Mainly, the uracil +H radicals were observed when 5-F-uracil was subjected to gaseous H atoms. Since replacement of F by H is not energetically possible, the impinging H atoms must first interact with the 5-F-uracil to form HF and a primary radical, which is converted to uracil by H atoms arriving later.

Upon bombardment of 5-Br-uracil or 5-I-uracil with OH free radicals and H atoms, a signal is observed like that obtained when uracil itself is bombarded with OH free radicals FIGURE 4). Either the OH replaces the Br or the I to form 5-OH-uracil, which then combines with H atoms to form radicals like (VII) above; or the H atoms first replace the halogens, and radicals like (VII) are then formed by interaction of the OH with uracil.

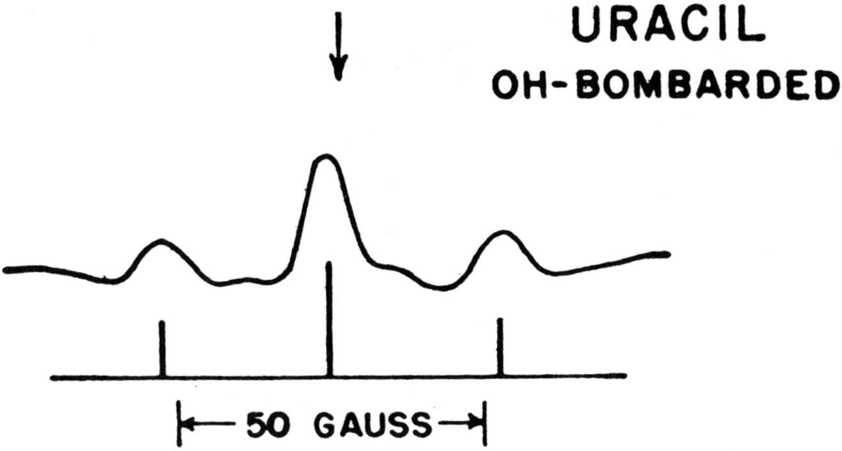

FIGURE 4. ESR pattern of uracil powder after bombardment with OH radicals at room temperature. (From Reference 14.)

Pyrimidine Single Crystals

Although it is tedious and difficult, work on single crystals can give specific and useful information about the free radicals when suitable crystals can be grown and a detailed analysis is possible. Pruden, Snipes and I succeeded first in obtaining the ESR spectra of irradiated single crystals of pyrimidines.[7] From the analysis of the results on thymidine, they concluded that the hydrogen-addition free radical (I) already mentioned gave rise to the observed spectra. Briefly, this is the evidence from the single crystal experiment: the hyperfine structure was found to be isotropic such as that expected from the CH_2 and CH_3 in radical (I), whereas the g factor had a dependence upon the orientation of the crystal in the magnetic field expected for an unpaired π electron on the rings. No nuclear coupling from the nitrogens was observed. The only resolvable hyperfine structure was that from the CH_2 and CH_3 protons, which have isotropic values essentially the same as those listed in TABLE 1.

In 1964, Snipes, Pruden and I began a study of the ESR spectra of irradiated single crystals of cytidine. Because of some doubt about the exact identity of the principal radical giving the observed spectra, we have withheld publication of our findings in the hope of clearing up the uncertainty. However, some of the results are reported in the Ph.D. thesis of Pruden (1965), together with a description of the radical which agrees best with these data. Snipes and Pruden are no longer at Duke, but this investigation is being continued with the assistance of Chester Alexander. I shall describe briefly the essential results and conclusions.

The principal radical is not an H-addition radical such as that in thymidine, although weak signals appearing in some crystals may arise from H-addition radicals. The surprising feature is that the predominant spectrum has a hyperfine structure, which seems definitely to arise from an almost isotropic coupling to only one N^{14} nucleus, giving a triplet with spacing of approximately 9 gauss for most orientations of the crystal. For orientations of the magnetic field along the a, b, or c axis, all molecules in the unit cell have equivalent orientations, and only one triplet appears, as in FIGURE 5. For

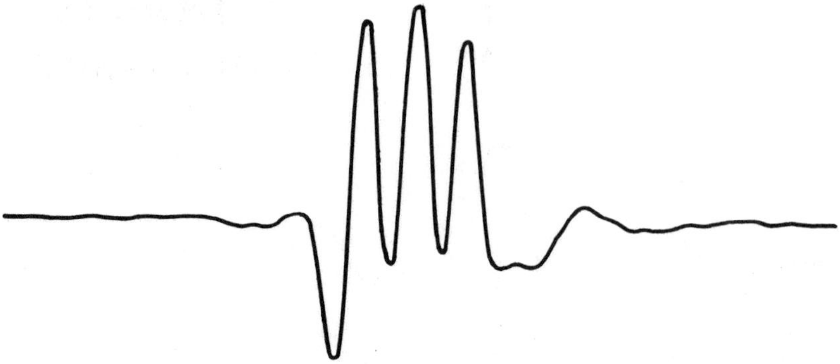

FIGURE 5. ESR pattern of a γ-irradiated single crystal of cytidine with the magnetic field parallel to the a axis of the crystal. (From Snipes, Pruden and Gordy, 1965.)

other orientations, two sets of triplets are observed because of variation in the g values for two inequivalent orientations of molecules of the unit cell.

The principal ESR spectrum of the irradiated cytidine crystal can be ascribed to the radical

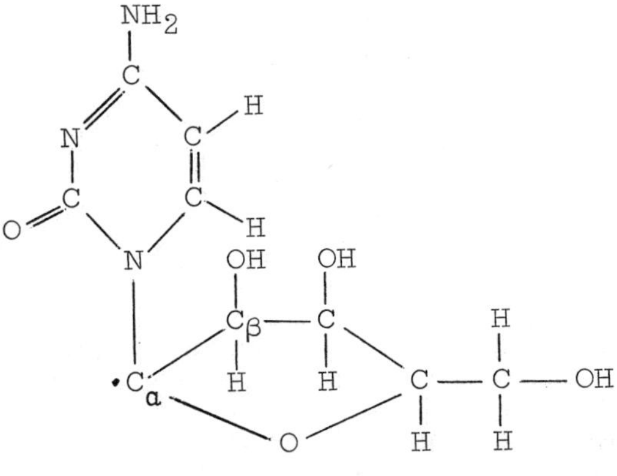

(IX)

formed by the loss of a hydrogen from the carbon of the ribose ring which links the ring to the base. The plane of the ribose ring is approximately at right angles to that of the x base ring, with $C\alpha$ approximately in both planes. The electron spin density is mainly in an sp_3 hybrid orbital directed almost in the plane of the base ring, and normal to that of the sugar. No noticeable coupling arises from the hydrogen on C_β because the C_β-H bond is approximately normal to the orbital of the unpaired electron. The triplet splitting arises primarily from exchange interaction of the unpaired electron with that of the $C\alpha$-N σ bond. There is little π-bonding of the unpaired electron with the N because of unfavorable orientation of the orbitals. The N-bonding orbital of the CN has approximately one-third 2s character, and it is this component which is responsible for most of the N^{14} coupling. The coupling of a 2s electron in N^{14} is 549 gauss. The observed isotropic coupling of 9 gauss indicates a 2s spin density of 0.016. With only one-third 2s character in the bonding orbital, this indicates 3 (0.016) or 4.8% spin density in the sp^2-bonding orbital of the N. This spin density would not cause significant anisotropy in the splitting because the coupling of a 2p electron of N^{14} is only 17 gauss and, with this small spin density, would give an anisotropic coupling constant **B** of only 0.18 gauss.

As this is being written, an interesting paper by Cook and collaborators[16] reports successful investigation of irradiated single crystals of cytosine. These researchers found the principal radical to be

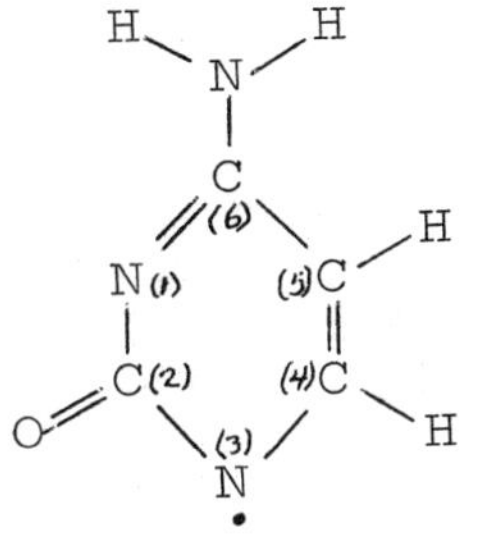

(X)

which is formed by loss of a hydrogen from $N_{(3)}$. Both $N_{(1)}$ and $N_{(3)}$ gave measurable hyperfine structure with anisotropic coupling constants of 2.5 gauss and 5 gauss (7 and 14 Mc). The corresponding spin densities are 0.15 and 0.29, respectively. In addition to the principal radical, Cook and coworkers observed lesser signals from H-addition radicals of the type earlier observed in the H-bombarded powder. These signals were about one-tenth the strength of the principal signals.

Although in our work on the cytidine single crystal we observed weak satellite signals, which may come from radicals such as those found by Cook and coworkers[15] in the cytosine crystal, the principal radicals found in the two crystals are basically different. This conclusion is in agreement with that reached from the original observations on powdered samples.

Bernhard and Snipes[17] have reported preliminary ESR studies of an irradiated single crystal of 3′-cytidylic acid, and have attributed the observed signals to a free radical having the form R–CH_βR–CH_α–R, in which R represents groups which have no appreciable hyperfine interactions.

Purine Single Crystals

The first ESR study of an irradiated purine single crystal to be reported is that on guanine hydrochloride, undertaken with my student, Chester Alexander.[18] The radical observed is one formed by hydrogen addition on $C_{(8)}$ and already identified by H-atom bombardment of the powdered sample. From the powdered samples, however, only the isotropic CH_2 coupling constants could be ascertained, whereas from the single crystal both the N^{14} nuclear coupling and the g tensor could be evaluated. In addition, an isotropic coupling was measured for an associated proton, apparently from the HCl and attached to $N_{(7)}$ of the guanine, mainly through electrostatic bonding. The observed radical is

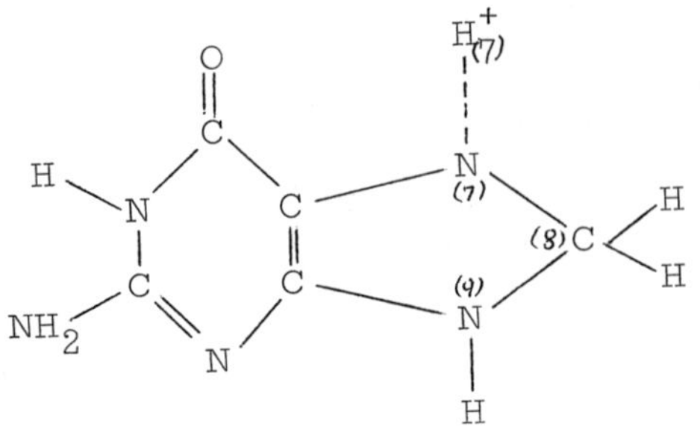

(XI)

Principal elements of the g tensor and the various nuclear couplings are given in TABLE 3. The direction cosines of the principal elements of g and the nuclear coupling tensor are in good agreement with those expected from the structure of the crystal, as determined by Iball and Wilson[19] from x-ray analysis. The coupling for the $H_{(7)}$ proton is also in agreement with this structural determination. From the N^{14} coupling, the spin densities of the p_π orbitals of $N_{(7)}$ and $N_{(9)}$ are found to be 0.38 and $\leq$ 0.08, in agreement with the theoretical value of 0.39 on $N_{(7)}$ and 0.08 on $N_{(9)}$, previously calculated by Pullman and Mantione[20] with the Hückel approximation.

FIGURE 6 shows ESR patterns obtained for three different orientations of the crystal in the magnetic field. For the crystal orientation corresponding to the top curve, only the isotropic CH_2 proton coupling is resolved. For the middle curve, the $H_{(7)}$ proton doublet is also resolved, but no N coupling is resolved. In the lower curve the $N_{(7)}$ nitrogen triplet is resolved, but not the $H_{(7)}$ doublet.

TABLE 3

ESR CONSTANTS OF H-ADDITION RADICALS IN SINGLE CRYSTALS OF GUANINE HYDROCHLORIDE DIHYDRATE[18]

Coupling Atom	Nuclear Coupling: Principal Values (gauss)	Direction in Guanine Molecule
Nitrogen $N_{(7)}$	21.0 ± 0.5	⊥ to plane of molecule
	1.5	∥ $N_{(7)}$–$H_{(7)}$ bond
	1.5	⊥ to above directions
Hydrogen $H_{(7)}$	−9.0 ± 0.5	⊥ to plane of molecule
	1.0	∥ $N_{(7)}$–$H_{(7)}$ bond
	−15.0	⊥ to above directions
Hydrogen $H_{(4)}$	−2.9	⊥ to plane of molecule
	−0.9	∥ $N_{(9)}$–$H_{(4)}$ bond
	−5.0	⊥ to above directions
Hydrogen CH_2	36.0 ± 0.5	Isotropic

g-Tensor: Principal Values	Direction in Guanine Molecule
2.0023 ± 0.0002	⊥ to plane of molecule
2.0048	∥ to $N_{(7)}$–$H_{(7)}$ bond
2.0048	⊥ to above directions

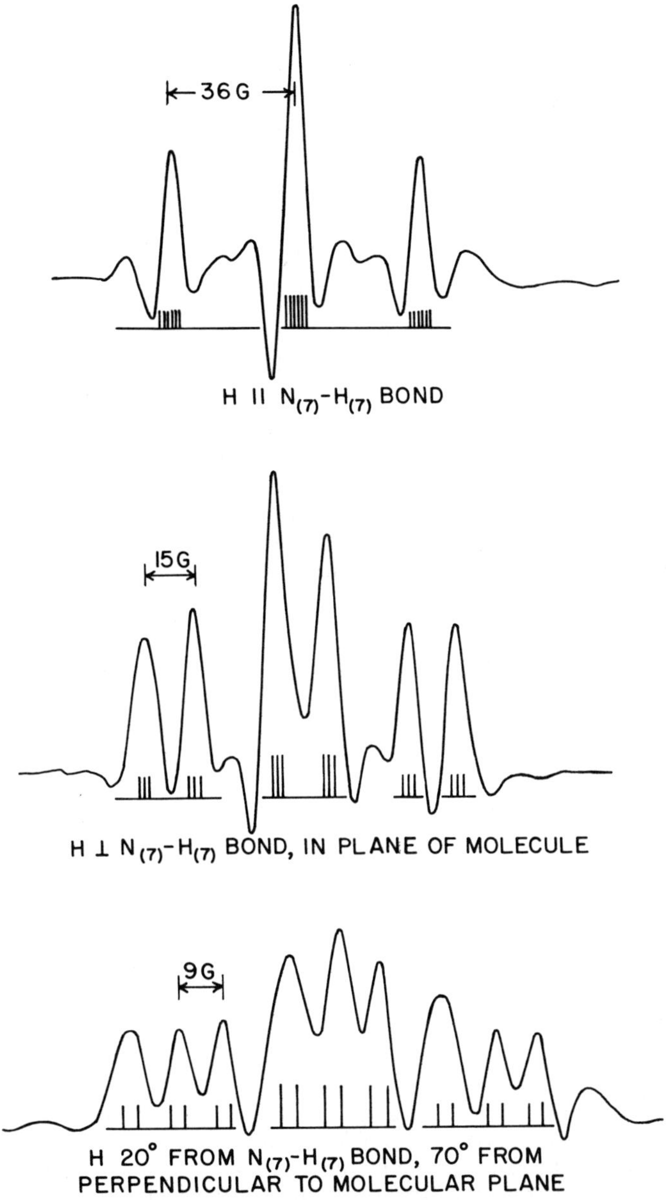

FIGURE 6. ESR patterns of a γ-irradiated single crystal of guanine hydrochloride dihydrate for different orientations of the crystal in the magnetic field. (From Reference 18.)

James Lichter and I are studying single crystals of deoxyadenosine. FIGURE 7 shows the ESR of a γ-irradiated single crystal of deoxyadenosine monohydrate for two orientations of the crystal in the magnetic field. There are evidently strong signals from two chemically different species of radicals. One

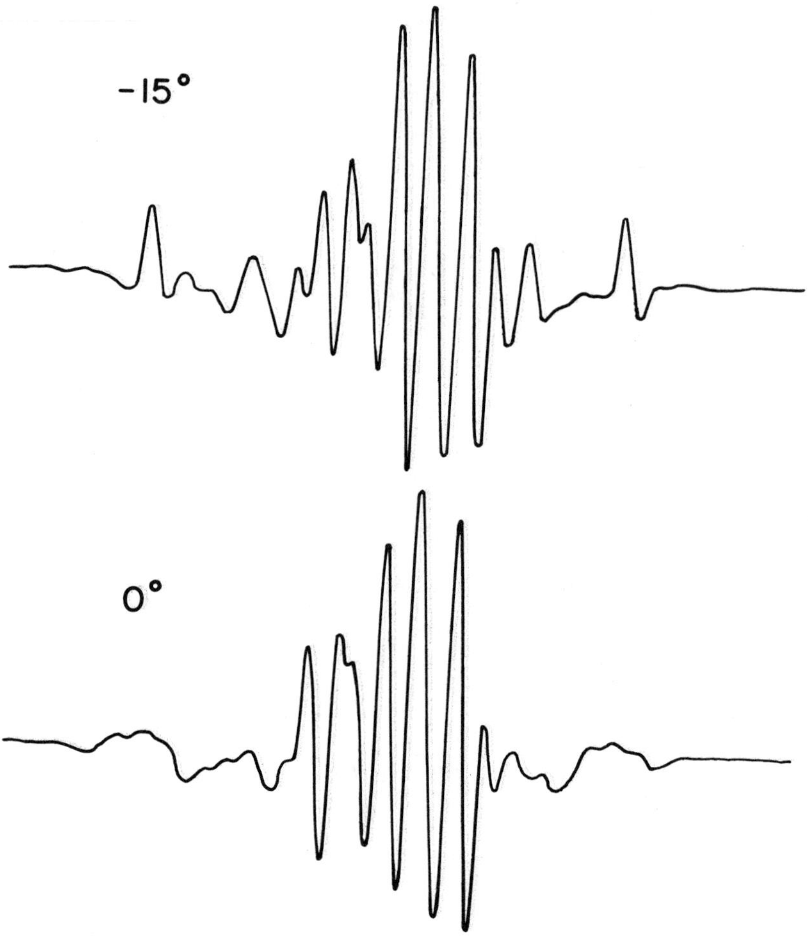

FIGURE 7. ESR patterns of a γ-irradiated single crystal of deoxyadenosine monohydrate for different orientations of the crystal. There are two chemically different radicals giving the patterns, and molecules having two different orientations in the unit cell. (From J. J. Lichter and W. Gordy. 1968.) Proc. Nat. Acad. Sci. **60,** 450–455.

of these is the H-addition radical of the basic ring structure, which was revealed by the earlier H-atom bombardment of the powder. The other is a radical formed in the ribose group by the loss of an H atom.

Fortunately, the isotropic triplet-splitting by the CH_2 protons is sufficiently great that the outer two components of the triplet are outside the range of the spectrum of the ribose radical. This allows resolution and analysis of the N^{14} hyperfine structure of these outer components from which the N^{14} coupling constants can be obtained. The analysis shows that there are two nitrogens in the radical that produce resolvable splittings. The coupling of each nitrogen is axially symmetric about the normal to the plane of the ring, and has maximum values when the field is normal to the rings. X-ray diffraction measurements by Watson and collaborators[21] show that there are two molecules in unit cell with the planes of their rings approximately 33° apart. These usually lead to radicals with two different orientations in the crystal, but for certain directions the orientations are magnetically equivalent. FIGURE 7 (lower curve) shows one recording for which the orientations are equivalent. At certain other orientations, the lines for one orientation are sufficiently sharper and stronger to be distinguishable from those of the other one.

TABLE 4 gives preliminary values for the coupling constants for the nitrogens and the hydrogens of the H-addition radical. The couplings of the two

TABLE 4

NUCLEAR COUPLING CONSTANTS FOR RADICALS IN SINGLE CRYSTALS OF DEOXYADENOSINE MONOHYDRATE*

Coupling Constant for	Principal Values (gauss)	Direction in Adenine Radical
Nitrogen $N_{(3)}$	19 ± 1	⊥ to radical plane
	≤ 1	In plane of radical
Nitrogen $N_{(1)}$	8 ± 1	⊥ to radical plane
	< 0.5	In plane of radical
Hydrogen CH_2	44 ± 1	Isotropic

* From Lichter, J. J. & W. Gordy. 1968. Proc. Nat. Acad. Sci. **60**: 450–455.

nitrogens are significantly different from those of the two nitrogens of the guanine single crystal. Likewise, the coupling of the CH_2 hydrogens is larger than in the guanine. These comparisons, together with a comparison between the observed spin densities and those predicted theoretically by Pullman and Mantione,[20] lead to the conclusion that the radical observed in the adenosine is formed by H addition to $C_{(2)}$ rather than to $C_{(8)}$ as it is in the guanine, i.e., that the radical has a structure similar to (VI) rather than (V).

The measurement and analysis of the radical found on the deoxyribose group is still incomplete. It is complicated by the superposition of the stronger central component of the H-addition radicals as well as by the two different orientations of molecules in the crystals. Nevertheless, observations for certain orientations of the crystal for which these complicating factors are minimized indicate that the hyperfine structure comes from an anisotropic coupling of a $C_\alpha H$ fragment combined with the isotropic coupling of about 6.5 gauss of a $C_\beta H$ proton. Tentative assignment of the structure of the radical is

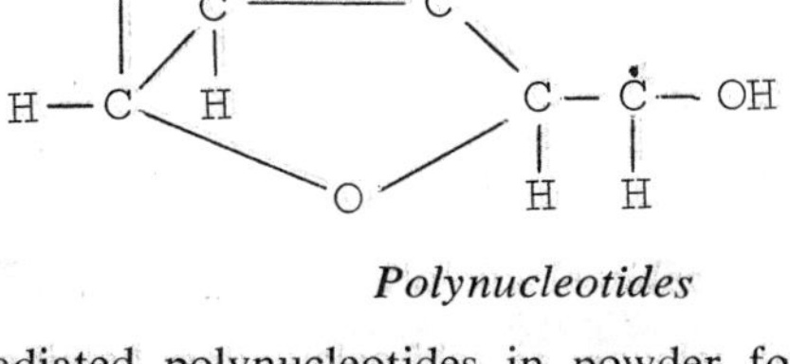

(XII)

Polynucleotides

Several irradiated polynucleotides in powder form[22] have been studied in our laboratory. These include poly U, poly C, and poly A and also the copolymers poly CU and poly AU. We were unable to obtain samples of poly T and poly G. Only γ-irradiation was used in these experiments.

Noticeable effects of moisture content on the formation of H-addition radicals on the basic rings of poly U and poly A were observed. These effects are illustrated in FIGURES 8 and 9. The patterns expected for H-addition radicals

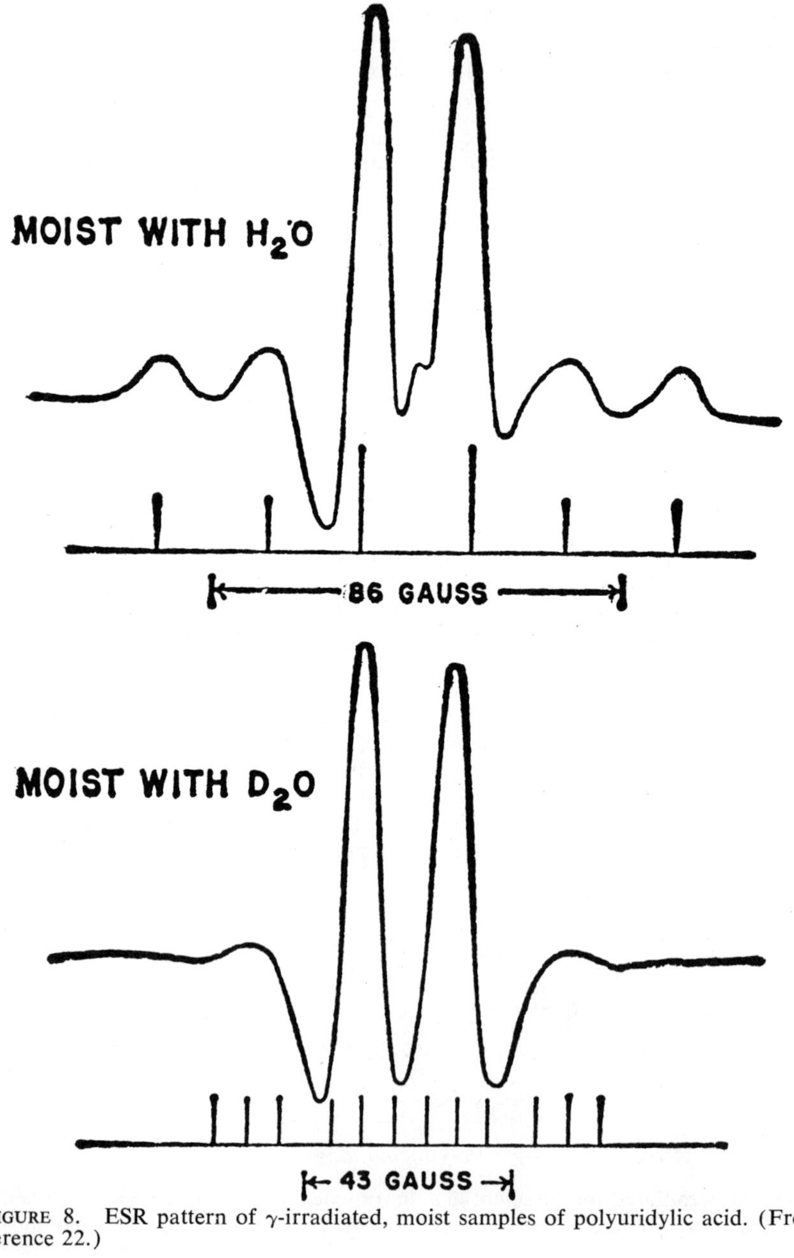

FIGURE 8. ESR pattern of γ-irradiated, moist samples of polyuridylic acid. (From Reference 22.)

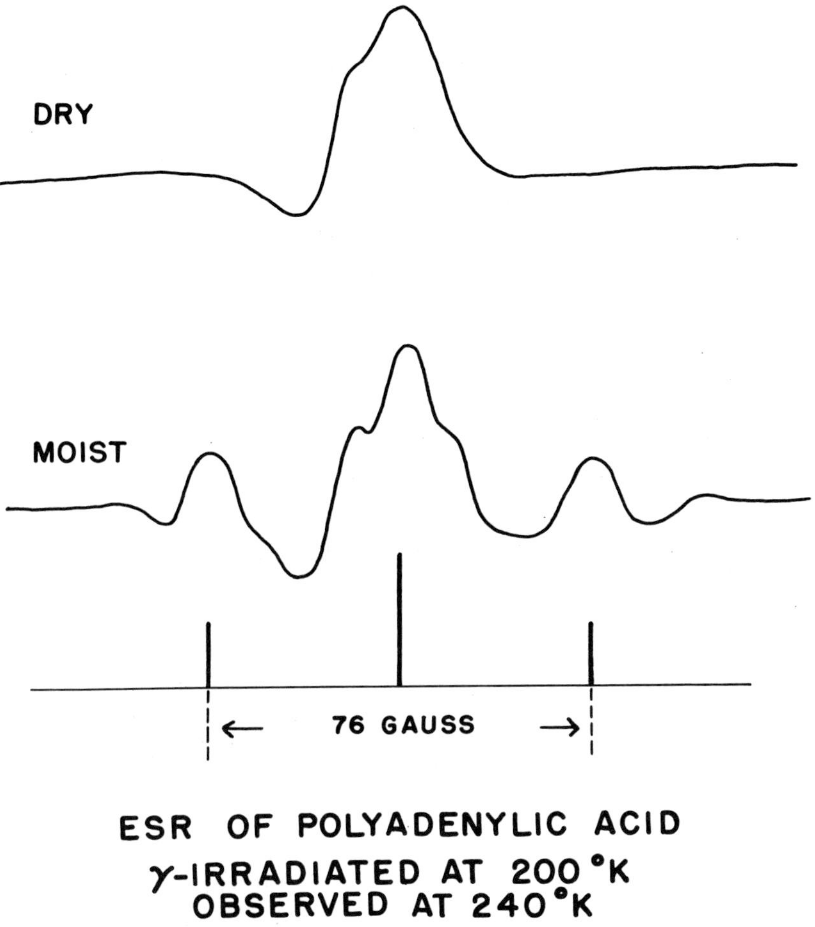

FIGURE 9. ESR patterns of γ-irradiated samples (dry and moist) of polyadenylic acid. (From Reference 22.)

are indicated by the bars in the lower graphs. In each polymer, considerable enhancement of the H-addition radicals was caused by the absorbed H_2O. That the H atoms which are added to the rings are produced from the H_2O is shown by the marked change in the pattern when D_2O is substituted for H_2O. These effects are similar to the enhancement of the thymidinelike resonance in DNA first observed by Pershan and coworkers.[8]

The strong doublet in the center of the poly U pattern, which is the same for samples moist with D_2O or H_2O, is believed to result from a radical formed by H abstraction from the ribose group. In agreement with the observations on cytidine powder, no evidence for significant formation of H-addition radicals was obtained for poly C even when the samples were moist when irradiated. The ESR pattern for γ-irradiated poly C resembles closely that of cytidine.

Müller[23] also observed the ESR of polynucleotides but did not report any study of moisture effects.

Purine and Pyrimidine Resonance in DNA and RNA

An important question to be considered is whether the various free radicals formed in the purines and pyrimidines described above are also formed by irradiation in DNA or RNA. Shields and I were surprised that the signals we observed for irradiated DNA and RNA were unlike any of the various signals we observed for their constituent purine and pyrimidine components. For both DNA and RNA irradiated with x-rays or γ-rays, we obtained a singlet resonance of 30 to 40 gauss in width but evidently having some unresolved structure. Although some people questioned the purity of our samples, it now appears that our samples may have been too pure or too dry to allow observation of H-addition radicals on the basic rings. We observed a number of different samples of DNA, but all of them were dry and evacuated. Several laboratories obtained results in agreement with ours. However, Salovey and collaborators[24] observed a thymidinelike component in DNA by large irradiation dosage at lowered temperature combined with postirradiation annealing of the sample. Ehrenberg and coworkers[25] obtained the thymidinelike resonance by special chemical treatment of the DNA samples before irradiation. Pershan and collaborators[8] obtained the thymidinelike resonance by irradiation of moist samples of DNA with U.V.

After our single crystal studies of thymidine revealed that the thymidine signal comes from H-addition radicals, it occurred to us that the difficulty in observation of thymidinelike signals in evacuated DNA may be due to the unavailability of H atoms at the proper sites. Consequently, we irradiated samples of DNA under pressure of hydrogen gas, and thereupon were able to produce relatively strong thymidinelike resonance[26] in dry DNA.

To my knowledge, no one has detected H-addition radicals either on the cytosine rings in DNA or, with certainty, on the purine rings in DNA. Gordy and coworkers,[26] however, observed a cytidinelike triplet, possibly from a radical such as (IX), in a sample of highly polymerized calf thymus DNA γ-irradiated and observed under vacuum at room temperature. Dorlet and collaborators[27] obtained a purinelike triplet in a sample of trout-sperm DNA containing 20% H_2O and 1/10% protein, which was irradiated and observed at room temperature.

When they subjected DNA to H atoms, Heller and Cole[12] obtained an unresolved resonance similar to that usually obtained for dry γ-irradiated DNA. Although we have been unable to produce definite signals from H-addition radicals such as those in the purine or pyrimidine bases by H bombardment of DNA, we did obtain a singlet resonance[10] similar to that shown by Heller and Cole.

On the other hand, we were able to produce both purine and pyrimidine signals when we subjected RNA to H atoms at lowered temperature (see FIGURE 10). Because of the similarity in patterns, it is not possible to learn whether the pyrimidine signals are from the cytosine group or the uracil group, or from both; nor can one tell whether the purine signals are from the adenosine group or the guanine group, or from both. However, the pyrimidine signal, like that of cytosine, is unstable at room temperature, whereas the purine signal remains after the sample is brought to room temperature. (See the lower curve of FIGURE 10).

An interesting recent paper by Ehrenberg and coworkers[28] reports the observation of definite orientation-dependence of the ESR resonance of strands of DNA irradiated at 77°, both when containing water and when dry. The ef-

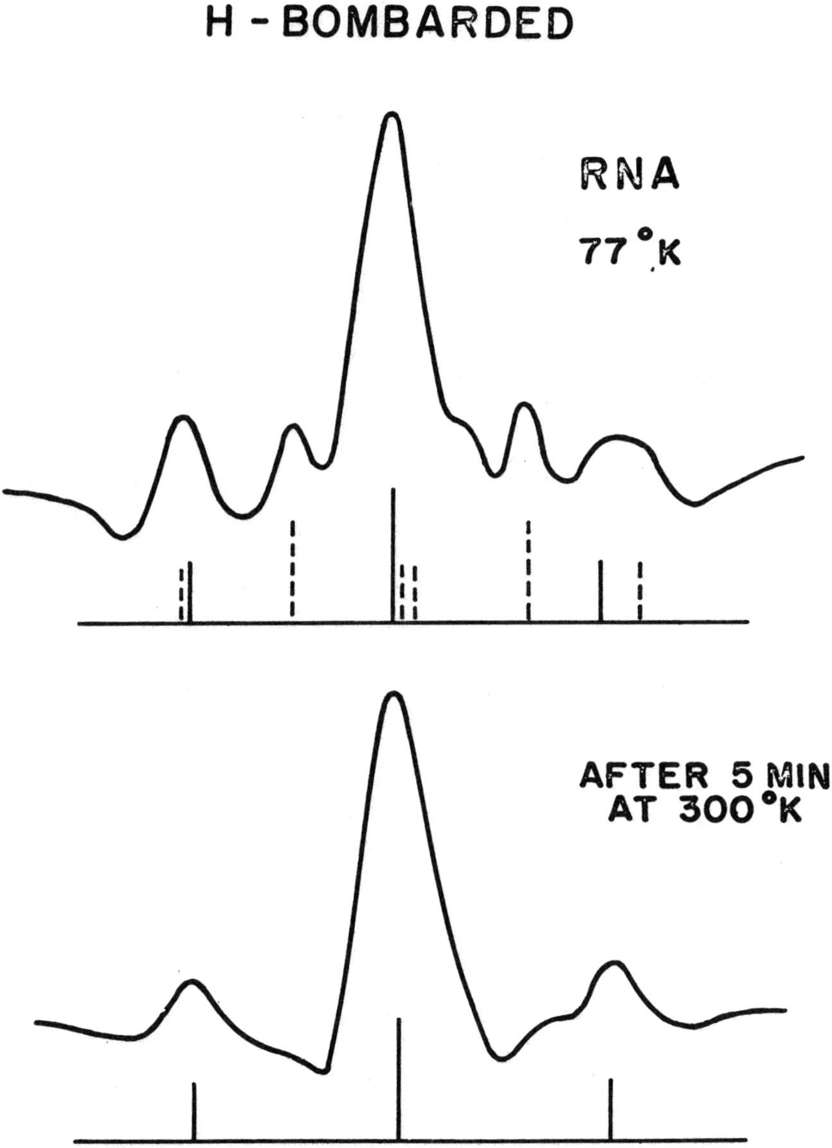

FIGURE 10. ESR patterns of RNA after exposure to gaseous H atoms at 77° K and then after warming. The dotted lines represent the pattern for the uracil H-addition radical at 77° K (see FIGURE 3), and the solid bars represent that for guanine or adenine (see FIGURE 2). (From Reference 10.)

fects are more pronounced in the moist strands than in the dry strands (see FIGURE 11). Note that the signals in the wet samples after annealing are predominantly the thymidinelike resonance, whereas the signals for the dry sample show no evidence of H-addition radicals even after annealing. Note also that the signals obtained for the moist samples show no structure such as that

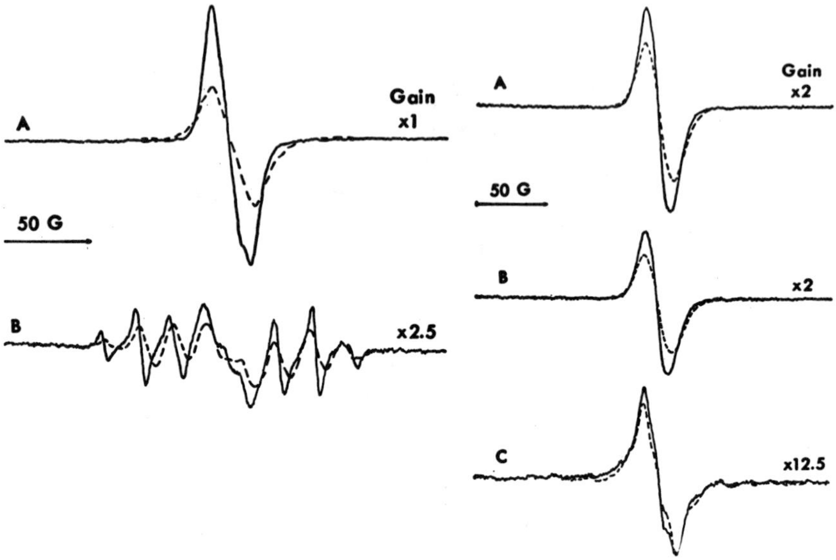

FIGURE. 11. (Top left) The ESR spectra from a moist sample of oriented calf-thymus lithium DNA after γ-irradiation at 77° K. (A) Signals obtained at 77° K with the DNA helices parallel with (----) and perpendicular to (——) the field; (B) signals obtained at 77° K after annealing of the sample at 199° K for 5 minutes. (The amplification, relative to that in (A) is 2.5.) (From Reference 28.)

from the H-addition radicals until the samples are annealed. This is consistent with the earlier work[29] on DNA + H_2O irradiated at 4.2° K, in which a singlet resonance for the DNA was obtained and separate signals from H atoms. The H atoms are produced by the irradiation at low temperature, but they evidently cannot move to attack the DNA rings until the sample is warmed.

Free Valencies and Spin Densities

It is reasonable to expect that the attack by H atoms or OH free radicals on the purine or pyrimidine rings would occur on the carbon having the highest free valence. In uracil and in the 5-halogen uracils (except 5-F-uracil) it has been possible to show that this is true. TABLE 5 gives the calculated

TABLE 5

CORRELATION OF FREE VALENCE WITH ATTACK BY H OR OH RADICAL[15]

Compound	Theoretical Free Valence		Atom Attacked (experimental)
	On $C_{(5)}$	On $C_{(6)}$	
Uracil	0.526	0.434	$C_{(5)}$
5-I-uracil	0.459	0.423	$C_{(5)}$
5-Br-uracil	0.446	0.438	$C_{(5)}$
5-Cl-uracil	0.435	0.443	$C_{(6)}$
5-F-uracil	0.400	0.434	F

free valences on $C_{(5)}$ and $C_{(6)}$, which have the highest values of the atoms of the ring. Also indicated is the carbon, which is found by ESR to be the point of attack by the H atom or OH radical. In 5-F-uracil, the attack occurs on F rather than on a carbon of the ring. For the other 5-halogen-uracils, the initial attack occurs on the carbon having the highest free valence. This is also true for 5-methyl-uracil (thymine).

In guanine, the H addition occurs on $C_{(8)}$, where calculations by Pullman and Pullman[30] predict the free valence to be highest, but spin densities on the nitrogens as derived from the single crystal measurements on adenosine (see comparisons in TABLE 6) indicate that the H addition occurs on $C_{(2)}$, whereas the predicted free valence is highest on $C_{(8)}$ for the free base adenosine.

TABLE 6 provides a comparison of observed and theoretical spin densities on certain atoms of H-addition free radicals derived from the measured nuclear coupling constants. The theoretical values are calculated with molecular orbital theory and with the Hückel assumption. The overall agreement is good in view of the approximations involved in the derivations.

Possible Significance for Radiation Damage and Mutations

The observed attack of H atoms at thermal velocities on all the information groups of the nucleic acids—the purine and pyrimidine rings—combined with the prevalent release of H atoms by radiation from H_2O and many other constituents of the biological cells already demonstrated by ESR studies, strongly indicates that attack by H atoms on the nucleic acids is one of the

TABLE 6

COMPARISON OF OBSERVED AND CALCULATED SPIN DENSITIES OF H-ADDITION RADICALS IN PURINES AND PYRIMIDINES

Radical Source	H-Addition on	Spin Density on	Spin Density: Observed at 300° K	Ref.	Calculated	Ref.
Thymine	$C_{(6)}$	$C_{(5)}$	0.70	7	0.72	d
Uracil	$C_{(5)}$	$C_{(6)}$	0.71	9	0.72	d
5-OH-uracil (radical)	$C_{(6)}$	$C_{(5)}$	0.64	14	0.67	14
5-Cl-uracil (radical)	$C_{(6)}$	$C_{(5)}$	0.80	15	0.77	14
Cytosine	$C_{(5)}$	$C_{(6)}$	0.71[a]	10	0.71	20
Deoxyadenosine (monohydrate)	$C_{(2)}$	$N_{(1)}$	0.15	b	0.12[c]	20
		$N_{(3)}$	0.37	b	0.38[c]	20
Guanine (hydrochloride dihydrate)	$C_{(8)}$	$N_{(7)}$	0.38	18	0.39	20
		$N_{(9)}$	0.08	18	0.08	20

[a] Derived from observed value of 0.75 at 300° K.
[b] From Lichter, J. J. & W. Gordy. 1968. Proc. Nat. Acad. Sci. 60: 450–455.
[c] Theoretical value for radical formed with adenine base by H addition on $C_{(2)}$. For H addition on $C_{(8)}$, predicted spin densities on $N_{(7)}$ and $N_{(9)}$ are 0.43 and 0.09, respectively.
[d] From Mantione, M. J. & B. Pullman. 1964. Biochim. Biophys. Acta 91: 387.

most important sources of radiation damage in biology. Many of the biochemicals which release H atoms when irradiated—H_2O, nucleoproteins, enzymes —are so closely associated with the DNA of the cell that H atoms released from them do not have to migrate far before they reach one of the sites where they readily add to the purine or pyrimidine rings. Of course, the H_2O or protein or other chemical which loses the H is also damaged, but such chemicals are more expendable and replaceable than is the DNA of the cell. The addition of an H atom to the base rings of DNA does not necessarily kill the cell nor constitute a mutation per se, but it could well be the initial step in a chain reaction which leads to either result.

We have demonstrated that the OH radical, also a radiation product of H_2O, will readily add to at least one of the pyrimidine rings, uracil. Thus far, our attempts to prove by the ESR method that gaseous OH likewise adds to other pyrimidine and purine groups have been negative, but this may be due to steric factors which prevent the OH from getting to the favorable sites of attack in the solid samples employed. Spectroscopic evidence has been obtained for OH addition to thymidine in solution. Although OH radicals are produced from H_2O, the ESR evidence indicates that they are not released as readily from other chemicals in the cell as are H atoms.

The evidence obtained for radical (IX) in irradiated cytidine suggests a possible cause of mutation. The existence of a radical with its unpaired electron mainly on the carbon that connects the base ring to the sugar group indicates that the formation of this radical might be the first step in the process of breaking off the cytosine base ring and replacing it with another group, perhaps a thymine ring.

References

1. SHIELDS, H. & W. GORDY. 1956. Bull. Amer. Phys. Soc. **1:** 267; GORDY, W. 1958. Electron spin resonance of free radicals in irradiated biochemicals. *In* Proc. Internat. Cong. Rad. Res. Burlington, Vt. (Suppl. 1, 1959. *Radiation Research*): 491–510. Academic Press. New York, N. Y.
2. SHIELDS, H. & W. GORDY. 1959. Proc. Nat. Acad. Sci. **45:** 269–281.
3. MÜLLER, A. 1967. The formation of radicals in nucleic acids, nucleoproteins, and their constituents by ionizing radiations. *In* Progress in Biophysics and Molecular Biology. **17:** 99–147. Pergamon Press. New York, N. Y.
4. SCHOFFA, G. 1964. Elektronenspinresonanz in der Biologie. G. Braun. Karlsruhe, Germany.
5. POOLE, C. P., JR. 1967. Electron Spin Resonance: A Comprehensive Treatise on Experimental Techniques. John Wiley & Sons. New York, N. Y.
6. MÜLLER, A. & W. KÖHNLEIN. 1964. Int. J. Rad. Biol. **8:** 121–130.
7. PRUDEN, B., W. SNIPES & W. GORDY. 1965. Proc. Nat. Acad. Sci. **53:** 917–924.
8. PERSHAN, P. S., R. G. SHULMAN, B. J. WYLUDA & J. EISINGER. 1965. Science **148:** 378–380.
9. HERAK, J. N. & W. GORDY. 1965. Proc. Nat. Acad. Sci. **54:** 1287–1292.
10. HERAK, J. N. & W. GORDY. 1966. Proc. Nat. Acad. Sci. **55:** 1373–1378.
11. HERAK, J. N. & W. GORDY. 1966. Proc. Nat. Acad. Sci. **56:** 7–11.
12. HELLER, H. C. & T. COLE. 1965. Proc. Nat. Acad. Sci. **54:** 1486–1490.
13. HOLMES, D. E., L. S. MYERS, JR. & R. B. INGALLS. 1966. Nature **209:** 1017–1018.
14. HERAK, J. N. & W. GORDY. 1966. Science **153:** 1649–1650.
15. HERAK, J. N. & W. GORDY. 1966. Proc. Nat. Acad. Sci. **56:** 1354–1360.
16. COOK, J. B., J. P. ELLIOTT & S. J. WYARD. 1967. Molec. Phys. **13:** 49–64.
17. BERNHARD, W. & W. SNIPES. 1967. Abstr. 15th Ann. Meet. Rad. Res. Soc. **15.** Academic Press, New York, N. Y.
18. ALEXANDER, C. JR. & W. GORDY. 1967. Proc. Nat. Acad. Sci. **58:** 1279–1285.
19. IBALL, J. & H. R. WILSON. 1965. Proc. Roy. Soc. (London) **A288:** 418–429.
20. PULLMAN, B. & M. J. MANTIONE. 1965. Compt. Rend. **260:** 5643–5645.

21. WATSON, D. G., D. J. SUTOR & P. TOLLIN. 1965. Acta Crystallogr. **19:** 111–124.
22. HERAK, J. N. & W. GORDY. 1966. Proc. Nat. Acad. Sci. **55:** 698–704.
23. MÜLLER, A. 1964. Akad. Wiiss. Lit. (Mainz) Abhandt. Math.-Nat. Kl. **5:** 143–261.
24. SALOVEY, R., R. G. SHULMAN & W. M. WALSH, JR. 1963. J. Chem. Phys. **39:** 839–840.
25. EHRENBERG, A., L. EHRENBERG & G. LÖFROTH. 1963. Nature **200:** 376–377.
26. GORDY, W., B. PRUDEN, & W. SNIPES. 1965. Proc. Nat. Acad. Sci. **53:** 751–756.
27. DORLET, C., A. VAN DE VORST & A. J. BERTINCHAMPS. 1962. Nature **194:** 767.
28. EHRENBERG, A., A. RUPPRECHT & G. STRÖM. 1967. Science **157:** 1317–1319.
29. PATTEN, R. A. & W. GORDY. 1964. Nature **201:** 361–363.
30. PULLMAN, B. & A. PULLMAN. 1963. Quantum Biochemistry: 683. John Wiley & Sons. New York, N. Y.

POLAROGRAPHY OF BIOLOGICAL PURINES AND PYRIMIDINES

Philip J. Elving
The University of Michigan
Ann Arbor, Mich.

Introduction

Since electron-transfer reactions are so important in biological systems, information which can be obtained in respect to the energy levels (electrical potentials) and reaction pathways involved should be helpful in the understanding, control and utilization of such reactions. Polarographically determinded half-wave potentials ($E_{1/2}$) and electrode reaction paths or mechanisms readily provide such data under conditions generally similar to those encountered in biological systems, e.g., electrolytic reductions and oxidations often occur under conditions resembling those of enzymatic transformations: electron-transfer at a heterogeneous interface, previous occurrence of adsorption and/or adduct formation, dilute aqueous solution, pH between 2 and 9, and moderate temperature.

Postulation of the extent of correlation that may exist between electrolytic and biological redox processes must at present be largely speculation. Nevertheless, to the extent that the two kinds of processes occur under similar conditions, information obtained from the examination by electrochemical techniques of the redox behavior of compounds of biological interest may help to clarify and explain biological processes with respect to the nature of the factors, such as pH, controlling the electron-transfer process.

The value of electrical measurement in elucidating redox behavior of biologically important organic compounds has long been recognized. However, due to the fact that few organic redox systems behave reversibly, valid potentiometric data have been obtained for only a limited number of compounds. Where such data have been systematically gathered and analyzed, the results have been fruitful, e.g., the work of Michaelis, Clark and their collaborators during the 1920's and 1930's. Since then, most studies of the redox behavior of organic compounds have been based on polarography, generally at the dropping mercury electrode (D.M.E.). Frequently, $E_{1/2}$ data on organic compounds so determined are the only energetic data readily obtainable by electrochemical measurement.

The present paper summarizes the results of polarographic examination of purines and pyrimidines in aqueous solution with emphasis on (a) the reaction path involved in electrochemical reduction and oxidation, (b) the effect of substituents and structure in altering the ease of reduction and the reaction path, and (c) the correlation of $E_{1/2}$ data with electronic and other indices. The stress on reduction is simply due to the fact that, until relatively recently, systematic study of the electrochemical behavior of organic compounds was largely restricted to their reduction at mercury electrodes due to the lack of an electrode suitable for studying oxidation.

In addition to classical direct-current constant-potential polarography at the D.M.E., derived techniques—controlled electrode potential electrolysis and coulometry, cyclic voltammetry, chronopotentiometry and alternating current polarography at mercury and graphite electrodes—have been used to obtain the data to be discussed.

The polarography of purines and pyrimidines was reviewed several years ago[1]; the present discussion largely assumes the availability of this review. Data for the polarographic reduction of selected pyrimidines and purines and for the oxidation of purines are summarized in TABLES 1 and 2.

GENERAL REACTION PATH

Elving and Pullman[2] proposed a general mechanistic pattern for organic electrode processes, based on the fact that the fundamental process in an organic electrochemical reduction is bond rupture, which requires only one electron to produce a free radical species; addition of a second electron completes rupture of the bond to give a carbanion. The pattern (FIGURE 1) assumes a generalized reaction site, R:X, where R represents the reactive carbon center in the molecule and X represents another carbon, oxygen, nitrogen, halogen or other atom; there may be more than one bond between R and X, for example, in a C=N linkage.

In the primary step of the electrode process, the reaction site accepts a single electron to form the electrode-activated complex, which can either revert to the original species or dissociate to give a free radical precursor and an anionic species; the latter, if a multiple bond was originally present between R and X, could form a single, free radical anion. The exact nature of these species will be modified by the extent of the participation of protons, solvent molecules and other solution constituents or even the electrode surface (such participation in subsequent steps is not explicitly indicated but may be involved).

The free radical precursor can either accept a second electron immediately on formation and be reduced to the equivalent of a carbanion, or can exist as a stable, free radical species, which may then either dimerize or, at more negative potential, be further reduced to a carbanion. The charge on the carbanion, formed by either path, is neutralized either by acceptance of a

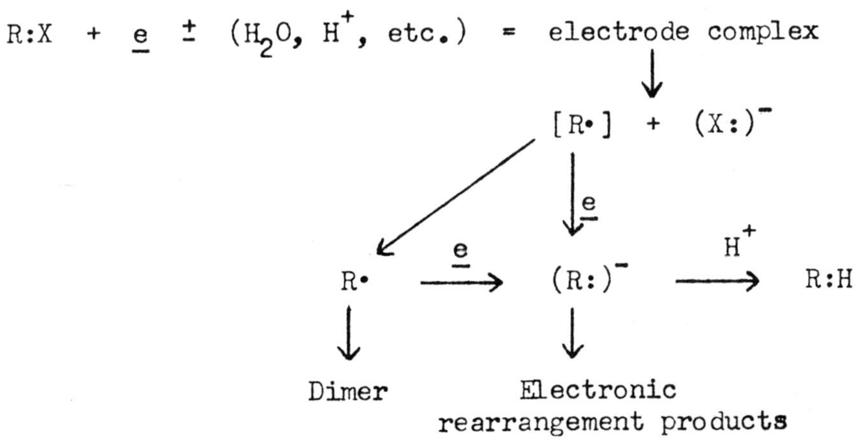

FIGURE 1. Generalized mechanistic path for an organic electrode reaction, in which R:X represents the reaction site; the individual steps are discussed in the text. Allowance may have to be made for (a) the participation in the various steps of protons, solvent, other solution constituents and the electrode surface, (b) the occurrence of chemical reactions preceding, accompanying and following charge-transfer, and (c) resulting modification of the species shown.

TABLE 1

POLAROGRAPHIC REDUCTION OF SELECTED PYRIMIDINES AND PURINES AT THE DROPPING MERCURY ELECTRODE[a]

Compound	pH	$E_{1/2}$[b] v.	I[c]
Pyrimidine	0.5–5	I −0.576–0.105 pH	2.0–2.5
	3–5	II −1.142–0.011 pH	2.2–2.7
	5–8	III −0.680–0.089 pH	4.3–4.7
	7–8	IV −1.000–0.005 pH	4.8
	9–13	V −0.805–0.079 pH	8.9[d]
2-Amino-	2–3	I −0.685–0.049 pH	2.0
	4–7	I −0.425–0.121 pH	2.1–2.4
	4–7	II −1.360–0.004 pH	2.0–2.4
	7–9	III −0.680–0.090 pH	4.0–4.3
2-Amino-4-methyl-	2–4	I −0.770–0.063 pH	2.0
	4–7	I −0.550–0.113 pH	2.1
	5–7	II −1.424–0.008 pH	2.0
	7–9	III −0.745–0.094 pH	4.0
2-Hydroxy-	2–8	−0.530–0.078 pH	2.1
4-Amino-2-hydroxy- (cytosine)	5.5		4.9
	4–6	−1.125–0.075 pH	
	5		6.4
4-Amino-6-hydroxy-	1.2	−1.18	
	6.8	−1.62	
4-Amino-2, 6-dimethyl	2–8	−1.130–0.073 pH	
	2–5		6.8
4-Amino-2, 5-dimethyl	3–6	−1.11–0.076 pH	4.8
4-Hydroxy-	1.2	−1.16	
	6.8	−1.60	
2, 4-Diamino-	1.2	−1.16	
	6.8	−1.52	
4, 5, 6-Triamino-	1.2	−1.17	
	6.8	−1.57	
1, 4-0-Dimethyl- (thymine)	1.2	−1.18	
	6.8	−1.62	
Purine	2–6	I −0.697–0.083 pH	3.8
	2–6	II −0.902–0.080 pH	6.3
6-Amino- (adenine)	1–3	e	10.2
	4–6	e	10.2
	2–6	−0.975–0.090 pH	5.6
6-Hydroxy- (hypoxanthine)	5.7	−1.61	2.75

[a] Data selected from TABLES 2 and 3 of Reference 1, where references to the original sources are given.

[b] Roman numbers indicate successive polarographic waves; potentials are vs. S.C.E.

[c] Diffusion current constant, $I = i_1/Cm^{2/3}t^{1/6}$; each electron transferred per molecule reduced or oxidized contributes a value of about 2. The values for purine and adenine are slightly high due to the presence of some concomitant hydrogen ion reduction (cf. References 4 and 22).

[d] At pH 13, I = 6.

[e] Dependence of $E_{1/2}$ on pH is similar to that given for pH range of 2–6, which is for McIlvaine buffers; these two sets of data are for chloride and acetate buffers, respectively.

TABLE 2

VOLTAMMETRIC OXIDATION OF SELECTED PURINES AT THE STATIONARY GRAPHITE ELECTRODE[a]

Compound	pH	$E_{p/2}$ v.	Ratio[b] i_p/C $\mu a/mM$
Purine		(no wave)	
6-Amino- (adenine)	2.3–5.7 5.5	 1.03 to 1.07	73[c] 48[d]
2-Amino-6-hydroxy- (guanine)	$2M\ H_2SO_4$	1.02	50
6-Amino-2-hydroxy- (isoguanine)	$2M\ H_2SO_4$	1.05	58
6-Hydroxy- (hypoxanthine)	2.3–5.7	1.25 to 1.04	62
2, 6-Dihydroxy-(xanthine)	$2M\ H_2SO_4$ 3.7–5.7	1.01 0.84 to 0.71	49
2, 6, 8-Trihydroxy- (uric acid)	$2M\ H_2SO_4$ 3.7 5.7	0.62 0.45 0.33	 31 34

[a] Data taken from Reference 22, with the exceptions noted in footnotes c and d.

[b] Current values are those obtained at a 0.25-inch diameter, wax-impregnated graphite rod.

[c] In the pH range of 2–5, E_p at a pyrolytic graphite electrode = 1.45–0.067 pH, with i_p/C being 68 for a 0.25-inch electrode (Reference 28).

[d] Obtained with a highly damped polarograph. (Reference 38).

proton from the solution or by electronic rearrangement that transfers the charge to another part of the molecule where it can be suitably handled.

Chemical reactions preceding, accompanying or following charge-transfer may—and often do—play significant roles in the overall process, as is subsequently indicated.

Reduction of the Pyrimidine Ring

The complex pattern observed for the reduction of pyrimidine at the D.M.E., in which five polarographic waves appear over the normal pH range (cf. TABLE 1), can be explained[3] on the basis of the general electrode reaction mechanism described (FIGURE 2): Wave I results from $1e$ reduction of the 3, 4 bond with the simultaneous acquisition of a proton to form a free radical, which may dimerize to 4,4'-bipyrimidine or be reduced at more negative potential in a further $1e$ process (wave II) to 3, 4- dihydropyrimidine. Since wave I is strongly pH-dependent and wave II is only slightly pH-dependent, the two wages merge at about pH 5 to form pH-dependent $2e$ wave III. Essentially pH-independent wave IV, which appears at higher pH, represents a $2e$ reduction at more negative potential of the dihydropyrimidine to a tetrahydropyrimidine. The difference in pH-dependency of waves III and IV result in their merging at about pH 9 to form pH-dependent $4e$ wave V.

Reduction Paths for Purines and Pyrimidines

Essentially, the reduction of pyrimidines, purines and their derivatives follows the course outlined for pyrimidine, i.e., the 3, 4 N=C bond in the

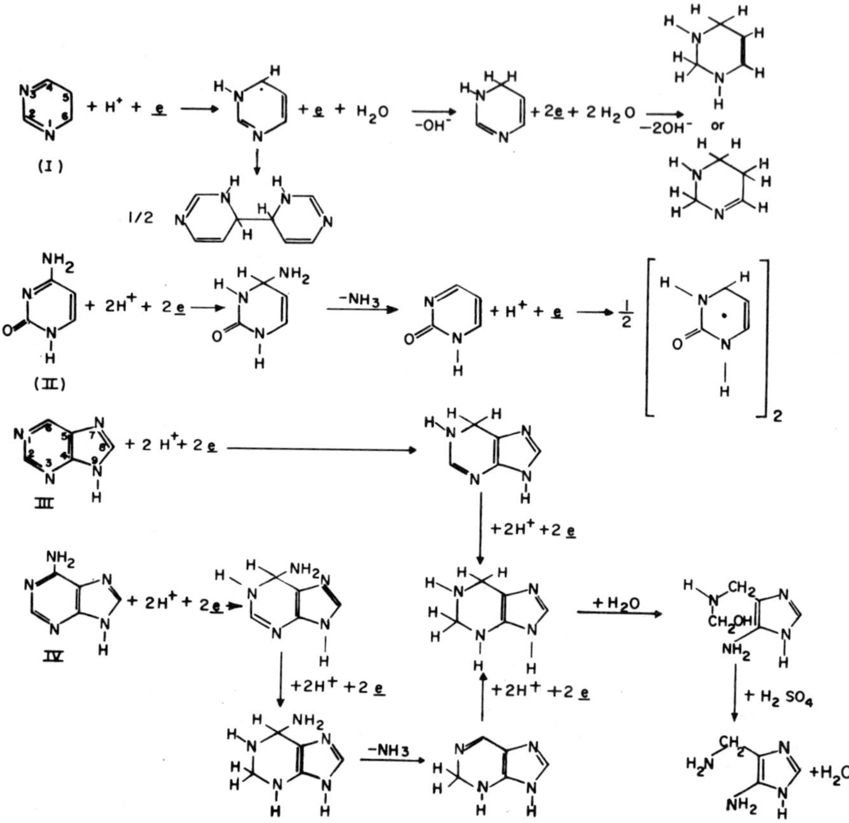

FIGURE 2. Interpretation of the electrochemical and chemical behavior observed on the polarographic reduction of pyrimidine (I), cytosine (II), purine (III), and adenine (IV). Protonation, dissociation and other acid-base and keto-enol equilibria, which may be involved, are not shown.

pyrimidine ring is usually the one most readily reduced, with possible modification resulting from structural and electron density alteration due to substituents: e.g., (a) fusing of consecutive electron-transfer steps or splitting of multiple-electron steps, (b) tautomeric shifts due to substituents having divalent sulfur or oxygen bonded to carbon with the resulting loss of reduction site, such as replacement of hydrogen by hydroxyl at the 2- or 4-position in pyrimidine results in removal of a double bond from the ring by ketonization, and (c) intramolecular chemical reactions accompanying electrode processes, such as deamination, which may generate electroactive species.

Thus, cytosine shows a single 3*e* polarographic wave at a potential more negative than that of waves I–III of pyrimidine (cf. TABLE 1), which is due to three successive processes (FIGURE 2): (a) 2*e* reduction of the 3, 4 N=C bond (this is a combination of the first two 1*e* processes seen in pyrimidine), (b) rapid deamination of the product to 2-hydroxypyrimidine, and (c) 1*e* reduction of the latter—similar to pyrimidine and the 2-aminopyrimidines—to a free radical, which dimerizes under the experimental conditions before it can be further reduced.[3]

Purine exhibits two pH-dependent waves in acidic solution (TABLE 1). Wave I is due to 2*e* reduction of the 1, 6 N=C double bond to 1, 6-dihydropurine; wave II is due to further 2*e* reduction, probably to 1,2,3,6-tetrahydropurine, which hydrolyzes to a 4-aminoimidazole.[4]

The electrolytic reduction of adenine parallels that of purine and cytosine for an overall 6*e* reduction: 2*e* hydrogenation of the 1, 6 N=C bond at a potential more negative than that of both purine waves is immediately followed by 2*e* reduction of the 2, 3 C=N bond, slow deamination at the 6-position, further 2*e* reduction of the regenerated 1, 6 N=C bond, and hydrolytic cleavage at the hydrogenated 2, 3 position to give the same product as the overall 4*e* purine reduction.[4] At the D.M.E., the extent of deamination of the reduced adenine is negligible, resulting in a single pH-dependent 4*e* wave.

Reaction Sites

Generalizations regarding oxidation and reduction sites in the bases are of obvious interest because of their biological importance. As indicated, the pyrimidine ring, for example, is involved in the electrochemical reduction of purines whereas the imidazole ring is untouched. On the other hand, the only two purines whose electrochemical oxidation has been thoroughly investigated (cf. subsequent discussion) are apparently attacked on oxidation at the double bond common to both rings.

EFFECT OF SUBSTITUENTS ON EASE OF REDUCTION

The effects of substituents, mainly amino and hydroxy groups, on the ease of electrochemical reduction of purines and pyrimidines are summarized in Reference 1 (largely on pages 151–153 and 160–161).

The effect of more elaborate substitution can be illustrated by the variation of $E_{1/2}$ values for the reduction of two interrelated series of compounds: a group of 6-substituted purines and one of adenine nucleosides and nucleotides. The 6-substituted purines were investigated[5] because the naturally occurring purines are, with few exceptions, substituted in that position: e.g., the major purine constituents of nucleic acids, adenine and guanine, as well as minor constituents such as 2-methyladenine, 6-methylaminopurine and 6-dimethylaminopurine. The nucleoside-nucleotide group was investigated[6] because, in spite of the fact that electrochemical reduction in nucleosides and nucleotides occurs primarily in the pyrimidine ring moiety, the sugar or sugar-phosphate group influences diffusion, adsorption, and electron density at reactive sites that generally manifests itself in potential shifts and possible alteration of the overall reaction path.

6-Substituted Purines

Only those 6-substituted purines (TABLE 3) were investigated,[5] whose substituent is unlikely to remove by tautomeric shift the 1, 6 N=C bond, which is one of two possible reduction sites in purines. Since $E_{1/2}$ of the one normal reduction wave of the 6-substituted purines is pH-dependent (a wave which may involve the reduced form of the purine appears at more negative potential in the case of a few compounds—6-methylpurine gives two ways); the potentials at pH 2.5 and 4.0 in McIlvaine buffer were selected for comparison.[5]

The diffusion current constant (TABLE 3) of the wave for all purines containing the 1, 6 and 2, 3 double bonds in the pyrimidine ring is approximately the same as that of adenine, whose polarographic reduction involves a 4*e* transfer; purine itself is reduced in two separate 2*e* waves. In this respect, 6-methylpurine resembles the parental purine, while the 6-alkylamino-, 6-dialkylamino-, and 6-methoxypurines resemble adenine (6-aminopurine). Similarly, the small change in the polarographic reduction of purine produced by introducing the 6-methyl group corresponds to small differences in total polar substituent constant, LEMO energies and other electronic indices, as subsequently discussed.

$E_{1/2}$ of 6-substituted purines becomes more negative in the following order (substituent in 6-position indicated): (at pH 2.5) H, CH_3, CH_3O, C_6H_5NH,

TABLE 3

POLAROGRAPHIC REDUCTION OF 6-SUBSTITUTED PURINES AT THE DROPPING MERCURY ELECTRODE[a]

Substituent	pH	$E_{1/2}$[b] V.	I[c]
6-Hydrogen	2–6 2–6	I −0.697–0.083 pH II −0.902–0.080 pH	10.1[d]
6-Methyl	1–4 4–6 1–2 2–6	I −0.825–0.069 pH I −0.725–0.095 pH II −0.965–0.063 pH II −0.870–0.085 pH	8.5[d]
6-Methoxy	1–2 2–4 4–6	−0.945–0.069 pH −0.835–0.103 pH −0.620–0.157 pH	8.5
6-Amino	1–6	−0.975–0.084 pH	9.8
6-Methylamino	1–6	−0.995–0.081 pH	9.8
6-n-Hexylamino	1–2.5 2–5–4 4–6	−0.995–0.076 pH −1.100–0.049 pH −0.995–0.076 pH	8.3
6-Benzylamino	1–2 2–4 4–6	−1.075–0.028 pH −1.000–0.065 pH −0.865–0.096 pH	9.8
6-Phenylamino	1–2 2–5	−0.885–0.097 pH −0.945–0.066 pH	8.3
6-Dimethylamino	1–2 2–4	−0.990–0.077 pH −1.025–0.067 pH	8.9
6-Amino-2-hydroxy	1–5 5–7	−0.995–0.071 pH −0.800–0.112 pH	4.6

[a] Data taken from References 1, 5 and 6, generally for the pH region of 1 to 6; the wave, which can be measured for some compounds to pH 8 or 9, shows some dependence on buffer system used. Data given are for chloride and McIlvaine buffers.

[b] Roman numbers indicate successive polarographic waves; potentials are vs. S.C.E.

[c] Diffusion current constant, $I = i_1/Cm^{2/3}t^{1/6}$, calculated from data for McIlvaine buffer usually between pH 2.5 and 4.5, where i_1 varied least with pH.

[d] Calculated from the total current of the two reduction waves.

$C_6H_5CH_2NH$, isoguanine, $n-C_6H_{13}NH$, $(CH_3)_2N$, NH_2 and CH_3NH, and (at pH 4.0) H, CH_3, C_6H_5NH, CH_3O, $C_6H_5CH_2NH$, isoguanine, $(CH_3)_2N$, $n-C_6H_{13}NH$, CH_3NH and NH_2. It is evident that reduction becomes more difficult as the basicity of the 6-substituent increases: for example, cf. order of increasing basicity of the corresponding amine.[7]

The mechanisms for the polarographic reduction of the 6-substituted purines do not differ essentially from those of the parental purine and adenine. This is apparent not only for the 6-alkylamino purines, whose $E_{1/2}$ are linearly related to the polar substituent constants (σ), but also for all 6-substituted purines examined, whose $E_{1/2}$ are linearly related to total polar substituent constants (σ_p) (FIGURE 3). The correlation of $E_{1/2}$ with σ and σ_p indicates either that no mesomeric and steric effects due to the substituents are involved, or that they are transmitted by an inductive mechanism.[8-10]

Correlation of $E_{1/2}$ with Electronic Indices

The ease of polarographic reduction, as represented by $E_{1/2}$, can be compared with electron-acceptor properties as represented by the energy of the lowest empty molecular orbitals (LEMO) calculated by the Hückel LCAO molecular-orbital approximation method[11] (FIGURE 4). Fairly linear relationships are obtained for purine, 6-methylpurine, adenine and 6-methoxypurine

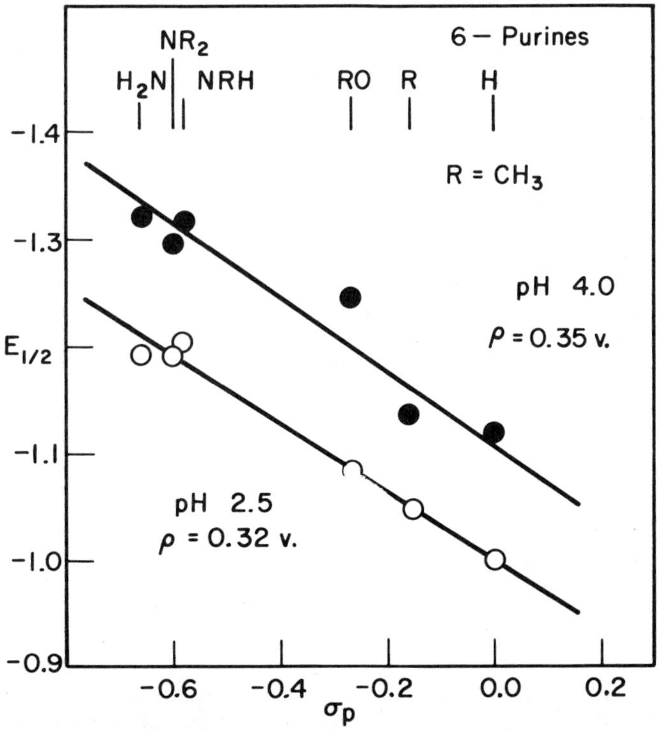

FIGURE 3. Variation of $E_{1/2}$ of the (first) reduction wave of 6-substituted purines with the total polar substituent constant, σ_p. Data for purine and adenine from References 25 and 6, respectively; data for other compounds from Reference 5.

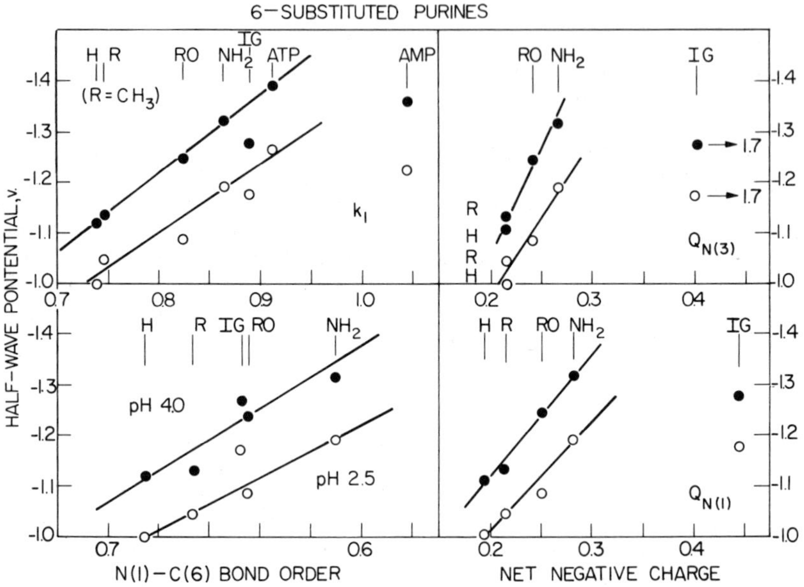

FIGURE 4. Variation of $E_{1/2}$ of 6-substituted purines with LEMO energies (k_1), N(1)-C(6) bond order, and net negative charges on N(1) and N(3). R = CH_3; IG = isoguanine; AMP = adenosine 5′-monophosphate; ATP = adenosine 5′-triphosphate. $E_{1/2}$ data for purine from Reference 25, for ATP and AMP from Reference 6, and for other compounds from Reference 5; quantum chemical data from Reference 11. Solid circles represent values measured at pH 4.0; open circles, at pH 2.5.

(data calculated for the hypoxanthine lactim form were used for the latter); ATP fits the correlation, but AMP does not. Isoguanine does not fit this or any of the subsequent correlations discussed.

Substitution in the 6-position influences mostly the N(1)-C(6) bond order and the electronic charge distribution on N(1) and N(3) which, in turn, largely determine the reducibility; $E_{1/2}$ correlates with these (FIGURE 4), but not with the C(2)-N(3) bond order and the charges on C(6) and C(2). These results are in accord with the previously suggested[4] association of the initial purine and adenine reduction steps with the 1, 6 N=C bond, which, moreover, seems more accessible for reduction than the 2, 3 C=N bond. For example, isoguanine (2-hydroxy-6-aminopurine) exhibits a well-defined wave, whereas hypoxanthine (6-hydroxypurine) only shows an ill-defined inflection on the background discharge,[4] and guanine (2-amino-6-hydroxypurine) is polarographically reduced only at potentials more negative than the background discharge by a different mechanism than adenine and its other derivatives.[4, 12, 13]

Since apparently only the protonated form of purine derivatives is polarographically reducible,[5] correlation of $E_{1/2}$ with acidic dissociation constants (pK_a values) may be expected. Adenine—and presumably other 6-substituted purines—is protonated first at N(1), i.e., at the most basic nitrogen.[11, 14, 15] Although the electronic density on the ring nitrogen cannot be taken alone as a measure of its basicity,[11] as a first approximation, the reducibility should be inversely proportional to the electronic density on N(1); $E_{1/2}$ does become more negative as the net negative charge on N(1) increases (FIGURE 4). Unfortunately, pK_a values are not available for all of the compounds tested and some had to be estimated from inflections in the *i*-pH and $E_{1/2}$-pH plots. Consequently, the correlations obtained are not too conclusive, although several 6-substituted derivatives do fit a straight line $E_{1/2}$-pK_a plot (FIGURE 5).

Behavior of Isoguanine

As noted, $E_{1/2}$ for the reduction of isoguanine deviates markedly from the linear correlations of $E_{1/2}$ with net negative charge on N(1) and N(3), and with pK_a shown by other 6-substituted purines. However, its $E_{1/2}$ deviates only slightly from the linear plots of $E_{1/2}$ *vs.* LEMO energy (k_1) and N(1)—C(6) bond order. This behavior may be correlated—at least to some extent—with the reduction site and the effect of protonation on the latter.

The diffusion current constant of isoguanine is about one-half that of adenine and related compounds, which is consistent with a 2*e* process based on only the 1, 6 double bond being reducible, since the 2, 3 double bond is unavailable due to the stability of the keto form. The agreement of isoguanine $E_{1/2}$ with LEMO energy and N(1)-C(6) bond order may then be ascribed to the connection of the latter with the reduction site. Protonation of isoguanine does not seem to play a decisive role in its polarographic reduction, i.e., the inflection point in the *i*-pH curve is at least 5 pH units higher than its pK_a compared to 2 to 3 units for other 6-substituted purines.[5] Even if apro-

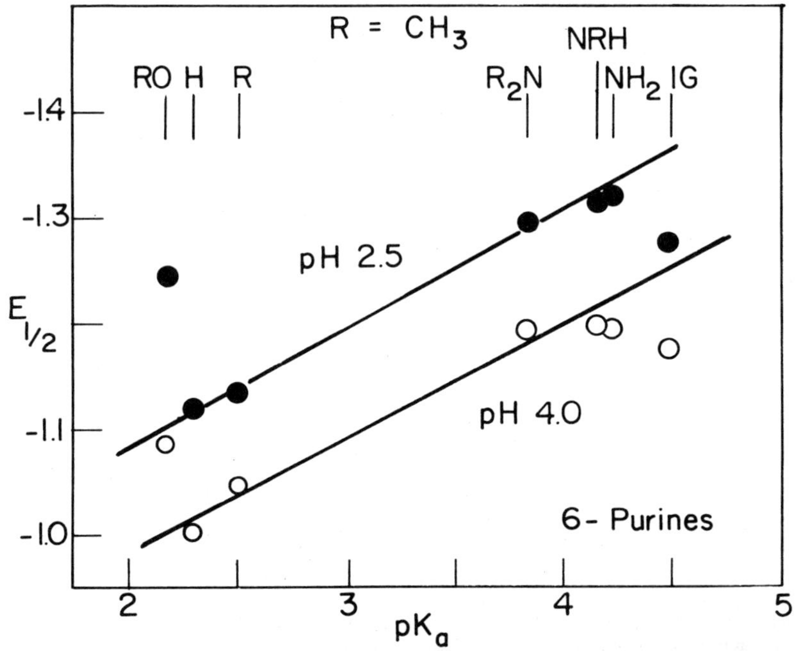

FIGURE 5. Variation of $E_{1/2}$ of 6-substituted purines with the acid dissociation constant pK_a. $E_{1/2}$ data for purine and adenine from References 25 and 6, respectively; $E_{1/2}$ data for other compounds from Reference 5; pK_a values from Reference 7. IG = isoguanine.

tonated species were involved in the reduction, the most probable protonation site based on comparison of N-charges[11] is N(7), which is not at the reduction site.

Adenine Nucleosides and Nucleotides

The polarographic behavior of adenine does not change drastically on attachment of a sugar or sugar-phosphate moiety; the current-controlling factors and the reduction mechanisms are common, in principle, for the whole series.[6] Each compound (TABLE 4) generally shows one well-defined cathodic polarographic wave, which may be distorted in the case of AMP, dAMP and ATP by the appearance of a second wave at more negative potential, probably due to the catalytic reduction of hydrogen. The overall behavior pattern is fundamentally similar to that observed for adenine itself.[4, 6]

The wave is relatively constant in height for all compounds up to pH 4 or 5, when it begins to decrease sharply and disappears by pH 6 or 7; the apparent diffusion current constants (TABLE 4) for the wave agree within 10% with that of the parent adenine, indicating a 4*e* process under polarographic conditions.[6] $E_{1/2}$ becomes more negative with increasing pH; $d(E_{1/2})/d(pH)$ varies from 0.04 to 0.08 volt per pH unit, compared to a theoretical value of 0.06 for a reduction involving the same number of electrons and protons in the potential-determining step of the electrode process.

The correlation of $E_{1/2}$ with structure in the series of a purine or pyrimidine base with its nucleosides and nucleotides is more complex than in the case of simple derivatives, e.g., purines or pyrimidines substituted only with alkyl, alkylamino or amino groups for which $E_{1/2}$ has been, on the whole, well correlated with electronic density at the reduction site and pK_a.[5] This is

TABLE 4

POLAROGRAPHIC REDUCTION OF ADENINE NUCLEOSIDES AND NUCLEOTIDES AT THE DROPPING MERCURY ELECTRODE[a]

Compound[b]	pH	$E_{1/2}$ v.	I[c]
Adenine	1–6.5	−0.975–0.084 pH	9.7
Adenosine	2–4.5 4.5–6	−0.040–0.070 pH −1.180–0.041 pH	10.2
Deoxyadenosine	2.5–4.6 4.6–6.5	−1.060–0.069 pH −1.205–0.037 pH	10.8
AMP	1–4 4–5.5	−1.015–0.083 pH −1.115–0.060 pH	10.2
dAMP	2–6.5	−0.985–0.080 pH	10.8
ATP	2.5–4.5 4.5–5.5	−1.035–0.083 pH −1.175–0.052 pH	d

[a] Data taken from Reference 6.

[b] AMP: adenylic acid or adenosine 5′-monophosphate; dAMP: deoxyadenylic acid or deoxyadenosine 5′-monophosphate; ATP: adenosine 5′-triphosphate.

[c] Diffusion current constant, $I = i_l/Cm^{2/3}t^{1/6}$, calculated from data for McIlvaine buffer between pH 2.5 and 4.5, where i_l varies least with pH or reaches a maximum.

[d] The wave height could not be measured meaningfully, due to merging with a subsequent catalytic wave.

probably due in large part, if not entirely, to the more complex structure in the nucleosides and nucleotides, resulting in increased adsorption and greater possibility for intramolecular association.

Attachment of a sugar or sugar-phosphate moiety to the adenine nucleus generally decreases the ease of reducibility of the parent compound; the exact order of reducibility is slightly pH and concentration-dependent, e.g., $E_{1/2}$ in pH 3.7 McIlvaine buffer becomes more negative in the order: dAMP $\leq$ adenine $<$ adenosine $<$ deoxyadenosine $<$ AMP $<$ ATP. The alternating current polarographic behavior of these compounds suggests a generally parallel order of increasing adsorbability; the general pattern is thus consistent with a frequently observed inhibition of the electrolytic process due to strong adsorption of the depolarizer with a consequent negative shift of the wave.[16]

Adsorbability, however, is obviously not the only factor influencing the reducibility in the adenine series. The electron-withdrawing effect of the ribose ring in nucleosides[17, 18] should promote nucleophilic attack on the heterocyclic ring, i.e., should increase its ease of reducibility. This prediction seems to be fulfilled in the case of the cytosine series, in which the reducibility increases in the order: base $<$ nucleoside $<$ nucleotide.[19, 20] In the adenine series, the distance between the sugar ring and the reduction sites in the pyrimidine ring is long enough to weaken electron withdrawal from the sites; other factors may also contribute to the decreased reducibility of nucleosides and nucleotides.[6] The fact that ATP is the most difficultly reducible of the group is due partially to the repulsion of the negatively charged phosphate groups from the similarly charged D.M.E. surface and partially to the remarkable stability of energy-rich ATP in water medium.[11] ATP assumes a more condensed structure than the other compounds, in which two terminal phosphate groups approach the relatively positive amino group and N(7), which are thus surrounded by a protective cloud of negatively charged phosphate groups.

Adenine and ATP fit the straight-line relation between $E_{1/2}$ and k_i (energy of LEMO) obtained for purine and some of its 6-substituted derivatives, whereas AMP deviates significantly (FIGURE 4). $E_{1/2}$ values for the cytosine series (bases, nucleosides and nucleotides) are more negative than those for the corresponding adenine derivatives, whereas the LEMO calculations predict the opposite.

The presence of the protonated species (with the proton most probably being on the N(1)), as indicated by NMR[17] and x-ray crystallography,[21] as the only polarographically reducible form is supported by a number of polarographic observations.[6] Since, to a first approximation, pK_a values of organic compounds are proportional to the electron density at the protonation site, ease of reducibility should decrease with increasing pK_a in the adenine series in which the protonation site, N(1), is also the reduction site. However, such agreement is observed only for adenosine, deoxyadenosine, AMP and ATP; adenine and dAMP strongly deviate in being more easily reduced than expected for an inverse pK_a-$E_{1/2}$ correlation.

Oxidation of Purines and Pyrimidines

None of the simpler pyrimidines investigated, e.g., those with only one or two amino or hydroxy substituents, give an oxidation wave at graphite or mercury electrodes[1, 22]; a polysubstituted pyrimidine such as dialuric acid does.[23] It was concluded[24] from a study of the polarographic oxidation of some 4, 5-dihydroxypyrimidines at a micro platinum anode in acetic acid solution that pyrimidines without a 5-OH group could not be oxidized, and that pyrimidines with an enediol structure (HOC:COH) could be oxidized polarographically to CO.CO.

All purines investigated,[1, 22, 25, 26, 27, 28] with the exception of purine itself, give an anodic wave at the graphite electrode (TABLE 2); the compounds, in order of decreasing ease of oxidation (increasingly more positive half-peak potential at constant pH), are: uric acid, xanthine, guanine, isoguanine, adenine, hypoxanthine and purine (the last, as mentioned, is not oxidized within the available potential range). Potentials become more positive (oxidation, more difficult) with decreasing pH; the ease of oxidation increases with the number of hydroxy groups (TABLE 2). Investigation of the electrolytic oxidation of purines prior to the work of the present author and his collaborators is apparently limited to a single study,[29] the significance of which is lessened by the probable occurrence of concommitant chemical oxidation due to oxygen evolution resulting from lack of control of the electrode potential. The author and his collaborators have thus far investigated in detail the oxidation of uric acid[27] and of adenine[28] at controlled electrode potential; in acid solution, uric acid gives a fundamental 2*e* anodic polarographic wave at graphite, and adenine gives a 6*e* anodic wave.

The chemical oxidation of uric acid, depending on experimental conditions, produces as the principal product either allantoin or alloxan, but not both. The electrochemical oxidation of uric acid involves a 2*e* oxidation to a primary short-lived dicarbonium ion, which undergoes simultaneous transformations including hydrolysis, leading to an allantoin precursor, alloxan, carbon dioxide and urea (there is some further oxidation of the ion to parabanic acid).[27] The plausibility of postulating an intermediate which can undergo transformation to either allantoin or alloxan suggests that the oxidation of uric acid by any method produces a common intermediate whose subsequent transformations—and consequently the ultimate products obtained—are determined by experimental conditions. An analogous reaction path has been postulated[30] to explain the results for the enzymatic uricase oxidation of uric acid, reflecting a parellelism between the two types of oxidation.

The electrochemical oxidation of adenine appears, initially, to follow the same path as the enzymatic oxidation with xanthine oxidase, but further oxidation and fragmentation of the purine ring occur[28]: i.e., adenine is oxidized in a process involving addition of oxygen to the two available carbon sites, C(2) and C(8), and removal of a total of 6 electrons per molecule to a dicarbonium ion intermediate, which is similar to that produced on uric acid oxidation except for having an NH_2 group instead of an OH group on the C(6) with the resulting presence of the 1,6 N=C bond. The dicarbonium ion is unstable and undergoes further reactions involving electrochemical oxidation and reduction as well as hydrolysis to yield parabanic, oxaluric and 4-aminopurpuric acids, allantoin, urea, carbon dioxide and ammonia. The fact that oxidation of adenine continues to the dicarbonium ion stage is due to the fact that 2-hydroxy- and 2, 8-dihydroxyadenine are probably more easily oxidized electrolytically than adenine itself and are consequently unstable in respect to oxidation at the potential at which adenine is oxidized (cf. TABLE 2).

CORRELATIONS INVOLVING POTENTIALS

Among the reasons for investigating in detail the electrochemical behavior—generally, the polarography—of biologically important compounds such as purines, pyrimidines and their derivatives, are the possible correlation between (a) the mechanistic paths involved and the characteristic potentials associated with them, and (b) chemical, biological and clinical activity.

Correlation of relatively readily measured polarographic $E_{1/2}$ values with numerical structural and reactivity characteristics is usually based on the postulation that the characteristic $E_{1/2}$ of a compound is a function of electron density and other factors that are also relatively simply related to some biological, physical or chemical property. The frequently resulting linear relationship between $E_{1/2}$ for a series of more or less closely related compounds and a suitably selected mathematical function of the values of the given property for that series of compounds permits: (a) prediction of the magnitude of the property of a compound from its readily measured $E_{1/2}$, and (b) the rapid comparative evaluation of a property based on comparison of $E_{1/2}$ values.

A large variety of experimental and theoretically calculated properties and phenomena have been compared to polarographically determined potentials, e.g., photoionization potentials, degree of carcinogenesis, wavelengths of spectrophotometric absorption maxima and antioxidant ability. The most extensively used correlations have involved various forms of the Hammett *sigma-rho* equation based on polar substituent quantities and the Taft modification (cf. reviews by Perrin[31] and Zuman[10, 32]); perhaps the most significant have involved quantum-mechanically calculated parameters (cf. reviews by Pullman and Pullman[11] and Zahradnik and Parkanyi[33]).

Correlations of molecular orbital (MO) calculations with polarographic data generally involve the quantum-mechnically calculated energies for adding an electron to the lowest empty MO (LEMO) or removing one from the highest occupied MO (HOMO). *A priori,* the optimum approach would seem to involve the use of electrochemical data based on initial 1*e* processes, since the MO data apply to such processes.

Since MO calculations have been correlated with various types of chemical and biochemical activity for a variety of molecules, a successful correlation with polarographic data will facilitate correlation of biochemical activity with polarographic data. The need for methods which experimentally measure the electron affinities or related properties of biological compounds has been emphasized.[11] The value of reliable polarographic potentials as tests of theoretical approaches to the electronic properties of biological molecules is typified by a recent paper[15] in which the calculated ionization potentials (electron-donor properties) and electron affinities (electron-acceptor properties) of the four nucleic acid bases (guanine, adenine, cytosine and uracil) were evaluated by comparing them with oxidation potentials determined at the graphite electrode and reduction potentials determined at the D.M.E. The correlation of $E_{1/2}$ data for the 6-substituted purines has been discussed.

Three frequently overlooked but important factors must be emphasized. The reliability of correlations of the type discussed depends on the calculations and measurements having been made on identical molecular species. It is for this reason, among others, that the details of the electrochemical redox reaction pathway—including the sites at which electron transfer occurs and their exact chemical nature—need to be elucidated, since only on this basis is it possible to assure that theoretical and experimental data are being compared for the same molecular species.

A second factor is the influence of the degree of reversibility of the electron-transfer process upon observed potential; whereas the potential observed for a completely reversible electrode process is directly relatable to the standard free energy of the process, that observed for one which is not so reversible contains a component due to the necessary energy of activation as well as components due to adsorption and other accompanying phenomena (cf. Reference 34).

Finally, account must be taken of the solvation energy contribution to the $E_{1/2}$. Theoretical calculations are frequently based on an idealized gas-phase molecule. Consequently, there has been the implicit assumption in many past correlations that the solvation energy term is constant, or varies in a regular fashion for the series of compounds studied. The latter assumption has to be examined for the purines, pyrimidines, and their nucleosides and nucleotides because of the variation, for example, in the nature, number and strength of the hydrogen-bonding donor and acceptor groups in the different compounds and in their reduction and oxidation products.

Adsorption on and Reversibility at Electrodes

As has been indicated, it is important to evaluate the roles of adsorption of reactants and products on the electrode, of reversibility of the electron-transfer step, and of accompanying chemical reactions, since these could seriously alter the potential that would be observed in their absence and would be the potential desired for comparison with calculated energies for the electron-transfer step.

Alternating current polarographic data strongly support the assumption that all of the purine-based compounds studied are adsorbed on mercury.[5, 6, 35] The fact that only cytosine of the four pyrimidines examined (pyrimidine, cytosine, and 2-amino- and 2-hydroxypyrimidine) showed any evidence for adsorption at mercury[35] suggests that the site of adsorption of purines lies in the imidazole ring, specifically—since position 9 is occupied in the adenosines—at either position 7 or 8. Since position 7 contains a heterocyclic nitrogen, adsorption is more likely to involve this position. Adsorption may also involve pi-bonding to the aromatic ring.

Significantly, Vetterl,[36, 37] who examined the effect of various purines and pyrimidines on the differential capacity at the D.M.E., found evidence for strong intermolecular interaction of adsorbed molecules only with the usual DNA and RNA components such as adenine, guanine, thymine, cytosine and uracil, but not with anomalous DNA components such as 5-methyl- and 5-hydroxymethylcytosine—at least not at the low concentrations for which effects were seen for the former compounds.

The data for adsorption on graphite electrodes are fragmentary; however, cyclic voltammetry indicates that purine and adenine are probably adsorbed on graphite.

Acknowledgments

The author thanks the National Science Foundation, which helped support the work described, as well as his past and present collaborators on the polarographic behavior of purines and pyrimidines: Glenn Dryhurst, Borivoj Janik, James E. O'Reilly, Conrad O. Schmakel, David L. Smith and William A. Struck.

References

1. Elving, P. J., W. A. Struck & D. L. Smith. 1965. Mises Point Chim. Anal. Org. Pharm. Bromatol. **14:** 141.
2. Elving, P. J., & B. Pullman. 1961. *In* Advances in Chemical Physics. I. Prigogine, Ed. **3:** 1–31. Interscience Publishers. New York, N. Y.
3. Smith, D. L. & P. J. Elving. 1962. J. Amer. Chem. Soc. **84:** 2741.
4. Smith, D. L. & P. J. Elving. 1962. J. Amer. Chem. Soc. **84:** 1412.
5. Janik, B. & P. J. Elving. To be published.
6. Janik, B. & P. J. Elving. To be published.
7. Perrin, D. C. 1965. Dissociation Constants of Organic Bases in Aqueous Solutions. Butterworth. London, England.
8. Zuman, P. 1960. Ric. Sci., Suppl. Contrib. Teor. Sper. Polarogr. **5:** 229.
9. Zuman, P. 1966. *In* Modern Aspects in Polarography. T. Kambara, Ed.: 102–16. Plenum Press. New York, N. Y.
10. Zuman, P. 1967. Substituent Effects in Organic Polarography. Plenum Press. New York, N. Y.
11. Pullman, B. & A. Pullman. 1963. Quantum Biochemistry. John Wiley & Sons. New York, N. Y.
12. Janik, B. & E. Palecek. 1966. Z. Naturforsch. **21b:** 1117.
13. Janik, B. & E. Palecek. 1966. Abhandl. Deut. Akad. Berlin, Kl. Med.: 513.
14. Dekker, C. A. 1960. Ann. Rev. Biochem. **29:** 463.
15. Berthod, H., C. Giessner-Prettre & A. Pullman. 1966. Theoret. Chim. Acta **5:** 53.
16. Volke, J. 1965. Talanta **12:** 1081.
17. Jardetzky, C. D. & D. Jardetzky. 1960. J. Amer. Chem. Soc. **82:** 222.
18. Broom, A. D., M. P. Schweizer & P. O. P. Ts'o. 1967. J. Amer. Chem. Soc. **89:** 3612.
19. Janik, B. & E. Palecek. 1964. Arch. Biochem. Biophys. **105:** 225.
20. Palecek, E. & B. Janik. 1962. Arch. Biochem. Biophys. **98:** 527.
21. Cochran, W. 1951. Acta Crystallogr. **4:** 81.
22. Smith, D. L. & P. J. Elving. 1962. Anal. Chem. **34:** 930.
23. Struck, W. A. & P. J. Elving. 1964. J. Amer. Chem. Soc. **86:** 1229.
24. Chiang, K. C. P. Chang. 1958, 1959. Hua Hsueh Hsueh Pao. **24:** 300; Chem. Abstr. **53:** 20080.
25. Smith, D. L. 1962. Ph.D. Thesis. University of Michigan. Ann Arbor, Mich.
26. Struck, W. A. 1963. Ph.D. Thesis. University of Michigan. Ann Arbor, Mich.
27. Struck, W. A. & P. J. Elving. 1965. Biochem. **4:** 1343.
28. Dryhurst, G. & P. J. Elving. 1968. J. Electrochem. Soc. **115:** 1014.
29. Fichter, F. & W. Kern. 1926. Helv. Chim. Acta **9:** 429.
30. Soberon, G. & P. P. Cohen. 1963. Arch. Biochem. Biophys. **103:** 331.
31. Perrin, C. L. 1966. *In* Progress in Physical Organic Chemistry. S. G. Cohen, Ed. **3:** 165–316. Interscience Publishers. New York, N. Y.
32. Zuman, P. 1964. Organic Polarographic Analysis. Pergamon Press. London, England.
33. Zahradnik, R. & C. Parkanyi. 1965. Talanta **12:** 1289.
34. Elving, P. J. 1963. Pure Appl. Chem. **7:** 423.
35. Dryhurst, G. & P. J. Elving. *Tallanta.* To be published.
36. Vetterl, V. 1966. Abhandl. Deut. Akad. Wiss. Berlin, Kl. Med.: 493.
37. Vetterl, V. 1966. Collection Czech. Chem. Commun. **31:** 2105.
38. Elving, P. J. & D. L. Smith. 1960 Anal. Chem. **32:** 1849.

IONIZATION POTENTIALS OF BIOLOGICAL MOLECULES

Ernst D. Bergmann
Department of Organic Chemistry
Hebrew University, Jerusalem

With the first attempts to use quantum-mechanical means for the calculation of the chemical and biochemical properties of compounds of biological importance, it became evident that not enough experimental data are available on the fundamental physical characteristics of these molecules. A verification of calculations on the charge distribution in the various types of compounds, for example, necessitates a knowledge of their dipole moments, which have been measured only in very isolated cases. Even more important are those parameters that are related to the ability of the compounds to interact with other molecules, because they permit an insight into the character of the forces that attract the reacting molecules to each other—the first step in complex biological processes. In particular, there is hope that the gathering of these data will explain the feature most typical of such processes, the specificity which expresses itself in an anomaly of a certain physico-chemical value. In this group of parameters defining the interaction of two different compounds belong the dispersion forces, i.e., the polarizability, the hydrogen bonding, the electron affinity and the ionization potential (which should more aptly be called ionization energy). The ionization potential has a bearing on the polarographic oxidation and the basicity of the molecules, on their ability to quench fluorescence and, most importantly, on the possibility of formation of charge-transfer complexes as well as on the more classical Van der Waals-London interactions.

From the theory developed by Mulliken,[1] we know that the binding energy of such a complex and the energy required for its transition to the excited state depend on the ionization potential of the donor I_D, the electron affinity of the acceptor E_A and a term Δ representing stabilization energy. One can easily see that I_D is closely related to the energy of the highest occupied orbital of the donor, E_A to that of the lowest empty orbital of the acceptor. As to Δ, as long as the other two factors are not known experimentally, this term must remain neglected, and this can be done with some justification if one studies a series of chemically related donors with one acceptor or a series of closely related acceptors with one and the same donor. Somewhat less important, perhaps, is the ionization potential for the knowledge of dispersion effects; it is easy to see that the magnitude of the influence of the electrons of one molecule on those of the other depends on the ionization potential of the former and the polarizability of the latter.[2] The knowledge of the ionization potentials is thus of some theoretical and practical interest.

A number of methods can be employed for the determination of ionization potentials. In the case of saturated hydrocarbons one can employ the quasi-Rydberg transitions in the far ultraviolet spectrum. In principle, the extrapolation of the quantum number for such a series will lead to the transition corresponding to the adiabatic ionization potential.[3] A second method[4] uses the photoionization current generated when the compound in the vapor phase is irradiated with monochromatic light. If the lowest vibrational level of the cation formed can be identified, one can determine the adiabatic ionization potential. In cases where both these methods have been used on the same substance, the values derived from them were in satisfactory agreement.

An entirely different method uses the mass spectrograph[5]. The compound is bombarded at low vapor pressure with electrons, the energy of which is varied by a potential drop and determines the energy at which cations are just formed. This is the appearance potential, closely related to the ionization potential. A source of some uncertainty lies in the energy spread of the electrons released from the heated filament of the instrument. Theoretically, a more serious problem is the difference between the values found by this method and the spectroscopic method, which is often in the neighborhood of 0.4 eV. This is generally[6] ascribed to the fact that the ionization by electron impact is of the Franck-London type, thus the potential is a vertical, not an adiabatic one: the vibrational level to which the transition is most probable is often above the zeroth level with which the UV method is concerned. This explanation of the difference, however, is not necessarily correct. It is also interesting that the photoionization method gives values for the ionization potentials, intermediate between those of the two other methods, though nearer to those of the UV method.[8]

In view of the fact that the calculations of ionization potentials are still in a state of low order of approximation, it seems that the differences between the methods and the interpretation of these differences are not very significant and that the results of any method will be sufficient for the verification of the calculations. We have, therefore, employed the mass-spectrometric method (good mass spectrometers are fortunately very plentiful) in our studies, using as an internal standard a rare gas—argon, krypton or xenon—for which the ionization potential is accurately known. One obtains a pair of lines as shown in FIGURE 1 for uracil and xenon. This method has been developed for a rapid determination of the ionization potentials that promises to give the desired result in about one minute's time, thus permitting the serial study of interesting compounds.[9] In conclusion, it should be mentioned that one can combine the advantages of the photoionization method—namely, the higher monochromaticity of the energy source—with those of the electron impact procedure, that permits a more exact definition of the cation formed. Obviously, this combined method requires a more complex instrumentation.[8]

Let us now consider some examples: first, the purine and pyrimidine bases. For these compounds, the energies of the highest occupied molecular orbitals as well as those of the lowest empty molecular orbitals have been calculated.[10] TABLE 1 shows the energy coefficients of these molecular orbitals (in β). We have measured the ionization potentials of some of these compounds;[11] the results are summarized in TABLE 2 and compared with the calculated values, expressed also in electron volts. These calculations have been made by Pullman and collaborators, using a refined semiempirical self-consistent field method.[12] It is gratifying that the sequence of the compounds in the two columns (measured and calculated) is practically identical, although the absolute figures in the two columns differ somewhat.

We learn from these figures that the purines can be expected to be moderately good donors, better in any event than the pyrimidines. The best donor properties are anticipated for uric acid (lowest energy of highest occupied molecular orbital). N-Methylation improves the donor properties of the purines and also, probably, of the pyrimidines. Equally, it can be predicted that these bases will not act as electron acceptors. Obviously, the results do not predict whether the purines and pyrimidines will in fact combine by charge transfer with any given electron acceptor; however, in a given series of compounds which may act as electron acceptors, one will be able to predict with

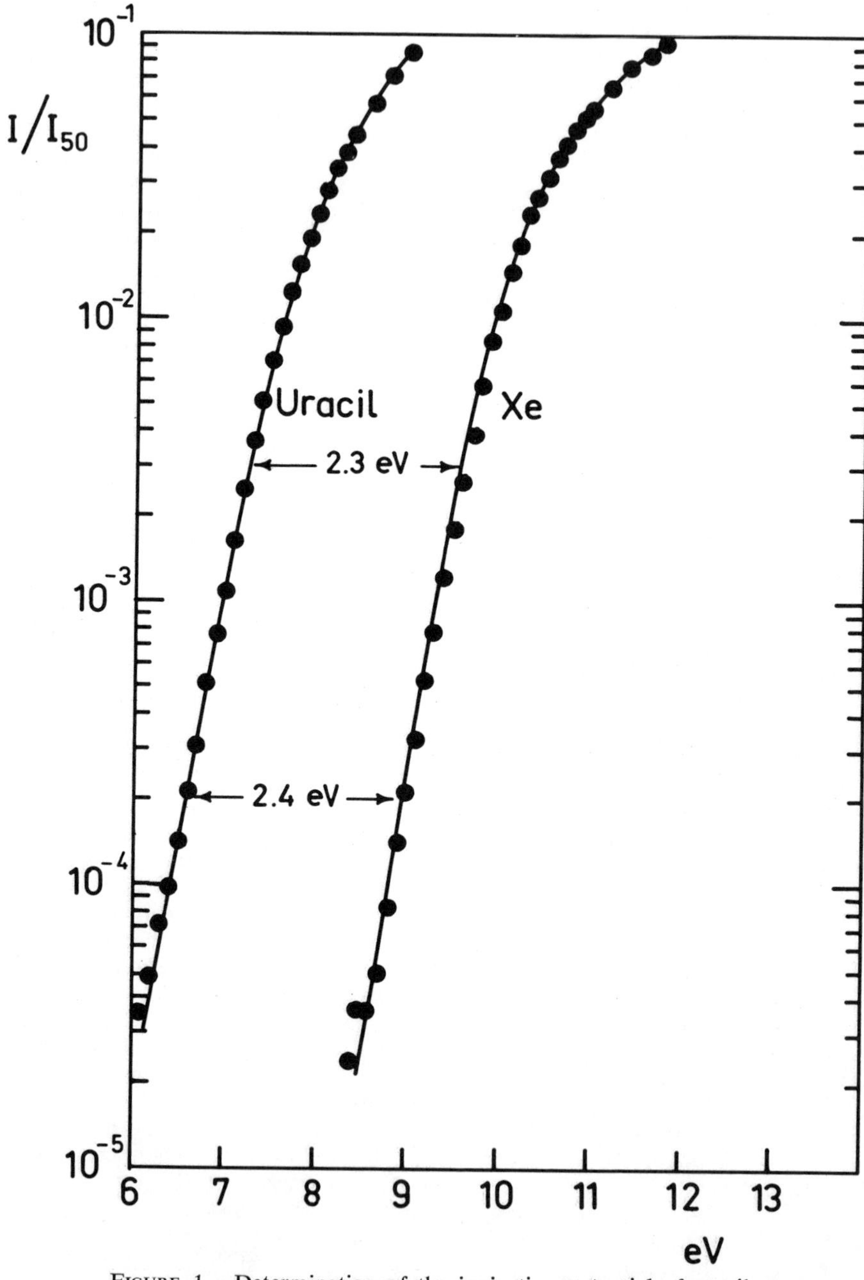

FIGURE 1. Determination of the ionization potential of uracil.

which of them the purines and pyrimidines are more likely to interact by charge transfer. Much has been said about the possibility that the carcinogenic activity of polycyclic aromatic hydrocarbons is related to their ability to

TABLE 1
COMPOUND ENERGY COEFFICIENTS OF MOLECULAR ORBITALS (IN β)

	HOMO	LEMO
Uracil	0.60	−0.96
Thymine	0.51	−.096
Cytosine	0.60	−0.80
5-Methylcytosine	0.53	−0.80
Adenine	0.49	−0.87
Guanine	0.31	−1.05
Hypoxanthine	0.40	−0.88
Xanthine	0.40	−1.20
Uric acid	0.17	−1.19
1-Methyluric acid	0.17	−1.20
3-Methyluric acid	0.15	−1.20
7-Methyluric acid	0.13	−1.20
9-Methyluric acid	0.16	−1.20

interact with purines and pyrimidines, perhaps by formation of charge-transfer complexes. This is not the place to discuss the carcinogenesis problem,[13] but there is an indication that these hydrocarbons do interact with purines and pyrimidines: the latter solubilize the former[14] (and equally the dibenzacridines[15], and the solubilizing efficiency runs parallel to the energy of the highest occupied molecular orbital. The solubilizing power of tetramethyluric acid is particularly high.[16] It has also been shown that the response of the polycyclic hydrocarbons to the influence of the purines and pyrimidines is a function of their electron affinity or rather of the energy of their lowest empty molecular orbital, which runs roughly parallel to the number of aromatic rings in a benzologous series of the hydrocarbons. The larger these molecules, the greater their electron affinity and the smaller their ionization potential.

A related case is the interaction of purines with isoalloxazines, compounds expected theoretically to be good electron acceptors.[17] Here, too, the purines are better donors than the pyrimidines,[18] and it is not impossible that the biological activity of the flavine-adenine-dinucleotide type of coenzyme is related to the interaction between the flavine and adenine moieties in some kind of charge transfer. This possibility is enhanced by the existence of a bridge (sugar-phosphate-sugar) between the two ring systems, and it may be useful to test the possibility of interaction of potential electron acceptors and

TABLE 2
IONIZATION POTENTIAL (IN eV)

Compound	Found	Calculated
6-Azauracil	10.18 ± 0.1	9.65
Uracil	9.82 ± 0.1	9.15
Purine	9.68 ± 0.1	8.87
Thymine	9.43 ± 0.1	8.80
Xanthine	9.30 ± 0.2	8.82
Hypoxanthine	9.17 ± 0.1	8.00
Adenine	8.91 ± 0.1	7.92
Cytosine	8.90 ± 0.2	8.16
Tetramethyluric acid	7.87 ± 0.1	~7

donors by bringing them together in the same molecule, so that the distance between them can be predetermined.

In view of the biological importance of the amino acids, it is regrettable that no experimental data exist on their ionization potentials. One must bear in mind that the methods for the determination of these potentials require that the compounds be vaporized without decomposition; but it is known that in the mass spectra of such amino acids as methionine, histidine, phenylalanine, tryptophan, lysine and arginine the molecular peaks do appear, so that it may be anticipated that their ionization potentials can be measured. Pullman and Pullman[19] have calculated the HOMO and LEMO energies of the four aromatic amino acids (or rather of the π-electron systems in them) and have obtained the results presented in TABLE 3. The four acids should be electron donors, but only tryptophan should be a relatively good one. Indeed, only tryptophan is known to give complexes with isoalloxazines or (substituted) pyridinium ions.[17, 20]

It may be of interest to compare with tryptophan a number of other indole derivatives for which the energies of the highest filled orbitals have been calculated.[21] The influence of substituents can be followed easily, and we hope to report on our results and conclusions in the near future. The energy calculated for indole (0.60 β) is reduced to 0.516 in tryptamine—which can thus be expected to be a better donor—but introduction of a 5-methoxy- or 5 hydroxy group into the latter does not affect the energy significantly ($k=0.512$ and 0.514, respectively). For 6-hydroxytryptamine, on the other hand, k is only 0.470. This difference is striking and may well be of biological interest.*

In this connection, a group of compounds should be mentioned which have recently aroused considerable interest as psychotropic agents: the phenothiazine derivatives. In fact, a relationship has been sought between the biological activity (which is not yet defined in terms of chemical interaction) and the electron-donor properties.[22] If one includes the d orbitals of the sulfur atom into the overall delocalization,[23] the energy coefficient k is 0.21 for phenothiazine, 0.19 for chlorpromazine (2-chloro-10-(γ-dimethylaminopropyl)-phenothiazine). If the experiment has shown[24] that the phenothiazines are good electron donors in charge-transfer complexes, this property cannot be (at least not by itself) responsible for the psychotropic activity, since the inactive phenothiazine has the same ionization potential as its highly active derivative. Another calculation of the HOMO and LEMO energies of 10-(γ-dimethylaminopropyl)-substituted phenothiazines[21] has been carried out in order to compare their electron-donating capacity with their efficiency as inhibitors of histamine methyl-transferase. It has been found that the two properties are

TABLE 3

COMPOUND ENERGY COEFFICIENTS OF MOLECULAR ORBITALS (IN β)

	HOMO	LEMO
Phenylalanine	0.91	−0.99
Tyrosine	0.79	−1.00
Histidine	0.66	−1.16
Tryptophan	0.53	−0.86

* For the tranquilizing drug, reserpine, which is also an indole derivative, the ionization potential was found to be 7.0.

parallel, so that the conclusion seems justified (if the few values available are sufficient evidence) that the phenothiazines act by combining with a part of the enzyme that is a good electron acceptor.

Finally, if it is permissible to consider the carcinogenic hydrocarbons as biological molecules, the ionization potentials which have been calculated in a particularly simple manner may be reported.[25] For aromatic hydrocarbons, it appears that the molecular electronegativity χ is a constant function of ionization potential and electron affinity ($\chi = \frac{1}{2}(I + E)$) with a value of 4.17 eV. If one then knows the electron affinity, the ionization potential follows. In TABLE 4, some such data are given. It is worthy of note that in one case, that of 1,2-benzanthracene, the ionization potential has been measured;[26] the experimental value of 7.54 ± 0.3 eV is in good accord with this calculation.[27]

A problem of some importance that arises in the determination of the ionization potentials is the nature or the site of the electron which is removed from the molecule (a problem discussed very frequently in connection with the interpretation of mass spectra). Although the answer is simple in hydrocarbons, especially in π-conjugated systems, the introduction of atoms with lone electron pairs creates considerable uncertainty, and almost all biological systems contain such atoms. Does the ionization of pyrimidine affect a π-electron or an electron of the nitrogen atom? Pyridine, for example, has been found to have practically the same ionization potential (9.23 eV) as benzene, and that of pyrimidine (9.47 eV) has a similar value. That this potential relates to a π-electron has been proven by a comparison of the influence of substitution on the potentials of benzene, toluene and pyridine[28] and by a careful study of the Rydberg series in the spectrum of pyridine.[29] It is more remarkable, then, that the charge-transfer complex of pyrimidine and iodine involves not a π-electron but an unshared electron of one of the nitrogen atoms.[30]

These factors may be of practical importance when the ionization potentials are related to the polarographic oxidation potentials. This oxidation involves a loss of electrons to the anode, and these electrons may be expected to come from the highest occupied molecular orbital. In fact, if one plots the half-wave potentials of a fairly large number of aromatic (alternant) hydrocarbons against the energy of the HOMO, a straight line is obtained.[31] Equally, the polarographic reduction potential is related to the electron affinity, i.e., to the energy of the lowest empty molecular orbital.[32] However, this need not be so

TABLE 4

IONIZATION POTENTIALS OF SOME POLYCYCLIC HYDROCARBONS (IN β)

Compound	Ionization Potential
	Carcinogenic Hydrocarbons
1, 2-Benzanthracene	7.67 ± 0.10
3, 4-Benzophenanthrene	7.84[a])
3, 4-Benzopyrene	7.62 ± 0.10
1, 2, 5, 6-Dibenzanthracene	7.70 ± 0.10
	Non-carcinogenic Hydrocarbons
Naphthacene (2, 3-Benzanthracene)	7.15[a])
Chrysene (1, 2-Benzophenanthrene)	7.90 ± 0.10
1,2-Benzopyrene	7.77 ± 0.10
1, 2, 7, 8-Dibenzanthracene	7.71 ± 0.10

[a] From D. D. Stevenson, quoted by A. Streitwieser. *In* Molecular Orbital Theory: 193. John Wiley & Sons. New York, N. Y.

in either case. The polarographic reduction and oxidation may not necessarily involve a delocalized electron, but a very specific one. Even in hydrocarbons, the situation is not always unambiguous. In dibiphenyleneethene, for example, the reduction is expected to affect the central double bond, and the unusually low value of the reduction potential has been ascribed to steric inhibition of planarity.[33] We have now determined the ionization potential of this hydrocarbon (8.5±0.2 eV)[34]. Does this figure, which is of the same order of magnitude as the ionization potential of similar polycyclic aromatic systems (phenanthrene 8.53 eV), relate to a π-electron of a benzene ring or to the central double bond? One could understand that by removal of the two

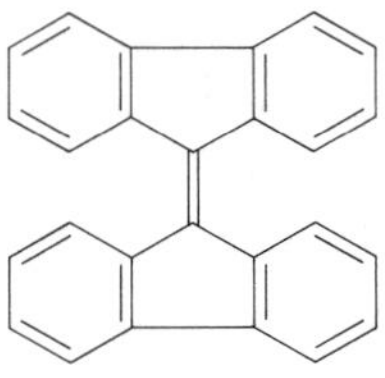

π-electrons of the central double bond the steric strain will be relieved. This type of uncertainty may be the reason for some irregularities which have been observed recently in studies of the correlation of polarographic oxidation and ionization potential.

The experimental data available on ionization potentials (and electron affinity) of biological molecules are still scanty. It appears, however, that these potentials are of sufficient interest to warrant their systematic study. I have attempted here to review the approaches so far made, to formulate the problems, and to justify the work which is now in progress toward their solution.

References

1. Mulliken, R. S. 1956. Rec. Trav. Chim. **75:** 845, and previous papers.
2. London, F. 1930. Z. Physik. **63:** 245; Z. Physik. Chem. (B) **11:** 222.
3. Herzberg, G. 1950. Spectra of Diatomic Molecules. 2nd edit.: 327 D. Van Nostrand Co., Inc. Princeton, N. J.
4. Watanabe, K. 1957. J. Chem. Phys. **26:** 542; Watanabe, K. & J. R. Mottl, J. Chem. Phys. **26:** 1773.
5. Warren, J. W. 1950. Nature. **165:** 830; M. E. Wacks *et al.* 1959, 1964. J. Chem. Phys. **31:** 1557; **41:** 1661, 3195; Lossing, F. P., A. W. Tickner & W. A. Bryce. 1951. J. Chem. Phys. **19:** 254.
6. Cf. Field, F. H. & J. L. Franklin. 1957. Electron Impact Phenomena. Academic Press, Inc. New York, N. Y.
7. Morrison, J. D. 1953. J. Chem. Phys. **21:** 1767; Nicholson, A. J. C. 1958. J. Chem. Phys. **29:** 1312.
8. Hurzeler, H., M. G. Inghram & J. M. Morrison. 1958. J. Chem. Phys. **28:** 76.
9. Kiser, R. W. & E. J. Galegos. 1962. J. Phys. Chem. **66:** 947.
10. Pullman, B. & A. Pullman. 1963. Quantum Biochemistry: 217. Interscience Publishers. New York, N. Y.
11. Lifschitz, C., E. D. Bergmann & B. Pullman. 1967. Tetrahedron Lett.: 4583.
12. Berthod, H., C. Giessner-Prettre & A. Pullman. 1966. Theor. Chim. Acta **5:** 53; 1967. Int. J. Quant. Chem. **1:** 123. Denis, A. & A. Pullman. 1967. Theor. Chim. Acta **7:** 110.
13. Cf. Bergmann, E. D. 1968. *In* Molecular Associations in Biology. Academic Press. New York, N. Y.
14. Weil-Malherbe, H. 1946. Biochem. J. **40:** 3511; Boyland, E. & B. Green. 1962. Brit. J. Cancer **16:** 507.

15. BOOTH, J. & E. BOYLAND. 1953. Biochem. Biophys. Acta **12:** 75.
16. MOLD, J. D., T. B. WALKER & L. G. VEASEY. 1963. Anal. Chem. **35:** 2071.
17. HARBURY, H. A. & K. A. FOLEY. 1958. Proc. Nat. Acad. Sci. U.S.A. **44:** 662; HARBURY, H. A., K. F. A. NOUE, P. A. LOACH & R. M. AMICK. 1959. Proc. Nat. Acad. Sci. U.S.A. **45:** 1708.
18. WEBER, G. 1958. J. Chim. Phys. **55:** 878.
19. PULLMAN, B. & A. PULLMAN. 1963. Quantum Biochemistry: 322. Interscience Publishers. New York, N. Y.
20. FUJIMORI, E. 1959. Proc. Nat. Acad. Sci. U. S. A. **45:** 133; CILENTO, G. & P. GIUSTI. 1959. J. Amer. Chem. Soc. **81:** 3801; CILENTO, G. & P. TEDESCHI. 1961. J. Biol. Chem. **236:** 907.
21. MERRIL, C. R., S. H. SNYDER & D. F. BRADLEY. 1966. Biochim. Biophys. Acta **118:** 316.
22. KARREMAN, G., I. ISENBERG & A. SZENT-GYORGYI. 1959. Science **130:** 1191.
23. ORLOFF, M. K. & D. D. FITTS. 1961. Biochim. Biophys. Acta **47:** 596.
24. KINOSHITA, M. 1962. Bull. Chem. Soc. Jap. **35:** 1609; BEUKERS, A. & A. SZENT-GYÖRGYI. 1962. Rec. Trav. Chim. **81:** 255.
25. BECKER, R. S. & E. CHEN. 1966. J. Chem. Phys. **45:** 2403.
26. WACKS, M. E. 1964. J. Chem. Phys. **41:** 1661.
27. For other methods for the calculation of ionization potentials of polycyclic hydrocarbons, see HUSH, N. S. & J. A. POPLE. 1955. Trans. Faraday Soc. **51:** 600.
28. BASILA, M. R. & D. J. CLANCY. 1963. J. Phys. Chem. **67:** 1551.
29. EL SAYED, M. F. A., M. KASHA & Y. TANAKA. 1961. J. Chem. Phys. **34:** 334.
30. KRISHNA, V. G. & M. CHOWDHURY. 1963. J. Phys. Chem. **67:** 1067.
31. HOIJTINK, G. J. 1958. Rec. Trav. Chim. **77:** 555.
32. HOIJTINK, G. J. 1955. Rec. Trav. Chim. **74:** 1525.
33. BERGMANN, E. D., G. BERTHIER, A. PULLMAN & B. PULLMAN. 1950. Bull. Soc. Chim. France **17:** 1079.
34. LIFSCHITZ, C. & E. D. BERGMANN. Unpublished data.

CHARGE-TRANSFER COMPLEXES IN BIOLOGICAL SYSTEMS

Sidney Shifrin
National Cancer Institute
National Institutes of Health
Bethesda, Md.

During the past several years, we have examined the interaction of amino acid side chains with the 3-carbamoylpyridinium ion as a model for enzyme-NAD^+ complexes. The studies were initiated by the observation that a new absorption band appeared when NAD^+ was added to solutions of apo-glyceraldehyde-3-phosphate dehydrogenase.[1] At the time Racker and Krimsky[1] reported this result, they suggested that the absorption band that appeared with an apparent maximum near 360 mμ suggested the presence of a quinoid-type structure in the nicotinamide moiety of NAD^+. Since the new absorption band disappeared on the addition of reagents such as iodoacetic acid, which are supposedly specific for sulfhydryl groups, the suggestion was made that the sulfhydryl group of a cysteine residue in the protein might form a covalent bond with some site on the nicotinamide ring of the coenzyme. This is shown schematically in FIGURE 1 in which the side chains of several amino acids of the protein are shown projecting into a cavity which also

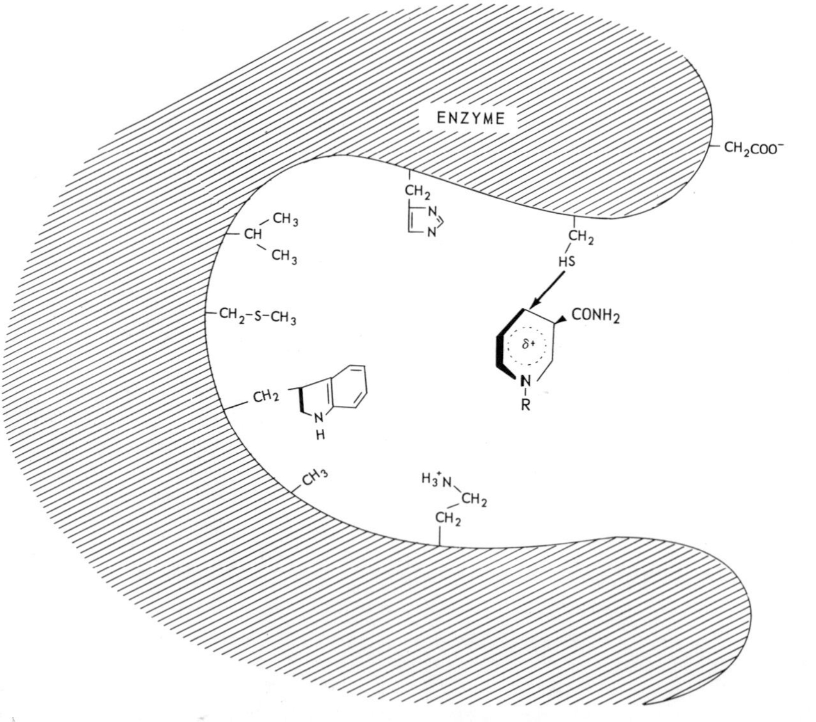

FIGURE 1. Schematic representation of a region of the enzyme in which the pyridinium ring of NAD^+ is covalently bonded to the sulfhydryl side chain of a cysteine residue.

contains the pyridinium ring of NAD^+. The sulfhydryl group is shown here to add to the most electrophilic portion of the pyridinium ring.

In addition to the covalent bond hypothesis, there have been some suggestions in recent years that the broad, diffuse absorption band which appears in the enzyme-coenzyme complex could be assigned to a charge-transfer transition.[2–4] Such a transition might arise as a result of the interaction of an efficient electron donor (such as the indole side chain of tryptophan) with a moderately efficient electron acceptor (such as the pyridinium ring of NAD^+). Several groups of investigators have observed that concentrated solutions of indole with NAD^+ or 1-alkyl-3-carbamoylpyridinium chloride produced an intensely yellow solution which was reminiscent of the properties of the enzyme-coenzyme complex.[3–5]

The schematic drawing in FIGURE 2 again shows the pyridinium ion in the presence of the amino acid side chains of the peptide chain. In this case, however, the indole side chain supplies electrons from a localized site (the 3 carbon atom[6]) to the pyridinium ring. Thus, the new transition cannot be associated with either component separately, but arises from the promotion of an electron in the highest occupied molecular orbital (HOMO) of the donor (indole) to the lowest empty molecular orbital (LEMO) of the acceptor (pyridinium ion). This transition is shown in FIGURE 3, in addition to the locally excited transitions associated with the individual and separated chromophores.

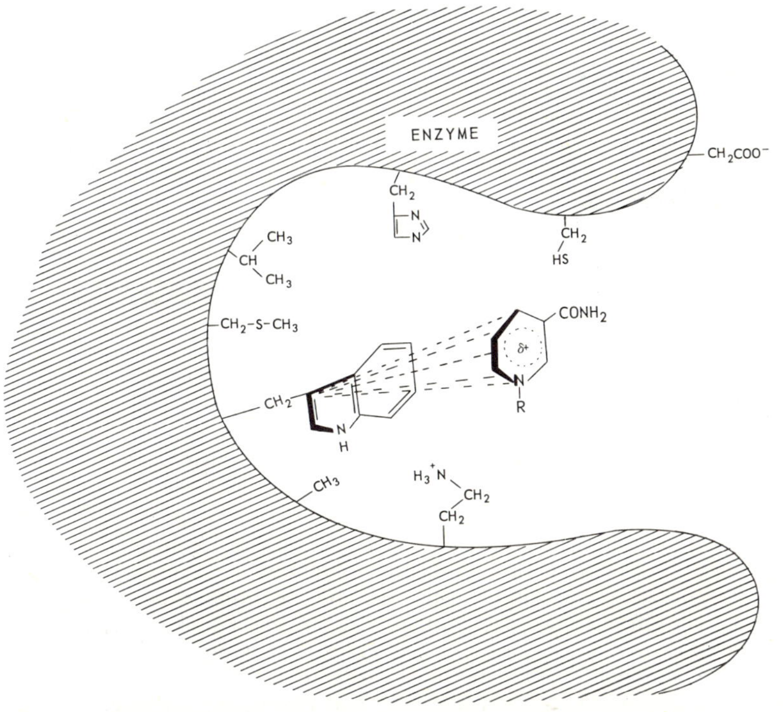

FIGURE 2. Schematic representation of a region of the enzyme in which the pyridinium ring of NAD^+ serves as an electron acceptor to the donor properties of the indole side chain of the protein.

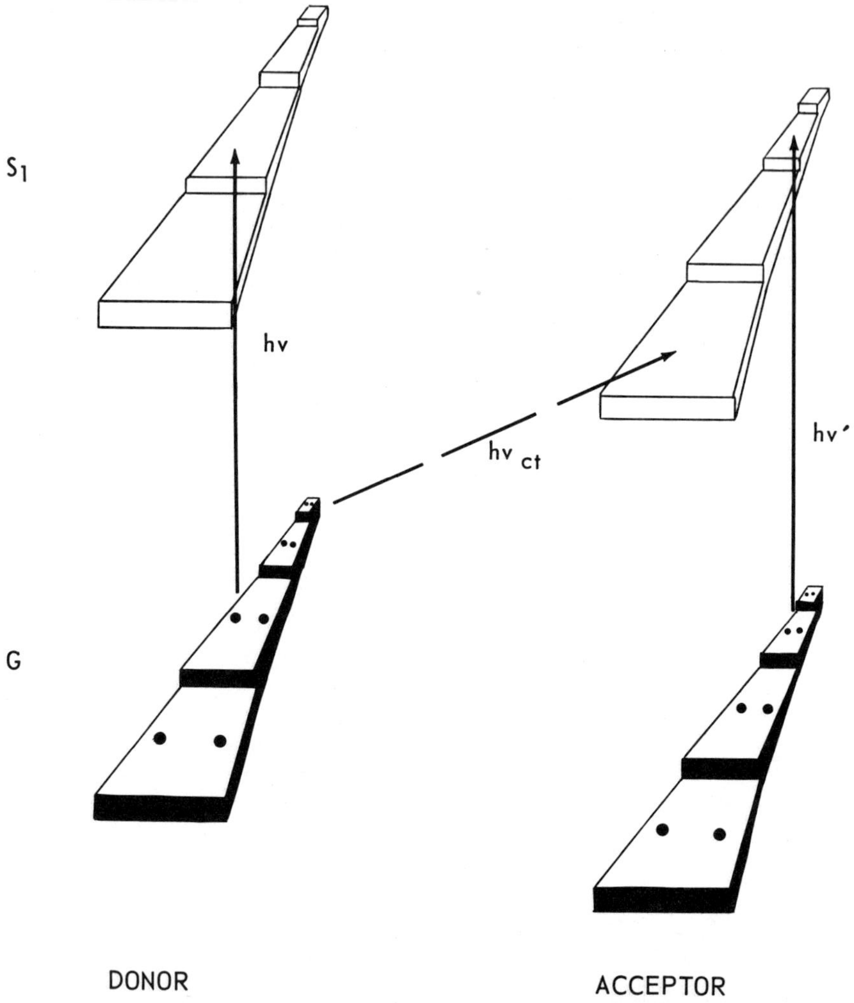

FIGURE 3. Diagrammatic presentation of ground states and first excited singlet states of the donor and acceptor transitions. The arrow labeled $h\nu_{ct}$ represents the charge-transfer transition in which an electron from the highest occupied orbital of the donor is promoted to the lowest empty orbital of the acceptor.

The most stable charge-transfer complexes should result from the interaction of molecules of relatively low ionization potential (i.e., not much energy required to remove an electron from the HOMO) with molecules of high electron affinity. Quantum chemical calculations of energies of highest occupied molecular orbitals of amino acid side chains indicate that indole is a relatively efficient electron donor,[7] although the 3-carbamoylpyridinium ion is only moderately effective as an electron acceptor when compared with groups such as tetracyanoethylene (TCNE).

Since both indole and 3-carbamoylpyridinium chloride have relatively large extinction coefficients and high concentrations of both molecules are required to see the charge-transfer complex, it was found most convenient to incorporate both groups into the same molecule, as shown by the structure in FIGURE 4. Here, the indole is separated from the pyridinium ion by two methylene groups, which function as an insulator to prevent transfer of electrons from one ring to another through the ethylene bridge, and also imposes steric restrictions on the two rings which minimizes intramolecular covalent bond formation. Intramolecular interaction does take place between the donor and acceptor portions of the model compound and results in a broad absorption band that is not associated with either chromophore alone. The band was assigned to an intramolecular charge-transfer transition.[4]

The charge-transfer transition should obey the following relationship:

$$h\nu_{ct} = I_D - E_A - \Delta$$

i.e., the frequency of the charge-transfer band is linearly related to the ionization potential of the electron donor (I_D) and the electron affinity of the acceptor (E_A). The electron-donor portion of the model system which has been described was modified to cover a range of ionization potential values, while the pyridinium portion was retained. The frequency of the new transition, as detected by difference spectroscopy, was linearly related to the ionization potential of the electron donor.[8, 9]

From the studies with the model compound, it is not possible to distinguish between sulfhydryl addition (covalent bond formation) and charge-transfer complex formation. Studies were initiated with the thionicotinamide analog which (theoretically) should be capable of distinguishing between the two possibilities. This analog contains the 3-thiocarbamoyl group in place of the 3-carbamoyl substituent. Previous studies[10] have shown that when sulfur replaces oxygen as part of the chromophore, as in 1-methyl-3-thiocarbamoyl-1, 4-dihydropyridine, the position of the absorption maximum is shifted by 50–60 mμ toward longer wavelengths (FIGURE 5). Wallenfels and Schüly[11] isolated the benzyl mercaptan adduct of N-(2, 6-dichlorobenzyl)-nicotinamide and studied its absorption spectrum (λ_{max} 335 mμ, ε 2400). If the benzyl mercaptan adduct of corresponding thionicotinamide analog were examined,

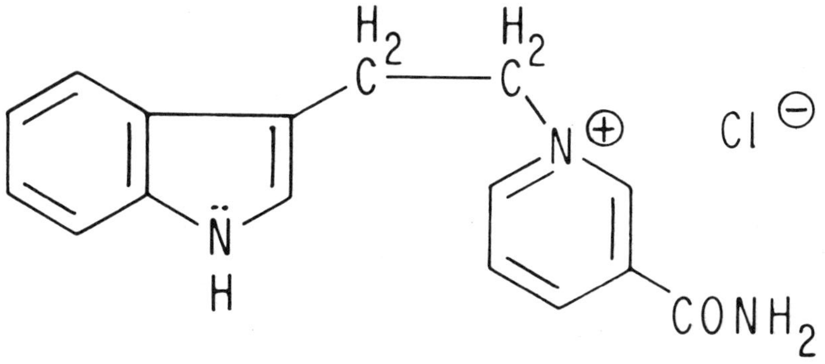

I

FIGURE 4. Structure of the model employed in the study of the interaction between indole and 3-carbamoylpyridinium chloride.

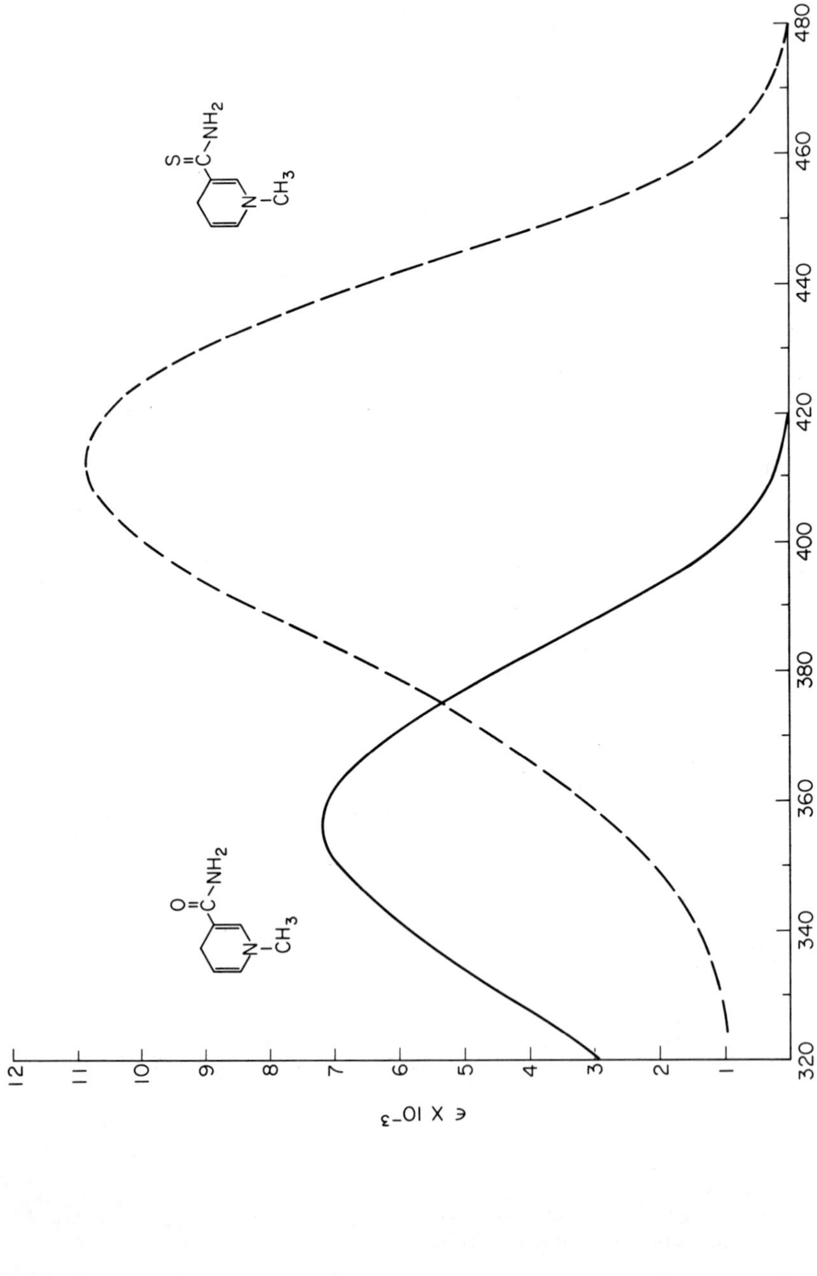

FIGURE 5. Comparison of the absorption spectrum of 1-methyl-3-carbamoyl-1, 4-dihydropyridine (solid curve) and the corresponding 3-thiocarbamoyl derivative (dashed curve.)

its absorption maximum would be expected to be at 385–395 mμ. The broad absorption band which is associated with the addition of coenzyme to glyceraldehyde-3-phosphate dehydrogenase should shift from 360 mμ with NAD^+ to 420 mμ with the thionicotinamide analog, if the new band results from addition of the protein sulfhydryl group to the 4-position of the pyridinium moiety of the coenzyme. On the other hand, let us suppose that the broad absorption band results from donor:acceptor interaction and is associated with a charge-transfer transition: what would be the effect of substituting the 3-thiocarbamoylpyridinium ion for the corresponding oxygen compound? The present investigation was initiated to answer this question, using the model designed to study such noncovalent interactions.

Synthetic Difficulties

The usual method of preparing N′-alkylnicotinamide halides is by refluxing nicotinamide with the alkyl halide in methanol. It is not possible to prepare N-alkylthionicotinamide halides by the same procedure, since the sulfur atom of the thiocarbamoyl group is alkylated more easily than the pyridine nitrogen. The S-alkyl group is readily solvolyzed, and one isolates a terrific stench and N-alkylnicotinamide halide. A modification of the method originally described by Lettré and coworkers[12] and used successfully with the nicotinamide derivatives was employed with thionicotinamide. The synthetic approach is shown in SCHEME 1. Thionicotinamide was heated with 2, 4-dinitrochlorobenzene, in the absence of solvent, in a hot water bath for several hours. The resulting mix was dissolved in methanol, and the product was precipitated with ether. After several recrystallizations, an orange powder was obtained which was characterized as N-(2, 4-dinitrophenyl)-3-thiocarbamoylpyridinium chloride. Subsequent reaction with the β-substituted ethylamine of the appropriate electron donor yielded the desired product. The products were purified by repeated crystallizations from methanol:ether, and were subjected

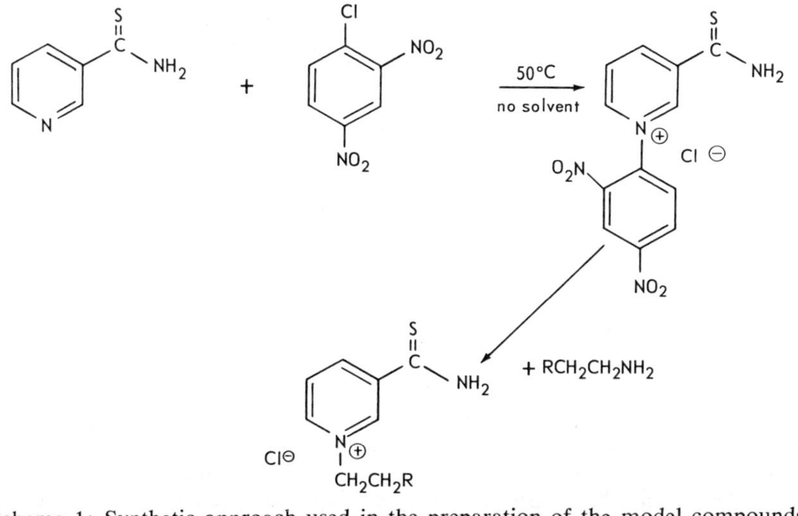

Scheme 1: Synthetic approach used in the preparation of the model compounds in which the 3-thiocarbamoylpyridinium ion is the electron acceptor.

to elemental analyses. In all cases, the experimental values were in agreement with the calculated values.

Absorption spectra were taken on the Cary recording spectrophotometer Model 15, and difference spectra were determined with tandem double cuvettes throughout a large range of concentrations and in cuvettes of varying path length as reported previously.[4] In every case the spectra obeyed Beer's law, and demonstrated that the broad band supported the assignment of an intramolecular charge-transfer transition.

Indolylethylthionicotinamide

The absorption spectrum of indolylethylthionicotinamide is given by the solid curve in FIGURE 6. The diffuse band that is characteristic of the charge-transfer band is present here, and extends nearly to 500 mμ. An additional absorption band present in the thionicotinamide derivatives that was absent in the oxygen counterpart is the one in the region of 297–305 mμ ($\epsilon \sim 6000$). This transition is assigned to the thiocarbamoyl group, and does add a complication to the detection of the weak charge-transfer band.

The dashed curve in FIGURE 6 represents the combined spectra of an equimolar mixture of tryptamine hydrochloride and 1-methyl-3-thiocarbamoylpyridinium perchlorate.

The difference spectrum is the subtraction of the separated chromophores from the spectrum of indolylethylthionicotinamide and, therefore, represents any new transition which arises from intramolecular interaction of the two chromophores. The difference spectrum in methanol is given by the solid curve in FIGURE 7. The apparent maximum of this band, which has been assigned to a charge-transfer transition, is around 357 mμ with an extinction coefficient of 900 M^{-1} cm^{-1}. The intensity of the band is similar to that found with the corresponding oxygen compound, but the apparent maximum of the band has shifted by 40 mμ to longer wavelengths. The difference spectrum in water is shown by the dashed curve in FIGURE 7, and the apparent maximum is now at 335 mμ with a higher extinction coefficient ($\epsilon \sim 1500$). Although the shift to longer wavelengths as the polarity of the medium is decreased has been suggested as diagnostic of a charge-transfer complex,[13] that does not appear to be the reason for the very large shifts found here. The sensitivity of the thiocarbamoyl absorption band to changes in polarity of the medium had previously been reported[14] and is found with thionicotinamide methochloride itself; the thiocarbamoyl absorption is at 298 mμ ($\epsilon \sim 5500$) in methanol, and is shifted to 284 mμ ($\epsilon \sim 6500$) in water. The magnitude of the frequency shift in the difference spectrum shown in FIGURE 7 and in thionicotinamide methochloride is almost the same: i.e., about 1700 cm^{-1}.

For the time being, let us continue with the properties of other electron donors and return to the complicating features of thiocarbamoyl absorption in the concluding remarks.

The usual fluorescence of the indole group which emits around 350 mμ upon excitation at 280 mμ cannot be detected in indolylethylthionicotinamide solutions even at low temperatures as had been observed in the corresponding oxygen compound. Shinitzky and collaborators[15] have employed this quenching by participation in charge-transfer complex formation to detect indole residues in lysozyme, using the imidazolium ion as the probe.

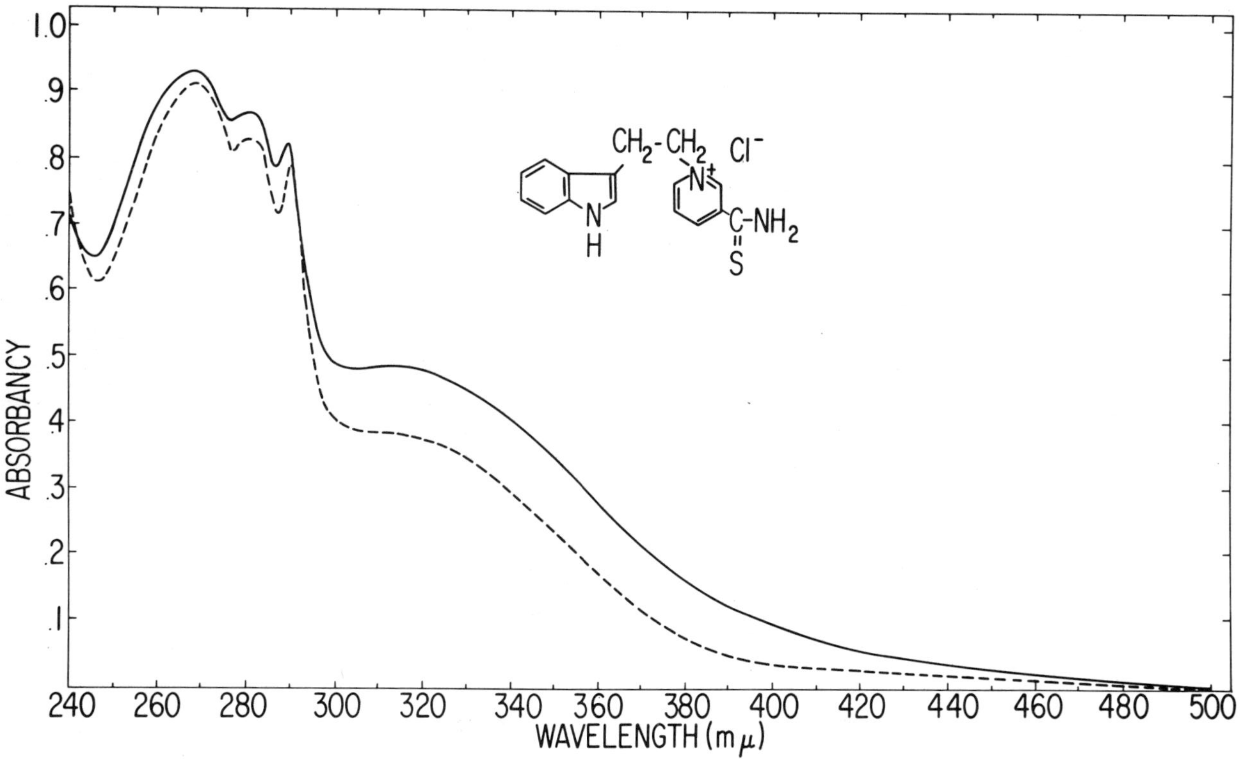

FIGURE 6. The absorption spectrum of indolylethylthionicotinamide in methanol (solid curve) and the combined spectra of equimolar solutions of tryptamine hydrochloride and 1-methyl-3-thiocarbamoylpyridinium perchlorate (dashed curve) in methanol. The concentration of all solutions was 8.4×10^{-5}M.

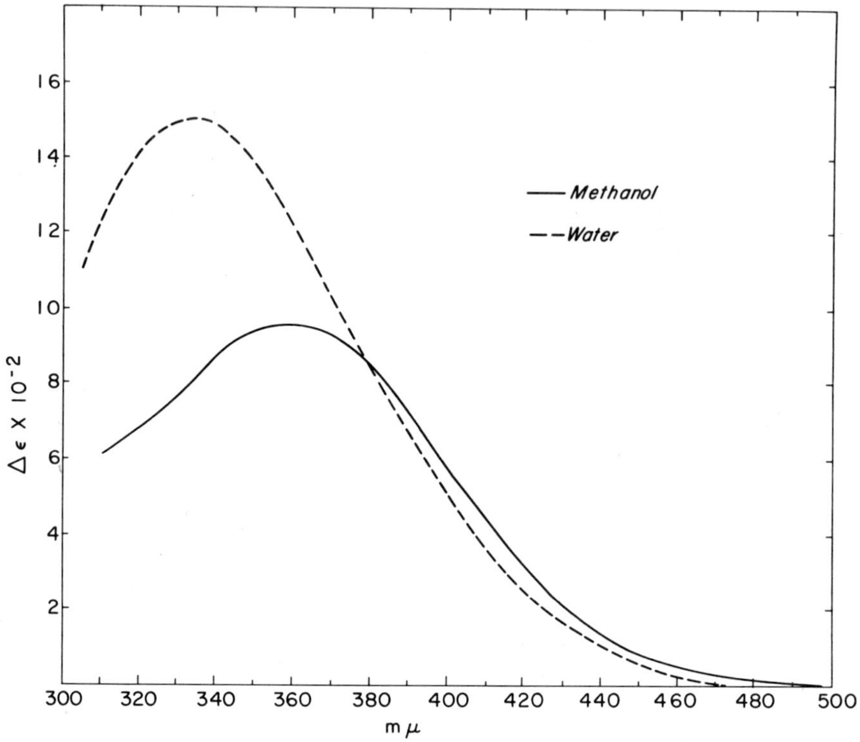

FIGURE 7. Difference spectrum obtained by subtracting the contribution of the individual chromophores from the total spectrum of indolylethylthionicotinamide. Solid curve obtained when all solutions were prepared in methanol: dashed curve for aqueous solutions.

Indolylethyldihydrothionicotinamide

Chemical reduction with sodium dithionite was carried out and yielded the corresponding 1, 4-dihydro derivative of indolylethylthionicotinamide. The absorption spectrum of the reduced product in methanol was completely coincident with the combined spectra of tryptamine and 1-methyl-3-thiocarbamoyl-1, 4-dihydropyridine, which indicates that if there is any kind of interaction between the two moieties it is not reflected by any absorbance properties. In the case of the corresponding dihydronicotinamide derivative, interaction between indole and the dihydropyridine was detected by the quantitative transfer of energy of excitation from the absorbing indole residue to the emitting dihydronicotinamide.[4] Since dihydrothionicotinamide is nonfluorescent, however, the analogous experiment could not be carried out. One of the outstanding features of the dihydrothionicotinamide group is its photosensitivity.[10] Brief exposures to light result in loss of the visible band and of the characteristic thionamide absorption band. A rather complicated series of experiments was set up to test whether exposure of solutions of indolylethyldihydrothionicotinamide to radiation at 280 mμ could bleach the compound to the same extent as was found on exposure to light near 400 mμ. Since 1-methyl-3-thiocarbamoyl-1, 4-dihydropyridine was also bleached by exposure to 280 mμ radiation, there was no purpose in carrying out the proposed experiments.

Amino Acid Side Chain—Thionicotinamide Interaction

Although indole is the most efficient electron donor among the amino acid side chains, other groups that formed a new transition as a result of their donor:acceptor interaction included benzene, phenol and imidazole. The apparent absorption maxima of the new transitions are summarized in TABLE 1. In every case, the extinction coefficient of the new transition is about 900 M^{-1} cm^{-1} in this series which is nearly identical with the value observed in the nicotinamide series ($\epsilon \sim 1000$). While the ionization potentials of indole and imidazole have not been published, the energies of the highest occupied molecular orbital of these have been determined by quantum chemical methods.[7] The frequencies of the intramolecular charge-transfer transitions for the nicotinamide and thionicotinamide compounds versus the calculated energies of the highest occupied molecular orbitals are plotted in FIGURE 8.

With the exception of indole, the apparent absorption maxima of the thionicotinamide derivatives are at shorter wavelengths than the corresponding nicotinamide compounds. A comment should be made concerning the large deviation of imidazole from this otherwise linear correlation. Since the transition which has been assigned to the charge-transfer band in imidazolylethylthionicotinamide disappears under conditions in which the imidazole nitrogen is protonated, it was assumed that the histidine side chain is primarily an n-donor. The calculations of the energy of the HOMO for the imidazole is based on its π-electron system, however, and does not consider the lone pair electrons which are the better electron donors.

Other Electron Donors

A large number of benzene derivatives whose ionization potentials are well known were incorporated as the electron donor in the N-substituted thionicotinamide, in the hope that we would be more confident of our assignment of a charge-transfer transition to the new band. The following benzene de-

TABLE 1

APPARENT ABSORPTION MAXIMA OF INTRAMOLECULAR CHARGE-TRANSFER TRANSITIONS OF AMINO ACID SIDE CHAINS WITH 3-THIOCARBAMOYLPYRIDINIUM CHLORIDE IN METHANOL

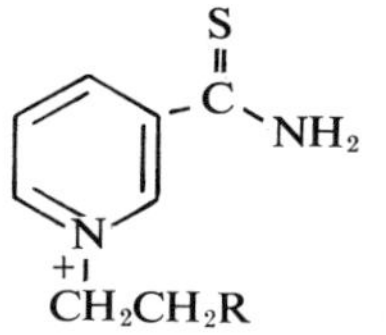

R	λ_{max} (mμ)	ϵ(M^{-1} cm^{-1})
Indole	357	950
Phenol	294	900
Imidazole	283	900
Benzene	276	920

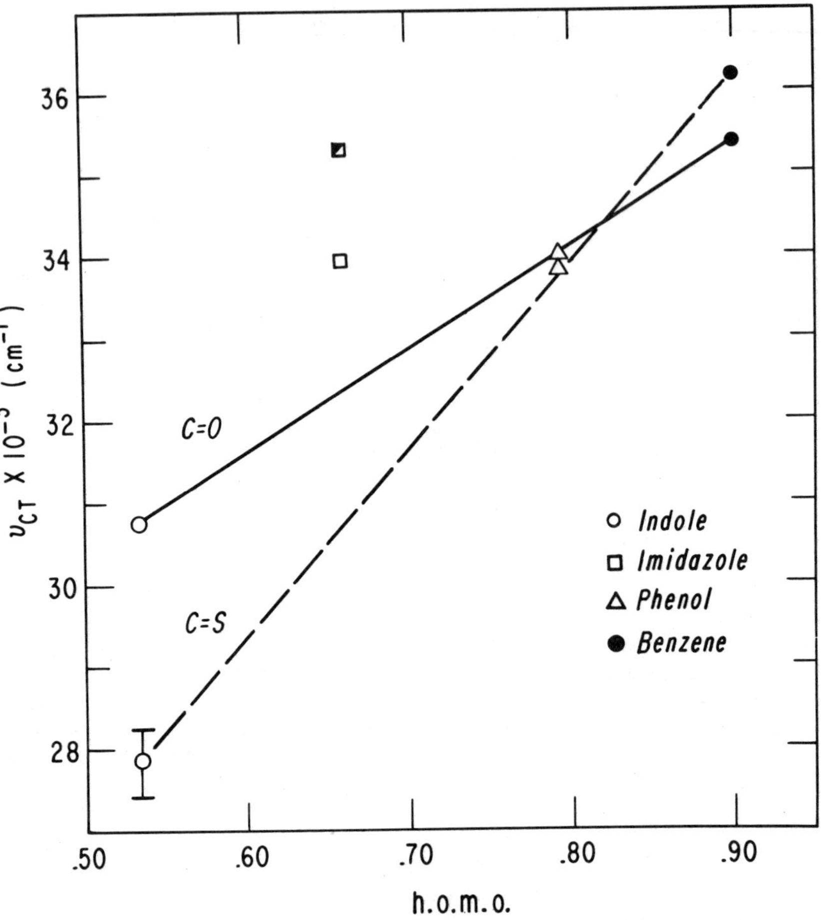

FIGURE 8. The frequencies of the charge-transfer transitions for thionicotinamide derivatives (dashed curve, c=s) compared with those for the corresponding nicotinamide derivatives (solid curve, c=o) plotted against the energies of the highest occupied molecular orbitals (Pullman and Pullman[7]).

rivatives were used: p-aminophenyl-, p-methoxyphenyl-, p-hydroxyphenyl-, p-tolyl-, p-chlorophenyl- and unsubstituted benzene. The frequency of the apparent absorption maxima of these new transitions versus the appropriate ionization potentials are shown by the solid line in FIGURE 9. The corresponding values obtained with the nicotinamide derivatives are represented by the dashed curve in the same figure.

In general, we may conclude from these studies that thionicotinamide is not as effective an electron acceptor as nicotinamide. The studies presented with these model compounds indicate that the proposed use of the thionicotinamide analog of NAD$^+$ as a probe into the nature of enzyme-coenzyme interaction would not be conclusive. Indole is the only amino acid side chain which gives a considerably longer wavelength band with thionicotinamide than with the oxygen-containing coenzyme model. The emission as well as the

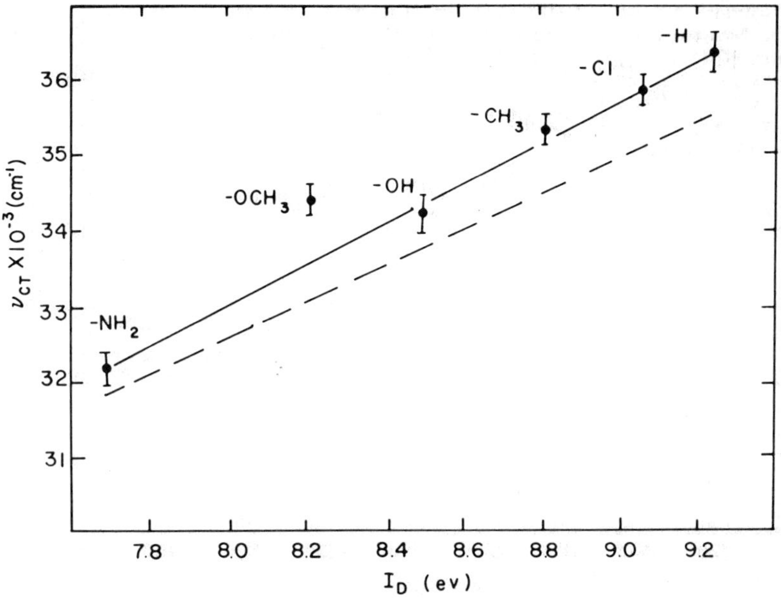

FIGURE 9. Frequencies of intramolecular charge-transfer transitions employing para-substituted benzenes as the electron donor, and 3-thiocarbamoylpyridinium ion (solid line) or 3-carbamoylpyridinium ion (broken line) as the electron acceptor plotted against ionization potentials of the benzene derivatives (from photoionization methods[16]).

absorption behavior of the enzyme-coenzyme complex implicates the indole nucleus as being the amino acid side chain that is most likely to interact with the coenzyme. The most serious complication is the sensitivity of the thionicotinamide absorption to the polarity of the medium, since a protein such as glyceraldehyde-3-phosphate dehydrogenase offers a broad spectrum of polarities from the hydrophobic regions of low polarity to the ionic environment of groups such as glutamic acid or lysine residues. Although the applicability of the thionamide compound to the present study may not have been as good as we had hoped, perhaps this group may serve as a probe in determining the polarity of hydrophobic regions in some NAD^+ -linked dehydrogenases.

References

1. RACKER, E. & I. KRIMSKY. 1952. J. Biol. Chem. **196:** 731.
2. CILENTO, G. & P. GIUSTI. 1959. J. Amer. Chem. Soc. **81:** 3801.
3. CILENTO, G. & P. TEDESCHI. 1961. J. Biol. Chem. **236:** 907.
4. SHIFRIN, S. 1964. Biochim. Biophys. Acta **81:** 205.
5. ALIVISATOS, S. G. A., F. UNGAR, A. JIBRIL & G. A. MOURKIDES. 1961. Biochim. Biophys. Acta **51:** 361.
6. GREEN, J. P. & J. P. MALRIEU. 1965. Proc. Nat. Acad. Sci. U. S. A. **54:** 659.
7. PULLMAN, B. & A. PULLMAN. 1958. Proc. Nat. Acad. Sci. U. S. A. **44:** 1197.
8. SHIFRIN, S. 1964. Biochemistry **3:** 829.
9. SHIFRIN, S. 1965. Biochim. Biophys. Acta **96:** 173.
10. SHIFRIN, S. 1963. Biochim. Biophys. Acta **69:** 1.
11. WALLENFELS, K. & H. SCHÜLY. 1959. Liebig. Ann. Chem. **621:** 86.

12. Lettre, H., W. Haede & E. Ruhbaum. 1953. Liebig Ann. Chem. **579:** 123.
13. Kosower, E. M. 1960. *In* The Enzymes. P. D. Boyer, H. Lardy & K. Myrback, Eds. **3:** 183. Academic Press, New York, N. Y.
14. Jenssen, M. J. 1960. Rec. Trav. Chim. **79:** 454.
15. Shinitzky, M., E. Katchalski, V. Grisaro & N. Sharon. 1966. Arch. Biochem. Biophys. **116:** 332.
16. Watanabe, K. 1959. Final Report on Ionization Potentials of Molecules from Photoionization Data.

SEMICONDUCTION IN PROTEINS AND LIPIDS—ITS POSSIBLE BIOLOGICAL IMPORT*

Barnett Rosenberg and Elliot Postow
Biophysics Department
Michigan State University
East Lansing, Mich.

INTRODUCTION

The application of the concepts of solid state physics to biology was first suggested by Szent-Györgyi in 1941.[1, 2] He proposed the existence of conduction bands in protein structures. The intervening years have seen a number of papers published which treat this suggestion from both theoretical and experimental views. The generality of solid state semiconduction in biochemical systems is now evident, and this provides a basis for a new class of models of biological function.

Substances whose electrical conductivity follows the relation:

$$\sigma(T) = \sigma_0 \exp(-E/2kT) \qquad (1)$$

where σ is the electrical conductivity; E is the activation energy for semiconduction; k is the Boltzmann constant; and T is the temperature in degrees Kelvin; are operationally defined as semiconductors. Employing this simple criterion, representative molecules of every class of biochemicals and even complex organelles have been demonstrated to be semiconductors. Several examples of biological materials exhibiting semiconduction are illustrated in FIGURE 1. A recent review by Gutmann and Lyons[3] lists 116 biochemicals and organelles, ranging from adenine to wool, upon which conductivity and semiconductivity activation energy measurements have been made. In all but three cases, the activation energy for semiconduction is in the range of 1–3 eV. The fact that all of these materials are semiconductors does not, of course, suggest that the conductivity mechanism or any of the parameters of conductivity are the same in all systems. Another experimental generalization is that similar effects have been observed with a variety of adsorbants and complexing agents with several different biochemicals, as discussed elsewhere. These results do indicate a basic similarity in the conductivity mechanisms of a diverse group of biological materials.

The dominant charge carrier in the substance may arise from an impurity or adsorbant (extrinsic), or it may be indigenous to the biological materal (intrinsic). Suard-Sender[4] has argued that, in proteins, an extrinsic semiconducting mechanism must apply. She reached this conclusion after calculating the energy band gap in a two-dimensional peptide network to be 5 eV. This is significantly higher than the measured value of the semiconduction activation energy in proteins, i.e., 2.4 eV. A possible explanation of this discrepancy will be considered later. Eley and Leslie[5] propose, for the hydrated protein system, that water acts as an electron donor. The interaction energy between

* This work has been supported in part by Contract ONR-2587 of the Office of Naval Research, Grant GM-10890 of the National Institute of General Medical Sciences of the United States Public Health Service, Grant No. NB-04145 of the National Institute of Neurological Diseases and Blindness of the United States Public Health Service, and Contract AT(11-1)1714 of the United States Atomic Energy Commission.

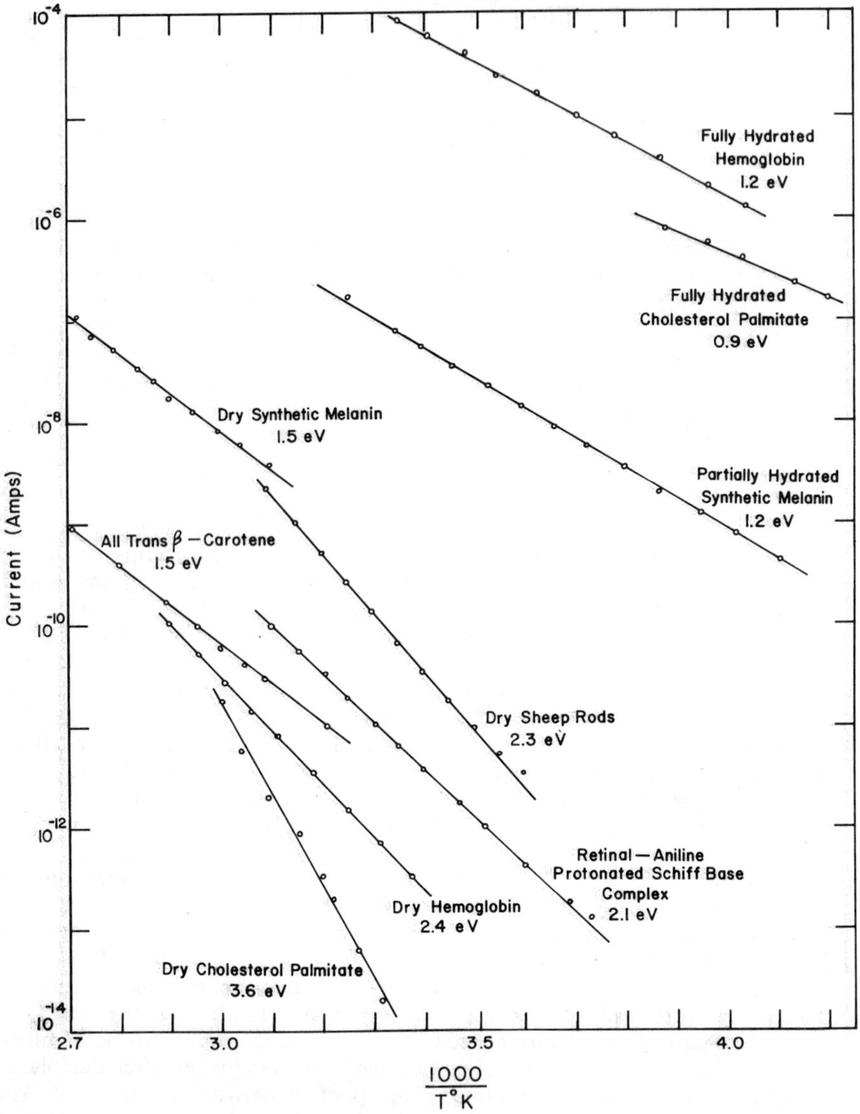

FIGURE 1. The log of the current plotted against 1/T°K for a variety of biological substances. The activation energies are calculated from the slopes of the lines using Equation 1.

impurity atoms is assumed to be inversely proportional to the distance between them. Therefore, the impurity mechanism predicts $E = E_0 - \alpha N^{1/3}$, where N is the number of impurity atoms (in the case under consideration, water). If only surface impurities are considered, then a square root dependence is predicted. In the intrinsic model (discussed elsewhere) a linear dependence of activation energy on hydration is assumed. Existing data can not definitely distinguish among these three possibilities.

Observed semiconductivity may be the result of either an electronic or an ionic current or both. The most general case for the conductivity of a given substance can be written in the form:

$$\sigma = [\sum_i Z_i n_i \mu_i + \sum_e n_e \mu_e]e \quad (2)$$

where i are the species of ions present of both signs; with a density n_i; with Z_i, the valence of the ions; μ_i, the mobility of the ion; e, the species of electronic charge carriers (electrons or positive holes) present with densities n_e and mobilities μ_e. All charge carrier species will make some contribution to the total conductivity. A major problem of solid state biophysics is to identify the densities and mobilities of each species in any given substance and thus evaluate the contribution of that species to the total conductivity.

Electrolysis will occur in ionic but not in electronic currents. Therefore, in order to distinguish between the two varieties of charge carriers, measurements of solid state electrolysis are essential. Either the increase in the evolved gas or the decrease of remanent water in a hydrated protein can be monitored. Conductivity is a very sensitive measure of the hydration state of a protein. Therefore, if the conductivity is primarily due to ions, the amount of adsorbed water will decrease as a current continues to flow through the sample, because electrolysis will convert some of the water to hydrogen and oxygen. This decreased hydration will manifest itself in a decreasing conductivity as a function of time. Hemoglobin, with 7.5% adsorbed water, was observed by Rosenberg[6] in such an experiment. The conductivity remained constant over a period of time in which ionic conductivity would have dropped by a factor of ten (as illustrated in FIGURE 2), and he concluded that at this hydration state at least 95% of the current was carried by electronic charge carriers. Maričič, and collaborators[7] corroborated this finding of electronic conductivity at low levels of hydration. In their experiment, evolved gas could not be detected when, for seven days, 150 volts were impressed across a sample of crystalline hemoglobin with 9.17% adsorbed water.

Reihl[8] reported the activation energy of gelatin, with somewhat less than 10% adsorbed water, to be 1.8 eV. Drawing on the similarity between this value and the activation energy for conduction in ice (which is now known to be lower), Reihl argued for protonic conduction in the icelike layer of water adsorbed on the protein. However, it is doubtful that an icelike array exists with less than two Brunauer-Emmet-Teller (B.E.T.) monolayers of water adsorbed on the protein. An activation energy of 1.8 eV for partially hydrated gelatin is consistent with the results of measurements on other proteins. Also, activation energies in proteins vary continuously with the quantity of adsorbed water (as illustrated in FIGURE 7) from a dry state value of approximately 2.4 eV to a minimum achievable value of about 1.1 eV.

Keratin films containing greater than 15% adsorbed water were examined by King and Medley.[9] These early investigators found the production of hydrogen sufficient to account for the conductivity as 100% ionic. Oxygen evolution was not detected, but oxygen may have been chemically sorbed onto the hemoglobin. The evolution of tritium in the solid state electrolysis of hemoglobin with 30% adsorbed tritiated water was observed by Rosenberg.[10] Tritium evolution at the observed rate could account for 44% of the conductivity by an ionic mechanism. In independent studies,[7] hemoglobin hydrated to 40–46% was found to exhibit large ionic conductivities. Maričič and coworkers[11] proposed that, at a hydration level of about 18%–22%, protonic conductivity

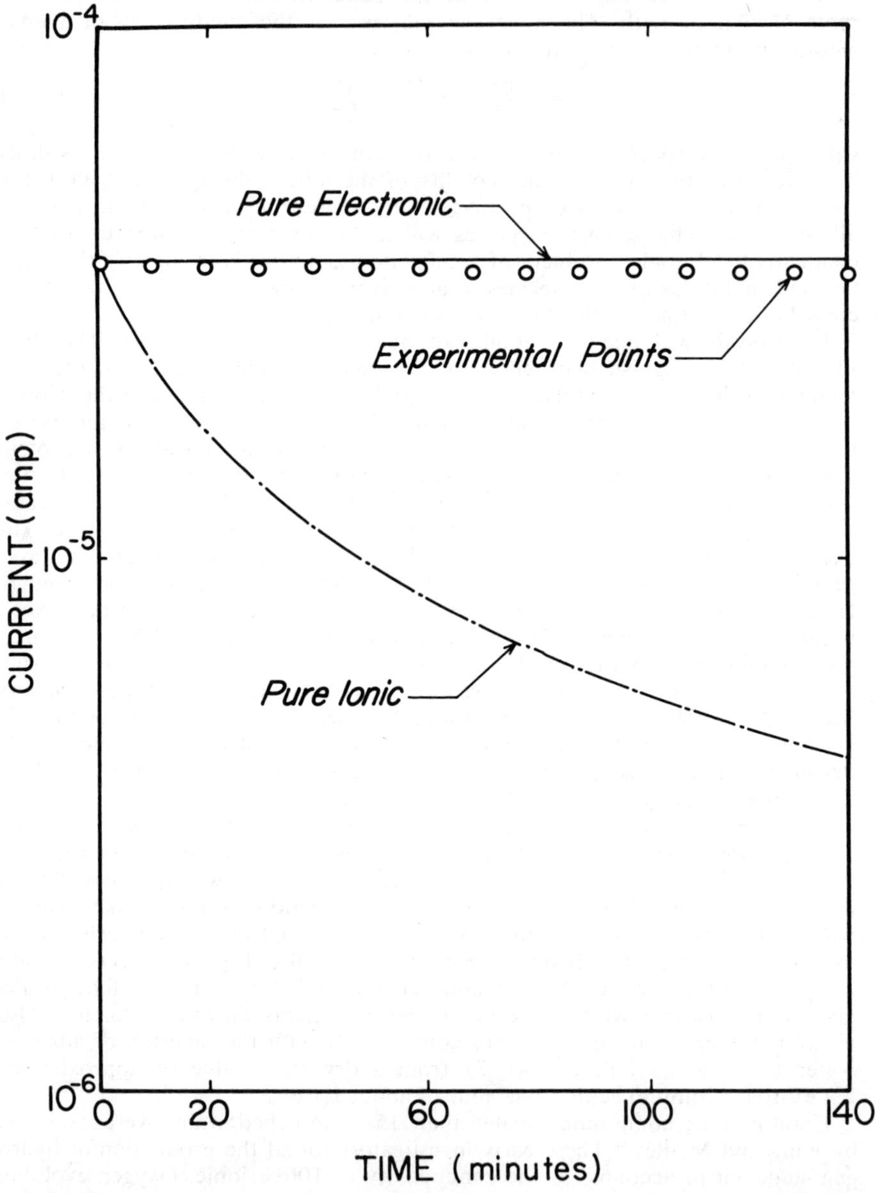

FIGURE 2. The time of a current through hemoglobin with 7.5% adsorbed water demonstrates the nature of the charge carrier. The time-independence of the current cannot be accounted for by ionic conductivity, which should decrease by an order of magnitude over the time period indicated.

becomes significant in hemoglobin. High-frequency dielectric measurements by Rosen[12] on bovine serum albumin and myoglobin exhibit curious breakpoints in the region of 20% hydration. This may be a result of the initiation of ionic conduction at this hydration state. For many proteins, this hydration level represents 3–4 B.E.T. monolayers of adsorbed water. At this hydration state, all of the water is no longer highly localized and oriented on the surface of the protein molecule but has begun to form a somewhat contiguous layer of water with extensive hydrogen bond bridges. Some conduction may take place through this layer of water. It now appears, in the case of proteins with small quantities of adsorbed water, that conductivity is predominantly, if not entirely, electronic; and, as the hydration is increased above a certain range, a contribution of ionic conductivity occurs and increases.

The Effect of Impurities on Semiconductivity

At present, biological substances are not obtainable in states of purity even approaching the electronic grade (one impurity molecule per 10^{10} substrate molecules) of certain inorganic semiconductors, although some organic crystals can be greatly purified by zone refining techniques. Electronic grade biochemicals, particularly of the polymeric type are not in the foreseeable future. This cannot, however, be a question of great importance in biophysics, for *in vivo* systems simply are impure. Therefore, a relative insensitivity of the conductivity mechanism to general impurities is demanded of semiconductive models postulated in biological systems.

There is a fundamental difference between inorganic and biochemical semiconductors. Covalent inorganic crystals possess long-range order, extending over as great a distance as 1000 unit cells, providing long-range interaction. Any local alteration in this order, such as the introduction of an impurity, will then have widespread ramifications. This is in contradistinction to biochemical crystallites which possess only relatively short-range order. Impurities, until their concentration becomes rather high, exhibit only local effects which do not statistically affect the short-range order of the biochemical molecular crystallite.[13]

Semiconduction curves for classic inorganic impurity semiconduction are illustrated in FIGURE 3A. At low temperatures, and hence low conductivity, the impurity conduction will dominate because of the lower activation energy needed to excite charge carriers to the conduction band from an impurity center (see FIGURE 4). All impurity centers which have not already been excited are assumed to be filled. At higher temperatures, the intrinsic conductivity of the host will dominate because of its larger activation energy and, therefore, faster rate of increase with temperature. As the impurity concentration is increased, the impurity conductivity will dominate over a larger temperature range. The activation energy for impurity conductivity will not markedly change with alteration of the impurity concentration, for only the number of carriers is affected by concentration alterations (unless impurity band conduction occurs). Hence, the two curves for different impurity concentrations are parallel indicating, not a change in activation energy, but a change in the preexponential factor. Semiconduction curves of hydrated crystalline hemoglobin, (FIGURE 7) are not of this form.

A heterogeneous system of mixed inorganic crystals may produce semiconduction curves of the form schematically illustrated in FIGURE 3B. In such a system, the increased concentration of a second component alters the activation energy. Folberth[14] has investigated one such example, In (As, P), while Larach and collaborators[15] discuss another, Zn (S, Se). In these cases

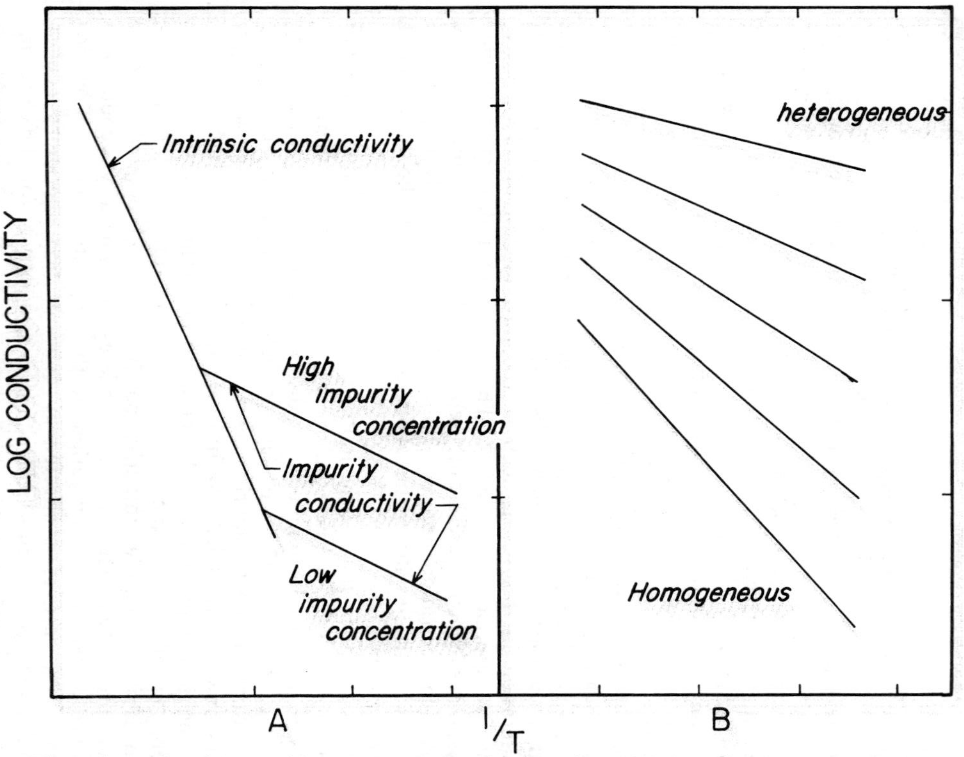

FIGURE 3. The schematic diagram illustrates two mechanisms in which a contaminant may influence the conductivity of its host: A—In a classical impurity mechanism, impurity conductivity dominates in one region and intrinsic conductivity in another. The impurity concentration does not affect the activation energy in the region of impurity-dominated conductivity. B—In a mixed system, the addition of a second component alters the activation energy. The change is proportional to the concentration of the second component.

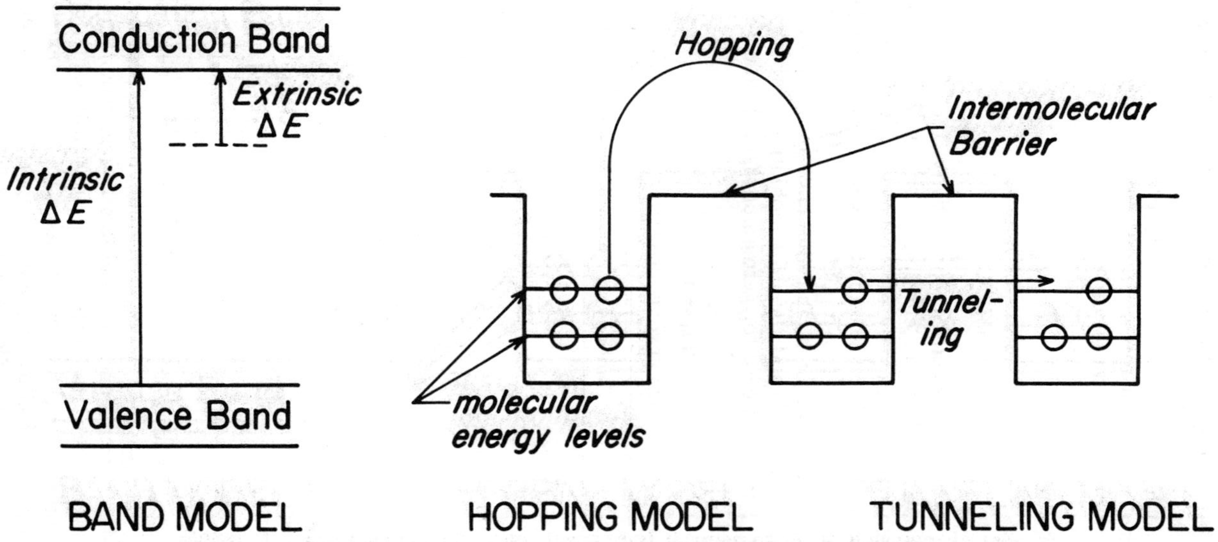

FIGURE 4. The diagram illustrates the several theories of semiconduction. In the band theory, the carriers are excited from either the valence band of the material (intrinsic) or the impurity center (extrinsic) to a conduction band. Conduction may also occur via a hopping of the charge carrier from one localized site, over a potential barrier, to a second localized site. The transport between localized sites may, however, occur via quantum mechanical tunneling.

and a number of others, a linear relationship is obtained between the activation energy and the relative concentration of the variable constituents.

In these examples, both constituents are present in relatively large concentrations; and, although mixing crystals does not add an additional mechanism of conductivity, it changes the conductivity properties of the system. The biochemical systems discussed in this paper exhibit semiconduction curves of this second type, rather than those of the impurity conduction type. A mechanism for the changes in the intrinsic conductivity properties of the system is discussed below.

Mobility

Three factors are involved in electrical conductivity: the charge, density and mobility of the carriers of electrical current, as shown in Equation 2. Conductivity measurements inform us only of the product of the number density and mobility of the carriers. These parameters can be separately determined from the Hall coefficient, where the product of the Hall coefficient and the conductivity indicates both the sign and the Hall mobility of the current carriers. It is assumed that Hall and the drift mobilities are both of the same order of magnitude. This is the case for germanium (see TABLE 1).

TABLE 1
REPRESENTATIVE MOBILITIES

Material	Mobility in $cm^2/(volt\text{-}sec)$	Type of Measurement
Indium antimonide	6.3×10^4	Hall
Germanium	2.6×10^3	Hall
Germanium	3.6×10^3	drift
Germanium	3.4×10^3	conductivity
Vitrius selenium	5×10^{-3}	drift
Semiconducting glass	5×10^{-2}	Hall
Li^+ or F^- ions in ice	$\ll 10^{-8}$	relaxation
H_3O^+ in water at 25° C	36×10^{-4}	drift
Li^+ in water at 25° C	4×10^{-4}	drift
Phthalocyanine (single crystals)	0.1 – 1.0	Hall
Anthracene (crystal)	0.3 – 2.0	drift
Poly(N-vinyl carbazole) - iodine (donor-acceptor complex)	0.5	AC Hall
Hemoglobin	2–3	Microwave Hall
DNA (hydrated)	0.5	Microwave Hall

Hall effects are produced when a transverse magnetic field is impressed across a conductor, thus yielding a potential difference perpendicular to both the direction of the current and the impressed magnetic field. This has proved a difficult experiment to perform on biological materials, and the literature contains only one claim of a successful experiment. Trukhan,[16] employing a microwave Hall effect apparatus, reports mobility measurements for proteins and nucleic acids. The sign of the charge carrier was found to vary from one system to another. It is problematical that the mobilities, about 1 $cm^2/(volt\text{-}sec)$, are applicable to the D.C. case. A list of representative mobilities of inorganic and organic substances is presented, for purposes of comparison, in TABLE 1. Neither DC Hall voltages nor magnetoresistive effects have been successfully detected in hemoglobin films or phospholipid films.[17] Recently, Hermann and Rembaum[18] have determined an AC Hall mobility for poly (N vinyl-carbazole)-iodine, a donor-acceptor complex, as 0.5 cm^2/(volt sec). These investigators employed the AC AC method of Hermann and Ham.[19]

Determination of charge mobility in biological semiconductors would be useful to distinguish between two proposed mechanisms of conductivity. Charge carriers may be localized on a given site for long periods of time and then, in a short period of time, "hop" or "tunnel" to a second site where, again, they would remain for a period of time. A second model visualizes the charge carriers drifting in a conduction band to which they have been thermally excited from either the valence band or from an impurity center. These several models are depicted in FIG. 4. In the first case, low mobilities, < 1 cm^2/(volt-sec), are anticipated, whereas in the second, higher mobilities, > 1 cm^2/(volt-sec), may be expected. Mobilities in the band structure are very dependent upon band width. As the band width decreases, the expected mobility likewise decreases. Eley[20] has shown that an electron possessing a mean free path of 70Å in a band 0.01 eV wide will have a mobility of $\sim$ 0.2 cm^2/(volt-sec).

An activation energy is interpreted, in the context of the band model, as that energy necessary to populate the conduction band; therefore, the mobility should be relatively temperature-insensitive. If only acoustic phonon scattering is considered, $\mu \propto T^{-n}$ where $n < 2$. n is a complex function of anisotropy and band width.[21] When—as is most often the case—only simple lattice scattering is considered, $n = 3/2$. If $\mu < 1$ cm^2/(volt-sec), the charge will remain localized on individual sites. A transfer of charge will occur via its hopping over or tunnneling through the potential barrier between molecules. Mobility, in this case, may be exponentially dependent on temperature, $\mu = \mu_0 \exp (E/kT)$. However, if the electron-lattice interactions are very small, the mobility may be relatively temperature-insensitive.[21] The temperature dependence of the mobility, therefore, may not provide a good means to distinguish between the band and the hopping models of conduction. Eley[20] has calculated that, at an intersite separation of 10Å, the hopping model is to be preferred whereas at smaller separations the tunnel model may be chosen. Calculations of DeVault and coworkers[22] show that, for a barrier height of 1 eV and a barrier width of 28Å, half times for electron tunneling are expected to be about 10^{-3} sec. When narrower or shorter barriers are considered, higher tunneling probabilities are calculated.

Temperature and Hydration Effects

A quarter of a century ago, Baxter[23] reported that some biological materials follow the operational definition of semiconduction, as in Equation 1. In the intervening period, the conductive properties of many other biological substances have been investigated.[3] These researches often were undertaken to substantiate the applicability of a semiconductive model of a biological function. Therefore, those classes of molecules which best lend themselves to such model building have been investigated most extensively. Electron transfer processes most often involve proteins, making them a logical system to study.

In our laboratory, conductivity and activation energy measurements were made on twice-crystallized hemoglobin pressed at 5,000 pounds per square inch to form a pellet. The pellet was made into a sandwich cell by placing it between metal electrodes. Our findings agree with those of Eley[20] that values of σ_o and E for proteins are independent of the electrode material. In order to investigate the effects of hydration, the sample was equilibrated over an appropriate saturated salt solution in a sealed chamber. Hydrated samples were cycled over the limited temperature range of +25 to −30° C to minimize desorption effects. The apparatus is shown in FIGURE 5.

At a constant temperature, the conductivity of a protein will increase with hydration, as found by King and Medley,[9] Eley and Spivey,[24] and Rosenberg.[25] In the region of hydration, where conductivity is believed to be principally electronic in nature, a good fit to the observed data is provided by:

$$\sigma(m) = \sigma_D \exp(\alpha m) \tag{3}$$

where σ_D is the dry state conductivity, m is the weight % water adsorbed onto the protein, and α is a constant. In the region where ionic contributions to the conductivity are significant, a saturation of conductivity with respect to hydration is observed. This effect is illustrated for two systems, a hydrated phospholipid and a hydrated protein, in FIGURE 6. Results described by Equation 3 were observed for methyl alcohol adsorbed on wool;[23] formic acid adsorbed on keratin;[9] and acetone, trimethylamine and ammonia, each adsorbed on β-carotene.[26]

The operational definition of semiconductivity, Equation 1, is still a valid description of the temperature dependence of the hydrated protein, as is demonstrated in FIGURE 7. However, as the hydration increases, the conductivity increases due to the decreasing value of the activation energy. The preexponential factor in Equation 1 is independent of the hydration state of the protein. Therefore, at any hydration state we may write:

$$\sigma(m, T) = \sigma_0 \exp(-E_H/2kT) \tag{4}$$

The applicability of this equation to the hydrated crystalline hemoglobin system is demonstrated in FIGURE 8, where the log of the relative conductivity at constant temperature is plotted against the activation energy for various hydration states. Equation 4, if plotted in this manner, should exhibit a slope of 1/2kT or 19.7 in this particular case, which compares well with the measured slope of 20.0. To a good first approximation, the only effect of hydration on the conductivity of proteins and other biological substances is to lower the activation energy for semiconduction. The mobility is independent of hydration. We may than combine Equations 1 and 3:

$$\sigma(T, m) = \sigma_0 \exp[-(E_D - \gamma m)/2kT] \tag{5}$$

where now:

$$E_H = E_D - \gamma m; \qquad \text{and} \qquad \gamma = 2kT\alpha \tag{6}$$

E, the activation energy for semiconduction, now depends both on the intrinsic properties of the material as manifest in E_D, and on its hydration state.

Some simple basic concepts of solid state theory may be used to explain these observations. Consider a charge removed from a neutral portion of the protein molecule and placed on a previously neutral portion of another, or a distant portion of the same molecule. If the charge is moved a considerable distance, then the coulomb interaction between charges may be neglected and the charges are essentially free. The energy required for such a process

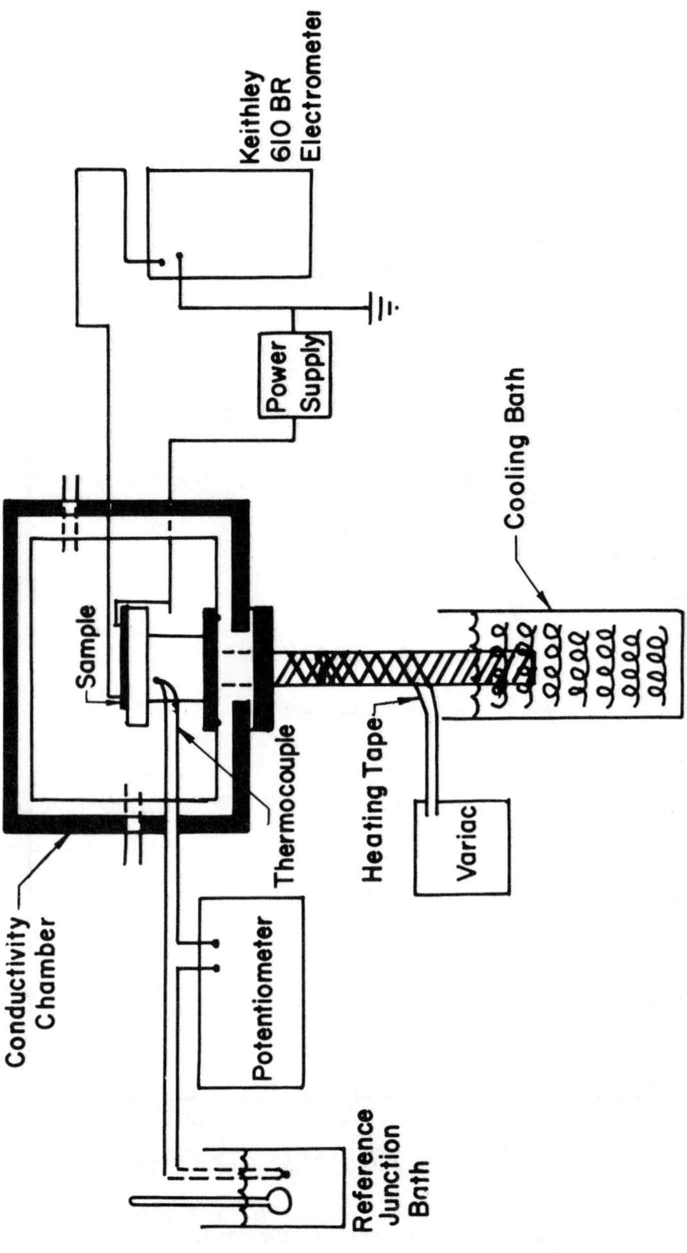

FIGURE 5. The diagram illustrates the apparatus used to make conductivity and activation energy determinations. With the chamber sealed, the sample is equilibrated over an appropriate saturated salt solution. Sample temperature is then cycled over a convenient range.

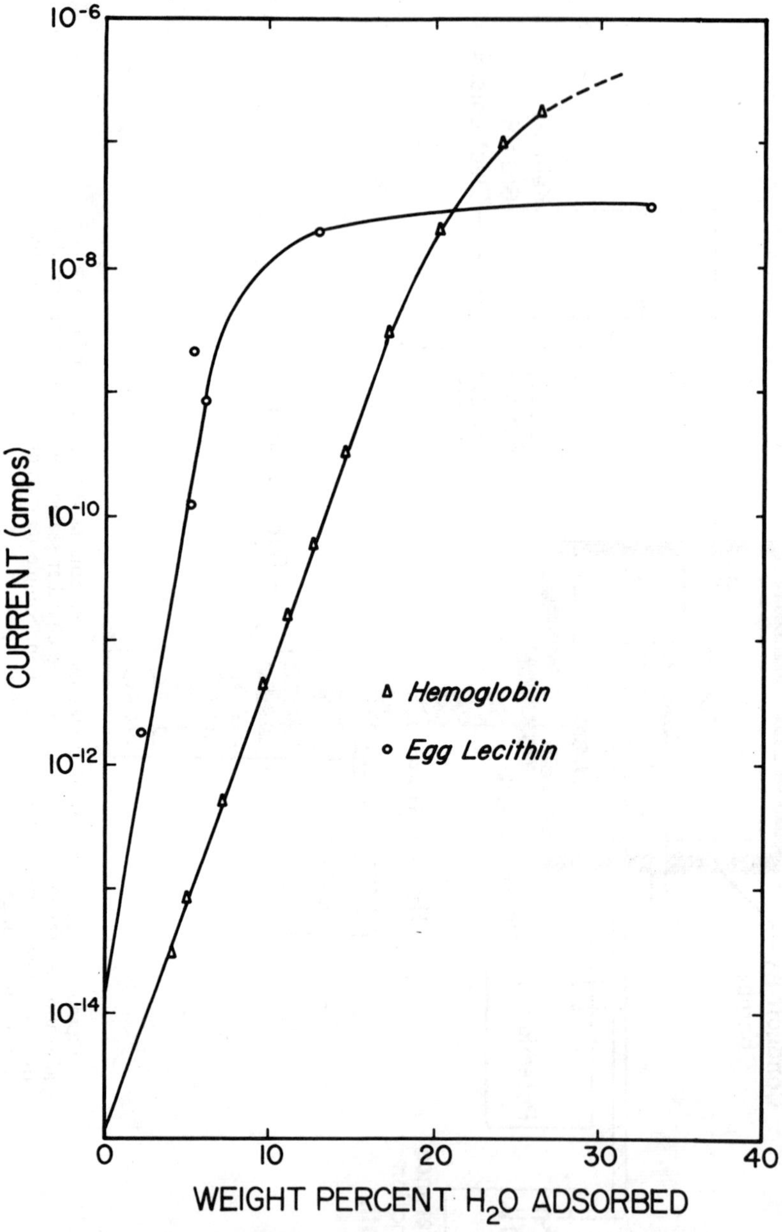

FIGURE 6. The log of the current plotted against the amount of adsorbed water for both a phospholipid and a protein. Saturation of the conductivity is found in the phospholipid and indicated in the protein.

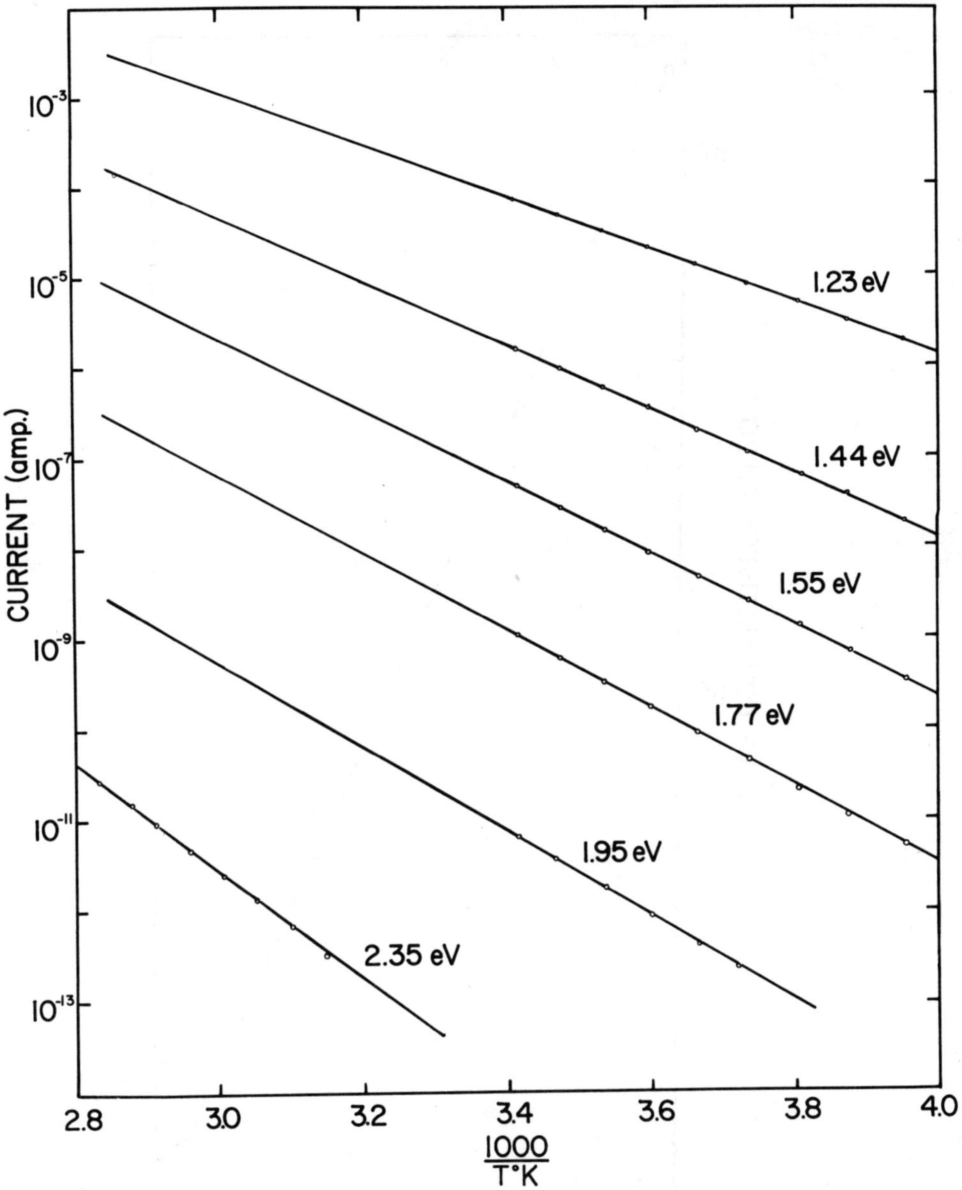

FIGURE 7. The log of the current plotted against 1/T for crystalline hemoglobin in various states of hydration. As the hydration increases the activation energy shows a decrease, but the preexponential factor in Equation 1 remains constant.

may be written as:

$$E = I_g - A_g - 2P \tag{7}$$

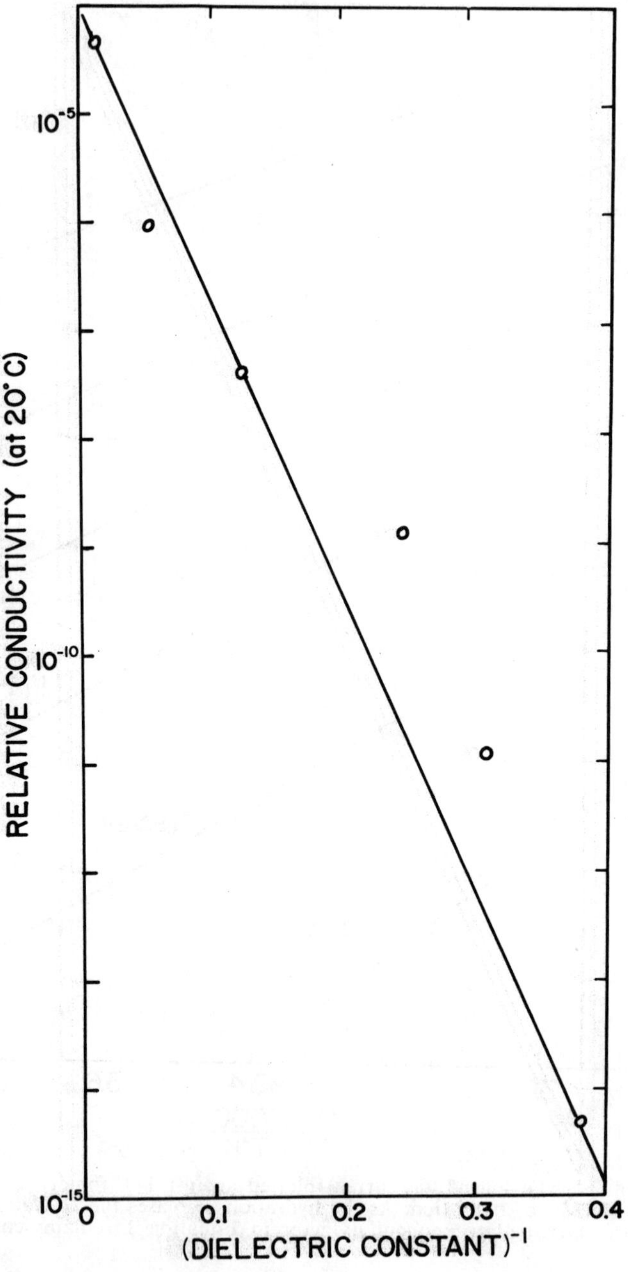

FIGURE 8. The log of the conductivity of hydrated crystalline hemoglobin is plotted against the reciprocal of the low-frequency dielectric constant.

where I_g is the gas state ionization potential of the substance, A_g is the gas state electron affinity, and P is the stabilization due to polarization relaxation at each site of ionization. The polarization stabilization is produced by relaxation of the dielectric media in a spherical region around each of the two newly created charges and is given by:

$$P = \frac{e^2}{2R}(1 - 1/\kappa) \quad (8)$$

where R is the cavity radius of the charged region and κ, the effective dielectric constant (considered as a bulk property) of the dry protein. Combining Equations 7 and 8, we have:

$$E_D = I_g - A_g - \frac{e^2}{R}(1 - 1/\kappa) \quad (9)$$

In the case of a hydrated protein, where the water of hydration increases the effective dielectric constant to a new value κ' ($>\kappa$):

$$E_H = I_g - A_g - \frac{e^2}{R}(1 - 1/\kappa') \quad (10)$$

Since hydration cannot alter either the gas state ionization potential or the gas state electron affinity of the protein, we may eliminate $I_g - A_g$ between Equations 9 and 10, resulting in the following:

$$E_H = E_D - \frac{e^2}{R}\left(\frac{1}{\kappa} - \frac{1}{\kappa'}\right) \quad (11)$$

Comparing this with Equation 6, yields the identity:

$$\gamma M = \frac{e^2}{R}\left(\frac{1}{\kappa} - \frac{1}{\kappa'}\right) \quad (12)$$

Finally, introducing this into Equation 5 yields the result:

$$\sigma(T, \kappa') = \sigma_0 \exp\left(\frac{-E_D}{2kT}\right) \cdot \exp\left[\frac{e^2}{2kTR}\left(\frac{1}{\kappa} - \frac{1}{\kappa'}\right)\right] \quad (13)$$

In this model, the water of hydration increases the conductivity by increasing the effective dielectric constant of the medium, thus decreasing the activation energy for semiconduction.

FIGURE 9 shows the frequency dispersion of the dielectric constant of hemoglobin crystals for various hydration states. There is a monotonic frequency dispersion for both the dielectric constant and the dissipation factor, i.e., both the real and imaginary parts of the complex permittivity of hydrated crystalline hemoglobin. These results agree with those of Maričič and coworkers.[11] More accurate low-frequency measurements are presently underway in our laboratory. Measurements of the dielectric constant of dry crystalline hemoglobin range from 2.7–3.0 Corrections for crystallite packing are made according to Böttcher's[27] method for dielectric constants of powders. Variations in packing, however, exist within a given sample as well as from pellet to pellet. It is believed that these variations cause the uncertainty in the dielectric constant. In the range $30-10^5$ Hz., the frequency dispersion of dry crystalline hemoglobin is very small, as illustrated in FIGURE 9.

Low-frequency values of the dielectric constant are taken as an approxi-

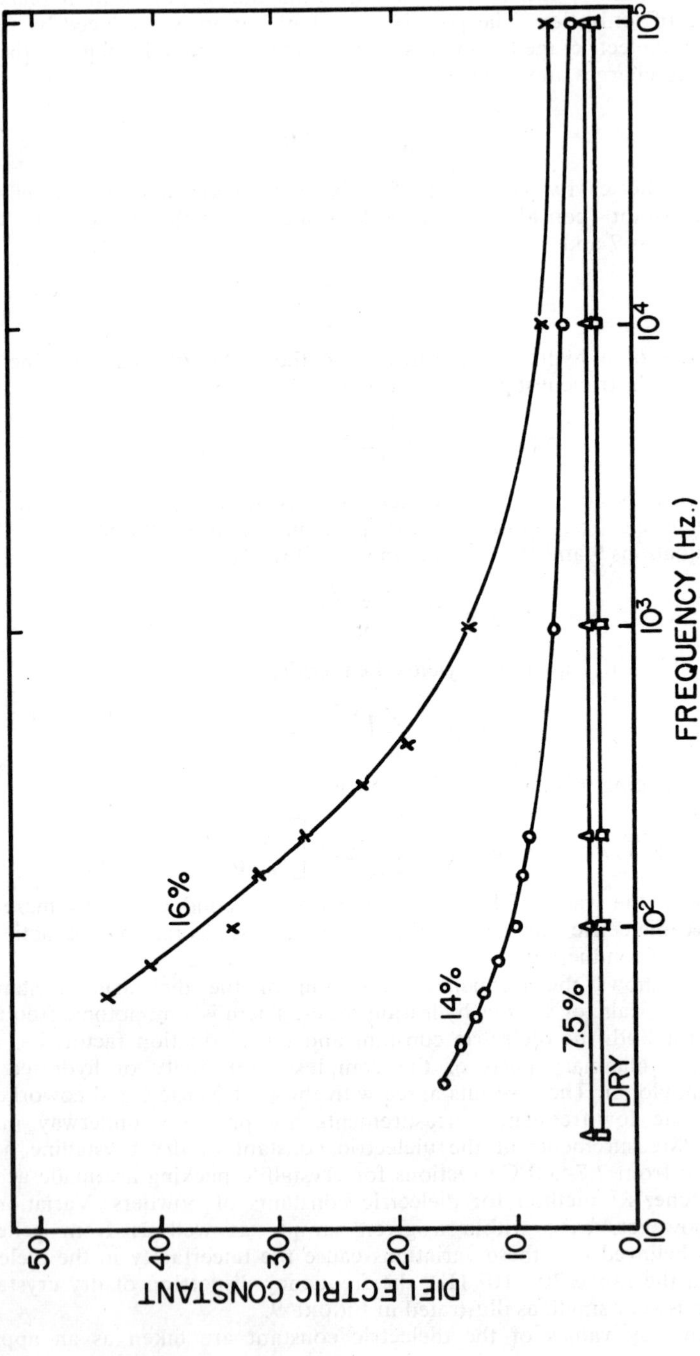

FIGURE 9. The frequency dispersion of the dielectric constant of hydrated crystalline hemoglobin is illustrated over the range 30 — 10^5 Hz. Over this range, the dielectric constant of dry hemoglobin is frequency-insensitive.

mation to the DC state. The good approximation to linearity obtained when the log of the conductivity is plotted against the inverse of the low-frequency dielectric constant for various hydration states (FIGURE 10) serves to verify Equation 13.

We have observed saturation of conductivity with increasing hydration at room temperature after it has increased by a factor of about 10^{11}. When the protein is fully hydrated, the dielectric constant is very large, and $1/\kappa \gg 1/\kappa'$. Therefore we have:

$$10^{11} = \frac{\sigma(\text{fully hydrated})}{\sigma(\text{dry})} = \exp\,(e^2/2kTR\kappa) \qquad \textbf{(14)}$$

Since dry hemoglobin crystals have a dielectric constant of about 3, Equation 14 gives a value of 3.6×10^{-8} cm. for the cavity radius, R. This is a very reasonable value. We can now evaluate $I_g - A_g$ by substituting this value of R and the measured dielectric constant, κ, of dry hemoglobin crystals in Equation 9:

$$I_g - A_g = 2.36\text{ eV} + \frac{e^2}{R}\left(1 - \frac{1}{\kappa}\right) = 4.9\text{ eV} \qquad \textbf{(15)}$$

Since the value of $I_g - A_g$ is known from Equation 15, we can solve the equations for the lowest value of the activation energy to be expected when hydration increases. This will correspond to the activation energy when current saturation has occurred. This occurs when $1/\kappa' << 1/\kappa$, and therefore we have:

$$E_{min} = E_D - \frac{e^2}{R\kappa} = 2.36 - 1.27 = 1.09\text{ eV} \qquad \textbf{(16)}$$

This value of about 1.1 eV agrees very well with the minimum value measured.

Comparison of Theory and Experiment

A number of theoretical calculations have been made to evaluate the possible band structure of energy levels in proteins. In all cases, the protein is treated as a repeating structure linked by hydrogen bonds across the peptide chains. The π electrons are delocalized across the hydrogen bonds. This is essentially the method of Evans and Gergely[28] who used a Hückel LCAO molecular orbital scheme. This method was modified by Yomosa[29] to extend this to an HMO SCF and ASMO SCF calculation. A further modification of Suard and collaborators[30] was made to include the oxygen lone-pair electrons as well. Suard-Sender[4] extended the calculation to an infinite two-dimensional network. Using the results of this latter calculation, a semiconductivity band gap of about 5 eV was calculated (as compared to 3 eV from the Evans and Gergely calculation). It was stated that this is too large a band gap for intrinsic electronic conductivity to be significant and, therefore, measured band gaps of 2.4 eV must refer to some extrinsic processes.

In Equation 15, we calculated a value of about 5 eV for the ionization energy minus the electron affinity for the protein. It is difficult to specify exactly what this means; presumably, it refers to vertical ionization and electron attachment processes in a small isolated polypeptide region of the protein.

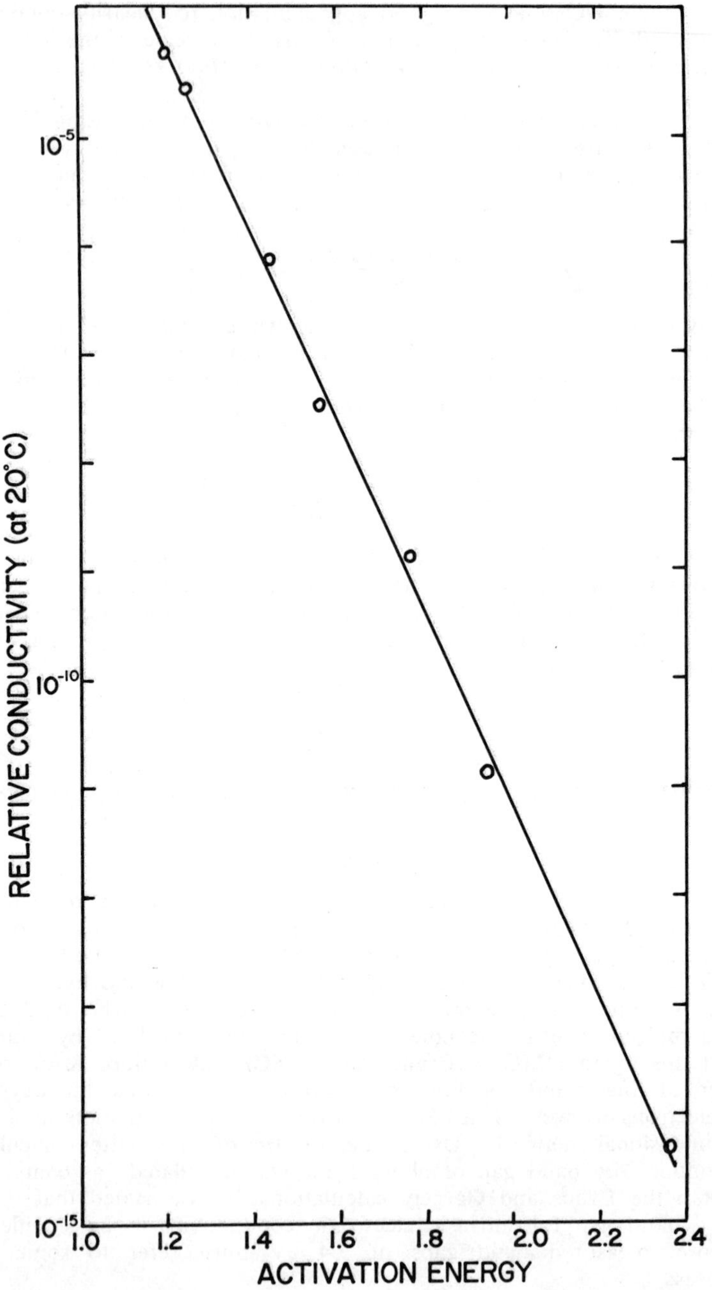

FIGURE 10. The log of the conductivity of hydrated crystalline hemoglobin, at constant temperature, is plotted against the activation energy. The slope of the line (1/2kT) should be 19.7, the experimental slope is 20.0.

This corresponds to the general usage of I_g and A_g as the gas values of a molecule. Considering an isolated amide group, Simpson[31a] has estimated that the ionization potential (I_g) is 8.5 eV, and that electron affinities are usually about 1-2 eV. This value of I_g is close to the reported I_g values[31b] for N,N-diethylacetamide (8.60 eV) and N-methylacetamide (8.9 eV), which we believe more closely resembles a peptide bond than formamide (10.25 eV). Suard and coworkers specified their expectation that, in going from a monopeptide linkage to a polypeptide linkage, the value of I_g would decrease by 1 eV and A_g would increase by about 0.6 eV. From these rough estimates, we can calculate a value for $(I_g - A_g)_{Protein}$ as 4.9 — 5.9 eV, which is in reasonable agreement with our value of 5 eV.

From band-theory we expect the semiconduction band gap, E, to be equal to $I_c - A_c$, where I_c and A_c are the solid state values of the ionization energies and electron affinities. The difference between the gas values and the solid state values are due to the polarization stabilization energy, P, arising from relaxation of the lattice around the new charge centers. Thus $I_c = I_g - P$, and $A_c = A_g + P$, and we have $E = I_c - A_c = I_g - A_g - 2P$ (as in our Equation 7).

Regarding quantum calculations, we quote M. Kasha,[32] "The fact that these are inherently vapor state calculations, with solvation effects neglected, is a worrisome point." The calculations of Evans and Gergely, Yomosa, Suard and coworkers and Suard-Sender do not explicitly take into account the polarization of the medium when charges are separated. In essence, their calculations are for a medium of dielectric constant 1, while our experiments are done in a medium with a dry-state dielectric constant of 3. This suggests that the value of 5 eV calculated by Suard-Sender should be compared to our value of $I_g - A_g$, and that when a proper accounting is made of the dielectric constant of the medium, the discrepancies between theory and experiment disappear.

If this suggestion is verified by further theoretical analysis, two results of value accrue: First, Dr. Szent-Györgyi was correct in 1941 and not in 1959; and second, we have a good piece of evidence, in the agreement between theory and experiment, that the experimentalists are indeed measuring intrinsic electron conductivity processes in proteins.

However, there are a number of points of difficulty to be considered. For example, there is still an element of ambiguity in this approach in that if one places an electron in the conduction band and leaves a positive hole behind, then, depending on the velocity of the charge carrier, it may be that P instead of 2P should appear in Equation 7. In this case, the only thing that would change in our development is the value of R, which will change from 3.6×10^{-8} cm to 1.8×10^{-8} cm.

A second point is that it is very questionable that band theory can be applied to protein semiconduction. Measurements of mobility are essential to decide this point.

A third difficulty is that as far as optical transitions are concerned, the Suard and coworkers theory is unchanged: that is, one does not expect an optical transition at 2.4 eV (or even lower energies for hydrated proteins) which is the measured band gap. Thus, we are led to the curious prediction that the exciton states of a protein lie at a higher energy than the conducting states. Although this seems to be the prevalent case in organic crystals, it is a point of controversy at the present time.

Conductivity of Lipids

As indicated above, similar results have been obtained for a host of other adsorbed gases and with other substrates.

It was first shown in 1961[33] that the semiconduction activation energy of β-carotene crystals was decreased when O_2 molecules were adsorbed on the crystallites. This decreased activation energy was exactly enough to account for the increased conductivity of the β-carotene in an O_2 atmosphere. This effect is reversible, as is the case of the hydration effects on proteins, and the binding energy of the O_2-carotene complex was evaluated as 0.17 eV. More recent work by Cherry and Chapman[34] has shown that a number of other gases when adsorbed on single crystals of β-carotene at 70° C increase the conductivity by factors of 2–50. Misra and collaborators[26] have shown in powder cells of β-carotene that vapors of methanol, propanol, acetone, trimethylamine, and oxygen, when adsorbed at room temperature and below, cause changes in conductivity of several orders of magnitude, and that these increments are consistent with measured changes in the activation energy, according to Equation 5. Again, σ_0 is found to be independent of both the quantity and variety of the adsorbed gas. In the two cases where low-frequency dielectric constants of the bulk system were measured, values of the activation energy were predicted with the aid of Equation 11. The calculated values of 1.25 eV and 0.78 eV compare favorably with the measured values of 1.25 eV and 0.74 eV for adsorbed oxygen and methanol, respectively. Misra and coworkers suggest that the increased dielectric constant may be the result of a donor-acceptor complex formed between the β-carotene and the adsorbed gas in which the partially dative ground state (D^+A^-) may contribute to the dipole moment. The adsorbed gas may, however, alter the polarizability of the system in some unknown manner, which would also serve to increase the dielectric constant.

The hypothesis that donor-acceptor complexes form between the adsorbed gas molecules and the carotenoid molecules, while logical, lacks independent experimental verification. Evidence for the appearance of spectral charge-transfer bands is still lacking.[35]

Leslie and collaborators[36] were the first to demonstrate the semiconductive properties of a variety of dry lipids. Anomalies in the conductivity results with temperature changes were attributed to phase transitions in the lipid. Rosenberg and Jendrasiak[37] have demonstrated semiconductive behavior in films (10–100 μ thick) of synthetic lecithin, egg lecithin, cholesterol and some cholesterol esters. Hydration of these films produced current increments of up to 10^{11} times the dry state values, and concomitant decreases in the activation energies. The dielectric constants of these materials were also observed to show the same large increase with hydration as did the proteins, and similar dispersion curves. Films of these substances exposed to iodine vapor were observed to follow the same pattern of increased conductivity, decreased activation energy and increased dielectric constant. Figure 11 illustrates the increased capacitance caused by adsorbed water or iodine in lecithin. It now appears that the effects of both water and iodine can be explained by the same basic solid state mechanism outlined above. In this instance, however, spectroscopic evidence of Bhowmik and coworkers[38] demonstrated the formation of donor-acceptor complexes between iodine and the lecithins, or cholesterol. The donor-acceptor complex serves to increase the effective dielectric constant of the bulk, which is then manifested in the increased conductivity and decreased activation energy.

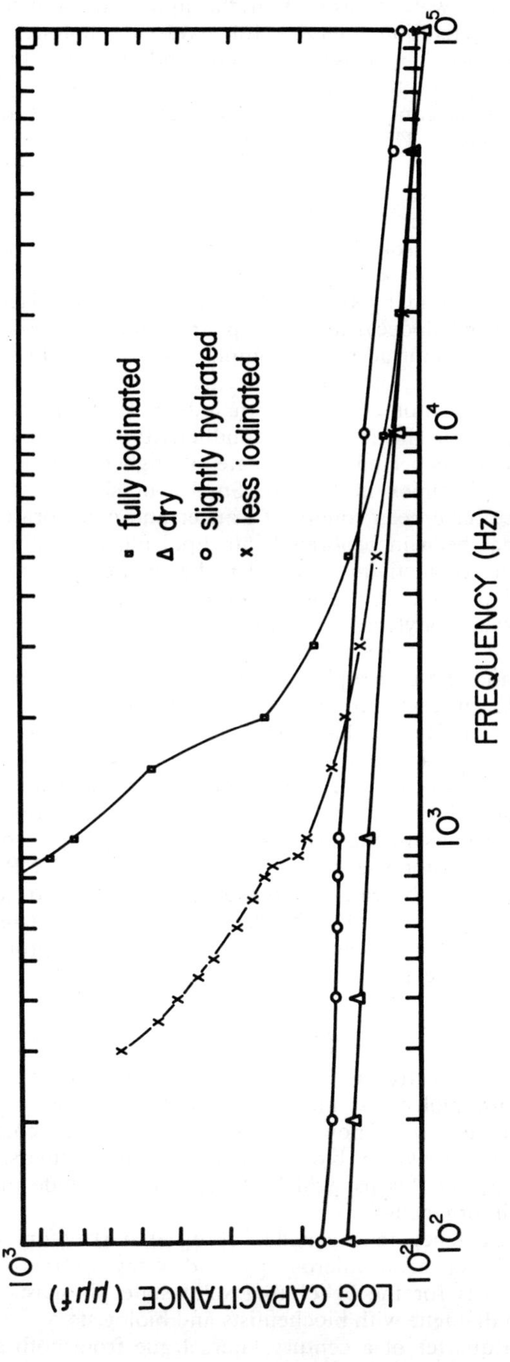

FIGURE 11. The log of the capacitance of egg lecithin with water or iodine adsorbed is plotted against the frequency.

The conductive properties of lipid bilayers, (70–100A thick) spread across a hole in a teflon cup, were measured in the apparatus shown in FIGURE 12. Bhowmik[39] found activation energies for oxidized cholesterol lipid bilayers similar to those reported by Rosenberg and Jendrasiak for the hydrated bulk lipid. The conductivity of the bilayer, however, is smaller by 10^6 than would be expected if the bulk conductance value of the film were extrapolated to the geometry of the bilayer. This result is still unexplained. Also, when iodine is added to one side of the bilayer, the conductivity increases by 4–5 orders of magnitude, and the activation energy decreases as expected. An asymmetric effect would be predicted if the iodine served to mediate the change from ionic conductivity in the solution to electronic conductivity in the bilayer by the injection of electronic charge carriers at the interface. Such an asymmetry could not be found by us, but has been found by Tien[40] in a bilayer film of cholesterol and dodecyl acid phosphate. The spectroscopic evidence of the formation of a donor-acceptor complex between iodine and the lipids strongly suggests that the conductivity of the bilayer is increased by the formation of a donor-acceptor complex with iodine. If the mechanism discussed above is responsible for the increased conductivity, then an increased bilayer capacitance would be expected in the state of higher conductivity, i.e., when the donor-acceptor complex is formed. Small but significant changes in the bilayer capacitance have been found by Läuger and collaborators.[41]

Beta-carotene has been incorporated into lipid bilayers by Leslie and Chapman.[42] The bilayer conductivity is found to be unaltered by the incorporation of the carotenoid pigment. Uncouplers of oxidative phosphorylation such as p-trifluoro-methoxycarbonylcyanidephenylhydrazone (FCCPO), m-chlorocarbonylcyanidephenyl-hydrazone (CICCP), tetrachloro-2-trifluoromethylbenzimidazol (TFB) and 2,4-dinitrophenol (DNP) recently have been shown by Skulachev and coworkers[43] to increase the conductivity of brain phospholipid bilayers. They postulate that this is a result of increased protonic conductivity, which is consistent with Mitchel's[44] hypothesis of the mechanism of action of uncouplers of oxidative phosphorylation. Bhowmik,[39] however, has found a conductance increase and a decrease in the activation energy of oxidized cholesterol bilayers in the presence of DNP, and spectroscopic evidence of the formation of a donor-acceptor complex between DNP and the lipids. This again suggests that the cause of the observed decreased activation energy and increased conductivity is by the same mechanism discussed above. Increases in the conductivity were found to be linearly proportional to the concentration of undissociated DNP.

Speculations on Semiconductive Models for Biological Systems

The transport of electronic charge carriers over large distances in biologically important molecules, membranes and organelles may play a functional role in biology. It is now certain that electronic charges can move through at least a number of biochemicals and biopolymers. Evidence now exists for believing that this list will be extended to include membrane model systems and certain organelles.

The extensive existence in organelles of ordered structure on a molecular level, as shown in electron microscopy and x-ray diffraction studies, provides a physical basis for the belief that solid state physicists may say something of value in a dialogue with biochemists and biologists.

We can now, a quarter of a century later, argue from both an experimental

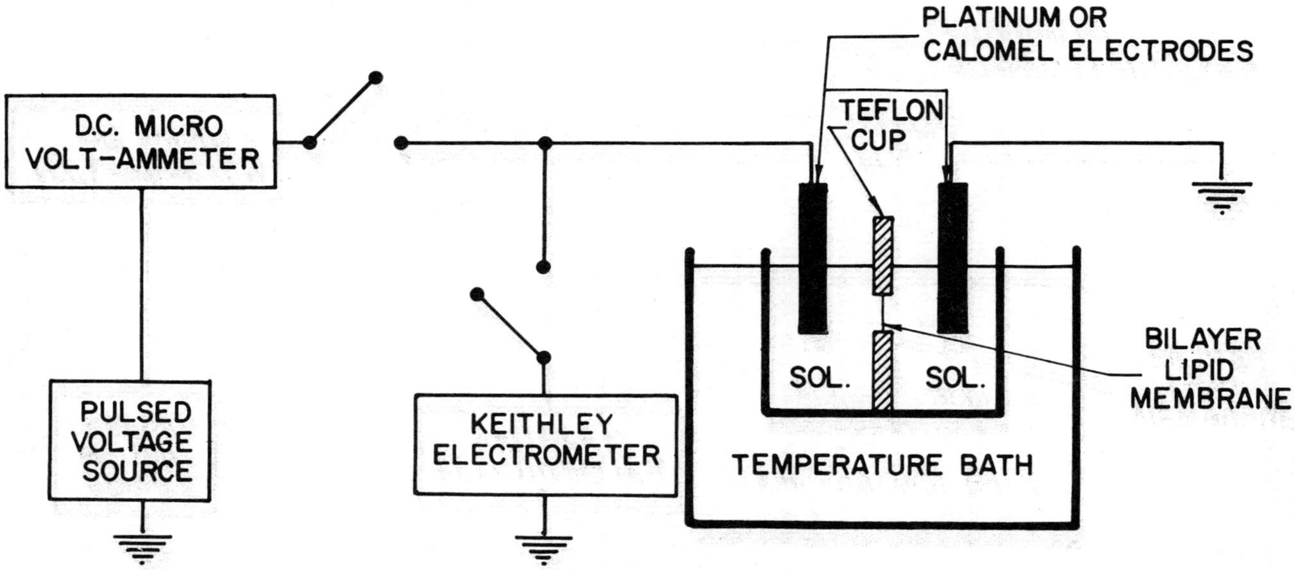

FIGURE 12. The apparatus used to make electrical measurements of lipid bilayers is illustrated. Either platinum (at currents $<10^{-7}$ amp) or calomel electrodes were employed.

and a theoretical viewpoint that Szent-Györgyi's curious (for 1941) suggestion of conduction bands in protein systems was quite correct. But we are in the even more curious position of being unable, in any single case, to prove the relevancy of this to biology. Since biologists in the main are conservative, it will require very forceful proof to allow them to accept such exotic mechanisms. Recognition of this necessity has forced a number of us to put forward at least tentative hypotheses concerning where, in biology, we think semiconduction is relevant. We shall briefly discuss four such cases.

Lipid Bilayers as a Model System for Cellular Membranes

Since the hypothesis of Danielli and Davson that a cellular membrane consists of a bimolecular layer of lipid coated on both sides with protein, attempts have been made to construct model systems suitable for laboratory manipulation. The most satisfying system is that of Mueller and collaborators.[45] A black lipid membrane of 50–100A thick may be formed in an aperture separating two solutions by slow dissolution of the lipid solvent painted over the hole. The membrane is surprisingly stable and is suitably arranged for optical or electrical measurements. The conductivity of such membranes is very low but, as mentioned above, it may be increased by a number of chemical additions to the solutions. This area has recently been reviewed by Tien and Diana.[46]

The point of interest we should like to emphasize is the nature of the charge carrier in the membrane. No experiment has yet been done which unambiguously identifies the dominant charge carriers in such bilayers. It is known that ions have some mobility in the membranes, for one can measure concentration potentials across the membrane. It is not known if these ions move through the intact membrane or through pores—either structurally stable or ephemeral—in the membrane. We have suggested that electronic charge carriers also have a reasonable density and mobility in these membranes, based upon the following indirect argument: iodine forms donor-acceptor complexes with these membranes; this D–A complex increases the conductivity and decreases the activation energy for semiconduction in bulk films; the D–A complex increases the conductivity and decreases the activation energy in lipid bilayers; and finally, all D–A complexes in which the nature of the charge carriers has been determined are known to be predominantly electronic semiconductors.

If, therefore, both ions and electrons can carry current through a bilayer, the remaining task is to evaluate the mobilities and the densities of each charge carrier to determine their relative significance. One such test might be as follows: If the membrane is permeable to an ion in the bathing solution, it can traverse the membrane with no necessity for an electrode reaction at the solution-membrane interface. If the dominant charge carriers in the membrane are electronic, then, since water solutions normally have an extremely small density of such charge carriers, there must be an electrode reaction at the interface injecting electrons and/or positive holes into the membrane. We are at present attempting to detect such an electrode reaction in our laboratory.

A Photoconductive Theory of the Visual Receptor Mechanism

The visual pigments which absorb the incoming light photons are found in the highly organized lamellar structures of the outer segments of rods and cones. The processes intervening between the absorption act and the depolarization (or hyperpolarization) of a neural membrane are not known. Photoisomerization of the retinal chromophoric group attached to the protein moiety of the pigment occurs with a quantum efficiency of about 0.5. Other processes to account for the other 50% of the excitation are largely conjectural. The relevance of photoisomerization and the succeeding dark chemical processes to the initiation of the nervous signal is also largely conjectural.

It has been proposed[47] that photoexcitation leads to the generation of a free charge carrier (electronic). This charge carrier is injected from the chromophore region into the protein, and drifts in the electric field direction or, at high light intensities, in a concentration gradient of charge carriers, and therefore constitutes a current (either photoconductive or photovoltaic). This current can change the potential across a neural membrane some distance away and initiate the depolarization (or hyperpolarization) of the membrane. Simplicity is the major value of this theory, since there are no intervening chemical events between excitation and charge carrier production. The ramifications of this physical approach have been reviewed recently.[48] The theory requires a direct electrical event (possibly of a biphasic nature) to occur in the outer segments of the receptor cells. Such events have been detected in recent years and are described as early receptor potentials (ERP)[49] and as photoelectric potentials (PEP).[50] However, verification of a prediction does not prove the precedent logic, but only indicates consistency, and a number of other somewhat ad hoc explanations of the ERP have now been proposed. None of these, however, has as yet received general acceptance. However, the integrity of the lamellar structure is known to be necessary for the appearance of the signals.

Photoconductivity and semiconductivity have now been shown to be quite general properties of carotenes; retinals; protonated retinal-Schiff base complexes; protonated retinal-enamine salt complexes; and extracted, dried rods of sheep eyes. Again, however, the relevancy of these properties to the biological photoreceptor process has not been proven.

One of the major successes of this theory has been an elucidation of a particularly simple model for the generation of the chromatic "S" potentials of color vision. A simple cell of a carotenoid pigment with a small DC voltage ($\sim$ 100 millivolts) across it is used, so that both photoconductive and photovoltaic effects of the same magnitude can occur. This reproduces, wavelength for wavelength, the complex biphasic signals reported by Svaetichin and MacNichol[51] for any given receptor type in fish retina.

Some years earlier, Arnold and Sherwood[52] had suggested a similar solid state photoconductive model for the chloroplast grana in the photosynthetic apparatus. Absorption of light by the ordered array of chlorophyll could generate free electrons and holes, which move independently of each other to different trapping sites where the dark chemistry is initiated, since these charge carriers are effective oxidizing and reducing entities.

A Semiconductive Mechanism for Olfactory Transduction

We have described above experimental results which indicate that gases may be adsorbed on the surfaces of β-carotene crystals and lead to marked changes in the effective dielectric constant, decreases in the activation energy for semiconduction, and increases in the conductivity. The interaction between the gas and the carotenoid molecules is postulated to be a weakly bound (binding energy, about 0.17 eV) donor-acceptor complex, and is, therefore, a reversible system. This phenomenon appears to have all the characteristics required for a model of olfactory transduction. Since carotenoids are known to be present in the olfactory patch (though the exact location is still in question), the following theory has been proposed[53]: (1) The pigment molecules in the olfactory receptors constitute the receptor sites. (2) These pigments exist to some degree in the limiting resistance membrane of the receptor cells. (3) The odorous molecules, when adsorbed on the receptor site, form weakly bound complexes (possibly donor-acceptor complexes) with the pigment molecule. (4) The conductivity of the membrane increases, due to an increase in the equilibrium number of charge carriers resulting from the D–A complex. (5) This increase in conductivity is an amplifying process, and leads to the depolarization of the membrane resulting in signal generation. (6) The D–A complexes are weakly coupled and break up, leading to the desorption of the gas molecule when the partial pressure of such molecules in the ambient atmosphere decreases. (7) The nature of the D–A complex determines the amount of increase in conductance and, therefore, the threshhold sensitivity to the odorous molecule. (8) The odorous molecule may form different strength D–A complexes with the different pigments of the various receptor types, and the resulting complex of signals defines the odor quality of that molecule. (9) Such D–A complexes may form to a lesser degree between some molecules and the phospholipid constituents of an unpigmented membrane (viz., the trigeminal nerve ending) and produce similar, though weaker, signals through the same mechanism.

We have tested the effects of some 26 gases on the conductivity of β-carotene. The results show that gases with no odor, or weak odor, cause no or little change in the conductivity. Gases with moderate odors cause a current increment of $10^2 - 10^3$; and gases with strong odors, with the exception of the esters, all cause large current increments ($10^4 - 10^7$) in the conductivity. Odorous esters, such as methyl or ethyl acetate, produce very small changes in the conductivity of β-carotene, but produce large changes (10^5) in vitamin A alcohol. Thus vitamin A, but not β-carotene, is sensitive to the esters, and a first example of differential sensitivity has been discovered. The theory rigorously requires that no gas with weak odor produce large changes in β-carotene conductivity. So far, this has been borne out in practice. If such a gas is found, this would be the strongest evidence that the theory is wrong.

Another feature of the experimental tests is the appearance of a fatigue effect in the conduction with gases such as NH_3 and H_2S. In these cases, the current may increase by a factor of 10^5 upon initial exposure of the β-carotene to the gas, and then slowly decrease with time to a final increment of only about a factor of 10. Repeated desorption and reexposure only reproduces this last value, unless adequate time is allowed for the cell to recover completely. An explanation in terms of two states of interaction between the gas and the carotene has been proposed, and experimental evidence in favor of this explanation has been derived. This effect may be of significance to fatigue effects in olfaction.

Intramolecular Electronic Conductivity as a Model of Enzymatic Activity

Several enzymes catalyze reactions which involve the transfer of an electron. It has been suggested that the protein molecule may act as the path of the electronic charge carrier between the site of reduction and the site of oxidation.

Calculations employing the conductivity parameters of dry hemoglobin were made by Cardew and Eley.[54] For a sea urchin egg, the respiration rate would be equivalent to a current of 1.68×10^{-10} amps. Assuming a redox driving potential of 1 volt, their calculation on a single fiber 50Å in diameter by 1 micron long leads to the prediction that the dry current value would be too small by a factor of 10^{16}. Also, the activation energy would be 1.4 eV as compared to the activation energy for respiration of 0.48 eV.

We should like to amend this calculation to take into account the hydrated conductivity and activation energy reported above. Assuming that the diameter of a cytochrome c molecule is 25Å, the length 36A, a 1 volt redox potential across the molecule, and the resistivity value of 10^8 (calculated from our hydrated hemoglobin data), we calculate a current per molecule of 10^{-15} amps. This corresponds to a maximum turnover rate of 10^4 electrons/sec, as compared to the 30 electrons/sec typical of cytochrome c. It would require at least 10^5 cytochrome molecules per cell to account for the total respiration rate. This appears to be a reasonable number. Using the activation energy of 1.1 eV (on a 1/2kT basis), we would predict an activation energy (on a 1/kT basis) of 0.55 eV. This compares favorably with the measured value of 0.48 eV. Thus, we conclude that the assumption of electronic conductivity in a protein molecule as the rate limiting step in electron transfer processes is entirely consistent with the biological data.

Cope[55] has examined the kinetics of electronic conduction through a particulate enzyme system. The kinetics predicted by this model are of the same form as observed in the cytochrome oxidase system.

Anomalous Arrhenius plots of enzymatic activity have recently been reported in several different enzymes.[56-59] In different enzymes, the transition temperature ranges from 13° C–24° C. Activation energies calculated at temperatures above the transition are in all cases smaller than those calculated below the transition temperature. If we hypothesize the rate limiting step of enzymatic activity (in these several cases) to be intramolecular electronic conduction, then the rate of enzymic activity will be proportional to the conductivity. Equation 1 may then be used to interpret the extant data producing the values shown in TABLE 2. These activation energy values are

TABLE 2

ACTIVATION ENERGIES (1/2kT BASIS) CALCULATED FROM ARRHENIUS PLOTS OF MAXIMUM TURNOVER RATES FOR ENZYMES SHOWING CONFIGURATIONAL TRANSITIONS

Enzyme	Transition Temperature	E(low temp.)	E(high temp.)	Reference
Myosin	16° C	2.1 eV	1.1 eV	56
D-amino acid oxidase (d-alamine substrate)	14°	1.5	0.9	57
D-amino acid oxidase (D-methione substrate)	24°	2.1	1.1	57
Glycogen phosphorylase b	13°	4.0(?)	1.6	58
Rabbit muscle pyruvate kinase (pH 7.8)	14°	1.7	1.0	59

similar to those we would expect for dry (or partially hydrated) and hydrated protein, respectively. Optical rotatory dispersion, ultraviolet difference spectra, fluorescence studies, and visible spectra all indicate the occurence of a conformational change at the same transition temperature.[57, 59] This conformational change may so alter one portion of the protein (site A in FIGURE 13) that it permits extensive hydration in one configuration while

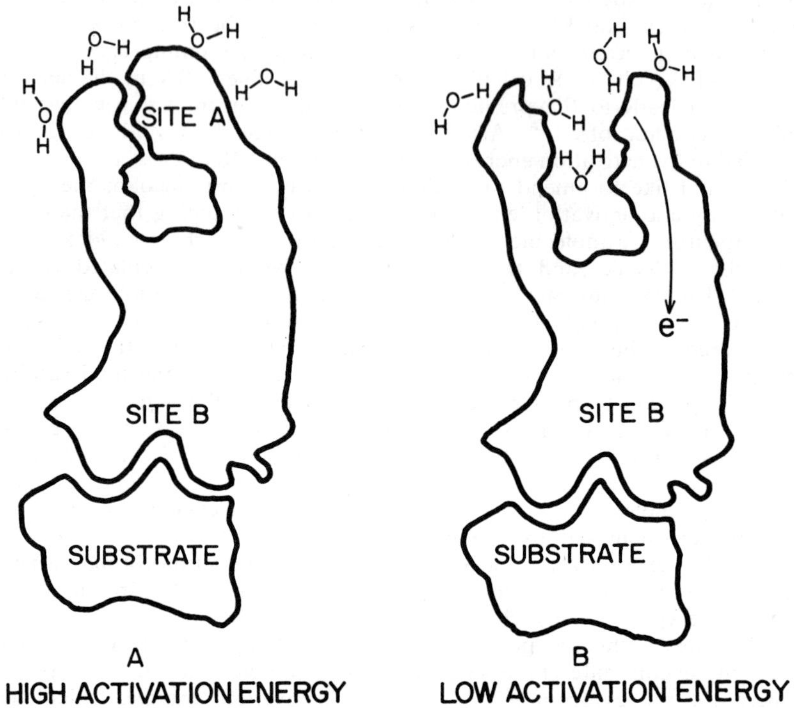

FIGURE 13. The diagram illustrates the semiconduction model of enzyme activity. When site A is in a hydrophobic environment, the activation energy for semiconduction will be high. If the protein conformation changes so that site A is placed in a hydrophilic environment, the activation energy for semiconduction will be lowered.

demanding a hydrophobic environment in the other conformation. When site A is in a hydrophobic environment, the activation energy for semiconduction is high. In a hydrophilic environment, after the conformational change, the activation energy will be greatly diminished.

REFERENCES

1. SZENT-GYÖRGYI, A. 1941. Towards a New Biochemistry? Science **93:** 609–611.
2. SZENT-GYÖRGYI, A. 1941. The Study of Energy Levels in Biochemistry. Nature **148:** 157–159.
3. GUTMANN, F. & L. E. LYONS. 1967. Organic Semiconductors. John Wiley & Sons. New York, N. Y.
4. SUARD-SENDER, M. 1965. Étude Théorique de la Délocalisation Électronique dans les Systemes Polypeptidiques I, II. J. Chim. Phys. **62:** 79–88, 89–98.
5. ELEY, D. D. & R. B. LESLIE. 1963. Adsorption of Water on Solid Proteins with Special Reference to Haemoglobin. *In* Structure and Properties of Biomolecules: 238–258. J. Duchesne, Ed. John Wiley & Sons. New York, N. Y.
6. ROSENBERG, B. 1962. Electrical Conductivity in Proteins. Nature **193:** 364–365.
7. MARIČIČ, S., G. PIFAT & V. PRAVDIČ. 1964. Proton Conduction in the Solid Hydrated Haemoglobin. Biochim. Biophys. Acta **79:** 293–299.
8. REIHL, N. 1957. Zum Zusammenhang zwischen Elektrischer Leitfähigkeit und Engergiewanderung in Proteinen. Kolloid Z. **151:** 66–72.
9. KING, G. & J. A. MEDLEY. 1949. The Influence of Temperature and Adsorbed

Salts on the D. C. Conductivity of Polar Polymer Adsorbate Systems. J. Colloid Sci. **4:** 9–18.
10. ROSENBERG, B. 1964. Preliminary Experiments to Determine the Nature of the Charge Carriers in the Electrical Conductivity of Wet Protein Crystals. Biopolymers Sympos. No. 1: 453–463.
11. MARIČIČ, S., G. PIFAT & V. PRAVDIČ. 1964. Hydration of Haemoglobin and its Reversible Oxygenation. Ber. Bunsenges. Physik. Chem. **68:** 787–793.
12. ROSEN, D. 1963. Dielectric Properties of Protein Powders with Adsorbed Water. Trans. Faraday Soc. **59:** 2178–2191.
13. GUTMANN, F. & L. E. LYONS. 1967. Organic Semiconductors: 123. John Wiley & Sons. New York, N. Y.
14. FOLBERTH, O. G. 1955. Mischkristallbildung bei $A^{III}B^{V}$-Verbindungen. Z. Naturforsch. **10a:** 502–503.
15. LARACH, S., R. E. SCHRODER & C. F. STOCKER. 1957. Anomalous Variation of Band Gap with Composition in Zinc Sulfo- and Seleno-Tellurides. Phys. Rev. **108:** 587–589.
16. TRUKHAN, E. M. 1966. Determination of the Mobility of Free Charged Carriers in Biological Compounds. Biofizika **11:** 412–419. Biophysics. **11:** 468–477.
17. JENDRASIAK, G. L., R. LEFFLER & B. ROSENBERG. 1967. Unpublished data.
18. HERMANN, A. M. & A. REMBAUM. 1967. Spin Resonance, Hall Effect and Transport Properties of Poly (N-vinyl-carbazole)—Iodine Complex. J. Polymer Sci. (C) **17:** 107–123.
19. HERMANN, A. M. & J. S. HAM. 1965. Apparatus for the Measurement of the Hall Effect in Semiconduction of Low Mobility and High Resistivity. Rev. Sci. Instrum. **36:** 1553–1555.
20. ELEY, D. D. 1967. Energy Gap and Pre-Exponential Factor in Dark Conduction by Organic Semiconductors. J. Polymer Sci. (C) **17:** 73–91.
21. GLARUM, S. H. 1963. Electron Mobilities in Organic Semiconductors. J. Phys. Chem. Solids. **24:** 1577–1583.
22. DEVAULT, D., J. H. PARKER & B. CHANCE. 1967. Electron Tunnelling in Cytochromes. Nature **215:** 642–644.
23. BAXTER, S. 1943. Electrical Conduction of Textiles. Trans. Faraday Soc. **39:** 207–214.
24. ELEY, D. D. & D. I. SPIVEY. 1960. Semiconductivity in Hydrated Haemoglobin. Nature **188:** 725.
25. ROSENBERG, B. 1962. Electrical Conductivity in Proteins. II. Semiconduction in Crystalline Bovine Hemoglobin. J. Chem. Phys. **36:** 816–823.
26. MISRA, T. N., B. ROSENBERG & R. SWITZER. 1968. The Effect of Adsorption of Gases on the Semiconductivity of All-Trans β-carotene. J. Chem. Phys. **48:** 2096.
27. BÖTTCHER, C. J. F. 1952. Theory of Electric Polarisation: 417 Elsevier. New York, N. Y.
28. EVANS, M. G. & J. GERGELY. 1949. A Discussion of the Possibility of Bands of Energy Levels in Proteins. Biochim. Biophys. Acta. **3:** 188–197.
29. YOMOSA, S. 1964. π Electronic Structure of Peptide Group and Hydrogen-Bonded Polypeptides. Biopolymers Sympos. No. 1: 1–34.
30. SUARD, M., G. BERTHIER & B. PULLMAN. 1961. Sur les États Électroniques des Protéins. Biochim. Biophys. Acta **52:** 254–265.
31a. SIMPSON, W. T. 1964. *In* Physical Processes in Radiation Biology. L. G. Augenstein, R. Mason & B. Rosenberg, Eds.: 125. Academic Press. New York, N. Y.
31b. GUTMANN, F. & L. E. LYONS. 1967. Organic Semiconductors: 675–676. John Wiley & Sons. New York, N. Y.
32. KASHA, M. 1962. Quantum Chemistry in Molecular Biology. *In* Horizons in Biochemistry. M. Kasha and B. Pullman, Eds.: 597 Academic Press, New York, N. Y.
33. ROSENBERG, B. 1961. The Effect of Oxygen Adsorption on Photo- and Semiconduction of β-carotene. J. Chem. Phys. **34:** 812–819.
34. CHERRY, R. J. & D. CHAPMAN. 1967. Effect of Gases on the Electrical Conductivity of β-carotene. Nature **215:** 956–957.
35. MISRA, T. N. & B. ROSENBERG. 1968. J. Chem. Phys. **48**: 5734.
36. LESLIE, R. B., D. CHAPMAN & C. J. HART. 1967. Physical Studies of Phospholipids. VII. The D.C. Electrical Conductivity Properties of Some Membrane Phospholipids. Biochim. Biophys. Acta **135:** 797–811.

37. ROSENBERG, B. & G. L. JENDRASIAK. 1968. Semiconductive Properties of Lipids and Their Possible Relationships to Lipid Bilayer Conductivity. Chem. Phys. Lipids. **2:** 47.
38. BHOWMIK, B., G. L. JENDRASIAK & B. ROSENBERG. 1967. Charge Transfer Complexes of Lipids with Iodine. Nature **215:** 842–843.
39. BHOWMIK, B. 1967. Personal communication.
40. TIEN, H. T. 1967. Personal communication.
41. LÄUGER, P., J. RICHTER and W. LESSLAUER. 1967. Electro-Chemistry of Biomolecular Phospholipid Membranes in Aqueous Iodine Solutions. Ber. Bunsen. für Phys. Chem. **71:** 906.
42. LESLIE, R. B. & D. CHAPMAN. 1967. Artificial Phospholipid Membranes and Bioenergetics. Chem. Phys. Lipids. **1:** 143–156.
43. SKULACHEV, V. P., A. A. SARAF & L. E. LIBERMAN. 1967. Proton Conductors in the Respiratory Chain and Artificial Membranes. Nature **216:** 718–720.
44. MITCHEL, P. 1961. Coupling of Phosphorylation to Electron and Hydrogen Transfer by a Chemi-Osmotic Type of Mechanism. Nature **191:** 144–148.
45. MUELLER, P., D. O. Rudin, H. T. TIEN & W. C. WESCOTT. 1962. Reconstruction of Excitable Cell Membrane Structure *In Vitro*. Circulation **26:** 1167–1172.
46. TIEN, H. T. & A. L. DIANA. 1968. Bimolecular Lipid Membranes: A Review and a Summary of Some Recent Studies. Chem. Phys. Lipids. **2:** 55.
47. ROSENBERG, B. 1962. Electronic Charge Transport in Carotenoid Pigments and a Primitive Theory of the Electroretinogram. Photochem. Photobiol **1:** 117–129.
48. ROSENBERG, B. 1966. A Physical Approach to the Visual Receptor Process. *In* Advances in Radiation Biology. L. G. Augenstein, R. Mason & M. R. Zelle, Eds. **2:** 193–241. Academic Press. New York, N. Y.
49. BROWN, K. T. & M. MURAKAMI. 1964. A New Receptor Potential of the Monkey Retina with no Detectable Latency. Nature. **201:** 626–628.
50. BROWN, J. E., J. R. MURRAY & T. G. SMITH. 1967. Photoelectric Potential from Photoreceptor Cells in Ventral Eye of Limulus. Science **158:** 665–666.
51. Svaetichin, G. & E. F. MACNICHOL, JR. 1958. Retinal Mechanisms for Chromatic and Achromatic Vision. Ann. N. Y. Acad. Sci. **74:** 385–406.
52. ARNOLD, W. & H. K. SHERWOOD. 1957. Are Chloroplasts Semiconductors? Proc. Nat. Acad. Sci. U. S. A. **43:** 105–114.
53. ROSENBERG, B., T. N. MISRA & R. SWITZER. 1968. Mechanism of Olfactory Transduction. Nature **217:** 423.
54. CARDEW, M. H. & D. D. ELEY. 1959. Semiconductivity of Organic Substances. Haemoglobin and Some Amino Acids. Discuss. Faraday Soc. (3) **29:** 115–128.
55. COPE, F. W. 1965. A Kinetic Theory of Electron and Ion Transport in Particulate and Membrane Systems, with Applications to the Cytochrome Oxidase, Melanin Free Radical, and Pyruvate Carboxylase Reactions and to Control of Enzymes by Hormones and Radiation. *In* Oxidase and Related Redox Systems. T. E. King, H. S. Mason and M. Morrison, Eds. **1:** 51–71. John Wiley & Sons. New York, N. Y.
56. LEVY, H. M., N. SHARON & D. KOSHLAND, JR. 1959. A Mechanism for the Effects of Dinitrophenol and Temperature on Hydrolytic Activity of Myosin. Biochim. Biophys. Acta **33:** 288–289.
57. MASSEY, V., B. CURTI & H. GANTHER. 1966. A Temperature-dependent Conformational Change in D-Amino Acid Oxidase and Its Effect on Catalysis. J. Biol. Chem. **241:** 2347–2357.
58. GRAVES, D. J., R. W. SEALOCK & T. H. WANG. 1965. Cold Inactivation of Glycogen Phosphorylase. Biochemical **4:** 290–296.
59. KAYNE, F. 1966. A Physical Analysis of the Effects of Temperature, Substrates and Cofactors on the Structural and Catalytic Properties of Rabbit Muscle Pyruvate Kinase. Ph. D. Thesis. Michigan State Univ. East Lansing, Mich.

SEMICONDUCTION IN NUCLEIC ACID AND ITS COMPONENTS

M. E. Burnel, D. O. Eley, and V. Subramanyan
Chemistry Department, University of Nottingham
Nottingham, England

INTRODUCTION

In earlier work[1] it was established that DNA and RNA in the dry state show a reproducible dark DC specific conductivity, σ, which followed the semiconduction equation

$$\sigma = \sigma_0 \exp(-\Delta\epsilon/2kT), \ \Omega^{-1}\ \mathrm{cm}^{-1} \quad (1)$$

The following values for $\Delta\epsilon$ ($\log_{10} \sigma_0$) have been reported for "dry" DNA (actually NaDNA) *in vacuo*: 2.42 eV (3.5),[2] 2.4 eV (~3),[3] 2.4 eV (~7).[4] A value of $\Delta\epsilon = 1.8$ eV[5] has been attributed to the effect of adsorbed water.[2] The view has been expressed that the charge carriers were electrons and holes passing along the axis of the parallel stacked bases within the DNA double helix.[2] Conflicting views have been expressed, in regard to whether heating NaDNA in oxygen lowers $\Delta\epsilon$[3] or leaves it unchanged.[6, 7] Photocurrents have been examined, but no action spectrum reported,[8] and a high frequency AC dark conduction value of $\Delta\epsilon = 0.2$ eV determined.[6] Attempts to discover an anisotropy in the conductivity of oriented dry films of LiDNA failed,[7] but this probably reflects a loss of base stacking following dehydration.[9] At least 75% humidity is required to maintain the double helix NaDNA structure with parallel stacking of bases. Eley and Leslie made a study of nucleic acid components.[10] The nucleotides showed $\Delta\epsilon = 2.0$ to 2.2 eV, with $\log_{10}\sigma_1 = 0.6$ to 2.7, but the nucleosides (except guanosine) showed $\Delta\epsilon$ values of 4.5 to 5.2 eV and $\log_{10}\sigma_0$ values from 15–22. Satisfactory data could not be established for the bases because of their very high resistivity and volatility. It was concluded that the phosphate groups lowered $\Delta\epsilon$ from nucleoside to nucleotide by playing an electron-bridging role between the base-deoxyribose molecules.

Exposure of a NaDNA film to 10% humidity increases the conductivity by a factor 10^6,[11] and in our laboratory we have shown that an adsorbed film of water molecules lowers $\Delta\epsilon$ for NaDNA from 2.33 to 1.5 eV;[12] similar results have been observed for K Poly A.[13] These results are analagous to earlier observations on proteins and, in the same way, we need to consider possible explanations in terms of an increased electron concentration due to increased dielectric constant,[14] or electron donation by water molecules into the conduction band of the DNA.[15] Proton conductivity is only considered to set in at relatively high degrees of hydration, i.e., greater than 3 BET monolayers.

In the following paper we report further dark conduction measurements on "dry" DNA (and RNA) and its components, and we extend the measurements to the free bases, to the homopolynucleotides and other related systems. Our object is to advance our knowledge of the conduction mechanism in DNA (and RNA) in the light of recent theoretical work on the electron energy band structure of DNA.[16] We shall restrict ourselves to data for DNA in the "dry" state and only incidentally consider the effects of hydration. Although the direct relevance of semiconduction to biological activity remains to be established for DNA and RNA, there has been a suggestion that electron mobility down the double helix of DNA may be a step in mitosis.[17, 18]

Experimental

The specimens examined were all compressed discs formed in a press mostly at 1000 Kg cm^{-2}, since single crystals of the substances to be studied were not available. The discs were held between platinum electrodes with a spring pressure of 80 Kg cm^{-2}, in a pyrex cell which could be pumped to 10^{-6} torr. The cell was constructed with silica supports to ensure a blank resistance of greater than 10^{17} ohms and was developed from an earlier model.[19] A current was passed through the cell and a standard resistor in series, and voltage drops across the cell and resistor were measured with a valve electrometer with an input impedance of about 10^{16} Ω. The samples were measured in a vacuum, except for the bases, which were volatile, in which cases an atmosphere of 150–200 torr of "white spot" nitrogen was used to restrain sublimation. Specimen thickness was of the order 1 mm, and measurements were usually made with 12 or 120 volts across the electrodes. Samples in the conductivity cell were warmed under evacuation within the limit of their heat stability for desiccation prior to electrical studies.

Materials

I. DNA

The following three high purity fibrous specimens were used: 1a) Calf thymus DNA from Worthington Biochemical Corporation, 1b) calf thymus DNA from British Drug Houses Ltd., 1c) salmon sperm NaDNA from BDH Ltd. Tests gave the following results: Ia) N 13.6%, hypochromic ratio 1.3, NaCl $< 1\%$; Ib) NaCl $= 5\%$; Ic N 12.6%, P 9.1%, hypochromic ratio 1.32, NaCl absent after dialysis, ϵ (P) max (260 mμ) 6730. These values may be compared with those for pure, native DNA: N 15.2%, P 9.2%,[20A] hypochromic ratio 1.35,[3] 1.49[6] and ϵ (P) max $=$ 6600.[20A] Id) was a technical grade powder, thymus NaDNA from BDH Ltd., N $=$ 13%, ϵ (P) max (260 mμ) $=$ 8270.

II. RNA

IIa) Highly polymerised yeast RNA from BDH Ltd. IIb) Technical grade yeast RNA from L. Light & Co.

III. Homopolymers

K Poly A, NH_4 Poly U, K Poly I, K Poly C, from the Miles Chemical Company, U.S.A., lyophilized felts of fine white fibers.

IV. Apurinic acid

The purine bases were removed from Ic) by Tamm's method.[20B] Maximum and minimum U.V. absorption were at 268 mμ and 238 mμ, to be compared with NaDNA, 259 mμ and 230 mμ. N 5.5% (N calc 6.0%). The product was dialyzed and freeze-dried to produce a white fluffy material.

V. Nucleotides

Adenylic and guanylic acids were from BDH Ltd., and guanosine 2′, 3′-monophosphate mixed isomers (Na salt) from the Sigma Chemical Company.

VI. Nucleosides

Adenosine, deoxyadenosine.½ H_2O, deoxyguanosine, deoxyuridine and deoxycytidine.HCl were all from the Mann Research Laboratories. Guanosine specimens were from BDH Ltd. and the Sigma Chemical Company.

VII. Bases

Adenine, guanine, xanthine and uracil were chromatographically homogeneous biochemical reagents from BDH Ltd. Purine and hypoxanthine were pure grade reagents from Koch-Light Laboratories Ltd. Cytosine and thymine were provided by L. Light & Co. and also by BDH Ltd.

VIII. Sugars

D-ribose and deoxy-D-ribose from L. Light & Co. and Ribose-5-phosphate (Ba salt) from BDH Ltd.

Oxygen, cylinder gas, from the British Oxygen Company was dried by passage over anhydrous calcium sulphate granules ("hidrite").

Results

DNA

In general, the temperature coefficient data gave good fit to the semiconduction Equation 1, as shown by the example in FIGURE 1, from which $\Delta\epsilon$ and σ_0 were calculated. A large number of runs were carried out on high purity DNA in the form of fibers, powdered films and dry gels, and technical grade powders were also investigated; the results are summarized in TABLE 1. Com-

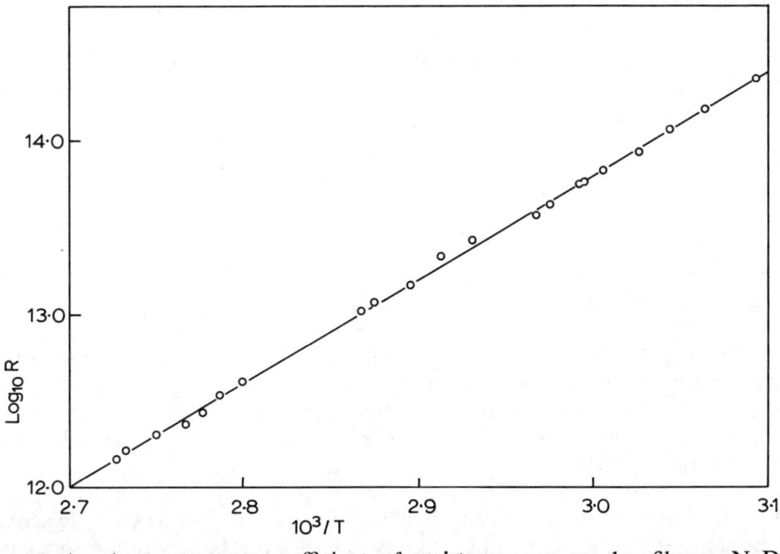

FIGURE 1. A temperature coefficient of resistance run on dry fibrous NaDNA, sample Ic, disc. D(2) (previously used in hydration studies).

TABLE 1

SEMICONDUCTION PARAMETERS FOR DNA

Material, Disc, Preparation Pressure kg cm^{-2}	Expt.	Temp. Range, ° C	$\Delta\epsilon$, eV	$\log_{10}\sigma_0$ Ω^{-1} cm^{-1}	$\log_{10}\rho 400$ Ω cm
Ia) D1, 1000	h, c*	40–80	2.15	1.12	12.08
Ia) D3, 10,000	h	30–70	2.2	1.31	10.80
Ia) D3, 10,000	c	70–30	1.98	1.10	11.36
Ia) D6, 100	h	80–115	2.33	0.95	13.00†
(Powdered D3)					
	eq*	90–125	2.30		
	Ar gas	90–125	2.30		
	O_2 gas	90–105	2.30		
	Air				
	h*	60–87	1.5	$\bar{4}.74$	12.34
Ic) D8, 1000	c, eq	105–80	1.95	$\bar{2}.7$	13.86
	h, eq	80–105	2.02		
	O_2 86° C		1.95	$\bar{2}.7$	13.86
Ic) D9, 1000	c, eq	85–60	2.38	1.94	13.0†
Id) D10, 1000	h, eq	90–130	2.46	2.86	13.15†
	Air†	100–126	2.40	3.18	12.63
Ic) D11, 100	c	95–50	2.33	2.85	11.82†
Ic) Gel 1	eq	70–100	2.30	2.92	11.78†
	Air, eq	70–100	2.30	2.92	11.78
Ib) Gel 2	eq	70–90	2.35	2.75	12.03†
	O_2 gas	65–87	2.18		
	vac	84–120	2.20	0.87	12.97
Ic) Gel 3	vac		2.36	2.20	12.65†
	O_2 gas, 16 days, 80° C, reevacuated	90–120	2.33		13.24

* h denotes heating run, c, cooling, and eq, thermal equilibrium at each temperature.
† subsequent O_2 gas addition gave no resistance change.

pressed discs from fibers showed initially low $\Delta\epsilon$ values, which slowly increased in value, and we associate this change with the slow loss of water from these discs and accept the final value of 2.3 to 2.4 eV as $\Delta\epsilon$ for the dry fibers. With this proviso, there is reasonably good agreement between all the specimens, and parameters were little changed from run to run except for a gradual shift of curves to higher resistivities from day to day. The seven results marked with a dagger have been dagger to give $\Delta\epsilon = 2.36$, $\log_{10}\sigma_0$ (Ω^{-1} cm^{-1}) $= 2.35$ and $\log_{10}\sigma_{400^\circ \mathrm{K}}$ (Ω^{-1} cm^{-1}) $= 12.49$.

Some current-voltage curves are shown in FIGURE 2. Truly dry specimens, such as those in FIGURE 2c), d), which are relatively loosely compacted, are found to obey Ohm's law, whereas the more highly compressed discs show deviations as in FIGURE 2a), b). These deviations we associate with the presence of absorbed moisture retained on the highly compacted specimens.

In a number of cases, it was found that admission of dry oxygen to DNA, even at temperatures up to 126° C, did not have an appreciable effect on $\Delta\epsilon$. Admission of laboratory air at temperatures less than 100° C decreased $\Delta\epsilon$ from 2.3 to 1.5 eV, an effect we attribute to the adsorption of moisture by the DNA. This supposition has been checked by direct experiments.[12] It seems at least possible that the effects observed by Snart[3] may be attributed to moisture in the oxygen used.

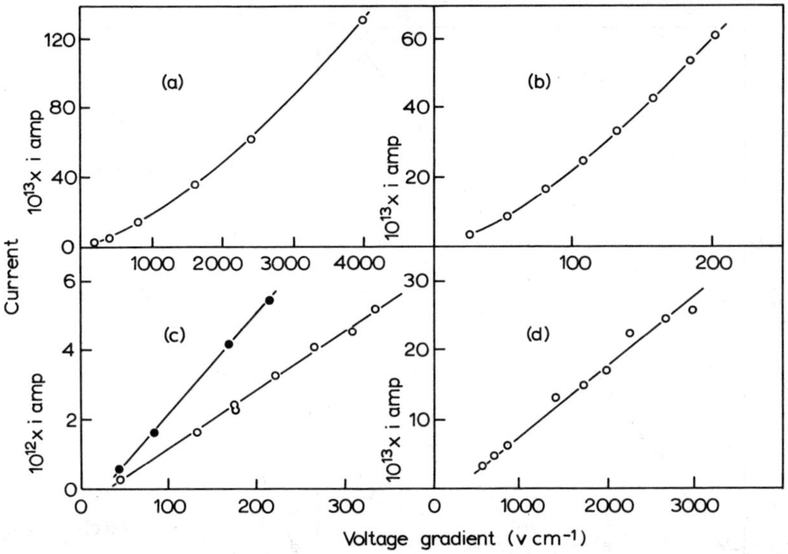

FIGURE 2. To show a), b) how highly compacted fibers of NaDNA retaining some adsorbed water deviate from Ohm's law and c), d) how loosely packed samples of NaDNA obey Ohm's law. a) a disc D(1) pressed at 1000 kg cm^{-2}, b) a disc D(3) pressed at 10,000 kg cm^{-2}, c) NaDNA, D6 pressed at 100 kg cm^{-2}, and d) a loose fiber sample. The disc in Fig. 2c), D(6), was made from DNA fibers previously used as D(3) and then finely cut, ground and repressed at the lower pressure, 100 kg.cm^{-2}. All data were recorded at temperatures above 73° C and *in vacuo* except for c) (●) which were for dry air (1 atmos.) at 91° C.

RNA, Homopolyribonucleotides and Apurinic Acid

Some typical data are shown in FIGURES 3 and 4 and collected data in TABLE 2. Ohm's law holds up to 3000 V cm^{-1} for apurinic acid (Fig. 3b) and other substances. According to these results, $\Delta\epsilon$ decreases over a series apurinic acid $>$ DNA $\simeq$ RNA $\simeq$ K Poly C $>$ K Poly A $>$ NH_4 Poly U $>$ K Poly I.

TABLE 2
SEMICONDUCTION PARAMETERS FOR POLYNUCLEOTIDES*

Polynucleotide	Disc, Preparation Pressure kg cm^{-2}	Temp. Range, °C	$\Delta\epsilon$, eV	$\log_{10}\sigma_0$ Ω^{-1} cm^{-1}	$\log_{10}\rho_{400}$ Ω cm
RNA	1000	83–118	2.36	2.25	12.6
	1000	96–130	2.3	0.2	14.2
K Poly A	10000	70–130	2.2	1.9	12.95
K Poly C	"	"	2.4	2.65	12.33
K Poly I	1000	"	1.8	$\bar{3}.49$	13.82
NH_4 Poly U	1000	78–133	2.0	$\bar{1}.66$	12.93
NH_4 Poly U	10000	60–130	2.06	1.23	11.98
NH_4 Poly U	gel	78–133	2.0	0.42	12.17
Apurinic acid	1000	96–127	2.9	4.45	13.8

*These were all temperature equilibrium runs.

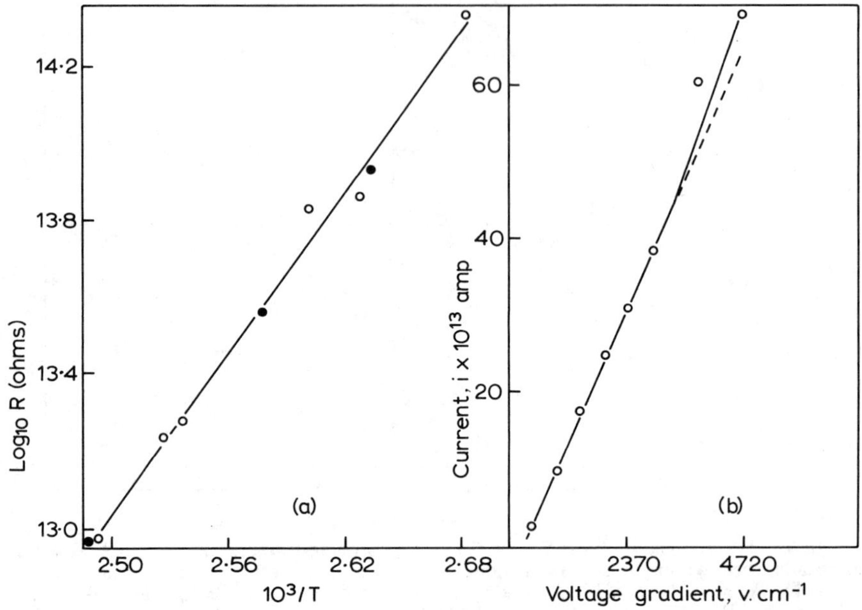

FIGURE 3. a) A temperature coefficient of resistance run on apurinic acid (● at 450 V cm^{-1}, ○ at 4700 V cm^{-1}). b) Ohm's law plot for apurinic acid at 120° C.

Nucleosides and Nucleotides

Some typical Ohm's law plots for this series in FIGURE 5 show that Ohm's law holds up to greater than 2000 V cm^{-1}, except in the case of deoxycytidine. HCl in which the deviations probably arose from ionic conduction. In support of this view, deoxycytidine. HCl showed markedly time-dependent currents after a change of voltage, whereas completely steady currents shown by all the other substances indicated obeyed Ohm's law. On this point, there is a strong contrast between the Ohm's law behavior of deoxyguanosine found here and earlier unpublished results of Eley and Leslie on guanosine, in which marked deviations from Ohm's law were found. The present results are gathered in TABLE 3 together with the earlier work of Eley and Leslie[10] on the ribo-derivatives for comparison. Eley and Leslie[10] data for adenosine and guanosine are confirmed; the present guanosine results are shown in FIGURE 6. The Liang and Scalco value[8] of $\Delta\epsilon = 4.52$ eV for adenosine is also in close agreement. The guanosine $\Delta\epsilon$ value of 2.1 eV was earlier observed to be much lower than the value for the other nucleosides, all of which had a value of about 4.5 eV. Our conduction data for two deoxynucleosides are displayed in FIGURE 7. Changing the sugar from D-ribose to deoxy-D-ribose seems to have little effect in this series.

Bases and Sugars

The conductivity values are low for the bases, which were all measured under a presence of nitrogen to avoid sublimation, in the working range 150–220° C. Although purine, xanthine and hypoxanthine are not nucleic acid

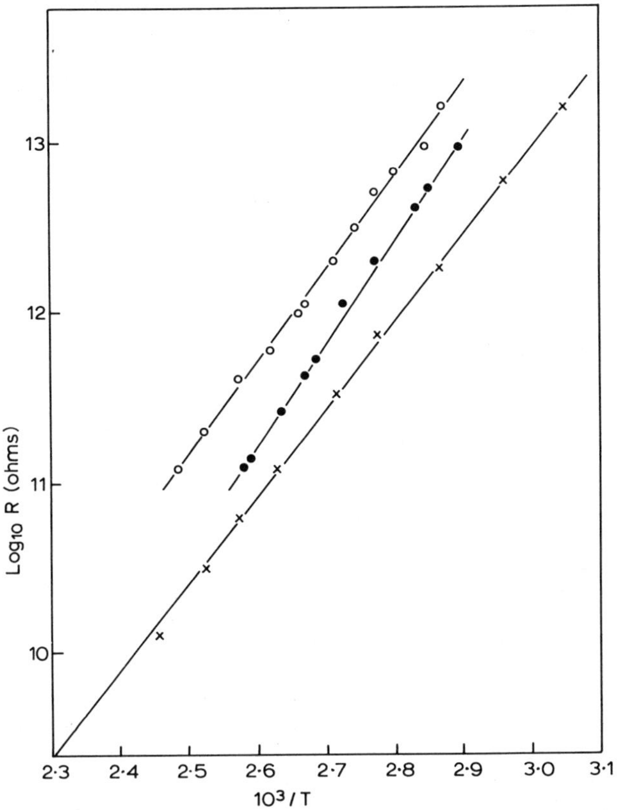

FIGURE 4. Temperature coefficient of resistance runs for (○) K Poly A, (●) K Poly C and (x) NH_4 Poly U.

bases, we have included them because of their related structure. Temperature coefficient graphs or adenine and uracil are shown in FIGURE 8. There is a small kink in the uracil graph at 435° K. The collected results are given in TABLE 4, and some theoretical values are included for convenience in later discussion.

We draw attention to the very marked effect of the phosphate group in lowering the $\Delta\epsilon$ for D-ribose. However, in contrast to the nucleoside and nucleotide results, there is an almost equally large lowering on going from D-ribose to deoxy-D-ribose and, unfortunately, we have no data for deoxy-D-ribose phosphate at present. Nevertheless, this proposed effect of phosphate on sugars has been found in several other cases, including glucose.[12, 13]

Discussion

Nucleic Acid and Polynucleotides

The conductivity parameters established here for dry DNA, $\Delta\epsilon = 2.36$ eV and $\log_{10}\sigma_0 = 2.35$, are very close to the earlier values of $\Delta\epsilon = 2.42$ eV, $\log_{10}\sigma_0$

TABLE 3

SEMICONDUCTION PARAMETERS FOR NUCLEOSIDES AND NUCLEOTIDES

Substance	Temp. Range, °C	$\Delta\epsilon$, eV	$\log_{10}\sigma_0$ Ω^{-1} cm^{-1}	$\log_{10}\rho_{400}$ Ω cm
Adenosine	140–173	3.9	10.6	14.1
Adenosine*		4.5	15	15.1
Deoxyadenosine. ½H_2O	>107	3.3	7.5	13.2
Guanosine	70–145	1.91	0.6	11.45
(BDH)		1.87		11.42
Guanosine (Sigma)	70–130	2.03	0.8	11.9
Guanosine*		2.1	2.6	10.9
Deoxyguanosine	100–130	2.6	4.3	12.8
"	110–150	2.3,2.6		
Deoxyridine	114–135	5.6	21.8	13.3
Uridine*		5.2	22.0	10.7
Deoxycytidine. HCl	76–113	4.5	18.0	10.1
Cytidine*		4.9	19.4	11.6
Adenylic acid	70–150	2.0	1.62	10.5
" *	60–160	1.8	2.7	
" *	60–160	2.0	2.0	
Guanylic acid	70–140	1.8	3.14	7.8
" *	60–120	1.5	1.8	
Uridylic acid*	70–120	1.3	0.6	
Cytidylic acid*	100–140	2.2	1.6	

* Values from Reference 10.

= 3.5. In the earlier work,[2] it was suggested that the conduction was intrinsic, electrons and holes being generated by thermal excitation in the nitrogen bases and passing down the axis of the double helix. It must, however, be admitted that the Crick-Watson helix is only stable above 75% relative humidity, and that our conduction results on dry DNA must correspond to a somewhat disordered system of bases. However, we shall assume for the moment that calculations and observations concerning the Crick-Watson helix are relevant to the present results.

The normal absorption band of DNA at 260 mμ corresponds to a first excited singlet state at 4.8 eV and the phosphorescence emission band at 450 mμ[21] to a triplet state at 2.75 eV, which, for molecular aggregates, is shifted to 2.6 eV.[22] There is evidence that the triplet state gives rise to an exciton energy band in the crystal,[21] since one paramagnetic ion will quench the phosphorescence of a large number of molecules. An exciton may be regarded as an electron-hole pair, and to separate electrons and holes a further coulombic force has to be overcome; on this basis we should expect $\Delta\epsilon > 2.6$ eV. This would give rise to an intrinsic semiconductor, with no particularly marked n or p character. Alternatively, the exciton may dissociate at an electron or hole trap, giving a p or n type conduction, respectively, with $\Delta\epsilon \simeq 2.6$ eV. Recently, Trukhan[23] has published Hall coefficient results, carried out on DNA at a frequency of 10^{10} cycle s^{-1}. DNA that had been denatured and dried by heating at 170° C for 3 hr showed no Hall voltage, whereas natural DNA, with normal hydration, showed p-typeness in both dark and photoconduction. It is not clear at present how far Hall measurements at such microwave frequencies refer to bulk DC conduction (cf. O'Konski's very low $\Delta\epsilon$ value at high frequency). Also, we have evidence that DNA and proteins at high degrees of hydration show proton conduction, and it is not clear whether

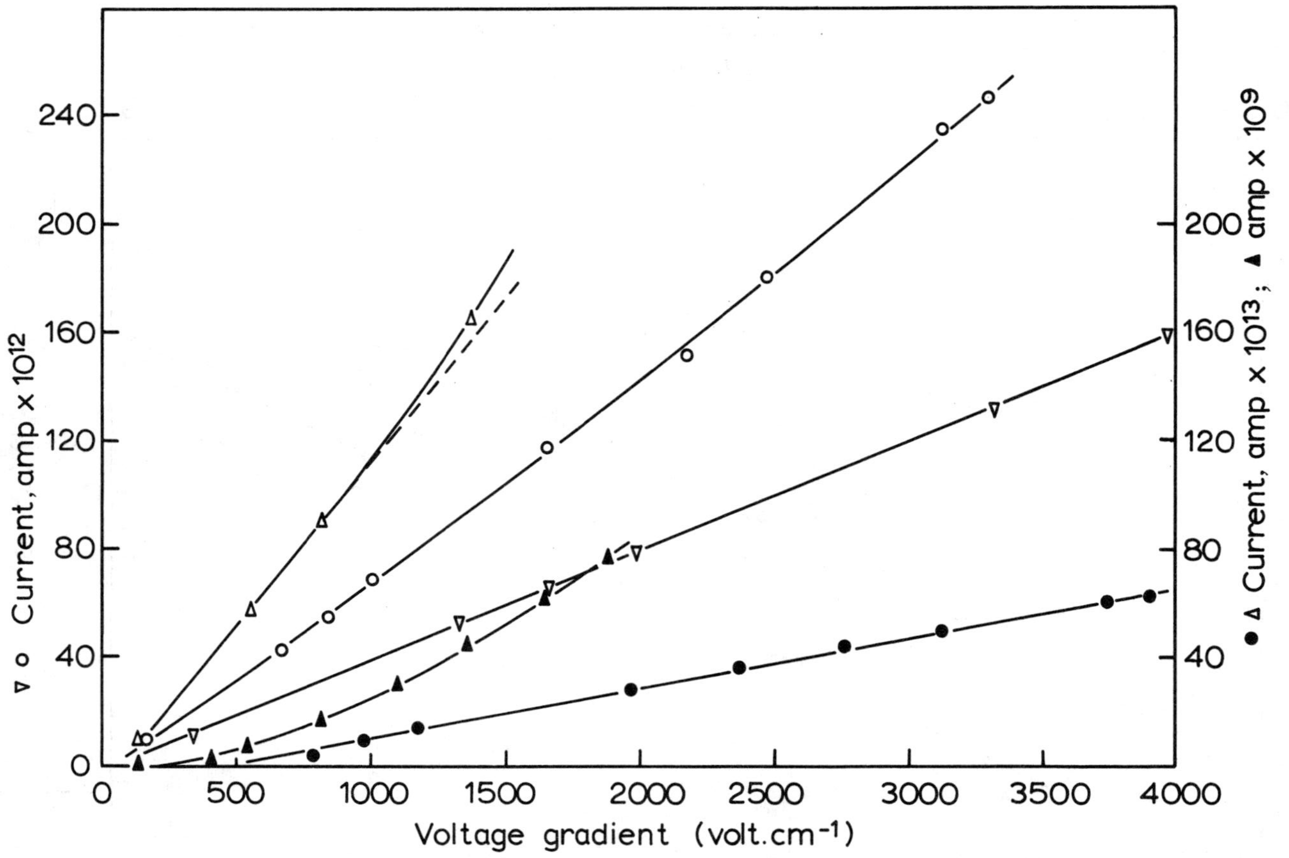

FIGURE 5. Ohm's law plots for (△) deoxycytidine HCl, 78° C, (○) deoxyuridine 129° C, (▽) deoxyadenosine.½H_2O, 153° C, (▲) deoxycytidine.HCl, 112° C, (●) deoxyguanosine, 116° C.

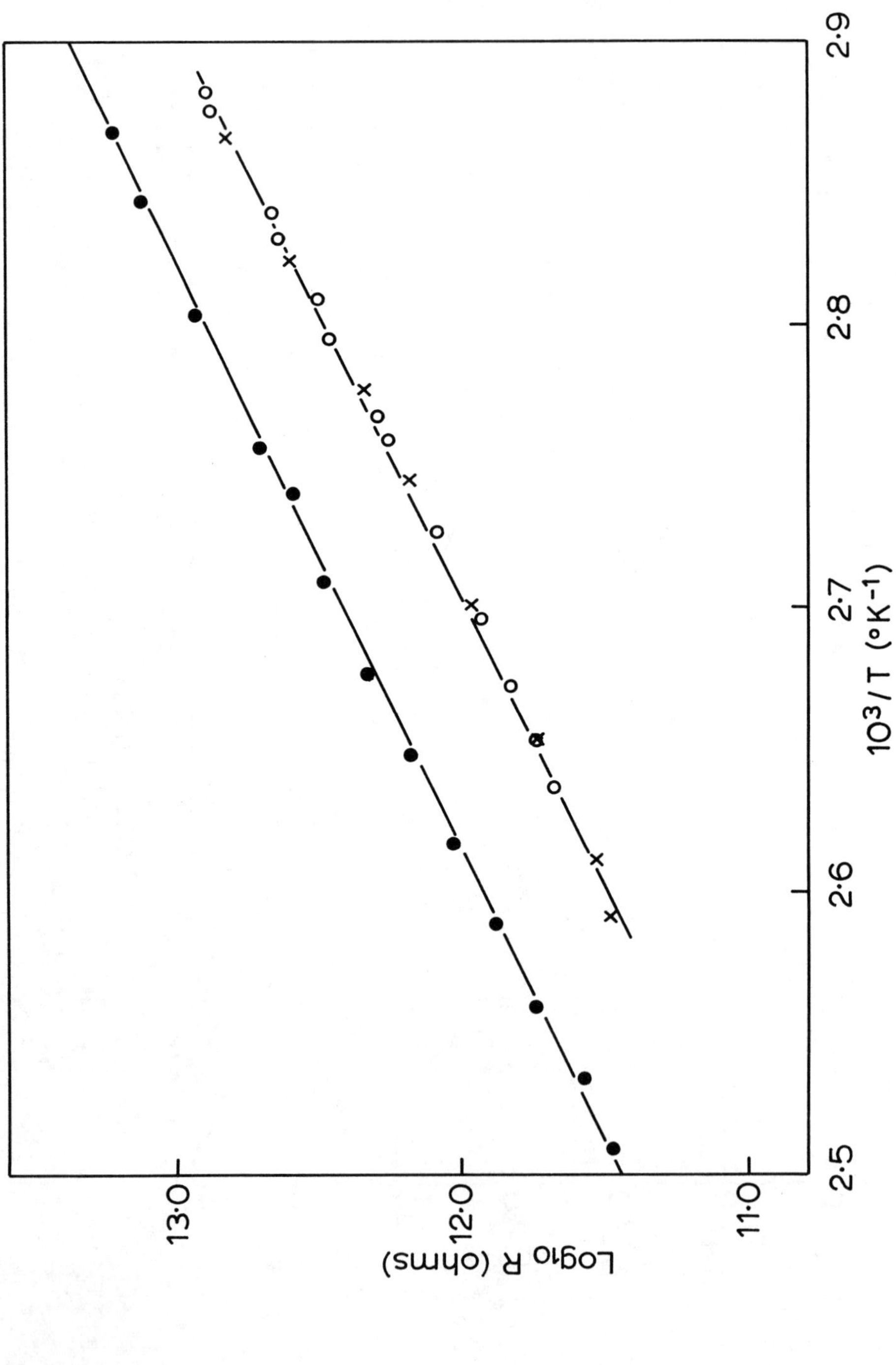

FIGURE 6. Temperature coefficient of resistance runs for guanosine, ◈, as compressed powder; ○, +, as compressed disc.

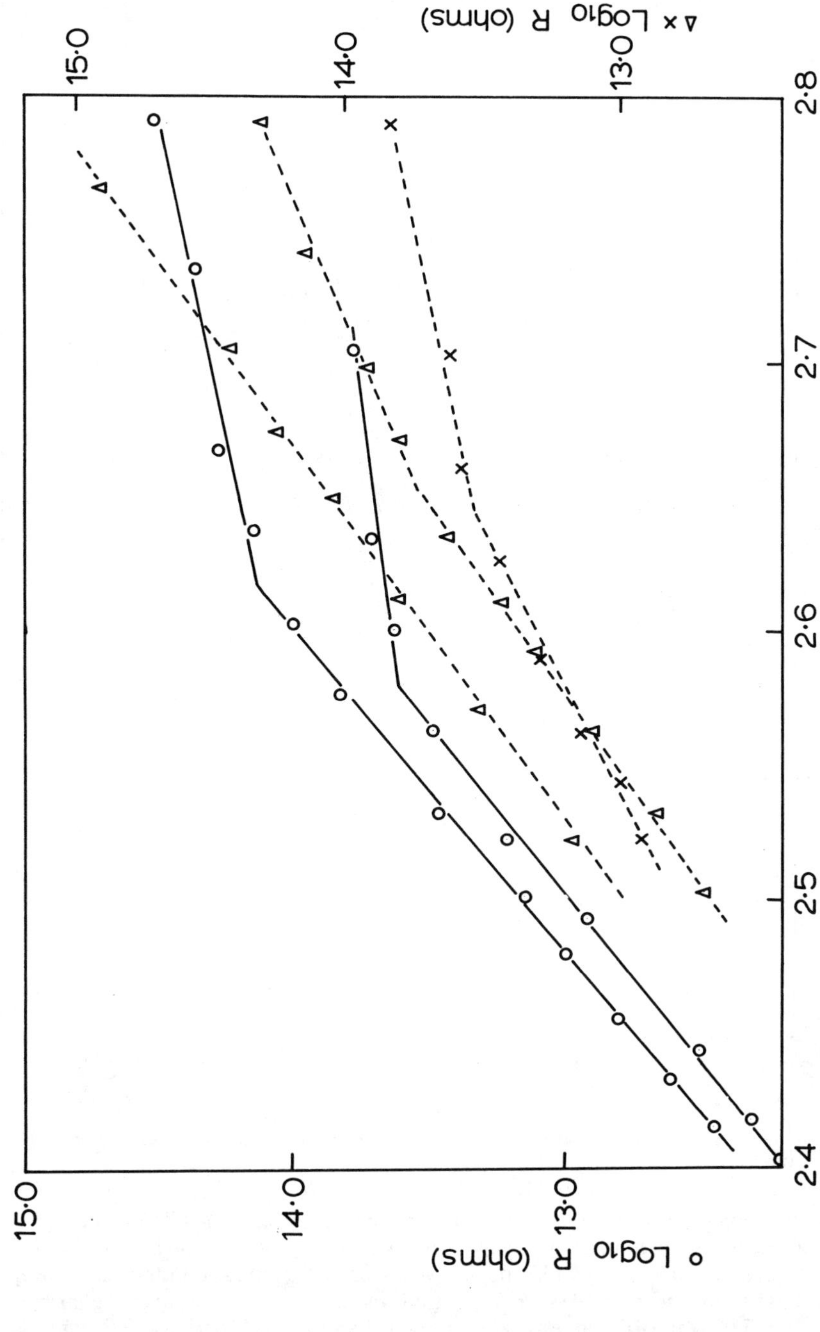

FIGURE 7. Temperature coefficient of resistance runs for (○) deoxyadenosine.½ H_2O and (◇, +) deoxyguanosine.

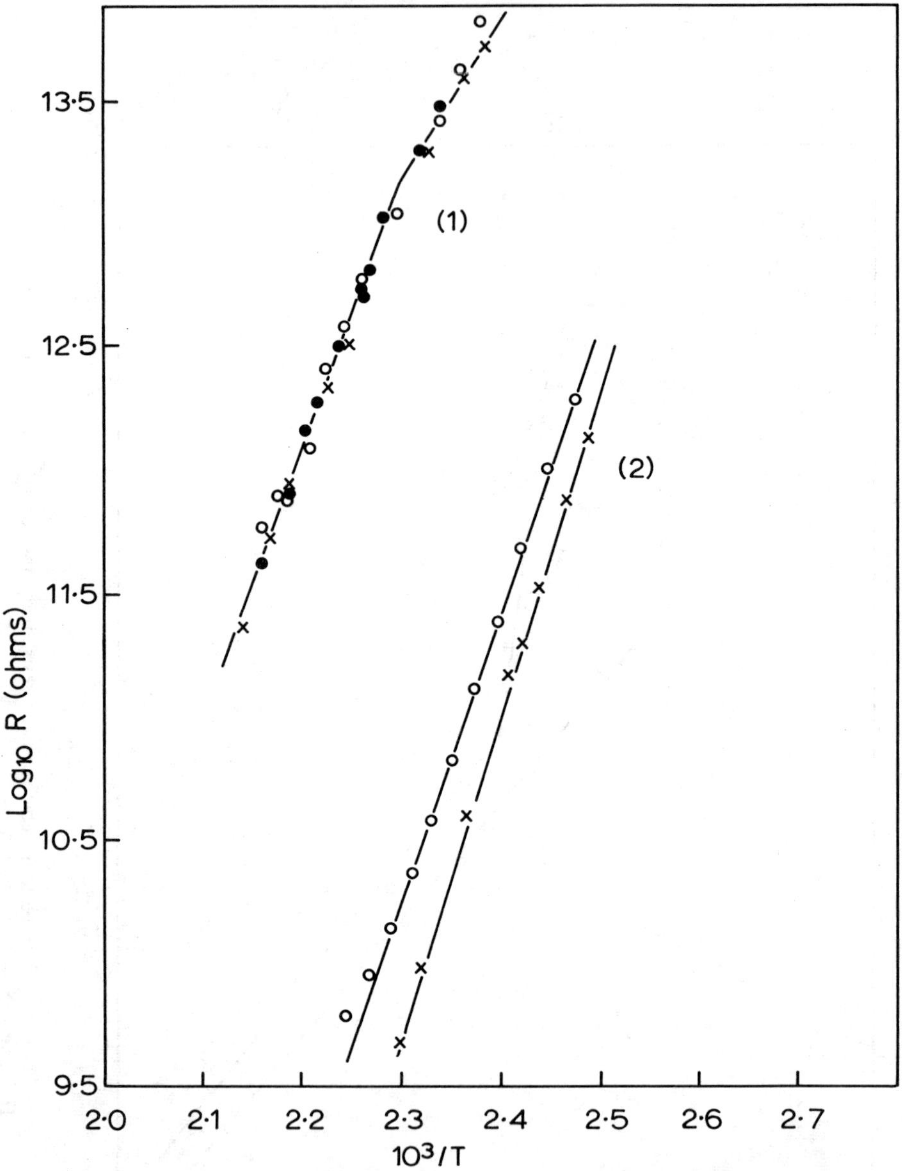

FIGURE 8. Temperature coefficient of resistance runs for (1) uracil (3 runs), (2) adenine (2 runs).

or not this stage has been reached in Trukhan's experiments. But the majority carriers in aromatic systems are usually positive holes; therefore, the Hall coefficient data would fit in with the view of a conduction band system based on the parallel array of thymine-adenine and cytosine-guanine base pairs. The importance of base contact for the conductivity is perhaps borne out by the higher $\Delta\epsilon$ value of 2.9 eV for apurinic acid, DNA from

TABLE 4

SEMICONDUCTION PARAMETERS FOR BASES AND SUGARS

Substance	Disc	$\Delta\epsilon$, eV	$\log_{10}\sigma_0$	$\log_{10}\rho_{400}$*	$\Delta\epsilon$ calc eV
Adenine	1	5.3	19.5	13.8	5.1
		4.8	16.9	14.1	
Uracil	1	4.5	11.5	16.8	5.8
	2	4.6, 2.8	12.0, 1.5	16.9, 16.1	
Guanine	1	3.5	4.45	17.6	4.7
	2	3.5	4.6	17.4	
Cytosine	1	4.9, 3.4	13.0, 4.6	17.7, 16.5	4.8
" (Light & Co.)	2	4.8, 3.2	11.8, 3.3	18.1, 16.8	
" (BDH)	3	4.0, 5.5	17.6, 9.2	17.25, 15.9	
Thymine (BDH)	1	4.0, 3.0	6.5, 1.1	18.7, 17.7	5.1
Thymine (Light & Co.)	2	0.53, 2.05	$\overline{11}.7$, $\bar{2}.8$	12.0, 12.6	
Xanthine	1	1.2	9.64	15.72	5.2
Hypoxanthine	1	1.5	7.3	16.1	4.6
"	2	1.6	7.3	16.5	
Purine	1	6.5, 3.75			
"	2	6.7, 3.4	29.3, 8.4	13.1, 12.9	
D-Ribose		3.6	16.6	14.0†	
Deoxy-D-Ribose		2.3	9.85	9.9†	
Ribose-5-phosphate		2.1	1.3	15.9†	

* All these values were calculated by extrapolation of the straight line relationship.

† These compounds decomposed before reaching 400° K and these are extrapolated 300° K values.

Two values of $\Delta\epsilon$ and $\log_{10}\sigma_0$ denote a kink in the activation energy graph, the higher temperature value coming first.

which the purine bases have been hydrolytically removed. Poly C[24] and Poly A[25] have double helix structures such as that of DNA,[26] but differ in that the double helices in each case are well maintained in the dry state. These polynucleotides (including Poly U) show very closely similar behavior to DNA, which suggests that the perfection of base stacking has only a small effect on the conduction. Poly I[27] has a markedly lower $\Delta\epsilon$ of 1.8 eV, although this lowering is overcompensated by a decrease in $\log_{10}\sigma_0$, so that its conductivity is less than that of DNA. Poly I is a triple helix, with hydrogen-bonded trimers of 9-methyl hypoxanthine in the keto form, and we should expect a lower excitation energy for charge carriers in these trimers over the dimers in DNA and the polynucleotide double helices. However, as we shall see, hypoxanthine itself has an anomalously low $\Delta\epsilon$ and this may be reflected in the low $\Delta\epsilon$ for Poly I. RNA shows similar results to DNA, judged by the rather scanty data available. RNA, compared with DNA, contains ribose in place of deoxyribose and uracil in place of thymine, but a number of RNAs contain a fair fraction of double-stranded helical form, so that the similarity in electrical behavior is perhaps understandable. As shown in TABLE 3, the electrical data for uracil are in the same range as for thymine. The difference between D-ribose and deoxy-D-ribose in this Table probably does not reflect differences in intrinsic conductivity, since an electrode injection process probably operates here.

Nucleic Acid Components

It will be convenient first to refer to the purine and pyrimidine bases. If we adopt the Riehl and Lyons approach, and approximate $\Delta\epsilon$ by[28]

$$\Delta\epsilon = I - E - 2P$$

where I is the ionization potential, E the electron affinity of the base, and P the polarization energy of the electron or hole, it is easily shown that $\Delta\epsilon$ values of >5 eV are to be expected. In TABLE 4 we show the calculated values using the latest I and E values,[29] and a $P = 1.7$ eV as given by Mesnard and collaborators.[30, 31] By these standards and, indeed, on the basis of semiempirical consideration based on the number of π electrons per base molecule, the values of Mesnard[30, 31] and Basu and Moore[32] are much too small, and the values found here (TABLE 4) are more in accord with theoretical expectation. The exceptions are xanthine and hypoxanthine with their very low $\Delta\epsilon$ values of 1.2 and 1.5 eV; and it is perhaps noteworthy that these molecules contain the C = O group conjugated to the NH group, which perhaps gives rise to an especially favorable hydrogen-bonded system in the crystals concerned. Referring again to TABLE 4: although many of the $\Delta\epsilon$ values for adenine, guanine, uracil, cytosine, thymine and purine are in the range 3 to 6 eV, there is a certain variability of results for a given specimen and, in the case of thymine, a very low $\Delta\epsilon$ of 0.53 eV. Furthermore, there is a compensation law between $\Delta\epsilon$ and $\log_{10}\sigma_0$, the higher $\Delta\epsilon$ values being accompanied by anomalously high $\log_{10}\sigma_0$ values. This is shown in FIGURE 9. The situation is one where the expected true energy gap is so high that the intrinsically generated electrons will be too few to account for the observed conductivity. In this case, the observed charge carriers must enter the crystal by electrode injection and, where the energy bands in the organic molecule remain straight to the crystal surface, we may expect an activation energy approximately equal to half the true band gap as found here. The high $\log_{10}\sigma_0$ values have been discussed for similar instances and attributed to a temperature-variable bending of energy bands associated with surface states.[33, 34]

If we now turn to the nucleosides, base + sugar, TABLE 3 shows $\Delta\epsilon$ values of 3.3 to 5.6 eV for three deoxyribose compounds, compared with Eley and Leslie's earlier results[10] for the corresponding ribose compounds of 4.5–5.2 eV. The guanosine derivatives, both deoxyribose and ribose, have anomalously low $\Delta\epsilon$ values of 2.0–2.6 eV. The presence of some very high $\log_{10}\sigma_0$ values suggests here again, apart possibly from the guanosine compounds, that we are dealing with an electrode-injection conduction process.

The present results confirm for the deoxyribose nucleotides what was earlier established for the ribose nucleotides, that attachment of the phosphate group to the base-sugar unit results in a strong decrease in $\Delta\epsilon$ to about 2 eV, with $\log_{10}\sigma_0$ values in the range expected for intrinsic conduction. This proposed effect of attached phosphate on conduction appears to extend to D-ribose, where $\Delta\epsilon$ and $\log_{10}\sigma_0$ (TABLE 4) appear to be brought into the intrinsic conduction region. As noted earlier, we do not regard the difference between D-ribose and deoxy-D-ribose recorded here as reflecting an intrinsic behavior, since the $\log_{10}\sigma_0$ values suggest we are in the electrode-injection, surface states region, and we have every reason to expect a true band gap of >5 eV. We shall discuss the case of sugars generally in another paper.

Taken together with the considerations of the first section, we can suggest the following intrinsic conduction mechanism for nucleotides, polynucleotides, DNA and RNA. The energy gap $\Delta\epsilon$ is associated with transfer of an electron from the purine or pyrimidine base to the phosphate group. The charge carriers are then positive holes moving through the bases, and the electrons moving over the phosphate-sugar system. We need to assume that

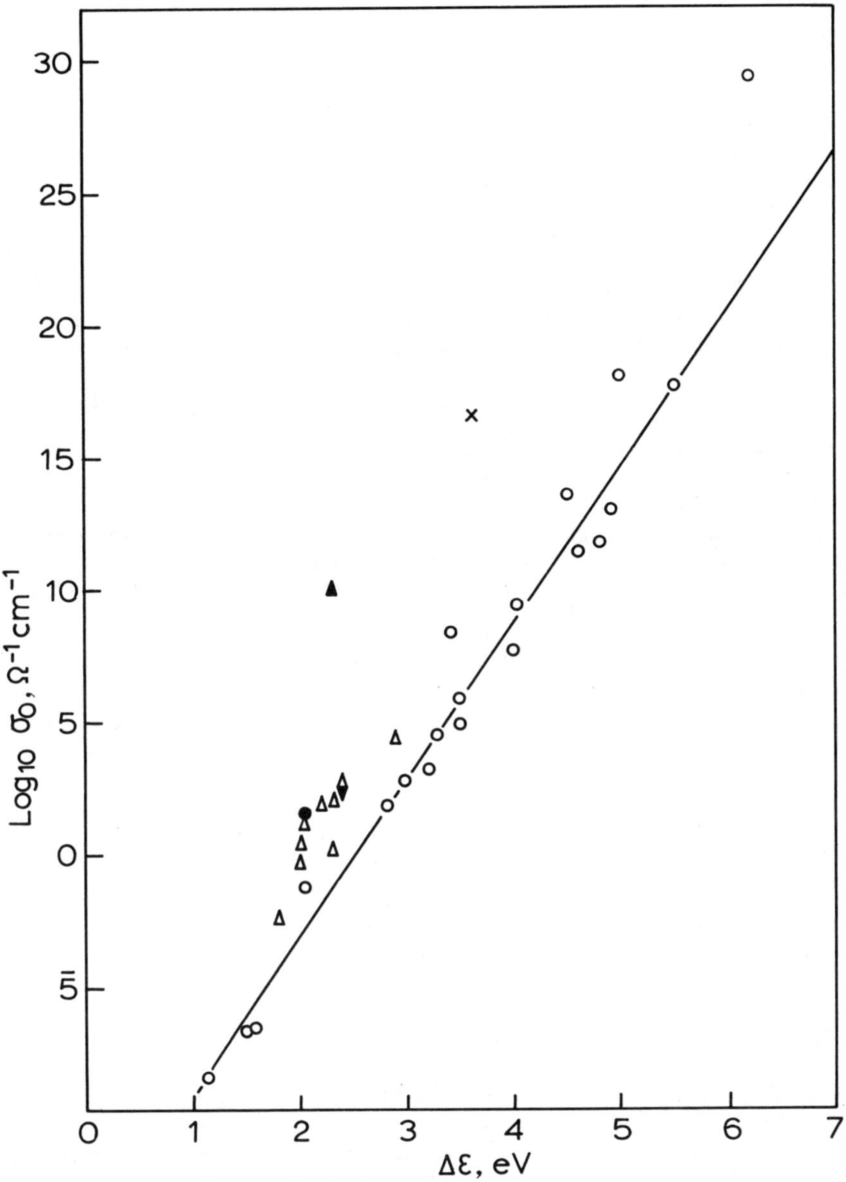

FIGURE 9. The Compensation Rule for $\Delta\epsilon$ and $\log_{10}\sigma_0$.

the electron and hole have comparable mobilities, to explain the observed Hall coefficient of zero.[23] The effect of low degrees of hydration is not easy to predict. In this case, water is expected to behave as an electron donor but, according to infrared evidence,[9] the first water goes to hydrate the phosphate groups and sodium ions. Normally, it would be expected to increase the n-type behavior, and if this is so, the observed p-typeness of damp DNA suggests the extent of hydration is sufficient for proton conduction to occur.

CONCLUSION

We express our results in a tentative model shown in FIGURE 10. The potential trough corresponds to the NaDNA double helix which may be disordered to some extent, separated from neighboring molecules by the potential energy barriers shown. The triplet and singlet energies of the nitrogen base system lie at 2.6 and 4.8 eV, respectively, and these may probably be regarded as exciton bands. The ground state of the model corresponds to the ground state of the CG-AT base system and constitutes the valence band. Dark conduction at $\Delta\epsilon = 2.36$ eV is attributed to excitation of an electron into the phosphate-deoxyribose chain, where it may be expected to be mobile, according to independent measurements on the sugar-phosphates themselves; and for convenience, we have designated this the charge-transfer (CT) band. This intramolecular charge transfer must be optically forbidden, since there is no evidence for a spectroscopic band corresponding to it in the nucleotides. If a triplet exciton band exists at 2.6 eV, it will be slightly higher than the charge-transfer conduction band, the reverse of that found for anthracene.[35]

There seems little doubt that a second conduction band (cf. also anthracene[35]) should exist at an energy somewhat higher than the singlet excitation level at 4.8 eV. This band would involve electron and hole movement within the CG-AT system and, based on the calculations of Pullman,[29,31] would lie somewhere around 4.7–5.8 eV. It should be noted that the latest molecular orbital calculations, using SCF LCAO methods,[36] lead to the concept of a conduction band at a gap of about 4–5.5 eV above the valence band. Basu and Moore[32] observed a photoconduction in purine and pyrimidine around 300 mμ (4 eV), which followed the absorption spectrum of the concentrated solution down to cut off at 300 mμ. This photocurrent was almost absent in vacuo, but clearly observable with air present, and it was greater when the sample was illuminated through the positive electrode. All the evidence supports the notion that this is a positive hole current in the valence band, subsequent to electron excitation by $h\nu_{II}$ to form an exciton in the singlet (S) level, with surface trapping of the electrons by an adsorbed oxygen molecule. If it proves possible to observe a photocurrent for the bases and for DNA in vacuo, this will probably involve excitation to, and electron movement in, the hypothetical band. The observations of Liang and Scalco on photoconduction in DNA and adenosine[8] are not too easy to fit into this picture. Using a lamp with a maximum emission at 1200 mμ (i.e., 1 eV) they found a photoconduction in both these systems, with markedly large photoconduction thermal activation energies, 0.89 eV for DNA and 1.8 eV for adenosine. The authors suggested that the charge carriers arise from impurity levels, and we may further note that these cannot be associated with phosphate, which is absent from adenosine. Accordingly, we have located some hypothetical impurity acceptor levels of unknown origin beneath our lower CT conduction band. The excitation of electrons by $h\nu_{I}$, about 1 eV, would then give electrons on the acceptor levels, from which further thermal activation may produce a kind of hopping from one level to the next via the CT band, this activation energy being related to the photoconduction activation energy of DNA of Liang and Scalco.[8] In the case of adenosine, such phosphate is absent; the CT band will also be absent and cannot be involved

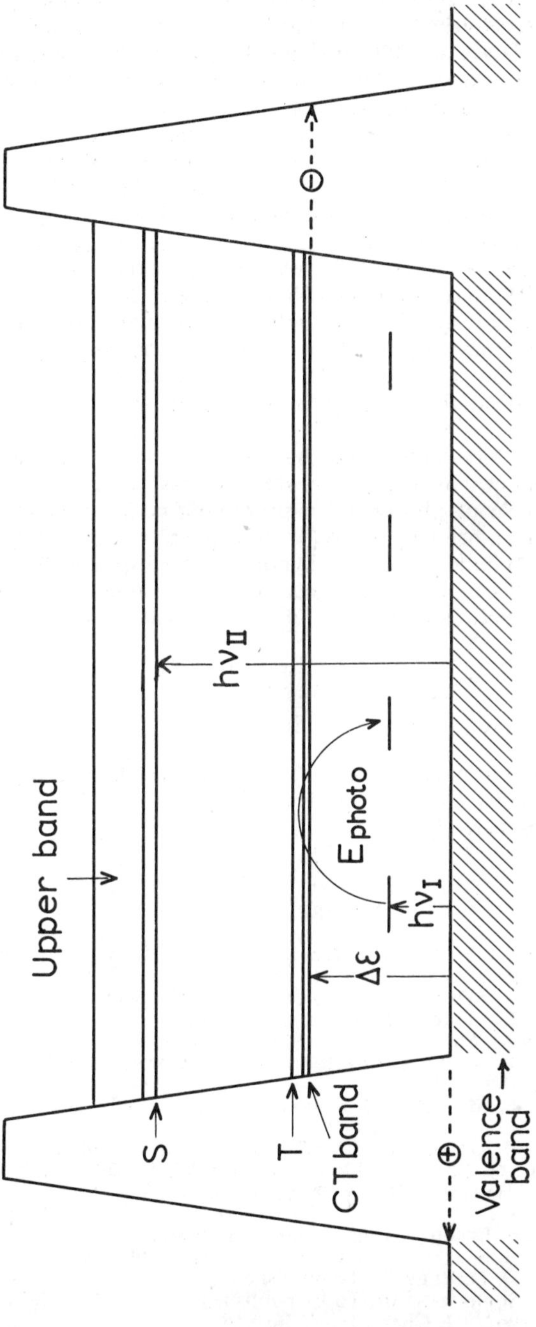

FIGURE 10. A postulated model for dark conduction and photoconduction in dry NaDNA. Dark conduction involves thermal excitation to the CT (charge transfer) band. Photoconduction occurs either (a) by electron excitation to corresponding levels at 1 eV, followed by thermal hopping, or (b) by excitation of an electron.

in the thermally activated hopping. This may perhaps be related to the much greater photoconduction activation energy found in this case. However, in preliminary work at Nottingham we have not so far been able to detect a photoconduction in DNA at 1200 mμ, and further work is required to decide the matter. Until this work has been undertaken, the remarks about the photoconduction process $h\nu_I$ and $h\nu_{II}$ are purely speculative.

Concerning the σ_o values for dark conduction, deformation potential calculations using the relatively wide band width predicted by Hückel LCAO calculations gave values of $10^5\ \Omega^{-1}cm^{-1}$ for Poly A[37] and DNA.[38] We should expect the narrower band widths arising by the SCF calculations to lead to smaller σ_o values, more in accordance with the experimental values around $10^2\ \Omega^{-1}cm^{-1}$.

The high-frequency $\Delta\epsilon$ values of 0.2 eV do not receive an obvious explanation on this model. We have estimated that a value of $\log_{10}\sigma_o = \bar{4}$ corresponds to this value of $\Delta\epsilon$, and it may be that the process is analogous to that observed in diphenyl picryl hydrazyl, where there is a DC conduction with $\Delta\epsilon = 1.6$ eV and an AC loss with $\Delta\epsilon = 0.2$ eV.[39] In the latter case, we have associated the loss with the free radical character of the DPPH; there is no such free radical character in DNA.

The present paper has emphasized the possible role of phosphate injecting holes by an intramolecular charge-transfer process. In an earlier note, we suggested that the role of phosphate in promoting conduction arose from an intramolecular electron-bridging action.[10] It cannot be claimed that we have been able to prove definitely the new hypothesis or disprove the old one. But the new hypothesis fits in with the basic chemical character of the phosphate group, and gives a qualitative account of the majority of facts in the field at the present time.

Acknowledgments

The authors thank the Science Research Council and the United Kingdom Commonwealth Scholarships Commission for scholarships to M. E. Burnel and V. Subramanyan, respectively.

References

1. Eley, D. D. 1962. Horizons in Biochemistry. M. Kasha & B. Pullman, Eds.: 341. Academic Press. New York, N. Y.
2. Eley, D. D. & D. I. Spivey. 1962. Trans. Faraday Soc. **58:** 411.
3. Snart, R. S. 1963. Trans. Faraday Soc. **59:** 754.
4. O'Konski, C. T. & M. Shirai. 1963. Biopolymers **1:** 557.
5. Duchesne, J., J. Depreux, A. Bertinchamps, N. Cornet & J. M. van der Kaa. 1960. Nature **188:** 405.
6. O'Konski, C. T., P. Moser & M. Shirai. 1964. Biopolymers Sympos. No. 1: 479.
7. Heden, C. G. & A. Rupprecht. 1966. Acta Chem. Scand. **20:** 583.
8. Liang, C. Y. & E. G. Scalco. 1963. Nature **198:** 86; **200:** 1319.
9. Falk, M., K. A. Hartman, Jr. & R. C. Lord. 1963. J. Amer. Chem. Soc. **85:** 391.
10. Eley, D. D. & R. B. Leslie. 1963. Nature **197:** 898.
11. Liang, C. Y. & E. G. Scalco. 1964. J. Chem. Phys. **40:** 919.
12. Burnel, M. E., & D. D. Eley. To be published.
13. Eley, D. D. & V. Subramanyan. To be published.
14. Rosenberg, B. 1962. J. Chem. Phys. **36:** 816.
15. Eley, D. D. & R. B. Leslie. 1966. Trans. Faraday Soc. **62:** 1002.

16. Ladik, J., G. Biczo & G. Elek. 1966. J. Chem. Phys. **44:** 483, and earlier papers cited herein.
17. Hoffmann, T. A. & J. Ladik. 1961. Cancer Res. **21:** 474.
18. Bozoky, L., G. Kiszely, T. A. Hoffmann & J. Ladik. 1963. Nature **199:** 1306.
19. Cardew, M. H. & D. D. Eley. 1959. Discuss. Faraday Soc. **27:** 115.
20. Chargaff, E. 1955. *In* The Nucleic Acids: A) 335, B) 341. Academic Press. New York, N. Y.
21. Bersohn, R. & I. Isenberg. 1964. J. Chem. Phys. **40:** 3175.
22. Douzou, P., J. C. Francq, M. Harss & M. Ptak. 1961. J. Chim. Phys. **58:** 926.
23. Trukhan, E. M. 1966. Biofizika **11:** 412.
24. Langridge, R. & A. Rich. 1963. Nature **198:** 725.
25. Rich, A., D. R. Davies, F. H. C. Crick & T. D. Watson. 1961. J. Molec. Biol. **3:** 71
26. Tomita, K. & A. Rich. 1964. Nature **201:** 1160.
27. Rich, A. 1958. Biochem. Biophys. Acta **29:** 502.
28. See Gutman, F. & L. E. Lyons. 1967. Organic Semiconductors: Chap. 6. John Wiley & Sons. New York, N. Y.
29. Pullman, B. 1964. C. R. Acad. Sci. **259:** 3101.
30. Mesnard, G. & D. Vasilescu. 1963. Compt. Rend. Acad. Sci. **257:** 4177.
31. Mesnard, G., D. Vasilescu & Y. Mathon. 1965. Phys. Stat. Sol. **11:** K137.
32. Basu, S. & W. J. Moore. 1963. J. Phys. Chem. **67:** 1563.
33. Eley, D. D. 1967. J. Polymer Sci. (C) **17:** 73.
34. Eley, D. D., A. S. Fawcett & M. R. Willis. 1968. Trans. Faraday Soc. In press.
35. Pope, M. 1967. Sci. Amer.: 88.
36. Ladik, J., D. K. Rai & K. Appel. 1966. Quantum Chemistry Group: (preprint). Uppsala University. Uppsala, Sweden.
37. Beleznay, F., G. Biczo & J. Ladik. 1964. Phys. Lett. **11:** 234.
38. Ladik, J., G. Biczo & G. Elek. 1966. J. Chem. Phys. **44:** 483.
39. Eley, D. D., K. W. Jones, J. G. F. Littler & M. R. Willis. 1966. Trans. Faraday Soc. **62:** 3192.

DNA-POLYLYSINE INTERACTION AS STUDIED BY POLARIZATION OF FLUORESCENCE*

Jay Evett and Irvin Isenberg
Department of Biochemistry and Biophysics
Oregon State University
Corvallis, Ore.

Introduction

In multicellular organisms, DNA exists in the form of a nucleoprotein complex. Most of these proteins are histones, which are basic and carry a large positive charge. The electrostatic interaction between negatively charged DNA and positively charged histone undoubtedly accounts for a considerable part of the binding. Other interactions may exist, however, and probably do.

In recent years, much attention has been given to the study of histone-DNA and basic polyamino acid-DNA complexes (Ohlenbusch *et al.*, 1967; Ohba, 1966 a, b; Olins *et al.*, 1967; Leng & Felsenfeld, 1966; Tsuboi *et al.*, 1966; Huang & Bonner, 1964; Huang *et al.*, 1964; Johns & Butler, 1964). In particular, the polylysine-DNA complex has been examined by a variety of techniques, and the following properties are known: a) At low salt concentrations the complex is irreversible in the sense that dynamic equilibrium does not exist (Tsuboi *et al.*, 1966). Alteration of the site of binding of the polylysine does not occur over relatively long periods of time. b) The complex has a definite stoichiometry of one lysine per one DNA phosphate (Tsuboi *et al.*, 1966; Olins *et al.*, 1967). This implies that a definite structural basis for the complex exists. c) The polylysine stabilizes the DNA. The complexed DNA melts at a considerably higher temperature than uncomplexed DNA (Ohba, 1966 b; Olins *et al.*, 1967; Tsuboi *et al.*, 1966). d) The binding shows a degree of cooperativity e) In the presence of NaCl, polylysine binds preferentially to A–T rich DNA, but the specificity is reversed in tetramethylammonium chloride solutions. (Leng & Felsenfeld, 1966; Olins *et al.*, 1967).

In this paper, we shall describe studies on the salt dissociation of polylysine-DNA by measurements of the intensity and polarization of fluorescence of dye-labeled polylysine and also report the results of turbidity measurements on such samples.

There has been surprisingly little use of polarization of fluorescence for quantitative investigations of DNA complexes. To our knowledge, the only prior quantitative study is an investigation of lysozyme—DNA and bovine serum albumin—DNA interactions (Steiner, 1953; Steiner & Edelhoch, 1962).

Materials and Methods

Poly-L-lysine was synthesized by the N-carboxyamino acid anhydride method (Becker & Stahmann, 1952; Katchalsky & Sela, 1958). The polylysine was analyzed by chromatography on a CM-cellulose column using an exponential sodium chloride gradient (Stewart & Stahmann, 1962). Most of

* This investigation was supported in part by National Science Foundation Research Grant No. GB-6185. Jay Evett was the recipient of a National Science Foundation Science Faculty Fellowship.

the work reported here was done on samples having a single range of molecular weights, centered around a degree of polymerization (D.P.) of 275. Some work was done on samples of 140 D.P. However, all comparisons of the effectiveness of different salts were based on results of samples with a D.P. of 275. Commercial salmon sperm DNA (Calbiochem) was used.

The dye was conjugated to polylysine by mixing an acetone solution of 1-dimethylaminonaphthalene-5-sulfonyl chloride (dansyl chloride) with an aqueous solution of polylysine. The mixture was permitted to stand for several hours, after which the acetone was removed by flash evaporation. The solution was dialyzed extensively against water and then passed through a Sephadex G-10 column. The lysine to dansyl ratio was 21.7.

The dansyl-polylysine was complexed to DNA by gradient dialysis (Huang *et al.*, 1964) in the following way. Dansyl-polylysine and DNA were mixed in 2.6 M NaCl to a final concentration of 1.92 mM phosphate and 0.442 mM lysine. In 2.6 M NaCl, the dansyl-polylysine and DNA are essentially uncomplexed. The mixture was dialyzed against successively lower concentrations of salt, reaching a final solution composition of 0.05 M NaCl and 0.1 M cacodylate buffer at pH 5.5. The solutions at this stage were turbid and contained visible precipitates. The precipitates were removed by centrifugation at 30,000 g for 90 minutes. The DNA concentration in the supernate was 1.02×10^{-3} M(P), and the phosphate to lysine ratio was 12. The concentration of dansyl was 3.82×10^{-6} M. This supernate was used for measurements of polarization of fluorescence, intensity of fluorescence, and turbidity. Samples were run at 25.0 ± 0.2^0 C.

Salts were added as powder and corrections for water of hydration were made, when necessary, by standard quantitive analysis of weighed amounts of material.

The polarization of fluorescence was measured using an instrument built in our laboratory. The instrument is a continuously recording polarization spectrometer having features in common with those described by Weber and Bablouzian (1966) and Deranleau (1966). Light from a 500 W Xenon lamp passes through a Jarrell-Ash ¼ M Ebert Monochromator and then through a Glan prism and an American Time Products 150 Hz tuning fork light chopper. This light excites the sample. The emission is detected by two EMI 9524B photomultipliers at right angles to the exciting beam on opposite sides of the sample. One photomultiplier senses light polarized parallel to the polarization of the exciting light. The intensity of this beam will be called I_E in this paper. The other photomultiplier senses light polarized in the direction of the exciting beam and perpendicular to the polarization of the exciting beam. The intensity of this beam will be called I_B. Filters before the photomultipliers block the passage of scattered exciting radiation.

The photomultiplier currents pass to the summing points of P25AU Philbrick operational amplifiers having 10^8 ohm feedback resistors. The output voltages are applied to lock-in amplifiers. A variable gain amplifier is in the I_E branch of the circuit.

$p = (I_E - I_B)/(I_E + I_B)$ is computed by an analog computer using a Leeds and Northrup No. 444185 Multiplier-Divider card. $I_E + 2\ I_B$ is computed with the use of a Philbrick P85AU operational amplifier and a standard adding circuit. $I_E + 2\ I_B$ is proportional to I, the intensity emitted by the sample (Weber, 1952), when the exciting beam is plane polarized. In practice, the polarizer in the exciting beam is first set for horizontally polarized light. With this setting $I_E = I_B$. The variable gain amplifier is set, therefore, so that $p = 0$. This adjustment compensates for mismatched sensitivities of the photomultipliers and the associated circuitry. Using rhodamine B as a test solution, we found that if p = 0 is set for one wavelength, the instrument reads p = 0 for all exciting wavelengths down to 270 nm.

After adjustment of the variable gain amplifier, the Glan prism in the excitation beam is set for vertically polarized light. With rhodamine B, we find that the instrument yields polarization values close to that reported by other workers in the literature (Weber, 1956; Deranleau, 1966), and we estimate our error to be about $\delta p = 0.002$.

Special precautions were taken because our samples were turbid and had weak emission. Consequently, the stray light from the monochromator was not negligibly small compared to the fluorescence intensity. Without precautions, this stray light would have raised the measured p above the actual p. The possibility of this artifact was eliminated by the use of a Corning 7–51 filter in the excitation beam. This use of complementary filters has been described by Weber (1952). Possible artifacts due to scattering of the emitted beam were checked by comparing results using samples in cuvettes of varying path length. The polarization of our samples was the same, to three significant figures, whether measured using 1 cm × 1 cm cuvettes or 2 mm × 2 mm cuvettes.

Turbidity was measured in a Cary Model 14 spectrophotometer at 500 nm.

Results

The polarization of fluorescence of the dansyl-polylysine DNA complex, excited at 355 nm. was 0.290. This value dropped upon the addition of salt (FIGURES 1, 2) reaching a final value of about 0.200 for most salts. Dissocia-

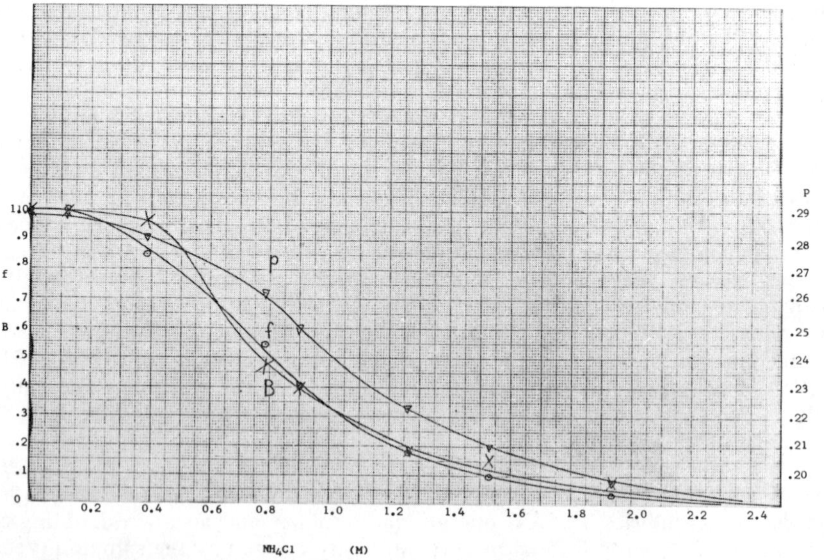

FIGURE 1. NH_4Cl dissociation of dansyl polylysine-DNA. Polylysine D. P. ≈ 275. f: fraction of dansyl polylysine bound to DNA, as determined by Equation 12. B: fractional decrement of turbidity. p: polarization.

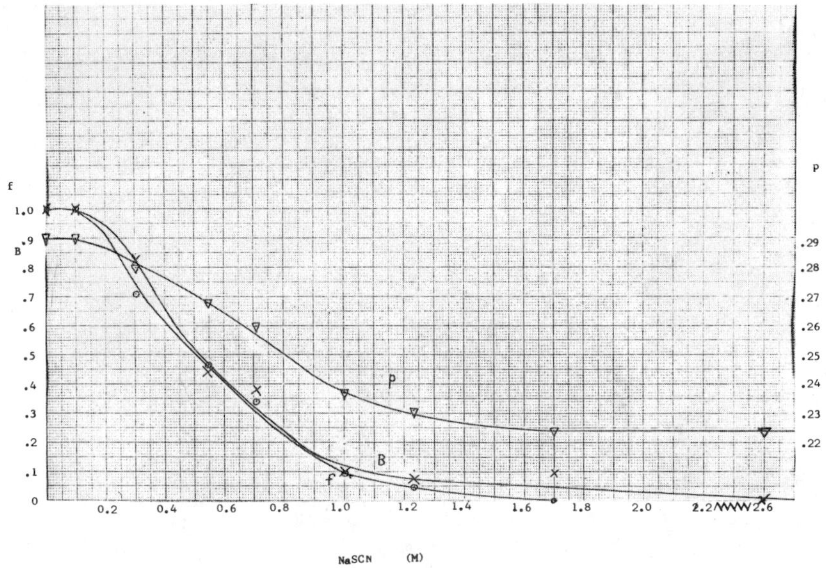

FIGURE 2. NaSCN dissociation of dansyl polylysine-DNA. Polylysine D. P. ≈ 275. f: fraction of dansyl polylysine bound to DNA, as determined by Equation 12. B: fractional decrement of turbidity. p: polarization.

tion by $NaClO_4$ and NaSCN resulted in final p values of 0.225 and 0.224, respectively.

FIGURE 3 shows the variation of intensity of fluorescence for dissociation by LiCl. Most salts showed the qualitative shape of the LiCl curve. The position of the intensity drop depended on the salt used, however.

The initial value of the turbidity was in the range 0.02–0.04 optical density units at 500 nm measured in a 1 cm cuvette. For salts containing monovalent cations, the turbidity decreased monotonically with increasing salt concentration. For Mg^{++} salts, the turbidity showed an initial rise followed by a subsequent decline (FIGURE 4), whereas p for $MgCl_2$ is monotonically decreasing (FIGURE 5). Low concentrations of other divalent cations, such as Mn^{++} or Cu^{++}, precipitated the complex.

A plot of percent change in p is markedly different from a plot of percent change in turbidity. However, the percent change in p has little or no theoretical significance. A more meaningful analysis of the data may be based on the use of the addition law for polarization (Weber 1952, 1953). This states that, for a multicomponent solution,

$$\frac{1}{p} - \frac{1}{3} = \frac{1}{\sum_i \frac{\phi_i}{\frac{1}{p_i} - \frac{1}{3}}} \tag{1}$$

where p_i is the polarization of the light emitted by the ith species; p is the measured polarizaion and ϕ_i is the fraction of the light emitted by the ith species.

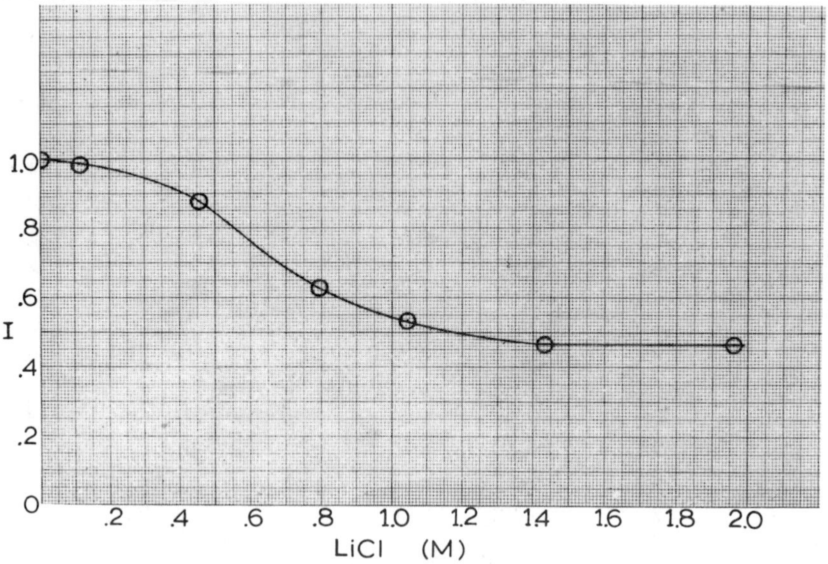

FIGURE 3. Intensity of fluorescence of dansyl polylysine-DNA vs LiCl concentration.

For an analysis of the data, we assume, essentially, that only two species are present—bound dansyl polylysine and free dansyl polylysine. In other words, we assume that the concentration of any other state is negligibly small compared to the concentration of these states. p_1, the polarization of the emission of bound dansyl polylysine, was taken to be the polarization at low salt concentrations. p_2 was taken to be the limiting polarization at high salt concentrations.

It should be noted that the accuracy of the present analysis is diminished if added salt appreciably raises the viscosity of the solution, so that the polarization is affected by viscosity alterations.

Under the assumption of essentially only two states

$$\phi_1 + \phi_2 = 1 \tag{2}$$

Let

$$\frac{1}{\mu} = \frac{1}{p} - \frac{1}{3} \tag{3}$$

$$\frac{1}{\mu_i} = \frac{1}{p_i} - \frac{1}{3} \tag{4}$$

Then, from Equations 1 through 4

$$\phi_1 = \frac{\mu - \mu_2}{\mu_1 - \mu_2} \tag{5}$$

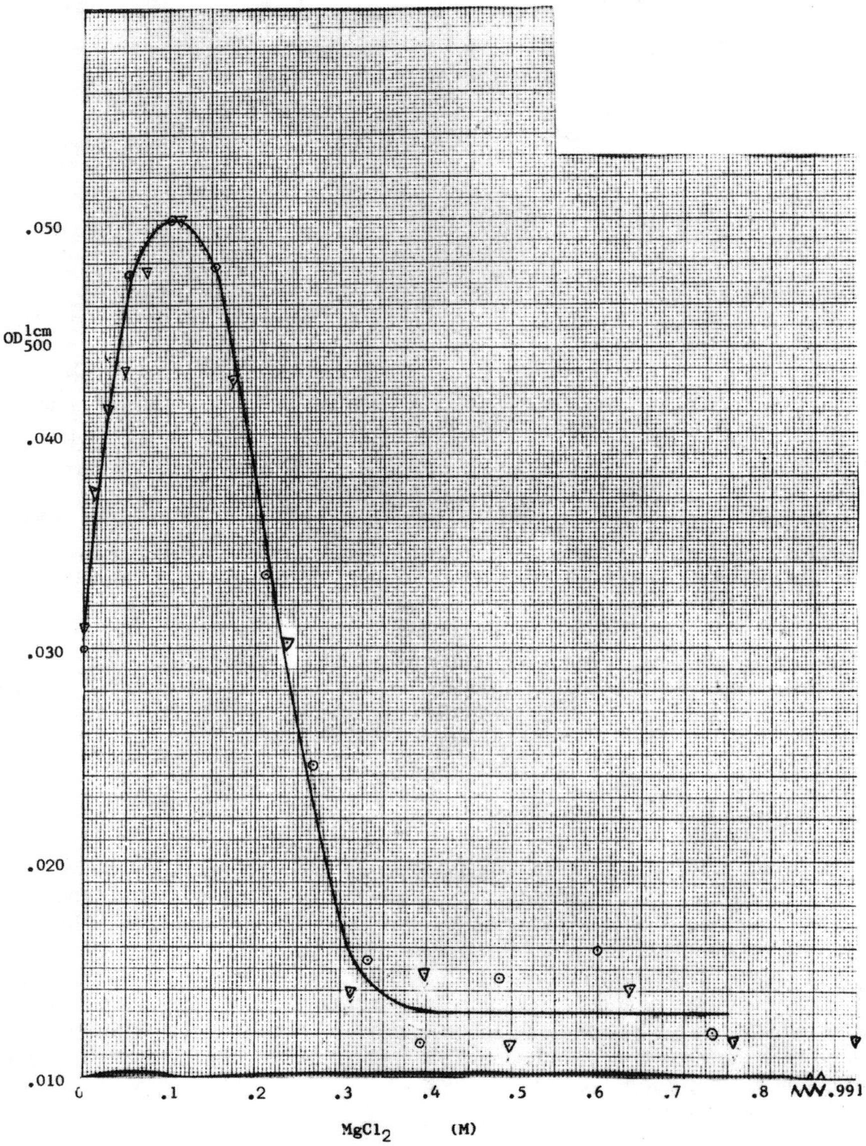

FIGURE 4. Turbidity versus $MgCl_2$ molarity for dansyl polylysine-DNA. Polylysine D. P. ≈ 275.

Let ϵ_1, ϵ_2 be the respective molar extinction coefficients, q_1, q_2 the quantum yields and I_1, I_2 the corresponding emitted intensities. $I = I_1 + I_2$. Let f be the fraction of molecules bound.

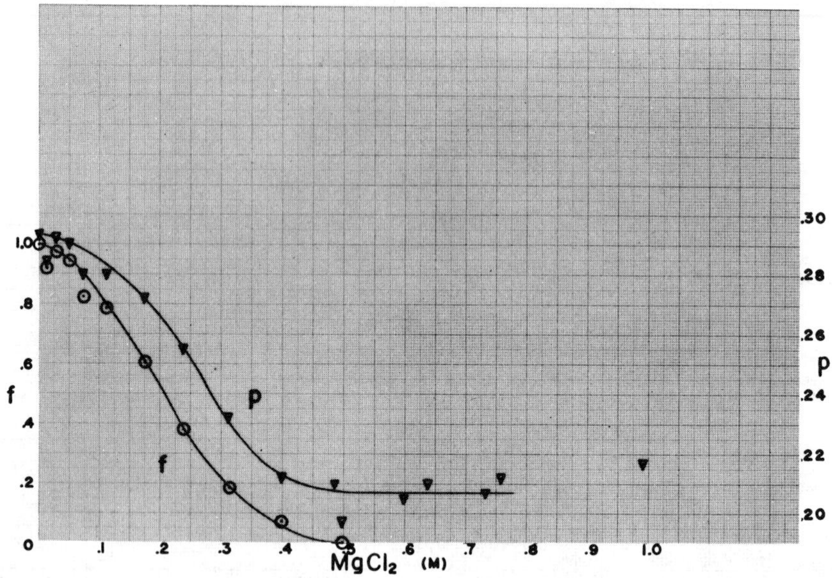

FIGURE 5. $MgCl_2$ dissociation of dansyl polylysine-DNA. Polylysine D. P. ≈ 275. f: fraction of dansyl polylysine bound to DNA, as determined by Equation 12. p: polarization.

$$\phi_1 = \frac{f\epsilon_1 q_1}{f\epsilon_1 q_1 + (1 - f)\epsilon_2 q_2} \tag{6}$$

$$f = \frac{\phi_1}{\phi_1 + (1 - \phi_1)\dfrac{\epsilon_1 q_1}{\epsilon_2 q_2}} \tag{7}$$

In general, the molar extinction coefficients and the quantum yields may vary with c, the salt concentration. It is possible, but unlikely, that such variations might be due to a direct interaction between salt and dye. What appears to be a more likely possibility is that variations would be due to indirect effects. Thus, the conformation of free dansyl polylysine could alter as the salt concentration changed, which in turn would place the dye in an altered environment, thus changing the spectral properties of the dye. Thus, we assume that the $\epsilon_4 q_1$ is independent of salt concentration, whereas $\epsilon_2 q_2$ may vary with salt concentration.

For the general case

$$I(c) = K\{\epsilon_1(c)q_1(c)f(c) + \epsilon_2(c)q_2(c)[1 - f(c)]\}$$

where K is a constant.

Since Tsuboi and collaborators (1966) showed that all of the polylysine is bound at low salt concentrations, f = 1 when c = 0. Therefore

$$I(c) = \frac{I(0)}{\epsilon_1(0)q_1(0)}\{\epsilon_1(c)q_1(c)f(c) + \epsilon_2(c)q_2(c)[1 - f(c)]\} \tag{8}$$

From Equations 7 and 8

$$f = \frac{I(c)}{I(0)} \frac{\epsilon_1(0)q_1(0)}{\epsilon_1(c)q_1(c)} \phi_1 \tag{9}$$

However, as discussed above, we assume that

$$\frac{\epsilon_1(0)q_1(0)}{\epsilon_1(c)q_1(c)} = 1 \tag{10}$$

With this assumption

$$f = \frac{I(c)}{I(0)} \phi_1 \tag{11}$$

$$f = \frac{I(c)}{I(0)} \frac{\mu - \mu_2}{\mu_1 - \mu_2} \tag{12}$$

Equation 12 permits the calculation of f from measurable parameters.

It is interesting to ask questions concerning the sensitivity of the calculated value of f to assumptions regarding the dependence of the quantities $\epsilon_i q_i$ on the salt concentration.

We may, for example, make the more stringent assumption that, not only does Equation 10 hold, but

$$\frac{\epsilon_2(c)q_2(c)}{\epsilon_2(\infty)q_2(\infty)} = 1 \tag{13}$$

also holds.

Under these assumptions

$$f = \frac{\phi_1}{(1 - \phi_1) \dfrac{I(0)}{I(\infty)} + \phi_1}$$

$$f = \frac{1}{1 + \dfrac{I(0)}{I(\infty)} \dfrac{\mu_1 - \mu}{\mu - \mu_2}} \tag{14}$$

Equation 14 may also be used to compute f from measurable quantities. In this case, it is necessary to measure the intensity at two salt concentrations only.

FIGURE 6 shows computed f values for LiCl dissociation, using both sets of assumptions. It may be seen that a computation of f for LiCl is insensitive to the validity of the assumption embodied in Equation 13.

However, if both Equations 10 and 13 are valid, it is possible to compute f from intensity measurements alone. From Equation 8

$$f = \frac{I(c) - I(\infty)}{I(0) - I(\infty)} \tag{15}$$

FIGURE 7 shows that, for LiCl, f(c) computed by Equations 12 and 15 agree with one another. This agreement cannot be taken to mean that the assumptions are strictly valid. What the agreement signifies is that the de-

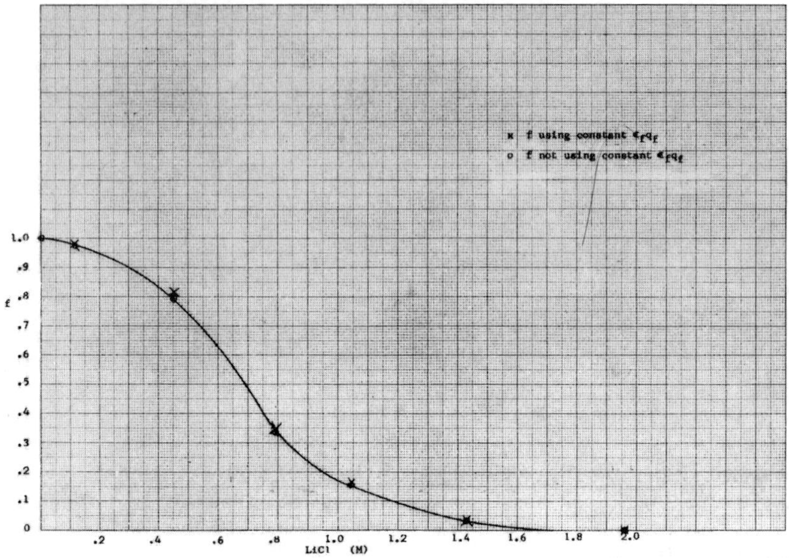

FIGURE 6. LiCl dissociation of dansyl polylysine-DNA. Polylysine D. P. ≈ 275. f: fraction of dansyl polylysine bound to DNA, as determined by Equation 12, ⊙, and Equation 14, ×.

crease in intensity upon the addition of salt is primarily due to the dissociation of the complex, and that other effects are small by comparison.

Let A = optical density measured at 500 nm.

$$B = \frac{A(c) - A(\infty)}{A(0) - A(\infty)}$$

We find, for salts containing monovalent cations, that a plot of B(c) vs c is very nearly the same as a plot of f(c) vs c (FIGURES 1, 2).

For Mg^{++} salts, however, there is an initial rise in B(c) that is not apparent in a plot of p or f (FIGURES 4, 5).

TABLE 1 gives a comparison of the salt concentrations for f = 1/2 and B = ½ for a variety of salts.

TABLE 1

SALT CONCENTRATIONS FOR f = 1/2 AND B = 1/2*

Salt	Salt Molarity f = 0.5	B = 0.5
$NaC_2H_3O_2$	1.24	1.06
NaCl	.86	.83
NaBr	.65	.68
$NaNO_3$	.64	.61
$NaClO_4$	.50	.42
NaSCN	.50	.52
NH_4Cl	.79	.77
KCl	.89	.97
LiCl	.69	.71
$MgCl_2$	.20	

* f was determined from Equation 12, and B is the fractional decrement in turbidity for the dissociation of dansyl polylysine-DNA. Polylysine D. P. ≈ 275.

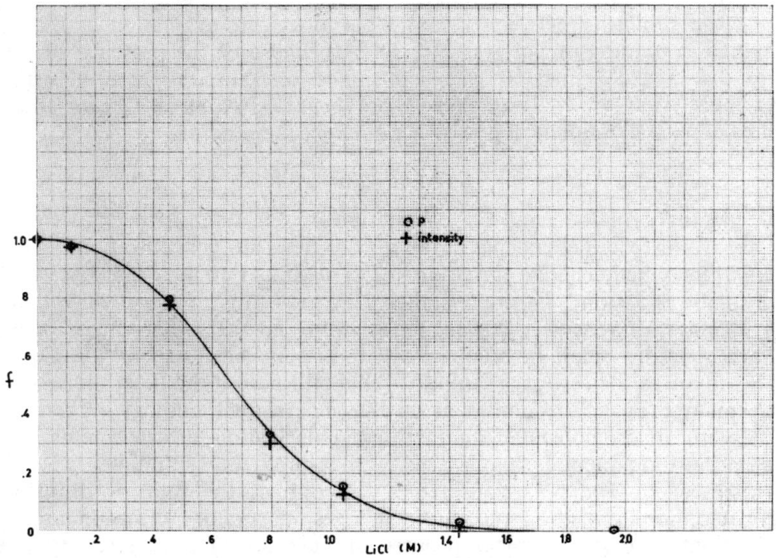

FIGURE 7. LiCl dissociation of dansyl polylysine-DNA. Polylysine D. P. $\approx$ 275. f: fraction of dansyl polylysine bound to DNA, as determined by Equation 12, $\odot$, and Equation 15, +.

TABLE 2 shows the order of ion effectiveness in dissociating the complex. For comparison, the order of effectiveness for conformational changes of a number of other systems is also shown.

TABLE 2

RELATIVE EFFECTIVENESS OF IONS*

	$\longleftarrow$ Helix Coil $\longrightarrow$ $\longleftarrow$ Complex Dissociate $\longrightarrow$
Collagen-Gelatin	$SO_4^{=} < CH_3COO^- < Cl^- < Br^- < NO_3^- < ClO_4^- < I^- < SCN^-$ $(CH_3)_4N^+ < NH_4^+ < Rb^+, K^+, Na^+, Cs^+ < Li^+ < Mg^{++} < Ca^{++} < Ba^{++}$ $(CH_3)_4N^+ < (C_2H_5)_4N^+ \ll (C_3H_7)_4N^+, (C_4H_9)_4N^+$
Ribonuclease	$SO^{=}_4 < CH_3COO^- < Cl^- < Br^- < ClO_4^- < SCN^-$ $(CH_3)_4N^+ NH_4^+, K^+, Na^+, < Li^+ < Ca^{++}$ $(CH_3)_4N^+ < (C_2H_5)_4N^+ < (C_3H_7)_4N^+ < (C_4H_9)_4N^+$
DNA	$Cl^-, Br^- < CH_3COO^- < I^- < ClO_4^- < SCN^-$ $(CH_3)_4N^+ < K^+ < Na^+ < Li^+$
Myosin	$Cl^- < Br^- < I^- < SCN^-$ $K^+ < Li^+$
Oligolysine-poly (A + U)	$(CH_3)_4N^+ < K^+, NH_4^+ < Li^+ < Na^+$
Oligolysine-poly (I + C)	$(CH_3)_4N^+ < Li^+ < NH_4^+ < K^+ < Na^+$
Polylysine-DNA	$CH_3COO^- < Cl^- < Br^- < NO_3^- < ClO_4^-, SCN^-$ $K^+ < Na^+, NH_4^+ < Li^+ < Mg^{++}$

*Relative effectiveness of ions in destabilizing the native form of collagen, ribonuclease, DNA, and myosin is taken from von Hippel & Wong (1964). Effect of ions on the binding of oligolysine to poly (A + U) and poly (I + C) is from Latt & Sober (1967).

The close similarity between B and f permitted the evaluation of the possible change in binding of polylysine to DNA because of the presence of a fraction of dye-tagged lysines. B was determined on samples prepared with untagged polylysine as well as dansyl polylysine. FIGURE 8 shows that the presence of a small amount of dye does not effect the binding.

Discussion

We find that, for most salts, a calculation of f is insensitive to the assumptions regarding the dependence of $\epsilon_i q_i$ on the salt concentration. Thus, it matters little whether only Equation 10 is assumed to be valid, or whether both Equations 10 and 13 are assumed. We take this to mean only that the major change in intensity is due to dissociation and that other causes of intensity variations are small in comparison. It is best, however, to use Equation 12. This involves the fewest assumptions that still permit the determination of f.

It seems appropriate to comment on the general methodology. When one is dealing with macromolecular interactions, polarization measurements appear to be more fundamental than intensity measurements although, in general, both are needed. The polarization is a function of the rotatory diffusion of the chromophore transition moment. Changes in rotatory diffusion are more directly related to the physical process of complexing than intensity alterations. In addition, there may be instances in which intensity changes might be minimal on complexing, while marked polarization changes would still occur. Furthermore, when studying macromolecules, it is necessary to measure the polarization, or its equivalent, in order to obtain the total intensity of emitted light.

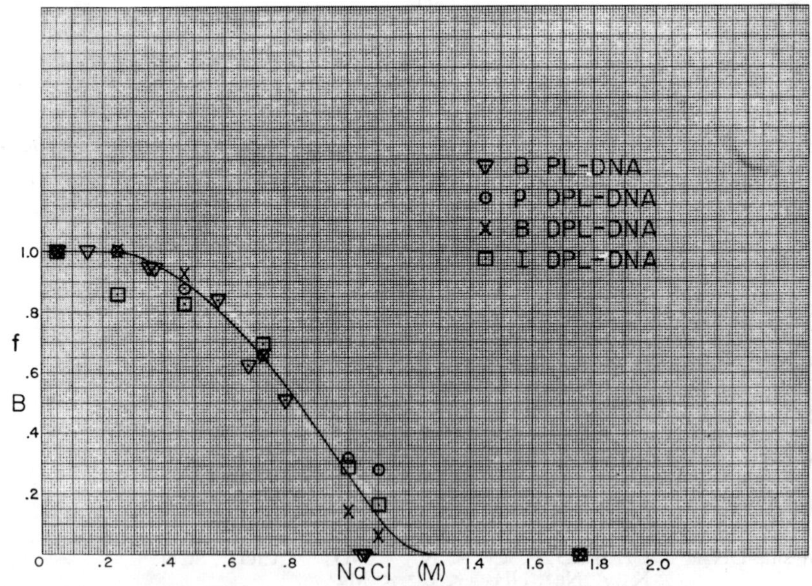

FIGURE 8. NaCl dissociation of polylysine-DNA. Polylysine without dye D. P. ≈ 140. ▽ : f determined by turbidity for unlabeled polylysine. ⊙, ×, ⊡ : f determined by Equation 12, turbidity, and Equation 15, respectively for dansyl polylysine.

The close agreement between B(c) and f(c) deserves comment. B(c) is the fractional decrement in turbidity. If the association between polylysine and DNA were random, B(c) would be weighted toward the larger aggregates and one would not expect a close agreement between B(c) and f(c). However, the available evidence (Tsuboi et al., 1966; Olins et al., 1967) indicates that the polylysine-DNA complex is stoichiometric and structurally well defined. If the scattering unit were either the complex, or a simple and well-defined association of complexes, then one would expect B to be proportional to the number of such scattering units. In this case, agreement between B and f would be expected. Our results are consistent, therefore, with the model of a well-defined complex between polylysine and DNA.

The Hofmeister series was found to be the order of effectiveness in denaturing a wide variety of biopolymers (von Hippel & Wong, 1964; von Hippel & Wong, 1965; Bello, 1965). Our work demonstrates that the salt dissociation of DNA-polylysine follows the same series. TABLE 2 summarizes the pertinent comparisons.

Recent discussions of the destabilization of proteins by salts have involved the consideration of the binding of ions and peptides and also the effect of salts on water structure (Schrier & Schrier, 1967; Robinson & Jencks, 1965; von Hippel & Wong 1964, 1965; von Hippel & Schleich, 1968, and references therein). The review of von Hippel and Schleich (1968) analyzes the pertinent evidence, and the reader is referred to that paper for a thorough discussion of the problems involved.

It appears premature, at present, to attempt a quantitative analysis of the polylysine-DNA dissociation by salts in terms of mechanism. However, it is of considerable interest that, as shown in TABLE 2, Latt and Sober (1967) reported that cations had a different order of effectiveness in dissociating oligolysine-poly (A + U) and oligolysine-poly (I + C) than that found by us in dissociating polylysine-DNA. Such differences seem to indicate that the complexes involve more than simple ionic interactions, and suggest that interesting specificities exist.

Acknowledgment

Much of the development of the polarization spectrometer was carried out by Spencer L. Baird, Jr. The machine shop work was done by John Archibald. Many of the electronic components were constructed by Dale Weeden. The authors thank these workers for their able assistance.

The authors wish to thank Drs. Peter von Hippel and Thomas Schleich for permitting them to read their review article prior to its publication.

References

BECKER, R. R. & M. A. STAHMANN. 1952. J. Amer. Chem. Soc. **74:**38.
BELLO, J. 1965. Biochim. Biophys. Acta **109:**250.
DERANLEAU, D. A. 1966. Annal. *Biochem.* **18:**438.
HUANG, R. C. & J. BONNER. 1964. *In* The Nucleohistones. J. Bonner & P. O. P. Ts'o, Eds.: 262. Holden-Day. San Francisco, Calif.
HUANG, R. C., J. BONNER & K. MURRAY. 1964. J. Molec. Biol. **8:**54.
JOHNS, E. W. & J. A. V. BUTLER. 1964. Nature **204:**853.
KATCHALSKY, E. & M. SELA. 1958. Advan. Protein Chem. **13:**394.
LATT, S. A. & H. A. SOBER. 1967. Biochemistry. **6:**3307.
LENG, M. & G. FELSENFELD. 1966. Proc. Nat. Acad. Sci. **56:**1325.
OHBA, Y. 1966. Biochim. Biophys. Acta **123:**76.

OHBA, Y. 1966. Biochim. Biophys. Acta **123**:84.
OHLENBUSCH, H. H., B. M. OLIVERA, D. TUAN & N. DAVIDSON. 1967. J. Molec. Biol. **25**:299.
OLINS, D. E., A. L. OLINS & P. H. VON HIPPEL. 1967. J. Molec. Biol. **24**:157.
ROBINSON, D. R. & W. P. JENCKS. 1965. J. Amer. Chem. Soc. **87**:2470.
SCHRIER, E. E. & E. B. SCHRIER. 1967. J. Phys. Chem. **71**:1851.
STEINER, R. F. 1953. Arch. Biochem. Biophys. **46**:291.
STEINER, R. F. & H. EDELHOCH. 1962. Chem. Rev. **62**:457.
STEWART, J. W. & M. A. STAHMANN. 1962. *In* Polyamino Acids, Polypeptides and Proteins. M. A. Stahmann, Ed:95. Univ. of Wisconsin Press. Madison, Wis.
TSUBOI, M., K. MATSUO & P. O. P. TS'O. 1966. J. Molec. Biol. **15**:256.
VON HIPPEL, P. H. & K. WONG. 1964. Science **145**:577.
VON HIPPEL, P. H. & K. WONG. 1965. J. Biol. Chem. **240**:3909.
VON HIPPEL, P. H. & T. SCHLEICH. 1968. *In* Biological Macromolecules. G. Fasman & S. Timasheff, Eds.: 2. Marcel Dekker. New York, N. Y.
WEBER, G. & B. BABLOUZIAN. 1966. J. Biol. Chem. **241**:2558.
WEBER, G. 1952. Biochem. J. **51**:145.
WEBER, G. 1953. Advan. Protein Chem. **8**:415.
WEBER, G. 1956. J. Opt. Soc. Amer. **46**:962.

THE ELECTROSTATIC FREE ENERGY OF MACROMOLECULAR SYSTEMS*

A. I. McMullen

Center for Theoretical Biology and Biophysics Department
State University of New York
Buffalo, N. Y.

The effect of the energy provided to a molecule by virtue of its having dissociable ionic groups, and thus a certain net electrostatic charge, is readily discernible in biological systems. The configuration and aggregation of proteins and the activity of some (perhaps all) enzymes, the phenomena of antibody-antigen interactions, the replication of DNA and RNA, the RNA triplet-triplet interaction involved in the coding mechanism for amino-acid sequence specification in proteins, the specificity of cell-cell aggregation and many other macromolecule interactions, such as drug-receptor recognition, appear to depend noticeably on electrostatic forces.

Fundamental experimental studies of the nature and extent of these forces have been made—not so much by biologists as by colloid scientists and physical chemists—and much effort has gone into interpreting the observed changes in electrical potentials at interfaces containing oriented monomolecular films of ionized macromolecules. At such asymmetric interfaces, the permanent molecular dipole contributes to the observed potential difference which, however, depends logarithmically on the ionic strength of the substrate

$$\Delta V = \frac{4\pi\mu d}{A} + Z_i F \psi_0$$

(where μd is the effective dipole change normal to the interface, A is the area of interface occupied per macromolecule and ψ_0 is the electrical potential on the boundary). It has been shown theoretically that such a logarithmic relationship also exists for the electrostatic free-energy change of polyelectrolyte micelles such as DNA by application of a statistical argument and also by using the Debye-Hückel derivation for ion distribution.[1] In these cases the geometry-dependent dipole contribution was assumed to be independent of ionic strength.

Attempts to calculate accurately the interfacial ψ_0, however, resulted in certain discrepancies, due largely to the highly nonlinear nature of the function describing the potential field near such an interface in the presence of mobile or diffuse-layer ions. Thus, the entropic randomizing of the spatial distribution of these ions is modified by electrostatic interactions in accordance with the Boltzmann exponential distribution law. This states that the charge density, σ, due to a potential field, ψ, is given by the probability difference factor $N_e(e^{-e\psi/kT} - e^{e\psi/kT})$ for the positive and negative mobile ions ($N_+ = N_- = N$) of charge e. Thus, $\sigma = -Ne \sinh(e_\psi/kT)$.

The electrostatic free energy $e\psi$, the work required to bring the ion from infinity to the location of ψ, is $W_e = \int_0^e \psi \cdot dq.$, and by employing Poisson's relation for the variation of potential due to a continuous charge density distribution σ, in a medium of dielectric constant D,

* This work was supported by Grant NSG-501 from NASA.

$$\nabla^2\psi = -\frac{4\pi\sigma}{D}$$

the Poisson-Boltzmann equation is derived. The form of this depends on the geometry of the application required and the choice of coordinate system for the Laplacian operator.

Validity of the Poisson-Boltzmann Equation

Since the use of this equation is a basic feature of the treatment described in this paper, a brief summary of the criticisms of, and the corrections to, this equation is necessary. An account is given by Falkenhagen[2] and by Fowler.[3] Kirkwood[4] objected to the application of this equation on the grounds that in the $e\psi$ term it is assumed that ψ remains constant as the ion is brought up from infinity. Clearly this will not be so, since the approach of the new ion must cause a redistribution of other ions in the vicinity. The exact magnitude of the error here has not been determined, but it has been suggested[5] that for a multicharged surface the error may be small.

Other corrections necessary include those for ion volume, dielectric saturation, ion self-atmosphere, polarization and electrostriction.[5] Since the potential at the surface under consideration is increased by the former two effects[6] and decreased by the second two,[7, 8] and since the final one is a small correction,[9] there is a tendency for the original equation to give an approximately correct value for the potential due to a given charge density at low ionic strength. A summary of the influence of these corrections on the diffuse layer equations indicates that the ionic volume effect is probably the most important and, at ion molarities $>10^{-2}$ and potentials >100 mV, could lead to errors (with the assistance of dielectric saturation effects) of up to 40% in the calculation of ψ.[5]

Corrections to the Poisson-Boltzmann equation for the ion volume effect have been made with some success using a hard sphere model of the ion, the resultant equation showing a marked increase in e_ψ/kT as the counter-ion radius rises above 2 Å, at 0.1 M concentration.[10] A statistical "cluster theory" approach to this problem[11] agrees with the Poisson-Boltzmann equation at low concentration; but when the double layer distance $(1/\kappa)$ becomes of the same order of magnitude as the ionic diameter (about 0.5 M, 1:1 electrolyte) then a differential-difference solution appears, indicating an alternation in space charge sign with distance from the surface and thus an extensive structured region in the diffuse layer.

The method of local thermodynamic balance[12] to determine the mean value of ψ has also been used.[8] This procedure divides the diffuse layer by a family of equipotential surfaces into subregions where $|e\Delta\psi| < kT$, and within which a statistically significant number of ions exists. Using this procedure to include the self-atmospheric effect[13] tends to demonstrate that, at the present time, such cluster-type procedures cannot yet be accurately applied at high concentrations and large potentials. Therefore the procedures used in the present work, with the unmodified Poisson-Boltzmann equation solutions, more readily produce an adequate result under moderate conditions of charge and ion concentration in which the discrete ion effect (self-atmospheric potential), in particular, is not excessive.

The discrete ion effects mentioned above are also important in the fixed-charge or inner region of the macromolecule electrostatic double layer. The finite size of the ion and of its self-atmospheric potential greatly influences the dielectric state of solvent molecules and their entropic contribution (from the number of possible arrangements of these and of the adsorbed ions). However, the theory dealing with this aspect is still in the very early stages of development,[14, 15] and this complication is ignored in the present work. Indeed, the following applications of solutions to the Debye-Hückel and Poisson-Boltzmann equations are also confined to the limit of zero concentration of macro-ions where the effects in which we are interested still exist but where the influence of other macromolecules is absent. In principle, however, the applications are still valid to multimacromolecular systems such as membranes, virus and protein subunit complexes, etc., if the energy differences between static systems of given geometry are being calculated. Such calculations for a number of alternative geometries for a given multisystem could, of course, give an indication of the energetically preferred conformations as a function of ionic strength and temperature. Thus the intermolecular potential energy is not independent of the intramolecular coordinates of the individual molecules and the collision, close approach or even relative reorientation of two adjacent molecules involves a highly complex distribution of energy states within the system as energy is transferred and exchanged via this long-range coulombic interaction process.

Linearized (Debye-Hückel) Approximation to the Electrostatic Energy

By assuming that the exponential factor $e_\psi/kT \ll 1$, it is legitimate to ignore all but the first term in the series expansion of the Poisson-Boltzmann equation. This is a simplification usually made in theoretical calculations of the potential, and in this manner Hill[16] found the electrostatic energy of a segment of an infinite cylinder of uniform charge density (representing a helical macromolecule format, Figure 1, I), using modified Bessel function expansions. We have improved upon this procedure by employing a more exact model, which takes into account the internal dielectric and the discreteness of the charged phosphate-sugar backbone (Figure 1, II). In addition, we consider the difference in energy between this geometry and that of a so-called random coil (this latter being equivalent to the Hill model for the helix, namely an infinite cylinder of uniform charge but with a diameter representative of the backbone dimensions).[17] Hill's resultant equation is similar to the first term in our Equation 1 which is obtained as $\kappa \rightarrow 0$ (i.e. at low ion concentration) and is independent of the internal dielectric of the helix. For higher ionic strengths, as the double layer limit moves towards the surface of the helix, the discreteness emerges and the polarizability of the interior becomes important. Our theory predicts that differences in the polarizability play an observable role in the melting characteristics. Thus we find

$$W = \frac{\pi b \sigma_0^2}{\epsilon_0} \left\{ \frac{K_0(\kappa b)}{\kappa L D_0 K_1(\kappa b)} + \sum_{n=1}^{\infty} \frac{L^2 \, \mathrm{Sin}^2 \frac{n\pi\delta}{L} K_0(\sqrt{\kappa^2 + k_n^2}\, b)\, I_0(k_n b)}{n^3 \pi^3 \delta^2 \left[D_0 \sqrt{1 + \left(\frac{\kappa}{k_n}\right)^2} K_1(\sqrt{\kappa^2 + k_n^2}\, b)\, I_0(k_n b) + D_i K_0(\sqrt{\kappa^2 + k_n^2}\, b)\, I_1(k_n b) \right]} \right\} \tag{1}$$

where

$\kappa^2 = 2ne^2Z^2/D_0\epsilon_0kT$ (the Debye factor)

I_0 and K_0 are modified Bessel functions

$k_n = 2\pi n/L$

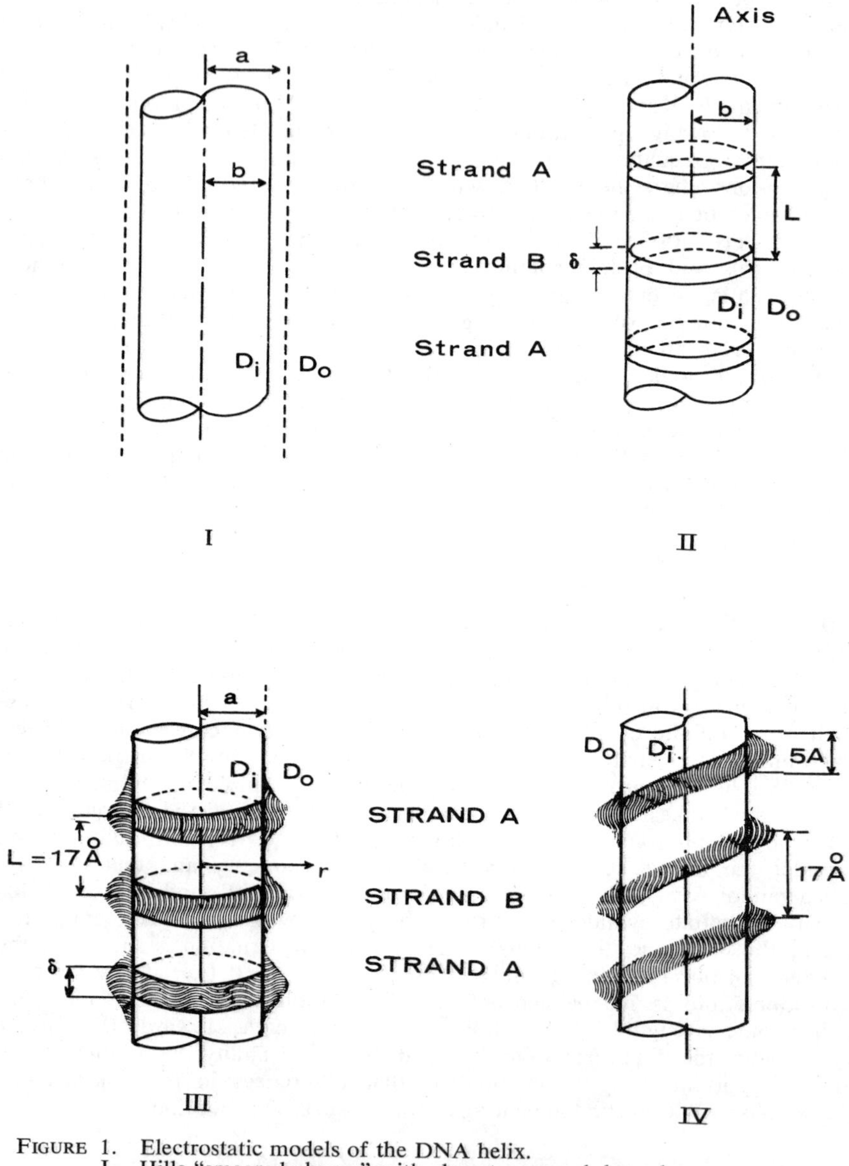

FIGURE 1. Electrostatic models of the DNA helix.
I. Hills "smeared charge" with closest approach boundary.
II. MacGillivray & McMullen's discretely banded format.
III. MacGillivray & McMullen's discretely periodic format.
IV. MacGillivray & McMullen's discrete helical periodicity.

FIGURE 2 illustrates a comparison between the energy (W) of the uniformly charged model, I, and the discretely charged model, II. At a concentration as low as 0.1 M, the difference in ΔW is fivefold; even at 0.01 M it is nearly twofold.

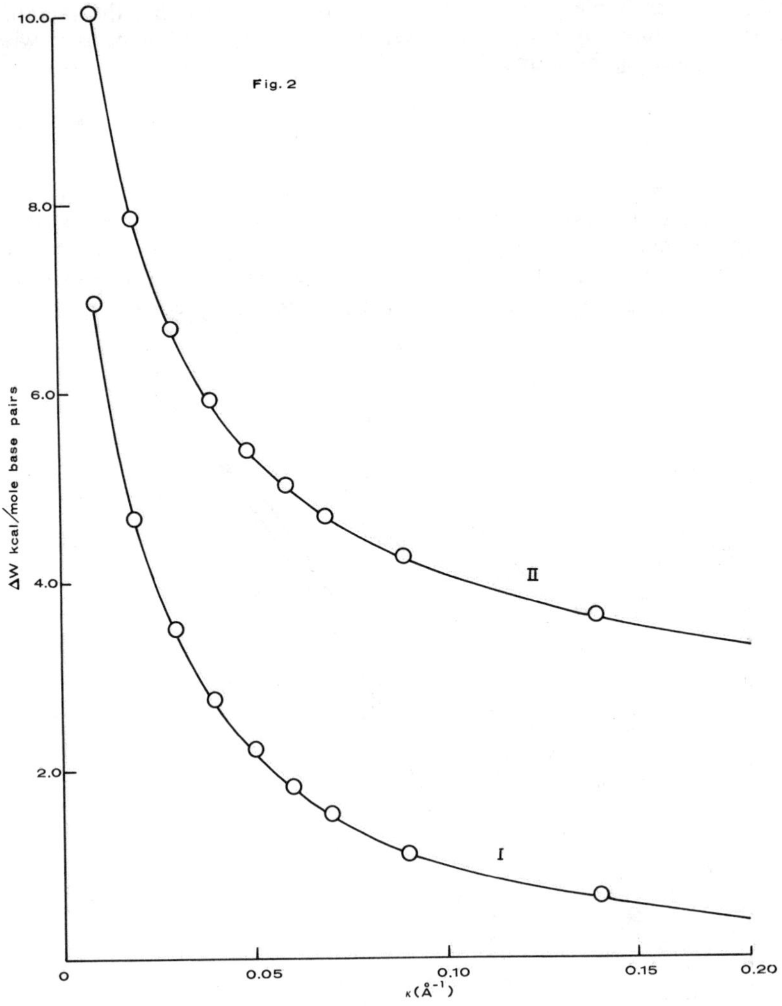

FIGURE 2. The effect of discreteness of charge on the linear theory of the helix energy.

I. Using the uniformly charged model I.
II. Using the discretely charged model II.

To investigate the effect of the energy differences on the DNA helix-coil transition, we employ throughout a simplified statistical theory which assumes: (1) that the electrostatic factor is the only one sensitive to ionic strength changes; (2) that the transition in question is in thermodynamic equilibrium; (3) that the transition can be treated as a phase change, i.e., that the temperature range over which the population of mainly double-helical complexes become mainly random coil (dissociated) molecules is small compared with the temperature differences observed by altering the ionic strength, or that the distribution of energy states within the transition region does not noticeably affect the T_m. (This latter assumption can be substantiated by a simple partition function argument); (4) that the random coil can be represented by a rigid rod over a length large in comparison with the distance separating the strands in the helix. We use the relation:

$$T_m = \frac{E^B + E^{ES}}{E^B} T_m', \tag{2}$$

where T_M' is melting temperature value at infinite salt ($E^{ES} \rightarrow 0$). If the value of E^B is taken as constant at 10 kcal/mole of base pairs,[18] we find the relationship between ionic strength and T_m as shown in FIGURE 3, curves A (for poly-dAT and dA$\overline{BU}$). The T_m' value is taken as 350° K from Inman and Baldwin[19] whose data are also shown, curves B. The theory correctly, albeit qual-

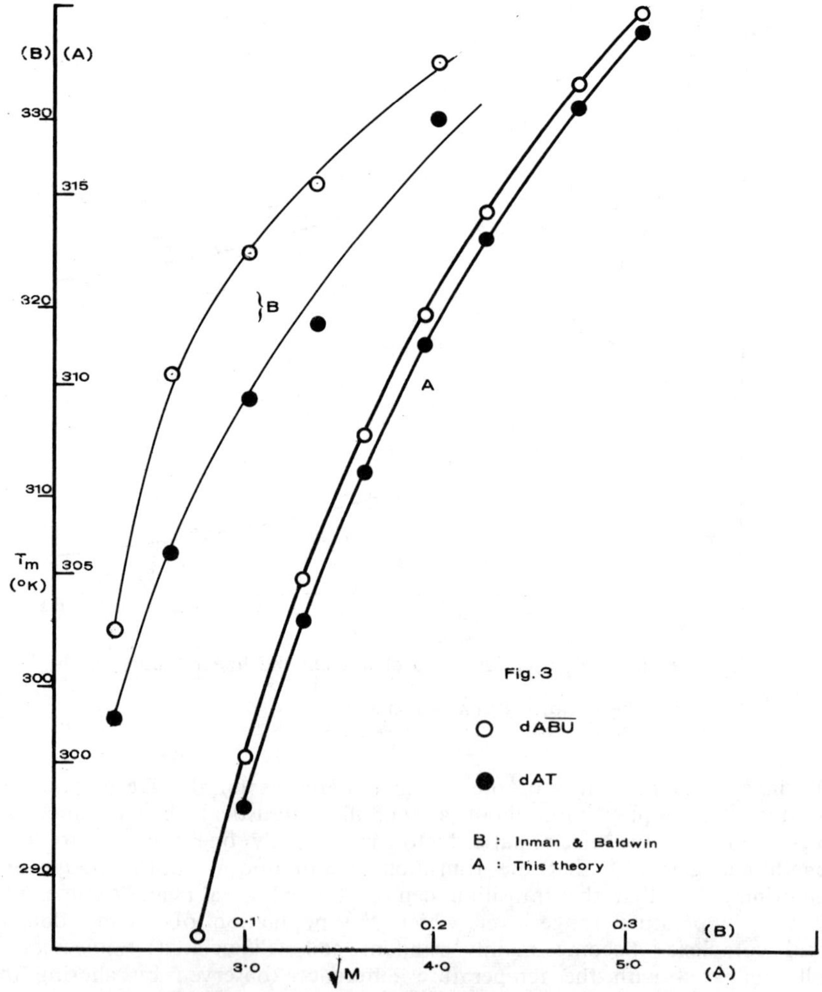

FIGURE 3. Comparison of linear theory applied to the discrete model II, showing the effect of the internal dielectric constant (A) and compared with experiment (B).

itatively, describes the behavior due to the difference in dielectric constant of the interior, but introduction of the nonlinear terms of the Poisson-Boltzmann expansion described in the next sections considerably improves the quantitative comparison with experiment.

Approximate Nonlinear Solutions

Asymptotic Procedures

An approximate, uniformly valid, asymptotic solution to the Poisson-Boltzmann equation is shown to be the solution of the Debye-Hückel equation —even when the molarity of the substrate is low and when $e\psi/kT \gg 1$.[20] However, this is only the case when the cylinder has a uniformly distributed charge of moderate density. The critical point above which the solution is not valid is given by $a/2l\sigma \approx 1.0$, where a is the cylinder radius and $l\sigma = kT\, D\epsilon_0/\sigma e$.

This result was obtained by matching the solution for the inner potential function to a valid approximation for the outer potential function, which in this case is the Debye-Hückel equation. Within the overlap domain in which these inner and outer approximations are asymptotically equal, such a matching procedure can be carried out.

$$\lim_{\epsilon \to 0} |\psi_{\text{inner}}^{+} - \psi_{\text{outer}}^{+}| = 0$$

This analytic result was confirmed by numerical integration for a value of $a/2l\sigma = 0.5$, and was shown in this case to give values for e_ψ/kT at the cylinder wall within 5% error, at the maximum charge of $\epsilon = 0.02$ ($\epsilon = a/l_n$, the ratio of the radius of the cylinder to the Debye length and the perturbation parameter in the asymptotic approximation). However, when the fully charged cylinder model of the DNA is used, with $a/2l\sigma$ approximately $= 2.87$ ($\epsilon = 0.28$), the error in 0.023 M salt is 65%. This particular asymptotic solution is, therefore, not suitable for the investigation of the electrostatic energy of highly charged, fully ionized polyelectrolytes such as DNA, RNA, etc., but might be appropriate for RNP, the polypeptide helix, etc. This approach is also valuable for providing qualitative insight into the behavior of the model as the environment is changed.

Variational Solutions

It was observed by Levine[21] and independently shown by MacGillivray[22] that the Poisson-Boltzmann equation can be derived from a variational principle. This is demonstrated by application of the procedure to a simple model of the potential distribution representing, for instance, the field between parallel plane potential surfaces or two model membranes on which the charge is uniformly distributed.

A simple trial function that satisfies the boundary conditions is chosen, substitution made into the variational functional and this integrated to give a pair of coupled differential equations. These may be approximated by two linear uncoupled equations for the unknown potentials and are solved—the unknown coefficients being attained by trial and error. FIGURE 4 illustrates that even a (very crude) straight line approximation to the potential between the plates gives a good solution and suggests that a family of such lines or a combination of simple functions would vastly improve the final result.[23]

In an application of this procedure to the DNA double helix, MacGillivray

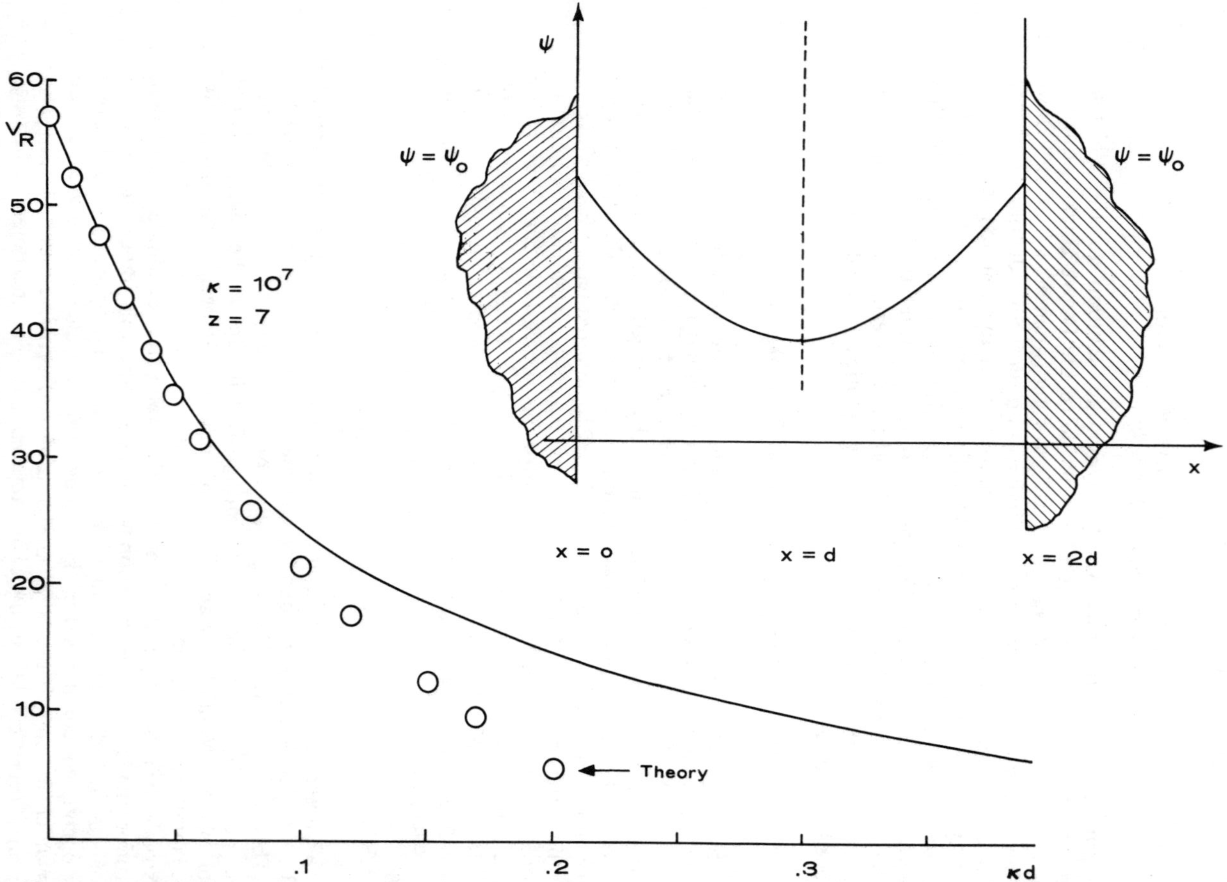

FIGURE 4. Result of using a very crude trial function in a variational theory applied to the potential between uniformly charged parallel plates (points) compared with the exact solution (curve).

and McMullen[24] again represented the DNA helix as a discrete banded model (FIGURE 1, III) but with an axially distributed surface charge having the periodicity,

$$\sigma = \sigma_0\left(1 + \cos\frac{2\pi Z}{L}\right).$$

Thus, the variational trial function chosen was $\psi_1(r) + \psi_3(r)\cos 2\pi Z/K$ (ψ_3 being the outer potential), and substitution into the variational functional

$$I[\psi] = \int_a^\infty \int_0^L \left\{\left(\frac{\partial\psi}{\partial r}\right)^2 + \left(\frac{\partial\psi}{\partial z}\right)^2 + \frac{4nkT}{D\epsilon_0}\left(\cosh\frac{e\psi}{kT} - 1\right)\right\} r\,dr\,dz + 2a\int_0^L \frac{\partial\psi}{\partial a}\cdot\psi\cdot(a, z)\,dz \qquad (3)$$

followed by integration over Z and independent variation of the two unknown functions, $\psi_1(r)$ and $\psi_3(r)$, leads to a pair of coupled nonlinear differential equations containing the modified Bessel functions I_0 and I_1, with boundary conditions

$$\frac{d\psi_1}{dr} = \frac{d\psi_3}{dr} = -\frac{\sigma_0}{D\epsilon_0}, \qquad \psi_1(\infty) = \psi_3(\infty) = 0$$

These were solved by approximating the Bessel and hyperbolic functions by their power series first term:

$$I_0\left(\frac{e\psi_3}{kT}\right) \approx 1, \quad I_1\left(\frac{e\psi_3}{kT}\right) \approx \frac{e\psi_3}{2kT}, \quad \sinh\left(\frac{e\psi_1}{kT}\right) \approx \frac{e\psi_1}{kT}, \quad \cosh\frac{e\psi_1}{kT} \approx 1,$$

where r is large; that is, about six Debye lengths from the surface; thus ψ_1 and ψ_3 are both small. This leads to two linear, uncoupled equations which give solutions satisfying the boundary conditions at infinity. These and their differentials, containing the two constants of integration α_1 and α_3, are used as initial values (at $r = 6 \times$ Debye length) for the Runge-Kutter solution of the nonlinear coupled equations. The values of α_1 and α_3, which are determined by the boundary conditions at the surface of helix, were found by trial and error on an IBM 7044 computer. These values were derived for a range of salt concentrations ranging from 1 M to .001 M, and over the temperature range 260–350° K. The charging parameter, σ_0, was also varied through the range 0.1, 0.5 and 1.0 times the value for one electronic charge per phosphate group. The choice of trial values for α_1 and α_3 becomes increasingly sensitive as $1/\kappa$ increases: i.e., the difficulty in matching the boundary conditions at the helix surface becomes much greater as the Debye length moves out toward infinity.

A similar procedure for the random coil was employed and the infinite cylinder of uniform charge (FIGURE 1, I) was used to determine the potential function ψ_4, from

$$\frac{1}{2}\cdot d/dr\left(2\frac{d\psi_4}{dr}\right) = \frac{2ne}{D\epsilon_0}\cdot\sinh\frac{e\psi_4}{kT}$$

for the usual boundary conditions. Again, initial values for ψ_4 were chosen at $6 \times$ Debye length and the integration constant α_4 determined by trial and error to satisfy boundary conditions at the surface, giving ψ_4.

Representative curves of ψ_1 and ψ_3 are shown in FIGURE 5 in relation to the charge parameter, and are compared to the equivalent linear Debye-Hückel solution. TABLE 1 shows the relationship between the salt concentration and the resulting potentials ψ_1 and ψ_3 for the value $\lambda = 1.0$ at different temperatures. It can be seen that the potential at the surface approximately doubles within the range studied, to over 200 mV at .001 M concentration. Clearly, the linear Debye-Hückel solution could not be expected to apply in the latter regions. The outer potential is nearly constant, as we anticipated. Integration of the potential-charge equations now provides the electrostatic energy for the helix according to the following relationship:

$$E = 2\pi a \sigma_0 \int_{\lambda=0}^{\lambda=1} \int_0^L \left[\psi_1(a, \lambda) + \psi_3(a, \lambda) \cos \frac{2\pi Z}{L} \right] \left[1 + \cos \frac{2\pi Z}{L} \right] dz$$

which gives

$$\frac{E}{L} = 1.602 \times 10^{-18} \int_{\lambda=0}^{\lambda=1} [\psi_1(\lambda) + 1/2\psi_3(\lambda)]\, d\lambda \quad \text{Joules/5 base pair.} \qquad (4)$$

TABLE 2 shows the resultant electrostatic free energy for the helix and coil and the T_m calculated from the difference, $\Delta E_{H/C'}{}^{ES}$, by Equation 2. Here, the assumption is made that E^B (where $E^{TOT} = E^B + E^{ES}$ for the phase change) has the value 10 kcal/base pair and that $T_m{}^\infty$ at infinite salt ($E^{ES} \rightarrow 0$) is 350° K. Equation 2 is a transcendental relation for T_m and, when both sides are plotted against T_m for several concentrations of salt, the intersection gives the desired value. This is shown, for the helix-coil configurations, in FIGURE 6, (taking $T_m{}^\infty = 350°$ K and, in this instance, $E_B = 7.0$ kcal).

In FIGURE 7, the T_m obtained in this way is plotted in comparison with some experimental data for dAT and with the result from the linear approximation. Clearly, this latter is hopelessly inadequate for deriving the DNA two-dimensional potential field.

This preliminary work has augmented the likelihood that a theory based entirely on the full nonlinear Poisson-Boltzmann equation will describe, qualitatively and quantitatively, the effect of salt on the melting transition of DNA, and provides the stimulus for developing the theory for application to more complex models.

TABLE 1

DEPENDENCE OF INNER AND OUTER HELIX POTENTIALS ON TEMPERATURE AND CONCENTRATION ($\lambda = 1.0$)

Ion Concentration (M)	Temperature (° K)	ψ_1 (mv)	ψ_3
0.001	290	195.7	30.7
	310	206.5	32.1
	330	218.2	33.4
0.010	310	152.0	35.0
	330	159.9	37.2
	350	167.6	38.3
0.100	260	84.3	33.0
	300	93.8	35.6
	340	102.8	37.8

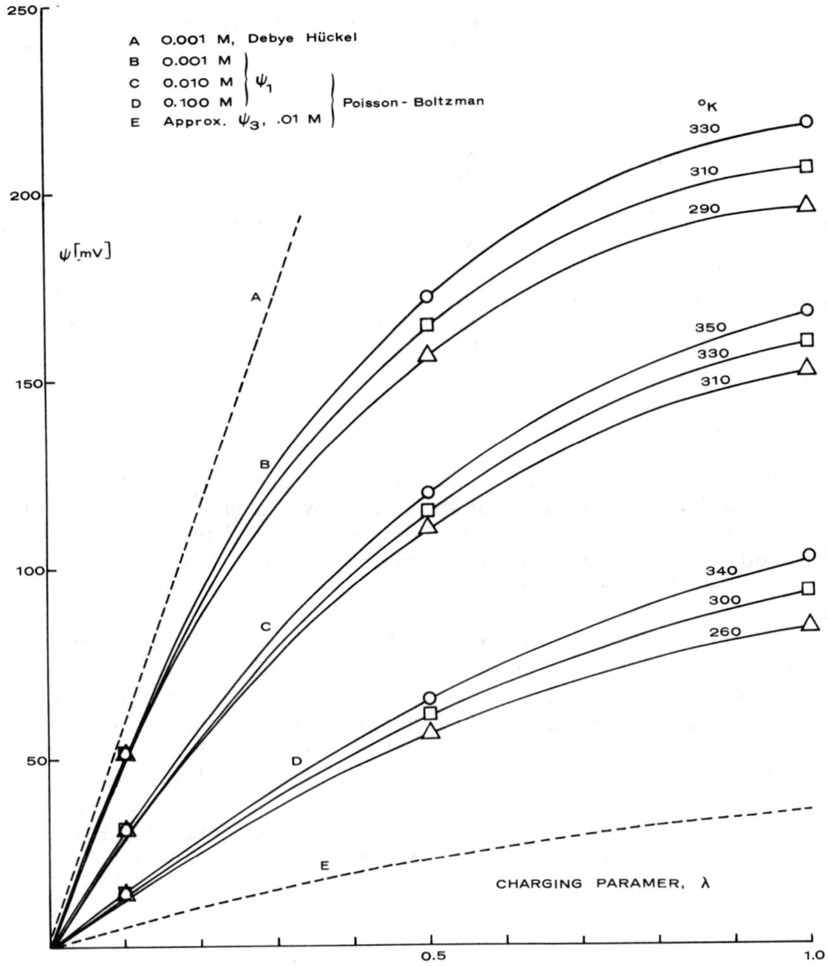

FIGURE 5. Potential-charge relationship for DNA using the nonlinear theory for various concentrations of supporting electrolyte at various temperatures.

FURTHER SOPHISTICATION OF THE MODEL

The banded models used so far have been a considerable improvement on a uniformly charged cylinder employed in other works and have already found application to other experimental data.[25] The periodic charge density function also offers the possibility of modification to the location and profile of the potential field in order to represent, in a simple manner, the penetration of counter-ions and other charged groups into radial distances less than that of the phosphate group, i.e., to within the DNA grooves.

In an attempt, however, to obtain even better correlation with the behavior of the macromolecule in question the model IV (FIGURE 1) is presently being employed. This model takes into account the helicity of the charge distribu-

TABLE 2

ELECTROSTATIC ENERGY OF HELIX AND COIL CONFIGURATIONS (K CAL/BASE PAIR)

Conc.	T(°K)	E_H	E_C	$\Delta E_{H/C}$	T_m (E_B = 10.0)	T_m' (Interpolation)
0.001	290	6.86	5.80	1.06	312.8	
	310	7.17	6.01	1.16	309.2	309.5
	330	7.49	6.21	1.28	305.0	
0.01	310	5.12	4.19	0.93	317.4	
	330	5.33	4.34	0.99	315.3	317.0
	350	5.53	4.43	1.10	311.5	
0.10	260	2.86	2.33	0.53	331.5	
	300	3.09	2.51	0.58	329.6	328.5
	340	3.33	2.69	0.64	327.8	
1.00	350	1.71	1.33	0.38	336.7	336.7

tion. This, however, is expected to alter the calculated energy very little, since the decrease due to distribution of the charge over a greater length of "ribbon" should be compensated by the closer approach of the charged regions to each other. On the other hand, the model employed is more realistic and consistent; therefore, results obtained from the theory will be more acceptable.

Neglect of the influence of the partial charges on the purine and pyrimidine ring—particularly of those on the H-bond-forming atoms—may be important in determining the differential energy, and future models must take into account the variation in such binding energy with temperature and ion concentration, at constant pH. This model will, however, involve a very complex sequence dependency of electrostatic forces within D_i and, therefore, a correspondingly more complex statistical treatment would be necessary if the sequence were not known. Such a model is being developed for known sequence interactions such as in the codon-anticodon complex, involving the model described herein.

OTHER MACROMOLECULAR SYSTEMS

It has recently been shown that the transfer RNA—messenger RNA—ribosome complex exhibits the characteristics of a reversible, temperature-induced, pseudo phase change[26] similar to the helix-coil melting discussed above. Although a little is known about the ribosome structure,[27] no complete model is presently available. However, the recent hypothetical geometry of the anti-codon loop and messenger strand[28] has allowed us to set up a provisional electrostatic model on which calculations have been initiated.[29] This is shown in FIGURE 8 in which a sequential quartet (α, β, γ, δ) of anti-codon loop arms form a super-helical repeating unit (L) within the infinitely extended array of transfer molecules. The messenger strand contribution to the free energy of this complex is three nucleotides per loop-arm unit, i.e., 3/17 of the total, and it forms an invert helix containing four triplets per complete pitch of length, L. Thus, in order to represent the loop-arm complex as two-dimensional (infinite in the third dimension), it is necessary and possible to

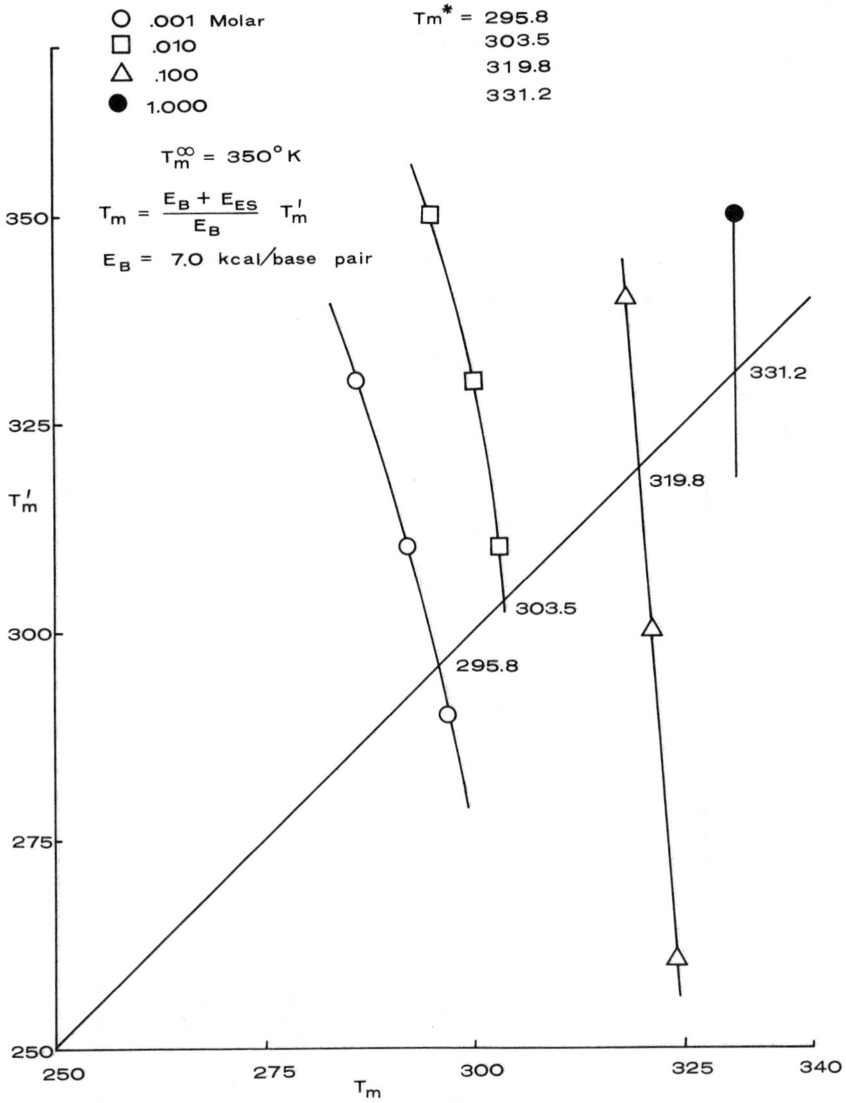

FIGURE 6. Interpolation curves for T_m, using the transcendental equation, at various salt concentrations. (In this instance, the value of 7.0 k cal/base pair has been used for the binding energy.)

orient the residue of the transfer RNA normal (or nearly so) to the super-helix axis and away from it ($\alpha\alpha$ in FIGURE 8). The contribution of these side arms to the stability of the complex, although probably important,[26] is presently being omitted from the theory as are the contributions from protein, water structure, etc.

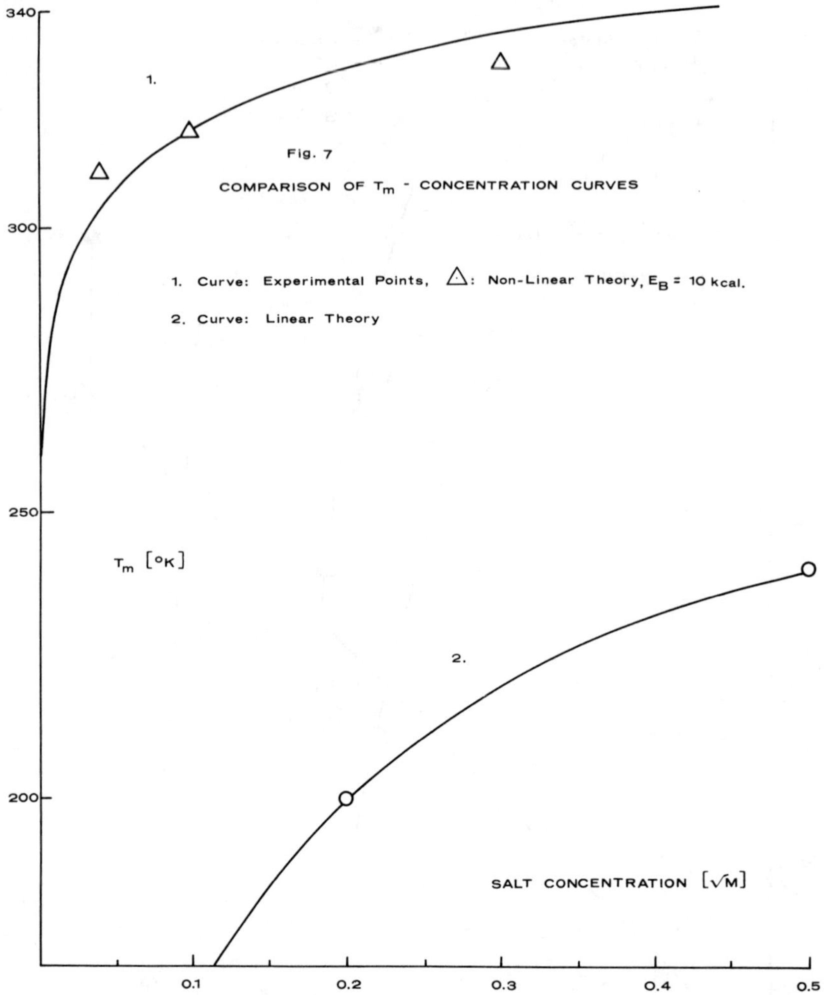

FIGURE 7. A comparison of T_m- salt concentration curves for dAT obtained experimentally (curve 1) compared with the theory (triangles) and the linear theory (curve 2).

DISCUSSION

Influence of Model Dimensionality on the Validity of the Theory

The work described herein has led to certain conclusions regarding the range of validity of the applications of the Debye-Hückel and Poisson-Boltzmann equations. These may be summarized briefly as follows, in the case of systems having uniform charge distribution all of one sign:

One Dimension (interfaces, membranes)

The solution of the Debye-Hückel equations diverges from the exact solu-

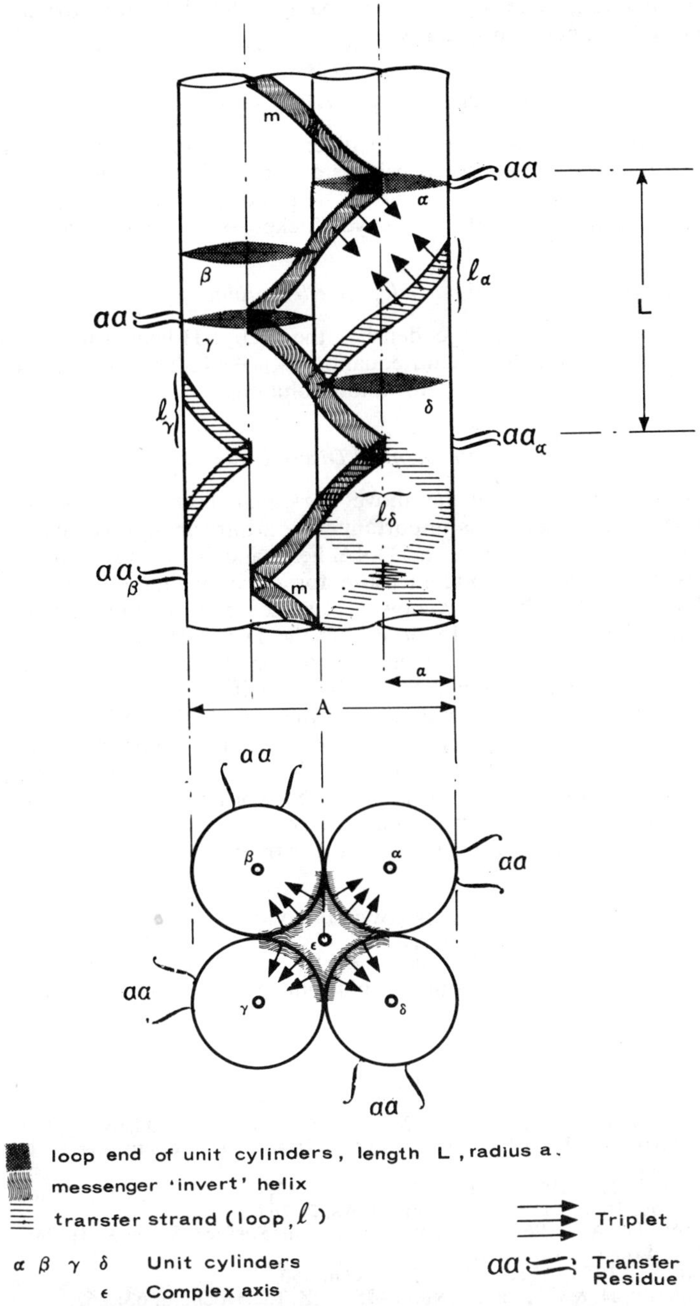

FIGURE 8. The hypothetical electrostatic model of the messenger-transfer RNA complex (based on the format described by Fuller & Hodgson). The charges are again discretely helical and periodic and repeat every four transfer units along a super-helical complex axis.

tion for all charge densities. It is probably valid, however, for neutral mosaics, but not if a net charge exists.

Two Dimensions (cylindrical format, DNA, α-helix, etc.)

The Debye-Hückel solution again diverges from that of the Poisson-Boltzmann treatment, if the charge density is above a critical value given by $a/21\sigma$. If there is overall neutrality, e.g. DNA + protons,[25] then for any charge density, and in the limit $\mu \rightarrow 0$, the Debye-Hückel → Poisson-Boltzmann solution.

Three Dimensions (spherical particle, micelles, globular protein)

No matter what the charge density, the Debye-Hückel solution converges to that of the Poisson-Boltzmann equation as $\mu \rightarrow 0$. This is true even if a net charge exists and if $e\psi/RT \gg 1$ for dilute solutions.

Problem of Discreteness

It is also concluded from the above work that the question of how discrete to make the charge source is important. The arbitrariness involved in selecting the diameter of the strand in the DNA helix and in the random coil, for example, is responsible in good measure for obtaining agreement with experiment. To proceed realistically, however, some criterion must be adopted for determining this parameter. In order for the Debye-Hückel equation to be a good solution to the Poisson-Boltzman equation, there is a dependence on the radius of the ion, and it is not clear that even if this → 0 the Poisson-Boltzmann equation will give a limit in agreement with the Debye-Hückel result. This is due to the uncertainty of whether or not the nonlinear terms detect an asymmetry of charge distribution on the particle over large distances, in the presence of intervening ions. In other words: Is this information lost completely by temperature randomization, or is it not? Such a question may be solved eventually by cluster theory or other treatments.

Acknowledgment

Thanks are due to my colleague, A. D. MacGillivray, who joined me in carrying out the research required to produce the findings discussed in this paper.

References

1. MacGillivray, A. D. & A. I. McMullen. 1966. J. Theoret. Biol. **12:** 260.
2. Falkenhagen, H. 1934. Electrolytes. Oxford University Press. New York, N. Y.
3. Fowler, R. H. 1927. Trans. Farad. Soc. **23:** 434.
4. Kirkwood, J. G. 1934. J. Chem. Phys. **2:** 767.
5. Haydon, D. A. 1964. Recent Progress in Surface Science. **1:** 94. Academic Press. London, England.
6. Levine, S. 1953. Proc. Phys. Soc. **A66:** 365.
7. Brodonsky, H. & H. Streblone. 1959. Z. Electrochem. **63:** 262.
8. Bolt, G. H. 1955. J. Colloid Sci. **10:** 206.
9. Sparnaay, M. J. 1958. Rec. Trav. Chem. **77:** 872.
10. Haydon, D. A. & F. H. Taylor. 1961. Phil. Trans. **A253:** 255.
11. Stillinger, F. H. & J. G. Kirkwood. 1960. J. Chem. Phys. **33:** 1282.

12. Prigogine, P., P. Mazur & R. Defay. 1953. J. Chem. Phys. **50:** 146.
13. Bell, G. M. & S. Levine. 1966. Chem. Physics of Ionic Solutions. B. E. Conway & K. G. Barradas, Eds.: 409. John Wiley & Sons. New York, N. Y.
14. Levine, S., J. Mingins & G. M. Bell. 1967. J. Electroanal. Chem. **13:** 280.
15. Bell, G. M., J. Mingins & S. Levine. 1966. Trans. Farad. Soc. **62:** 949.
16. Hill, T. L. 1955. Arch. Biochem. Biophys. **57**(1): 229.
17. MacGillivray, A. D. & A. I. McMullen. 1966. J. Theoret. Biol. **12:** 75.
18. Nash, H. A. & D. F. Bradley. 1965. Biopolymers **3:** 261.
19. Inman, R. B. & R. L. Baldwin. 1962. J. Molec. Biol. **5:** 172.
20. MacGillivray, A. D. & J. J. Winkleman. 1966. J. Chem. Phys. **45:** 2184.
21. Levine, S. 1939. J. Chem. Phys. **7:** 831.
22. MacGillivray, A. D. 1966. Theoret. Biol. Center Preprint No. 9.
23. MacGillivray, A. D. & J. Swift. 1967. Submitted for publication.
24. MacGillivray, A. D. & A. I. McMullen. 1966, 1968. 40th Nat. Colloid Sympos. Wisconsin; J. Theoret. Biol. **19:** 159.
25. Gilbert, M. & P. Claverie. 1967 J. Theoret. Biol. **18:** 330.
26. McLaughlin, C., J. Dondon, M. Grunberg-Monago, A. Michelson & G. Saunders. 1966. Sympos. Quant. Biol. **31:** 601. Cold Spring Harbor Lab. Quant. Biol. New York, N. Y.
27. Cantor, C. R. 1967. Nature **216:** 513.
28. Fuller, W. & A. Hodgson. 1967. Nature **215:** 817.
29. McMullen, A. I. & D. de Gweck. 1968. Unpublished data.

CHARGE FLUCTUATION FORCES IN BIOLOGICAL SYSTEMS*

Herbert Jehle
Physics Department
George Washington University
Washington, D. C.

Charge fluctuations are due to two different effects: (1) the thermal motion of charges, be it (1a) thermally excited jumps of electrons over their available quantum levels, or (1b) thermally excited protons as envisaged by Kirkwood and Shumaker; (2) the quantum-mechanical random motion of electrons inherent in the quantum mechanical uncertainty principle. The latter kind of charge fluctuation interaction energies are, in the case of atoms, called correlation energies. In the case of intermolecular interaction they are called London interaction, or dispersion interaction, or polarizability-polarizability interaction; they represent only one of the types of van der Waals interactions.

These interaction energies, though weak, may play an important role: although electrical charges which are usually attached to molecules may be neutralized if appropriate gegenions are available, charge fluctuation interactions generally cannot be neutralized. They lead to interesting specific association phenomena between identical molecules, phenomena to which Hamaker had already drawn attention 30 years ago and which our group, in particular Bade, Yos and Parke, has calculated and discussed on several previous occasions.

We should like to draw attention to some physical and structural aspects of charge fluctuation interactions, and to raise questions in regard to the biological implications of those interactions.

Intermolecular interactions are due to a diverse variety of mechanisms (Hirschfelder, 1954, 1965; Mulliken, 1962; London, 1936; Landau & Lifshitz, 1958, 1960; Löwdin, 1960; Slater, 1963; Sinanoğlu, 1965.) Charge fluctuation interactions between molecules (or atoms) arise when the distribution of charge is subject to random fluctuations in the interacting molecules. Let us consider a pair of molecules in interaction with each other. Two basic mechanisms are responsible for charge fluctuation interactions.

First, the well-known Brownian motion causes, whether it be in the framework of classical mechanics or in the framework of quantum mechanics, fluctuations of the spatial distribution of carriers of electric charge. Considering electrons as charge carriers, their fluctuations may be described in terms of a Boltzmann distribution over the energy states that the electrons may adopt. Each quantum state of the pair of molecules is associated with an electric interaction energy which is an R-dependent interaction energy (R the distance between the two interacting molecules). As the interacting molecules are considered to be imbedded in a medium which provides a temperature bath for them, a Boltzmann distribution characterizes their average states. Brownian motion causes the electrons to make jumps between the various quantum states which are in thermal reach, and a Boltzmann distribution is maintained even while R may change. Thus, averaging the interaction

* Research formerly supported by United States Public Health Service grants CA 04989 and GM 12054 and a fellowship from the National Cancer Institute, and presently supported by National Science Foundation grant GB 6783 and by the George Washington University Committee on Research.

over all states of the combined set of electrons of the first and the second molecules gives the resultant R-dependent interaction free energy and the (attractive) force.

It seems, at first sight, a complex matter to carry through such calculations. It becomes, however, almost trivially simple if done in terms of the convenient Drude model of molecular oscillators, i.e., in terms of the model which considers the electrons bound to their atoms or molecules as simple harmonic oscillators.

Before carrying through this calculation, one may well ask whether ions or protons loosely attached to a macromolecule may also be considered as charge carriers, implying a similar interaction mechanism. Indeed, Kirkwood and Shumaker (1952) have made such a calculation; a review of the application of it to proteins in solution has been given by Oncley (1965) and Scheider (1965); they have discussed the relationship of ionic versus protonic charge carriers in such mechanisms.

It is worthy of note that, in these protonic or ionic fluctuation discussions, not only a fluctuation of charge distribution on each of the interacting molecules is under discussion, but also, or most of all, the fluctuation of net charge on each of the molecules which is of prime importance for that interaction. One speaks of charge fluctuation interactions between molecules when one simply considers fluctuations in the individual charge distributions while the net charge on each of the interacting molecules is zero (or constant), whereas the mechanisms of fluctuations of net charge would fall under the terminology of charge-transfer interactions (Mulliken, 1950, 1951, 1952, 1962).

We turn now to the second mechanism responsible for charge fluctuation interactions that are due to quantum mechanical fluctuations, both zero point fluctuations and those in any other state. These fluctuations are an inherent part of quantum mechanics—in simplest terms—of the quantum mechanical uncertainty principle: even if an electron or set of electrons belonging to a molecule is in a stationary quantum state, their motion has a fluctuating component.

The ensuing instantaneous interactions of one electron with another in the same atom (or molecule), when the fluctuation interactions are averaged over all electron configurations, would fall under the terminology of correlation energy.

The instantaneous interactions of electrons in one molecule with those of another molecule are called polarizability—polarizability interactions, or dispersion force interactions, or London-van der Waals interactions. Indeed, London (1936) has been responsible for the profound understanding of that type of interaction, discovered by London (1930), Eisenschitz (1930) and Wang (1927), and he has given a classic report in his Faraday Discussion contributions.

This London force is one of the three types of van der Waals forces, the most important and significant type, a force quite distinct from the orientation effect (Keesom, 1912) and from the induction effect (Debye-Falkenhagen, 1920), which are the other two types of van der Waals forces of attraction. Much confusion has arisen through misuse of the term van der Waals forces. The two van der Waals attractive forces mentioned in this paragraph often merge with other charge interactions, including H bond interactions; they are experimentally and theoretically often difficult to separate from the latter.

The London-van der Waals forces are very distinct. Weak as they are, they are often drowned imperceptibly among the much stronger nonfluctuating charge interactions, not to mention covalent bond interactions (Pauling, 1960; Eyring, Walter & Kimball, 1944; Slater, 1963; Davydov, 1966).

In situations in which the charges on molecules are neatly neutralized by gegenions, (Debye & Hückel, 1923; Scatchard 1931, 1937) and where there is no other dominant interaction such as bond formation or breakage, the London force comes in the foreground; it stands immutably, little influenced by changes in the surroundings. The London force is also, to a very good approximation, additive, i.e., not saturated (London, 1930).

The London force is sometimes called a long-range force. This term is used to mean an R^{-6} dependence of interaction energy rather than an exponentially, i.e., much faster, falling-off interaction. Considering two equal spheres in interaction, at, for example, a distance equal to five times their radii, the interaction energy, proportional to the square of each sphere's volume, i.e. $[(4\pi/3)(R/5)^3]^2$, times R^{-6}, is independent of R, thus the term "long range." Casimir and Polder (1948), Lifshitz (1955, 1961), Abrikosov (1957, 1959, 1963), Deryagin (1956, 1960), Dzyaloshinskii (1957, 1959), Gorkov, Pitayevskii, Rytov (1963) calculated retardation effects for large bodies in such interaction and arrived at a different R dependence. In the instances which interest us most of all about London forces—i.e., their specificity—only intimately close distances, R, which correspond to side chains almost in contact, are relevant to the discussion, and no retardation effects need be considered.

If larger macromolecules are in London-van der Waals interaction, we should consider a small side-chain of one of the macromolecules interacting with one or several small side-chains of the other macromolecule, and do this pair by pair for all such nearest neighbor pairs of side chains in an additive fashion.

As mentioned previously, the London interactions come into the foreground when other, nonfluctuating charges are neutralized; they are, essentially, interactions between apolar side-chains. What are simply lumped together as "apolar interactions" (hydrophobic bonds, Frank 1957, 1958; Klotz 1960, 1962; Tanford 1961; Kauzmann; Nemethy & Scheraga, 1963) should be carefully subdivided into London (and perhaps other) van der Waals contributions, H-bonding, and entropy contributions. For a general review of the intermolecular forces we refer to Hirschfelder's lecture at the Squaw Valley Symposium (1965).

Drude Model Calculations

Since we plan to subdivide the interaction between two macromolecules into those of pairs of adjacent side-chains or side groups, we might best use the Drude oscillator model for evaluating the interaction between each such pair. This has been done by Bade (1954), Yos (1954–1957) and Jehle (1963). The more general quantum-mechanical treatment, beyond the Drude model, has been discussed by London (1936), Yos (1958) and, for other purposes, in a large number of papers of other authors. These calculations include the effects of the Brownian motion and of quantum-mechanical fluctuations of electrons in the pair of molecules.

It would not be appropriate to repeat the calculations already reported (Jehle, Yos, Bade, Parke & Salyers, 1958, 1963, 1964, 1965) and reviewed; therefore, we note only some of the results. The Drude model considers a pair of molecules, each represented by a set of electronic oscillators. The normal modes l of the set of all oscillators of the pair of molecules may have normal mode frequencies, denoted by ω_l, which depend on the intermolecular distance, R.

In the Drude model, we are enabled to carry through the second order quantum mechanical perturbation theory in a particularly simple way: we search for the classical normal mode frequencies ω_l, i.e., for the perturbations $(\omega_l - \tilde{\omega}_l)$ from their unperturbed values $\tilde{\omega}_l$ (which refer to the intermolecular distance, i.e., perturbation parameter, $R = \infty$) by simple classical oscillator techniques (i.e., diagonalization of the potential energy matrix). Once the normal mode frequencies are known as a function of R, the quantum levels are known too, and the interaction free energy is calculated by straightforward statistical mechanics.

The Helmholtz free energy of this set of oscillators is

$$
\begin{aligned}
A &= -kT \ln Z \\
&= -kT \ln \sum_{n_1=0}^{\infty} \cdots \sum_{n_l=0}^{\infty} \cdots \sum \prod_{l} \exp\left(-(n_l + 1/2)\hbar\omega_l/kT\right)
\end{aligned}
\tag{1}
$$

$$
\left(\frac{\partial A}{\partial R}\right)_T = \sum_{n_1=0}^{\infty} \cdots \sum_{n_l=0}^{\infty} \cdots \sum \frac{\partial E_{n_1 n_2 \cdots n_l \cdots}}{\partial R} \frac{\exp\left(-E_{n_1 n_2 \cdots n_l \cdots}/kT\right)}{Z} = F
\tag{2}
$$

is the attractive force. Let us assume $(\omega_l - \tilde{\omega}_l)/\tilde{\omega}_l \ll 1$. The closed form expression for Z is

$$
Z = \prod_{l} \left[2 \sinh (\hbar\omega_l/2kT)\right]^{-1}
\tag{3}
$$

and gives, by expansion,

$$
\Delta A = \sum_{l} kT \left\{ \frac{\hbar\tilde{\omega}_l}{2kT} \frac{\omega_l - \tilde{\omega}_l}{\tilde{\omega}_l} \coth \frac{\hbar\tilde{\omega}_l}{2kT} - \frac{1}{2}\left(\frac{\hbar\tilde{\omega}_l}{2kT}\right)^2 \left(\frac{\omega_l - \tilde{\omega}_l}{\tilde{\omega}_l}\right)^2 \Big/ \sinh^2 \frac{\hbar\tilde{\omega}_l}{2kT} \right\}
\tag{4}
$$

For isotropic, single three-dimensional oscillators representing the molecules, I, II each, we get, in the classical limit $\hbar\tilde{\omega}_l \ll kT$ (cf London)

$$
\begin{aligned}
\Delta A_{I\,II} &= -kT\left[\ln \prod_{l} (kT/\hbar\omega_l) - \ln \prod_{l} (kT/\hbar\tilde{\omega}_l)\right] \\
&= \sum_{l} kT\{(\omega_l - \tilde{\omega}_l)/\tilde{\omega}_l - (1/2)[(\omega_l - \tilde{\omega}_l)/\tilde{\omega}_l]^2\} \qquad (5) \\
&= -3R^{-6}\alpha_I\alpha_{II}kT
\end{aligned}
$$

and in the quantum limit $(\hbar\tilde{\omega}_l \gg kT)$

$$
\begin{aligned}
\Delta A_{I\,II} &= -kT\left[\ln \prod_{l} \exp(-(1/2)\hbar\omega_l/kT) - \ln \prod_{l} \exp(-(1/2)\hbar\tilde{\omega}_l/kT)\right] \\
&= \sum_{l} (1/2)\hbar\tilde{\omega}_l(\omega_l - \tilde{\omega}_l)/\tilde{\omega}_l \qquad (6) \\
&= -(3/2)R^{-6}\alpha_I\alpha_{II}\hbar\tilde{\omega}_I\tilde{\omega}_{II}/(\tilde{\omega}_I + \tilde{\omega}_{II})
\end{aligned}
$$

The more general case of molecules whose Drude oscillators imply anisotropy in their polarizabilities—polarizabilities which are distributed over an arbitrary frequency range (in particular, in the extreme ultra-violet)—was covered by a matrix calculation to obtain normal modes, cf. Yos, Bade and Jehle (1957),

$$\Delta A_{I\,II} = -(1/2)kT \sum_{s=-\infty}^{+\infty} \text{trace } W_{sI} W_{sII} \tag{7}$$

(s covering all negative and positive integers), where (with N_I = number of oscillator modes of the molecule I, and u_{lx}, u_{ly}, u_{lz} = direction cosines of the lth oscillator with respect to the coordinate system x, y, z of molecule I)

$$W_{sI} = -R^{-3} \sum_{l=1}^{N_I} \frac{\alpha_l}{1 + (2\pi kT/\hbar\tilde{\omega}_l)^2 s^2} \begin{bmatrix} u_{lx}u_{lx}, & u_{lx}u_{ly}, & \sqrt{2}u_{lx}u_{lz} \\ \cdot & \cdot & \cdot \\ \sqrt{2}u_{lz}u_{lx} & \cdot & 2u_{lz}u_{lz} \end{bmatrix} \tag{8}$$

W_{sI} is a dynamical polarizability

$$\alpha(\omega) = \sum_{l} \alpha_l u_l u_l / [1 - (\omega_l/\tilde{\omega}_l)^2] \tag{9}$$

analytically continued into the domain of purely imaginary arguments

$$\omega = is2\pi kT/\hbar \tag{10}$$

(Bade, Yos, Jehle, 1958; McLachlan, 1963; Linder, 1960).

We are writing these formulas again so that we may recognize: (1) that for the small side-chains to which these detailed, anisotropic frequency-dependent polarizabilities may apply, the distances R are so small that no retardation effects need be considered; (2) that any specificity effects, depending on anisotropy and frequency dependence of polarizability can only be of importance at nearest neighbor distance interactions between side-chains; (3) that the energies are of the order kT for the classical limit and $\hbar\tilde{\omega}$ for the quantum limit. In other words, the interaction energy naturally is of the order of the equipartition energy or of the zero point energy, respectively; (4) that, as was shown (Jehle, Yos & Bade, 1958), the classical and quantum limit results in Equations 5 and 6 can easily be seen to follow from the general result (Equations 7, 8) as special cases; (5) that the interaction energy is proportional to a bilinear function $-\alpha_I\alpha_{II}$ of the polarizabilities.

The latter circumstance, as observed by Hamaker (1937), leads to a most important property of these London interactions: If the ionic conditions are such as to neutralize the nonfluctuating charge interactions, an arrangement of two pairs of molecules in the form

I II
I II

is energetically more advantageous, by an amount

$$\Delta_4 A_{I\,II} = \Delta A_{I\,I} + \Delta A_{II\,II} - 2\Delta A_{I\,II} \leq 0 \tag{11}$$

than an arrangement

I I
II II

This rearrangement of I, I and II, II to I, II and I, II is equivalent to a rearrangement of I, I, I, II, II, I, I to I, I, II, I, II, I, I or similar two- or three-dimensional patterns and this rearrangement free energy $\Delta_4 A_{I\,II}$ is negative definite because the $\Delta A_{I\,II}$ is a bilinear function $-\alpha_I \alpha_{II}$ of the polarizabilities. Indeed, from Equation 5 follows

$$\Delta_4 A_{I\,II} = -3R^{-6}kT(\alpha_I - \alpha_{II})^2, \tag{12}$$

and a similar result follows from Equations 6 and 7. Equation 11 evaluated for the general formulas (Equations 7 and 8) leads to

$$\Delta_4 A_{I\,II} = -\frac{kT}{2} \sum_{s=-\infty}^{+\infty} \sum_{\mu,\nu=1}^{3} (W_{s\mu\nu I} - W_{s\mu\nu II})^2 \leq 0 \tag{13}$$

Different molecule types, e.g. I, II, have different distributions of their polarizabilities αl over frequency $\tilde{\omega} l$ (i.e., $W_{s\nu\mu}$ over s), and over anisotropy (i.e., $W_{s\mu\nu}$ over μ, ν). A molecule type is thus characterized by a multiparametric manifold of $W_{s\mu\nu}$ values. Given the order of magnitude of the interaction energy $\Delta A_{I\,II}$, most discriminations $|\Delta_4 A_{I\,II}|$ against dissimilar molecules are of the order of magnitude of $\Delta A_{I\,II}$ itself; they are not just differences on a linear energy scale. In evaluating $\Delta_4 A_{I\,II}$ Equation 13, as outlined in our earlier papers, we must essentially evaluate the square of a distance in a multidimensional space (s, μ, ν). What this multiparametricity (multidimensionality) means in relation to specificity has been graphically illustrated (Jehle, Bade & Yos, 1958, 1963; Biopolymers, 1964): it implies a high degree of specificity.

Let us now consider the interaction of macromolecules with several small apolar side-chains each. Consider two such macromolecules whose side-chain sequence is the same in both molecules, and consider them as coming next to each other. Such nearby association may permit the pairwise identical side-chains of the two macromolecules to come to lie side by side, which implies a cumulative effect of association energies of identical pairs of side-chains. This, of course, means an enormously high specificity, i.e., a strong preference for identical pairs of molecules to associate as nearest neighbors. This specificity is thus multiparametrical, i.e., similar to a complicated lock and key situation; it is, however, not dependent on complementarity but on identity of the interacting side-chains.

It is important to realize that the statement (Equation 11) of preferential association does not say that a molecule I rather associates with a second identical molecule I than with a dissimilar molecule II. It is a statement about the rearrangement, as indicated above; it is thus a statement readily applicable to a population of molecules rather than a pair. It says that under the stated conditions similar molecules tend to aggregate and cluster together rather than to intermingle freely. This clarification has been particular emphasized by Steinberg (1962, 1963) in the context of preferential associations of cells. It should also be remarked that the issue of entropy of mixing of molecules has to be applied to the particular situation at hand. As this entropy of mixing assumes very different quantitative aspects in the case of mixing of molecules and in the case of the mixing of cells, we shall omit entropy calculations here. In the context of the mixing of cells, we may presumably neglect these entropy terms.

We repeated these formulas and the statements about specificity because of their fundamental importance of some instances of biological specificity, and because the existence of this property of the London force is still widely ignored.

Quantitative Estimates of the Forces

What really matters is the order of magnitude of the London forces in the situation under consideration. Fowkes (1964, 1966, 1967) and Vold (1961) have made careful estimates of London forces between apolar side-chains. For the understanding of specificity, one needs to know the frequency distribution of polarizabilities. In this respect, the Thomas-Reiche-Kuhn Sum rule applied to electrons in the valence shells, and the extrapolation of measured UV polarizabilities into the extreme UV by means of dispersion formulas, have lead to estimates of polarizability distributions over the entire frequency spectrum (Platzman, 1962). It is to be noted that the frequency region most important for the London forces, i.e., the relevant frequency regions for polarizabilities or f values, are mostly in the extreme UV region, far beyond the usually available 2000 Å to 3000 Å region. It is the combination $\tilde{\omega}(\Sigma\alpha)^2$ which characterizes the interaction energy; this quantity is proportional to $\tilde{\omega}^{-3}(\Sigma f)^2$. The total Σf is, by the Thomas-Reiche-Kuhn rule (Kramers-Kronig, 1928, 1956) limited by the number of electrons. A shift of the essential oscillator strengths, f, towards lower frequencies therefore intensifies the interaction energy. The overall effect for the interaction of a pair of identical vs unidentical side-chains, i.e. $\Delta_4 A_{I\ II}$, may certainly be larger than the noise level, kT. The cumulative effect of many side-chains on a macromolecule will bring about highly specific discrimination.

There is at present much work in progress which may, for particular types of side-chains, pin down their polarizabilities as a function of frequency and of orientation, and will thus make it possible to give more accurate statements about the interaction. A most important avenue to get the necessary data may be through the study of optical properties of molecular aggregates, as investigated by De Voe (1962, 1963, 1967), Bradley (1959, 1964), Tinoco (1960, 1963, 1964), Davydov (1966), Simpson (1957), Rhodes (1962), Linder (1960, 1962, 1964), Kasha (1964, 1967), Moffit, Mulliken (1950, 1951, 1962), Eyring (1944) and London (1936). But the largest gap in the application to biology is certainly the information needed about the biochemical circumstances of the interactions, e.g., in regard to the surface layers of the cells that are making specific contacts with surface layers of other cells, or concerning the corresponding biochemical nature of specific attachments between intracellular structures such as chromosomes.

The medium in which specifically interacting cells are imbedded is a matter of special concern in two respects: (1) in the biochemical investigations of a particular biological phenomenon (in order to get to know all the accompanying relevant reactions) and also (2) from the physicochemical point of view, apart from any further chemical reactions. Recent investigations by Sinanoğlu (1964, 1966), Abdulnur and others have laid the groundwork for understanding the significance of different types of media for the interaction of biological macromolecules.

Preferential Association of Similar Molecules and Molecular Mechanisms Accounting for It

Muller (1922, 1947), from cytological and genetical considerations, postulated a mechanism of specific interactions between identical pairs of molecules, and Haurowitz (1950, 1963), from biochemical considerations, reached a similar conclusion for certain interactions between proteins. Later, we shall discuss some biological phenomena which ask pointedly for possible mechanisms that may account for specific association of similar structures and, by inference, of similar molecules as next nearest neighbors.

Because of the urgency (for widely different molecules) to arrive at a possible understanding of why similar molecules may associate as nearest neighbors, it becomes desirable to look for every imaginable mechanism to bring about such association; the first one is the general property of the London force.

A second mechanism to be kept in mind may be found in nucleic acid homologies. When, in synapsis of homologous chromosomes in meiosis (and strikingly evidenced in inverted synapsis), corresponding chromosome sections come to a close alignment without fail, there may be single-strand nucleic acids hanging loose from the chromosomes. If they belong to exactly corresponding sections of homologous chromosomes, respectively, exactly complementary strands may meet and join into nucleic acid double strands which then hold the two chromosomes together because one of the strands was attached to one chromosome and the other strand to the other chromosome (Weiss, 1967). In other words, association of corresponding homologous sections of chromosomes may occur by means of complementarity of two single-strand nucleic acids. It may, however, be the London force mechanism which may be responsible for this effect in the first instance.

A third mechanism of specific attraction of similar macromolecules, based again on self-complementary structures, has been proposed by Blotnick (1967). Applied to the issue of synapsis of homologous chromosomes, his proposal might be formulated in simplified terms, suggesting that the bands (visible band structures, marking the classical genetic loci in chromosomes) have electrostatic dipole moments in a direction (and opposite direction) perpendicular to the line which marks the chromosome's layout at the time of synapsis. The dipole moments might be about coplanar, i.e., lying in the surface of a ribbon which characterizes the electric polarization of the chromosome. The polarity of the dipole moments of subsequent bands on the chromosome might define some $+ + - + - + - - - +$ pattern, a code. It is easy to see that two such ribbon dipole-coded chromosomes that are exactly homologous may come to lie side by side, lining up in a specific manner in order to bring homologous sections next to each other. A little electrostatics will show varieties of possible side-by-side alignments of the two polarized coded bands. (A similar mechanism was proposed by Blotnick to operate on a macromolecular level, rather than on the much more macroscopic level of bands of chromosomes.)

Biological Implications of the London Force

This is a chapter of questions, suggestions, and more questions. We should like to consider here the specificity of cellular association as evidenced in morphological movements of cells in embyrogenesis, or, to start with a more simple phenomenon, the reaggregation of fully differentiated cells after an artificial disarraying disturbance of the orderly arrangement of a manifold of different cells has occurred. Or, in a still more simple setting, the *in vitro* sorting out of a mixture of cells from different tissues: starting with a random mixture of different cell types or tissue fragments, cells of the same type tend to lump together (Steinberg 1962, 1963).

How do cellular rearrangements come about? Before definitive cellular attachments are established, cells are usually moving about. Tentatively, they make contacts with other cells; these contacts are often initiated by processes reaching out from the surface layer of one cell to tentatively touch another cell or still another cell. These cellular contacts, through bridgelike processes, either break loose again, or lead to a firmly established attachment, if the neighbor cell is compatible with the outreaching cell (i.e., if the two cells are of similar type). Tissue specificity of cells denotes this compatibility.

Is this process formation a phenomenon such as the well understood and similar looking phenomenon of formation of bridges when a phase transition occurs between melt and solid state of organic materials? (Keith, Padden & Vadimsky, 1965.) Is the matter of specificity of cellular association simply a matter of biochemically specific response of the surface layer of one cell to the surface layer of the other cell, so that the matter of specific cellular association may be discussed on the basis of interface energy of contact between the surface layers of the two cells. Can the specificity of cellular contacts be discussed as if the status of differentiation of the contacting cells were fixed, i.e., a given condition? How, on the other hand, is it to be understood that the status of cellular differentiation changes with morphogenetic movements depending upon what neighbor cells confront the differentiating cell? How may contact inhibition be understood on the basis of cellular contacts?

One should be perfectly aware of the distinction between such specialized late formations as tight-junctions and desmosomes on the one hand, and the phenomenon of initial, specific cellular contacts leading to specific intercellular attachment on the other. We intend, in the discussion of morphogenesis of embryos, to refer to the latter phenomenon only. Let us assume, for the following comments, that it is indeed simply the surface layer of the cell which, because of its molecular constitution, implies a specificity of attachment toward the surface layer of an adjacent cell, and that it is thus permissible to express the tissue specificity of cellular attachment in terms of specificity of interface energy.

It is interesting to note that though the nature of the forces responsible for intercellular interactions is very far from being clarified, one may understand why the ensuing morphogenesis of embryos implies a high degree of bilateral symmetry in animals (Jehle preprint). This circumstance somewhat resembles the status of elementary particle physics. There, too, we are confronted with gaps in the understanding of the forces responsible for elementary particle interactions which are studied in high energy physics. Without having to know the force laws, we may, however, from known data about elementary particles, infer much about symmetries which they and their interactions exhibit.

We may try not only to understand symmetry in morphogenesis of embryos, we may also venture to suggest mechanisms of intercellular interactions that may yield some understanding of tissue specific cellular association. Of the three types of specific interactions between identical macromolecules listed earlier in this paper, the London force seems to be the most interesting candidate to account for tissue specific cellular attachment.

As was emphasized in the discussion of association of molecular sidechains, here too, the specific cellular association is a population issue. It is not that a pair I,I of cells attract each other more strongly than a pair I,II; it is the rearrangement effect of I,II and I,II into I,I and II,II which is favorable. Also, similar molecules preferentially associate, compared with dissimilar ones; one may be able to understand highly specific morphogenetic movements on this basis.

Precondition for such specific interaction is a neutralization of ionic or other nonfluctuating charge interactions, so that side-chains attached to the surface layer of a cell, not interfered with by nonfluctuating electrostatic interactions nor by hydration, may interact in an apolar manner with the side-chains belonging to a neighbor cell. One may want to think of macromolecules, perhaps mucopolysaccharides, attached to the surface of one cell. If the same types of macromolecules are attached to a second cell, the variety of side-chains of a macromolecule of the first cell may come to lie side by side with the corresponding side-chains of one of the macromolecules of the other cell. Identical pairs of side-chains associating may permit one to understand the high degree of specific attachment of a pair of identical cells to each other. It has been observed that in a population of cells of a few different types similar cells tend to aggregate. The attraction may thus be highly specific; however, a repulsion between cells, when it occurs, may be an entirely nonspecific phenomenon. All that is needed is a change in the ionic condition of the medium which implies a lack of neutralization; similar or equal types of cells are then apt to repel each other.

Although we may be far from understanding the issue of morphogenetic movements, and even though an enormous amount of biochemical research lies before us in that field, it may be not too ambitious to hope that the physics of intermolecular forces may contribute to the resolution of this most fascinating biological problem.

References

ABRISKOSOV, A. A., L. P. GORKOV & I. E. DZYALOSHINSKII. 1959. Zh. Eksperim. i Teor. Fiz. **36:** 900; 1957. **33:** 799.

ABRISKOSOV, A. A., L. P. GORKOV & I. E. DZYALOSHINSKII. 1963. Methods of Quantum Field Theory in Statistical Physics. R. A. Silverman, Ed. Prentice-Hall. Englewood Cliffs, N.J.

BADE, W. L. 1957. J. Chem. Phys. **27:** 1280; **28:** 282; 1954. Ph.D. Thesis. University of Nebraska. Lincoln, Neb.

BADE, W. L. & J. G. KIRKWOOD. 1957. J. Chem. Phys. **27:** 1284.

BERNAL, J. D. 1958. Proc. Roy. Soc. **A247:** 421, 534, 536.

BLOTNICK, S. 1967. Personal communication.

BRADLEY, D. F. & M. K. WOLF. 1959. Proc. Nat. Acad. Sci., **45:** 944.

BRADLEY, D. F., S. LIPSON & B. HONIG. 1964. *In* Electronic Aspects of Biochemistry B. Pullman, Ed.: 77. Academic Press, New York, N. Y.

BRIEGLEB, G. 1961. Elektronen-Donator-Acceptor-Komplexe. Springer, Berlin, Germany.

CALLEN, H. B. & T. A. WELTON. 1951. Phys. Rev. **83:** 34.

CASIMIR, H. G. B. & D. POLDER. 1948. Phys. Rev. **73:** 360.

CASIMIR, H. G. B. 1948. Konink. Ned. Akad. Wetenschap. Proc. (Ser. B.) **60:** 793.

CALVIN, M. 1956. Amer. Scient. **44:** 284.

DAVYDOV, A. S. 1965. Quantum Mechanics. Schensted trans. Neo Press. Ann Arbor, Mich.; Ter Haar, Trans. Pergamon Press, Oxford, England.

DE BOER, J. H. 1936. Trans. Farad. Soc. **32:** 21.

DE BOER, J. H. & G. HELLER. 1937. Physica. **4:** 1045.

DEBYE, P. 1920. Physik. Z. **21:** 178; **22:** 302.

DEBYKE, P. & E. HÜCKEL. 1923. Physik. Z. **24:** 185.

DERYAGIN, B. V. & I. I. ABRIKOSOV. 1956. J. Exp. Theor. Phys. **30:** 993; **31:** 3.

DERYAGIN, B. V., I. I. ABRIKOSOV & E. M. LIFSHITZ. 1960. Sci. Amer. **203:** 47. 1956 Quart. Rev. Chem. Soc. (London). **10:** 295.

DEVOE, H. 1963. Nature **197:** 1295; Biopolymers Sympos. M. Weissbluth, Ed.: 251. Interscience. New York, N.Y.; 1967. Discuss. Farad. Soc.

DEVOE, H. & I. TINOCO. 1962. J. Molec. Biol. **4:** 500.

DOTY, P. & R. D. LUNDBERG. 1957. Proc. Nat. Acad. Sci. **43:** 213.

DZYALOSHINSKII, I. E. 1957. Sov. Phys. JETP (Eng. trans.) **3:** 977.

DZYALOSHINSKII, I. E. & L. P. PITAYEVSKII. 1959. Sov. Phys. JETP (Eng. trans.) **9:** 912.
DZYALOSHINSKII, I. E., E. M. LIFSHITZ & L. P. PITAYEVSKII. 1959. Zh. Eksperim. i. Teor. Fiz. **37:** 229.
EIGEN, M. & L. DE MAYER. 1958. Proc. Roy. Soc. **A247:** 505.
EYRING, H. 1931. J. Amer. Chem. Soc. **53:** 2537; **54:** 3191.
EYRING, H. & M. POLANYI. 1931. Z. Phys. Chemie. **B12:** 279.
EYRING, H., J. WALTER & G. E. KIMBALL. 1944. Quantum Chemistry. John Wiley & Sons. New York, N.Y.
FELSENFELD, G. 1965. J. Molec. Biol. **13:** 407.
FEYNMAN, R. P. 1939. Phys. Rev. **56:** 340.
FÖRSTER, T. 1951. Fluoreszenz organischer Verbindungen. V. & R. Goettingen, Germany; 1959. Discuss. Farad. Soc. **27:** 7; 1963. Rev. Mod. Phys. **35:** 572.
FOWKES, F. M. 1964. Ind. Eng. Chem. **56:** 40; 1966. *In* Treatise on Adhesives and Adhesion. R. A. Patrick, Ed.: 325. Marcel Dekker. New York, N. Y.; 1967. Surfaces and Interfaces Burke, Reed, Weiss, Eds. **1:** 197–224. Syracuse University Press. New York, N.Y.; 1966. Society of Chemical Industry. **25:** 3.
FRANK, H. S. 1958. Proc. Roy. Soc. **A247:** 481.
FRANK, H. S. & W. T. WEN. 1957. Discuss. Farad. Soc. **24:** 133.
GINSBERG, V. L. & L. P. PITAYEVSKII. 1958. Soviet Phys. (Eng. trans.). **34:** 1240.
HAMAKER, H. C. 1937. Physica. **4:** 1058; 1938. Chem. Weekblad. **35:** 47; 1948. *In* Theory of the Stability of Lyophobic Colloids. E. J. W. Verwey & J. T. G. Overbeek, Eds.: 161. Elsevier. Amsterdam, Holland.
HAUROWITZ, F. 1950. The Chemistry and Biology of Proteins. Academic Press. New York; 2nd edit. 1963. The Chemistry and Function of Proteins. Academic Press, New York, N.Y.
HIRSCHFELDER, J. O. 1941. J. Chem. Phys. **9:** 645; 1963. Rev. Mod. Phys. **35:** 616; 1964. Univ. Wisconsin (Madison) Theoret. Chem. Rept. No. WIS-TCI-66; 1965. *In* Molecular Biophysics. M. Weissbluth & B. Pullman, Eds.: 325. Academic Press. New York, N.Y.
HIRSCHFELDER, J. O. & M. A. ELIASON. 1957. Ann. N.Y. Acad. Sci. **67:** 451.
HIRSCHFELDER, J. O., C. F. CURTISS & R. B. BIRD. 1954. Molecular Theory of Gases and Liquids. John Wiley & Sons. New York, N.Y.
HIRSCHFELDER, J. O. & P.-O. LÖWDIN. 1959. Molec. Phys. **2:** 229.
JEHLE, H. 1965. Advan. Quant. Chem. **2:** 195; 1963. Proc. Nat. Acad. Sci. **50:** 516.
JEHLE, H., W. C. PARKE, *et al.* 1964. Biopolymers Sympos. M. Weissbluth, Ed. **1:** 209. Interscience Publishers. New York, N.Y.
JEHLE, H., W. C. PARKE & A. SALYERS. 1964. Biofisika. **9:** 401; Biophysics **9:** 433; 1964. *In* Electronic Aspects of Biochemistry. B. Pullman, Ed.: 313. Academic Press. New York, N.Y.
JEHLE, H., J. M. YOS & W. L. BADE. 1958. Phys. Rev. **110:** 793.
JORDAN, P. 1947. Eiweissmolekule. Stuttgart, Germany.
KASHA, M. 1964; 1967. Studies in Quantum Chemistry. Institute of Molecular Biophysics. Tallahassee, Fla.
KAUZMANN, W. 1957. Quantum Chemistry. Academic Press. New York, N.Y.
KEESOM, W. H. 1912. Commun. Phys. Lab. University of Leiden. Leiden, Holland. Suppl. 24–26.
KEITH, H. D., F. J. PADDEN & R. G. VADIMSKY. 1965. Science **150:** 1026.
KELLY, H. P. 1963. Phys. Rev. **131:** 654; 1966. Many-Body Perturbation Theory Calculation of Atomic Polarizabilities. Phys. Rev. **152:** 62; 1968. Advan. Chem. Phys.; 1968. Int. Journ. Quant. Chem.
KELLY, H. P. & H. S. TAYLOR. 1964. J. Chem. Phys. **40:** 1478.
KESTNER, N. R. & O. SINANOĞLU. 1963. J. Chem. Phys. **38:** 1730.
KIRKWOOD, J. G. & J. B. SHUMAKER. 1952. Proc. Nat. Acad. Sci. **38:** 855; 863.
KLOTZ, I. M. 1953. *In* The Proteins. Neurath & Bailey, Eds. Academic Press. New York, N.Y.; 1962. *In* Horizons of Biochemistyr. M. Kasha & B. Pullman, Eds.: 523. Academic Press. New York, N.Y. 1960. *In* Brookhaven Sympos. Biol. **13:** 25.
KRAMERS, H. A. & R. DE L. KRONIG. 1928. Z. Physik. **48:** 174; 1956. *In* Collected Scientific Papers of Kramer's: 382.
KRUYT, H. R. & J. T. G. OVERBEEK. 1964. Introduction to Physical Chemistry. Holt. New York, N.Y.
LANDAU, L. D. 1958. Zh. Eksperim. i Teor. Fiz. **34:** 262.

LANDAU, L. D. & E. M. LIFSHITZ. 1958. Statistical Physics. Addison-Wesley. Reading, Mass.; 1960. Electrodynamics of Continuous Media. Addison-Wesley. Reading, Mass.
LERMAN, L. S. 1963. Proc. Nat. Acad. Sci. **49:** 94.
LIFSHITZ, E. M. 1955. Zh. Eksperim. i Teor. Fiz. **29:** 94.
LIFSHITZ, E. M., I. E. DZYALSHINSKII & L. P. PITAYEVSKII. 1961. Advan. Phys. **10:** 165.
LINDER, B. 1960. J. Chem. Phys. **33:** 688; 1962. **37:** 963; 1964. **40:** 622, 2003.
LINDERBERG, J. 1962. Phys. Lett. **1:** 272; 1964. Uppsala Reports. Uppsala, Sweden.
LINDERBERG, J. & H. SHULL. 1960. J. Molec. Spectry. **4:** 30; **5:** 1.
LÖWDIN, P.-O. 1955. Phys. Rev. **97:** 1474; 1956. Texas J. Sci. **8:** 163; 1957. J. Phys. Chem. **61:** 55; 1960. Ann. Rev. Phys. Chem. **11:** 107; 1962. Rev. Mod. Phys. **34:** 80, 520; 1963. **35:** 702.
LONDON, F. 1930. Z. f. physik. Chemie. **B11:** 222; 1936. Trans. Farad. Soc. **33:** 8; 1942. J. Chem. Phys. **46:** 305.
LONGUET-HIGGINS, H. C. 1956. Proc. Roy. Soc. **A235:** 537.
MCLACHLAN, A. D. 1963. Proc. Roy. Soc. **A271:** 387.
MARGENAU, H. 1939. Rev. Mod. Phys. **11:** 1.
MULLER, H. J. 1922. Am. Naturalist **56:** 32; 1937. Sci. Month. **44:** 210; 1941. Cold Spring Harbor Sympos. Quant. Biol. **9:** 290; 1947. Proc. Roy. Soc. **B134:** 1; 1950. *In* Genetics in the 20th Century. L. C. Dunn, Ed.: 77. Macmillan. New York, N.Y.
MULLIKEN, R. S. 1950. J. Amer. Chem. Soc. **72:** 600; 1951. J. Chem. Phys. **19:** 514; 1952. J. Amer. Chem. Soc. **74:** 811.
MULLIKEN, R. S. & W. B. PERSON. 1962. Ann. Rev. Phys. Chem. **13:** 107.
NEMETHY, G. & H. A. SCHERAGA. 1963. Biopolymers **1:** 43.
NYQUIST, H. 1928. Phys. Rev. **32:** 110.
ONCLEY, J. L., W. SCHEIDER, H. W. DINTZIS & N. R. S. HOLLIES. 1965. *In* Protides of the Biol. Fluids. Vol. **12:** Elsevier. Amsterdam, Holland.
ONSAGER, L. 1933. Chem. Rev. **13:** 73; 1936. J. Amer. Chem. Soc. **58:** 1486.
OVERBEEK, J. T. G. 1948. *In* Theory of Lyophobie Colloids. E. J. W. Verwey & J. T. G. Overbeek, Eds.: 161. Elsevier. Amsterdam, Holland; 1952. *In* Colloid Science. H. R. Kruyt, Ed.: **1:** 276. Elsevier. Amsterdam, Holland.
PAULING, L. 1933. J. Chem. Phys. **1:** 280; 1955. Aspects of Synthesis and Order in Growth. Princeton University Press. Princeton, N. J.; 1957. Probability of Errors in the Process of Synthesis of Protein Molecules. Stoll Festschrift: 597. Birkhäuser. Basel, Switzerland; 1960. The Nature of the Chemical Bond. 3rd edit. Cornell University Press. Ithaca, New York; 1960. *In* Aspects of the Origin of Life. M. Florkin, Ed.: 132. Macmillan (Pergamon). New York, N. Y. 1961. Science **134:** 17.
PAULING, L. & M. DELBRÜCK. 1940. Science **92:** 77.
PAULING, L. & R. HAYWARD. 1964. The Architecture of Molecules. Freeman. San Francisco, Calif.
PAULING, L. & H. A. ITANO. 1957. Molecular Structure and Biological Specificity. Am. Inst. Biol. Sci. Washington, D. C.
PAULING, L. & E. B. WILSON, JR. 1935. Introduction to Quantum Mechanics McGraw-Hill, New York, N. Y.
PIMENTEL, G. C. & A. L. MCCLELLAN. 1960. Hydrogen Bond. Freeman. San Francisco, Calif.
PLATZMAN, R. L. 1962. Vortex. **28:** 372.
PULLMAN, A. & B. PULLMAN. 1963. Quantum Biochemistry. Interscience Publishers. New York, N. Y.
PULLMAN, B. 1964. Biopolymers Sympos. M. Weissbluth, Ed.: **1:** 141. Interscience Publishers. New York, N. Y.
RABINOWITCH, E. & L. F. EPSTEIN. 1941. J. Amer. Chem. Soc. **63:** 69.
RHODES, W. 1962. J. Chem. Phys. **37:** 2433.
ROSENBERG, M. 1960. Biophys. J. **1:** 137.
RYTOV, S. M. 1963. Theory of Electromagnetic Fluctuations (in Russian). Academy of Sciences. Moscow, U.S.S.R.
SALEM, L. 1962. J. Chem. Phys. **37:** 2100; 1962. Canad. J. Biochem. & Physiol. **40:** 1287; 1964. *In* Electronic Aspects of Biochemistry. B. Pullman, Ed.: 293. Academic Press. New York, N. Y.
SCATCHARD, G. 1931. Chem. Rev. **8:** 321; 1937. Trans. Farad. Soc. **33:** 160. 1952. Am. Scientist. **40:** 61.
SCHEIDER, W. 1965. Biophys. J. **5:** 617.

SERBER, R. 1934. Phys. Rev. **45:** 461.
SIMPSON, W. T. & D. L. PETERSON. 1957. J. Chem. Phys. **26:** 588.
SIMPSON, W. T. 1962. Theories of Electrons in Molecules. Prentice-Hall. Englewood, Cliffs, N. J.
SINANǦLU, O. Ed. 1965. Modern Quantum Chemistry. Academic Press. New York, N. Y.
SINANǦLU, O., S. ABDULNUR & N. R. KESTNER. 1964. *In* Electronic Aspects of Biochemistry. B. Pullman, Ed.: 301. Academic Press. New York, N. Y.
SLATER, J. C. 1963. Quantum Theory of Molecules and Solids. Vol. 1. McGraw-Hill. New York, N. Y.
STEINBERG, M. S. 1962. Proc. Nat. Acad. Sci. **48:** 1577, 1769; 1963. Exptl. Cell Res. **30:** 257; 1962. Science **141**: 401; 1964. *In* Cellular Membranes in Development. M. Locke, Ed.: 321. Academic Press. New York, N. Y.
SUSSMAN, M. & R. R. SUSSMAN. 1961. Exptl. Cell Res. (Suppl.) **8:** 91.
TANFORD, C. 1961. Physical Chemistry of Macromolecules. John Wiley & Sons. New York, N. Y.
TINOCO, I. 1960. J. Amer. Chem. Soc. **82:** 4785; 1960. J. Chem. Phys. **33:** 1332; 1964. *In* Elementary Aspects of Biochemistry. B. Pullman, Ed.: 7. Academic Press. New York, N. Y.
TINOCO, I. & H. DEVOE. 1962. J. Molec. Biol. **4:** 518.
TINOCO, I., A. HALPERN & W. T. SIMPSON. 1962. *In* Polyomino Acids, Polypeptides and Proteins. M. Stahman, Ed. University of Wisconsin Press. Madison, Wis.
TINOCO, I., R. W. WOODY & D. F. BRADLEY. 1963. J. Chem. Phys. **38:** 1317.
VAN VLECK, J. H. & A. SHERMAN. 1934. Rev. Mod. Phys. **7:** 167.
VERWEY, E. J. W. & J. T. G. OVERBEEK. 1948. Theory of the Stability of Lyophobic Colloids. Elsevier. Amsterdam, Holland.
VINOGRAD, J. R. 1935. *In* Thixotropy. H. Freundlich, Ed.: 267. Herman. Paris, France.
VOLD, M. J. 1961. J. Colloid. Sci. **16:** 1.
WADDINGTON, C. H. 1939. Nature **144:** 637.
WANG, S. C. 1927. Physik. Z. **28:** 663.
WEISS, L. 1967. Personal communication.
WEISSBLUTH, M. 1961. Optical Properties of Polymers. Biophys. Lab. Rept. No. 19. Stanford University Press. Stanford, Calif.
WIGNER, E. 1934. Phys. Rev. **46:** 1002; 1938. Trans. Farad. Soc. **34:** 678.
YOS, J. M. 1956. Ph.D. Thesis. University of Nebraska. Lincoln, Neb. 1958. Phys. Rev. **110:** 800.
YOS, J. M., W. L. BADE & H. JEHLE. 1957. Proc. Nat. Acad. Sci. **43:** 341.

Appendix A

The behavior of hydrophobic and hydrophilic colloids in an electrolyte medium has been excellently discussed by Kruyt and coworkers.

Particles or molecules which carry electric charges may have part of their charges neutralized by gegenions, i.e., by the formation of electric double layers, depending on the nature and concentration of the electrolytes.

Added to this static electric interaction there is, in the case of hydrophilic colloids, the interaction with the aqueous medium through hydrogen bonding. This implies both enthalpy and entropy terms in the interaction. Even though there are wide discrepancies among different research groups in the estimation of those enthalpy and entropy contributions, it would be a good idea if a precise terminology were agreed upon to separate what so often has been lumped together into hydrophobic bond energy.

For these hydrophilic colloids (polyelectrolytes) the hydrogen-bonding interaction depends, of course, again on the medium: i.e., on the dehydrating or rehydrating effect of electrolytes or other dehydrating agents—an effect which is not very critically sensitive to their concentrations.

In the case of either hydrophilic or hydrophobic colloids there are, in addition to those static interactions, the charge fluctuation interactions. Let

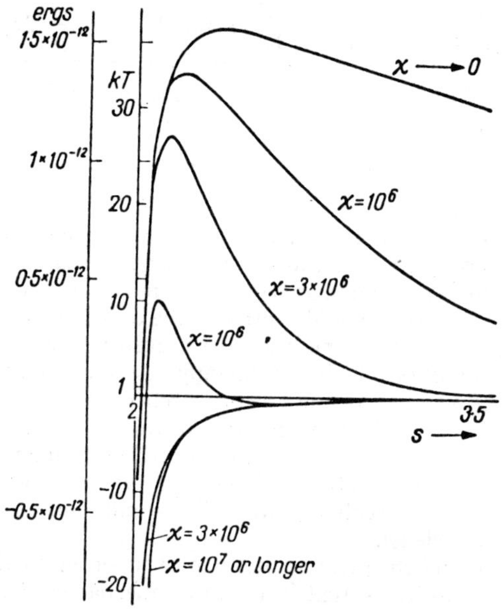

FIGURE 1. H. C. Hamaker's plots of charge fluctuation interactions for varying electrolyte concentrations (χ). These curves depict the quantitative influence of electrolyte concentrations upon the total potential energy of interaction (London attraction plus electrostatic repulsion modified by Debye-Hückel-Onsager gegenion layers). The s represents the center distance divided by the radius of two spherical particles. An approaching particle bearing the energy of Brownian motion is unlikely to exceed the barrier. (From Kruyt, 1952. Colloid Science. Elsevier. New York, N.Y.)

us mention here only the London force. The sharp R^{-6} dependence of the interaction energy of the London force between two particles, together with the much less sharp, static electric interaction energies (modified by gegenions) bring about a resultant potential which has been drawn by Hamaker (FIGURE 1). Stability of the hydrophobic colloid exists if the potential maximum is large compared with the kinetic energy 3kT/2, so that colliding particles have difficulty penetrating this wall (in the Figure, it would mean $\chi \geq 10^6$).

Appendix B

In order to present the simple idea of charge fluctuation forces, we may quote London's fundamental review (Trans. Farad. Soc., 1936) for a description of a simplified model of the dispersion effect.

Let us take two spherically symmetrical systems, each with a polarizability, α, say two three-dimensional isotropic harmonic oscillators, with no permanent moment in their rest position. If the charges, e, of these oscillators are artificially displaced from their rest positions by the displacements

$$\vec{r}_I = (x_I, y_I, z_I) \qquad \text{and} \qquad \vec{r}_{II} = (x_{II}, y_{II}, z_{II})$$

respectively, we obtain for the potential energy:

$$V = \underbrace{\frac{e^2 r_I^{\,2}}{2\alpha} + \frac{e^2 r_{II}^{\,2}}{2\alpha}}_{\text{Elastic Energy}} + \underbrace{\frac{e^2}{R^3}(x_I x_{II} + y_I y_{II} - 2 z_I z_{II})}_{\text{Dipole Interaction Energy}} \qquad (\mathbf{0})$$

Classically the two systems in their equilibrium position

$$(x_I = x_{II} = \cdots = z_{II} = 0)$$

would not act upon each other and, when brought into finite distance ($R > \sqrt[3]{2\alpha}$), remain in their rest position. They could not influence a momentum in each other.

However, in quantum mechanics, as is well known, a particle cannot lie absolutely at rest on a certain point. That would contradict the uncertainty relation. According to quantum mechanics our isotropic oscillators, even in their lowest states, make a so-called zero-point motion which one can only describe statistically, for example, by a probability function which defines the probability with which any configuration occurs, although one cannot describe the way in which the different configurations follow each other. For the isotropic oscillators, these probability functions give a spherically symmetric distribution of configurations around the rest position. (The rare gases, too, have such a spherically symmetrical distribution for the electrons around the nucleus).

We need not know much quantum mechanics in order to discuss our simple model. We only need to know that in quantum mechanics the lowest state of a harmonic oscillator of the proper frequency ν has the energy

$$E_0 = (1/2)h\nu \qquad (\mathbf{1})$$

the so-called zero-point energy. If we introduce the following coordinates (normal coordinates):

$$\vec{r}_+ \equiv \begin{cases} x_+ = \dfrac{1}{\sqrt{2}}(x_I + x_{II}) \\ y_+ = \dfrac{1}{\sqrt{2}}(y_I + y_{II}) \\ z_+ = \dfrac{1}{\sqrt{2}}(z_I + z_{II}) \end{cases} \qquad \vec{r}_- \equiv \begin{cases} x_- = \dfrac{1}{\sqrt{2}}(x_I - x_{II}) \\ y_- = \dfrac{1}{\sqrt{2}}(y_I - y_{II}) \\ z_- = \dfrac{1}{\sqrt{2}}(z_I - z_{II}) \end{cases}$$

the potential energy (0) can be written as a sum of squares such as the potential energy of six independent oscillators (although the kinetic energy does not change its form):

$$V = \frac{e^2}{2\alpha}(r_+^{\,2} + r_-^{\,2}) + \frac{e^2}{2R^3}(x_+^{\,2} + y_+^{\,2} - 2z_+^{\,2} - x_-^{\,2} - y_-^{\,2} + 2z_-^{\,2}).$$

$$= \frac{e^2}{2\alpha}\left[\left(1 + \frac{\alpha}{R^3}\right)(x_+^{\,2} + y_+^{\,2}) + \left(1 - \frac{\alpha}{R^3}\right)(x_-^{\,2} + y_-^{\,2}) + \left(1 - 2\frac{\alpha}{R^3}\right)z_+^{\,2} + \left(1 + 2\frac{\alpha}{R^3}\right)z_-^{\,2}\right] \qquad (\mathbf{0'})$$

The frequencies of these six oscillators are given by

$$\nu_x^{\pm} = \nu_y^{\pm} = \nu_0\sqrt{1 \pm \alpha/R^3} \approx \nu_0\left(1 \pm \frac{\alpha}{2R^3} - \frac{\alpha^2}{8R^6} \pm \cdots\right)$$
$$\nu_z^{\pm} = \nu_0\sqrt{1 \mp 2\alpha/R^3} \approx \nu_0\left(1 \mp \frac{\alpha}{R^3} - \frac{\alpha^2}{2R^6} \mp \cdots\right) \qquad (2)$$

Here $\nu_0 = e/\sqrt{m\alpha}$ is the proper frequency of the two elastic systems, if isolated from each other ($R \to \infty$), and m is their reduced mass. Assuming $\alpha \ll R^3$, we have developed the square roots in Equation 2 into powers of (α/R^3).

The lowest state of this system of six oscillators will therefore be given, according to Equation 1, by:

$$E_0 = \frac{h}{2}(\nu_x^+ + \nu_y^+ + \nu_z^+ + \nu_x^- + \nu_y^- + \nu_z^-)$$
$$= \frac{h\nu_0}{2}\left[6 + \left(\frac{1}{2} + \frac{1}{2} - 1 - \frac{1}{2} - \frac{1}{2} + 1\right)\frac{\alpha}{R^3} - \left(\frac{4}{8} + \frac{2}{2}\right)\frac{\alpha^2}{R^6} + \cdots\right]$$
$$= 3h\nu_0 - \frac{3}{4}\frac{h\nu_0\alpha^2}{R^6}$$

The first term $3h\nu_0$ is, of course, simply the internal zero-point energy of the two isolated elastic systems. The second term, however,

$$U = -\frac{3}{4}\frac{h\nu_0\alpha^2}{R^6} \qquad (3)$$

depends upon the distance, R, and is to be considered as an interaction energy which, being negative, characterizes an attractive force. We shall presume that this type of force, which is not conditioned by the existence of a permanent dipole or any higher multipole, will be responsible for the Van der Waals attraction of the rare gases and also of the simple molecules H_2, N_2, etc. These forces are called the dispersion effect.

CONTRIBUTION OF NUCLEAR MAGNETIC RESONANCE TO THE STUDY OF THE STRUCTURE AND ELECTRONIC ASPECTS OF NUCLEIC ACIDS

P. O. P. Ts'o,* M. P. Schweizer,† and D. P. Hollis‡

Department of Radiobiological Sciences and Department of Physiological Chemistry, Johns Hopkins University, Baltimore, Md.

About ten to twenty years ago, physicochemical studies of nucleic acids were concerned mostly with the problems of the molecule as a whole: the molecular weight, size, and shape. Therefore, light scattering, viscosity, sedimentation and other hydrodynamic and thermodynamic techniques were most commonly used. During the last five years, attention has been focused on the problems of short-range properties within the molecule, such as the interaction of the bases, and the precise description of the conformation. Thus, the application of spectroscopic techniques such as uv and infrared absorption, optical rotatory dispersion, and circular dichroism, became more prevalent. Advances in theory and in instrumentation (in both sensitivity and resolution) of nuclear magnetic resonance (n.m.r.) have made this technique much more promising for studies of biological macromolecules. A brief report will be made here on the contribution of n.m.r. to the study of the structure and electronic aspects of nucleic acid and its constituents. Since the pioneering work of the Jardetzkys published in 1960,[1, 2] the number of publications in this field has increased rapidly, especially during the last two years. This summary then, will not be exhaustive or complete, and will be concerned with the interests and contributions of our laboratories. Moreover, most of the magnetic resonance studies deal with the proton, rather than with other nuclei.

Assignment and Calculation of the Chemical Shifts of the Base Protons in Bases and in Nucleosides

The first task of the p.m.r. study is the assignment of the various spectral lines to the appropriate protons in the molecule. Based on existing theories, the following factors which are known to influence the positions of the proton resonances were enumerated in one of our early papers[3]: (1) electron densities at various carbon atoms bearing the proton; (2) the ring current effect associated with the mobile π-electron cloud; (3) the magnetic anisotropy of the heteroatoms in the aromatic rings; (4) solvent effects; (5) solute-solute interaction. The problem of solute-solute interaction of the bases, nucleosides and nucleotides will be discussed extensively in a later section. The question of solvent effects has not been explored adequately, except as one of the variables in relation to the study of solute-solute interaction. The main reason for this is the problem of solubility: the bases, nucleosides and nucleotides are sparingly soluble in very few solvents, and usually they are soluble only in water (or D_2O for p.m.r. studies). We shall report our attempt in re-

* Work supported in part by National Science Foundation grant GB-5483 and United States Public Health Service grant 10802-05.
† Present address: Department of Experimental Therapeutics, Roswell Park Memorial Institute, Buffalo, N. Y.
‡ Work supported in part by NSF grant GB-6682.

lating the observed chemical shifts of the base protons to the electronic structure of these heterocyclic compounds in a semiquantitative fashion.

A linear correlation between the observed chemical shifts and the calculated π-electron charge densities in the aromatic homocyclic and heterocyclic systems can be established with a certain degree of satisfaction, as notably shown by the work of Schaefer and Schneider,[4] Veillard[5] and, more recently, by the work of Lynch and Dou[6] on protonated nitrogen heterocyclic compounds. These papers pointed out as well the significant contributions of ring current and nitrogen atom magnetic anisotropy which will be considered here. In following the method developed in our previous paper,[3] the calculated excess π-charge densities at each atom of the base ring are handled in terms of a field effect upon the proton chemical shifts by the following equation:

$$\Delta\sigma = 12.5 \times 10^{-6} \sum_i \frac{\Delta\rho_i}{R_i^2} \cos\Theta_i - 17.0 \times 10^{-6} \left(\frac{\sum_i \Delta\rho_i}{R_i^2\ \Delta\rho_i} \right)^2 \qquad (1)$$

where σ is the screening constant (ppm), $\Delta\rho i$ is the excess π-electron density on the ith atom of the base, R_i is the distance (Å) from the ith atom to the proton in question and Θ_i is the angle in degrees of the field vector with respect to the C-H bond axis for the appropriate proton. R_i and Θ_i were obtained from scale drawing of the bases according to appropriate x-ray diffraction results. Equation 1 takes into account the calculated π-electron density at each atom of the base, rather than just that at the carbon atom at which the proton is bonded. This expression was obtained from the familiar equation for field effect calculations:

$$\Delta\sigma = -aE_2 - bE^2 \qquad (2)$$

For our case a has been chosen to fit the linear correlation found experimentally by Schaefer and Schneider.[4] This value of a is 2.60×10^{-12}, which is close to the value of 2.0×10^{-12} obtained by Buckingham[7] and 2.9×10^{-12} obtained by Musher.[8] Musher's value for b, was obtained from Marshall and Pople's calculation, was used. The adoption of several sets of the π-charge density calculations for the bases will be discussed later in greater detail.

The contribution to the screening constants due to ring currents was calculated with the following equation from Schaefer and Schneider:[4]

$$\Delta\sigma(\text{ppm}) = -12.0 \sum_i \left(\frac{A_i^2}{R_i^2} \times \text{RING CURRENT INTENSITY} \right) \qquad (3)$$

Where A and R in angstrom units are, respectively, the radius of each ring and the distance of the proton being considered from the center of each ring. Fortunately, ring current intensities of various bases relative to benzene have been calculated by Giessner-Prettre and Pullman.[9]

The final problem is the effect of nitrogen atom magnetic anisotropy. For pyrimidine, this effect was also evaluated in our earlier papers.[3, 10] It was noticed that only slightly more than half of the shift difference between H_2 and H_6 (0.50 ppm)[11] could be accounted for by the difference in charge densities calculated by two different groups.[12, 13] If the remaining 0.21 ppm (based on charge densities calculated from Reference 12) or 0.24 ppm (based on charge densities calculated from Reference 13) can be attributed to the difference in the effects of the nitrogen magnetic anisotropy at the two protons, one can compute a magnetic anisotropy for the nitrogen atoms in the pyrimidine ring by the use of the following general equation based upon the dipole approximation[14]:

$$\Delta\sigma = \sum_i \frac{\Delta\chi_i}{3R_i^3}(1 - 3\cos^2\gamma_i) \quad \textbf{(4)}$$

where R_i is the distance between N_i and the proton in question, $\Delta\chi_i$ is the anisotropy of the susceptibility tensor and γ_i is the angle between the axis of symmetry in N_i and the N_i-H line. $\Delta\chi$ was computed to be $+2.72 \times 10^{-6}$ and $\Delta\sigma$ for H-2 due to N_1 in purine or adenine was computed to be -0.183 ppm. Considering the uncertainties and assumptions involved in both calculations, this value is in reasonable agreement with the -0.25 ppm calculated by Gil and Murrell[15] as the effect of the magnetic anisotropy of the N atom on the α protons in pyridine. As in the treatment by these authors, our reference for calculation was sp^2 carbon. But the actual comparison between the bases of the nucleosides (see later section) is the difference in magnetic anisotropy between pyridine-type nitrogen (N_1 in adenine and cytosine) and cyclic amide nitrogen (N_1 in hypoxanthine, guanine, and N_3 in uracil). At present, we have no reliable evaluation of the magnetic anisotropy of the cyclic amide nitrogen, so that the value of -0.183 ppm may be either an over- or underestimate of the difference in the anisotropic effect exerted on the adjacent hydrogen by these two different types of nitrogen atoms.

We shall attempt to provide a theoretical basis to account for the observed chemical shifts of the ring protons of these heterocyclic compounds based on the summation of the effects calculated from Equations 1, 3 and 4.

Purine and Purine Nucleosides

Though the unsubstituted purine is not a base component of nucleic acid, because of its relatively simple structure and its high solubility, it is an excellent model for the properties of 6-amino purine (adenine), 6-keto purine (hypoxanthine) and 2-amino, 6-keto purine (guanine)—the bases present in nucleic acid (FIGURE 1). There are three resonance lines for the protons H-2, H-6 and H-8, and the correct assignment of these lines to the appropriate protons was achieved independently by Matsuura and Goto,[16] by Schweizer and collaborators,[3] and by Bullock and Jardetzky.[17] This achievement was made possible by selective deuteration of the molecule: 2-deuterio purine and 6-deuterio purine were synthesized by Matsura and Goto; and 2-deuterio purine and 8-deuterio purine were synthesized by Schweizer and coworkers and by Bullock and Jardetzky. This is an important experimental finding, since the result is different from the two previous attempts based on more speculative grounds.[1, 18]

The calculated values for the proton chemical shifts of purine based on Equations 1, 3 and 4 are listed in TABLE 1. These values were calculated using four sets of excessive π-charge density calculations.[12, 13, 19a, 19b, 20] From four sets of ring current values reported by Giessner-Prettre and Pullman,[9] the two that were results of most recent calculations were adopted for comparison. It can be seen that the major contributions to the calculation of the chemical shifts comes from the excess π-charge density and the ring current effect, whereas the contribution of the nitrogen magnetic anisotropy is relatively small. TABLE 2 provides a comparison between the observed differ-

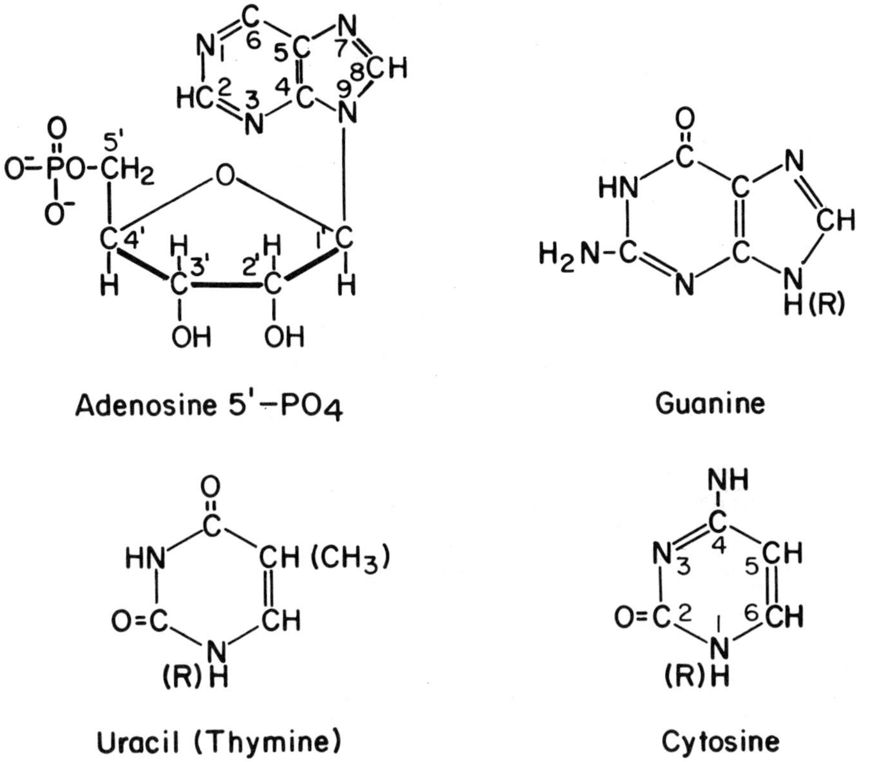

FIGURE 1. The structural formula of the bases in nucleic acids and 5'-AMP in syn conformation.

ences among the chemical shifts of the three protons in purine and the calculated values. The observed values in D_2O, dimethyl sulfoxide (DMSO) and dimethylformamide were from our work,[21] and the observed values in chloroform were from the work of Reddy and coworkers.[18] It can be seen that the calculated values of set I agree semiquantitatively with the experimental values. These results encourage us to continue our efforts in comparing the calculated values of the base protons among various nucleosides. Recently, two sets of x-ray data have been obtained for purine.[22a] These dimensions are slightly different from those adopted in our calculation, based on the model of adenine from Cochran[22b] and the CH bond length of 1.08 for aromatic systems. One reason why these values are not recalculated is that these two sets of data differ significantly in the C–H bond length, for instance, varying from 0.95 to 1.06Å in C_8–H. It is felt that the values previously adopted for our calculations are sufficiently close for the purpose of a preliminary attempt.

The carbon-13 resonance of purine has been studied by Pugmire and collaborators,[23a] by the aid of deuterated compounds and the decoupling technique. The C-13 chemical shift values for the 2, 6, and 8 carbons in purine were assigned unequivocally. The two remaining peaks found at the lowest and highest field positions are assigned to carbons 4 and 5, respectively, on

TABLE 1

CALCULATIONS OF THE PROTON CHEMICAL SHIFTS FOR PURINE (PPM)[a]

	$\Delta\sigma\Delta\rho$	$\Delta\sigma\pi$[b]	$\Delta\sigma_{\chi N}$	Summation
H-8				
I.[c]	−1.202	−1.532, −1.306	−0.206	−2.940, −2.714
II.[d]	−1.464	−1.532, −1.306	−0.206	−3.202, −2.976
III.[e]	−0.994	−1.532, −1.306	−0.206	−2.732, −2.506
IV.[f]	−2.328	−1.532, −1.306	−0.206	−4.066, −3.840
H-2				
I.[c]	−1.194	−1.952, −1.766	−0.383	−3.529, −3.343
II.[d]	−0.326	−1.952, −1.766	−0.383	−2.661, −2.475
III.[e]	−1.427	−1.952, −1.766	−0.383	−3.762, −3.576
IV.[f]	−0.685	−1.952, −1.766	−0.383	−3.020, −2.834
H-6				
I.[c]	−1.469	−2.062, −1.850	−0.210	−3.741, −3.529
II.[d]	−0.509	−2.062, −1.850	−0.210	−2.781, −2.569
III.[e]	−1.922	−2.062, −1.850	−0.210	−4.194, −3.982
IV.[f]	−1.002	−2.062, −1.850	−0.210	−3.274, −3.062

[a] Calculations are based on Equations 1, 3 and 4.
[b] Ring current intensity values from Reference 9 (see text).
[c] Excess π-charge density values from References 13 and 19a.
[d] Excess π-charge density values from Reference 19b.
[e] Excess π-charge density values from Reference 12.
[f] Excess π-charge density values from Reference 20.

the strength of the theoretical prediction that the highest π-electron density is at C-5. They also observed that a gross correlation of C-13 chemical shift data with theoretical estimates of charge distribution in purine does exist. They pointed out that, in an increasing magnetic field, the resonance pattern for C-13 (2, 8, 6) differs from that for the corresponding directly bonded hydrogens (6, 2, 8). This is perhaps to be expected, in view of the large contribution from the ring current magnetic anisotropy (TABLE 1). The H-6 proton

TABLE 2

COMPARISON OF THE OBSERVED DIFFERENCES AMONG THE CHEMICAL SHIFTS OF THE THREE PROTONS IN PURINE WITH THE CALCULATED VALUES (PPM)[a]

	$H_8 - H_2$	$H_2 - H_6$
Observed values		
D_2O, infinite dilution[b]	0.36	0.18
DMSO, 0.2 m[b]	0.29	0.22
DMF 0.2 m[b]	0.24	0.21
CH Cl_3, uncertain[c] conc.	0.55	0.17
Calculated values		
I.[d]	0.589, 0.629	0.212, 0.186
II.[d]	−0.541, −0.501	0.120, 0.094
III.[d]	1.029, 1.070	0.432, 0.406
IV.[d]	−1.046, −1.006	0.254, 0.228

[a] The calculated values are computed from values in TABLE 1.
[b] From Reference 21.
[c] From Reference 18.
[d] See TABLE 1 for the references.

is subjected to the deshielding effect from both the six-membered ring and the five-membered ring, and thus is moved substantially downfield.

In the course of preparing the deuteropurine, it was found that the H-8 proton of the purine and the purine nucleosides is exchangeable at elevated temperature.[3, 17, 23a] By this method, the resonance lines of H-2 and H-8 of many purine nucleosides were assigned.[17] For the adenine nucleoside and nucleotides, this procedure was checked independently.[23b] TABLE 3 sum-

TABLE 3

PROTON CHEMICAL SHIFTS FOR NUCLEOSIDES IN D_2O AT 30–35° C PPM FROM TMS CAPILLARY

	Molal Conc.	H-2	H-5 or H-8	H-6	H-1′	CH_3
Ribosylpurine	0.0	9.425	9.162	9.627	6.700	
	0.1	9.303	9.088	9.477	6.598	
Ribosyl-6-chloropurine	0.027	9.258	9.258		—	
	0.05	9.203	9.203		6.663	
1-Methylinosine	0.0	8.870	8.802		6.560	4.151
	0.1	8.773	8.773		6.483	4.091
6-Thioinosine	0.027	8.810	8.933		6.590	
	0.05	8.791	8.921		6.570	
Adenosine	0.0	8.730	8.820		6.533	
	0.1	8.483	8.667		6.467	
N-6-Methyladenosine	0.0	8.733	8.733		6.491	3.550
	0.1	8.308	8.502		6.323	3.311
Inosine	0.0	8.728	8.830		6.608	
	0.1	6.641	8.756		6.518	
N-6-Methyl-2′-deoxyadenosine	0.0	8.710	8.728		6.900	3.578
	0.1	8.343	8.503		6.720	3.363
2′-O-Methyladenosine	0.0	8.686	8.760		6.582	3.858
	0.1	8.528	8.678		6.498	3.845
2′-Deoxyadenosine	0.0	8.686	8.756		6.930	
	0.1	8.435	8.585		6.765	
3′-Deoxyadenosine	0.0	8.683	8.761		6.513	
	0.1	8.420	8.611		6.353	
N-6-Dimethyladenosine	0.0	8.628	8.686		6.513	3.886
	0.1	8.253	8.483		6.308	3.543
Ribosyl-2, 6-diaminopurine	0.027		8.423		6.353	
	0.05		8.401		6.350	
1-Methylguanosine	0.025		8.418		6.375	3.916
Cytidine	0.0		6.508(H-5)	8.280	6.355	
	0.1		6.497	8.275	6.347	
Uridine	0.0		6.333(H-5)	8.278	6.346	
	0.1		6.325	8.275	6.342	
Thymidine	0.0			8.075	6.723	2.313
	0.1			8.067	6.702	2.313

marizes the pertinent information on the 17 nucleosides which have been studied in our laboratory.

Up to the present time, no serious attempt has been made to account quantitatively for the effect of ring substiuents upon base proton chemical shifts in the purine nucleosides. Coburn and coworkers[24] have reported a correlation of proton chemical shifts of 6-substituted purines with the reactivity parameters (Brown's electrophilic substituent constants) of the substituents. Diminution of ring currents by polar substituents has been proposed by Jardetzky,[25] to explain the reduction of $\Delta\delta$ and intrinsic δ of anions of purine and sustituted purines. This explanation may be invoked in the case of ribosylpurine vs adenosine, but fails to account for the almost identical shifts observed for adenosine and inosine (TABLE 3). Inosine, existing in the lactam form, should have less ring current in the pyrimidine ring than does adenosine, which exists in the lactim form shown in the calculation.[9] Thus, according to this ring-current argument, one would expect H-2 in inosine to be shifted upfield significantly, contrary to what has been observed.

Additional uncertainty is encountered in applying Equations 1 and 3 for the quantitative estimation of the chemical shifts of the base protons in the nucleosides, since the theoretical values of the excess π-charge densities and the ring current were calculated on the free bases and not on the pentosyl bases, i.e., the nucleosides. The comparison of experimental δ's of purine and ribosylpurine at infinite dilution in water indicates that H-6 and H-2 are deshielded by about 0.16 ppm and H-8 by about 0.25 ppm, owing to the N-9 ribosyl substitution. This observation is anticipated from the electron-withdrawing effect of this group. It is reasonable, as a first approximation, to consider that the effect of pentosyl substitution at N-9 on all the atoms in the base is the same for each of the several nucleosides in question. Thus, we assume that a comparison of the calculated π-charge densities of the bases can represent the comparison of the π-charge densities of the bases in the nucleosides. At present, we shall not attempt to compare the observed difference in δ values of the H-2 and the H-8 protons to the calculated difference based on the computed values for the free bases because of uncertainty about the effect of the pentosyl substitution. Concerning the problem of ring current, the validity of employing the figures for the five-membered ring is again somewhat questionable since they were calculated for the bases and not for the nucleosides. Fortunately, the calculated ring-current differences for various five-membered rings among these bases is rather small.[9] In regard to, the problem of nitrogen magnetic anisotropy, the contribution in this category to H-8 is likely to be the same for all the nucleosides and, therefore, not important in the comparison. However, in comparing the H-2 of adenosine and ribosyl purine with the H-2 of inosine, the N-1 is changed from the pyridine type to that of the amide type. As mentioned above, we have estimated that this change of bonding to the nitrogen atom in N-1 position may bring about a positive contribution of about 0.183 ppm to the H-2 of the inosine in comparison to the H-2 of adenosine or ribosyl purine because of the reduction in the magnetic anisotropy. The anisotropic effect of N-1 upon H-8 is sufficiently small to be neglected. The results of the calculation of the chemical shifts of the base protons are listed in TABLE 4. In TABLE 5, the observed differences of the H-2 protons as well as the H-8 protons among several nucleosides are compared to the calculated differences based on values enumerated in TABLE 1 (for ribosyl purine) and in TABLE 4 (for adenosine, inosine and guanosine). The experimental results are those taken in D_2O at in-

TABLE 4

CALCULATIONS OF THE BASE PROTON CHEMICAL SHIFTS FOR THE PURINE NUCLEOSIDES (PPM)[a]

	$\Delta\sigma\Delta\rho$	$\Delta\sigma\pi$[b]	$\Delta\sigma_{\chi N}$
A. Adenosine			
H-8			
I.[c]	−1.073	−1.470, −1.254	Same[d]
II.[e]	−0.976	−1.470, −1.254	Same[d]
IV.[f]	−1.792	−1.470, −1.254	Same[d]
H-2			
I.[c]	−1.155	−1.715, −1.540	Same[d]
II.[e]	−0.063	−1.715, −1.540	Same[d]
IV.[f]	−0.460	−1.715, −1.540	Same[d]
B. Inosine			
H-8			
I.[c]	−0.984	−1.159, −1.032	Same[d]
II.[e]	−0.489	−1.159, −1.032	Same[d]
IV.[f]	−1.158	−1.159, −1.032	Same[d]
H-2			
I.[c]	−1.721	−0.557, −0.575	+0.183-
II.[e]	−2.264	−0.557, −0.575	+0.183-
IV.[f]	−2.742	−0.557, −0.575	+0.183-
C. Guanosine			
H-8			
I.[c]	−0.817	−1.140, −1.012	Same[d]
II.[e]	−0.168	−1.140, −1.012	Same[d]
IV.[f]	−0.904	−1.140, −1.012	Same[d]

[a] Calculations are based on Equations 1, 3 and 4.
[b] Ring current intensity values from Reference 9. (See text.)
[c] Excess π-charge density values from References 13 and 19a.
[d] $\Delta\sigma_{\chi N}$ value is the same as that listed for the appropriate protons of purine listed in TABLE 1.
[e] Excess π-charged density values from Reference 19b.
[f] Excess π-charged density values from Reference 20.
[g] The N_1 atom in hypoxanthine is changed from the pyridine type to cyclic amide type. A contribution of +0.183 ppm was calculated to compensate this change in comparison to purine. (See text.)

finite dilution (TABLE 3). Since guanosine is insoluble for measurement, the δ value for H-8 of 1-methyl guanosine is used instead. The justification for this substitution is that δ of H-8 is the same for both inosine and 1-methylinosine (TABLE 3). It should be mentioned also that the value for H-8 for 1-methyl guanosine is not extrapolated to infinite dilution because of solubility limitations, and therefore likely to be about 0.05 ppm closer to the purine than listed (TABLE 5). In general, it appears that the calculated values from Set I are in better agreement with the observed values.

Pyrimidines and Pyrimidine Nucleosides

The assignment of the high-field doublet to H_5 and the low-field doublet to H_6 of the uracil (or uridine) and of the cytosine (or cytidine) was first made by the Jardetzkys.[1] This assignment was substantiated by studies on a large number of 5- and 6- substituted uracils[26] as well as by the studies on methyl derivatives of cytosine involving the use of N^{15} and spin coupling data.[27] In

TABLE 5

COMPARISON OF THE OBSERVED DIFFERENCES OF THE CHEMICAL SHIFTS OF THE BASE PROTONS AMONG SEVERAL PURINE NUCLEOSIDES WITH THE CALCULATED DIFFERENCES BASED ON THE VALUES IN TABLES 1 AND 4 (PPM)

A. H-2			
	P-A	P-I	
Observed values[a] (D$_2$O, Infinite dilution)	−.695	−0.697	
Calculated values			
I.[b]	−0.276, −0.265	−1.051, −0.847	
II.[b]	−0.500, −0.489	+0.360, +0.564	
IV.[b]	−0.462, −0.451	+0.479, +0.683	
B. H-8			
	P-A	P-I	P-G (1-MG)
Observed values[a] (D$_2$O, Infinite dilution)	−0.342	−0.332	−0.744
Calculated values			
I.[b]	−0.191, −0.181	−0.591, −0.492	−0.777, −0.679
II.[b]	−0.550, −0.540	−1.348, −1.249	−1.688, −1.590
IV.[b]	−0.598, −0.588	−1.543, −1.443	−1.816, −1.718

[a] From Reference 10 and TABLE 3.
[b] See TABLE 4 for the references.

DMSO, Kokko and collaborators[26] reported that the chemical shifts of H_6 N_3–H, and N_1–H of the uracil are related approximately linearly to the group dipole moment of the 5-substituents ranging from nitro to methyl groups. Similarly, the data of the average chemical shifts of N_3–H and N_1–H can be correlated linearly also with the Hammett σ-constants of the 5- substituents; groups with high positive values (electron-withdrawing) such as nitro, cause the shift to go downfield and groups with low or negative values (electron-releasing) such as methyl, cause the shift to go upfield.

We have employed Equations 1, 3, and 4 for the computation of the chemical shifts of H-5 and H-6 of uracil and cytosine with two sets of excess π-charge density calculations.[28, 29] Again, two sets of ring current values from Gissner-Prettre and Pullman[9] were adopted. The results of these computations are given in TABLE 6. Because of the long distance, the contribution of the magnetic anisotropy of N_6 to H-5 or H-6 of cytosine is very small. Comparison between the observed and the calculated differences in the chemical shifts of the H-5 and H-6 of C (cytosine or cytidine) and those of U (uracil or uridine), i.e., H_6 of C–H^2 of U, etc., is shown in TABLE 7. The observed values are those of the bases in DMSO (I)[26] and those of the nucleosides in water (TABLE 3). These two sets of experimental data are very close to each other (~0.05 ppm) except for the difference between H-6 and H-5 of U (~0.3 ppm). Both sets of calculations agree with the experimental results that the H-6 proton should be downfield from the H-5 proton; the agreement is better with C than with U. One set of the calculated results, (I), is also very close to the observed difference between the δ of H-5 of C and the δ of H-5 of U. It is somewhat surprising that, experimentally, the H-6 of C is very close to the H-6 of U, whereas in both sets of calculation, the difference is about 0.50 ppm. In terms of the diamagnetic contribution from the excess π-charge density to the calculated shift, H-5 of U is less than H-5 of C, but this difference

TABLE 6

CALCULATIONS OF THE BASE PROTON CHEMICAL SHIFTS OF THE PYRIMIDINE NUCLEOSIDES[a]

	Calculation I.[b] H-5	H-6	Calculation II.[c] H-5	H-6
1. Uracil[d]				
$\Delta\sigma\Delta\rho$	+0.105	−0.990	+0.292	−0.824
$\Delta\sigma\pi$	−0.098, −0.140	−0.107, −0.153	−0.098, −0.140	−0.107, −0.153
	+0.007, −0.035	−1.097, −1.143	+0.194, +0.152	−0.931, −0.977
2. Cytosine[e]				
$\Delta\sigma\Delta\rho$	+0.323	−1.141	+0.930	−1.006
$\Delta\sigma\pi$	−0.402, −0.439	−0.398, −0.435	−0.402, −0.439	−0.398, −0.435
$\Delta\sigma_{\chi N}$	−0.050	−0.036	−0.050	−0.036
	−0.129, −0.166	−1.575, −1.612	+0.478, +0.441	−1.440, −1.477

[a] Calculations were based on Equations 1, 3 and 4. Ring current intensity values were from Reference 9. (See text.)
[b] Excess π-charge density values from Reference 28.
[c] Excess π-charge density values from Reference 29.
[d] Dimensions from calcium thymidylate, Reference 84.
[e] Dimensions from 3′ cytidylic acid, Reference 85.

is minimized to about 0.13 ppm by the larger paramagnetic contribution of the ring current in C. On the other hand, the greater paramagnetic contribution from the excess π-charge density to H-6 of C compared with H-6 of U is amplified by the large paramagnetic ring current effect of C, causing H-6 of C to be computed significantly downfield from H-6 of U—a result contrary to the experimental observation. Clearly, more work is needed in this area, since much can be learned from these relatively simple molecules.

In conclusion, chemical shifts of the base protons of the bases and the nu-

TABLE 7

COMPARISON OF THE DIFFERENCES AMONG THE CALCULATED CHEMICAL SHIFTS OF THE PYRIMIDINE NUCLEOSIDE BASE PROTONS WITH THE OBSERVED VALUES (PPM)[a]

	C_{H-5}—U_{H-5}	C_{H-6}—U_{H-6}	C_{H-6}—U_{H-5}	U_{H-6}—U_{H-5}
Observed[b] values I.	−0.172	+0.03	−1.760	−1.668
II.	−0.175	−0.02	−1.772	−1.945
Calculated[c] values I.	−0.136, −0.131	−0.478, −0.469	−1.446[d], −1.446[d]	−1.104[d], −1.108[d]
II.	+0.284, +0.289	−0.509, −0.500	−1.918,[d] −1.918[d]	−1.125,[d] −1.129

[a] The calculated values were obtained from TABLE 6.
[b] Values in I were obtained from Reference 26, and values in II were obtained from TABLE 3.
[c] See TABLE 6 for the corresponding references.
[d] A correction factor of about −0.15 ± 0.05 ppm should be added to all the calculated differences. When compared to the observed difference of set I (bases), this factor is due to the omission of the differential contribution of N-3 magnetic anisotropy to H-6 vs that to H-5. When compared to the observed differences of set II (nucleosides), this factor is due to the omission of the differential deshielding effect of the N-3 pentosyl substitution on H-6 vs that on H-5.

cleosides all have been properly assigned. A preliminary attempt to account for these assignments on theoretical and quantitative bases has been presented here. Undoubtedly, n.m.r. spectra contain pertinent and much needed information about the electronic structure of these important heterocyclic bases in the ground state. This information is most valuable, not only for the quantum mechanical studies of these types of compounds, but also for the theoretical prediction of other properties of these molecules such as hydrogen-bonding and vertical stacking. Obviously, better theoretical treatments of the observed n.m.r. spectra of these compounds are urgently needed. We hope that our preliminary effort will bring about more interest and more significant advances in these directions.

Tautomerization, Protonation, Methylation and other Structure Assignments

Effective application of n.m.r. has provided decisive information about various important but subtle structural features such as tautomerization, site of protonation and methylation, etc. Some of the outstanding examples in relation to nucleic acids will be briefly described here.

In comparing the p.m.r. spectra of 1, 9-dimethylguanine and guanosine in DMSO, Miles and coworkers[30] have properly assigned the resonance for the protons of the 2-amino group, thereby eliminating the possibility of a 2-imino structure. The assignment of N_1–H in the p.m.r. spectra together with other pertinent infrared data allow them to determine the correct tautomeric structure of guanine or guanosine (Figure 1). In comparing the ^{14}N and ^{15}N spectra of 1-methyl-cytosine in DMSO, Becker and collaborators[27] have established the chemical shift of the 4-amino protons and thereby proved the amino form to be the correct tautomeric structure (Figure 1). The work of Kokko and coworkers[26] has also contributed to the establishment of the keto form as the correct form for the 4-oxo group in uracil or thymine.

An elegant quantitative study has been made by Read and Goldstein[31] on the rather complex question concerning the site of protonation of purine. They found that the δ's of H_6, H_2 and H_8 were affected by the change of pD to about the same extent deshielding at lower pD), indicating that N-1, N-3 and N-7 are all affected. However, the change of the ^{13}C–H coupling constants versus the change of pD was found to be in the following order: $H_2 > H_6 > H_8$. Analyses of these data led them to conclude that the percent of protonation at each site is: N-1, 54 ± 12%, N-3, 17 ± 12%, and N-7 (or N-9), 29 ± 7%. In a study of the site of protonation for cytosine derivatives, Becker and collaborators[27, 32] compared the spectrum of 1-methylcytosine hydrochloride (and hydroiodide) with its ^{15}N derivatives in DMSO at 23° and SO_2 at −60°. They observed a splitting of the H-5 (by 2.5 cps) due to the long-range coupling of N_3–H, which they have located at 11.43 ppm (downfield from TMS internal standard) in SO_2 at −60°. These data unequivocally established the site of protonation for cytosine. In the studies of the δ values of the pyrimidines in anhydrous trifluoroacetic acid, Jardetzky and coworkers[33] proposed that the order of basicity in pyrimidines is N ring > N amino > oxygen.

Confirmation of the site of methylation in 7-methylinosine versus 1-methylinosine was made possible by the observation that the methyl resonance of 7-methylinosine occurs at about 0.55 ppm downfield from that of 1-methylinosine in D_2O, indicating the location of the methyl group at a positively charged nitrogen atom.[34] In addition, the fact that the H-8 of the 7-methylinosine is located about 1 ppm downfield from the H-8 of 1-methylinosine in DMSO, and that this proton cannot be found in D_2O due to rapid exchange,[35] further supports the assignment of the site of methylation for the 7-methylinosine. Comparison of the data on 1-methylinosine with inosine and other nucleosides reveals some interesting features. 1-Methylinosine is the only 6-substituted nucleoside to have δ of H-2 at a lower field than δ of H-8. H-2 of 1-methylinosine is shifted downfield by 0.14 ppm as compared to H-2 of inosine, whereas the H-8 proton of 1-methylinosine is unchanged as compared to inosine (TABLE 3).

In view of the large downfield shift (1 ppm) of the H-8 in 7-methylinosine in comparison to 1-methylinosine due to quaternization of the imidazole ring, we propose[10] that the substantial and selective deshielding of H-2 in 1-methylinosine is due to a more extensive degree of quarternization occurring at N-1 in the 1-methyl inosine as compared with inosine itself. The electron-releasing inductive effect of the methyl group will tend to stabilize the positive charge on the N-1 nitrogen.

Similar methyl-stabilized resonance forms can be adopted as an explanation for the difference in base proton chemical shifts of adenosine, N-6-methyladenosine and N-6-dimethyladenosine (TABLE 3). At infinite dilution, H-2 and H-8 are shifted progressively to higher fields as methyl groups are added to the N-6 amino position. H-2 and H-8 of adenosine are 8.730 and 8.820 ppm, those of the monomethyl compound, 8.733 and 8.333, and those of the dimethyl derivative 8.628 and 8.686. On the other hand, the methyl proton resonance shifts downfield from monomethyl to dimethyl compound, 3.550–3.886 ppm. These observations suggest that a progressively greater degree of resonance donation of electrons from the amino group to the ring takes place as hydrogen is being replaced by CH_3, due to methyl inductive stabilization of positive charge on N-6.

A comprehensive survey of chemical shifts of N-methyl derivatives has been published by Ma and Warnhoff.[35] Comparison of data on monomethyl and dimethyl N-substituted aromatic compounds, such as N-methylaniline vs N, N-dimethylaniline, shows a similar deshielding of the methyl protons in the dimethylated compounds. In saturated systems, methyl protons are more shielded in N, N-dimethyl compounds, as compared with monomethyl derivatives.

The resonance spectra of the pentosyl substituents of the nucleosides have also provided valuable assistance in difficult structural assignments. In an examination of a variety of 2′-deoxy-D-ribofuranosyl derivatives of purines of known anomeric configuration, Robins and Robins[36] have found that the resonance patterns of H-1′ of the α anomers are multiplets of four with apparent coupling constants $J_{H_1'}$, of 3.1 $\pm$ 0.4 and 7.2 $\pm$ 0.3 cps; and the resonance patterns of H-1′ of the β-anomers are "pseudo-triplet" with apparent $J_{H_1'}$ of 6.8 $\pm$ 0.3 cps. We have also noticed[10] that the chemical shifts for H-1′ of the adenine ribonucleosides occur at about 0.4 ppm upfield from that of the adenine deoxynucleosides. This phenomenon has been observed previously in dimethyl sulfoxide solutions and was attributed to shielding of H-1′ by the cis oxygen atom in the 2′ position.[37] This explanation is in accord with the following two observations: (1) The δ of H-1′ of 3′-deoxyadenosine has a similar value to that of adenosine, and is 0.42 ppm upfield from 2′-deoxyadenosine. (2) The δ for H-1′ of arabinosylcytosine, which has a 2′-OH group trans to H-1′, has a value .27 ppm downfield from the δ of cytidine H-1′ in which a 2′-OH group is cis to the H-1′.[38] The observation with the arabinosyl compound definitely establishes that the shielding effect of the cis-OH on the H-1′ of the ribose is a magnetic effect of the oxygen atom and not an inductive effect, since it does not occur with the trans-OH group. Fromageot and coworkers have concluded that, for the ribose nucleosides, the H-1′ resonance is at a lower field for the 2′-substituted isomers (phosphate, acetyl, etc.) than for the 3′-substituted isomers,[39]) $J_{H_1'-H_2'}$ is greater for the 3′- than for the 2′-isomer.

Conformation and Intramolecular Interaction

During the early sixties, Jardetzky made a substantial effect to study the pentose conformation of the nucleosides and nucleotides[2,40,41] by measuring the coupling constants, especially the $J_{H_1'-H_2'}$, and by the application of the Karplus analysis[4] of the H–C–C–H system. Though the application of this Karplus relationship between the vicinal coupling constants and the dihedral angle of a H–C–C–H system to the analyses of sugar conformation is subject to the influence of other effects such as substituent perturbations, $C_{1'}$-$C_{2'}$ bond lengths, etc.,[43,44] it is generally recognized that this analysis provides a valuable guide. The coupling constants of various nucleosides and nucleotides are shown in Table 8. These values differ slightly from those previously published by the Jardetzkys,[1,40,41] probably because

Table 8

The Coupling Constant, $J_{H_1'-H_2'}$, for Various Nucleosides and Mononucleotides[a]

A. Ribose Derivatives	$J_{H_1'-H_2'}$ (cps)
Adenosine	6.1
3′-Deoxyadenosine	2.2
2′-0-Methyladenosine	5.3
5′-AMP	5.3
5′-AMP Monomethyl ester	5.1
3′-AMP	5.8
2′-AMP	5.9
2′-AMP Monomethyl ester	5.1
1-Methylguanosine	5.7
5′-GMP	6.2
3′(2′)-GMP	5.4
Inosine	5.6
5′-IMP	5.5
Cytidine	3.7
5′-CMP	3.2
3′-CMP	3.4
2′-GMP	4.6
Uridine	4.2
5′-UMP	4.5
5-Bromouridine-5′-phosphate	4.4
3′(2′). UMP	3.5
B. Deoxyribose Derivatives[b]	
2′-Deoxyadenosine	6.5
Thymidine	7.0
5′-dAMP	7.0
5′-dCMP	6.8
5′-dUMP	7.0
5′-TMP	7.0

[a] Solution conditions: neutral D_20, 0.02-0.1M.
[b] $J_{H_1'-H_2'} = 1/2 (J_{H_1'-H_2'} + J_{H_1'-H_2''})$.

of the improved quality of the spectra obtained from 60 and 100 mc instruments. It can be seen that, although all of the average $J_{H_{1'}-H_{2'}}$ values for the deoxyribose compounds are similar to each other, the $J_{H_{1'}-H_{2'}}$ of the ribosyl purine compounds (5.5 cps) are significantly higher than that of the ribosyl pyrimidine compounds (4.0 cps). Based on these observations, Jardetzky has proposed that in the ribose nucleosides, the $C_{2'}$ is endo for the purine compounds while the $C_{3'}$ is endo for the pyrimidine compounds. Though she could not exclude the possibility of a $C_{3'}$ exo conformation for the purine compounds, her arguments appear to be consistent, especially in the study of cyclic 3′–5′ AMP.[41] Her conclusion, however, received very little support from the x-ray diffraction data of these compounds in the crystalline state.[45,46] Adenosine (in a complex with 5-bromouridine), 5′-adenylic and 3′-adenylic acid all have the $C_{3'}$ instead of the $C_{2'}$ in endo conformation. As for the pyrimidine compounds, the x-ray results show that the cytidine has the $C_{3'}$ in endo form as determined by Jardetzky, but 3′-cytidylic acid has the $C_{2'}$ in endo form instead; both compounds have about the same $J_{H_{1'}-H_{2'}}$ values (3 .4–3 .7 cps). It appears that an open question, at present, is whether this difference of $J_{H_{1'}-H_{2'}}$ values between that of the ribosyl purine compounds and that of the ribosyl pyrimidine compounds is due to the difference in spatial arrangement (differences in dihedral angle) or to the electronic effect of having different substituents at the $C_{1'}$ position, because it is not entirely clear why the ribose conformation will be changed by having different substituents at the $C_{1'}$ position. If this difference, however, is due to the electonic effect of different substituents at the $C_{1'}$ position, then this effect is not observed in the average values of $J_{H_{1'}-H_{2'},H_{2''}}$ of deoxyribose compounds. Nevertheless, we feel that under certain conditions the influence of the dihedral angle must be decisive, as in the case of comparing the value of $J_{H_{1'}-H_{2'}}$ of 3′-deoxyadenosine (2.2 cps) to that of adenosine (6.1 cps).[10] In this case, the substituent at the $C_{1'}$ is the same (both adenine), and there is no change of the groups at $C_{2'}$ either. The only difference between these two compounds is a change of OH by H at $C_{3'}$, two carbon atoms removed from the $C_{1'}$. Therefore, we feel that this large difference in the $J_{H_{1'}-H_{2'}}$ value must reflect a difference in the dihedral angle between $H_{1'}$ and $H_{2'}$ if the Karplus relationship can be applied at all to this type of system.

Attempts have been made by Tsuboi and coworkers[47,48] to ascertain the conformation of the H–C–O–P group in nucleotides or nucleic acid by analyzing the J_{HP}, the proton-phosphorus spin coupling constant, in a manner similar to the H–C–C–H system just discussed. It is believed that the value of J_{HP} is sensitive to its dihedral angle, and it was further assumed that the internal rotation around the C–O single bond in the CH_3–O–P group or C–CH_2–O–P group has mainly two kinds of potential minima, a trans or a gauche relation between the proton and the phosphorus (or between the C in C–CH_2–O–P and the phosphorus). The value of J_{HP} in the gauche relation was assigned to be 1.5 cps and the value of J_{HP} in the trans relation was assigned to be 28 cps, from the analyses of the data of J_{HP} of a series of model compounds including some cyclic phosphates. Experimentally, the J_{HP} values in the H–$C_{5'}$–O–P group were measured to be about 4.5 cps for both 5′-IMP and 5′-GMP.[48] These authors conclude that the phosphorus atom in these two nucleotides is mostly (estimated to be ~80%) trans to C-4′. This approach and the results are of great interest and should be confirmed by measurements with other model compounds and be extended to di- or polynucleotides. We have observed a splitting of the $H_{5'}$ and $H_{5''}$ resonance of the nucleosides into a doublet of about 3 cps that is independent of field strength, probably indicating that this splitting is due to the coupling with $H_{4'}$. Substitution of a phosphate group at the 5′-position further splits this doublet into a quartet with a $J_{H_{5'}}$C–O–P value of 4.0–5.0 cps for the following compounds in agreement with the observation of Tsuboi[48] on 5′-IMP and 5′-GMP: 5′-TMP, 5′-AMP, 5′-AMP methyl ester, 5′-dAMP, 5′-dCMP, 5′-dUMP as well as 5′-IMP.

Based on the available x-ray crystallographic data and a hard-sphere model, Ramachandran's group[49] has analyzed the allowable conformation of the nucleosides and nucleotides. Because of the restriction due to the contact between the 5′-P atom and the 4′-C atom, they also reached the conclusion that the P atom must rotate away from the 4′-C, and therefore be in a trans position to the 4′-C.

Hindered rotation of the 4-amino group in protonated cytosine derivatives has been observed by Becker and collaborators,[27] especially in SO_2 at −40–−60°. The existence of the geometric isomers can be demonstrated by the splitting of the 7-H or 7-CH_3 resonance being cis or trans to the N_3H^+. Again, the use of ^{15}N compounds and the application of decoupling techniques have been very helpful in the assignment of resonance lines.

It is interesting to note that the ring protons of adenine ribonucleosides are downfield several cycles per second from the corresponding adenine 2′-deoxy- or 2′-substituted nucleosides (TABLE 3). This observation strongly suggests the existence of hydrogen bonding from the 2′-OH group of the pentose to the N-3 of the purine ring. Such a hydrogen bond has received support from studies of ultraviolet absorption spectroscopy[50] and of infrared spectroscopy,[51, 52] on nucleosides and nucleotides. Preliminary potentiometric titration experiments done in our laboratory (0.05 M nucleoside, 0.15 N NaCl, 25°) indicate that 2′-deoxyadenosine has a pK_a 0.1 pH unit higher than that of adenosine. We have also found that H-2 and H-8 of 2′-deoxyadenosine are shifted .16 ppm downfield going from neutral solution to pH 3.6, whereas H-2 and H-8 of adenosine are shifted only .08 ppm to lower field over the same pH range. Thus, the base of 2′-deoxyadenosine is more readily protonated, indicating a higher pK_a. These results again are in accord with the concept of intramolecular hydrogen bonding.

Differences in chemical shifts between the adenine ribose and deoxyribose nucleotides were also found.[53] The chemical shifts of the adenine nucleotides at infinite dilution are listed together with the corresponding nucleosides for comparison. Regardless of the state of ionization, the δ's of the H-2 and H-8 of the 5′-AMP are at lower field than those of the 5′-dAMP. Hence, these data suggest that there is also an intramolecular hydrogen bonding of 5′AMP

TABLE 9

CHEMICAL SHIFTS OF THE ADENINE NUCLEOSIDES AND NUCLEOTIDES AT INFINITE DILUTION

	H-8	H-2	H-1′
Adenosine	8.820	8.730	6.533
2′-Deoxyadenosine	8.756	8.686	6.930
5′-AMP·Na	8.957	8.705	6.578
5′-dAMP·Na	8.861	8.640	6.922
5′-MeAMP·Na	8.883	8.717	6.605
5′-AMP·Na_2	9.055	8.717	6.587
5′-dAMP·Na_2	8.960	8.672	6.945
3′-AMP·Na	8.805	8.697	6.530
2′-AMP·Na	8.773	8.653	6.610
2′-AMP·Na_2	8.810	8.700	6.597

similar to that in adenosine discussed above. The chemical shift of the H-2 proton of the 3′-AMP is very close to that of the 5′-AMP, and the chemical shift of the H-2 proton of the 2′-AMP, which has no free 2′-OH group, is very close to the 2′-deoxy AMP. These data also suggest that an intramolecular hydrogen bonding may exist in 3′-AMP as well. This interpretation is far less certain, however, as compared to that concerning the 5′-AMP. The main reason is that data on 3′-dAMP are not easily obtainable, and therefore no direct comparison was made. A recent paper by Ts'o and coworkers[54] suggests that this intramolecular hydrogen bonding is responsible for the differences in conformation between the polyribonucleotides and the polydeoxyribonucleotides as studied by optical rotatory dispersion and other methods.

As shown in TABLE 9, the δ of H-8 of the 5′-nucleotides are substantially downfield from those of the corresponding nucleosides, whereas the δ of H-2 of the nucleosides and the 5′-nucleotides are similar to each other. Such a phenomenon of specific deshielding of a base proton due to the presence of the 5′-phosphate was found to exist in all 5′-nucleotides, as shown in TABLE 10. In TABLE 10, the chemical shifts of all the adenine derivatives are ob-

TABLE 10

INFLUENCE OF THE PHOSPHATE GROUP AS SHOWN BY THE COMPARISON OF THE CHEMICAL SHIFTS OF THE NUCLEOSIDES AND NUCLEOTIDES (pD 5.9): CHEMICAL SHIFTS MEASURED FROM TMS CAPILLARY

	H-8	H-2	H-6	H-5	H-1	H-5′, H-5″
5′-AMP[a]	8.957	8.705			6.578	4.602
Adenosine[a]	8.820	8.730			6.533	4.353
	.137	−.025			.045	.249
Adenosine-5′-methyl hydrogen phosphate[a]	8.883	8.717			6.605	4.572
Adenosine[a]	8.820	8.730			6.533	4.353
	.063	−.013			.072	.219
5′-dAMP[a]	8.861	8.640			6.922	
2′-Deoxyadenosine[a]	8.756	8.686			6.930	
	.105	−.046			−.008	
3′-AMP[a]	8.805	8.697			6.530	
Adenosine[a]	8.820	8.730			6.533	
	−.015	−.033			.003	
2′-AMP[a]	8.773	8.653			6.610	
Adenosine[a]	8.820	8.730			6.533	
	−.047	−.077			.077	
5′-GMP[b]	8.544				6.381	
1-Methyl-guanosine	8.418				6.375	
	.126				.006	
5′-IMP[c]	8.888	8.662			6.592	4.603
Inosine[c]	8.762	8.653			6.542	4.367
	.126	.009			.050	.236

TABLE 10 (CONT'D)

	H-8	H-2	H-6	H-5	H-1	H-5′, H-5″
5′-CMP[c] Cytidine[c]			8.424 8.292	6.546 6.513	6.402 6.367	4.587 4.333
			.132	.033	.035	.254
Cytidine-5′-methyl hydrogen phosphate[c] Cytidine[c]			8.383 8.292	[d] 6.513	6.463 6.367	4.625 4.333
			.091		.096	.292
5′-UMP[b] Uridine[c]			8.403 8.275	6.370 6.327	[d] 6.343	[d] 4.295
			.128	.043		
Uridine-5′-methyl hydrogen phosphate Uridine[c]			8.352 8.275	6.372 6.327	6.406 6.343	4.566 4.295
			.077	.045	.063	.271
3′-CMP[c] Cytidine[c]			8.303 8.292	6.533 6.513	6.372 6.367	4.325 4.333
			.011	.023	.005	−.008
5′-TMP[c] Thymidine[c]			8.190 8.087	2.350[e] 2.318[e]	6.774 6.715	4.486 4.283
			.103	.032	0.059	.203

[a] Extrapolated infinite dilution shifts.

[b] 0.02M, in mixture with 0.02M 3′(2′)-UMP. 1-methyl guanosine was used because of solubility problem with guanosine. Since the chemical shift of the H-8 proton is the same for inosine and 1-methyl inosine, this substitution of guanosine was considered justifiable, (see Reference 8).

[c] 0.09M.

[d] These resonances not discernible.

[e] Methyl protons.

tained by extrapolation to infinite dilution, and the chemical shifts of the other compounds at the low concentration are not sensitive to concentration, as shown in later sections. Therefore, the influence of the intermolecular stacking is essentially eliminated from the data in TABLE 10. In this Table, the influence of the phosphate group is shown by comparing the nucleoside with the corresponding nucleotide in monoanion. Only the effect on the base protons will be discussed here.[53] First, if the monoanionic phosphate group is substituted at the 3′-position, no difference in chemical shift can be found for the base protons (H-8 and H-2 of purine, H-5 and H-6 of pyrimidine) between the nucleoside and the corresponding 3′-nucleotide, as exemplified by the adenosine vs 3′-AMP and the cytidine vs 3′-CMP. If the phosphate group is substituted at the 5′-position, the H-8 protons of the purine nucleotides such as 5′-AMP, 5′-dAMP, 5′-GMP and 5′-IMP, are deshielded specifically by about 0.12 ppm, although the H-2 protons are unaffected. In an analogous manner, and with similar magnitude, the H-6 protons of the pyrimidine nucleotides such as 5′-CMP, 5′-UMP and 5′-TMP are deshielded to a much greater extent than the H-5 protons. The deshielding effect on the H-8 (for purine) or H-6 (for pyrimidine) of the 5′-phosphate is strongest when it is dianionic as anticipated (TABLES 9 and 11), weaker when it is monoanionic (TABLES 9, 10 and 11), and weakest when it is in the form of a monomethyl ester (TABLES 9 and 10). The probable reason for the deshielding effect being stronger when the phosphoryl group is in the monoanionic form than when it is in the monomethyl ester form is that the methyl group on the phosphate may provide a steric hindrance in reducing the deshielding effect.

The influence of the phosphate group on the base protons was studied a function of pH (or pD). The effect of pD on the chemical shifts of 5′-AMP and 5′-AMP monomethyl ester at 0.09M is shown in FIGURE 2. At the region of pD 4.5–6.0, the effect of the pD is on the deprotonization of the base. The loss of the proton from the adenine moiety causes the upfield shift of the base protons both by the removal of the intrinsic deshielding effect of the positive charge and by the increase in the intermolecular association of the bases. This interpretation is confirmed by the identical results obtained from both the

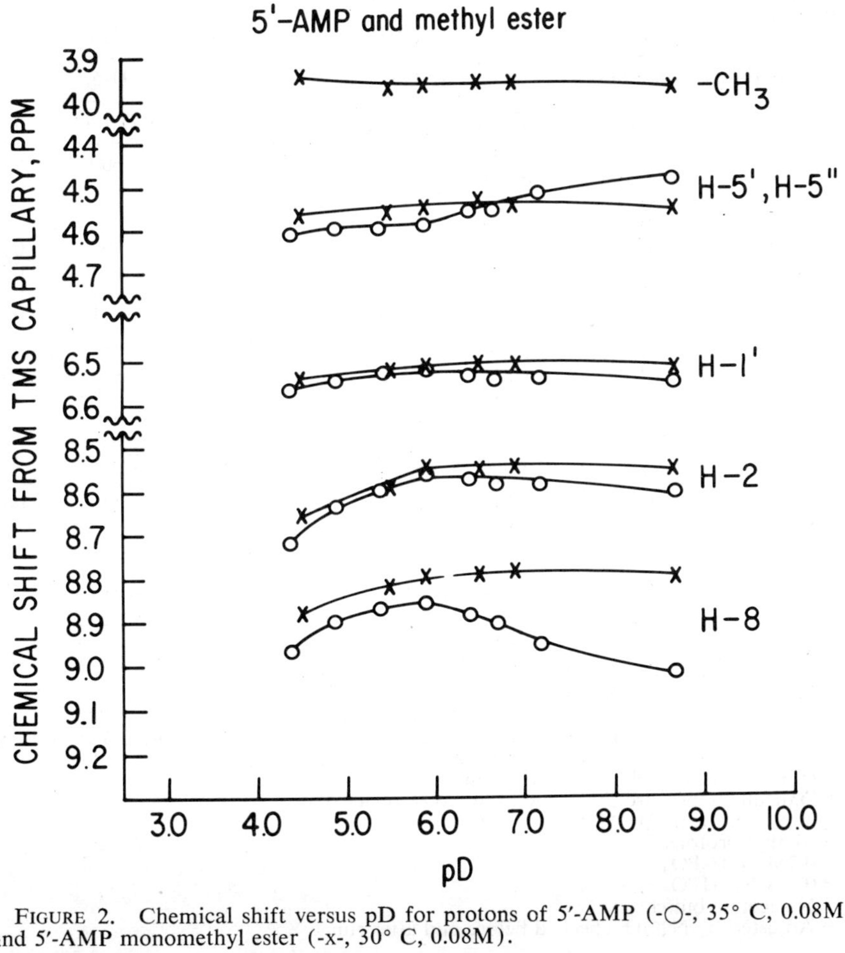

FIGURE 2. Chemical shift versus pD for protons of 5′-AMP (-○-, 35° C, 0.08M) and 5′-AMP monomethyl ester (-x-, 30° C, 0.08M).

TABLE 11

THE EFFECT OF THE SECONDARY PHOSPHATE IONIZATION (FROM pD 5.9 TO pD 7.4) ON THE CHEMICAL SHIFT OF VARIOUS MONONUCLEOTIDES
($\Delta\delta = \delta$pD 5.9 − δpD 7.4)[a]

A. Purine Nucleotides			δ[a] H-8,			δ[a] H-2,	
	Conc (M)	pD 5.9	pD 7.4	Δδ	pD 5.9	pD 7.4	Δδ
5′-AMP	(0.08)	8.853	8.950	.097	8.567	8.588	.021
5′-AMP	(0.25)	8.792	8.895	.103	8.425	8.442	.071
5′-MeAMP	(0.08)	8.795	8.795	0	8.550	8.553	.003
3′-AMP	(0.09)	8.717	8.737	.020	8.547	8.562	.015
2′-AMP	(0.09)	8.733	8.780	.047	8.508	8.608	.100
2′-MeAMP	(0.09)	8.758	8.758	0	8.628	8.625	+.003
5′-IMP	(0.09)	8.888	9.000	.112	8.645	8.662	.017
5′-GMP[b]	(0.02)	8.500	8.613	.113			
5′-MeGMP	(0.09)	8.462	8.465	.003			
3′-GMP[c]	(0.02)	8.393	8.423	.030			
5′-dAMP	(0.08)	8.788	8.883	.095	8.533	8.562	.029
Tubercidin-5′-phosphate	(0.1)	8.000	8.008	.008	8.510	8.513	.003
B. Pyrimidine Nucleotides			δ[a] H-6,			δ[a] H-5,	
	Conc (M)	pD 5.9	pD 7.4	Δδ	pD 5.9	pD 7.4	Δδ
5′-CMP	(0.02)[d]	8.424	8.504	.080	6.588[e]	6.600	.012
5′-MeCMP	(0.09)	8.383	8.383	0		[f]	
3′-CMP	(0.03)	8.303	8.287	+.016		[g]	
2′-CMP	(0.03)	8.241	8.233	+.008		[g]	
5′-UMP[h]	(0.02)	8.403	8.533	.130	6.370	6.398	.028
5′-MeUMP	(0.01)	8.352	8.357	.005	6.372	6.378	.006
5′-dUMP	(0.09)	8.443	8.527	.084	6.400	6.430	.030
5-TMP	(0.095)	8.190	8.240	.050	2.361[i]	2.371	.010
5, 6 dihydro-5′-UMP	(0.1)	4.097	4.115	.018	3.220	3.235	.015
5′-dCMP	(0.09)	8.411	8.472	.061	6.551	6.554	.003
C. Nucleosides			δ[a] H-6,			δ[a] H-5,	
	Conc (M)	pD 5.9	pD 7.4	Δδ	pD 5.9	pD 7.4	Δδ
Uridine	(0.1)	8.370[j]	8.368[k]	+.002	6.398[j]	6.393[k]	+.005
			δH-8			δH-2	
Inosine	(0.05M)	8.762[l]	8.755[m]	+.007	8.653[l]	8.642[m]	+.011

[a] Measured from TMP capillary; Δδ values negative unless indicated.
[b] In mixture with 0.02M 3′-AMP.
[c] In mixture with 0.02M 5′-AMP.
[d] In mixture with 0.02M 2′(3′)-CMP. H-5 not discernible
[e] In 0.09M concentration measured with 60 mc instrument. The absolute δ value is not as accurate as that quoted in TABLE 10, but Δδ is accurate.
[f] H-5 was not unambiguously determined.
[g] Difficult to measure shifts due to broad resonances.
[h] In mixture with 0.02M 3′(2′)-UMP.
[i] Methyl protons.
[j] 0.2M NaH_2PO_4.
[k] 0.2M Na_2HPO_4.
[l] Na-acetate buffer.
[m] Adjusted by NaOD, checked before and after run.

5′-AMP and 5′-AMP monomethyl ester. In the region of pD 6.0–8.7, the secondary phosphate is being ionized and thus increases its electron density. This is illustrated by the increase in shielding of the H-5′, H-5″ protons of the 5′-AMP at higher pD, whereas the H-5′ proton on the methyl ester is unchanged as expected. At this region, the H-8 proton of the 5′-AMP is specifically and substantially deshielded (~0.1 ppm), although the H-8 and H-2 protons of the corresponding methyl ester are unaffected. There is a slight downfield shift (~0.02 ppm) of the H-2 proton of the 5′-AMP. This shift is most likely due to the small effect of the ionization of the secondary phosphate on the stacking of the 5′-AMP and to the fact that the H-2 proton is most sensitive to the degree of stacking, as will be described herein. Therefore, since the deshielding effect due to the increase of pD from 6 to 8 occurs only in the 5′-AMP and not in its monomethyl ester, and since this deshielding effect occurs only in H-8 and not in H-2, this effect must be a direct result of the ionization of the secondary phosphate on the H-8 proton.

In FIGURE 3, the effect of pD on the chemical shifts of the 3′-AMP is shown. When the phosphate group is moved from the 5′-position to the 3′-position, the specific effect of ionization of the secondary phosphate essentially disappears. The small deshielding effect upon increase in pD from 6 to 9 observed for the H-2, H-8 and H-1′ protons (0.01–0.02 ppm) is probably due to a slight decrease in stacking because of the increase in the charge of the phosphate group (as explained below) for the similar effect on the H-2 proton of the 5′-AMP. The shielding effect upon increase in pD from 4.5 to 6, due to the deprotonation of the adenine ring, is also observed here.

TABLE 11 shows the effect of the secondary phosphate ionization (from pD 5.9, 10% dianion to pD 7.4, 90% dianion on the chemical shift of various mononucleotides. For the purine nucleotides, the change of pD from 5.9 to

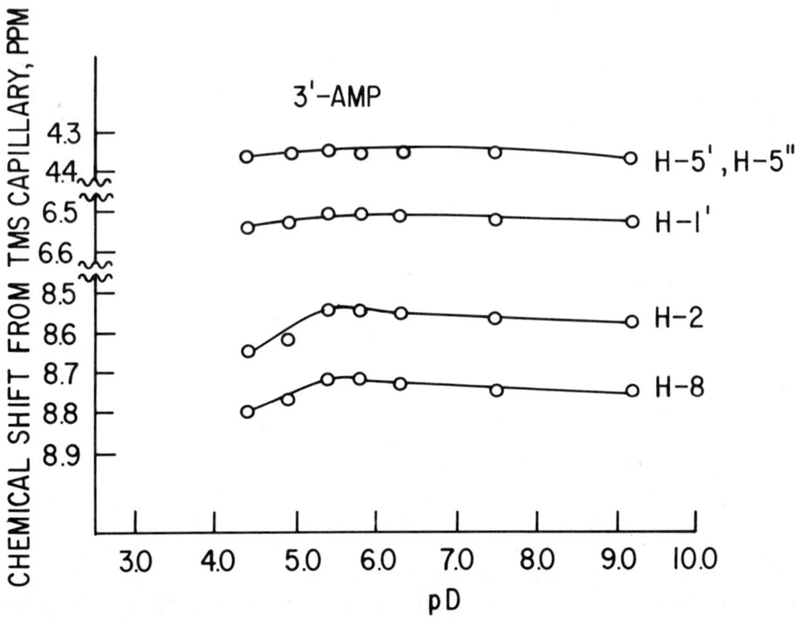

FIGURE 3. Chemical shift vs pD for protons of 3′-AMP (0.09M, 30° C).

7.4 has virtually no effect on the H-2 protons save that of the 2′-AMP, which is discussed in the original paper.[53] As controls, this change of pD has no effect on the H-2 or H-8 protons of all the monomethyl esters of 5′-AMP, 2′-AMP and 5′-GMP nor on the nucleoside, inosine. Little or no effect on the H-2 can also be observed for the dianion formation of the 3′-phosphate of the AMP and GMP. The ionization of the secondary phosphate has a large effect (0.1 ppm) on the H-8 protons of the 5′-AMP, 5′-deoxy AMP, 5′-IMP and 5′-GMP. This ionization has no effect on the H-8 or H-7 protons of tubercidin-5′-phosphate, which will be discussed later in relation to the mechanism. As for the pyrimidine nucleotides, this change of the pD from 5.9 to 7.4 has virtually no effect on the H-5 protons. As controls, this increase of pD has no effect on the H-5 or H-6 protons of the methyl esters of the 5′-CMP and 5′-UMP. This ionization of the secondary phosphate has a specific and substantial effect ($\sim$0.08 ppm) on the H-6 proton of the 5′-CMP, 5′-dUMP, 5′-TMP and 5′-dCMP. The ionization has no effect on the H-6 of 3′-CMP or 2′-CMP or on the H-6 proton of the 5, 6 dihydro-5′-UMP, as will be discussed later. We may conclude therefore, by analogy to the 5′-purine nucleotides, that the 5′-phosphate group of the pyrimidine nucleotide also has a direct and specific effect on the H-6 proton and not on the H-5 proton.

All these p.m.r. results are directly related to the overall conformation of the nucleotides. For convenience in discussing the conformation of the sugar relative to the base, Donohue and Trueblood[55] first defined the sugar-base torsion angle, ϕ_{cn}, as "the angle formed by the trace of the plane of the base with the projection of the C–O bond of the furanose ring when viewed along the C–N bond. This angle will be taken as zero when the furanose-ring oxygen atom is anti-planar to C_2 of the pyrimidine or purine ring, and positive angles will be taken as those measured in a clockwise direction when viewing from C to N." They further concluded that there are two ranges of ϕ_{cn} for the nucleosides; ca $-$ 30° for the anti conformation, and ca $+$ 150° for the syn conformation. All the x-ray data and stereochemical analysis based on x-ray data[45, 46] indicated that most of the purine and pyrimidine nucleosides and nucleotides exist in the solid state with the anti conformation including 5′-AMP[56] and 3′-AMP,[57] except the case of deoxyguanosine (syn conformation) in a mixed crystal with 5-bromodeoxycytidine.[58] The situation about the conformation of nucleosides or nucleotides in solution is far less clear. Analyses of the x-ray data[45, 46] clearly indicate the existence of a substantial rotation barrier; therefore, a rapid conversion between syn and anti conformation in solution is most unlikely. The attempts to provide an answer by optical rotatory dispersion measurement in an empirical approach have not been successful (see Reference 53). The specific deshielding of the H-8 proton of the purine nucleotide and of the H-6 proton of the pyrimidine nucleotide by the 5′-phosphate indicates that the 5′-nucleotides must be in anti conformation. Only in this anti conformation (and not in the syn conformation, see FIGURE 1) can the H-8 proton (purine) or the H-6 proton (pyrimidine) of the 5′-nucleotide be in juxtaposition to the 5′-phosphate as depicted for 5′-AMP in FIGURE 4.

Cushley and collaborators have compared the chemical shifts of the acetyl group of various uracil nucleosides (both pyranose and furanose) and that of the corresponding dihydrouracil nucleoside in DMSO.[59] They concluded that there is an anisotropic effect of the 5, 6 double bond on these acetyl groups. Therefore, they also proposed that there is a restriction of the rotation around the glycosyl bond of these uracil nucleosides, and that these com-

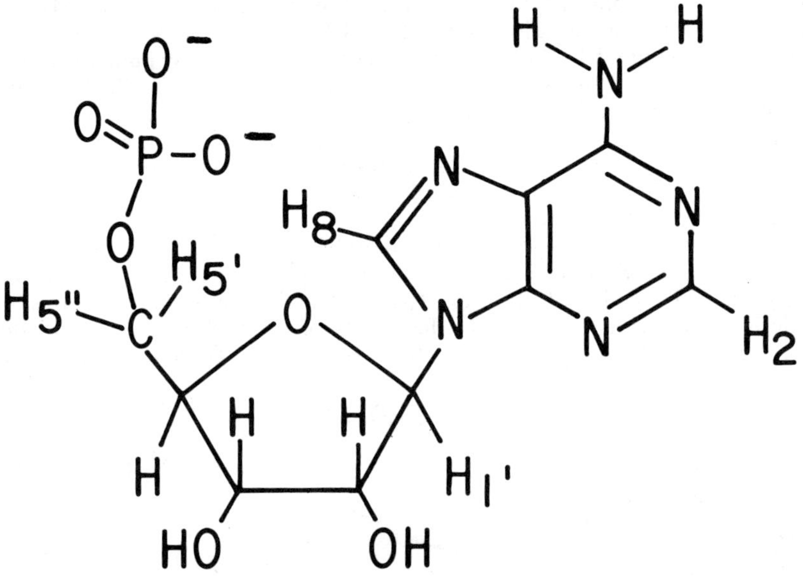

FIGURE 4. The 5′-AMP disodium salt depicted in anti conformation with the H-8 proton in juxtaposition with the phosphate group.

pounds have an anti conformation in DMSO.[59] The mechanism of the deshielding effect of the 5′-phosphate on the H-8 proton of the purine nucleotides or on the H-6 proton of the pyrimidine nucleotides deserves further inquiry. One possible mechanism is the paramagnetic effect of the anisotropy of the phosphoryl group which may be spatially oriented in a proper manner toward the sensitive protons (H-8 or H-6) in order to produce the deshielding effect. It should be noted, however, that the phosphoryl group presents a complex case with regard to its magnetic anisotropy: not only does the P–O bond resonate between the three oxygen atoms (FIGURE 4), but the P–O ester bond can also rotate freely. This consideration leads us to expect that the anisotropic effect of the phosphoryl group on the H-8 or the H-6 proton may be minimized on a time average basis. Another possible mechanism is the direct electrostatic field effect of the negatively charged phosphate. This mechanism hypothesizes that the electrostatic field of the negative charge tends to attract the positive proton and thus polarizes the C–H bond to a greater extent, resulting in lower electron density at the proton and hence a deshielding effect. In other words, the former mechanism emphasizes the influence of the magnetic field effect of the phosphate, whereas the latter emphasizes the electrostatic field effect of the phosphate on the proton. One way to distinguish these two proposals is to compare the deshielding effect of the phosphate group on the sensitive protons which have different degrees of acidity. It is also important for the success of this experiment that the spatial relationship of the phosphate group to the sensitive protons of these various analogs remain essentially constant.

Following this line of reasoning, one can examine the data on 5′-TMP and 5′-dUMP in TABLE 11. The 5′-TMP, bearing an electron-releasing methyl group at the C-5 position, produces a chemical shift of the H-6 proton about 0.25 ppm upfield in comparison to the H-6 of the 5′-dUMP, as expected. The less acidic H-6 of the 5′-TMP is shifted only 0.05 ppm downfield over the pD 5.9–7.4 range compared with the 0.084 ppm for the more acidic H-6 of the 5′-dUMP. If the 5, 6 double bond of the 5′-UMP is saturated as in 5, 6 dihydrouridine-5′-phosphate, the effect of pD change is practically eliminated (0.018 ppm, TABLE 11.) Concerning the 5′-purine nucleotides, the H-8 proton is well known for being acidic, judging from its rate of exchange with deuterium as described above. In regard to the change of the acidity of the H-8 proton, we have studied the effect of pD on tubercidin-5′-phosphate (4-amino-7-β-D-ribofuranosyl-5′-phosphate-7H-pyrrolo-(2, 3-d) pyrimidine) which is a 7-deaza adenosine-5′-phosphate (TABLE 11 and FIGURE 5). The acidity of the H-8 (purine numbering system) of this molecule is decreased as compared to the acidity of the H-8 of the adenine, due to the replacement of the electronegative N-7 with C–H in the five-membered

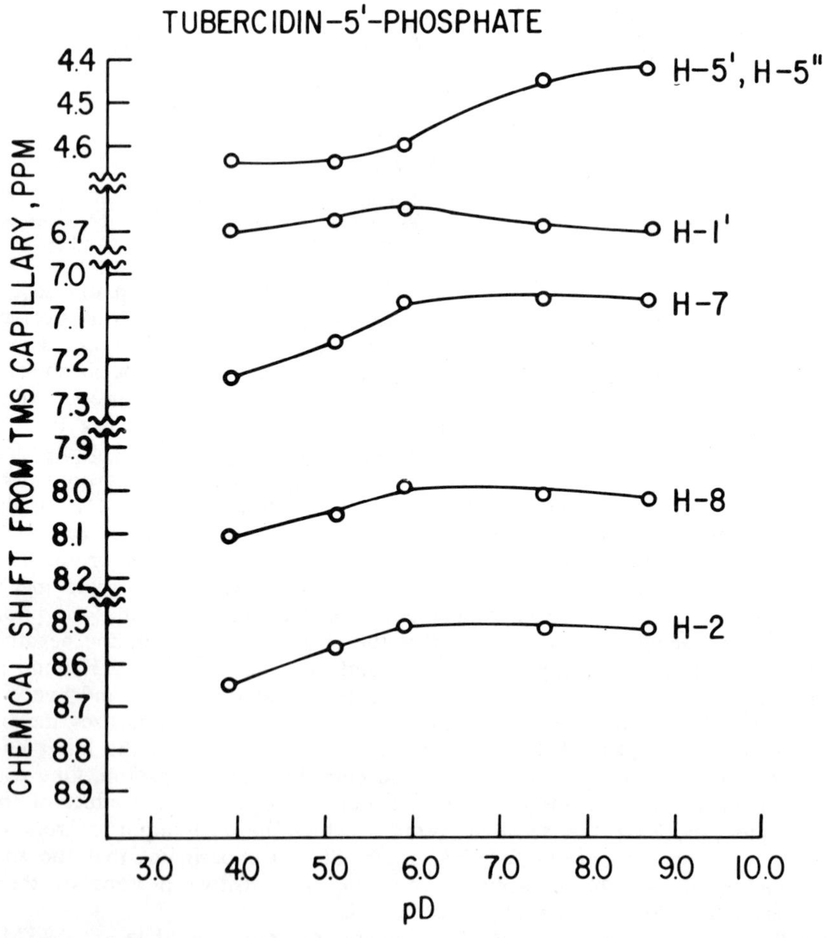

FIGURE 5. Chemical shift vs pD for protons of tubercidin-5′-phosphate 0.1M, 32° C.

ring of the adenine. This is evidenced by the fact that the H-8 resonance of the tubercidin-5′-phosphate is moved upfield to 8.00 ppm (TABLE 11) as compared to H-8 of 5′-AMP (8.85 ppm.). As is clearly shown in FIGURE 5 and TABLE 11, neither the pyrrole ring protons H-8 and H-7 nor H-2 in the pyrimidine ring are deshielded upon dianion formation of the phosphate. The effect of deprotonation on the ring protons and the effect of the secondary phosphate ionization on the H-5′, H-5″ are shown in FIGURE 5, as anticipated. We expected that the general conformation of the tubercidin-5′ phosphate would be similar to that of the 5′-AMP since the five-membered rings of the base remain aromatic (therefore, planar) in both molecules. There is evidence from optical rotatory dispersion measurement to support this view.′[5]

The foregoing experiments on analogs of 5′-pyrimidine and 5′-purine nucleotides do provide some reliable evidence that this dishielding effect of the phosphate is reduced when the acidity of the sensitive protons is decreased. Unfortunately, no experimental data are yet available to prove or to disprove the reverse situation. Nevertheless, we view these data as favoring the electrostatic mechanism over the paramagnetic mechanism, since the latter mechanism should not be concerned with the acidity of the sensitive protons.

INTERMOLECULAR INTERACTIONS

Interaction of the Bases and Nucleosides in Organic Solvents

Interaction of the base derivatives and nucleosides in organic solvent is of great interest. Recently, this interaction has been studied by infrared spectroscopy[60–62] and by p.m.r. In DMSO, Katz and Penman[63] have observed a large downfield shift of the donor protons (N_1–H and 2–NH_2 of guanosine, and 4–NH_2 of cytosine) when both guanosine and cytosine are present, indicating a hydrogen-bonding interaction. Such a phenomenon can be found also for the solution of adenine and uracil derivatives in chloroform, though not in solution of DMSO, apparently because of the competition of the solvent with the bases for the acceptance of the hydrogen bond. Interaction of the guanosine and cytosine appears to have a stoichiometry of 1:1, whereas the stoichiometry of the interaction with A and U is probably 1:2. In an equal volume mixture of DMSO and benzene, guanosine was found to interact only with cytidine, and uridine only with adenosine, identical to the Watson-Crick base-pairing scheme for the nucleic acids. At the same time, and independently, similar results were obtained by Shoup and coworkers.[64] They used DMSO as well as 1:1 mixtures of DMSO and dimethyl formamide as solvents. They also observed the downfield shift of the NH and NH_2 of the base pairs that increases with concentration and decreases with temperature. The specificity of the base pairing was also confirmed (thymine was used in this study). As will be shown later, base pairing through horizontal hydrogen bonding cannot be found in aqueous solution.

Work in the early sixties on the properties of nucleic acids in organic solvents, including that contributed from our laboratory,[65–70] indicated that organic solvents such as DMSO and dimethylformamide are effective denaturants for helical nucleic acids. It was proposed then that the hydrogen bonding of the base pairs can not be the major force in maintaining the stability of the hellical nucleic acids. At that time, it was reasoned that the hydrogen bonding of the base pairs should be strengthened in organic solvents as compared to the hydrogen bonding of the base pairs in water. This reasoning is now borne out completely by these recent studies of the interaction of the bases in organic solvents and in aqueous solution by p.m.r. and other techniques.

Interaction of the Bases, Nucleosides and Nucleotides in Aqueous Solutions

Vapor pressures of solutions of purine, 6-methyl purine and 14 pyrimidine and purine nucleosides have been measured thermoelectrically at varying concentrations in our laboratory.[10, 71, 72] Osmotic coefficients, ϕ were calculated from the data, and activity coefficients of purine, 6-methyl purine, uridine, 5-bromouridine and cytidine were also computed from the osmotic coefficients by the Gibbs-Duhem relationship.[71, 72] Values of both osmotic coefficients and activity coefficients of these compounds are much below unity, indicating that these bases and nucleosides do associate extensively in aqueous solution. After further analyses for their congruence to different models for multiple equilibria, the thermodynamic data were found to be incompatible with the model which assumes that only dimers are formed.[71] Thus, the degree of association of these compounds may go beyond the dimers stage to a higher degree of polymerization. Most of the results are consistent with the model which assumes that the association process continues through many successive steps (at least above five steps) with the same equilibrium constant. These apparent equilibrium constants (ranging from 0.6–15 M^{-1}) for the association of these bases and nucleosides in aqueous solutions were calculated.[71, 72, 10] In addition, the distributions of the population of the associated species at varying concentrations of purine, 6-methylpurine and 5-bromouridine were computed from the knowledge of the activity coefficients and the apparent equilibrium constants. The first general conclusion is that the tendency of purine to associate is much greater than that of the pyrimidine nucleosides, which in turn is greater than that of urea. The second general conclusion is that methylation at the base (and not at the pentose) enhances the association. These two conclusions strongly suggested that these compounds do not self-associate by means of horizontal hydrogen bonding in aqueous solutions.

More direct information about the mode of association of the bases and nucleosides in solution was obtained by the p.m.r. studies. The p.m.r. spectra of purine and 6 methylpurine have been measured over the concentration range of 0.05–1 M as reported in one of our previous papers.[21] Independently, Jardetzky has reported the measurement of purine spectra up to 2M concentration.[25] The resonance of all the protons of these two compounds are shifted significantly to higher field as the solute concentration is increased. The values of these concentration shifts (ppm) to higher field at 25° over the range 0.0–1.0 M are: purine: H-6 (0.69), H-2 (0.62) and H-8 (0.48); 6-methylpurine: $-CH_3$ (0.71), H-2 (0.78) and H-8 (0.53). Shifts to high fields with concentration are well known for aromatic systems and are generally attributed to the magnetic anisotropy associated with the ring currents in neighboring molecules. At higher temperature, or when the purine is dissolved in organic solvent such as DMSO and dimethylformamide, such concentration-dependent chemical shifts for the purine protons are greatly reduced.[21] Furthermore, when the purines are protonated by hydrochloride so that they cannot associate because they carry a positive charge, such concentration-dependent chemical shifts are again almost eliminated.[21] These data clearly suggest that the mode of association of purine is by the vertical stacking of rings in a partial overlapping fashion. As described above, the osmotic coefficients and activity coefficients of purine and 6-methylpurine have been interpreted in terms of multiple equilibria and, on this basis, populations of various associated species at varying concentrations were computed. Based on these population distributions of the associated species, we can calculate the concentration dependence of the chemical shifts. As shown in our original paper,[21] the calculated and the experimental values are in very satisfactory agreement. Therefore, a numerical correlation between the p.m.r. data and the osmotic data has been obtained successfully in the sense that they reinforce and support the interpretations of each other quantitatively. The temperature dependence of the chemical shifts of 1 M purine solution in ethanol-water mixture or glycerine-water mixture has been studied recently by Helmkamp and Kondo[70] over a range of $-50°$ to $50°$. In agreement with the concentration-dependence measurement at 25° cited above, the δ value of H-8 is less sensitive to temperature change (or to concentration change) than the H-2 and the H-6 protons. Similar results were observed for the nucleosides and nucleotides, and are explainable by a model of stacking for these compounds proposed in later paragraphs.

The concentration dependence of the chemical shifts for eleven purine nucleosides in D_2O at 25–32° over 0.0–0.2 M is shown in TABLE 12.[10] As shown in our original paper,[10] there is a close correlation between the magnitudes of $\Delta\delta$ (the concentration dependence of the chemical shifts) and the values of ϕ (osmotic coefficients) and k (apparent equilibrium constants). This correlation again establishes that stacking is the mode of association of these solutes, and the usefulness of p.m.r. as a tool for studies of association. The differentials in the magnitude of $\Delta\delta$ for various protons of a given nucleoside may provide additional information about the average geometry of the stacks in solution. In FIGURE 6, the concentration dependence of protons of 2′-deoxyadenosine is shown. The H-2 proton of the six-membered ring of

TABLE 12

CONCENTRATION DEPENDENCE OF CHEMICAL SHIFTS FOR 11 PURINE NUCLEOSIDES (0.0–0.2 m) IN D_2O

Compound	Temp. °C	H-2	H-8	H-6	H-1′	CH_3
Inosine	32	6.4	5.3		7.1	
1-Methylinosine[a]	33	8.9	6.4		6.8	5.3
Ribosylpurine	30	10.7	6.4	13.1	8.8	
Purine[b]	25–27	12.6	9.6	14.2		
2′-O-Methyladenosine	31	13.7	7.5		8.8	
6-Methylpurine[b]	25–27	19.4	13.3			17.0
2′-Deoxyadenosine	30	19.8	13.0		13.6	
N-6-Methyl-2′-deoxyadenosine	32	26.0	15.8		14.0	15.2
N-6-Dimethyladenosine	28	27.2	14.5		14.4	25.5
N-6-Methyladenosine	26	32.6	17.5		12.6	18.1
2′-Deoxyadenosine[c]	30	14.8	10.0		9.8	
Adenosine[c]	32	14.8	8.3		6.9	
3′-Deoxyadenosine[c]	25	15.8	9.0		9.6	

[a] Peak positions of H-8 and H-2 are reversed with respect to the other 6-substituted nucleosides studied.

[b] See Reference 21.

[c] Differences measured over the concentration range 0–0.10 m because of solubility limitation.

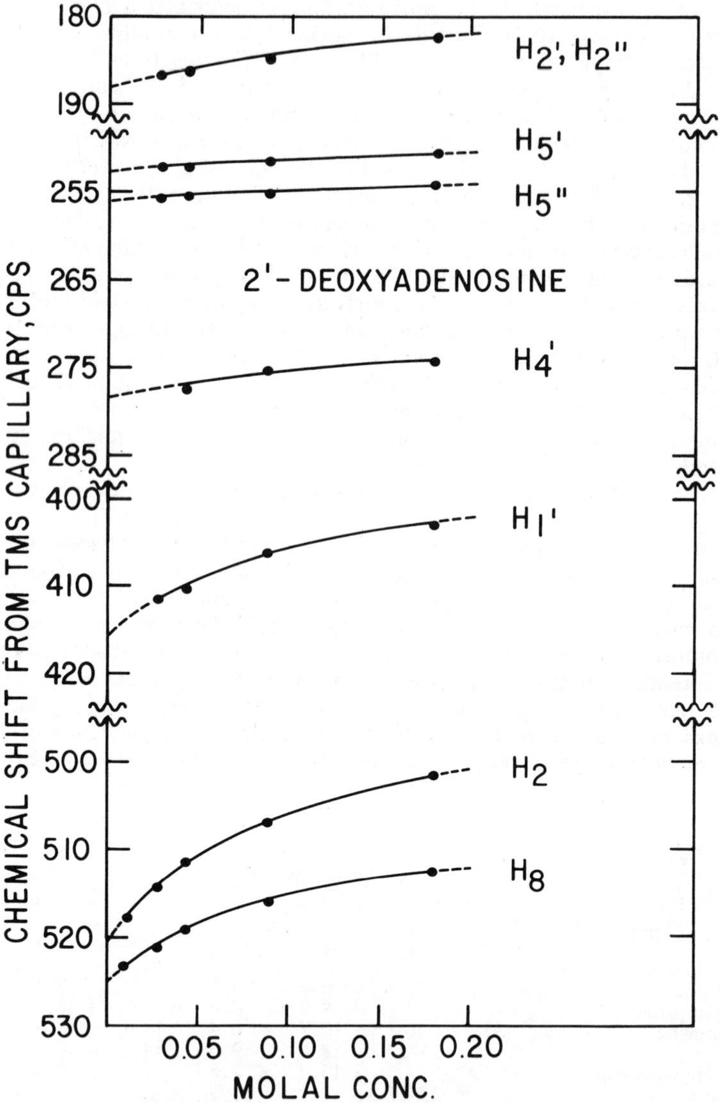

FIGURE 6. Concentration dependence of proton chemical shifts for 2′-deoxyadenosine in D_2O.

the adenine has a larger Δδ value than the H-8 proton in the five-membered ring. This indicates that the six-membered ring of the adenine does participate to a greater extent in the stacks than the five-membered ring of the adenine nucleosides. The pentose protons of H-1′ are also shifted considerably to higher fields when concentration is increased, although the pentose protons of H-5′ are hardly affected. As one proceeds around the pentose ring from the C-1′ to the C-5′, there is a progressive decrease in the magnitude of these concentration-dependent chemical shifts. This indicates that the adenine nucleoside interaction is preferentially localized at the purine base of the nucleoside, so that the ring current magnetic anisotropy is principally felt by the base protons. Similar phenomena are observed for all the purine nucleosides (TABLE 12 and Reference 10). From this study, therefore, we can not only obtain the general picture about the mode of association, we can even get down to the detailed molecular geometry of the stacks. Two models for the preferred average orientation of the nucleosides in the stacks have been proposed to account for the results observed.[10] One of the models which is favored currently, especially in view of the results on the nucleotides, is shown in FIGURE 7. In this dimer model, one can see that the H-2 proton will be shielded strongly by the six-membered ring of the neighboring bases most of the time. The H-8 proton and the H-1′ proton will be shielded mainly by the 5-membered ring. In addition, according to this model, H-8 and H-1′ will spend less time, on the average, in the proximity of the five-membered ring than will H-2 in the proximity of the six-membered ring. In this

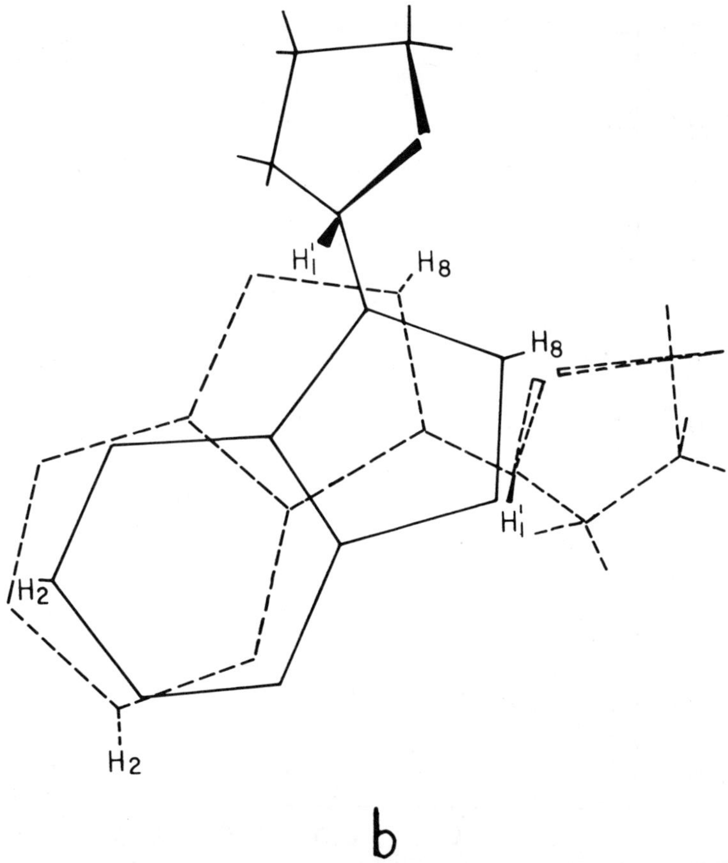

FIGURE 7. Model illustrating the proposed arrangements for two nucleosides in alternate stacks (face to face and back to back); one of the nucleosides is rotated by 180° along an axis in the plane bisecting the C_4-C_5 bond. The pentosyl substituents are opposite each other in the stack.

model, the base stacking arrangement is face to face (or back to back); and the two ribosyl moieties at the N-9 site are opposite each other in the dimer, resulting in an alternating arrangement (alternate stack). The other proposed model is related to the present one by symmetry considerations. The base stacking arrangement for the other model is face to back and the two ribosyl substituents at N-9 will be on the same side of the dimer (straight stack).

As shown in TABLE 13 and FIGURE 8,[53] the concentration dependence of various protons of these 5′-adenine nucleotides is very similar to that of the

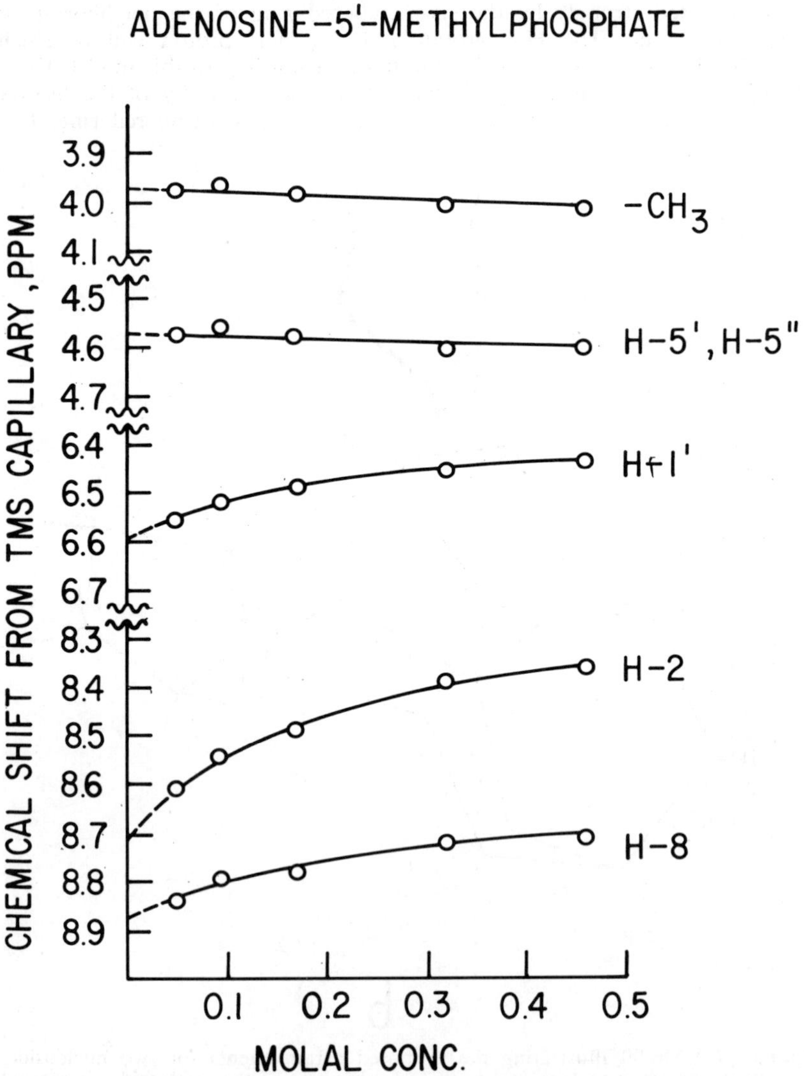

FIGURE 8. Chemical shift vs molal concentration for protons of adenosine-5′-methyl phosphate (5′-MeAMP (Na)) 31° C, D_2O, pD 5.9.

TABLE 13

EFFECT OF CONCENTRATION UPON THE CHEMICAL SHIFTS OF VARIOUS PROTONS OF THE MONONUCLEOTIDES[a,b]

A. Mononucleotides	Conc. (Molal)	ppm from TMS Capillary				
		H-8	H-2	H-1′	H-5′, H-5″	H-2′, H-2″, $-CH_3$
5′-AMP·Na	0.0	8.957	8.705	6.578	4.602	
	0.3	8.805	8.412	6.463	4.658	
	Δδ	.152	.293	.115	−.056	
5′-AMP·Na_2	0.0	9.055	8.717	6.587	4.483	
	0.3	8.897	8.392	6.472	4.580	
	Δδ	.158	.325	.115	−.097	
5′-Me AMP·Na	0.0	8.883	8.717	6.605	4.575	3.990 ($-CH_3$)
	0.3	8.730	8.408	6.447	4.585	4.020
	Δδ	.153	.309	.158	−.010	−.030
5′-dAMP·Na	0.0	8.861	8.640	6.922		
	0.3	8.720	8.375	6.730		
	Δδ	.141	.265	.192		
5′-dAMP·Na_2	0.0	8.960	8.672	6.945		
	0.3	8.803	8.395	6.753		
	Δδ	.157	.277	.192		
3′-AMP·Na	0.0	8.805	8.697	6.530		
	0.3	8.613	8.347	6.407		
	Δδ	.192	.350	.123		
2′-AMP·Na	0.0	8.773	8.653	6.610		
	0.3	8.697	8.328	6.555		
	Δδ	.076	.325	.055		
2′-AMP·Na_2	0.0	8.810	8.700	6.597	4.323	
	0.3	8.730	8.462	6.562	4.365	
	Δδ	.080	.238	.035	−.042	
5′-dGMP·Na_2	0.049	8.568		6.712	4.373	3.133
	0.90	8.520		6.598	4.480	3.073
	Δδ	.048		.104	−.110	.060

B. Mononucleotides	Conc. (Molal)	p.p.m. from TMS Capillary				
		H-6	CH_3	H-1′	H-5′, H-5″	H-2′, H-2″
5′-TMP·Na_2	0.052	8.272	2.392	6.812	4.518	2.838
	0.98	8.280	2.438	6.830	4.580	2.912
	Δδ	−.008	−.046	−.018	−.062	−.074

[a] Temperature 28–31° C.

[b] Δδ values are all positive unless otherwise noted, indicating upfield shifts with increase in concentration. Values of chemical shifts at 0.0 m were obtained from extrapolations.

adenine nucleosides. Again, the δ value of the sugar protons located far away from the adenine base, such as the H-5′ and H-5″, are not sensitive to concentration changes. For the base protons, Δδ is largest for H-2 and about the same for H-8 and the anomeric proton, H-1′. Similar observation for the concentration dependence of the 5′-AMP protons at pH 5.7 has also been reported by Jardetzky.[25] These results suggested that the mode of association of the 5′-AMP is probably very similar to that of the purine nucleosides. It is interesting to compare the Δδ of the H-8, H-2 and H-1′ of the monosodium 5′-AMP (pD 5.8), the monomethyl-5′-AMP and disodium 5′-AMP (pD 7.4) in TABLE 13.[53] Di-ionization and methylation of the 5′-phosphate have very little effect on the Δδ of these protons. This observation suggests to us that the model of the alternate stack in FIGURE 7 is preferred over the straight stack model.[53] The alternating arrangement in separating the ribosyl-phosphate substituents will result in the reduction of electrostatic and steric repulsion. This may be the reason why the increase in the charge of the phosphat group by further ionization has very little effect on the Δδ values. The chemical shifts of the methyl protons of the adenosine-5′-methyl phosphate (FIGURE 8) are not sensitive to concentration. This is another indication that the phosphate groups of the nucleotide stacks are far away from diamagnetic moieties such as the purine rings and the hydroxyl groups. Comparison of the Δδ value of the 5′-dAMP at a range of 0.02 M with that of the 2′-deoxyadenosine, does indicate a reduction in the extent of interaction of about 40% at H-8 and about 30% at H-2 and H-1′.

Comparison of the Δδ of the protons of the 2′-AMP and 3′-AMP with the Δδ of the protons of the 5′-AMP reveals some very interesting effects of the position of the charged phosphate group. When the charged phosphate group was moved from the 5′-position to the 2′-position, which is much closer to the five-membered ring and the H-1′, the Δδ values of the H-8 and of the H-1′ were reduced by about 50% (TABLE 13.) The Δδ value for the more distant H-2 proton located at the six-membered ring remains unaffected by this 2′-phosphate group, until the phosphate is doubly ionized. Then, there is a reduction of Δδ value of about 30% for the H-2, 50% for the H-8 and 70% for the H-1′, as compared to the Δδ value of the 5′-AMP. Thus, placement of the phosphate near the site of the interaction results in a different stacking orientation for 2′-AMP. Na, chiefly involving overlap of the six-membered rings. When the phosphate is moved from the 5′-position to the 3′-position the Δδ values appear to be higher, especially for the H-8 proton. Examination of the molecular model indicates that now the 3′-phosphate group is distant from the base rings regardless of the rotation around the glycosyl bond (N_9–C_1'). Thus, the specific interaction of the 5′-phosphate group to the H-8 proton that occurs when the nucleotide is in an anti conformation is abolished. This is undoubtedly the reason for the enhancement of the Δδ value of the H-8 proton of the 3′-AMP as compared to the H-8 proton of the 5′-AMP. The H-8 proton of the 3′-AMP can now be overlapped closer to the neighboring molecules in the stack.

The chemical shifts of the base protons (H-5, H-6, or 6-CH_3) of the pyrimidine nucleosides[74] or nucleotides[53] (TABLE 13) are not concentration-dependent even though these compounds have all been shown to associate in aqueous solutions by osmotic pressure lowering.[71, 10] Therefore, we should interpret this result on the basis that these pyrimidine nucleosides do not support ring currents as do the aromatic purine bases, thus, their interactions can not be monitored by p.m.r. via the ring-current magnetic anisotropy. Interaction of pyrimidine nucleosides with purine or purine nucleosides, however, can be shown by p.m.r.; for example, over the purine concentration range 0.0-1.0 M (D_2O, 35°), H-6 and CH_3 of thymidine are shifted upfield by 0.40 and 0.34 ppm, respectively. This effect falls off progressively as the proton distance from the ring increases, i.e., H-1′ by 0.31 and H-5′ by 0.08-0.10 ppm. This phenomenon, which is similar to that observed for the self-interaction of purine nucleosides, again indicates that the purine-pyrimidine nucleoside interaction is preferentially localized at the pyrimidine base of the nucleoside, and the mode of interaction is vertical stacking of the bases. The same effect is observed for the interaction between thymidine and adenine nucleoside. For example, a mixture of 0.2 M 2′-0-methyl adenosine and 0.1 M thymidine results in the following upfield shifts (ppm) of the thymidine protons: 0.135 ($-CH_3$), 0.15 (H-6) and 0.12 (H-1′). On the other hand, the strong self-association of purine in stacks can be reduced by addition of these nonaromatic pyrimidine nucleosides, presumably by insertion or destacking.[74] For instance, in mixtures containing 0.97 M purine and 0.1 M cytidine, thymidine or uridine, the purine proton resonances are generally shifted 0.08–0.11 ppm to lower field compared to a 0.97 M purine solution.

At the conclusion of this section, it should be indicated that the extensive and systematic research done on the intramolecular and intermolecular interaction of the bases, nucleosides and nucleotides provides the foundation upon which the p.m.r. studies of the dinucleotides are to be interpreted correctly.

Interaction of the Monomeric Units in the Dinucleotides and Polynucleotides

In early 1965, we reported the preliminary results of the p.m.r. studies of ten 3′–5′ linked diribonucleoside monophosphates (XpY) with a 100 Mc instrument.[75] It was evident then that these spectra contain a wealth of information about these molecules which cannot be obtained by any other method at the present time, but it was also realized immediately that, in order to interpret these data properly, much more work on the mononucleosides and mononucleotides was required. Now, there is a fair amount of information on the monomers, some of which was described above, except in the area of temperature effect. Precise study on the temperature dependence of various spectral properties of the monomers is much needed for a more thorough understanding of the spectra and the properties of the dimer.

Since these data have not been published elsewhere and the presentation of these results in detail will be beyond the scope of this paper, only very broad conclusions are stated briefly here. In TABLE 14, the spectral information and assignments of 15 3′-5′ ribodinucleoside monophosphates, ($A_{2'P5'}C$), and one 3′–5′ deoxyribodinucleoside monophosphate are given. The assignments were made on the basis of the known chemical shifts and the spin coupling constants of the 3′-nucleotides and 5′-nucleotides, and on the studies of various 5′-phosphorylated and 2′, 3′ phosphorylated dinucleoside monophosphates such as pXpY, or, Xp, $Yp_{(2',3')}$. Some of the assignments are tentative (see footnote in TABLE 14), especially those of the H-1′. TABLES 15 and 16 provide a comparison of the chemical shifts of all the base protons at 28° to that at 61. In FIGURES 9 and 10, the actual spectra of UpC, CpU, CpA, ApC, UpA, ApA, ApG and GpA in D_2O, pD 6.4, 0.02 M are shown. Based on this information, the following general considerations can be stated.

TABLE 14

CHEMICAL SHIFTS OF BASE AND H-1′ PROTONS OF DINUCLEOSIDE MONOPHOSPHATES (0.02 M, D_2O, pD 7.4, 28° C, PPMTMS CAPILLARY)

	A_{H-8}	G_{H-8}	H-2	C_{H-6}	U, T_{H-6}	C_{H-5}	U_{H-5}	H-1′(1)	H-1′(2)
A_PC	8.753		8.548	8.132		6.113		6.452(A)	6.158(C)
C_PA	8.823		8.632	8.111		6.238		6.512(A)	6.126(C)
A_PU	8.754		8.599		8.181		6.057	6.470(A)	6.182(U)
U_PA	8.830		8.634		8.151		6.177	6.514(A)	6.131(U)
A_PG	8.636	8.325	8.493					6.336(A)	6.218(G)
G_PA	8.738	8.310	8.582					6.488(A)	6.104(G)
A_PA	8.637(5′) 8.596(3′)		8.500(5′) 8.360(3′)					6.376(5′)	6.250(3′)
G_PC		8.440		8.234		6.127		6.313(C)	6.288(G)
C_PG		8.431		8.164		6.311		6.318(G)	6.187(C)
G_PU		8.405			8.270		6.170	6.330(G)	[c]
U_PG		[b]			8.203		6.263	6.332(G)	6.224(U)
C_PU				8.313	8.342	[c]	[c]	[c]	[c]
U_PC				8.348	8.331	6.447	6.280	6.365(C)	6.263(U)
C_PC				8.343(5′) 8.293(3′)		[c]		[c]	[c]
U_PU					8.344(5′)[a] 8.335(3′)		6.292	6.370(5′)	6.310(3′)
T_PT					8.117(5′)[a] 8.088(3′)		(CH_3) 2.318	6.750(5′)	6.665(3′)
A2′p5′C	8.725		8.397	7.765		6.113		6.589(A)	[c]

[a] Assignment tentative.
[b] Not observed at 28° C, a broad peak of 14 cps width was found at 8.52 ppm at 61° C.
[c] Indiscernible.

TABLE 15

EFFECT OF TEMPERATURE ON THE CHEMICAL SHIFTS OF THE PURINE BASE PROTONS IN DINUCLEOSIDE MONOPHOSPHATES

		$\Delta\delta._T$(ppm) = δ28° C − δ61° C (all negative)									
		ApC	CpA	ApU	UpA	ApG	GpA	ApA	ApC 2′–5′	Ap	pA
A	H-8	.075	.087	.078	.080	.114	.112	3′ .126 / 5′ .173	.085	.080	.089
A	H-2	.167	.138	.146	.136	.187	.148	3′ .189 / 5′ .250	.193		.140
		GpC	CpG	GpU	UpG	ApG	GpA				
G	H-8	.058	.090	.077	[a]	.145	.075				

[a] G_{H_8} too broad to see at 28°.

1. The δ values of the pyrimidine dimers (i.e., UpU, UpC, etc.) are rather similar to those of the corresponding monomers. On the other hand, in the purine dimers (i.e., ApA, ApG, etc.), or the mixed dimers with both pyrimidine and purine (i.e., ApU, ApC, etc.), the δ values of the units neighboring a purine unit—especially an adenyl unit—are substantially shielded as compared to those of the corresponding monomers. All the results on the dimers are entirely consistent with the two general conclusions derived from the studies on the monomers: (a) Bases of the nucleosides (or nucleotides) stack in aqueous solution with the tendency to associate in the following order: adenine and purine ≫ cytosine uracil; and (b) the magnitudes of ring current magnetic anisotropy of the bases are in the following order: adenine > guanine (its five-membered ring) > cytosine > uracil.

2. The H-8 protons of the purine 5′-monomeric (-pY) unit in the dimer and the H-6 protons of the pyridine 5′-monomeric unit in the dimer are at

TABLE 16

EFFECT OF TEMPERATURE ON THE CHEMICAL SHIFTS OF THE PURINE BASE PROTONS IN DINUCLEOSIDE MONOPHOSPHATES

		$\Delta\delta._T$(ppm) = δ28° C − δ61° C (all negative)							
		CpC	UpC	CpU	ApC	CpA	ApC 2′–5′	GpC	CpG
C	H-6	.048 / .032	.043	.030	.143	.090	.160	.089	.058
C	H-5	[a]	[a]	[a]	.257	.182	.157	.243	.145
		UpU	UpC	CpU	ApU	UpA	TpT	GpU	UpG
U	H-6	.036 / .019	.015	.030	.113	.079	(T) .060 / .045	.068	.051
U	H-5	[a]	[a]	[a]	.208	.153	(Me) .090	.180	.092

[a] Unable to analyze.

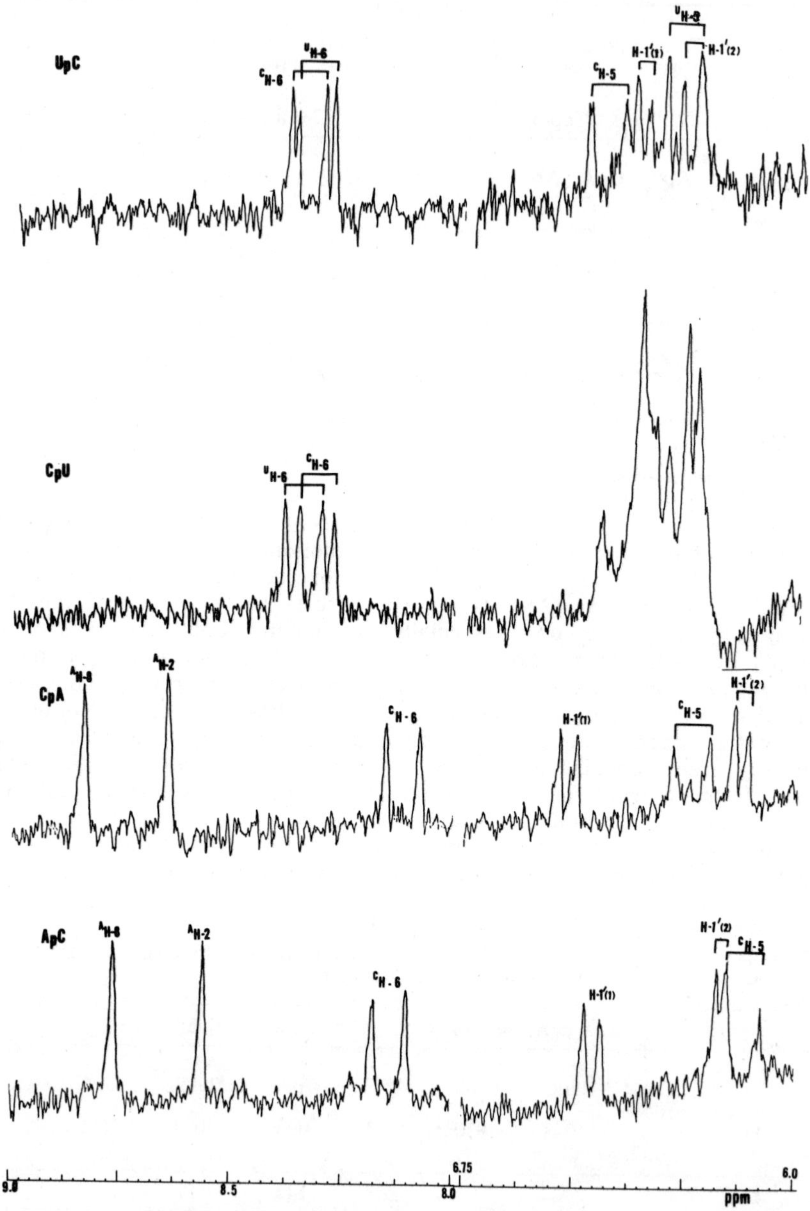

FIGURE 9. 100 Mc spectra of dinucleoside monophosphates, UpC, CpU, CpA and ApC in D_2O, pD 7.4, 0.02M.

lower field than the corresponding protons of the 3′-monomeric unit (Yp-) in the dimer. This observation is in accord with the conclusion derived from the study on the specific deshielding effect of the 5′-phosphate on the H-8 or H-6 of the purine or pyrimidine nucleotides. This indicates that the 5′-units (-pY)

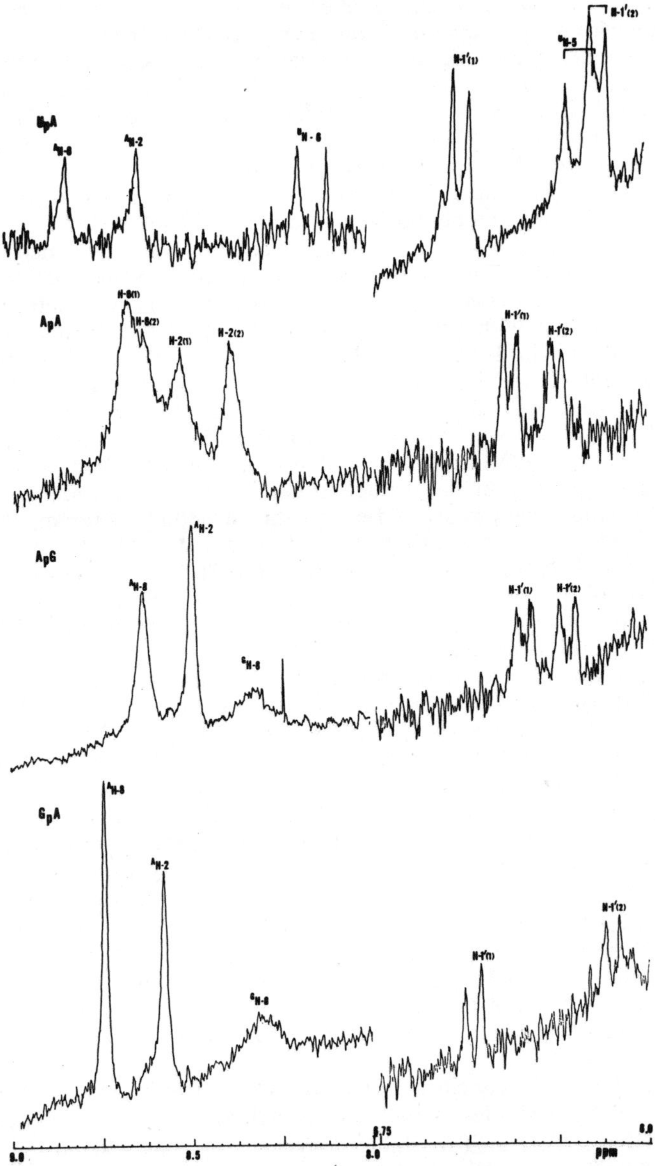

FIGURE 10. 100 Mc spectra of dinucleoside monophosphates, UpA, ApA, ApG and GpA in D_2O, pD 7.4, 0.02M.

have the anti conformation. Studies on the 5′-phosphorylated dimers (pXpY) indicate that the 3′-units (Xp-) are also in anti conformation, since the H-8 (purine) or H-6 (pyrimidine) protons of the 3′-unit are now deshielded by added 5′-phosphate in the form of (pXp-).

3. All the pairs of dimers having the same bases but with reverse sequences (XpY vs YpX, i.e., UpA vs ApU) have different spectra. This se-

quence effect on spectra is to be expected for a structure of right-handed helical stack with both 3′-unit and 5′-unit in anti conformation.

4. The spectral line-width of the purine units are usually two-to threefold broader than those of the pyrimidine units. This phenomenon appears to be related to the interdimeric association, probably by means of intercalation.

Recent advances in both experimental and theoretical studies of the optical rotory dispersion of the dinucleotides[76–78] indicate that the stack of the dinucleotides has a right-handed turn. Based on the studies of the nucleotides[53] and the dinucleoside monophosphates and 5′-phosphorylated dinucleoside monophosphates (pXpY) as mentioned above, it was concluded that both nucleoside units in the dimer are in anti conformation. Stacks of dinucleotides constructed with these two basic guiding principles have structural features which are consistent with practically all of the spectral information listed in TABLES 14–16 and in FIGURES 9 and 10. A schematic diagram of the spatial arrangement of the bases of a trinucleoside diphosphate, ApUpA, in a right-handed stack with all the nucleosides in anti conformation is shown in FIGURE 11. This diagram shows the structural features responsible for the spectral differences between ApU and UpA, and will be discussed as an example. The uridyl unit in this trimer is both 5′ to A (bottom, broken line) and 3′ to A (top, heavy line). Based on this structural diagram, the following spectral properties are anticipated and observed: (1) H-5 of U will be shielded by the 3′-A, but not by 5′-A; therefore H-5 of (–pU) is at a higher field than H_5 of (Up). (2) H-6 of U will not be shielded substantially by either 3′-A or 5′-A, but H-6 of U in the 5′-unit (pU) will be deshielded by the 5′-phosphate group as compared to the H-6 of U in the 3′-unit (Up). (3) The H-1′ of U will be shielded by the five-membered ring of 5′-A, but not by 3′-A; therefore, H-1′ of (Up-) is at a higher field than the H-1′ of (-pU). (4) H-8 of (-pA) is located at a lower field than H-8 of (Ap-) because of the phosphate deshielding effect. (5) H-2 of the A will be shielded by the 5′-U, but not by the 3′-U. The difference is small (0.03 ppm) because of the low magnitude of the ring-current magnetic anisotropy of uracil. This difference is much larger (0.08 ppm) between the H_2 of (Ap-) in ApC vs the H_2 of (-pA) in CpA. The H-2 of (pA-). (6) The H-1′ of A will be shielded by 5′-U but not by the 3′-U. Again, this difference in 6 values is larger between the H-1′ of A in ApC vs that in CpA (0.06 ppm). The H-1′ of (Ap-) is located at higher field than the H-1′ of (-pA)- (7) The structure and the above arguments are also in accord with the temperature-dependent results (TABLES 15 and 16); i.e., $\Delta\ \delta_{28^\circ-61}$ is larger for H-5 than for H-6, and larger for H-2 than for H-8. Since U is shielded more by 3′-A than by 5′-A, it is anticipated that the $\Delta\delta_{28^\circ-61^\circ}$ is also larger for the H-5 of U in ApU than for the H-5 of U in UpA.

Basically, the same conclusion was reached recently by McDonald and collaborators in their studies of the deoxydinucleoside monophosphates.[79] They observed that the CH_3 of T is shielded by the 3′-purine (or purine neighbor at the 5′-side in their notation, d–XpT), but not by the 5′-purine (d–TpX). They showed further that such an observation can be used to explain the observed splitting of the methyl protons of T in the DNA at high temperature, if the dimers or trimers (dApTpA is shown in their paper[79]) are stacked in a conformation similar to the helical DNA. The conformation of a helical DNA is a right-handed helix with the nucleosides in anti conformation.

The spectral properties of TpT, TpdU, dUpT, and the interaction of these compounds with purine in aqueous solution have been studied by Chan and

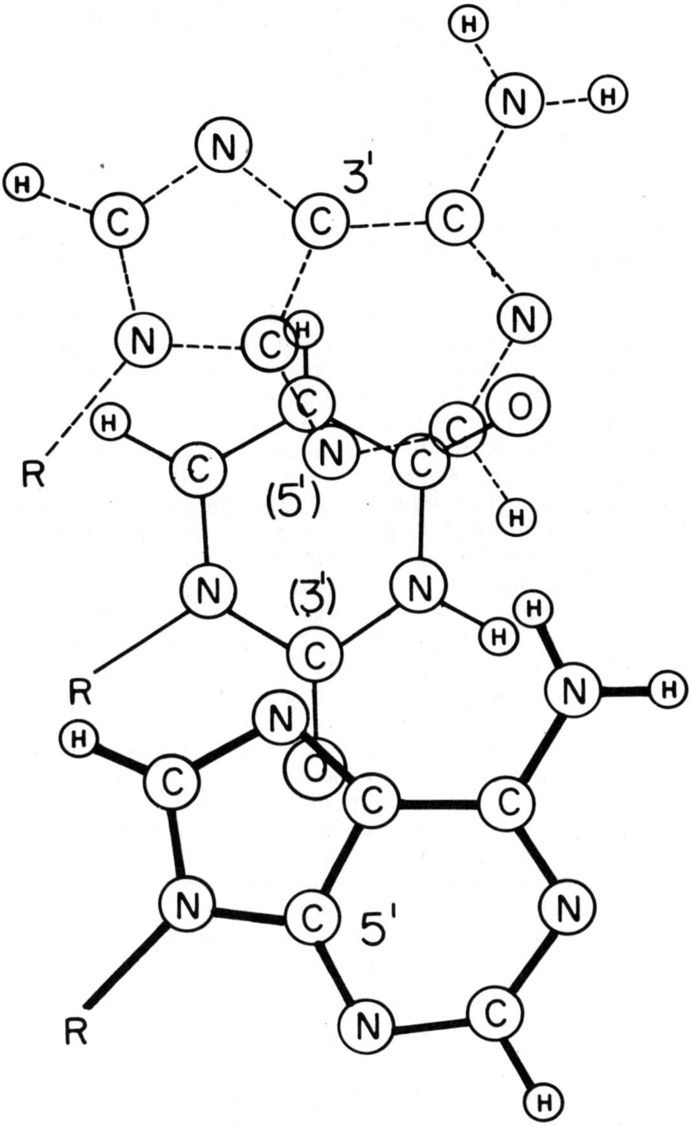

ApUpA

FIGURE 11. Schematic diagram of the spatial arrangement of the bases of a trinucleoside diphosphate, ApUpA, in a righthanded helical turn and with all the nucleosides in anti conformation. This diagram shows the structural features responsible for the spectral differences of ApU vs UpA. The heavy line signifies the base (A) on top, and the broken line signifies the base (A) at the bottom.

coworkers.[80] The spectral lines of the H-6, H-1 and CH_3 protons of these dimers are broadened, shifted, and split specifically in the interaction of these dimers with purine. Also, the resonance lines of the purine are broadened specifically by interacting with the dimer. They came to the conclusion that the purine molecule can be inserted or intercalated between two stacking bases in the dimers, and is experiencing the dipolar relaxation by the hydroxyl groups inside the bend of the stack. Therefore, their results are also relevant to the study of the intermolecular interaction of the dimers, since insertion of intercalation may take place in this situation.

It may be concluded that the basic principles for the conformation of the stacked dinucleotides or trinucleotides have now been established by p.m.r and other studies. These stacks are right-handed, and the nucleoside units in them have an anti conformation. However, we do not yet know the population distribution of the stacked, half-stacked and unstacked species of these dimers or trimers at a given condition in quantitative terms. The precise spatial description of these dinucleotides at a given temperature requires much more extensive investigation on the temperature effect and of various relevant model compounds. Some of the assignments are still tentative, especially those of the homodimers. Chemical synthesis of the appropriate deutero compounds are needed. The conformation of pyrimidine dimers such as UpU is unlikely to be investigated effectively by p.m.r. because of the low magnitude of the ring-current magnetic anisotropy. A more definitive knowledge about the relative magnitudes of the ring-current magnetic anisotropy of these bases will be most helpful. This knowledge is needed to differentiate the contribution due to stacking (or unstacking) from the contribution due to ring-current magnetic anisotropy, since certain bases, such as uracil, have a low value of ring-current anisotropy as well as a small tendency to stack as compared with others.

The p.m.r. studies of the polynucleotides can be classified into two categories. In the first category, the chemical shifts were studied, especially in comparison to the monomers and to the dimers. The elegant study of McDonald and collaborators has already been mentioned.[81] They have observed the splitting of the methyl protons of the thymine in the DNA at elevated temperatures in a 220 Mc instrument. Comparing this result with those of the appropriate dimers, they concluded that these different magnetic environments around the CH_3 group represent the distribution frequency of the purine and pyrimidine in a 5′-neighbor position (XpT) to thymine. This conclusion is supported also by our previous study on the interaction of the thymidine with pyrimidine or purine nucleosides.[74] The p.m.r. spectra of polynucleotides such as $r(A)_n$, $r(U)_n$, $r(I)_n$ and $r(C)_n$ have been measured independently by several laboratories at about the same time,[25, 81, 82] Jardetzky[25] compared the δ values of the base protons and the H-1′ with that of the 5′-nucleotides. As was anticipated from the studies of the interaction of the monomers, this difference, which is described as polymerization shift, is largest with $r(A)_n$ vs AMP and lowest with $r(U)_n$ vs UMP. We have reported[53] that the difference of δ of the H-8 proton of the $r(A)_n$ (8.287 ppm, measured at neutral pH) to the intrinsic δ of the H-8 of 3′-AMP is 0.52 ppm, and to the intrinsic δ of the H-8 of 5′-AMP it is 0.67 ppm. The reason for the larger difference in the δ value of H-8 between $r(A)_n$ and 5′-AMP is that the H-8 proton is specifically deshielded by the 5′-phosphate in the 5′-AMP described above. The difference between the δ value of the H-2 proton of the poly A (8.167 ppm) and the intrinsic δ of the H-2 proton in 3′ or 5′-AMP is 0.53–0.55 ppm. This value of

0.5–0.6 ppm due to polymerization is about twice the value of the shift due to dimerization, i.e., comparison of δ of Ap or pA to that of (-Ap) or (Ap-) in ApA.

In the second category, the main concern is on the line-widths of the spectral line. Since the intra- and intermolecular motions of the atoms and groups at the helical region of the nucleic acid polymer are sufficiently slow, the resonance lines of the protons situated in this helical conformation are broadened by nuclear dipole-dipole interaction. These lines can be so broad that they are virtually undetectable in the high resolution p.m.r. spectra. When the motions of the atoms and the groups of the polymer are more rapid, as is evident in the case of the random coil form, the resonance lines become narrower and detectable in the spectrum. In this fashion, p.m.r. can be used to study the helix-coil transition of the polynucleotides. By measuring the appearance of resonance lines (normalized intensity) versus temperature, the melting profiles of $r(A)_n + r(U)_n$,[81, 82] $r(C)_n + r(I)_n$,[82] thymus DNA,[81] and S-RNA[82, 83] were obtained. Because of the problem of sensitivity and resolution and of the rapid exchange of the H-8 protons of purine bases with D_2O at elevated temperatures, only qualitative results were obtained in these early attempts. With improved instrumentation and better knowledge of the monomers and dimers, much more information can probably be gained from the natural nucleic acids through this approach.

References

1. Jardetzky, C. D. & O. Jardetzky. 1960. J. Amer. Chem. Soc. **82:** 222.
2. Jardetzky, C. D. 1960. J. Amer. Chem. Soc. **82:** 229.
3. Schweizer, M. P., S. I. Chan, G. K. Helmkamp & P. O. P. Ts'o. 1964. J. Amer. Chem. Soc. **86:** 696.
4. Schaefer, T. & W. G. Schneider. 1963. Canad. J. Chem. **41:** 966.
5. Veillard, A. 1962. J. Chim. Phys. **59:** 1056.
6. Lynch, B. M. & H. J. Dou. 1966. Tetrahedron Lett.: 2627.
7. Buckingham, A. D. 1960. Canad. J. Chem. **38:** 300.
8. Musher, J. I. 1962. J. Chem. Phys. **37:** 34.
9. Giessner-Prettre, C. & B. Pullman. 1965. Compt. Rend. **261:** 2521.
10. Broom, A. D., M. P. Schweizer & P. O. P. Ts'o. 1967. J. Amer. Chem. Soc. **89:** 3612.
11. Gronowitz, S. & R. A. Hoffman. 1960. Arkiv Kemi. **16:** 459.
12. Miller, R. L., P. G. Lykos & H. N. Schmeising. 1962. J. Amer. Chem. Soc. **84:** 4623.
13. Veillard, A. & B. Pullman. 1961. Compt. Rend. **253:** 2277.
14. Pople, J. A., W. G. Schneider & H. J. Bernstein. 1959. High Resolution Nuclear Magnetic Resonance: 178. McGraw-Hill. New York, N. Y.
15. Gil, V. M. S. & J. N. Murrell. 1964. Trans. Faraday Soc. **60:** 248.
16. Matsuura, S. & T. Goto. 1963. Tetrahedron Lett. **22:** 1499.
17. Bullock, F. J. & O. Jardetzky. 1964. J. Org. Chem. **29:** 1988.
18. Reddy, G. S., L. Mandell & J. H. Goldstein. 1963. J. Chem. Soc.: 1414.

19a. Veillard, A. & B. Pullman. 1963. J. Theoret. Biol. **4:** 37.

19b. Pullman, P. & A. Pullman. 1963. Quantum Biochemistry: 764. Interscience Publishers. New York, N. Y.

20. Fernandez-Alonso, J. I. 1964. Advan. Chem. Phys. **7:** 1.
21. Chan, S. I., M. P. Schweizer, P. O. P. Ts'o & G. K. Helmkamp. 1964. J. Amer. Chem. Soc. **86:** 4182.

22a. Watson, D. G., R. M. Sweet & R. E. Marsh. 1965. Acta Crystallogr. **19:** 573.

22b. Cochran, W. 1951. Acta Crystallogr. **4:** 81.

23a. Pugmire, R. J., D. M. Grant, R. K. Robins & G. W. Rhodes. 1965. J. Amer. Chem. Soc. **87:** 2225.

23b. Fox, J. R. 1965. Ph.D. Thesis, University of Illinois. Urbana, Illinois.

24. COBURN, W. C. JR., M. C. THORPE, J. A. MONTGOMERY & K. HEWSON. 1965. J. Org. Chem. **30:** 1114.
25. JARDETZKY, O. 1965. Biopolymer Sympos. **1:** 501.
26. KOKKO, J. P., L. MANDEL & J. H. GOLDSTEIN. 1962. J. Amer. Chem. Soc. **84:** 1042.
27. BECKER, E. D., H. T. MILES & R. B. BRADLEY. 1965. J. Amer. Chem. Soc. **87:** 5575.
28. LADIK, J. & K. APPEL. 1966. Theoret. Chim. Acta **4:** 132.
29. PULLMAN, A., C. GIESSNER-PRETTRE & H. BERTHOD. 1967. Personal communication.
30. MILES, H. T., F. B. HOWARD & J. FRAZIER. 1963. Science **142:** 1458.
31. READ, J. M. & J. H. GOLDSTEIN. 1965. J. Amer. Chem. Soc. **87:** 3440.
32. MILES, H. T., R. B. BRADLEY & E. D. BECKER. 1963. Sciences **142:** 1569.
33. JARDETZKY, O., P. PAPPAS & N. G. WADE. 1963. J. Amer. Chem. Soc. **85:** 1657.
34. TS'O, P. O. P., N. KONDO, A. D. BROOM & R. K. ROBINS. Unpublished data.
35. MA, J. C. N. & E. W. WARNHOFF. 1965. Canad. J. Chem. **43:** 1849.
36. ROBINS, M. J. & R. K. ROBINS. 1965. J. Amer. Chem. Soc. **87:** 4934.
37. GATLIN, L. & J. C. DAVIS. 1962. J. Amer. Chem. Soc. **84:** 4464.
38. WECHTER, W. J. 1969. J. Org. Chem. **34:** 244.
39. FROMAGEOT, H. P. M., B. E. GRIFFIN, C. B. REESE, J. E. SULSTON & D. R. TRENTHAM. 1966. Tetrahedron **22:** 705.
40. JARDETZKY, C. D. 1960. J. Amer. Chem. Soc. **83:** 2919.
41. JARDETZKY, C. D. 1962. J. Amer. Chem. Soc. **84:** 62.
42. KARPLUS, M. 1959. J. Chem. Phys. **30:** 11.
43. LEMIEUX, R. V., J. D. STEVENS & R. R. FRASER. 1962. Canad. J. Chem. **40:** 1955.
44. LEMIEUX, R. V. & J. D. STEVENS. 1965. Canad. J. Chem. **44:** 249.
45. HASCHEMEYER, A. E. V. & A. RICH. 1967. J. Molec. Biol. **27:** 369.
46. DAVIES, D. R. 1967. Ann. Rev. Biochem. **36:** 321.
47. TSUBOI, M., F. KURIYAGAWA, K. MATSUO & Y. KYOGOKU. 1967. Bull. Chem. Soc. (Japan) **40:** 1813.
48. TSUBOI, M., M. KAINOSHO & A. NAKAMURA. 1968. Recent Developments of Magnetic Resonance in Molecular Biology. S. Fujiwara and L. H. Piette, Eds. Hirokawa Company. Tokyo, Japan.
49. SASISEKHARAN, V., A. V. LAKSHMINARAYANAN & G. N. RAMACHANDRAN. 1967. *In* Conformation of Biopolymers. G. N. Ramachandran, Ed. **2:** 641. Academic Press. New York, N. Y.
50. WITZEL, H. 1960. Ann. Chem. **635:** 182.
51. PITHA, J., S. CHLADEK & J. SMRT. 1963. Coll. Czech. Chem. Comm. **38:** 1622.
52. MICHELSON, A. M. 1963. Ann. Rev. Biochem. **30:** 133.
53. SCHWEIZER, M. P., A. D. BROOM, P. O. P. TS'O & D. P. HOLLIS. 1968. J. Amer. Chem. Soc. In press.
54. TS'O, P. O. P., S. A. RAPAPORT & F. J. BOLLUM. 1966. Biochemistry **5:** 4153.
55. DONOHUE, J. & K. N. TRUEBLOOD. 1960. J. Molec. Biol. **2:** 363.
56. KRAUT, J. & L. H. JENSEN. 1963. Acta Crystallogr. **16:** 79.
57. SUNDARALINGAM, M. 1966. Acta Crystallogr. **21:** 495.
58. HASCHEMEYER, A. E. V. & H. M. SOBELL. 1965. Acta Crystallogr. **19:** 125.
59. CUSHLEY, R. J., K. A. WATANABE & J. J. FOX. 1967. J. Amer. Chem. Soc. **89:** 394.
60. PITHA, J., R. N. JONES & P. PITHOVA. 1966. Canad. J. Chem. **44:** 1045.
61. KYOGOKU, Y., R. C. LORD & A. RICH. 1967. J. Amer. Chem. Soc. **89:** 496.
62. KUCHLER, E. & J. KERKOSCH. 1966. Z. Naturforsch. **21B:** 209.
63. KATZ, L. & S. PENMAN. 1966. J. Molec. Biol. **15:** 220.
64. SHOUP, R. R., H. T. MILES & E. D. BECKER. 1966. Biochem. Biophys. Res. Commun. **23:** 194.
65. HERSKOVITS, T. T., S. J. SINGER & E. P. GEIDUSCHEK. 1961. Arch. Biochem. Biophys. **94:** 99.
66. HERSKOVITS, T. T. 1962. Arch. Biophys. Biochem. **97:** 433.
67. HELMKAMP, G. K. & P. O. P. TS'O. 1961. J. Amer. Chem. Soc. **83:** 138.
68. MARMUR, J. & P. O. P. TS'O. 1961. Biochem. Biophys. Acta **51:** 32.
69. TS'O, P. O. P., G. K. HELMKAMP & C. SANDER. 1962. Biochim. Biophys. Acta **55:** 584.
70. TS'O, P. O. P., G. K. HELMKAMP, C. SANDER & F. W. STUDIER. 1963. Biochim. Biophys. Acta **76:** 54.

71. Ts'o, P. O. P., I. S. Melvin & A. C. Olson. 1963. J. Amer. Chem. Soc. **85:** 1289.
72. Ts'o, P. O. P. & S. I. Chan. 1964. J. Amer. Soc. **86:** 4176.
73. Helmkamp, G. K. & N. S. Kondo. 1967. Biochim. Biophys. Acta **146:** 27.
74. Schweizer, M. P., S. I. Chan & P. O. P. Ts'o. 1965. J. Amer. Chem. Soc. **87:** 5241.
75. Schweizer, M. P., D. P. Hollis & P. O. P. Ts'o. 1965. Abstr., 9th Ann. Meet. Biophys. Soc.: 16. San Francisco, California.
76. Warshaw, M. M., C. A. Bush & I. Tinoco, Jr. 1965. Biochim. Biophys. Res. Commun. **18:** 633.
77. Bush, C. A. & J. Brahms. 1967. J. Chem. Phys. **46:** 79.
78. Warshaw, M. M. & I. Tinoco, Jr. 1966. J. Molec. Biol. **19:** 29.
79. McDonald, C. C., W. D. Phillips & J. Lazar. 1967. J. Amer. Chem. Soc. **89:** 4166.
80. Chan, S. I., B. W. Bangerter & H. H. Peter. 1966. Proc. Nat. Acad. Sci. **55:** 720.
81. McDonald, C. C., W. D. Phillips & S. Penman. 1964. Science **144:** 1234.
82. McTague, J. P., V. Ross & J. H. Gibbs. 1964. Biopolymers **2:** 163.
83. McDonald, C. C. & W. D. Phillips. 1965. Biopolymers **3:** 609.
84. Trueblood, K. N., P. Horn & V. Luzzati. 1961. Acta Crystallogr. **14:** 965.
85. Sundaralingam, M. & L. H. Jensen. 1965. J. Molec. Biol. **13:** 930.

THE THEORY OF HYPOCHROMISM OF BIOPOLYMERS: CALCULATED SPECTRA FOR DNA

Howard DeVoe*

Laboratory of Neurochemistry
National Institute of Mental Health
Bethesda, Md.

THEORY

Hypochromism is a decrease in the absorption of light by a chromophore. The best known example in biochemistry is the hypochromism of the near UV† absorption band of the purine and pyrimidine bases in an ordered, helical nucleic acid, compared to the absorption band of partially or randomly oriented bases.

The hypochromism of an absorption band is defined as the fractional decrease in its integrated intensity (or its oscillator strength) per chromophore. The integrated intensity is the area under a plot of the extinction coefficient of the band versus the wavenumber. The oscillator strength is found by multiplying the intensity, in units of liter $mole^{-1}$ cm^{-2}, by 4.32×10^{-9}. Point hypochromism is the fractional decrease in the extinction coefficient at a given wavelength. Hyperchromism refers to the opposite phenomenon—an increase in absorption.

The hypochromism of the band seen in the near UV absorption spectrum of a solution of helical calf thymus DNA, with absorption maximum at 258 mμ, is about 0.37 relative to the constituent mononucleotides (FIGURE 1). The exact value depends upon how one divides the spectra into band contributions in the region around 230 mμ, where the first and second band systems overlap. The point hypochromism at the position of the absorption maximum of DNA has about the same value because the polymer and monomer spectra have similar band shapes and a negligible band shift. A small point hyperchromism is seen between 290 and 300 mμ.

The longest wavelength bands of some other biopolymers and molecular aggregates have a similar extent of hypochromism relative to the monomer form of the chromophores. Examples are: the near UV band of double-strand helices of synthetic polyribonucleic acids, the amide band at 190 mμ of the α-helix form of polypeptides, and the visible absorption band of aggregated species of cationic dye molecules such as acridine orange.

Tinoco[1, 2] and Rhodes[3] independently derived a general theory of the hypochromism of ordered polymers by first-order perturbation methods. In this theory, the Coulomb interaction of an electronic transition moment with the transition moments of higher transitions in other chromophores, oriented in a side-by-side geometry (as for the $\pi\pi^*$ base transitions in DNA), causes the band associated with the first transition moment to be hypochromic relative to randomly oriented chromophores (for which the Coulomb interactions average out to zero). The intensity that is lost by the long wavelength band in the polymer is gained by bands at shorter wavelengths, in agreement with the Kuhn-Thomas sum rule which states that the summed oscillator strength of

* Present address: Department of Chemistry, University of Maryland, College Park, Md.

† Abbreviations used: UV, ultraviolet; DNA, deoxyribonucleic acid; A, adenine; T, thymine; G, guanine; C, cytosine.

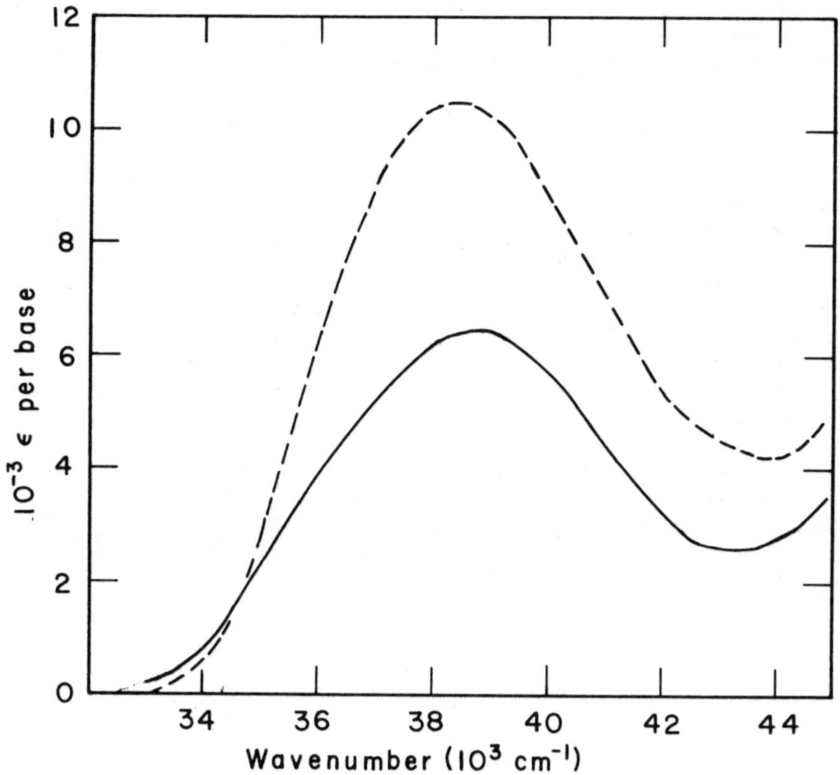

FIGURE 1. Near UV absorption band of helical DNA and of the constituent bases. Solid curve: spectrum of calf thymus DNA (Sigma) in 2.4 mM $NaClO_4$, measured with a Cary 14 recording spectrophotometer; the values of the extinction coefficient ϵ were determined by setting the value at the peak equal to 6.54×10^3, as measured by R. B. Inman and D. O. Jordan in 1960 (Biochim. Biophys. Acta **42:** 530). Dashed curve: spectrum of a mixture containing 0.29 mole fraction of A and of T and 0.21 mole fraction of G and of C, calculated from solution spectra of the individual deoxynucleosides containing these bases at neutral pH.

all bands of a molecule is conserved. A quantitatively similar theory was derived by Hoffmann using second quantization formalism.[4, 5] DeVoe[6] presented a local field interpretation of the Tinoco-Rhodes result: the polarizability due to the higher transitions of the base groups in DNA reduces the amplitude of the local electric field of the light at near UV frequencies, thus decreasing the absorption.

A limitation of these theories is that they do not predict the shape or position of the band in the polymer. To do this, one must make simplified assumptions about the effect of nuclear vibrations. The appropriate model for DNA, with its small band shift relative to the band width, is weak coupling in which the electronic and vibrational parts of the monomer wavefunctions remain separable in the polymer. DeVoe[7] extended the Tinoco-Rhodes theory to the interaction of vibronic transition moments and derived the spectrum of a polymer with weak coupling in terms of the monomer spectra to first order in the interaction energies. The amount of band hypochromism is the same as that predicted by Tinoco and Rhodes, but the bands can shift position and change shape.

The most recent treatments have been based on a local field approach in which each chromophore responds to the local oscillating electric field (averaged over electron motions) coming from the incident light and the other chromophores. Essentially equivalent results, valid for the weak coupling case and correct to all orders in the interactions between chromophores, have been obtained by classical models[8–12] and by various versions of time-dependent perturbation theory.[13–19] The results agree in first order with the hypochromism and band shifts predicted by the first-order theories, and the sum rule is obeyed.

The following sections describe DNA spectra calculated by a classical oscillator model.[10] This is probably the simplest of the all-order local field pictures to visualize. Each transition of a chromophore in the polymer is represented by a one-dimensional electronic oscillator located at the position of the chromophore and oriented in the direction of the transition moment (the direction in which linearly polarized light must be polarized for maximum absorption). The oscillator has an intrinsic frequency-dependent complex polarizability which determines the optical properties of the isolated chromophore at a given frequency of incident light according to the classical theory of optics. The imaginary part of the polarizability describes the amplitude of the oscillator's component of polarization which oscillates out-of-phase with the local electric field. This polarization dissipates energy, so that the imaginary part of the polarizability is largest in magnitude at the frequency of maximum absorption. The real part of the polarizability describes the in-phase polarization, which is responsible for the oscillator's contribution to the optical refraction and has a damped Drude-type dispersion with reversal of sign in the absorption region.

The polymer is treated as a rigid array of the oscillators, each seeing a local field coming from the incident light and the polarization of the oscillators in the other chromophores. Thus, the polarizations of the oscillators are coupled by Coulomb interactions, and the polarization equations can be solved simultaneously to give a self-consistent solution. The polymer absorption is given by the amplitude of the component of the total polarization which is out-of-phase with the incident light.

Rhodes and Chase[19] have shown what approximations are necessary in a quantum treatment to derive the results of the classical oscillator model. A partial decorrelation of the motions of electrons in different chromophores must be assumed, resulting in the neglect of transitions between excited states of chromophores.

All of these theories ignore the possibilities of electron exchange and charge transfer between adjacent chromophores in the polymer. Koutecký and Paldus[20] and Hoffmann and Ladik[21] have suggested that these effects may be largely responsible for the hypochromism of the near UV band of DNA, but no calculations for DNA have been made. Although it is not clear how important these effects may be, hypochromism of the right order of magnitude can be predicted without including them.

Calculations

Method

The classical oscillator theory was used to calculate the spectra of long molecules of poly AT and of poly ATGC, each molecule having a sequence of base pairs that repeats itself once in every turn of the double helix. Such a polymer can be treated as a one-dimensional crystal consisting of a row of identical unit cells related by translation along the helix axis.

The equation for the extinction coefficient of the polymer per mole of base groups is [11]

$$\epsilon = -0.00688\,\tilde{\nu} \sum_{i,j} \mathrm{Im}\, A_{ij} \cos \theta_{ij}/N$$

where $\tilde{\nu}$ is the wavenumber of the light in cm^{-1}, the indices i and j label the oscillators in one unit cell, Im A_{ij} is the imaginary part of a complex element of a matrix A defined below, θ_{ij} is the angle made by the positive directions of oscillators i and j, and N is the number of bases in a unit cell (N = 20 for the present calculations). The matrix A is formed by inverting a symmetric complex matrix B

$$A = B^{-1}$$

nsing standard mathematical methods, where B has elements

$$B_{ij} = \delta_{ij}/\alpha_i + \sum_b G_{ai,bj}.$$

Here, δ_{ij} is the Kronecker delta; α_i is the complex one-dimensional polarizability of oscillator i (in units of A^3) at wavenumber $\tilde{\nu}$; $G_{ai,bj}$ in the dipole-dipole approximation used here is the instantaneous Coulomb interaction energy (in units of A^{-3}) between point unit dipoles along the positive directions of oscillators i and j in unit cells a and b, respectively; and the sum over b includes unit cell a (unless oscillators i and j belong to the same base group) and many other unit cells in both directions along the helix from a. In the present work, interactions were included between bases separated by up to 39 base pairs. All calculations were performed by Fortran programs written for an IBM/360 computer.

Oscillator Polarizabilities

Each base group was considered to have one or, at most, two mutually perpendicular oscillators lying in the plane of the base, located at the position which DeVoe and Tinoco[22] used for transition moments. Each oscillator was used to represent one or two of the $\pi\pi^*$ transitions seen in the mononucleotide spectrum in the 260 mμ or 200 mμ region. The imaginary part of the polarizability α_i of each oscillator i at wavenumber $\tilde{\nu}$ was evaluated from the molar extinction coefficient $\epsilon_i(\tilde{\nu})$ of the corresponding absorption band or bands at this wavenumber by[10,11]

$$\mathrm{Im}\,\alpha_i = -145.3\,\epsilon_i(\tilde{\nu})/\tilde{\nu}$$

using deoxynucleoside spectra divided into bands as given by DeVoe and Tinoco.[22] The real part of the polarizability at $\tilde{\nu}$ contributed by the band or bands was evaluated by[10,11]

$$\mathrm{Re}\,\alpha_i = 92.5 \int \frac{\epsilon_i(\tilde{\nu}')\,d\tilde{\nu}'}{(\tilde{\nu}')^2 - \tilde{\nu}^2}.$$

The integration for each oscillator was performed numerically over the entire band or bands using wavenumber intervals of 200 cm^{-1} at wavenumbers below 48×10^3 cm^{-1} and larger intervals at higher wavenumbers. The interval where $\tilde{\nu}' = \tilde{\nu}$ was omitted to give the principal value of the integral.

The only polarizability contributed by far UV transitions in the polymer to be considered was the in-plane polarizability of the base groups. This additional polarizability, when included, was assumed to be isotropic in the plane of each base and to add a contribution to Re α_i at wavenumber $\tilde{\nu}$ for both of the mutually perpendicular oscillators of the base given by a Drude formula

$$\mathrm{Re}\,\alpha_i = C/(\tilde{\nu}_i^{\,2} - \tilde{\nu}^2).$$

The characteristic wavenumber $\tilde{\nu}_i$ was estimated from dispersion data to be 70×10^3 cm^{-1} for the purines and 84×10^3 cm^{-1} for the pyrimidines.[23] The values used for the coefficients C were (in units of A^3 cm^{-2}) 6.4×10^{10} for adenine, 7.1×10^{10} for thymine, 4.9×10^{10} for guanine and 5.8×10^{10} for cytosine; these values give an average total in-plane polarizability at $\tilde{\nu} = 0$ for each base agreeing with estimates based on atomic refractions.[23]

Oscillator Directions

The directions of the oscillators within the base groups were chosen on the basis of experimental data for the corresponding transition moments where available. In the following list, the band positions are described by the wavelength of maximum absorption, and the angle Θ describing the oscillator directions within the bases refers to the convention given by DeVoe and Tinoco.[23]

Adenine—first band at 259 mμ: $\Theta = -3°$, as determined by Stewart and Jensen[24] from polarized absorption spectra of crystals of 9-methyladenine crystals. Second band at 207 mμ: assumed perpendicular to first band ($\Theta = 87°$), in agreement with data of Stewart and Davidson.[25]

Thymine—first band at 267 mμ: $\Theta = -19°$, as determined by Stewart and Davidson[25] from polarized absorption spectra of 1-methylthymine crystals. Second band at 206 mμ: assumed perpendicular to the first band ($\Theta = 71°$), in approximate agreement with the theoretical molecular orbital calculations of Denis and Pullman.[26]

Guanine—first band at 276 mμ: $\Theta = -70°$, as calculated theoretically by Berthod and coworkers[27] using self-consistent field molecular orbitals with configuration mixing. Second band at 252 mμ: assumed perpendicular to the first band ($\Theta = 20°$), in agreement with measurements by Callis and collaborators[28] of the polarization of fluorescence from guanine. Third band at about 187 mμ: assumed parallel to the first band ($\Theta = -70°$), in rough agreement with theoretical calculations of Berthod and coworkers.[27]

Cytosine—first band at 271 mμ: $\Theta = 9°$ as measured by Callis[29] from polarized reflection spectra of crystalline cytosine monohydrate and 1-methylcytosine. Second band at 230 mμ: assumed parallel to the first band ($\Theta = 9°$), in agreement with the data of Callis[29] on the polarized fluorescence of 5-methylcytosine. Third band at 197 mμ: assumed perpendicular to the first and second bands ($\Theta = 99°$); Berthod and collaborators[27] calculate $\Theta = 136°$, which is closer to the perpendicular direction than to the parallel one.

Polymer Structure

The base groups were assumed to be assembled in rigid, straight double-strand DNA helices with the geometry and dimensions of the B form of fibrous DNA lithium salt. The base pairs are in planes perpendicular to the helix axis, separated by 3.36 A. The sequences considered were: (1) Poly AT (nonalternating sequence). One strand of the helix contains adenine groups and the other contains thymine groups. (2) Poly ATGC (random sequence). An arbitrary sequence of base pairs was chosen that includes equal numbers of the four bases and repeats after every ten base pairs. The sequence along one of the strands (reading from left to right in the direction of phosphodiester links from the 3′ carbon on one sugar to the 5′ carbon on the adjacent sugar) is

A A G C C A T C G T.

The sequence of the opposite strand is the Watson-Crick complement.

Results and Discussion

Figures 2 and 3 show the calculated extinction coefficients of poly AT and poly ATGC, respectively, at various wavenumbers in the first near UV band. The circles are values calculated using only the $\pi\pi^*$ transitions in the 260 mμ and 200 mμ regions of the monomer spectra. The triangles are values calculated when the additional in-plane polarizability of each base

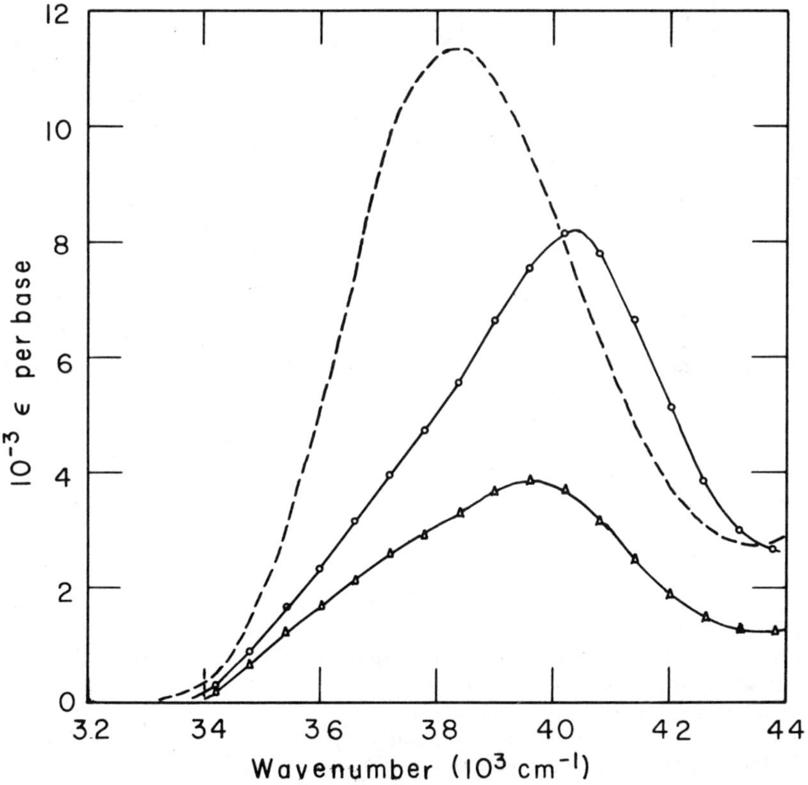

Figure 2. Near UV absorption band of helical poly AT (nonalternating sequence) and of the constituent bases. Circles: calculated for the polymer using the 260 mμ and 200 mμ transitions of the bases. Triangles: calculated for the polymer using all in-plane transitions of the bases. Dashed curve: spectrum of a mixture containing equal concentrations of A and T deoxynucleosides.

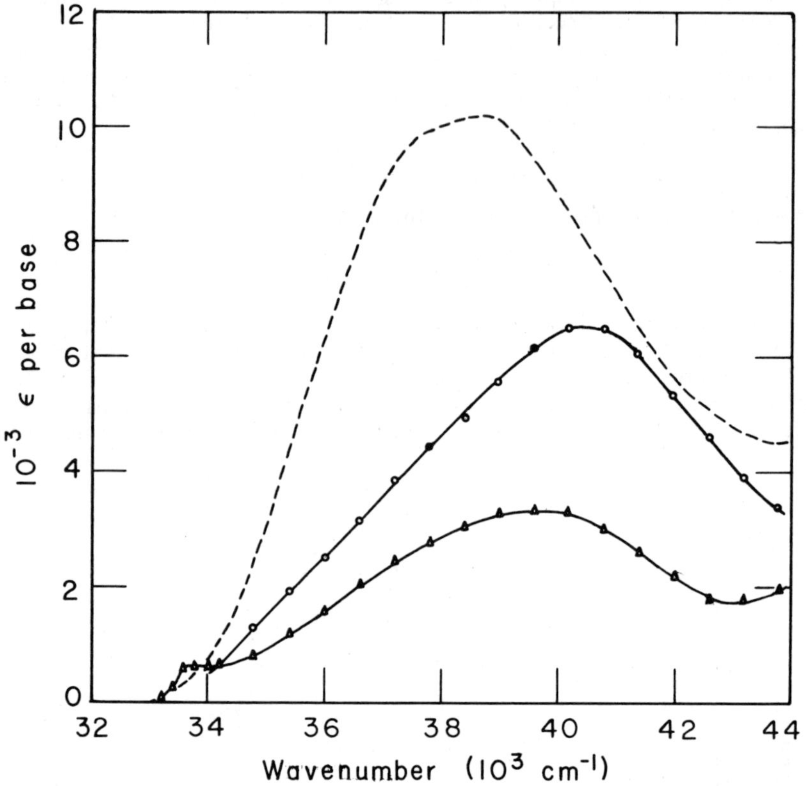

FIGURE 3. Near UV absorption band of helical poly ATGC (random sequence) and of the constituent bases. The circles and triangles have the same meaning as in FIGURE 2. Dashed curve: spectrum of a mixture containing equal concentrations of A, T, G, and C deoxynucleosides.

group coming from transitions in the far UV was also included. The out-of-plane base polarizability and the polarizability of sugar and phosphate groups and the solvent were not considered.

Hypochromism

The inclusion of the in-plane far UV transitions is seen to approximately double the calculated hypochromism, because these transitions contribute as much polarizability at frequencies in the 260 mμ region as do the bands in the vicinity of 200 mμ. Experimentally, helical poly AT (non-alternating sequence) has a band maximum of $\epsilon = 6.0 \times 10^3$ at 259 mμ (38.6×10^3 cm^{-1}),[30] midway between the two calculated values. Helical *E. coli* DNA, with the same base composition as poly ATGC, has a band maximum of $\epsilon = 6.7 \times 10^3$ at about 258 mμ,[31] approximately equal to the higher of the two calculated values for poly ATGC.

For both molecules, too much hypochromism is predicted when the full in-plane polarizability of the bases is used. One reason for this is probably that the higher excited states of the bases are more delocalized than the lower π^*

states, so that the dipole-dipole approximation overestimates the Coulomb interactions involving the far UV oscillators. Another reason is that the solvent polarizability, which was ignored in the present calculations, decreases the hypochromism of DNA.[6, 22]

The effect of the solvent polarizability on the DNA extinction coefficient can be estimated as follows within the framework of the all-order local field theory. The solvent is treated as a continuum with a real polarizability α_v per unit volume, and the DNA helix as a long cylinder which excludes the solvent. Since an internal field correction for the solvent was omitted in obtaining the oscillator polarizabilities from the absorption spectra of the approximately spherical monomers in solution,[11] the DNA calculation should include only the solvent within a spherical boundary around the DNA molecule. It can be shown mathematically that the polarization of solvent contained outside a cylinder, but inside a sphere whose center is any point within the cylinder, adds a quantity $2\pi\alpha_v E^\circ/3$ to the component of the local field at that point along any direction perpendicular to the cylinder axis. Here, E° is the component of the incident field in the same direction. The effect of the solvent is, then, to multiply the extinction coefficients calculated without it by the coefficient

$$(1 + 2\pi \alpha_v/3)^2.$$

With water as the solvent, the value of α_v in the near UV is estimated from the refractive index to be 0.054 making the coefficient equal to 1.24. The solvent correction alone is not enough to increase the calculated band maxima to the experimental values (the corrected values are 4.8×10^3 for poly AT and 4.2×10^3 for poly ATGC).

Band Shifts

The positions of the calculated polymer band maxima are blue-shifted (moved to higher wavenumbers) from the monomer solution bands by 1000–2000 cm^{-1}, much more than found experimentally. The calculated shift is primarily caused by a redistribution of intensity in the near UV band, due to the interactions between the vibronic transition moments (or classically, the polarizations) of this band in different monomers. Herzenberg and Modinos[18] and also Rhodes and Chase[19] point out that the polarizability from higher transitions tends to suppress this blue shift, but the present calculations show that the suppression is not sufficient to prevent a sizable shift.

The classical calculations should use oscillator polarizabilities appropriate to the monomers in the time-average (static) field of the polymer environment. If the near UV bands of some of the monomers are red-shifted in this environment compared to the solution spectra actually used, the result of using the red-shifted spectra in the calculations would be to predict a more satisfactory polymer band shift. For instance, if the permanent moment of the excited state of a chromophore is greater than the ground state, the excited state will be preferentially stabilized by dipole induced-dipole interactions when the chromophore is moved to a more polarizable environment, such as the interior of the DNA helix. Shifts of different extents and directions were observed by Clark and coworkers[32] for bases in various solvents and the vapor phase.

Point Hyperchromism at Long Wavelengths

The most remarkable feature of the calculated spectra is the small peak appearing at about 33.7×10^3 cm^{-1} (297 $m\mu$) in the spectrum of poly ATGC when the full in-plane polarizability of the bases is included (FIGURE 3). A narrow region at the long wavelength edge of the near UV band has borrowed intensity from the far UV transitions. This finding suggests that the point hyperchromism observed in DNA in this region (FIGURE 1) is caused by absorption derived from the $\pi\pi^*$ transitions of the bases instead of from $n\pi^*$ transitions as suggested by Rich and Kasha.[33] This interpretation is consistent with the dichroism measurements made by Gellert[34] and Wada[35] on oriented DNA molecules. Point hyperchromism is not predicted by the calculations for poly AT (nonalternating sequence) (FIGURE 2), and apparently none is observed experimentally.[30]

Using red-shifted monomer spectra in the calculations, as suggested above, would also tend to produce point hyperchromism at the long wavelength edge of the near UV band. Drobnik and Kleinwächter[36] have suggested that the observed point hyperchromism could represent weak $\pi\pi^*$ bands hidden in the solution spectra of the monomers which red-shift in the environment of the helix.

REFERENCES

1. TINOCO, I., JR. 1960, 1961. Hypochromism in polynucleotides. J. Amer. Chem. Soc. **82:** 4785–4790; **83:** 5047.
2. TINOCO, I., JR. 1960, 1961. Optical and other electronic properties of polymers. J. Chem. Phys. **33:** 1332–1338; **34:** 1067.
3. RHODES, W. 1961. Hypochromism and other spectral properties of helical polynucleotides. J. Amer. Chem. Soc. **83:** 3609–3617.
4. HOFFMANN, R. 1963. Exciton theory by second quantization. Rad. Res. **20:** 140–148.
5. SINANOĞLU, O. 1963. On the theories of hypochromism in polynucleotides. Rad. Res. **20:** 149–153.
6. DEVOE, H. 1964. Hypochromism as a local field effect. Biopolymers Sympos. **1:** 251–258.
7. DEVOE, H. 1962. Effect of weak coupling on the absorption spectrum of an aggregate of chromophores. J. Chem. Phys. **37:** 1534–1540.
8. BOLTON, H. C. & J. J. WEISS. 1962. Hypochromism in the ultra-violet absorption of nucleic acids and related structures. Nature **195:** 666–668.
9. DEVOE, H. 1963. Polarizability theories of polynucleotide hypochromism. Nature **197:** 1295–1296.
10. DEVOE, H. 1964. Optical properties of molecular aggregates. I. Classical theory of electronic absorption and refraction. J. Chem. Phys. **41:** 393–400.
11. DEVOE, H. 1965. Optical properties of molecular aggregates. II. Classical theory of the refraction, absorption, and optical activity of solutions and crystals. J. Chem. Phys. **43:** 3199–3208.
12. BULLOUGH, R. K. 1965. Theory of hypochromism. J. Chem. Phys. **43:** 1927–1933.
13. NESBET, R. K. 1964. Theory of hypochromism. Molec. Phys. **7:** 211–221.
14. NESBET, R. K. 1964. Interaction of paired bases in polynucleotides. Biopolymers Sympos. **1:** 129–139.
15. FOWLER, G. N. 1964. On the theory of hypochromism. Molec. Phys. **8:** 383–386.
16. MCLACHLAN, A. D. & M. A. BALL. 1964. Hypochromism and optical rotation in helical polymers. Molec. Phys. **8:** 581–595.
17. THIÉRY, J. 1965. Verification of the Kuhn-Thomas sum rule in the framework of some recent polarizability theories for molecular aggregates. J. Chem. Phys. **43:** 553–560.
18. HERZENBERG, A. & A. MODINOS. 1966. Co-operative effects in a polymer rod. Proc. Phys. Soc. **87:** 597–617.

19. RHODES, W. & M. CHASE. 1967. Generalized susceptibility theory. I. Theories of hypochromism. Revs. Mod. Phys. **39:** 348–361.
20. KOUTECKÝ, J. & J. PALDUS. 1963. A study of interaction of two ethylene molecules by the semiempirical complete configuration interaction method in π-electron approximation. Theoret. Chim. Acta **1:** 268–281.
21. HOFFMANN, T. A. & J. LADIK. 1964. Some remarks on the hypochromicity of polynucleotides. J. Theoret. Biol. **6:** 26–32.
22. DEVOE, H. & I. TINOCO, JR. 1962. The hypochromism of helical polynucleotides. J. Molec. Biol. **4:** 518–527.
23. DEVOE, H. & I. TINOCO, JR. 1962. The stability of helical polynucleotides: base contributions. J. Molec. Biol. **4:** 500–517.
24. STEWART, R. F. & L. H. JENSEN. 1964. Crystal structure of 9-methyladenine. J. Chem. Phys. **40:** 2071–2075.
25. STEWART, R. F. & N. DAVIDSON. 1963. Polarized absorption spectra of purines and pyrimidines. J. Chem. Phys. **39:** 255–266.
26. DENIS, A. & A. PULLMAN. 1967. Theoretical study of the electronic properties of biological purines and pyrimidines. III. The representation of the methyl group and the structure of thymine. Theoret. Chim. Acta **7:** 110–116.
27. BERTHOD, H., C. GIESSNER-PRETTRE & A. PULLMAN. 1967. Theoretical study of the electronic properties of biological purines and pyrimidines. II. The effect of configuration mixing. Internat. J. Quant. Chem. **1:** 123–137.
28. CALLIS, P. R., E. J. ROSA & W. T. SIMPSON. 1964. Search for accidental degeneracy in purines. J. Amer. Chem. Soc. **86:** 2292–2294.
29. CALLIS, P. R. 1966. Transition moment studies on the DNA bases. The transition moments of cytosine. Diss. Abstr. **B27:** 773.
30. RILEY, M., B. MALING & M. J. CHAMBERLIN. 1966. Physical and chemical characterization of two- and three-stranded adenine-thymine and adenine-uracil homopolymer complexes. J. Molec. Biol. **20:** 359–389.
31. MAHLER, H. R., B. KLINE & B. D. MEHROTRA. 1964. Some observations on the hypochromism of DNA. J. Molec. Biol. **9:** 801–811.
32. CLARK, L. B., G. G. PESCHEL & I. TINOCO, JR. 1965. Vapor spectra and heats of vaporization of some purine and pyrimidine bases. J. Phys. Chem. **69:** 3615–3618.
33. RICH, A. & M. KASHA. 1960. The n $\rightarrow$ π^* transition in nucleic acids and polynucleotides. J. Amer. Chem. Soc. **82:** 6197–6198.
34. GELLERT, M. 1961. On the assignment of n $\rightarrow$ π^* transitions in polynucleotides. J. Amer. Chem. Soc. **83:** 4664–4665.
35. WADA, A. 1964. On the parallel absorption of DNA helices in the ultraviolet region. Biopolymers Sympos. **1:** 476–477.
36. DROBNIK, J. & V. KLEINWÄCHTER. 1965. On the nature of hyperchromicity in polynucleotide complexes. Biochem. Biophys. Res. Commun. **21:** 366–372.

SOLVENT EFFECTS ON CIS-TRANS AZOBENZENE ISOMERIZATION: A DETAILED APPLICATION OF A THEORY OF SOLVENT EFFECTS ON MOLECULAR ASSOCIATION*

Timur Halicioğlu and Okatay Sinanoğlu

Sterling Chemistry Laboratory
Yale University, New Haven, Conn.

INTRODUCTION

The free energy of a reaction—enthalpy and entropy as well—is modified by solvents. In a physical or chemical association of two molecular groups, or in a conformational change, solvent effects are usually significant. Recently, a quantitative and general theory for contribution of solvent to the forces between molecular groups in solution (solvophobic forces) has been formulated and outlined.[1] In the present work, the theory is applied in detail to a specific case: the effect of various solvents on the cis-trans isomerization reaction of azobenzene, which involves molecular groups more or less similar to those that occur in biopolymers and whose association influences the conformation. The calculation procedure is presented in some detail and should be useful in indicating the relative magnitudes of the various effects involved, and how the theory may be applied in other contexts.

Azobenzene Cis-Trans Isomerization

Azobenzene is usually found in the trans form that is considerably more stable than the cis form. Cis-trans isomerization of azobenzene has been investigated by Hartley.[2] This isomerization is a unimolecular reaction; its rate constant has been measured by several investigators 2–4 in different solvents.† Isomerization can be formulated as‡

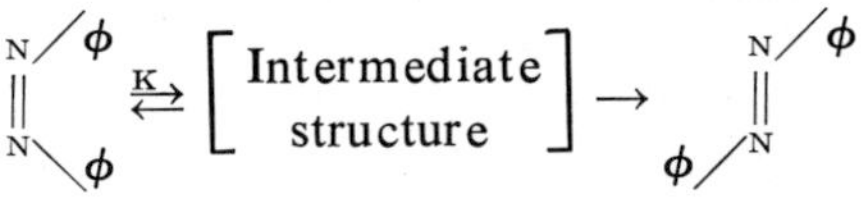

According to the absolute rate theory, we assumed that transitions state molecule is in quasi-equilibrium with the reactant, i.e., the cis form. Therefore, we have the relation between the rate constant, k_r, and the free energy of activation, $\Delta F^{\dagger}$, as

$$\Delta F^{\dagger} = -RT \operatorname{Ln} k_r + RT \operatorname{Ln} \kappa \frac{kT}{h} \tag{1}$$

where κ is the transmission coefficient which is usually equal to unity, k is the

* This work supported by grants from the National Science Foundation and the Alfred P. Sloan Foundation.

† According to the general theory, solvent should play no catalytic role on the reaction mechanism. We included only inert solvents, considering the investigation by Schulte-Frohlinde,[5] who studied the catalytic influence of various compounds on the cis-trans conversion of azobenzene.

‡ As an intermediate structure, one may assume that one of the phenyl group is rotated around the nitrogen double bond for about 90°. (See Reference 5.)

Boltzmann factor, and h is the Planck constant. Thus, the last term results in a constant. For the reaction occurring in the solvent $\Delta F^{\dagger}$ has two parts;[1]

$$\Delta F^{\dagger} = \Delta F^{\dagger}(\text{gas}) + \Delta F^{\dagger}(\text{solv. eff.}) \tag{2}$$

$\Delta F^{\dagger}$ (gas) is the free energy of activation of the same reaction in the gas phase, which is constant for a given reaction. Consequently, the dependence of $\Delta F^{\dagger}$ on the solvent is due to $\Delta F^{\dagger}$ (solv. eff.) alone. Now, the $\Delta F^{\dagger}$ (solv. eff.) will be calculated using the formulation given in Reference 1. For a unimolecular reaction of smaller molecules, $\Delta F^{\dagger}$ (solv. eff.) is given by[§]

$$\Delta F^{\dagger}(\text{solv. eff.}) = \Delta F_{int} + \Delta F_{c} + \Delta F_{red} \tag{3}$$

ΔF_{int} is the contribution coming from the solute-solvent intermolecular forces. It is the interaction term. The ΔF_c is the difference of the free energies for creating cavities in the solvent to accommodate the trans- and cis-forms of the solute. ΔF_{red} is the change in the reduction of free energies of interaction of the solute molecular groups due to solvent.

The ΔF_{int} has two parts:

$$\Delta F_{int} = \Delta F_{vdw} + \Delta F_{e.s.} \tag{4}$$

ΔF_{vdw} and $\Delta F_{e.s.}$ are the free energy differences due to the dispersion and the electrostatic forces, respectively.

a) Dispersion part

ΔF_{vdw} is defined as:

$$\Delta F_{vdw} = F_{vdw}{}^{\dagger} - F_{vdw}{}^{(cis)} \tag{5}$$

where, $F_{vdw}{}^{A}$ is the free energy of interaction—due to the dispersion forces—of the particle A (i.e., cis-azobenzene or the transition molecule) with the solvent molecules around it, and given by[1]:

$$F_{vdw}{}^{A} = -f(\varphi_{1A}, \bar{l}_{1A})\, \Delta_{1A}\, D_1\, D_A\, B_{1A} \tag{6}$$

where,

$$\Delta_{1A} = \mu(I_A I_1)/(I_A + I_1) \quad \text{with} \quad \mu = 1.35 \tag{7}$$

I_1 and I_A are the ionization potentials of solvent and solute molecules, respectively. We considered that the ionization potential of the solutes were equal to 10 e.v. (This value is estimated from the magnetic susceptibility measurement.[7]) D_1 and D_A are the Clausius-Mosotti functions for pure solvent and for pure liquid A.

$$D_i = \frac{n_i^2 - 1}{n_i^2 + 2} = \frac{4\pi}{3V_i} N\bar{\alpha}_i \tag{8}$$

n_i, V_i, and $\bar{\alpha}_i$ are the refractive index, molecular volume, and the average polarizability of pure liquid i, respectively. In calculating the Clausius-Mosotti function for solutes, we used polarizabilities of cis- and trans-azobenzene[‖] that are meas-

§ This equation is for the specific case under consideration. The general form is given in Reference[1] by Equation 37 of that paper, and should be consulted for other reactions.

‖ The polarizabilities of cis- and trans-azobenzenes are estimated as 2.4×10^{-23} and 2.54×10^{-23} cm^3, respectively, using the distortion polarizations given in Reference.[8] Transition state molecule is considered to have a polarizability equal to the ured by Bullock and coworkers.[8] For solvents, D_1 is calculated from the measured refractive indices.

The function f times B_{1A} is given by:

$$-f(\varphi_{1A}, \bar{l}_{1A})B_{1A} = \frac{27}{8\pi}(1 - x)(Q' + Q'') \qquad (9)$$

where, x is a proportionality constant that relates the entropy of interaction to the energy of interaction. For various liquids—polar and nonpolar—it has been found to be quite constant and equal to $x \approx 0.436$.[9] Q' and Q'' are dimensionless functions; they are obtained by integrating the effective pair potential (between the solute and the solvent molecules) over the total volume. Details are given in the Appendix. Integral equation for Q' (Equation A6) yields

$$Q' = \left[V_A \frac{\bar{\sigma}_{1A}{}^6}{(R - l_{1A})^9}\left(\frac{t^2}{11} + \frac{t}{5} + \frac{1}{9}\right) - \frac{1}{(R - l_{1A})^3}\left(\frac{t^2}{5} + \frac{t}{2} + \frac{1}{3}\right)\right] \qquad (10)$$

(The meaning of the symbols are explained in the Appendix.) An analytic solution of the integral equation for Q'' (Equation A7) would be difficult since it contains a fairly complicated function, L_{AB}'. This is a function which occurs in the effective intermolecular potential in a liquid We solved the integral equation numerically for each solvent, using the effective intermolecular potential formulas given in Reference 10 (TABLE 1).

Molecular volume of the solutes, V_A, (i.e., cis-azobenzene and the transition molecule) are calculated as 250 A^3 and 270 A^3, respectively from the X-ray structures reported by Robertson.[11] The volume of the transition molecule has been considered approximately equal to the molecular volume of the trans form.[12] In Equation 10, $\bar{\sigma}_{1A}$ and $\bar{l}_{1A}$ are estimated from the acentric factor, w, as explained in the Appendix. The value of w for cis-azobenzene and for the transition state molecule are considered to be 0.35 and 0.36, respectively. These are obtained from nonpolar model compounds.

b) Electrostatic part

The free energy difference coming from the electrostatic forces is given as

$$\Delta F_{e.s.} = F_{e.s.}{}^{\dagger} - F_{e.s.}{}^{(cis)} \qquad (11)$$

where $F_{e.s.}{}^A$ is the free energy of interaction due to the electrostatic forces of the particle A (i.e., cis-azobenzene, or the transition molecule) with the solvent. An approximate estimate of $F_{e.s.}{}^A$ is obtained from the Onsager reaction field.[13]

$$F_{e.s.}{}^A = -\frac{1}{2}\left(\frac{\mu_A{}^2}{V_A}\right)\mathfrak{F}(\epsilon) \qquad (12)$$

$$\mathfrak{F}(\epsilon) = \frac{\mathfrak{D}}{1 - (\bar{\alpha}_A/r_A{}^3)}$$

with

$$\mathfrak{D} = 2(\epsilon - 1)/(2\epsilon + 1).$$

Where ϵ is the dielectric constant of the pure solvent, μ_A and r_A are the dipole moment and the average radius of the solute A. $\bar{r}_A$ is calculated from the molecular

trans form. An intermediate value for the polarizability of the transition molecule does not affect the result greatly.

volume as $r_A = (3V_A/4\pi)^{1/3}$. The dipole moment of cis- and trans-azobenzene are 3.08 and 0.52 D, respectively[8]. The dipole moment of the transition molecule is expected to have an intermediate value. Isomerization presumably occurs from either (i) the rotation of one phenyl group around N‖N for about 180°, or (ii) by displacement of one phenyl group for about 120° staying always on the same plane. From the geometry, as an intermediate value of dipole moment we found for case (i) $\mu^\dagger = 2.1$ D corresponding to a rotation for about 90°; and for case (ii) $\mu^\dagger = 1.7$ D corresponding to a displacement for 60°. In calculating $F_{e.s.}^\dagger$: we considered $\mu^\dagger = 1.9$ D, which is the average value of intermediate dipole moments.

In Equation 3, ΔF_c corresponds to the free energy difference due to the surface forces.[1] It is given by:

$$\Delta F_c = F_c^\dagger - F_c^{(cis)} \tag{13}$$

where F_{cA} is the free energy required to create a cavity inside the liquid which accommodates the solute molecule A (i.e., cis-azobenzene or the transition molecule). F_{cL} is calculated from:

$$F_c^A = \kappa_1^e(\varphi_{1A})4.836\,V_A\gamma_1(1 - W_{1A}) \tag{14}$$

$$W_{1A} = (1 - \eta_{1A})\left(\frac{d\ \mathrm{Ln}\ \gamma_1}{d\ \mathrm{Ln}\ T} + \frac{2}{3}\,\mathfrak{A}_A T\right)$$

$$\eta_{1A} = \frac{\kappa_1^s(\varphi_{1A})}{\kappa_1^e(\varphi_{1A})}$$

where, γ_1 is the ordinary surface tension of pure solvent. $\mathfrak{A}_A$ is considered here as $\mathfrak{A}_A \approx (d\ \mathrm{Ln}\ V_1/d\ \mathrm{Ln}\ T)$.¶

$\kappa_1^e(\varphi_{1A})$ and $\kappa_1^s(\varphi_{1A})$ are the constants dependent on the volume fraction $\varphi_{1A} = V_1/V_A$, and adjust the planar surface energy and the surface entropy to highly curved microscopic dimensions. For nonpolar molecules, the function $\kappa_1^e(\varphi_{1A})$ has been obtained empirically from the solubility and the mixing data of asymmetric systems[9]. It approaches unity as the size of solute relative to solvent becomes larger. For a nonpolar liquid $\kappa_1^e(\varphi_{1A})$ is approximately given by:

$$\kappa_1^e(\varphi_{1A}) = 1 + \varphi_{1A}^{2/3}(\kappa_1^e(1) - 1) \tag{15}$$

where $\kappa_1^e(1)$ is the microscopic cavity factor for the pure liquid (the solvent alone), i.e., for a cavity the size of a solvent molecule in the pure solvent itself. $\kappa_1^e(1)$ can be calculated using the physical constants of pure liquid by Equations 16 and 19 of Reference 1. For polar liquids $\kappa_1^e(\varphi_{1A})$ and $\kappa_1^s(\varphi_{1A})$ are usually somewhat above 1. However, it is expected to approach 1 as φ_{1A} becomes larger. In calculating κ_1^e and κ_1^s, we used equation 15 for polar liquids as well as for nonpolars.

The $\kappa_1^e(1)$ and $\kappa_1^s(1)$ alone, with some physical constants of the various pure solvents that are used in the computations, are tabulated in TABLE 1.

¶ A_A denotes a coefficient of thermal expansion appropriate to the cavity (see also Equation 20 of Reference 1) that must be dependent on both solute and solvent expansivities. It is expected to have a value somewhere between the values of the thermal expansion coefficients of solute and solvent molecules. Calculations indicate that it is closer to the solvent expansion coefficient than to the solute expansivity. In this calculation, we used solvent expansivities.

TABLE 1
PURE SOLVENT PROPERTIES*

Solvents	$\kappa_1^e(1)$	$\kappa_1^s(1)$	D_1	γ (25° C) Surface Tension dyn/cm	Dielectric Constant $\epsilon_{25°}$	$-\frac{d\gamma}{dT}$	ω Nonpolar Part	Expansion Coeff × 10^3
1) Heptane	0.687	0.542	0.234	19.80	1.92	0.100	0.348	1.250
2) Isooctane	0.672	0.527	0.238	18.32	1.91	0.089	0.313	1.207
3) CCl_4	0.629	0.475	0.272	26.15	2.23	0.126	0.255	1.220
4) Cy-Hexane	0.621	0.466	0.254	24.38	2.01	0.120	0.262	1.200
5) Benzene	0.629	0.469	0.293	28.20	2.27	0.139	0.215	1.220
6) Toluene	0.679	0.529	0.291	27.92	2.37	0.121	0.256	1.066
7) Anilin	0.972	1.127	0.335	42.79	6.85	0.105	0.256	0.850
8) n-BuOH	1.089	0.931	0.241	24.20	17.10	0.108	0.252	0.940
9) EtOH	1.543	1.508	0.220	21.85	24.44	0.084	0.147	1.080
10) Nitromethane	0.808	0.580	0.231	36.47	38.20	0.168	0.192	1.192
11) MeOH	1.776	1.609	0.202	22.20	32.63	0.086	0.100	1.190
12) Water	1.277	1.235	0.205	72.00	77.46	0.157	0.023	0.257

* Data taken from Landolt-Börnstein, Zahlenwerte und Funktionen (6. Auflage); International Critical Tables and Physical and Chemical Constants of Pure Organic Compounds (Vols. I, UU). In some cases, extrapolated values for desired temperature.

ΔF_{red}, the reduction part, is considered to be quite small and relatively constant.** It is not included in the calculations, though it would be fairly easy to do so (cf. the ΔF_{red} formulas in Reference 1).

Results and Discussions

The result of the calculations for ΔF_{vdw}, $\Delta F_{e.s.}$, ΔF_c and ΔF(solv. eff.) are separately given in Table 2 with the experimental values, i.e., RT Ln k_r. A plot of ΔF(solv. eff.) against RT Ln k_r is shown in Figure 1. The dielectric constant and the surface tension of pure solvents does not show any satisfactory correlation with the experimental values. These are demonstrated graphically in Figure 2. In both cases there are some scattered points, belonging mostly to the polar liquids.

Solvent dependence of ΔF_{vdw} is small, whereas ΔF_c and $\Delta F_{e.s.}$ vary considerably from one solvent to another in a complementary way. The larger dipole moment of the cis form results in a $\Delta F_{e.s.}$ part which is positive. The two main parts of the solvent effect that have been classified as solvation (or inverse volume forces) and the surface forces[1] are quite apparent in this example. Consideration of both forces is essential for a satisfactory quantitative agreement with experiment (cf. Figure 1). The other effects, e.g. ΔF_{red}, would be of secondary importance.

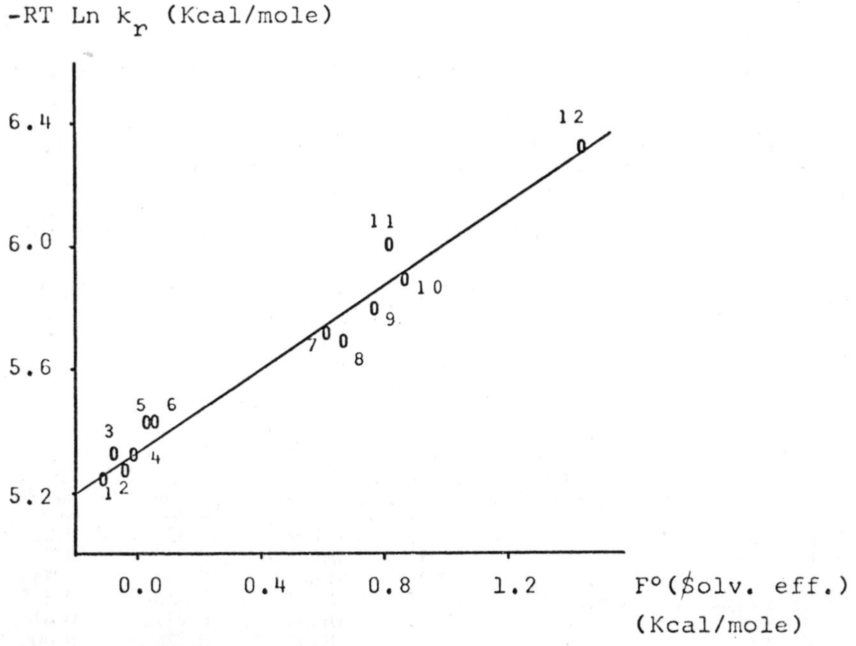

Figure 1. Cis-trans isomerization of azobenzene. Calculated F° (solv. eff.) vs —RT Ln k_r (k_r = rate constant).

** In estimating solvent effects on the denaturation process of DNA, Sinanoğlu and Abdulnur[14] found that ΔF_{red}, i.e., reduction in the interaction free energy between the bases due to the neighboring solvent molecules—is quite small and stays relatively unchanged in various solvents. In the case of cis-azobenzene, with the parts having smaller dipoles, ΔF_{red} is expected to contribute less.

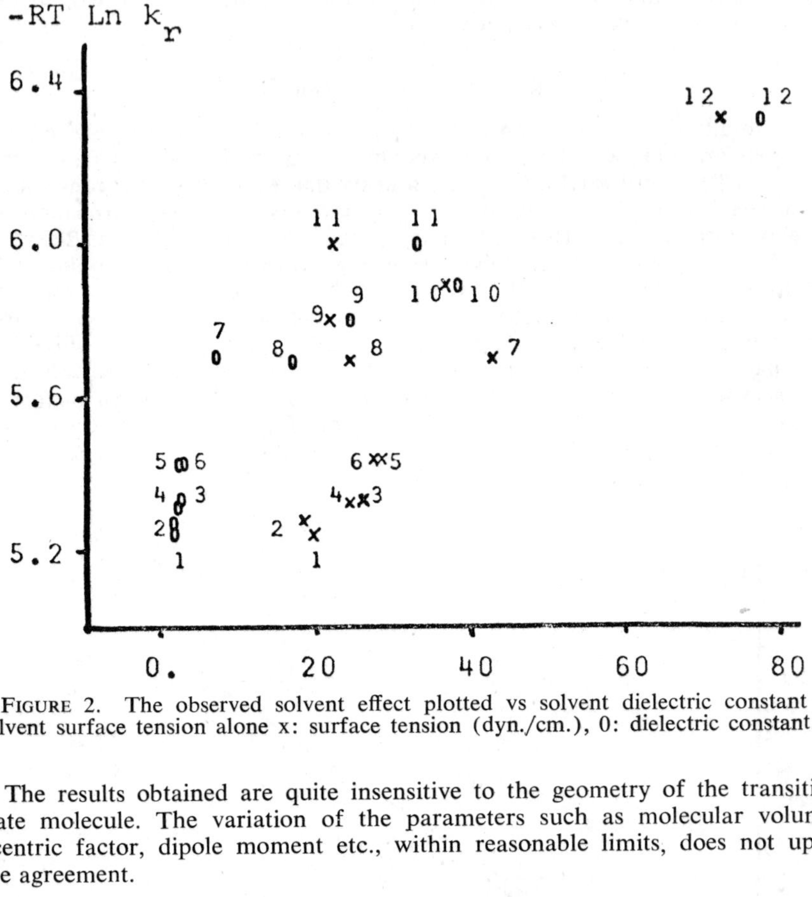

FIGURE 2. The observed solvent effect plotted vs solvent dielectric constant or solvent surface tension alone x: surface tension (dyn./cm.), 0: dielectric constant.

The results obtained are quite insensitive to the geometry of the transition state molecule. The variation of the parameters such as molecular volume, acentric factor, dipole moment etc., within reasonable limits, does not upset the agreement.

TABLE 2
CIS-TRANS ISOMERIZATION OF AZOBENZENE IN VARIOUS SOLVENTS

Solvents	$-RT \ln k_r$ (25° C) Kcal/mole	$\Delta F°$ (solv. eff.) (calc'd) Kcal/mole	ΔF_{vdw} Kcal/mole	$\Delta F_{e.s.}$ Kcal/mole	ΔF_c Kcal/mole
1) Heptane	5.241	−0.108	0.729	0.333	0.288
2) Isooctane	5.269	−0.054	0.651	0.330	0.266
3) CCl_4	5.333	−0.079	0.868	0.408	0.380
4) Cy-Hexane	5.324	−0.012	0.723	0.356	0.355
5) Benzene	5.436	0.033	0.794	0.417	0.410
6) Toluene	5.431	0.046	0.798	0.438	0.406
7) Anilin	5.719	0.612	0.881	0.870	0.622
8) n-BuOH	5.697	0.680	0.753	1.076	0.352
9) EtOH	5.803	0.772	0.670	1.123	0.318
10) Nitromethane	5.894	0.860	0.836	1.165	0.530
11) MeOH	6.020	0.814	0.662	1.152	0.323
12) Water	6.327	1.440	0.811	1.205	1.047

We have presented a detailed application of the theory of solvent effects on molecular associations given in Reference 1. The effect of different solvents on the isomerization of azobenzene was treated by the theory. A quantitative estimate of the solvent effects results without the use of any adjustable parameters. In most cases the inverse volume forces and the surface forces both strongly affect the molecular association equilibrium or rate constants. The size of the molecular groups treated in this paper is quite typical of purine and pyrimidine bases as well as amino acid side groups. The association of such groups—crucial in the resulting conformation of bipolymers—is affected by the solvent medium available, in the same ways as in the example above. The solvent effect theory given is applicable to the biopolymers problem and requires mainly macroscopic properties such as surface tension, refractive index, dielectric constant, and the vapor pressure of solvents at a given reduced temperature.

APPENDIX

The energy of interaction, e_{int}, of a solute molecule with the surrounding liquid can be evaluated by using an effective pair potential,[10] $v^{eff}(r)$, that contains corrections to the gas phase potential, in a form:

$$e_{int} = \rho \int_0^\infty v^{eff}(r) g^{(2)}(r) 4\pi r^2 \, dr \qquad \textbf{(A1)}$$

where ρ is the number density of the liquid, $g^{(2)}(r)$ is the radial distribution function for the liquid molecules about a central solute molecule. Considering

$$g^{(2)}(r) = \begin{cases} 0 & \text{for } r < R \\ 1 & \text{for } r \geq R \end{cases} \qquad \textbf{(A2)}$$

where $R = r_1 + r_A$; r_1 and r_A are the radii of the solute and solvent molecules estimated from their molecular volumes. The effective pair potential between two interacting molecules, A and B, in a solvent of C is given in Reference 10 as

$$v^{eff}(r) = C_{AB}\left[\frac{\sigma_{AB}^{6}}{(r - l_{AB})^{12}} - \frac{1}{(r - l_{AB})^{6}}\right] + \frac{\Delta' D_1' L_{AB}'}{n(r - l_{AB})^{6}} \qquad \textbf{(A3)}$$

where C_{AB} is the London coefficient, and is given by:

$$C_{AB} = \frac{27}{32\pi^2} \Delta_{AB} D_A D_B V_A V_B$$

D_A, D_B and Δ_{AB} are given by Equations 8 and 7, respectively. V_A and V_B are the corresponding molecular volumes.

$$\bar{l}_{AB} = (\bar{l}_A + \bar{l}_B)/2; \qquad \bar{\sigma}_{AB} = (\bar{\sigma}_A + \bar{\sigma}_B)/2$$

These are core size parameters, which may be evaluated from the semiempirical relations[10,15]

$$\bar{l}_A = \frac{1}{\beta}\left(\frac{3V_A}{4\pi}\right)^{1/3}\left(\frac{1}{3.24 + 7\bar{\omega}_A}\right)$$

$$\bar{\sigma}_A = \frac{1}{2^{1/6}\beta}\left(\frac{3V_A}{4\pi}\right)^{1/3}\left(\frac{2.24 + 7\bar{\omega}_A}{3.24 + 7\bar{\omega}_A}\right)$$

$\bar{\omega}_A$ is the acentric factor[16] of A. For polar substances, $\bar{\omega}$ should be taken from a nonpolar model compound with similar geometry.

$$\bar{\omega}_A = -\log P_r - 1$$

P_r = reduced vapor pressure, P/P_c of pure liquid A at a reduced temperature of $T/T_c = T_c = 0.7$.

$$\Delta' = \frac{I_C(I_A + I_B + I_C)}{(I_A + I_C)(I_B + I_C)}$$

for solute solvent interactions we have B = C = 1. Thus,

$$\Delta' = \frac{I_A + 2I_1}{2(I_A + I_1)} \quad \textbf{(A4)}$$

$$D_1' = D_1/(1 + D_1)$$

and

$$n = \begin{cases} 3 \text{ for pure liquids, } A = B = C \\ 2 \text{ for solute solvent interaction, } A \neq B = C \\ 1 \text{ for solute-solute interaction in solvent, } A \neq B \neq C \text{ or } A = B \neq C \end{cases}$$

L_{AB}' is a dimensionless function which contains the three-body potential integrated over the discrete solution layers and the volume of the liquid with respect to the position of molecules, C. It is described in a detailed way, in Reference 10.

Combining Equations A1, A2 and A3, we obtain:

$$e_{int} = D_A\, D_1\, \Delta_{1A}\phi \quad \textbf{(A5)}$$

$$\phi = \frac{27}{8}(Q' + Q'')$$

(Compare with Equation 6; subscripts A and 1 refer to the solute and solvent molecules, respectively) with:

$$Q' = V_A \int_R^{\infty} \left(\frac{\bar{\sigma}_{1A}{}^6}{(r - l_{1A})^{12}} - \frac{1}{(r - l_{1A})^6} \right) r^2\, dr \quad \textbf{(A6)}$$

$$Q'' = V_A \int_R^{\infty} \frac{D_1' L_{AB}'}{n(r - l_{1A})^6}\, r^2\, dr$$

REFERENCES

1. SINANOĞLU, O. 1968. Solvent Effects on Molecular Associations. *In* Proc. Internat. Conf. Molec. Assoc. Biol. B. Pullman, Ed. Academic Press. New York, N. Y.
2. HARTLEY, G. S. 1938. J. Chem. Soc. :633.
3. HALPERN, J., G. W. BRADY & C. A. WINKLER. 1950. Canad. J. Res. **28**(B): 140.
4. LE FEVRE, R. J. W. & J. NORTHCOTT. 1953. J. Chem. Soc.: 867.
5. SCHULTE-FROHLINDE, D. Ann. Chem. **612:** 138.
6. ZIMMERMAN, G., L. CHOW & U. PAIK. 1958. J. Amer. Chem. Soc. **80:** 3528.
7. FRANÇOIS, H. 1962. Bull. Soc. Chim.: 506.
8. BULLOCK, D. J. W., C. W. N. CUMPER & A. I. VOGEL. 1965. J. Chem. Soc.: 5316.

9. Halicioğlu, T. & O. Sinanoğlu. To be published.
10. Sinanoğlu, O. 1967. Advan. Chem. Phys. **12:** 283: Chem. Phys. Lett. **1:** 340.
11. Robertson, J. M. 1939., 1941. J. Chem. Soc.: 232: 409.
12. Hartley, G. S. & R. J. W. Le Fevre. 1939. J. Chem. Soc.: 531.
13. Onsager, L. 1936. J. Amer. Chem. Soc. **58:** 1486.
14. Sinanoğlu, O. & S. Abdulnur. 1965. Fed. Proc. **24**(2): S-12.
15. Danon, F. & K. S. Pitzer. 1962. J. Chem. Phys. **36:** 425.
16. Pitzer, K. S. 1955. J. Amer. Chem. Soc. **77:** 3427.

ELECTRONIC ASPECTS OF CATALYSIS OF THE OXYGENASES*

Osamu Hayaishi

Department of Medical Chemistry
Kyoto University, Faculty of Medicine
Kyoto, Japan

Introduction

The term oxygenase refers to a group of enzymes which catalyze the incorporation of molecular oxygen into various organic and inorganic substrates.[1] Two subclasses may be defined according to the following equations:

$$\text{Dioxygenases:} \quad \text{Substrate} + O_2 \rightarrow \text{Substrate } O_2 \qquad (1)$$

$$\text{Monooxygenases:} \quad \text{Substrate} + O_2 + H_2X \rightarrow \text{Substrate } O + H_2O + X \qquad (2)$$

Dioxygenases catalyze the incorporation of both atoms of molecular oxygen into a molecule of substrate, and monooxygenases are responsible for the incorporation of a single atom of oxygen into the substrate—the other oxygen atom being reduced to water in the presence of an electron donor.

For example, tryptophan is known to undergo a variety of metabolic transformations; among them, two most important metabolic pathways are initiated by a dioxygenase and a monooxygenase, respectively. Tryptophan 2, 3-dioxygenase catalyzes the insertion of two atoms of molecular oxygen into the pyrrole moiety of tryptophan forming formylkynurenine as a product. Hence, the enzyme is sometimes referred to as tryptophan pyrrolase. This reaction is the initial step in a metabolic sequence which leads to the biosynthesis of DPN from tryptophan in mammals as well as in microorganisms. It is probably a rate limiting step and a likely site of regulation in this pathway. Tryptophan also serves as a precursor for the biosynthesis of serotonin, a potent vasoconstrictor substance and a neurohumoral agent. The enzyme, tryptophan 5-monooxygenase, which catalyzes the initial step of this metabolic transformation has recently been found and purified from the brain stem of various species of mammals in our laboratory.[2] It catalyzes the insertion of one atom of molecular oxygen to tryptophan forming 5-hydroxytryptophan, which is then decarboxylated to serotonin.

The reaction mechanisms of both dioxygenases and monooxygenases have recently been the subject of intensive studies in our laboratory in Kyoto. In this paper, however, I would like to confine myself to the discussion of some of our recent experiments with highly purified dioxygenases, and to summarize major developments concerning the reaction mechanism of dioxygenases.

The dioxygenases are ubiquitously distributed in nature, and catalyze a wide variety of physiologically important reactions in which molecular oxygen serves either as a biosynthetic or a biodegradative device.[1,3] The metabolic importance of dioxygenases in the transformation of aromatic amino acids and phenolic compounds has been recognized for a long time. More recently,

* This investigation was supported in part by United States Public Health Service Research Grants CA-04222, from the National Cancer Institute; AM-10333, from the National Institute of Arthritis and Metabolic Diseases, National Institutes of Health; and grants from the Jane Coffin Childs Memorial Fund for Medical Research, the Squibb Institute for Medical Research, and the Scientific Research Fund of the Ministry of Education of Japan.

several mammalian dioxygenases have been shown to participate in the biosynthesis of hormones, vitamins and other physiologically active substances. For example, the formation of bile pigments from hemoglobin,[4] the biosynthesis of vitamin A from β-carotene,[5, 6] and the formation of prostaglandins from unsaturated fatty acids[7] are all catalyzed by specific dioxygenases. However, the amount of these enzymes in tissues is rather limited and, therefore, it is usually difficult to obtain mammalian dioxygenases in large quantities. On the other hand, a number of dioxygenases in bacteria are inducible and thus serve as a much better starting material for enzyme studies. In fact, several dioxygenases of microbial origin have been extensively purified, and some of them have recently been crystallized. The experimental results which I shall discuss here are obtained with these highly purified dioxygenase preparations of bacterial origin: the names of these enzymes and some of their properties are given in TABLE 1.

Pyrocatechase, protocatechuate 3,4-dioxygenase and metapyrocatechase are all concerned with cleavage of an aromatic double bond of catechol and related compounds. These three enzymes contain either ferric or ferrous ion as a sole cofactor and, therefore, belong to the so-called non-heme iron proteins. On the other hand, tryptophan 2,3-dioxygenase is a hemoprotein. These enzymes range in molecular weight from 95,000 for pyrocatechase to almost 700,000 for protocatechuate 3,4-dioxygenase; the iron content per mole of enzyme protein also varies from 2 to 8. Interestingly enough, the number of iron atoms present roughly coincides with the number of subunits of the enzyme protein, indicating that each subunit may contain one atom of iron. Since iron (organic or inorganic) is the only constituent of these typical dioxygenases beside enzyme protein, and since iron has been known to combine with or activate molecular oxygen, it seems reasonable to assume that iron is in the active center of these dioxygenases and plays a major role in the catalysis.

In 1964, when I presented a plenary lecture at the Sixth International Congress of Biochemistry in New York, it was proposed that iron in the active center of oxygenases forms a ternary complex with oxygen and organic substrate.[8] Within this ternary complex, both organic substrate and oxygen are activated in some way and react together to form an oxygenated end product. Since that time, intensive studies have been carried out in a number of laboratories and the results seem to be in accord with this hypothesis. However, such a complex has never been isolated nor has it been detected as a discernible entity, and the question of whether the complex formation proceeds in a concerted or a successive manner was left unresolved. In the present paper I would like to consider first the nature of the interaction of iron with organic substrate and second, that of iron with oxygen, and finally to

TABLE 1
SOME PROPERTIES OF MICROBIAL DIOXYGENASES

Enzyme	Cofactor	Molecular Weight	Fe/mole
		$\times 10^3$	
Pyrocatechase	Fe^{3+}	95	2
Protocatechuate 3, 4-dioxygenase	Fe^{3+}	700	7–8
Metapyrocatechase	Fe^{2+}	140	2–3
Tryptophan 2, 3-dioxygenase	Heme	130	2

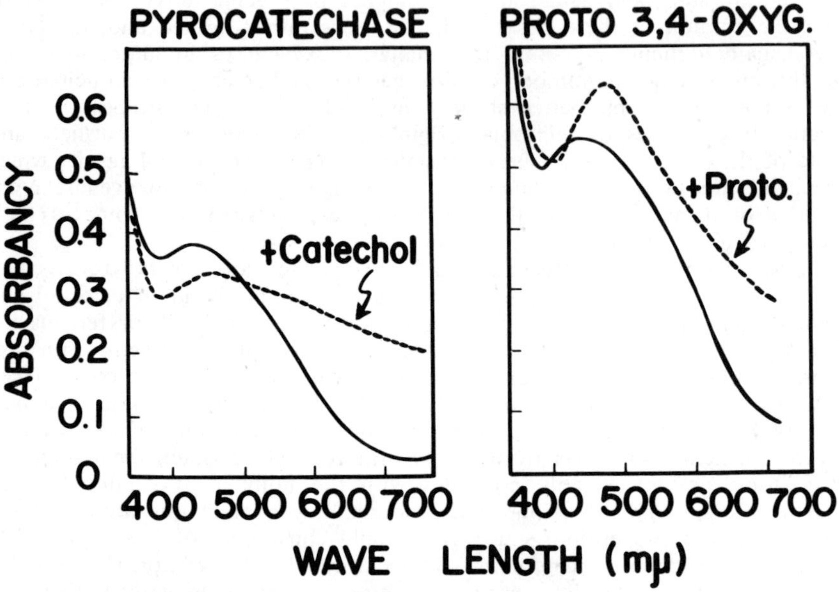

FIGURE 1. Spectra of E-S complex.

discuss recent experimental evidence for the presence of the ternary complex as an intermediate in a dioxygenase reaction.

Pyrocatechase and Protocatechuate 2,3-Dioxygenase

Pyrocatechase is the first dioxygenase to be characterized by experiments with the heavy oxygen isotope.[9] It cleaves catechol in between the two hydroxylated carbon atoms, forming muconic acid as a product (Equation 3).

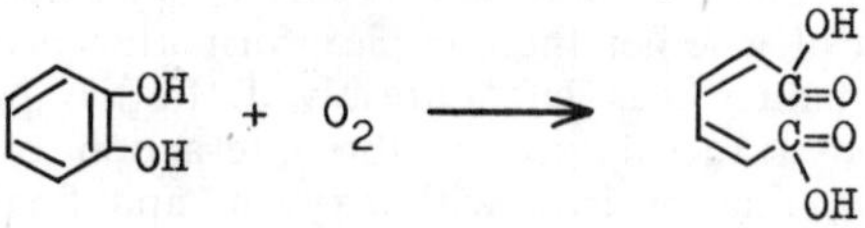

---- (3)

The most purified preparation of pyrocatechase is homogeneous upon ultracentrifugation and electrophoresis, but it has not yet been obtained in a crystalline form.[10]

Protocatechuate 3,4-dioxygenase catalyzes a reaction identical to pyrocatechase except that the substrate is a carboxylated catechol (Equation 4). This enzyme was recently obtained in a crystalline form in our laboratory.[3]

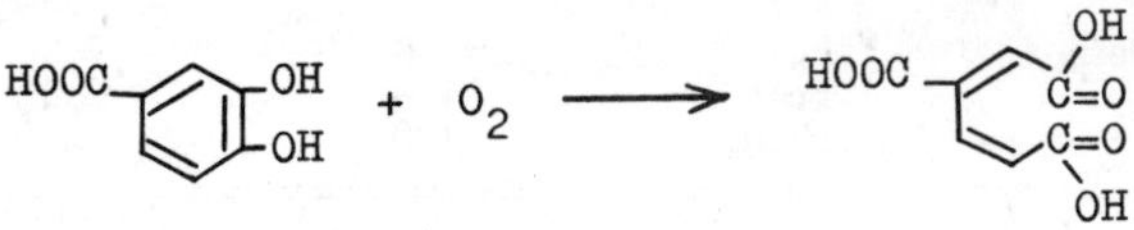

---- (4)

These two enzymes are very similar, not only in their catalytic properties but also in their appearance. Both of them are maroon-red, whereas metapyrocatechase, which will be discussed later, is completely colorless. The spectra of pyrocatechase and protocatechuate 3,4-dioxygenase are shown in FIGURE 1. The solid lines in these figures represent the absorption spectra of these two red enzymes. Although the extinction coefficients are considerably different, the absorbances per atom of iron at 450 mμ are almost identical in both enzymes. Upon the addition of each substrate to the native enzyme under anaerobic conditions, as shown by the dotted lines, the visible absorption spectra of the enzymes showed an increase in absorbance, which by difference spectroscopy expressed itself as a broad peak at around 710 mμ. When oxygen was admitted, no further change of spectra was observed until all the substrate was exhausted; then the spectra were reversed to the original state, and these changes could be observed repeatedly by the alternative addition of catechol and oxygen.[10]

FIGURE 2 shows the ESR spectra of native pyrocatechase. A sharp signal was observed at a g value of 4.2, which was interpreted as due to the presence of trivalent iron in the enzyme preparation. Again, upon the addition of substrate catechol under anaerobic conditions the ESR signal disappeared, but when oxygen was admitted and the substrate was exhausted the ESR signal appeared again. These changes could be observed repeatedly by the alternative addition of oxygen and substrate.[11] Essentially similar results were obtained with protocatechuate 3,4-dioxygenase. Since the color as well as the ESR signal appears to be due to the mode of chelation of ferric ion in the active center to the amino acid residues, the appearance of a new absorption band in the visible range as well as the disappearance of the ESR signal may be attributable to a modification of the ligand structure of the iron caused by its interaction with organic substrate and may well indicate the formation of an enzyme substrate complex. On the other hand, when catechol was not included in the reaction mixture, no significant differences in the optical and ESR spectra were observed in either the absence or presence of oxygen. Although these results do not necessarily prove that these complexes are intimately involved as an integral part of the overall reaction, nor do they establish unequivocally the order of the addition of catechol and oxygen to the active center, it seems reasonable at this point to propose as a working hypothesis that in these dioxygenase reactions the organic substrate combines with the enzyme first to form a binary complex, which subsequently reacts with oxygen to produce an oxygenated end product.

Metapyrocatechase

Metapyrocatechase is the first dioxygenase to be crystallized. Since this enzyme was crystallized in our laboratory in 1963,[12] it has been a favorite subject for investigation of the mechanism of action of dioxygenase. As shown in Equation 5, metapyrocatechase cleaves the bond adjacent to a hydroxyl group of catechol with the incorporation of two atoms of molecular oxygen to form α-hydroxy-muconic semialdehyde.

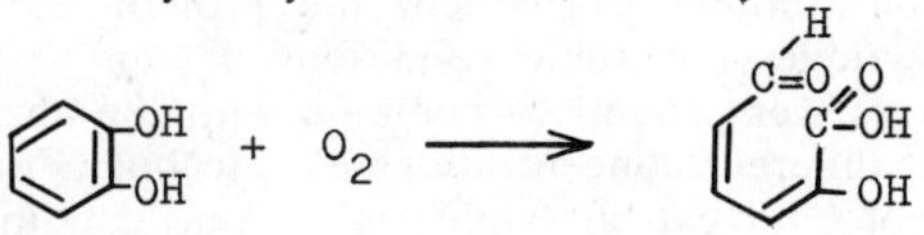

---- (5)

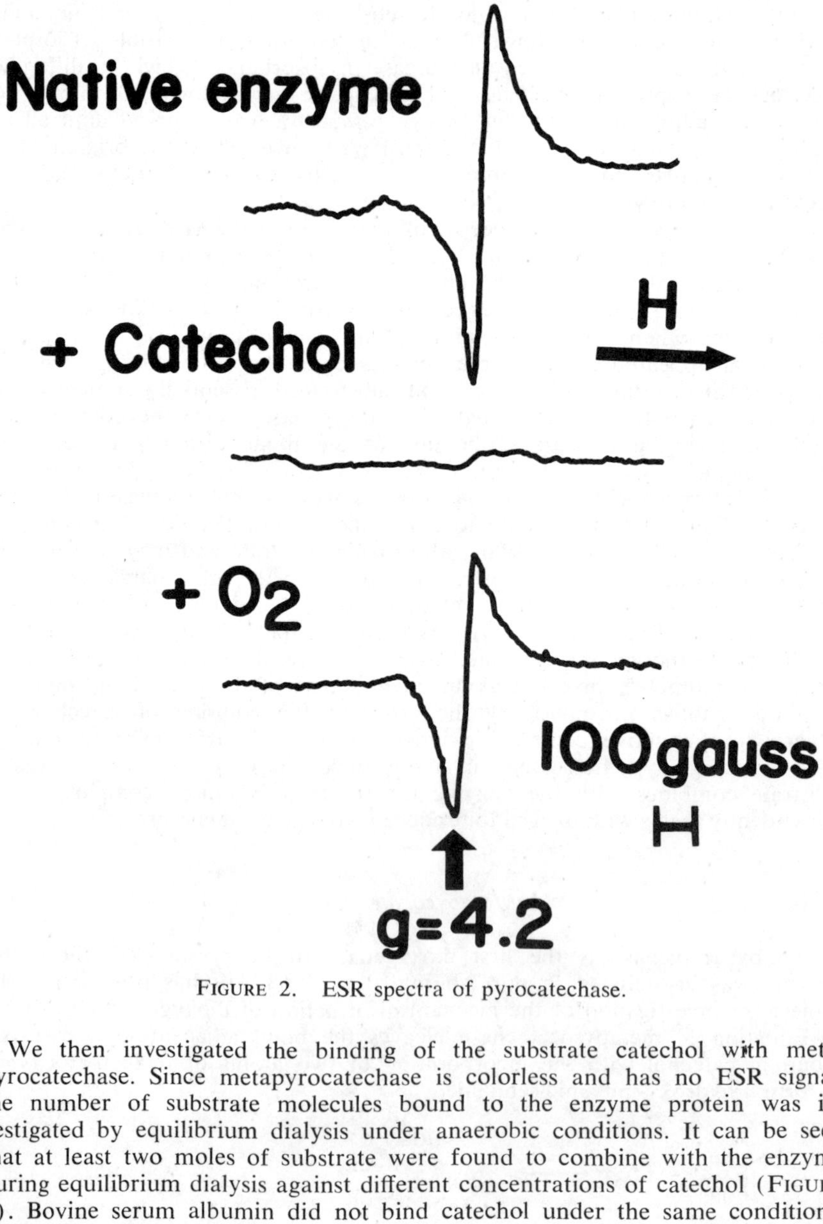

FIGURE 2. ESR spectra of pyrocatechase.

We then investigated the binding of the substrate catechol with metapyrocatechase. Since metapyrocatechase is colorless and has no ESR signal, the number of substrate molecules bound to the enzyme protein was investigated by equilibrium dialysis under anaerobic conditions. It can be seen that at least two moles of substrate were found to combine with the enzyme during equilibrium dialysis against different concentrations of catechol (FIGURE 3). Bovine serum albumin did not bind catechol under the same conditions,

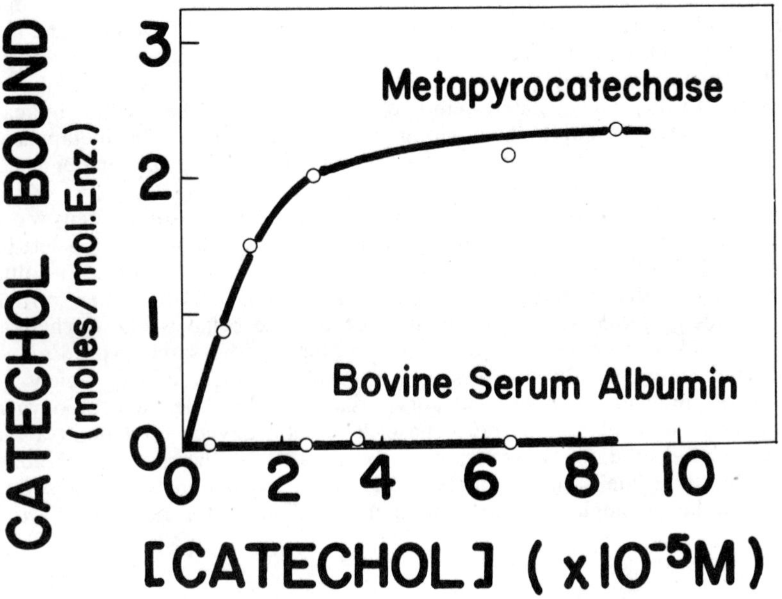

FIGURE 3. Equilibrium dialysis of metapyrocatechase.

indicating that the binding is due to a specific complex formation rather than to nonspecific adsorption. Determination of the N-terminal amino acid revealed that the enzyme contains about two moles of serine per mole of the enzyme, indicating that it consists of at least two peptide chains. Ultracentrifugal and diffusion analyses of the enzyme suggested that the enzyme was dissociated in dilute alkali into two or three subunits. The number of iron atoms in metapyrocatechase thus coincided with the number of subunits and with the number of substrate binding sites. These results could possibly be interpreted to mean that the iron may be related to the substrate binding site. However, this interpretation was shown not to be valid, because when the enzyme preparation was made almost free of iron by oxidation and dialysis, the apoenzyme was still able to bind the same number of substrate as the holoenzyme. Furthermore, the dissociation constant of substrate with the apoenzyme thus determined appears to be in the same order as that of the holoenzyme. These results are interpreted to mean that the presence of iron is not obligatory for the binding of the substrate catechol. Indeed, several lines of evidence that were published previously strongly indicate that these aromatic substrates are held tightly in the hydrophobic crevasse in the enzyme protein.[13]

In contrast to pyrocatechase and protocatechuate 3,4-dioxygenase, the iron in the native metapyrocatechase was shown to be in a divalent state. Since the property of combining reversibly with molecular oxygen is considered to be characteristic of a divalent—rather than a trivalent—state of iron, we then attempted to demonstrate the presence of an oxygenated form of metapyrocatechase.

First, oxyhemoglobin was used as a control. Oxyhemoglobin contains one mole of oxygen per mole of heme. Accordingly, the total oxygen content in an oxyhemoglobin solution which is equilibrated with air at a certain temperature should be the sum of dissolved oxygen and the oxygen bound to the heme. When sufficient quantities of metapyrocatechase and catechol were added to a solution of oxyhemoglobin in a closed system, all the oxyhemoglobin was converted to the deoxygenated hemoglobin as judged by the spectra, indicating that the oxygen bound to hemoglobin can be utilized for the metapyrocatechase reaction. Since the product of the reaction, α-hydroxy-muconic semialdehyde, has a rather high extinction coefficient at 375 mμ ($\epsilon_{375\ m\mu} = 44{,}000$), it is possible to determine the total oxygen content of a solution by sepctrophotometric determination of the product formed. As shown in the left-hand figure of FIGURE 4, the total oxygen content in an oxyhemoglobin solution determined by this method was proportional to the amount of the oxyhemoglobin added. If the oxygenated metapyrocatechase behaves like oxyhemoglobin, it should be possible to demonstrate this by the same procedure. The right-hand figure of FIGURE 4 shows a result of such an experiment. The dotted line indicates a theoretical curve assuming that one mole of oxygen is bound to a mole of metapyrocatechase. The total oxygen content in a metapyrocatechase solution, however, was not parallel to the amount of enzyme added but was the same as that of dissolved oxygen in a buffer solution. Thus, unlike hemoglobin, free metapyrocatechase does not appear to be

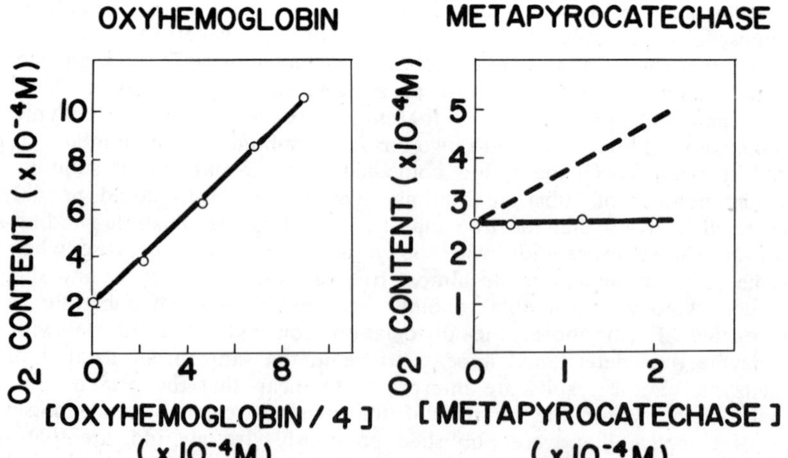

FIGURE 4. Total oxygen content in solutions of oxyhemoglobin and metapyrocatechase.

oxygenated. Further attempts to demonstrate an oxygenated form of the enzyme in the presence of a substrate analogue or a competitive inhibitor such as o-aminophenol, o-phenylene diamine, or metaphenanthroline have also been uniformly unsuccessful.

These experimental results obtained with three non-heme iron-containing dioxygenases, together with other data not discussed here,[13] indicate the following scheme as a tentative hypothetical mechanism of the interaction of organic substrate and oxygen with the enzyme and iron (FIGURE 5).

The organic substrate combines with the enzyme protein to form an enzyme substrate complex irrespective of the valency state of iron. Although the spectral and ESR experiments with pyrocatechase and protocatechuate 3,4-dioxygenase indicate a definite interaction between the substrate and iron, the primary site of this binding does not seem to involve the iron itself. The interaction between iron and organic substrate may either be due to a direct chemical bonding or of indirect nature through an allosteric effect on the protein part.

Since typical dioxygenases contain either organic or inorganic iron, it has been tacitly assumed that oxygen binds with iron and is activated in some way. However, there has been no positive evidence that these dioxygenases bind oxygen in the absence of organic substrate. Perhaps by virtue of the initial binding of the organic substrate with the enzyme, iron becomes accessible to oxygen, which may then be bound to iron and be activated. An alternative hypothesis is that the substrate may be activated in a binary complex, and molecular oxygen, without being activated itself, may simply react with the activated substrate. Although the latter assumption is less likely, the above experiemnts have not provided any positive evidence for the direct interaction of oxygen and iron. We therefore proceeded to investigate the interaction of oxygen and heme of tryptophan 2,3-dioxygenase, because the physicochemistry of oxygenated heme has recently been advanced a great deal and tryptophan 2,3-dioxygenase appears to serve as an excellent material to study this problem.

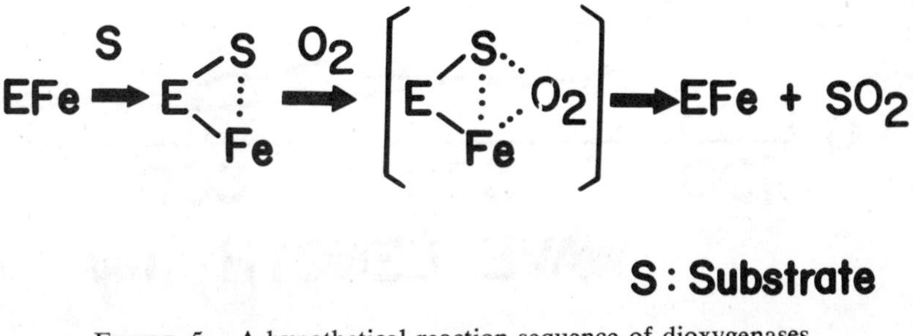

FIGURE 5. A hypothetical reaction sequence of dioxygenases.

Tryptophan 2,3-Dioxygenase

As mentioned previously, this enzyme cleaves the pyrrol moiety of indole ring of tryptophan with the insertion of two atoms of oxygen resulting in the formation of formylkynurenine as a reaction product (Equation 6).

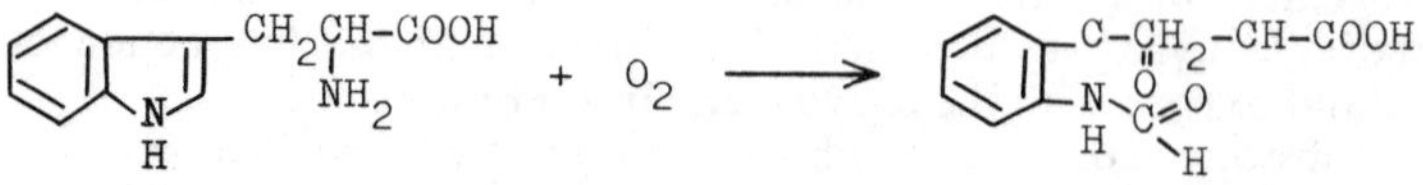

---- (6)

The enzyme has recently been purified from *Pseudomonas* to a state of near homogeneity both in Dr. Feigelson's laboratory and in our laboratory, but it has not yet been obtained in a crystalline form. As FIGURE 6 illustrates, the purified enzyme showed absorption spectra characteristic of a hemoprotein both in its ferric and ferrous states.

It was recently reported by Drs. Maeno and Feigelson, and subsequently confirmed in our laboratory, that when the substrate tryptophan was added either to the ferric or ferrous state of the enzyme under anaerobic conditions,

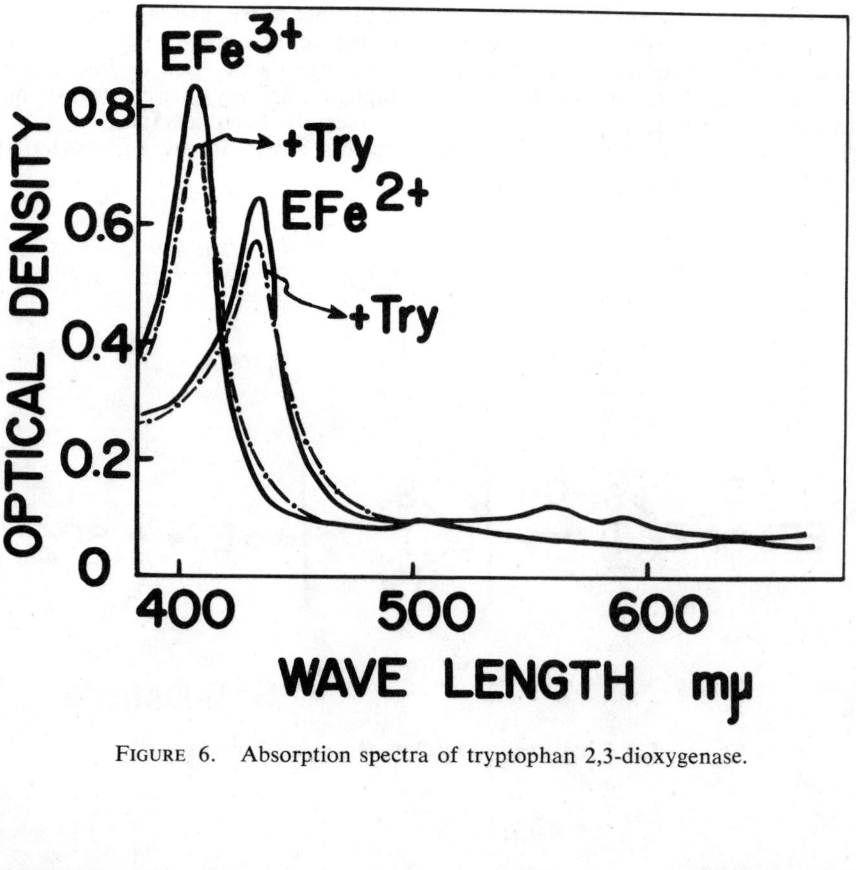

FIGURE 6. Absorption spectra of tryptophan 2,3-dioxygenase.

slight shifts of the Soret band were observed accompanied by some hypochromicity.[14] This observation seems to indicate that tryptophan combines with the enzyme irrespective of the valency state of the heme (FIGURE 6). On the other hand, when tryptophan was not present, these spectra were not altered at all by the presence or absence of oxygen, nor was there any evidence to indicate the existence of an oxygenated state of the heme of tryptophan 2,3-dioxygenase in the absence of the substrate tryptophan. These findings are certainly in good agreement with those observed with non-heme iron containing dioxygenases.

In order to observe whether the binding of substrate has any influence on the reactivity of the heme, the binding of cyanide and CO was first examined. When the amount of cyanide complex was plotted against a minus logarithm of cyanide concentrations in both the presence and absence of tryptophan, the affinity of the ferric enzyme toward cyanide was markedly augmented by the presence of tryptophan; almost a hundredfold difference in affinity was observed, as shown in FIGURE 7. The concentrations required for half-maximal conversion of the ferric enzyme to cyanide complex were 1.5×10^{-6} M and 2.8×10^{-4} M in the presence and absence of tryptophan, respectively. When the affinity of the ferrous enzyme towards carbon monooxide was examined, the concentrations required for half-maximal conversion of ferrous enzyme to CO complex were found to be 5×10^{-6} M and 2.8×10^{-4} M in the presence and absence of tryptophan, respectively. These results certainly indicate that in the presence of tryptophan the state of heme is altered in such a way that the reactivity of heme is greatly increased towards heme binding substances, and suggested the possibility that, in the presence of tryptophan, the existence of an oxygenated state of heme may be demonstrable by close

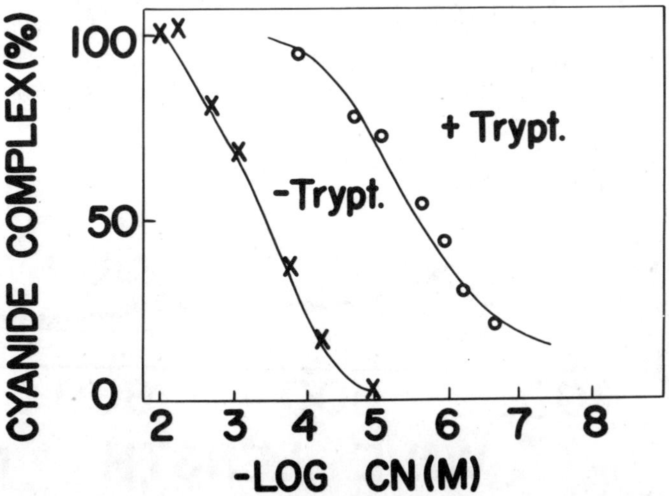

FIGURE 7. Increased affinity toward CN^- in the presence of tryptophan.

examination of its absorption spectra. In collaboration with Drs. Tamura and Yamazaki of Hokkaido University, we then performed a series of experiments in which incubations were carried out at 5° to slow down the rate of the reaction; a special cuvette was used, which enabled us to obtain a continuous supply of oxygen through bubbling without interference in the optical measurements.[15]

As shown in FIGURE 8, when oxygen was bubbled into the mixture of ferrous enzyme and tryptophan, a new spectral species appeared immediately with absorption maxima at 415, 545 and 580 mμ. When the supply of oxygen was discontinued, the spectrum reverted almost instantaneously to the ferrous state; this process could be repeated until all the tryptophan in the system was consumed. With the ferric enzyme in the presence of tryptophan and oxygen, no such spectral changes were observed. However, with ferric enzyme in the presence of ascorbic acid and tryptophan a similar spectral species was observed. It should be emphasized that when oxygen was introduced to the ferrous enzyme in the absence of tryptophan, the spectrum changed very slowly to that of ferric enzyme showing an isosbestic point at about 415 mμ in contrast to the immediate oxygenation in the presence of tryptophan. Thus the formation of this new species is dependent on the simul-

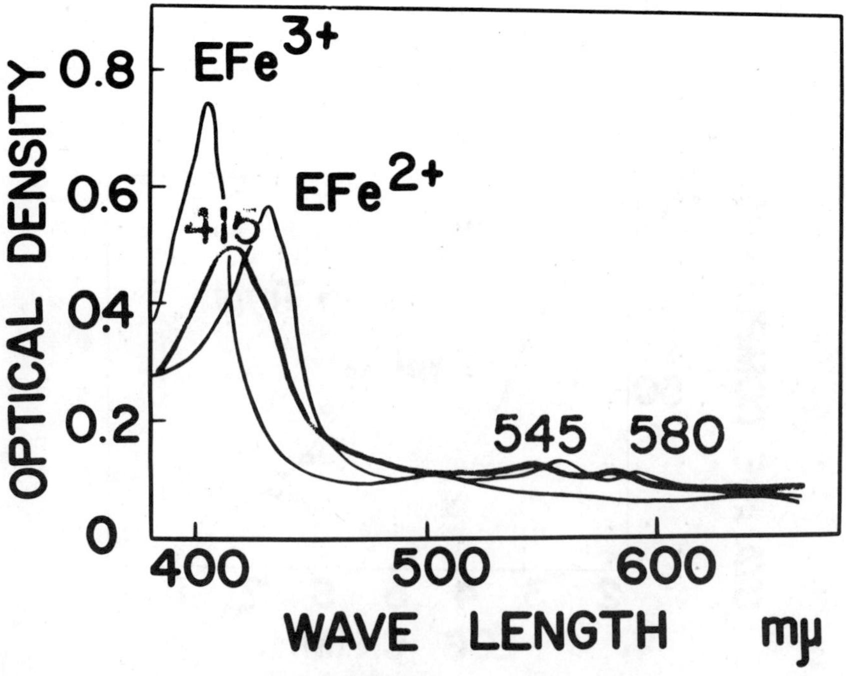

FIGURE 8. A new spectral species during the reaction.

taneous presence of ferrous heme, the substrate tryptophan and oxygen. The absorption maxima of the new species were found to be similar to those of the known oxygenated heme proteins such as hemoglobin, myoglobin and peroxidase, as shown in TABLE 2. It can be seen that the absorption maxima which were observed in the presence of tryptophan and oxygen are very similar to the maxima of α, β and γ bands of oxyhemoglobin, oxymyoglobin or peroxidase compound III, which is believed to be the ferrous oxygenated state of peroxidase. Taken together, these results strongly indicate that only in the presence of tryptophan may the heme coenzyme of tryptophan 2,3-dioxygenase be oxygenated, and that the ternary complex of heme, tryptophan and oxygen could be an intermediate of the catalysis during the tryptophan 2,3-dioxygenase reaction.

In order to establish that this oxygenated form of tryptophan 2,3-dioxygenase is the compulsory intermediate of the overall reaction, kinetic studies were carried out with the use of a flow apparatus, in collaboration with Drs. Yamazaki, Nakamura and Tamura of Hokkaido University. The principle of these experiments is illustrated in FIGURE 9. The ferrous enzyme and tryptophan were placed in one syringe under anaerobic conditions. The other syringe held a buffer solution containing desired amounts of oxygen. These were injected rapidly into a mixing chamber and, by observing the reaction at different wavelengths, the spectra of short-lived intermediates could be recorded within a few milliseconds after mixing.

FIGURE 10 shows that when optical densities thus determined at different wavelength were plotted, a continuous difference spectrum in the entire Soret region was obtained. The absolute spectrum of the intermediate which was reconstructed from this figure and the spectrum of the reduced enzyme is shown in FIGURE 11. It can be seen that when the difference spectrum was superimposed on the spectrum of ferrous enzyme, the reconstructed spectrum is almost identical to that observed in the previous experiments during the continuous supply of oxygen (FIGURE 8), indicating that this spectral species detected by the flow technique is indeed the oxygenated form of enzyme.

Since 433 mμ is the peak of the difference spectrum, the appearance of this oxygenated complex was determined by the change in absorbancy at 433 mμ. The upper curve in FIGURE 12 represents the formation and decomposition of this intermediate, and the lower curve represents the rate of the overall reaction as determined by the formation of formylkynurenine at 321 mμ recorded in a parallel experiment under identical conditions. When the amounts of this complex at different time intervals were plotted against the rate of reaction a linear relationship was obtained, indicating that the complex is the intermediate of the reaction (FIGURE 12).

Although the above experiment was performed with a fixed concentration

TABLE 2
ABSORPTION MAXIMA OF OXYGENATED HEME PROTEINS

	Absorption Maxima (mμ) γ	β	α
Oxyhemoglobin	415	542	576
Oxymyoglobin	418	544	582
Peroxidase compound III	418	546	581
Intermediate of tryptophan pyrrolase	415	545	580

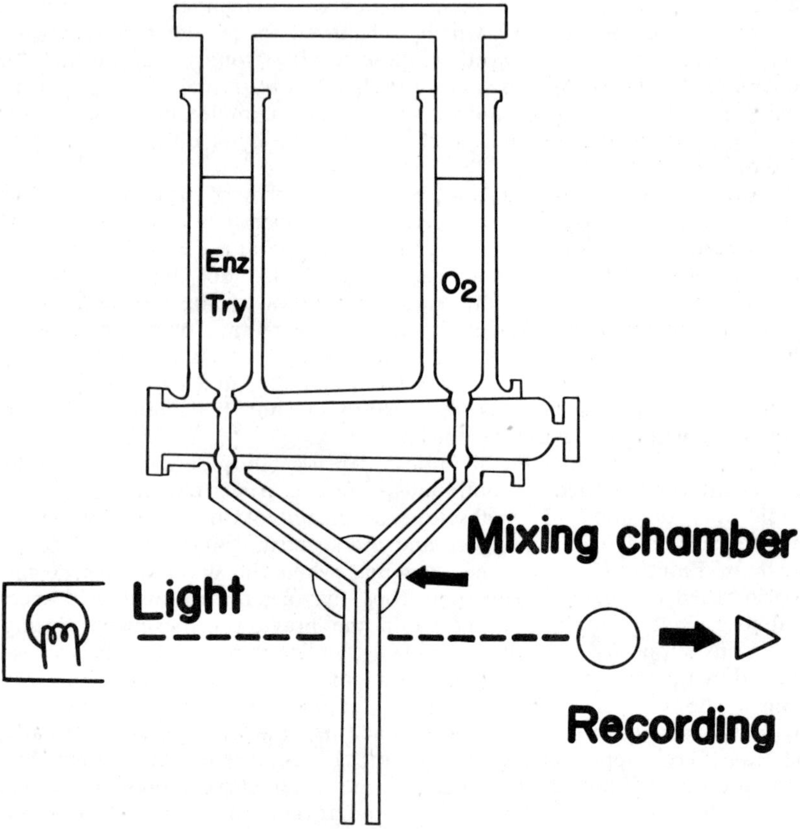

FIGURE 9. Principle of flow method.

of oxygen, FIGURE 13 illustrates the results of experiments in which the concentration of oxygen was varied. The numbers represent concentrations of oxygen expressed in terms of μM concentrations. It should be noted that the area under each curve increased proportionally to the initial concentrations of oxygen. When the amounts of intermediate[16] were plotted against different concentrations of oxygen, a linear relationship was again obtained. The rate constant of the intermediate decomposition computed from these experiments using Chances equation[16] was found to be about 20 per sec, which is in good agreement with the turnover number as determined from the overall reaction. Furthermore, the affinity constant, 5×10^{-5} M for oxygen calculated from these results is in good agreement with the affinity constant of oxygen in the overall reaction as determined by more conventional procedures. These results are consistent with the interpretation that the complex observed is indeed the obligatory intermediate of the overall reaction.

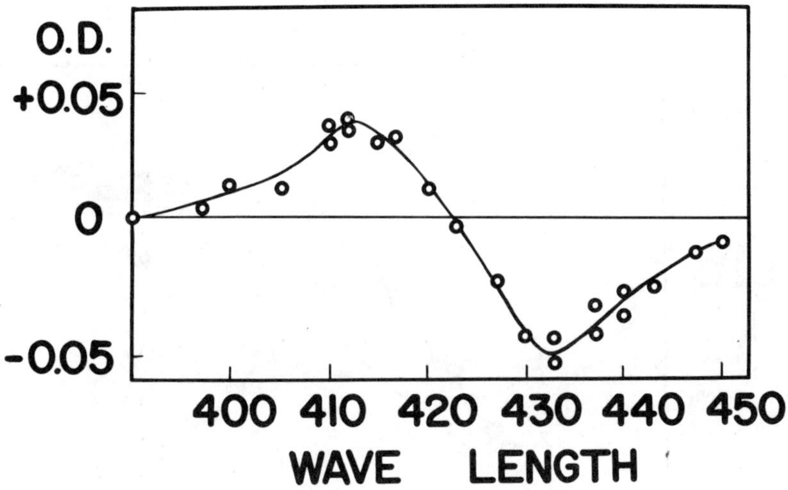

FIGURE 10. Difference spectrum obtained by flow method.

These experimental results are, therefore, consistent with the reaction sequence which is shown in FIGURE 14. First, the organic substrate tryptophan combines with the enzyme, which may evoke a conformational change of the enzyme protein and the increase of the reactivity of the heme moiety. The oxygen molecule is then bound to the heme to form a ternary complex of tryptophan, heme and oxygen. Within this ternary complex, oxygen is presumably activated and reacts with the substrate to form an oxygenated product. The only enzymatically active species of oxygenated heme so far known is compound III of peroxidase, in which case ferrous ion in the heme is oxygenated in the absence of its organic substrate. By way of contrast, in the case of tryptophan 2,3-dioxygenase, the organic substrate is necessary in order to form an oxygenated intermediate. It is not clear, however, whether this first reaction of tryptophan with the enzyme is at the site which is involved in the catalysis or whether this is due to the combination of tryptophan with some other site of the enzyme. In fact, there is some evidence from Dr. Feigelson's laboratory[17] and my own as well that the first combination of tryptophan with the enzyme is not on the active site but rather on the allosteric site of this enzyme.

These experimental observations with tryptophan 2,3-dioxygenase provide further evidence to support the hypothetical reaction mechanism which was proposed on the basis of experimental findings with the non-heme iron containing dioxygenases; in addition, they clearly establish that a ternary complex of iron, oxygen and organic substrate is formed as an intermediate of a dioxygenase reaction. Although it may still be premature to propose a generalized reaction mechanism, the scheme depicted in FIGURE 14 may be

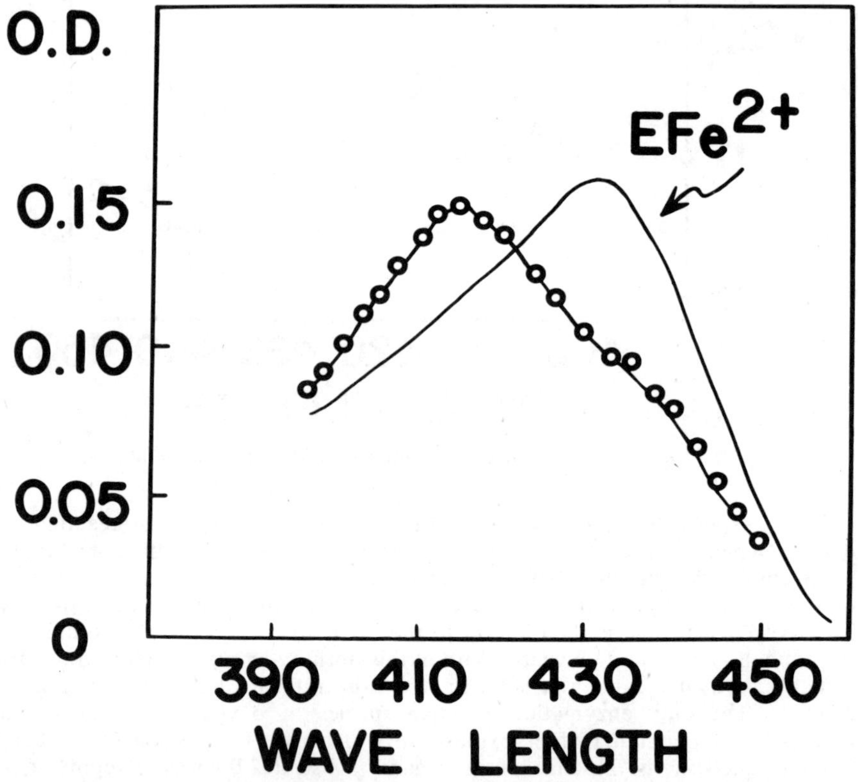

FIGURE 11. Reconstructed spectrum of the initial intermediate.

applicable to other dioxygenases as well. The exact physicochemical characterization of the electronic state of heme, oxygen and tryptophan in this ternary complex and, in particular, the nature of "active oxygen" remain questions to be answered.

Recent studies from a number of laboratories indicated that the oxygenation reaction of hemoglobin, myoglobin and peroxidase involves partial migration of an electron from the ferrous heme iron to the oxygen molecule. Dr. Peisach for example, presented a detailed study concerning the electronic structure of oxyhemoglobin.[18] If an analogy is permitted, the oxygenated heme in tryptophan pyrrolase may be written as shown in FIGURE 15. The activated species of oxygen in this case resembles that proposed by us about three years ago for the non-heme iron containing dioxygenase.[8] On the

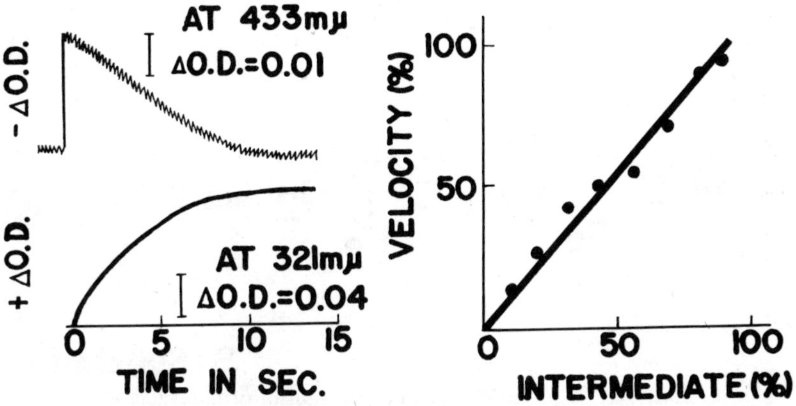

FIGURE 12. Stopped flow analysis of the intermediate.

other hand, the exact role of tryptophan and its electronic state have not yet been understood. Further studies on the role of tryptophan and the physicochemical characterization of the state of iron, oxygen and tryptophan in the complex are currently in progress in our laboratory, and are expected to contribute much to the understanding of the general mechanism of dioxygenase reactions.

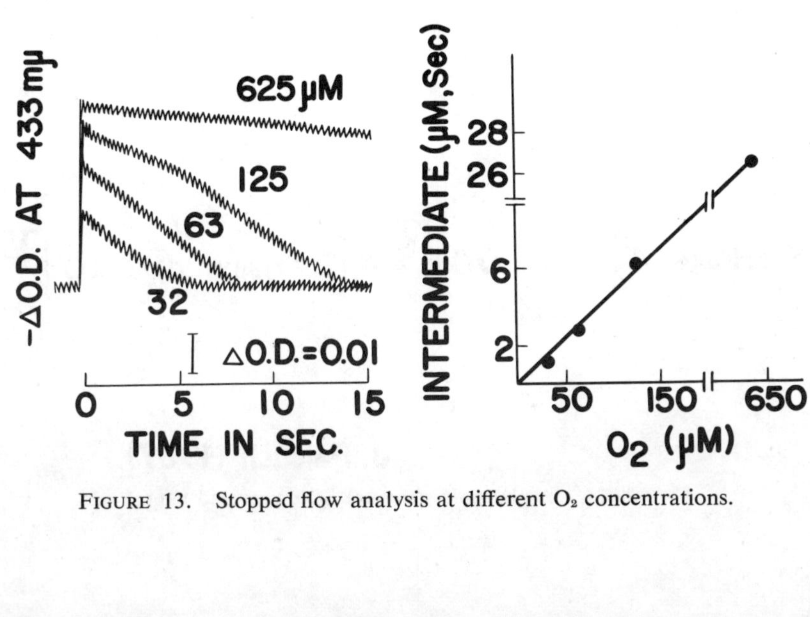

FIGURE 13. Stopped flow analysis at different O_2 concentrations.

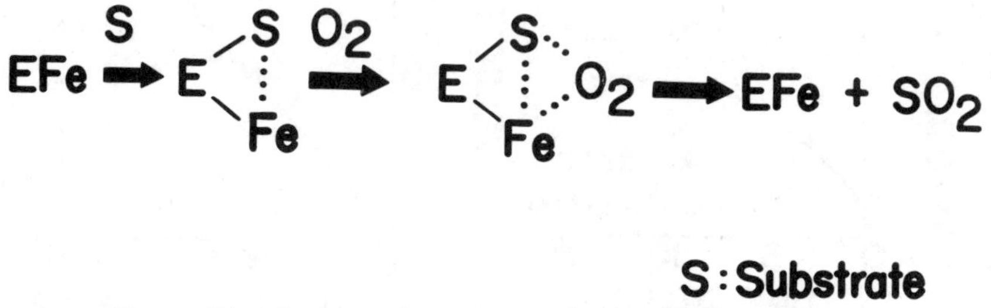

FIGURE 14. A proposed reaction mechanism of dioxygenases.

Acknowledgments

I am indebted to Professor I. Yamazaki for invaluable advice and collaboration during the course of experiments concerning tryptophan 2,3-dioxygenase, and for his criticism during the preparation of this manuscript. A number of experiments with tryptophan 2,3-dioxygenase have been carried out in collaboration with Drs. I. Yamazaki, T. Nakamura and M. Tamura in the Laboratory of Biophysics Division, Research Institute of Applied Electricity, Hokkaido University. Experiments reported in this paper have been performed in collaboration with Drs. M. Nozaki, Y. Kojima, Y. Ishimura, T. Nakazawa and H. Fujisawa. I would like to express most sincere thanks to Drs. P. Feigelson and B. Wittenberg for many stimulating discussions during the course of this work, and to Dr. J. Peisach for making available to us his unpublished manuscript.

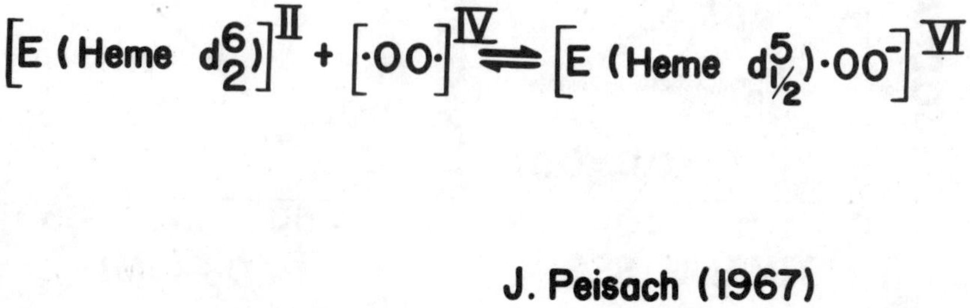

FIGURE 15. A plausible structure of oxygenated heme.

References

1. HAYAISHI, O. 1962. History and scope. *In* Oxygenases. O. Hayaishi, Ed.: 1–29. Academic Press. New York, N. Y.
2. NAKAMURA, S., A. ICHIYAMA & O. HAYAISHI. 1965. Purification and properties of tryptophan hydroxylase in brain. Fed. Proc. **24:** 604.
3. HAYAISHI, O. 1966. Crystalline oxygenases of pseudomonads. Bact. Rev. **30:** 720–731.
4. NAKAJIMA, H. 1963. Studies on heme α-methenyl oxygenase. II. The isolation and characterization of the final reaction product, a possible precursor of biliverdin. J. Biol. Chem. **238:** 3797–3801.
5. OLSON, J. A. & O. HAYAISHI. 1965. The enzymatic cleavage of β-carotene into vitamin A by soluble enzymes of rat liver and intestine. Proc. Nat. Acad. Sci. **54:** 1364–1370.
6. GOODMAN, D. S., H. S. HUANG, M. KANAI & T. SHIRATORI. 1967. The enzymatic conversion of all-*trans* β-carotene into retinal. J. Biol. Chem. **242:** 3543–3554.
7. BERGSTRÖM, S. 1967. Prostaglandins: members of a new hormonal system. Science **157:** 382–391.
8. HAYAISHI, O. 1964. Oxygenases. Proc. Plen. Sess. Sixth Internat. Cong. Biochem.: 31–43. New York, N. Y.
9. HAYAISHI, O., M. KATAGIRI & S. ROTHBERG. 1955. Mechanism of the pyrocatechase reaction. J. Amer. Chem. Soc. **77:** 5450–5451.
10. KOJIMA, Y., H. FUJISAWA, A. NAKAZAWA, T. NAKAZAWA, F. KANETSUNA, H. TANIUCHI, M. NOZAKI & O. HAYAISHI. 1967. Studies on pyrocatechase. I. Purification and spectral properties. J. Biol. Chem. **242:** 3270–3278.
11. NAKAZAWA, T., Y. KOJIMA, H. FUJISAWA, M. NOZAKI & O. HAYAISHI. 1965. Studies on the mechanism of action of pyrocatechase by electron spin resonance spectroscopy. J. Biol. Chem. **240:** PC3224–PC3226.
12. NOZAKI, M., H. KAGAMIYAMA & O. HAYAISHI. 1963. Metapyrocatechase. I. Purification, crystallization and some properties. Biochem. Z. **338:** 582–590.
13. NOZAKI, M., Y. KOJIMA, T. NAKAZAWA, H. FUJISAWA, K. ONO, S. KOTANI, O. HAYAISHI & T. YAMANO. 1966. Studies on the reaction mechanism of dioxygenases. *In* Biological and Chemical Aspects of Oxygenases. K. Bloch & O. Hayaishi, Eds.: 347–367. Maruzen Company. Tokyo, Japan.
14. MAENO, H. &. P. FEIGELSON. 1967. Spectral studies on the catalytic mechanism and activation of *Pseudomonas* tryptophan oxygensae (tryptophan pyrrolase). J. Biol. Chem. **242:** 596–601.
15. ISHIMURA, Y., M. NOZAKI, O. HAYAISHI, M. TAMURA & I. YAMAZAKI. 1967. Evidence for an oxygenated intermediate in the tryptophan pyrrolase reaction. J. Biol. Chem. **242:** 2574–2576.
16. CHANCE, B. 1943. The kinetics of the enzyme-substrate compound of peroxidase. J. Biol. Chem. **151:** 553–577.
17. FEIGELSON, P. & H. MAENO. 1967. Studies on enzyme-substrate interactions in the regulation of tryptophan oxygenase activity. Biochem. Biophys. Res. Commun. **28:** 289–293.
18. PEISACH, J. 1969. A proposed mechanism for subunit interaction in hemoglobin. This monograph.

ELECTRON-NUCLEAR AND ELECTRON-ELECTRON SPIN INTERACTIONS IN THE STUDY OF ENZYME STRUCTURE AND FUNCTION*

Helmut Beinert and William H. Orme-Johnson
Institute for Enzyme Research, University of Wisconsin, Madison, Wis.

Introduction

The past decades have witnessed an astounding development in the area generally referred to as biological chemistry, a development in volume and in depth. An increasing number of colleagues trained in the more basic physical sciences feel the challenge to apply concepts and theory which have proven their value in the long established areas of chemistry to problems of the new biological branch. However, there have been and still are serious obstacles to communication across boundaries of traditionally separated disciplines. The most serious are probably the difference in language and the very characteristics of the objects of investigation—biological substances. They are often not easily available, hard to reproduce, poorly defined and so bulky that any intrinsic specific property that one may want to investigate is diluted out by the bulk of the material with which it is by necessity associated. We see, therefore, at least one of the missions of the biochemists represented herein in presenting examples to our theoretically oriented colleagues, where macromolecular substances have been brought to a state of definition so that theory, albeit in simple form, has led to unique and decisive answers.

Nuclear Hyperfine Interaction (hfs) in EPR of Biological Macromolecules

General Considerations

In accord with our field of interest, we propose to choose these examples from electron paramagnetic resonance (EPR) studies of metal proteins carried out in several laboratories including our own.

Initially, the fact that resonances could be observed at all in biological materials was of interest; since then more sophisticated approaches have been attempted and applied. Among these are rapid reaction methods[1, 2] and combined optical and EPR observation techniques.[3-5] Hyperfine interactions of the unpaired electrons, either with nuclei naturally present or after substitution of suitable isotopes, have been observed and successfully exploited in favorable instances.[6-11] Spin relaxation properties of unpaired electrons, either naturally present[12-14] or artificially introduced in macromolecules,[15] have been studied.

We will first and mainly consider electron-nuclear hyperfine interactions (hfs). They originate from the local magnetic fields created by the nuclear spins which are forced to orient themselves in the external magnetic field ap-

* The experimental work from our own laboratory discussed here was supported by the National Institutes of Health, Grant GM-12394, by a Public Health Service Research Career Award (GM-KG-12, 442) to Helmut Beinert, and a Public Health Service Career Development Award (K3-GM-10236) to W. H. Orme-Johnson, both from the Institute of General Medical Sciences.

plied in the EPR experiment. These local fields lead to a splitting of the EPR lines, the size of which depends on the nuclear magnetic moment and the strength of the interaction (coupling). The number of lines is determined by the spin of the nucleus and the number of interacting nuclei. The number of lines produced from equivalent nuclei equals $2nI + 1$, where n is the number of nuclei interacting with an unpaired electron and I is the nuclear spin in multiples of $h/2\pi$.

The study of the hyperfine interaction of nuclei of nonzero spin with unpaired electrons is a well-established technique of structural organic chemistry.[16] Organic free radicals give complex EPR signals that can be explained in terms of Fermi contact interaction between the unpaired electron and nuclei of hydrogen, carbon, and nitrogen isotopes in the molecule. An example of this sort of study which is of interest to biochemists is the investigation by Ehrenberg and his collaborators[10] of the hfs of flavin semiquinone signals at room temperature. From these well-resolved spectra, the distribution of unpaired spin density over the tricyclic aromatic isoalloxazine nucleus can be determined.

The extension of this type of study to macromolecular systems has been hindered by the fact, successfully exploited by McConnell and coworkers in the spin-labeling technique,[15] that attachment of a spin system to a macromolecule restricts the rapid tumbling required to average out anisotropic interactions. The resulting broadened spectra have not exhibited the resolved hfs needed for the type of work so successful on low molecular weight organic radicals.

In addition to this, many studies on biochemical materials are conducted at low temperatures in the frozen state for reasons of instrument sensitivity, relaxation rates, or in order to fix intermediate reaction states in kinetic studies. The result is, of course, additional restriction on the tumbling of paramagnetic species. Only the envelope of the hfs is seen in these situations. Nevertheless, changes of line width may remain as a useful measurable parameter.

The nuclei of principal interest in biological materials, and their spin and magnetic moments, are listed in TABLE 1. Since the most abundant natural isotopes of C, O, S, Mg, Ca, Fe, and Mo lack a nuclear spin, replacement with suitable isotopes (see TABLE 1) is necessary to observe hfs. In other instances, when a nucleus such as H^1 or N^{14} does produce hfs, and an isotope is available (D or N^{15}) that has a sufficiently different nuclear spin and magnetic moment, replacement by this isotope and observation of ensuing changes in hfs can help to identify the origin of the hfs.

Nature of the Light-Induced Resonance in Photosynthetic Materials

One of the oldest observations in the brief history of EPR applications to biological materials is that when light shines on a photosynthetic material such as algae or photosynthetic bacteria, a resonance typical of free radicals can be detected.[17, 18] The origin of this resonance has been the matter of much experimentation and speculation. Even at low temperature, this signal appears very rapidly. It has, therefore, been considered likely that it stems from an unpaired electron at or near the site of the primary photoact.

An attack on this problem became feasible when methods for the growth of algae and bacteria on deuterated media had been elaborated, so that almost complete replacement of hydrogen by deuterium could be effected.[19] I_H is $\frac{1}{2}$, I_D is 1, and the

TABLE 1
ISOTOPES OF ELEMENTS OF POTENTIAL INTEREST IN BIOLOGICAL EPR WORK

Isotope Non-metals	Abundance %	Spin I $\frac{h}{2\pi}$	Magnetic Moment μ Magnetons	Isotope	Abundance %	Spin I $\frac{h}{2\pi}$	Magnetic Moment μ Magnetons
H^{1}	99, 984	1/2	2.793	H^{2}	0.016	1	0.857
C^{12}	98.892	0	0	C^{13}	1.108	1/2	0.702
N^{14}	99.635	1	0.404	N^{15}	0.365	1/2	−0.283
O^{16}	99.76	0	0	O^{17}	0.037	5/2	−1.893
F^{19}	100.	1/2	2.627				
P^{31}	100.	1/2	1.131				
S^{32}	95.06	0	0	S^{33}	0.74	3/2	0.643
Cl^{35}	75.4	3/2	0.821	Cl^{37}	24.6	3/2	0.683
I^{127}	100.	5/2	2.794				
metals							
Na^{23}	100.	3/2	2.216				
Mg^{24}	78.6	0	0	Mg^{25}	10.05	5/2	−0.855
K^{39}	93.08	3/2	0.391	K^{41}	6.91	3/2	0.215
Ca^{4}_{0}	96.92	0	0	Ca^{43}	0.13	7/2	−1.315
V^{51}	100.	7/2	5.139				
Mn^{55}	100.	5/2	3.461				
Fe^{56}	91.52	0	0	Fe^{57}	2.245	1/2	0.090
Co^{59}	100.	7/2	4.639				
Cu^{63}	69.09	3/2	2.221	Cu^{65}	30.91	3/2	2.379
$_{64,66}$							
Zn^{68}	95.20		0	Zn^{67}	4.12	5/2	0.874
$_{92,94}$		0					
$_{96,98}$							
Mo^{100}	75.2	0	0	Mo^{95}	15.78	5/2	−0.910

nuclear moments are 2.792 and 0.857 nuclear magnetons, respectively. Hfs from one H should produce 2 lines and from one D, 3 lines, with $\frac{1}{2}/2.792 \times 0.857/1 = 0.153$ times the splitting between individual lines.

When algae and bacteria were grown in deuterated media, a decrease in line width by a factor of 2–3 of the light-induced resonance (FIGURE 1) was indeed achieved.[6] Theoretically, this factor should be 4. Replacement of exchangeable protons only produced no change in line width. It was, therefore, concluded that the hydrogens producing the hfs must be bound to carbon. Consideration of the g value of the resonance ($g = 2.002$), which is very close to that of the free electron, the absence of major anisotropy and any effect of substitution by N^{15}, and the distinct line sharpening on deuterium substitution led to the conclusion that the unpaired electron observed in the resonance was not likely to be near a heavy metal, nitrogen or sulfur atom. It may be recalled that iron and sulfur in ferredoxins, iron in cytochromes, copper in plastocyanin, and manganese in an unknown structure, are components of the photosynthetic system.

The observed hyperfine effect suggested[6] that "the wave function of the unpaired electron does not extend over more than a few hundred atoms as it would if it were in a conduction band of a semiconducting region of appreciable extent." This latter conclusion is of interest since aggregates of chlorophyll molecules may have the properties of semiconductors, and it had been suggested that the resonance observed on illumination might be attributable to conduction electrons.[20]

It was also possible with the narrowed resonance of deuterium-grown bacteria to resolve an otherwise overlapping weaker signal.[6] Thus, the struc-

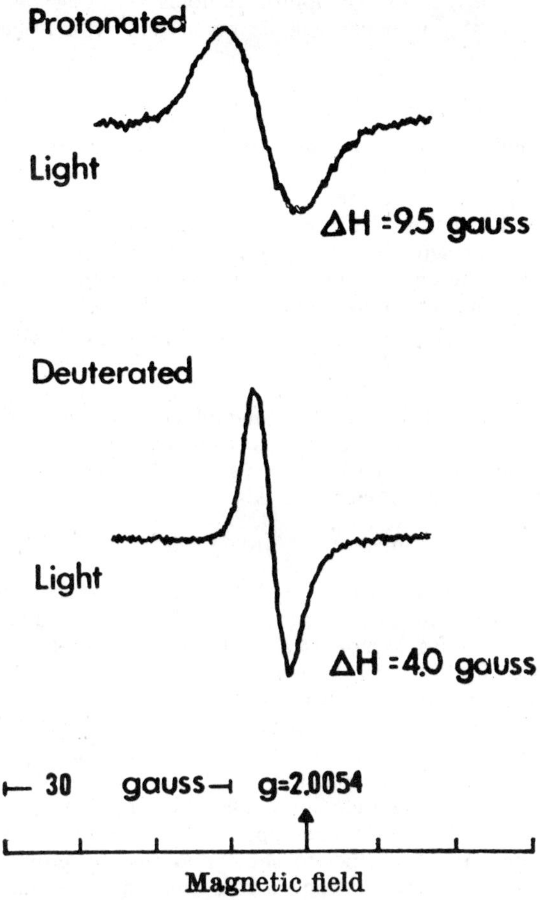

FIGURE 1. Influence of growth in totally deuterated medium on the dominant electron-spin resonance response (signal I) in the light. The effect of deuterium substitution is shown for *Rhodospirillum rubrum,* a purple non-sulfur bacterium. The spectra were recorded at 16° C. The line width, measured peak to peak of the derivative spectrum, narrows by a factor of 2.4 as a result of deuterium substitution. A low modulation amplitude, 0.75–1G (gauss), was used in each case. (From Kohl, *et al.,* Reference 6.)

tures of both signals (so-called signals I and II) could be studied. Analysis of the resonance at two different microwave frequencies by Mauzerall and collaborators[21] confirmed the line width effect previously observed. Analogous effects were observed with porphyrin model compounds. These authors found that the rise and decay time of the light-induced signal in *Rhodospirillum rubrum* increased only twofold between 1.3 and 80° K. On the basis of this small temperature coefficient, the authors suggest that the free radical is formed and decays by an electron tunneling process.

The example briefly discussed above still remains the classical example in which hfs, or at least its consequences, could be usefully studied and its effects exploited in material as crude as whole cells. Most of the conclusions are admittedly tentative, but the approach holds challenge as well as promise. The remainder of this paper will be concerned with isolated proteins of high purity.

Environment of Molybdenum in Xanthine Oxidase

Despite this statement, the means of incorporating a suitable isotope may take us far into the realm of biology. This certainly applies to the next example we wish to present, which is concerned with the elucidation of the molybdenum site of the enzyme xanthine oxidase.[22] In this case, a cow was injected with Mo^{95} and the milk containing the labeled enzyme collected.[23] The enzyme is widely found in animals—in liver and in milk—in birds, in insects, and in microorganisms.

It contains flavinadeninedinucleotide, molybdenum and iron in a molecule of a weight of approximately 300,000. Part of the molybdenum can be detected by EPR as Mo(V) when the enzyme has accepted electrons from the substrate. The kinetics of intramolecular electron transfer have been studied by rapid reaction methods,[24,25] and it appears that the path of electrons is:

$$\text{Substrate} \longrightarrow \text{Mo} \longrightarrow \text{Flavin}$$

Normally, the Mo(V) signal observed shows the hfs expected for the mixture of isotopes present in natural abundance, of which 25% have a nuclear spin of 5/2, namely six lines symmetrically disposed around the principal absorption, each showing 5% of the intensity of the main line. It was only with considerable effort that this hfs was detected in unlabeled xanthine oxidase as well as in the related enzyme aldehyde oxidase,[26, 27] proving that the observed signal was indeed due to Mo. However, in addition to the expected anisotropy the Mo signals showed additional structure in the principal lines, which first appeared to preclude an explanation of the spectrum in terms of a single species of Mo. Two lines appeared where one line was expected. Bray and his colleagues were able to show that this structure collapses when deuterium is substituted for hydrogen.[25] In this case, exchangeable protons were involved. The resolution of the lines achieved by Bray and his colleagues by labeling with Mo^{95} and D is seen in FIGURE 2. Rapid reaction experiments showed that when 8-deuteroxanthine was supplied to the enzyme, a deuterium type Mo spectrum was observed at early reaction times, which changed to the hydrogen type with a half time of 100–200 milliseconds at 20° C.[28] This indicates that hydrogen from the 8- position in the substrate finds its way quickly to the site where it is "seen" by Mo. The point at which this hydrogen is bound has not been established. Bray and Knowles, arguing that the hydrogen transferred rapidly from the substrate must have located itself at a reducible site in the enzyme, suggest that it is located at the flavin while interacting with Mo. As will be discussed later, electron spin relaxation of the flavin semiquinones in metal flavoproteins has been found to be more efficient, in some cases by orders of magnitude, than in metal-free flavoproteins,[12, 14, 29] thus providing independent evidence for metal-flavin interaction in these complex enzymes. It has now been shown, however, that xanthine oxidase from which the flavin component has been removed is still reduced by substrate with appearance of the Mo signal and proton hfs. Therefore, the proton cannot be located on the flavin.

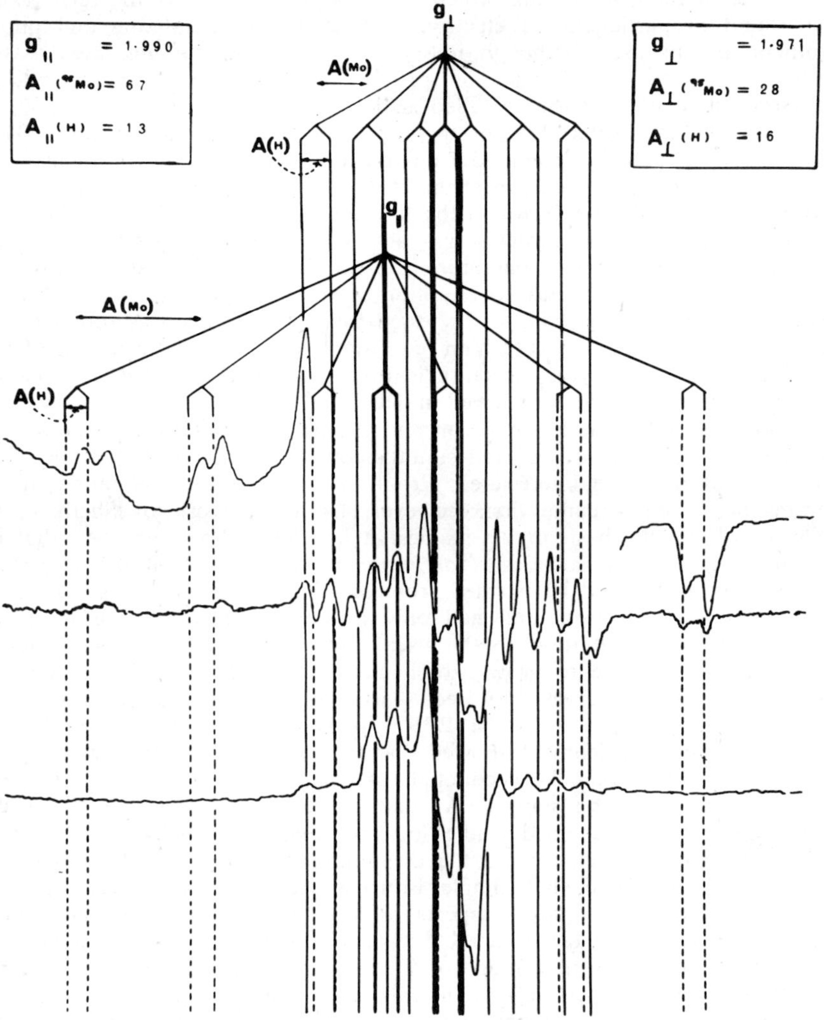

FIGURE 2. EPR signal from xanthine oxidase: bottom trace: normal enzyme; center trace: Mo^{95} enzyme; upper trace: Mo^{95} enzyme run at higher gain and modulation (center of trace omitted). The enzyme at pH 10 was reduced with formaldehyde for 1 min. Signals recorded at $-150°$. (From Bray and Meriwether. Reference 23).

Structure of the Iron Site in Iron-Sulfur (Non-Heme Iron) Proteins

In attempts to dissect the electron transfer system of mitochondria, careful analytical work revealed that the iron content of the fractions obtained exceeded the heme content several fold.[30] It was shown that much of this non-heme iron was not due to adventitiously bound iron.[31] At about the same time, several nonmitochondrial enzymes, including xanthine oxidase, aldehyde oxidase, and dihydroorotate dehydrogenase, were shown to contain iron bound to the protein in the absence of a porphyrin ring, and a few years later, a class of proteins which contains non-heme iron, the ferredoxins, was found to participate in electron transfer in nitrogen-fixing and photosynthetic organisms.[32] Although initially a relationship among these classes of non-heme iron proteins was not apparent, the first property common to all was soon discovered in the so-called acid labile sulfur or labile sulfide (32), which is readily displaced from these proteins on mild acidification. Then flavin-free iron proteins prepared from the non-heme iron flavoproteins were shown to have an optical spectrum very similar to the plant-type ferredoxins,[33] and finally it was found that the typical EPR spectrum of the mitochondrial and iron flavoproteins was also shown by the ferredoxins at sufficiently low observation temperature (20–50° K).[34, 35] This signal, which is seen after chemical reduction or addition of substrate, is characterized by the g values, $g = 2$ and $g = 1.94$. In tested cases, this signal was found to appear and dissappear in a fashion consistent with a kinetically significant function of the underlying structure in these enzymes.[24, 27, 36–38] The matters sketched in here have been reviewed in detail.[5, 39]

As in all instances non-heme iron and the paramagnetic center responsible for the $g = 1.94$ signal occurred simultaneously, it was widely assumed that the two features were interrelated. Proof that iron atoms are bound in the paramagnetic center came first, however, from the work of Shethna and colleagues,[40] on the basis of hfs studies. It had been shown earlier[41] that nitrogen-fixing bacteria, such as *Azotobacter vinelandii,* exhibit the $g = 1.94$ signal. A protein could be isolated from azotobacter that exhibited the $g = 1.94$ signal on reduction, and had only iron and acid labile sulfur as detectable entities in addition to the usual protein constitutents. Shethna and coworkers[40] were able to grow azotobacter on a medium in which the natural isotope of iron, Fe^{56}, had been partically replaced with Fe^{57} (nuclear spin, ½). A comparison of the EPR signals from proteins prepared with and without Fe^{57} enrichment showed that the enriched protein gave a broadened signal which could be accounted for by assuming a 22 gauss hfs from the Fe^{57} nuclei in the sample. At that time, the low ($\sim$ 60–70%) enrichment achieved precluded studies on how many Fe nuclei were involved in the paramagnetic center, and the assumption was made in the calculation of the expected signal that simple isotropic hyperfine interaction operated on *one* nucleus. Quantitative aspects aside, the importance of the experiment lay rather in the fact that the broadening of the EPR signal could only come from the higher percentage of $I = ½$ nuclei in the enriched sample. This established the fact, at least in this case, that iron, and therefore non-heme iron, was part of the paramagnetic center responsible for the $g = 1.94$ EPR signal. Recently, it has become possible to remove and replace the iron atoms of a number of these proteins.[42, 43] This has opened the possibility of enriching proteins from organisms that it would be impractical to grow on enriched media with Fe^{57}. Thus, Palmer[44] has shown that enriched spinach ferredoxin exhibits a broadening, and we shall discuss the effects of incorporating Fe^{57} into a non-heme iron protein of beef and pig adrenals as well as studies on the (+) -camphor hydroxylase iron protein putidaredoxin from *Pseudomonas putida.* Furthermore, we have recently observed broadening from Fe^{57} nuclei in the paramagnetic protein[45] of *Clostridium pasteurianum.*

From these studies, it appears that what was surmised on the basis of composition studies is likely to be true for all systems, i.e., that the $g = 1.94$ paramagnetic center contains iron atoms.

The observation was made early by Massey[46] and confirmed by others, (cf. Reference 39) that on acidification a number of non-heme iron-containing proteins release hydrogen sulfide. The origins of this acid labile sulfide are not entirely clear, but it has often been suggested that the g = 1.94 paramagnetic center is a complex containing both iron and sulfur. That sulfur atoms are indeed involved in this center was shown by Hollocher and collaborators[47] with azotobacter cells and by DerVartanian and coworkers[8] with purified proteins from azotobacter and pseudomonas. They were able to demonstrate broadening of the g = 1.94 signal when the bacteria were grown on media enriched in S^{33} (nuclear spin = 3/2). In these experiments, it was not possible to distinguish among potential sulfur-bearing ligands in the protein. These include cysteine, cystine, methionine, sulfate, and sulfide. Recently, Tsibris and colleagues[9] have attacked the problem by exchanging the acid labile sulfide of *Pseudomonas putida* (+) -camphor hydroxylase. Cells grown on the normal S^{32} isotope were used to prepare a protein that was enriched by exchange with S^{33} sulfide (48% enrichment). The broadening observed, illustrated in FIGURE 3, serves to prove the participation of acid labile sulfide in the g = 1.94 paramagnetic center. It should be noted that further examination of selectively enriched proteins will be needed to determine which, if any, of the other possible sources of sulfur ligands participate in the g = 1.94 center.

The proteins for which accurate data are available seem to contain two or

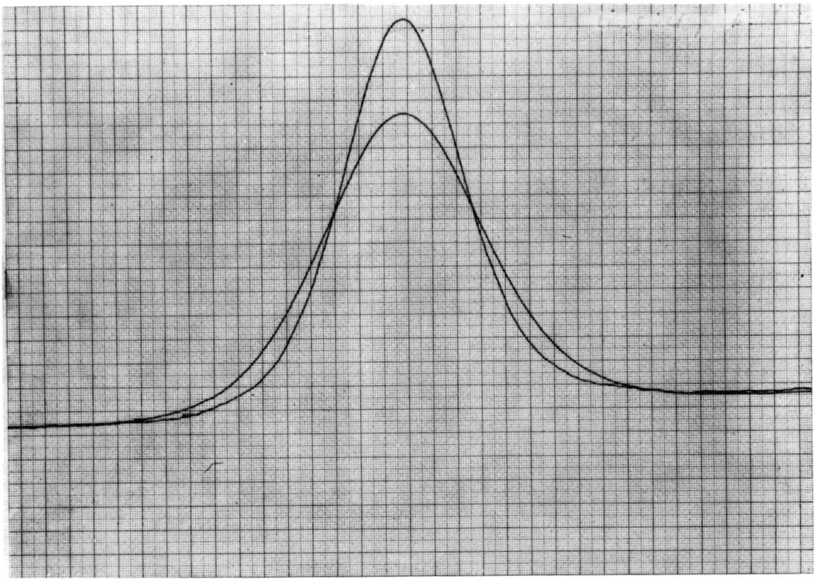

FIGURE 3. EPR spectra of reduced putidaredoxin in its native form (upper curve), and after exchange with S^{33}-sulfide (lower curve); the enrichment of sulfur was 48.5% S^{33}. The conditions of EPR spectroscopy were: microwave power, 27 mW; frequency 9,248 MHz; modulation amplitude, 5G, scanning rate, 400G per min; time constant, 0.5 sec; temperature, 100° K. The two curves represent equal numbers of unpaired spins. The ordinate is an arbitrary measure of the first derivative of the EPR absorption curve. This figure shows only the low-field (g $\approx$ 2) portion of the signals, which is located at 3,271 gauss at 9,248 MHz. The magnetic field is increasing from left to right. (From Tsibris, *et al.*, Reference 9.)

more iron atoms per molecule, and integrations of the EPR signal of the reduced g = 1.94 proteins always yield fewer spins than the presence of one spin per iron atom would require. Thus, the question presents itself: Are the iron atoms associated in multiple units, each unit accepting one electron, or is a fraction of the iron atoms simply inert and not participating in oxidation reduction processes?

The pseudomonas protein has been obtained with a known and reasonably high (> 90%) enrichment in Fe^{57}, and the results seem unequivocal[9]: in view of the enrichment, the shape of the spectra can only be accounted for if one assumes that a single electron interacts with two iron nuclei. This conclusion is based on comparisons of spectra calculated from the spectrum of the Fe^{56}-containing protein, using different assumptions about hyperfine splittings and enrichment, with the spectrum of the Fe^{57}-exchanged protein. The comparison with a calculated spectrum (A = 14 gauss, 94% Fe^{57} is given in FIGURE 4. The conclusion is supported by the finding that on anaerobic titration with dithionite, the protein accepts only one electron per two iron atoms for maximal reduction. In passing, it is interesting to note that this protein, (containing two iron atoms) as a component of the camphor hydroxylase, must turn over twice if it is to interact as a monomer with any of the substrates—TPNH, oxygen, or camphor. Thus, one may find substrate radicals in studies of rapid reaction kinetics of this system.

Recently, we have studied the properties of a mammalian iron-sulfur protein known as adrenodoxin. This protein is a component of the corticosteroid oxygenase of adrenal cortex.[48, 49] Proteins obtained from both beef and pig adrenals were titrated anaerobically with dithionite plus catalytic quantities

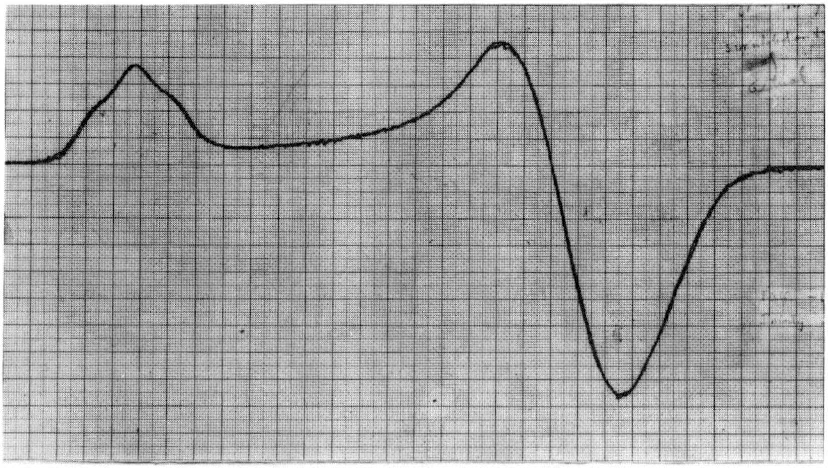

FIGURE 4. Computer simulation of EPR spectrum of Fe^{57}-substituted reduced putidaredoxin, based on the spectrum of the reduced native protein and interaction of the unpaired electron with 2 iron nuclei. The enrichment in Fe^{57} was assumed to be 94% and the splitting, 14G. The spectrum of the reduced protein, in which iron has been exchanged with Fe^{57}, is superimposed on the computed spectrum. The conditions of EPR spectroscopy were: microwave power, 27 mW; frequency 9,248 MHz; modulation amplitude, 5G; scanning rate, 200G per min; time constant, 0.5 sec; temperature, 107°K. The ordinate is an arbitrary measure of the first derivative of the EPR absorption curve. The peaks of the derivative curve are located (left to right) at 3,271, 3,401, and 3,433G. (From Tsibris, *et al.*, Reference 9.)

of methyl viologen, and, in contrast to earlier reports,[49] we found that the uptake of $1e^-/2Fe$ produced maximal EPR signal and bleaching of the visible spectrum. The results of such a titration of the pig protein can be seen in FIGURE 5. This shows that one electron per protein (containing two iron atoms) is accepted, by the criterion of EPR spectroscopy. A study of the changes in the visible spectrum leads to the same conclusion. Integration of signals from maximally reduced preparations indicated that one electron per molecule was represented in the EPR spectrum. Experiments aimed at exchanging the native Fe^{56} of the protein for Fe^{57} were carried out by a modification of the Malkin-Rabinowitz method.[43] Chemical and radio-chemical (Fe^{59} tracer in the Fe^{57} solution) iron determinations were in agreement, indicating that the final enrichment of Fe^{57} in the protein was near that ($\sim$ 91%) in the Fe^{57} solution.

Comparison of the EPR spectra of the Fe^{56} (native) and Fe^{57} (enriched) proteins are seen in FIGURE 6. It is evident that this case is analogous to that of putidaredoxin; according to computer simulations, both iron nuclei par-

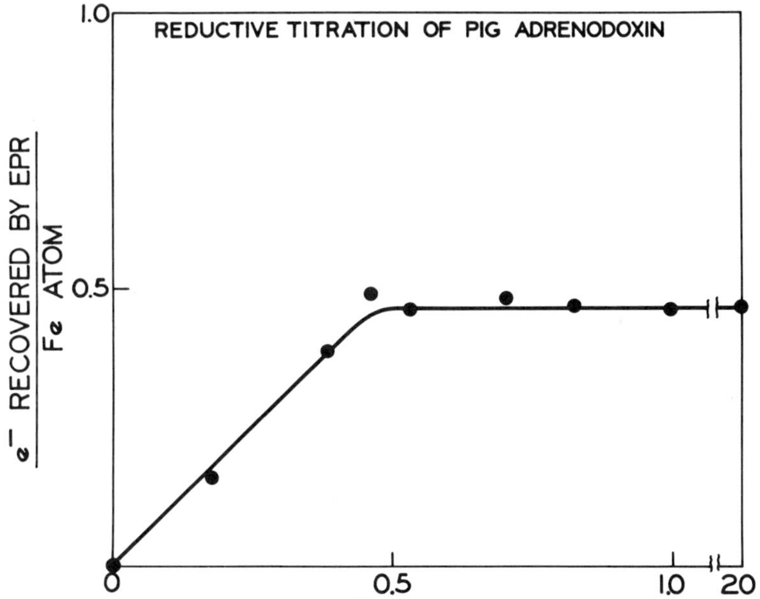

FIGURE 5. Results of reductive anaerobic titration of pig adrenodoxin with dithionite. Samples of protein solution, containing 315 nanomoles of iron (adrenodoxin) plus 1 nanomole of methyl viologen and 40 μmoles of potassium phosphate, pH 7.4, in a volume of 400 μl, were made anaerobic in a Thunberg-type EPR tube. Graded amounts of solid-diluted dithionite[81] were added to a series of these samples and, after they were frozen, the integrated intensity of their g = 1.94 signal was determined. Comparison to a Cu EDTA standard allowed the determination of the number of unpaired spins per liter of sample. This number, divided by the iron concentration, is plotted as the ordinate, whereas the electron equivalents per iron atom, added as dithionite, are plotted as the abscissa of each point. The conditions of EPR spectroscopy were: microwave power, 2.7 mW; frequency, 9,230 MHz; modulation amplitude 6 G; scanning rate, 400 G per min; time constant, 0.5 sec; temperature, 107° K.

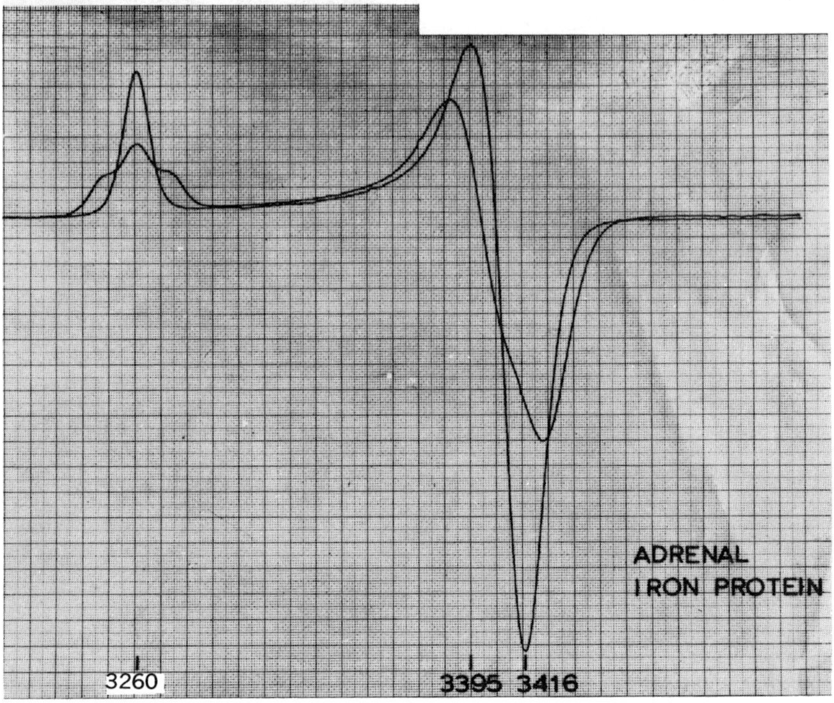

FIGURE 6. Comparison of EPR spectra of Fe^{56} (native) and Fe^{57} (enriched) pig adrenodoxin. The Fe^{57} enriched sample was prepared as follows[43]: the color of the adrenodoxin was bleached with a slight excess of mersalyl in 0.1 M Tris buffer at pH 8, at room temperature. The bleached solution was dialyzed against 1,000 volumes of mM EDTA in 0.05 M Tris, pH 8, at 0°C, under N_2 for 12 hr. The solution was then dialyzed 5 hr against 0.01 M potassium phosphate, pH 7.4. To the resulting protein solution was added a twofold molar excess each of Fe^{57}-ferric citrate, pH 7, and sodium sulfide, plus 2-mercaptoethanol to 0.14 M. After incubation at 37° C for 10 minutes, the solution was decanted to a 3 mm × 10 mm DEAE column. The column was washed with 0.05 M tris- 0.01 M citrate, pH 7, until no iron could be detected in the effluent by orthophenanthroline plus dithionite. The reconstituted protein was eluted with 0.5 M KC1 in small volume, and reduced for EPR spectroscopy by the addition of about 1 mol % methyl viologen plus excess sodium dithionite. The (broader) Fe^{57} spectrum shown was obtained from material which had been taken through two complete cycles of iron removal and replacement. For this sample, the radiochemical (Fe^{59} tracer in the Fe^{57}) and chemical iron values agreed to within the variation of the analytical methods used, so that the enrichment achieved is near that (91%) of the Fe^{57}-ferric citrate. The Fe^{56} material was reduced and the spectrum was taken in the same fashion. Conditions of EPR spectroscopy: microwave power, 9 mW; frequency 9,231 MHz; modulation amplitude, 1.2 G; scanning rate, 100G per min; time constant, 0.5 sec; temperature, 84° K. The field markers along the abscissa are in gauss. The two curves represent equal numbers of unpaired spins.

ticipate in the paramagnetic center. In this instance, the assumption of a single hfs parameter will not suffice to produce a calculated Fe^{57} spectrum agreeing with the experimental one. The $g_{\perp}$ and $g_{\parallel}$ (high- and low-field) portions of the spectrum appear to have different hyperfine coupling constants between the unpaired electron and the iron nuclei.

The results obtained to date on quantitative aspects of the $g = 1.94$ signal in the bacterial protein putidaredoxin and the mammalian protein from adrenals may be summarized as follows: The proteins can accept one electron per two iron atoms and thus per molecule. This electron appears to interact with both iron nuclei and, in the case of the bacterial protein, the acid labile sulfur and perhaps other sulfur atoms participate in the paramagnetic center.

A number of theories have been proposed to account for the $g = 1.94$ signal (cf discussion in Tsibris and coworkers),[9] but whether present experimental studies prove or disprove any of them is not readily apparent. What is apparent so far is that in even the simplest cases of these non-heme iron proteins with the smallest number of iron atoms and no other detected prosthetic groups per molecule, there is a multinuclear inorganic complex responsible for the EPR, optical, and presumably enzymatic properties. To our knowledge, a structure of this nature has thus far not been known to chemists, or, if known, its significance has not been recognized.

How these results, obtained with bacterial and mammalian proteins of low molecular weight and similar functional characteristics, may be generalized to the multiiron bacterial ferredoxins, the iron-molybdenum flavoproteins, and finally to the components of the terminal oxidation system of mitochondria, (where the $g = 1.94$ signal was first seen) remain questions for future studies to settle.

Environment of Copper in Blue Copper Proteins

A variety of copper proteins had attracted the attention of biochemists for some time because of their unusually deep blue color.[50] The intensity per copper atom of their optical absorption exceeds that of ordinary copper complexes by at least two orders of magnitude. In 1960, Malmström and Vänngård[51] conducted a comparative investigation of copper proteins and complexes, and noted that those copper proteins that showed enzymatic activity as oxidases were characterized by this unusually strong optical absorption. Simultaneously, the expected hyperfine splitting stemming from their Cu nuclei was only approximately one-half of that generally seen with copper complexes with various ligands (four lines of equal intensity spaced approximately 150 gauss apart at X band frequency), including peptides and amino acids. Considerable effort has since been expended in the study of these and related proteins,[50] but progress was hampered by the fact that most of these copper proteins may contain not only one but as many as eight copper atoms per molecule. In addition, the copper atoms of one molecule are not equivalent. There is strong evidence that when several Cu atoms are present, some are in the cuprous state. Thus, abnormalities in the properties and behavior of these proteins might be attributed to interactions between adjacent atoms in the cupric state or in the cupric and cuprous states, respectively. It was, therefore, clearly desirable to find and investigate copper proteins of this class which had only one copper atom per molecule. Fortunately, several of these proteins, of plant as well as bacterial origin, have been found in recent years[52–56]; they are generally known as blue proteins with the source mentioned first, i.e., "pseudomonas blue protein." Their molecular weights lie in the range of 10–20,000. For one of these, which is also known as azurin, the complete amino acid sequence is now known.[57] When it was established from molecular weight and metal determinations that these proteins had indeed only one copper atom per molecule and had, nevertheless, the unusual properties of high optical absorption and narrow hfs (although generally lacking oxidase activity), the idea that copper-copper interaction might be responsible for these features had to be abandoned. On the other hand, optical and EPR spectroscopic studies, mainly on model complexes, pointed to a highly asymmetric copper site as a source of the observed anomalies (cf discussions in References 58–62). In a beautiful combination of theoretical and experimental studies, Peisach and colleagues[63] have recently been able to support strongly an explanation for the peculiarities of the blue proteins based on considerations of the symmetry of the copper site. They studied a blue protein by *Rhus vernicifera,* the Japanese lacquer tree, which they called Stellacyanin. This protein has a molecular weight of 20,000, and contains a single copper atom per molecule. Forty percent of the molecular weight is accounted for by carbohydrate; the remainder is made up of 108 amino acid residues.

In a theoretical study, Blumberg had previously addressed himself to the problem of constructing models of Cu(II) complexes on the basis of physical measurements, which are related to structure by established physical theory.[61] He based his approach on magnetic susceptibility, spectroscopic splitting factors (= g values) and hfs parameters of the EPR spectra; and the positions and strengths of the optical transitions and optical rotatory dispersion. Cu(II) complexes seemed well suited to such a study, since the great majority of them can be represented in terms of distortions of the basic square planar model well known in the coordination chemistry of Cu(II). Blumberg's approach in constructing simplified models was based principally on electrostatic considerations. These models illustrate what kinds of distortions from the square planar model can lead to certain physical properties such as were observed with the blue copper proteins.

Drawing on these previous considerations, Blumberg postulated for Stellacyanin two types of distortions of the ligands from square planar geometry, one to produce rhombic character and one to lead to what is called odd distortion (i.e., FIGURE 7). Peisach and Levine, on the other hand, were able to support such a model with the results of stepwise alkaline and acid denaturation of the protein. When the pH was raised beyond 8.3, the rhombic distortions were relaxed with the result that the narrow hfs in the EPR spectrum were replaced by the usual axial spectrum with wide hfs pattern, as seen in the biuret complex (i.e., FIGURE 8). Simultaneously, the optical absorption moved to shorter wavelengths (FIGURE 9), although the intensity of the optical absorption still remained high. Up to pH 11.5, these changes were reversible. At higher pH, the odd distortions became relaxed and the intensity of the optical absorption dropped to the range of values typical for ordinary copper complexes. This change was irreversible. It did not affect the principal features of the EPR spectrum. However, super hfs (stemming from ligand nitrogen nuclei) was now seen on the principal absorption (FIGURE 8), as is usually observed with Cu(II)—peptide complexes at high pH. The environment of the copper in these stages is shown schematically in FIGURE 7. Denaturation at low pH (<2), however, proceeded in a different fashion. Here the odd distortions were relaxed first with a dramatic drop in optical absorption intensity. At this stage, the copper was still not available to chelating agents such as EDTA, and partial renaturation was possible. It has been suggested that the striking optical absorption of these blue proteins is due to charge transfer.[50] Peisach and colleagues[63] propose, however, that the observed transitions are d-d transitions,

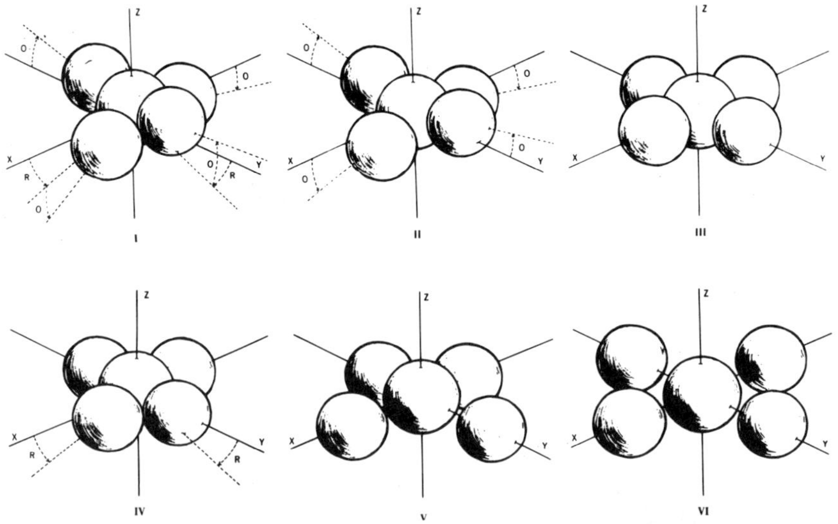

FIGURE 7. Diagramatic sketch of the four strong ligand atoms of the copper-binding site of stellacyanin. Structure I is the native site. The central sphere represents the divalent copper atom, the surrounding four spheres the ligand atoms to which the copper is attached. The two types of displacement from a square planar configuration are denoted by R (rhombic) and O (odd). Structure II is the intermediate stage in high pH denaturation (pH 8.3–11.5), where only the R displacement has been relaxed. Structure III is the final stage in high pH denaturation above 11.5, where both R and O have been relaxed. Structure IV is the first stage of acid denaturation, pH below 2.0, in which the O displacement has been relaxed, but the copper is not accessible to chelating agents. Structure V is the second stage in acid denaturation in which the copper, although renaturable, is accessible to chelating agents. Structure VI is the last stage in acid denaturation in which the copper is not renaturable and is accessible to chelators. (From Peisach *et al.,* Reference 63.)

which are forbidden in ordinary symmetrical copper complexes. Odd components in the ligand field, would, however, partially allow these transitions, and these odd components are maintained by constraints on the ligands posed by the structure of the protein. As these constraints become relaxed on partial unfolding of the protein (denaturation), the odd components disappear and the transitions become forbidden.

It has been argued from the standpoint of coordination chemistry that the Cu(I)—Cu(II) couple cannot be expected to be an efficient oxidation-reduction system as would be required for an enzyme, since Cu(I) is found largely in tetrahedral coordination, whereas Cu(II) prefers a square planar ligand environment.[50, 61] Reshuffling of the coordination sphere would be far too slow and expensive in terms of energy to permit efficient electron transfer. Returning to the original observation of Malmström and Vänngård,[51] namely that only proteins with the unusual features of deep blue color and narrow hfs are efficient oxidases, and considering the explanation of Blumberg and his colleagues for these features, we realize that a distorted ligand field around Cu(II) is apparently a requirement for a copper protein to be an efficient oxidase. Thus it would seem that the distortions of the ligands in the cupric state bring the environment sufficiently close to a tetrahedral one,

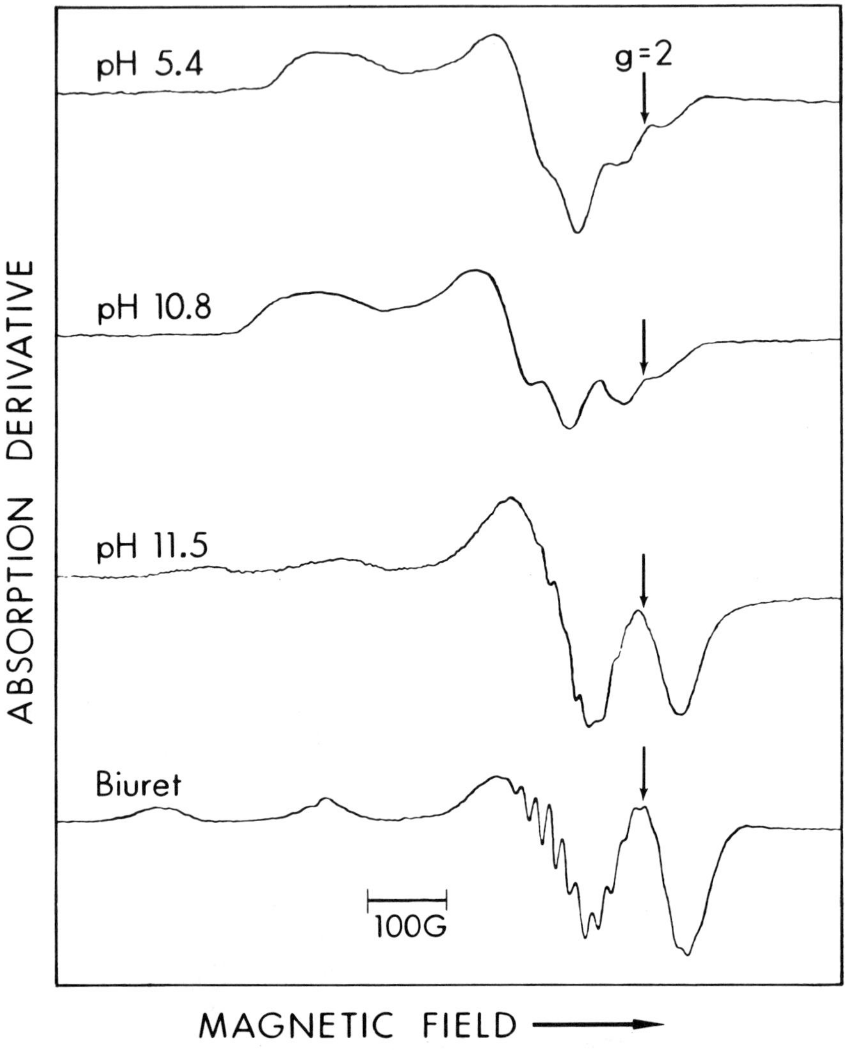

FIGURE 8. X band EPR spectra for stellacyanin at various values of pH. The sample was 0.5 ml of stellacyanin (1.35 mM) containing 85 μg of copper per ml in 0.05 M Tris-acetate buffer, pH 5.4. The sample was frozen in liquid nitrogen, and was examined at pumped liquid helium temperature (approximately 1.5° K). After EPR observations were made, the pH was adjusted to 10.8 with 6 M NaOH, and the sample was quickly refrozen. The same procedure was followed for pH 11.5. For the pH 12.0 sample, NaOH was added at 0° until the solution was an intense pink, and the sample was immediately frozen. After the EPR observation was made, the sample was thawed upon which rapid decolorization occurred. The pH was then found to be 12.0, as measured at room temperature. Upon refreezing of this solution, the EPR spectrum was found to be unchanged and was identical to that of bis-biuret copper complex in basic solution. (From Peisach *et al.*, Reference 63.)

as required by Cu(I), so that electron transfer can be accomplished without complete reorientation of ligands.

We mentioned previously that the blue proteins of low molecular weight have the physical but not the catalytic properties of the larger proteins con-

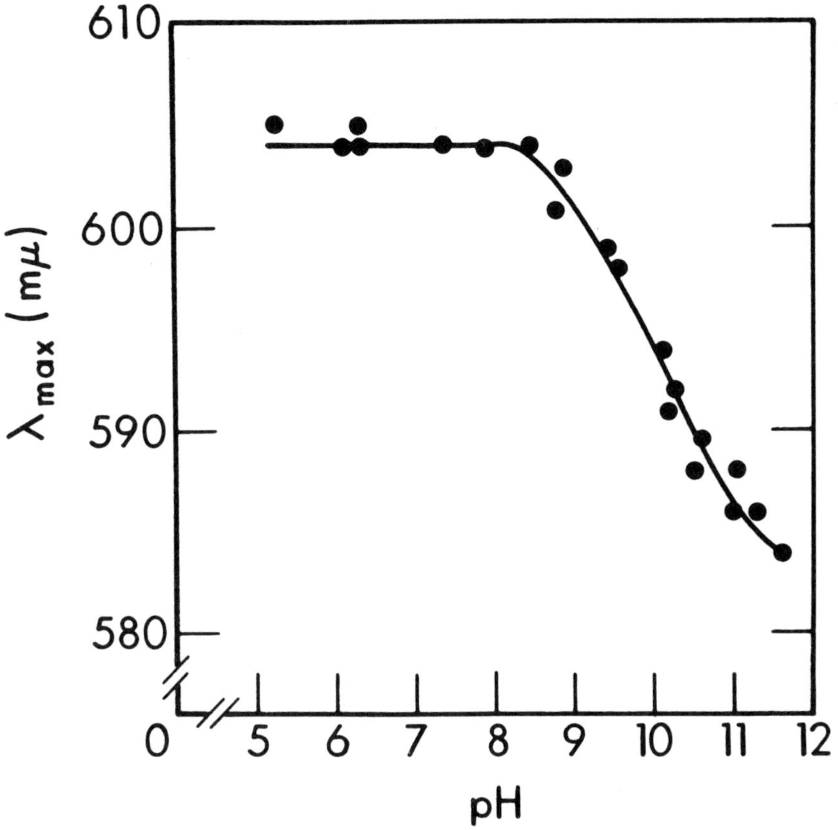

FIGURE 9. pH dependence of the position of the major visible optical absorption of stellacyanin. Three ml of stellacyanin, 0.175 mM, in 0.05 M Tris-acetate buffer, pH 5.4, were contained in a cuvette with 1 cm light path. The pH was adjusted by adding concentrated NaOH with a syringe microburet so that dilution effects were insignificant. After pH adjustment, the position of the major visible peak was measured. (From Peisach *et al.*, Reference 63.)

taining several copper atoms. Nakamura and Ogura[64] have carefully studied the ability of various copper proteins to accept electrons from donors such as ascorbate, hydroquinone, and p-phenylenediamine, and to donate electrons to oxygen. They found that the two blue proteins of low molecular weight that they studied were very efficient acceptors but poor donors to oxygen, whereas the three larger proteins reacted more efficiently with oxygen. An optical absorption band of 330 mμ was characteristic of those proteins that reacted rapidly with oxygen. These interesting observations will have to be extended to a larger sample of copper proteins before further conclusions can be drawn.

Electron Spin-Spin Interaction in EPR of Biological Macromolecules

Electron Spin Relaxation as Indicator of Intramolecular Interactions between Components of Oxidative Enzymes

Examination of power saturation curves for EPR signals of flavin radicals in flavoproteins and metal flavoproteins showed that the spin systems giving rise to signals in metal-containing proteins were better relaxed than was the case in a simple flavoprotein.[12] This suggests that interactions between paramagnetic components in proteins might reveal themselves in relaxation phenomena. Indeed, it has been observed with proteins containing flavin and iron (dihydroorotic dehydrogenase) and additionally molybdenum (xanthine and aldehyde oxidases)[13, 14] that the rather easily saturated radical and molybdenum signals can be seen to change (by orders of magnitude) their saturation behavior with time in kinetic experiments and with oxidation state of the components in titration experiments. The saturation behavior also reflects the nature of the reactants interacting with the enzyme. These and other aspects have recently been discussed at length by Beinert and Orme-Johnson.[14] We wish here only to draw attention to these intricate but potentially rewarding phenomena.

Enhancement of electron-spin relaxation will, in the extreme case, lead to uncertainty broadening and the effective disappearance of signals. The EPR spectroscopic properties of the enzyme discussed in the following pages may possibly be explained by such an interaction, although we favor other explanations at the moment.

Electron Spin-Spin Interactions Interfering with Observation of EPR Signals from Paramagnetic Species

The enzyme cytochrome c oxidase, ubiquitous in aerobic creatures, is distinguished by a long history of controversy and obscurity concerning its nature. Keilin and Hartree,[65] in their classical studies on the cytochrome system, found it necessary to describe the spectral properties of this enzyme in terms of two distinct cytochrome components called a and a_3. More recently, evidence has revealed that a copper component also plays a vital role in the function of cytochrome c oxidase,[66–68] and it is now likely that at least two different copper components are involved.[69, 70] The simplest unit of the enzyme may, therefore, be described as: a a_3 $Cu_\alpha Cu_\beta$, which has a molecular weight in the range of 200,000. The molecular weight of the enzyme is not known, since complicated aggregation phenomena are involved. The history of this enzyme has been lucidly summarized,[71] and more recent developments pertaining to the copper components are reviewed[69] in recent symposium volumes.

The optical absorptions of the a and a_3 components of cytochrome c oxidase overlap to such an extent that the spectral properties of the individual cytochromes can only be inferred by experiments involving differential ligand binding and have been the subject of much discussion and controversy.[72, 73] The optical absorptions of the copper components are completely overwhelmed by the contributions of the hemes, except at wavelengths beyond 700 mμ. The picture in the EPR spectra is the inverse, however, where the sharp Cu(II) absorption is dominant[5] (FIGURE 10, upper trace). At high protein concentrations, the EPR absorptions due to the heme components can, however, be resolved.[74] Fortunately, these absorptions occur over such a wide field range ($g = 6$ to $g = 1.5$) that overlap never obscures all the individual bands of a composite spectrum.

Cytochrome c oxidase in the oxidized, resting state shows an EPR spectrum typical of Cu(II) with a narrow hfs similar to the blue proteins discussed previously. In addition, the spectrum of a low-spin heme compound with anisotropic g values at 1.5, 2, and 3.0 can be seen. This spectrum is

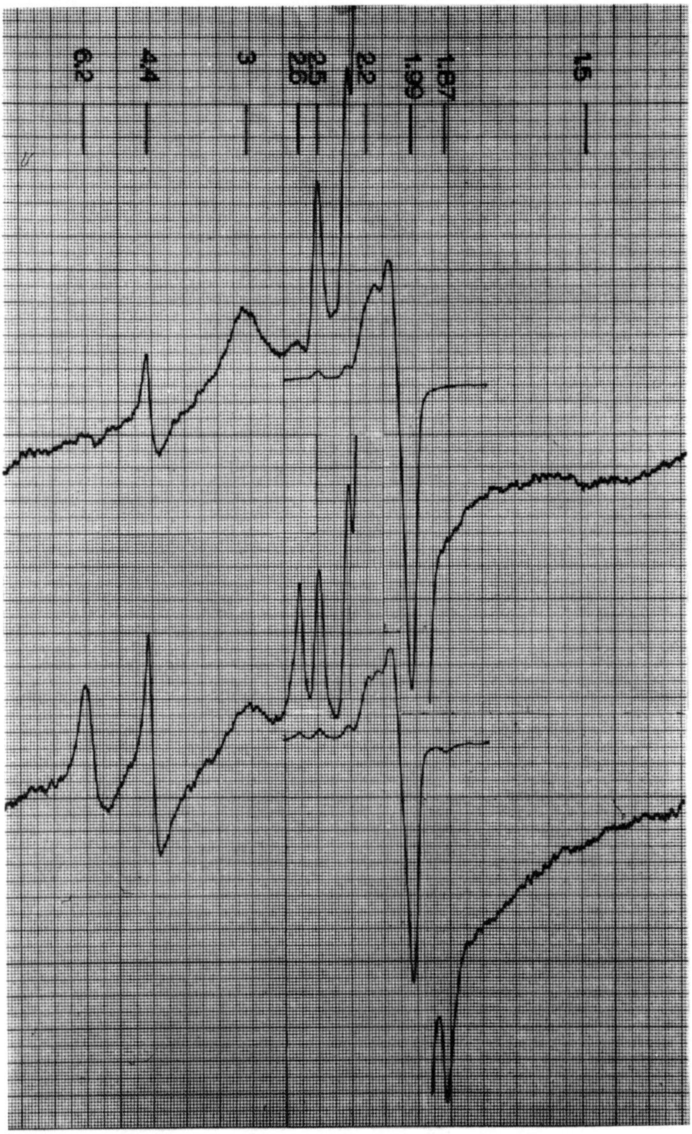

FIGURE 10. EPR spectra of cytochrome *c* oxidase, oxidized form (upper curve) and after addition of 0.95 reducing equivalents per mole of heme (lower curve). Cytochrome *c* oxidase (heme), 645 μM, was reduced anaerobically with 305 μM DPNH and 3μM phenazine methylsulfate. Samples were frozen after 15 min at room temperature. The conditions of EPR spectroscopy were: microwave power, 91 mW; frequency 9,250 MHz; modulation amplitude, 18 G; scanning rate, 1,000 G per min; time constant, 1 sec; temperature, 88° K. The wings of the signals were recorded at 25 times the instrument sensitivity used for the center. The markers on the figure labeled with g values correspond to the following field values in gauss; 1055, 1498, 2195, 2540, 2665, 3000, 3322, 3530, and 4445. (From van Gelder, *et al.*, Reference 74.)

attributed to cytochrome a in agreement with its optical properties, which are those of a low-spin heme compound.[75] Quantitatively, the heme and the copper signal do not account for more than one-half of the total heme or copper present in the enzyme according to chemical analysis. No signals have been found in the oxidized enyzme, either at liquid nitrogen or helium temperature, which could be attributed to the remainder of the oxidase components. With the reduced enzyme, naturally, EPR is not likely to be of much use, since Cu(I) as well as low-spin Fe(II) are diamagnetic, and high-spin Fe(II) is usually hard to detect because of its rapid spin relaxation. One peculiar observation was, however, known, namely that denaturation of cytochrome oxidase leads to a two- to threefold increase in the Cu(II) signal.[76] During denaturation, a mercury compound must be present to prevent reduction by exposed SH-groups. The newly appearing Cu(II) is, therefore, either the oxidized form of an originally present Cu(I), or is released from an interaction with another component which abolishes its EPR spectrum. That the latent copper of the native enzyme is indeed cupric was strongly suggested by the consumption of two reducing equivalents per heme in reductive titrations.[70]

Until recently, however, no component had been observed in the native enzyme other than those mentioned. We have discovered, during stepwise anaerobic titrations with various reducing agents, that as electrons are taken up by the enzyme, a new heme component is exposed,[74] (FIGURE 10, lower trace). This component manifests itself by the appearance of a signal ($g_{\perp} = 6$) typical of high-spin heme compounds such as acid metmyoglobin.[75]

This signal reaches maximal intensity at approximately 50% reduction and disappears as reduction proceeds to completion. Since optical absorption[77] as well as magnetic susceptibility data[78] indicated that cytochrome a_3 must be a high-spin heme compound, it is reasonable to assign the new EPR signal to this cytochrome c oxidase component. It had previously been concluded from studies of optical absorption that dithionite reduces the a component much more efficiently than the a_3 component.[79] In agreement with this, it was found that the high-spin EPR signal was particularly intense on partial reduction with dithionite (FIGURE 11). It should be mentioned here that, concomitant with the signal at $g = 6$, a low-spin signal ($g = 1.87$, 2.2, and 2.6) also appears. However, its intensity is not strictly related to the signal at $g = 6$. It may represent a low-spin form of cytochrome a_3.

There are several ligands, such as fluoride, azide and cyanide, which bind tightly to the fifth and/or sixth coordination positions of the iron porphyrin system.[72, 73] Their effects on the optical spectra and the spin state of heme compounds in general and of cytochrome c oxidase are well known.[72, 73, 80] In agreement with this available knowledge, we found that flouride stabilizes the high-spin state, represented by the signal at $g = 6$, whereas azide, cyanide, and carbon monoxide prevent the formation of the high-spin intermediate.[74] During reduction in the presence of azide, a new signal appears at intermediate states of oxidation with the g values 1.67, 2.2, and 2.9, typical of a low-spin intermediate. This indicates that in the presence of azide, cytochrome a_3 is converted into a low-spin form from its latent state in the oxidized enzyme.

The course of an anaerobic titration of cytochrome ocidase by DPNH and phenazine methylsulfate according to van Gelder[70] is shown schematically in FIGURE 12. We are following here the increase in optical absorption measured at room temperature and the disappearance or appearance of EPR signals measured at low temperature (ordinate) with increasing amounts

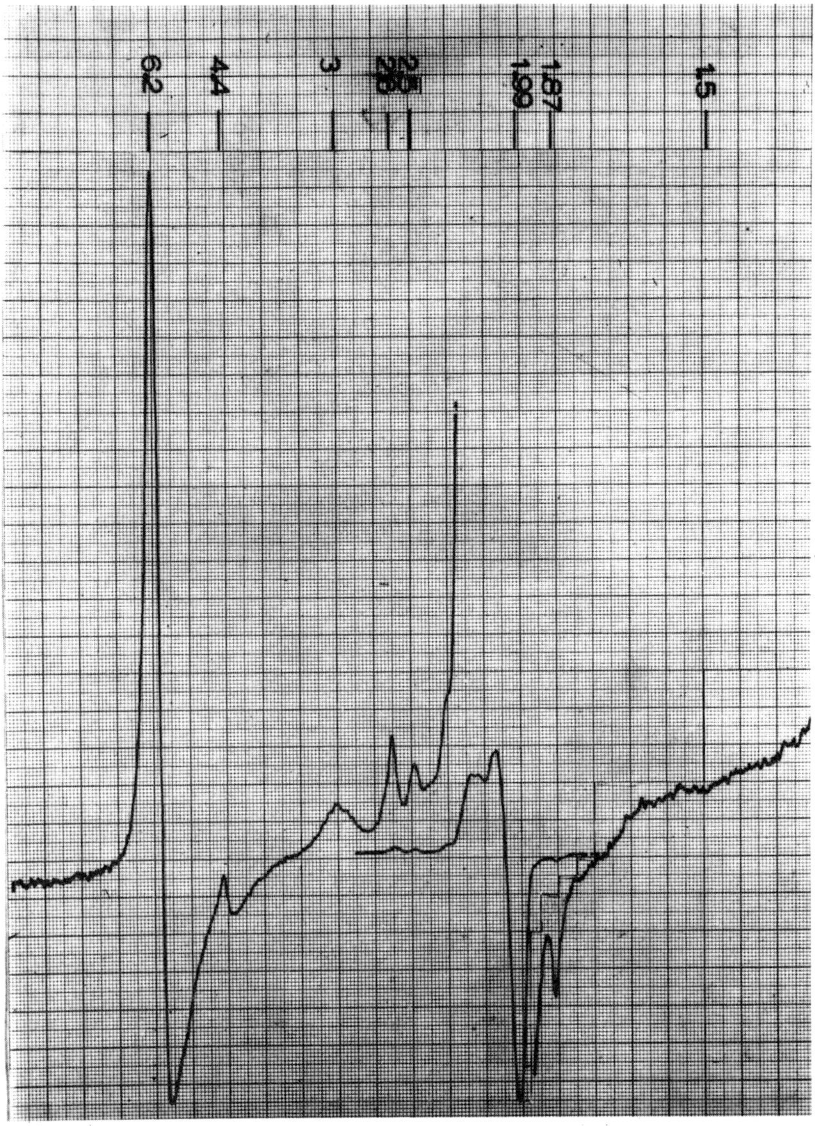

FIGURE 11. EPR signals of cytochrome *c* oxidase after partial reduction with dithionite. The enzyme, as in FIGURE 10, was reduced anaerobically with an amount of solid dithionite corresponding to two reducing equivalents per heme and frozen after 20 minutes at room temperature. The conditions of EPR spectroscopy were: microwave power, 27 mW, frequency, 9,250 MHz; modulation amplitude, 18 G; scanning rate, 1000 G per min; time constant, 0.5 sec; temperature, 86° K. The wings of the signal were recorded at 20 times the instrument sensitivity used for the center.

of reductant (abscissa) in the absence of ligands. It is remarkable that the optical absorption (605 mμ) and the high-spin signal of cytochrome a_3 increase, and the initially observed low-spin signal of cytochrome a disappears in a linear fashion, whereas the Cu(II) signal of the enzyme disap-

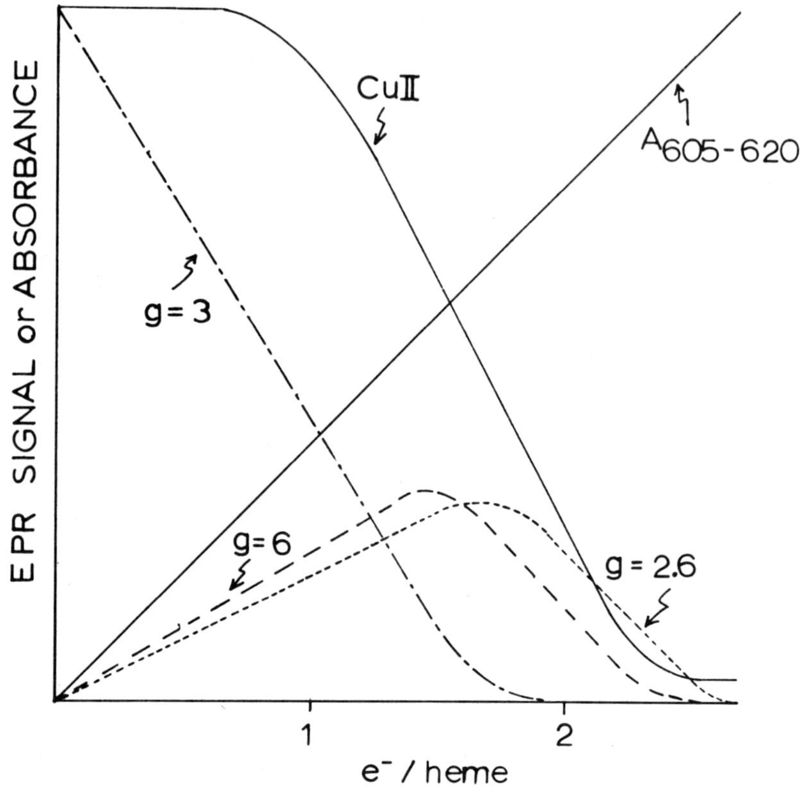

FIGURE 12. Plot of EPR signal heights vs reductant added during titration of cytochrome *c* oxidase, as in FIGURE 10. The abscissa shows reducing equivalents added per mole of heme, and the ordinate height of EPR signals with the indicated g value or optical absorbance in arbitrary units. It is assumed according to quantitative estimations (cf Ref. 74) that the concentration of cytochrome *a* (g = 3) and the EPR detectable copper are approximately equal and that the maximum concentration of cytochrome a_3 represented in the signal at g = 6, as reached in this experiment, is approximately 25% of this value. Therefore, if quantities of heme represented by absorbance values or signals are to be compared, the ordinate is expanded roughly threefold for Cu(II), g = 6, and g = 3, as compared to the optical absorbance scale and tenfold for g = 2.6.

pears only after a considerable lag. A new copper signal for a previously latent Cu(II) never appears, however. If one were to explain these observations in the simplest terms, considering only interactions within the smallest active unit, one might represent the state of the components of the oxidized resting enzyme as follows:

$$a_{l.s.}^{III} \quad Cu_{\alpha}^{II}$$

$$[a_{3\,h.s.}^{III} Cu_{\beta}^{II}]$$

Interacting components are indicated by ◌, species not detectable by EPR are enclosed in brackets, and the spin state is indicated by h.s. or l.s., respectively. The first two electrons would be accepted by a^{III} and Cu_{β}^{II} and the copper-heme interaction consequently broken. Thus the high-spin species appears whereas the Cu(II) signal remains unaltered:

$$\xrightarrow{+2e^-} \begin{matrix} [a_{1.s.}{}^{II}]\ Cu_\alpha{}^{II} \\ a_{3\,h.s.}{}^{III}[Cu_\beta{}^{I}] \end{matrix}$$

On further reduction we obtain:

$$\xrightarrow{+2e^-} \begin{matrix} [a_{1.s.}{}^{II}]\ [Cu_\alpha{}^{I}] \\ [a_{3\,h.s.?}{}^{II}][Cu_\beta{}^{I}] \end{matrix}$$

Quantitative data on signal intensities indicate, however, that the system may be more complex and that interactions between the smallest units (a a_3 Cu_α Cu_β) may have to be invoked in order to explain the observed events satisfactorily.

It is, therefore, premature to attempt any definitive explanation. The reported observations, however, represent the strongest support yet adduced for the presence of two different cytochromes in cytochrome c oxidase, one of high (a_3), and one of low spin (a) and for the involvement of conformational changes in its oxidation-reduction, as previously suggested from less direct evidence.

As pointed out at the end of the foregoing section, electron spin-spin interactions between copper and heme, or between two heme groups or two copper atoms, could interfere with the observation of an EPR absorption. The three possibilities to be considered are: first, that mentioned above, i.e., an increase in the electron-spin relaxation rate to the extent that signals are broadened beyond detection (lifetime broadening); second, the static component of magnetic dipolar interaction between neighboring electron spins could bring about similar broadening; and third, antiferromagnetic coupling of electron spins could occur. In this last instance, not only is detection by EPR spectroscopy interfered with, but the underlying paramagnetism is cancelled. In the first and second instances, bulk magnetic susceptibility should still be measurable.

In the case at hand, namely the absence of EPR signals from components of cytochrome c oxidase which can be expected to be paramagnetic, rapid electron-spin relaxation is not likely to be the explanation, because even at liquid helium temperature these signals are not seen. At this temperature, the relaxation rate should have increased sufficiently so that signals might be detected. Concerning the possibility of antiferromagnetic interaction, it must be noted that measurements of the magnetic susceptibility of cytochrome c oxidase at room temperature[78] indicate a substantial contribution by the a_3 component. Antiferromagnetic interactions have a characteristic complex dependence on temperature: above the Néel transition temperature, the spins are uncoupled and the system exhibits the $1/T$ dependence of susceptibility of paramagnetic substances, whereas, below the Néel temperature, an ever larger proportion of the spins are coupled so that the susceptibility drops as the temperature is lowered. The room temperature observation of a susceptibility contribution from a_3, and our EPR observations at liquid nitrogen temperature would be compatible with antiferromagnetic coupling if the Néel temperature of the system lay between 77° and 300° K. The resolution of the EPR spectra of cytochrome c oxidase at room temperature is, unfortunately, completely unsatisfactory. Accurate susceptibility measurements at low temperature should enable us to decide the question of whether dipolar broadening or antiferromagnetic interaction is the reason for the absence of EPR signals for cytochrome a_3 and one of the copper components in the oxidized form of cytochrome c oxidase.

REFERENCES

1. BRAY, R. C. 1961. Biochem. J. **81:** 189.
2. BORG, D. C. 1964. Nature **201:** 1087.
3. PIETTE, L. H., G. BULOW & I. YAMAZAKI. 1964. Biochem. Biophys. Acta **88:** 120.
4. PALMER, G. & H. BEINERT. 1964. Anal. Biochem. **8:** 95.
5. BEINERT, H. & G. PALMER. 1965. Advan. Enzymol. **27:** 105.
6. KOHL, D. H., J. TOWNSEND, B. COMMONER, H. L. CRESPI, R. C. DOUGHERTY & J. J. KATZ. 1965. Nature **206:** 1105.
7. BRAY, R. C., P. F. KNOWLES & L. S. MERIWETHER. 1967. Magnetic Resonance in Biological Systems. A. Ehrenberg, B. G. Malmström & T. Vänngård, Eds.: 249. Pergamon Press. Oxford, England.
8. DERVARTANIAN, D. V., W. H. ORME-JOHNSON, R. E. HANSEN, H. BEINERT, R. L. TSAI, J. C. M. TSIBRIS, R. C. BARTHOLOMAUS & I. C. GUNSALUS. 1967. Biochem. Biophys. Res. Commun. **26:** 569.
9. TSIBRIS, J. C. M., R. L. TSAI, I. C. GUNSALUS, W. H. ORME-JOHNSON, R. E. HANSEN & H. BEINERT. 1968. Proc. Nat. Acad. Sci. (U. S. A.) **59:** 959.
10. MÜLLER, F., A. EHRENBERG &. L. E. G. ERICKSSON. 1967. Magnetic Resonance in Biological Systems. A. Ehrenberg, B. G. Malmström & T. Vänngård, Eds.: 281. Pergamon Press. Oxford, England.
11. BLUMBERG, W. E. & J. PEISACH. 1965. J. Biol. Chem. **240:** 870.
12. BEINERT, H. & P. HEMMERICH. 1965. Biochem. Biophys. Res. Commun. **18:** 212.
13. BEINERT, H. 1966. Flavins and Flavoproteins (BBA Library). E. C. Slater, Ed.: **8:** 49. Elsevier. Amsterdam, Holland.
14. BEINERT, H. & W. H. ORME-JOHNSON. 1967. Magnetic Resonance in Biological Systems. A. Ehrenberg, B. G. Malmström & T. Vänngård, Eds. 221. Pergamon Press. Oxford, England.
15. MCCONNELL, H. M. 1967. Magnetic Resonance in Biological Systems. A. Ehrenberg, B. G. Malmström & T. Vänngård, Eds.: 313. Pergamon Press. Oxford, England.
16. INGRAM, D. J. E. 1958. Free Radicals as Studied by Electron Spin Resonance, Butterworth. London, England.
17. COMMONER, B., J. J. HEISE & J. TOWNSEND. 1956. Proc. Nat. Acad. Sci. (U. S. A.) **42:** 710.
18. CALVIN, M. & P. B. SOGO. 1957. Science **125:** 499.
19. CRESPI, H. S., S. M. CONRAD, R. R. UPHAUS & J. J. KATZ. 1960. Ann. New York Acad. Sci. **84:** 648.
20. CALVIN, M. 1961. Light and Life. W. D. McElroy & G. Glass, Eds.: 317. Johns Hopkins Press. Baltimore, Md.
21. MAUZERALL, D., G. FEHER & J. MCELROY. 1967. Abstr. Seventh Internat. Cong. Biochem. **H-49:** 893. Tokyo, Japan.
22. BRAY, R. C. 1963. The Enzymes. P. D. Boyer, H. Lardy & K. Myrbäck, Eds.: **7:** 533–556.
23. BRAY, R. C. & L. S. MERIWETHER. 1966. Nature **212:** 467.
24. BRAY, R. C., G. PALMER & H. BEINERT. 1964. J. Biol. Chem. **239:** 2667.
25. BRAY, R. C., P. F. KNOWLES & L. S. MERIWETHER. 1967. Magnetic Resonance in Biological Systems. A. Ehrenberg, B. G. Malmström & T. Vänngård, Eds.: 249. Pergamon Press. Oxford, England.
26. PALMER, G., R. C. BRAY & H. BEINERT. 1964. J. Biol. Chem. **239:** 2657.
27. RAJAGOPALAN, K. V., P. HANDLER, G. PALMER & H. BEINERT. 1968. J. Biol. Chem. **243:** 3784.
28. BRAY, R. C. & P. F. KNOWLES. 1968. Proc. Roy. Soc. A. **302:** 351.
29. KNOWLES, P. F. 1967. Magnetic Resonance in Biological Systems. A. Ehrenberg, B. G. Malmström & T. Vänngård, Eds.: 265. Pergamon Press. Oxford, England.

30. GREEN, D. E. 1956. *In* Enzymes, Units of Biological Structure and Function. O. H. Gaebler, Ed.: 465. Academic Press. New York, N. Y.
31. BEINERT, H. 1965. *In* Non-Heme Iron Proteins: Role in Energy Conversion. A. San Pietro, Ed.: 23. Antioch Press. Yellow Springs, Ohio.
32. Non-Heme Iron Proteins: Role in Energy Conversion. 1965. A. San Pietro, Ed. Antioch Press. Yellow Springs, Ohio.
33. RAJAGOPALAN, K. V. & P. HANDLER. 1964. J. Biol. Chem. **239:** 1509.
34. PALMER, G. & R. H. SANDS. 1966. J. Biol. Chem. **241:** 253.
35. PALMER, G., R. H. SANDS & L. E. MORTENSON. 1966. Biochem. Biophys. Res. Commun. **23:** 357.
36. BEINERT, H., G. PALMER, T. CREMONA & T. P. SINGER. 1965. J. Biol. Chem. **240:** 475.
37. ALEMAN, V., P. HANDLER, G. PALMER & H. BEINERT. 1968. J. Biol. Chem. **243:** 2569.
38. DERVARTANIAN, D. V., C. VEEGER, W. H. ORME-JOHNSON & H. BEINERT. 1967. Fed. Proc. **26** (2): 732.
39. MALKIN, R. & J. C. RABINOWITZ. 1967. Ann. Rev. Biochem. **36:** 113.
40. SHETHNA, Y. I., P. W. WILSON, R. E. HANSEN & H. BEINERT. 1964. Proc. Nat. Acad. Sci. (U. S. A.) **52:** 1263
41. NICHOLAS, D. J. D., P. W. WILSON, W. HEINEN, G. PALMER & H. BEINERT. 1962. Nature **196:** 433.
42. LOVENBERG, W., B. B. BUCHANAN & J. C. RABINOWITZ. 1963. J. Biol. Chem. **238:** 3899.
43. MALKIN, R. & J. C. RABINOWITZ. 1966. Biochem. Biophys. Res. Commun. **23:** 822.
44. PALMER, G. 1967. Biochem. Biophys. Res. Commun. **27:** 315.
45. HARDY, R. W. F., E. KNIGHT, JR., C. C. MCDONALD & A. J. D'Eustachio. 1965. *In* Non-Heme Iron Proteins: Role in Energy Conversion. A. San Pietro, Ed.: 275: Antioch Press. Yellow Springs, Ohio.
46. MASSEY, V. 1957. J. Biol. Chem. **229:** 763.
47. HOLLOCHER, T. C., F. SOLOMON & T. E. RAGLAND. 1966. J. Biol. Chem. **241:** 3452.
48. OMURA, T., E. SANDERS, R. W. ESTABROOK, D. Y. COOPER & O. ROSENTHAL. 1966. Arch. Biochem. Biophys. **117:** 660.
49. KIMURA, T., & K. SUZUKI. 1967. J. Biol. Chem. **242:** 485.
50. The Biochemistry of Copper. 1966. J. Peisach, P. Aisen & W. E. Blumberg, Eds. Academic Press. New York, N. Y.
51. MALMSTRÖM, B. G. & T. VÄNNGÅRD. 1960. J. Molec. Biol. **2:** 118.
52. OMURA, T. 1961. J. Biochem. (Tokyo) **50:** 394.
53. SUTHERLAND, I. W. & J. F. WILKINSON. 1963. J. Gen. Microbiol. **30:** 105.
54. SHICHI, H. & D. P. HACKETT. 1963. Arch. Biochem. Biophys. **11:** 195.
55. BLUMBERG, W. E., W. G. LEVINE, S. MARGOLIS & J. PEISACH. 1964. Biochem. Biophys. Res. Commun. **15:** 277.
56. HORIO, T. 1958. J. Biochem. (Tokyo) **45:** 195.
57. AMBLER, R. P. & L. H. BROWN. 1967. Biochem. J. **104:** 784.
58. WILLIAMS, R. J. P. 1964. J. Polymer Res. Sympos **I:** 515.
59. MALMSTRÖM, B. G. 1965. *In* Oxidases and Related Redox Systems. T. E. King, H. S. Mason & M. Morrison, Eds.: 207. John Wiley & Sons. New York, N. Y.
60. MASON, H. S. 1965. Ann. Rev. Biochem. **34:** 595.
61. BLUMBERG, W. E. 1966. *In* The Biochemistry of Copper. J. Peisach, P. Aisen & W. E. Blumberg, Eds.: 49. Academic Press. New York, N. Y.
62. WÜTHRICH, K. 1966. Helv. Chim. Acta **49:** 1400.
63. PEISACH, J., W. G. LEVINE & W. E. BLUMBERG. 1967. J. Biol. Chem. **242:** 2847.
64. NAKAMURA, T. & Y. OGURA. 1968. J. Biochem. (Tokyo) **64:** 267.
65. KEILIN, D. & E. F. HARTREE. 1939. Proc. Roy. Soc. **B 127:** 167.
66. SANDS, R. H. & H. BEINERT. 1959. Biochem. Biophys. Res. Commun. **1:** 175.
67. PALMER, G. & H. BEINERT. 1964. J. Biol. Chem. **239:** 1221.
68. GIBSON, Q. H. & C. GREENWOOD. 1965. J. Biol. Chem. **240:** 2694.
69. BEINERT, H. 1966. *In* The Biochemistry of Copper. J. Peisach, P. Aisen & W. E. Blumberg, Eds.: 213. Academic Press. New York, N. Y.
70. VAN GELDER, B. F. 1966. Biochem. Biophys. Acta **118:** 36.
71. SLATER, E. C., B. F. VAN GELDER & K. MINNAERT. 1964. Oxidases and Related Redox Systems. T. E. King, H. S. Mason & M. Morrison, Eds. **2:** 667. John Wiley & Sons. New York, N. Y.

72. Haematin Enzymes. 1961. J. E. Falk, R. Lemberg & R. K. Morton, Eds. Pergamon Press. London, England.
73. Hemes and Hemoproteins. 1966. B. Chance, R. W. Estabrook & T. Yonetani, Eds., Academic Press. New York, N. Y.
74. Van Gelder, B. F., W. H. Orme-Johnson, R. E. Hansen & H. Beinert. 1967. Proc. Nat. Acad. Sci. (U. S. A.) **58:** 1073.
75. Ehrenberg, A. 1962. Arkiv för Kemi **19:** 119.
76. Beinert, H. & G. Palmer. 1964. Oxidases and Related Redox Systems. T. E. King, H. S. Mason & M. Morrison, Eds. **2:** 567. John Wiley & Sons. New York, N. Y.
77. Williams, R. J. P. 1956. Chem. Rev. **56:** 299.
78. Ehrenberg, A. & T. Yonetani. 1961. Acta. Chem. Scand. **15:** 8.
79. Gilmour, M. V., D. F. Wilson & R. Lemberg. 1967. Biochem. Biophys. Acta **143:** 487.
80. Structure and Function of Cytochromes. 1967. K. Okunuki, M. D. Kamen & I. Sekuzu, Eds. University of Tokyo Press. Tokyo, Japan.
81. Orme-Johnson, W. H. & H. Beinert. In preparation.

Acknowledgments

We would like to express our appreciation to our colleagues Drs. I. C. Gunsalus, J. C. M. Tsibris, R. L. Tsai, and B. F. van Gelder for permission to present unpublished results of joint work and for their comments and discussions; to Drs. R. C. Bray, D. L. Kohl, D. Mauzerall, and J. Peisach for permission to discuss examples from their work and for supplying figures; to Drs. T. Vänngård, R. H. Sands, and G. Palmer for clarifying discussions, and to Mr. R. E. Hansen for his continuing assistance and advice in problems of instrumentation. We are particularly grateful to Dr. T. Kimura for advice and information, in advance of publication, on the purification of the non-heme iron protein from adrenals.

MEASUREMENTS OF SUBNANOSECOND FLUORESCENCE LIFETIMES WITH A CROSS-CORRELATION PHASE FLUOROMETER*

Richard D. Spencer and Gregorio Weber
Department of Chemistry and Chemical Engineering
University of Illinois
Urbana, Ill.

Introduction

The methods for the direct determination of fluorescence lifetimes may be discussed by considering each single fluorescent species as a detector in which the response to an infinitely narrow pulse of light decays in time, t, according to the exponential law $I(t) = I(0) \times \exp - (kt)$. From the relations of the exciting light with the light emitted by such exponential detector, the rate constant k or its reciprocal τ, the lifetime of the excited state may be determined. Figure 1 shows the Fourier spectrum characteristic of an exponential detector (cf. McLachlan, 1963). The detector responds without attenuation or change of phase to all frequencies from zero to those approaching k, while frequencies of this order or exceeding k are progressively more attenuated. The phase of the emitted light lags behind that of the excitation by 45° when $\omega = k$, and tends to 90° lag towards complete attenuation. It follows that, for the determination of k, the fluorescence must be excited by light of one or more frequencies in the neighborhood of k (hatched area of Figure 1). The former is practically realized by excitation with sinusoidally modulated light, and the latter by excitation with light pulses the frequency spectrum of which is made up of a narrow band of frequencies.

Classical electrodynamics shows that, for emission in the visible and ultraviolet regions of the spectrum, k is of the order of 10^8 sec^{-1} (or τ of order 10^{-8} sec). Therefore, the frequencies to be employed in the excitation must be of the order of $10^8/2\pi$ or in the region of 1-50 MHz. Light modulated at a single frequency in this range may be produced by various electro-optical methods, (Gaviola, 1927; Maerks, 1938; Bauer & Rozwadowski, 1959; Müller *et al.*, 1965), whereas techniques for the production of approximately Gaussian pulses of half-width 0.3 to 3 nsec (D'Alessio *et al.* 1964, Hundley *et al.* 1967) have been described. Each type of method has its own advantages and disadvantages. The pulse method is particularly useful when several modes of decay are possible, although the methods employing a single frequency are undoubtedly the more accurate because of the extreme frequency selection attainable by electronic techniques. They are also better adapted to the measurement of lifetimes in the subnanosecond region, and because we had this object in mind we have chosen to employ sinusoidally modulated light of fixed frequency in our measurements.

The theory of the fluorometer, so named by Gaviola who constructed the first apparatus of this kind in 1926, has been given in detail by Dushinsky (1933). If a fluorescent species is illuminated with light modulated with frequency f, describable by the expression

$$E(t) = A + B \cos 2\pi ft$$

* This research was supported by United States Public Health Service Grant GM 11223.

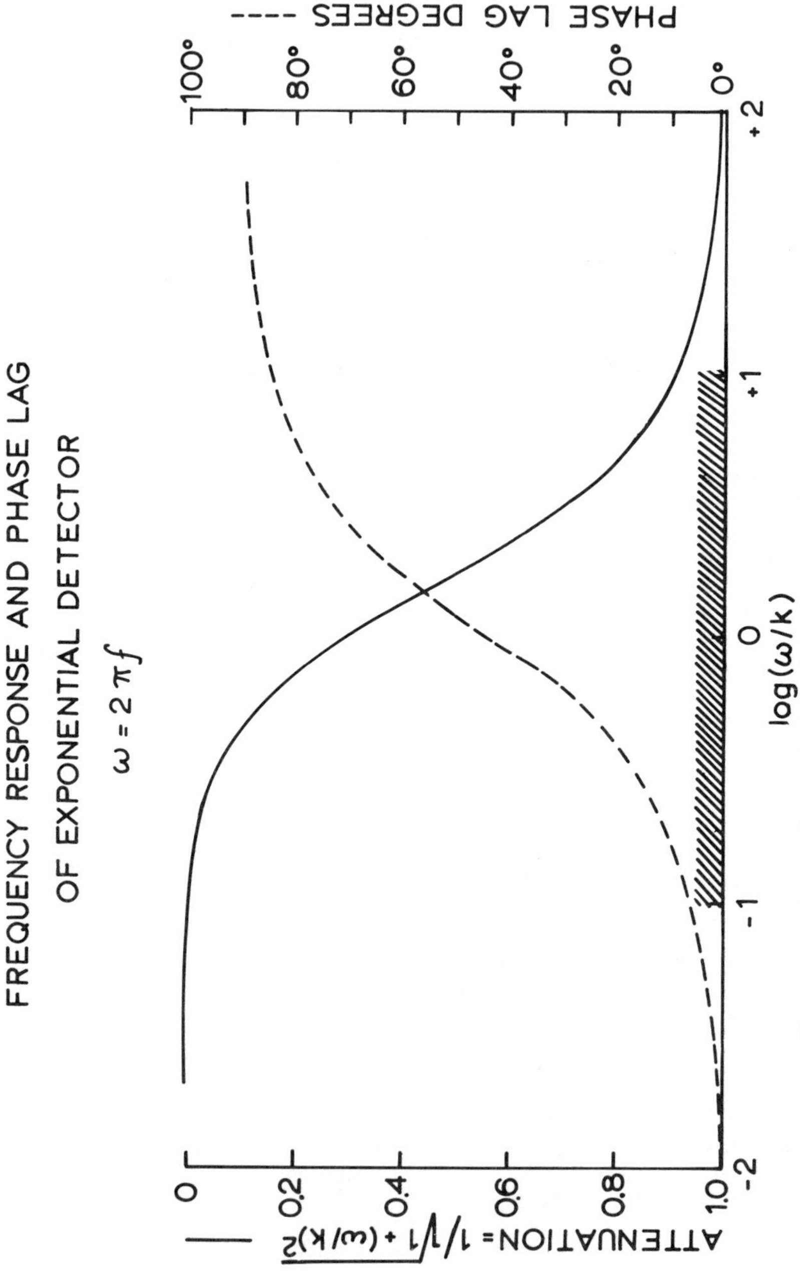

FIGURE 1. Attenuation and phase lag of exponential detector as a function of $\omega/k = 2\pi f/k$.

where $A \geq B$, the modulation of the exciting light is given by B/A. The fluorescent light due to emission by a population with exponential decay e^{-t}/τ is then described by the expression

$$F(t) = A + B \cos \delta \cos (2\pi ft - \delta) \quad (1)$$

where

$$\tan \delta = 2\pi f\tau \quad (2)$$

$$\text{Relative Modulation D} = \frac{\text{Modulation of Fluorescence}}{\text{Modulation of Excitation}} \quad (3)$$

$$= \cos \delta = (1 + 4\pi^2 f^2 \tau^2)^{-1/2}$$

Thus, it is possible to determine the lifetime either by a measurement of the phase lag, δ, or of the relative modulation of the emitted light. (FIGURE 2). The above equations were derived on the assumption of a single homogeneous emitting population with a unique decay constant, and it is often cited as one of the shortcomings of the single frequency method that the existence of a unique decay is presupposed but not demonstrated by the measurements. This is, indeed, the case if only one of the two quantities mentioned above is measured. If both are measured, the existence of an exponential decay may be demonstrated. In a heterogeneous emitting population, the lifetime measured by the degree of modulation will almost always be longer than the weighted average of the component lifetimes, whereas the lifetime determined from the phase lag will always be shorter than the weighted average. This fact is graphically demonstrated in FIGURE 3. It is only when there is a single decay that both methods give the same results, so that the obtention, within the experimental error, of the same value of τ by the two methods is sufficient proof of the simple exponential character of the decay and, indirectly, of the homogeneity of the emitting population.

The Cross-Correlation Method

The measurements of phase differences are simplified and the reliability of the measurements increased if the photocurrent produced by the fluorescence is mixed with a voltage of fixed frequency near, but not equal to, the modulating light frequency and the phase is measured in the amplified difference signal (Bailey and Rollefson, 1953; Schmillen, 1953). In these heterodyning procedures, the DC levels are disregarded, so that the degree of modulation which represents an important source of information is usually lost. Birks and Little (1953) first introduced an alternative method by which the phenomena may be transferred from the original high frequency to any desired low frequency while preserving in the latter the phase and the degree of modulation of the former. To obtain this result, an AC voltage of the light-modulating frequency having a known fixed phase difference, ϕ, is applied to one or more of the dynodes. The result is the modulation of the phototube response according to the equation:

$$R(t) = a + b \cos (2\pi ft - \phi)$$

The photocurrent is then the cross-correlation product $\overline{R(t)F(t)}$ integrated over a period, and equals

ALTERNATE METHODS OF MEASUREMENT OF τ

1. PHASE DIFFERENCE WITH SCATTERER.
2. RELATIVE MODULATION.

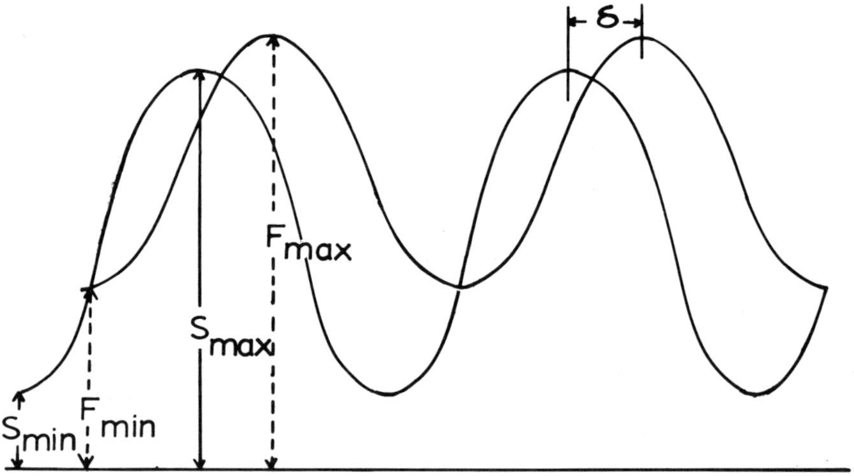

MODULATION FREQUENCY = f

δ = PHASE DIFFERENCE; $\tan\delta = 2\pi f\tau$

$$D_F = F_{max} - F_{min} \,/\, F_{max} + F_{min}$$

$$D_S = S_{max} - S_{min} \,/\, S_{max} + S_{min}$$

D = RELATIVE MODULATION =

$$D_F \,/\, D_S = 1 \Big/ \sqrt{1 + 4\pi^2 f^2 \tau^2} = \cos\delta$$

FIGURE 2. Schematic diagram showing the phase lag and demodulation of the photocurrents due to scatter, S, and a fluorescent solution, F.

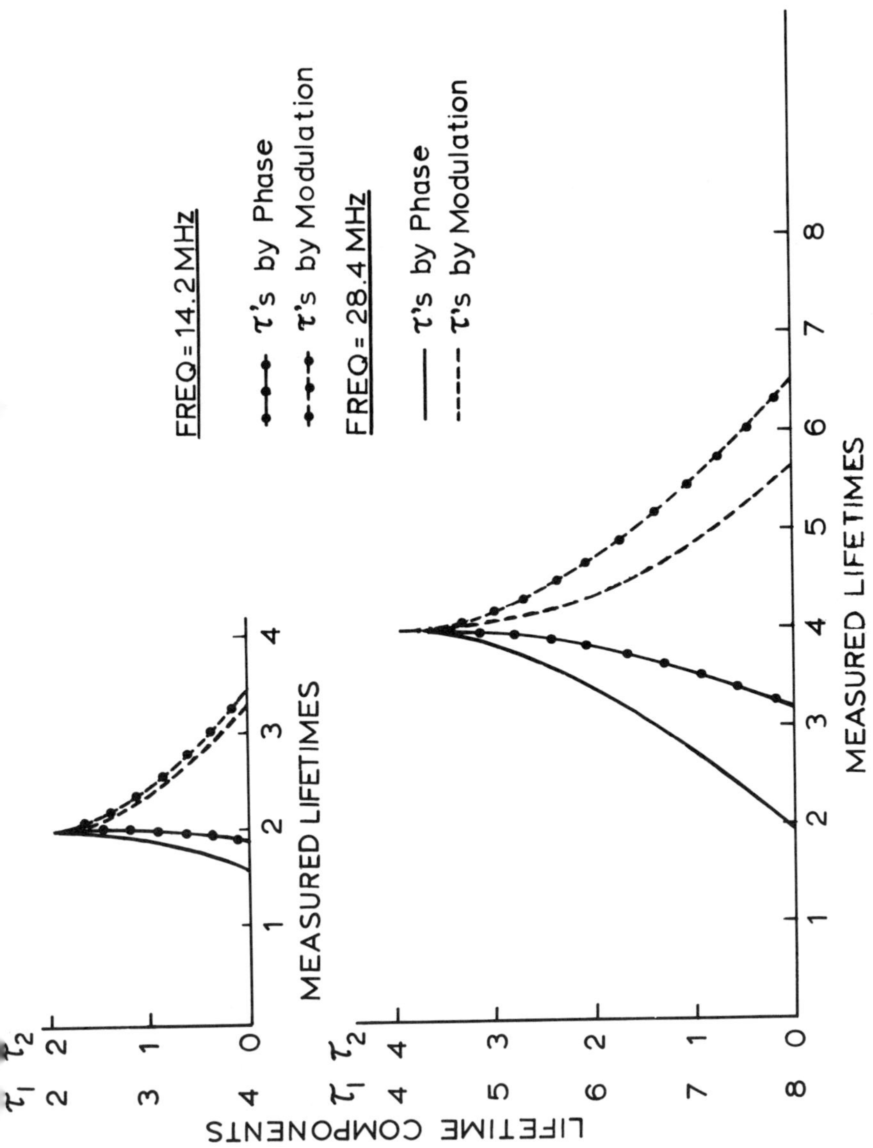

FIGURE 3. In a heterogeneous system of two components of equal intensity the two methods—phase and demodulation—give divergent results with respect to the expected mean value of the lifetime.

$$\overline{R(t)F(t)} = aA + bB\frac{\cos\delta}{2}\cos(\phi - \delta) \qquad (4)$$

Birks and Little determined δ by the value of ϕ necessary to get maximum photocurrent. We chose to translate the phenomenon to a lower frequency, Δf, by varying ϕ linearly with time so that $\phi = 2\pi\Delta ft$. In such case, if $\Delta f \ll f$,

$$\overline{R(t)F(t)} = aA + Bb\frac{\cos\delta}{2}\cos(2\pi\,\Delta ft - \delta) \qquad (5)$$

Thus, the low-frequency response preserves the phase difference δ and the relative modulation of the high-frequency photocurrent.

The advantages of the procedure utilized are several: (1) Since mixing of the high frequencies f and $f+\Delta f$ takes place only inside the phototube, and the low-frequency component is desired, the photomultiplier may be used with any practical anode load or even as a current device with a great improvement in sensitivity. (2) All frequencies above Δf may be filtered off with great increase in the signal/noise ratio and signal isolation. (3) With Δf less than 100 Hz, numerical time-interval counting may be used to determine the phase difference between the exciting and fluorescence light. Such a procedure is particularly well adapted to increase the accuracy through averaging.

Description of the Fluorometer

The features that make for the high sensitivity and wide spectral range of the instrument are to be found in the light modulation technique, the cross-correlation electronics and the phase measuring device employed.

Optics

The excitation optics is shown in FIGURE 4. The light source is a direct-current 150-watt xenon arc powered by storage batteries to reduce to a minimum the noise in the light source, and to eliminate the inherent 1–5% a–c ripple present in high-current power supplies.

The ultrasonics unit and lens system are similar to those described by Debye and Sears (1932) and Bailey and Rollefson (1953). The ultrasonics tank is constructed of heavy stainless steel, to achieve a high damping factor. An interchangeable x-cut quartz crystal is mounted at one end of the tank and a polished stainless steel reflector at the opposite end. The plane of the reflector may be adjusted through several degrees, to produce the optimum ultrasonic standing wave across the tank. Optical stability of the standing wave is provided by using a solution of 19% absolute alcohol and 81% glass-distilled water, since the temperature coefficient of the velocity of sound in this mixture at room temperature is nearly zero (Demtroeder, 1962). The major cause of phase instability appears to be the unavoidable, swirling suspended particles. This "phase-noise" appears to be quite random.

The ultrasonics crystal is driven in the 3rd harmonic by a 65-watt crystal-excited radio transmitter (Johnson Viking Ranger II). Two driving frequencies presently used are: 7.0994 MHz and 14.1988 MHz. The fre-

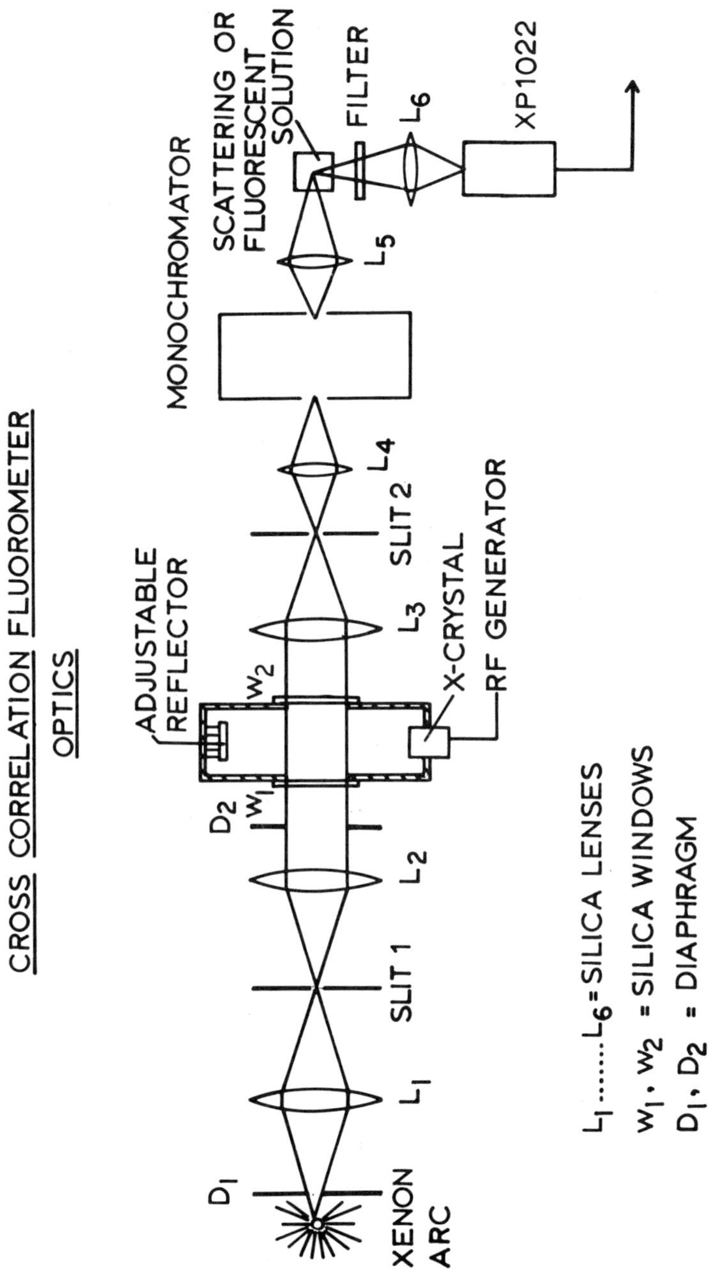

FIGURE 4. Plan of the optics of fluorometer.

quencies have been accurately measured and have been found to be stable within 5 parts in 10^7 over periods of 15 minutes, and within 5 parts in 10^6 over periods of weeks.

Lens 1 gathers light and focuses an image of the xenon arc at slit 1. Lens 2, placed at focal length distance from this slit, forms a nearly parallel beam of light through the ultrasonics tank. The long optic axis (large focal lengths) reduces the beam's divergence, which occurs to some extent because the lamp is not an ideal point source of light. The ultrasonic standing wave perpendicular to the light wave front creates planes of higher refractive index which collapse and build with the ultrasonic wave. The result is that the wave front of the emerging parallel beam is modulated in phase according to the modulation of the refractive index across the light path in the tank, just as occurs when a parallel beam strikes an ordinary grating. When this interference pattern is focused at slit 2 by lens 3 to form the image of slit 1, the image appears in the zero order as well as in several higher orders of diffraction. Each order is modulated at twice the frequency of the standing wave, i.e., at 14.2 MHz or 28.4 MHz. The zero order and first order images are the highest in intensity and in modulation (as great as 45% for the first order), and one or the other is used by adjusting slit 2 to select the desired image. This image of modulated light is then focused upon the input slit of the monochromator, so that any wavelength in the interval 240–1,000 nm may be chosen for excitation of a fluorescence sample.

Cross-Correlation Electronics

Cross correlation is accomplished by modulating the gain of the photomultiplier tube with an RF signal of 14,200,036 Hz (or 28,400,072, depending upon the excitation frequency used). Since the fluorescent light is modulated at 14,200,000 Hz (or 28,400,000 Hz), the signal detectable at the anode contains the cross-correlation frequency 36 Hz (or 72 Hz).

A Phillips XP1022 photomultiplier is used as the photodetector because of its high gain (up to 10^9) and fast rise time of 1.7 nanoseconds (manufacturer's specifications). This tube contains an anode screen grid that can conveniently be used to modulate the overall gain of the photomultiplier by applying to it an AC signal.

It should be pointed out that if the RF signal of the fluorescence were detected directly at the anode of the photomultiplier, the anode load (and thus the output impedance) would be limited to about 50 ohms due to parasitic capacitance. Also, the frequency bandpass, and thus the effective Johnson noise bandwidth, would have to be 100 MHz or greater in order to preserve the relative modulation. However, by heterodyning inside the photomultiplier and by detecting the audio frequency, large anode loads (20,000–100,000 ohms) and current detection amplifiers may be used, thus optimally utilizing the electrical characteristics of the photomultiplier tube. Typically, the audio signal at the anode is 1,000 times greater than the RF signal that would be obtained at low anode loads. Also, by using low-pass filter amplifiers with a high roll-off gain above 36 Hz (or 72 Hz), the effective noise bandwidth is reduced by a factor of 10^{-6}. In general, the sensitivity is so increased that it is safe to say that lifetime measurements may be obtained of any fluorescent solution having an intensity detectable in present-day spectrofluorometers.

The key to the translation from high- to low-frequency output is the addition of a constant known audio frequency Δf to an RF signal f. The difficulty of performing this addition successfully is apparent when it is realized that the sum $(f + \Delta f)$ must be absolutely locked in frequency and in phase to f, even though they differ by only about 5 parts in 10^5, and that other frequencies apart from $(f + \Delta f)$ must be absent.

The unique addition is accomplished by a Variogon Phase Shifting Transducer (Nilson Manufacturing Company, Haines City, Fla.), which is basically a rotating capacitor originally described by Morrison (1937), and subsequently improved (Holmes, 1949). The important feature of the phase shifting capacitor is that the phase angle between the input and the output is linearly dependent upon the angular position of one of its plates. Thus, turning the capacitor's rotor one revolution increases the phase of the output sine wave by 360 degrees, or one full cycle.

In the fluorometer, a damped hysteresis synchronous motor drives the rotating plate of the Variogon at 36 revolutions per second, thereby adding 36 Hz to the RF signal connected to the input. The period of this audio signal is 27.78 msec and, with the present motor, is stable within $\pm$ 0.01 msec. A phase reference signal, also 36 Hz, is obtained photoelectrically from holes in a disk mounted on the rotating shaft of the capacitor.

FIGURE 5 shows the electronic block diagram for measuring both phase angle and relative modulation of a fluorescence signal excited by either 14.2 MHz or 28.4 MHz. Since the phase shifting capacitor operates at only one frequency, 14.2 MHz, the reference RF signal from the ultrasonics crystal must be doubled previous to or following the phase shifter's addition of 36 Hz, depending upon the excitation frequency desired, thus producing 14,-200,036 Hz or 28,400,072 Hz for the photomultiplier gating frequency.

Phase Measurement

The actual phase measurement is accomplished by a two-channel frequency counter (Hewlett-Packard Model 5223L) that can measure time intervals to 0.01 msec. The counter is turned on by the rise of the phase reference square wave from the phase shifter, and it is turned off by the passage through zero of the audio signal from the photomultiplier tube. The counter displays or prints the time interval in milliseconds, so that the phase is calculated by:

$$\alpha = \frac{\text{time interval}}{\text{period}} \times 360 \text{ degrees}$$

A phase measurement of the light scattered by a water suspension of glycogen is used to correct for phase shifts in the electronics and the optics. Therefore the phase shift, δ, due to fluorescence is:

$$\delta = \alpha_{\text{fluorescence}} - \alpha_{\text{scatter}}$$

In all measurements, the intensity of the signal from the glycogen scatter is adjusted to be nearly equal to the intensity of the signal from the fluorescent sample. This precaution prevents possible systematic errors due to differences in gain, light intensity and noise, since phase resolution of better than 0.5 degrees is desired.

With the standard deviation of the time interval measurements within 0.01 msec, the smallest phase difference detectable (with a 72 Hz cross cor-

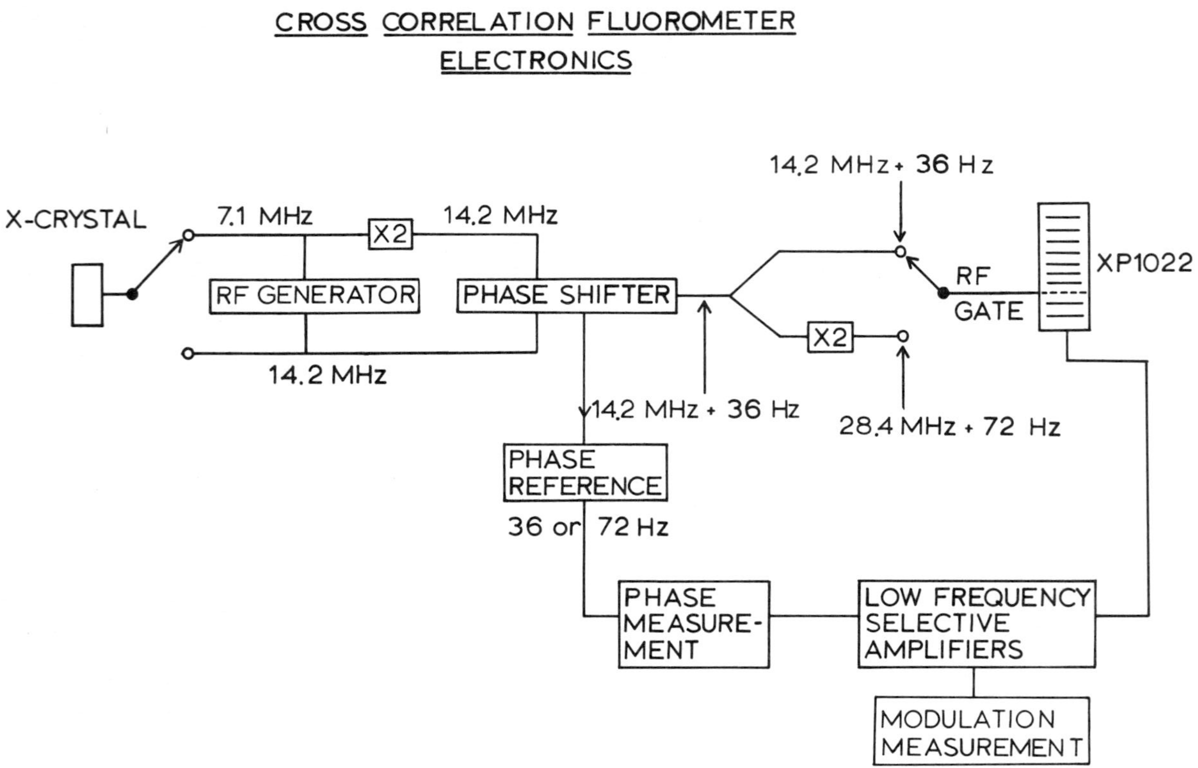

FIGURE 5. Block diagram of electronics of cross-correlation fluorometer.

relation frequency) is 0.35°. Therefore, with the 28.4 MHz excitation frequency, fluorescence decay times of less than 1 nsec can be measured with an expected accuracy of ± 0.03 nanoseconds.

Performance

Working with light modulated at 28.4 MHz a phase lag of 1° is equivalent to 0.1 nsec delay, and such an interval should be directly resolved by the apparatus. Although many fluorometers have been described in the literature, there have been few attempts to determine directly the ultimate time resolution of the instrument.

For this purpose, we have used two different methods. As shown in FIGURE 6, a known delay may be introduced in the signal arriving to the photocathode by lengthening the path of light after modulation. A lengthening of 30 cm results in a delay of 1 nsec, so that a measured delay of 0.1 nsec may be introduced with great accuracy. Similarly, replacement of 10 cm of air path by 10 cm of water (refractive index = 1.334) introduces a delay of approximately 0.11 nsec. The results of both types of experiments are shown in TABLE 1. It appears certain that the instrument can resolve directly 0.1 nsec. None of the delays measured differed from the actual introduced delays by more than 0.03 nsec.

The discrimination between lifetimes in the subnanosecond region was

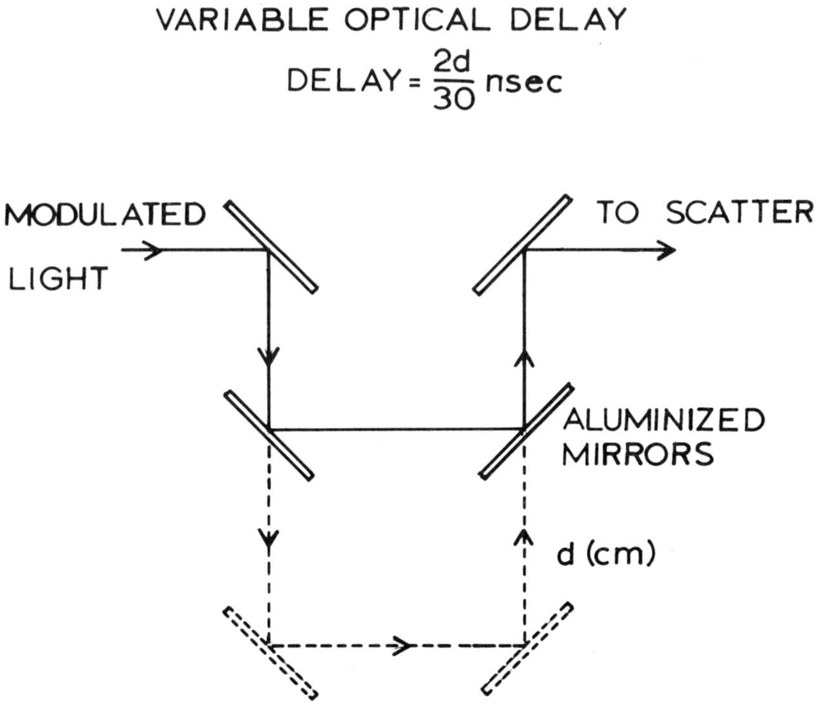

FIGURE 6. Plan of variable optical delay. The delay is introduced by sliding two aluminized mirrors in order to increase the light path by a known distance.

TABLE 1
OPTICAL DELAY MEASUREMENTS

Increase in Path Length in Air	Expected Delay (nsec)	Observed Delay (nsec)
10 cm	0.333	0.33
20 cm	0.667	0.70
40 cm	1.334	1.31
60 cm	2.001	2.03
Increase in Refractive Index of Path		
10 cm water	0.11	0.12

demonstrated by measurements in solutions of fluorescein in 0.01 M NaOH, quenched by the addition of KI. For an ideally collisional quenching process (Perrin, 1929; Wavilov, 1936), the relation $F/F_0 = \tau/\tau_0$ is expected to obtain. Here, F_0 and τ_0 are the fluorescence yield and lifetime of the solution in the absence of quencher, F and τ are the corresponding quantities in the presence of quencher. The classical observations of Perrin (1929) on the polarization, and of Szymanowsky (1936) on the actual lifetimes have substantiated the validity of this relation. As TABLE 2 shows, the difference in lifetime between two solutions quenched to 1/11 (τ = 0.49 nsec) and 1/19 (τ = 0.39 nsec) of the initial fluorescence yield could be determined. From these observations, we conclude that the instrument is capable of determining directly a difference of 0.1 nsec between two lifetimes each less than a nanosecond long.

The Fluorescence Lifetime of NADH (Nicotinamide-Adenine Dinucleotide)

The only direct measurement of NADH lifetime is given in a recent publication by Chen and coworkers (1967) as 4.5 nsec. The value experimentally found by us for the lifetime of the fluorescence of NADH (shown in TABLE 3) is 0.38 ± 0.03 nsec, an order of magnitude smaller than that of Chen and coworkers and in very good agreement with the value of 0.35 nsec calculated from oscillator strength and quantum yield (Weber, 1958). In 90% propylene glycol, the relative fluorescence yield and the lifetime of NADH increased by

TABLE 2
DECAY TIMES OF FLUORESCEIN SOLUTIONS IN 0.01 M NAOH QUENCHED BY POTASSIUM IODIDE

KI Molarity	F/F_0	τ_{nsec}	τ/τ_0
0	1.	4.7*	1.
0.1	0.48	2.26	0.45
0.2	0.26	1.40	0.30
0.5	0.093	0.49	0.10
0.8	0.052	0.39	0.083

Fluorescein concentration: 10 μgm/ml, 25° C.
Excitation: 480 nm.

* The value of 4.7 nsec, obtained at a concentration of 10 μgm/ml, is higher than the value of 4.2 (FIGURE 7) measured at higher dilution due to radiative transfer, as shown by Schmillen (1953) and by Bailey and Rollefson (1953).

TABLE 3

DECAY TIMES OF FLUORESCENCE OF SOLUTIONS OF NICOTINAMIDE-ADENINE DINUCLEOTIDE AT 17° C

Excitation at 340 nm	
0.1 M Phosphate Buffer, pH 7.5	0.38 ± 0.03 nsec
90% Propylene glycol—pH 7.5 Buffer	1.01 ± 0.03
Ratio of Decay Times	2.66 ± 0.2
Ratio of Fluorescence Yields	2.77 ± 0.05
Excitation at 280 nm	
0.1 M Phosphate Buffer, pH 7.5	0.38 ± 0.03

the same factor (~2.7). The closeness of this correlation also gives a measure of the reliability of the lifetime determinations.

FIGURE 7 gives a direct demonstration that the lifetime of NADH fluorescence is approximately one-tenth of the lifetime of fluorescein in 0.01 M NaOH (4.2 nsec). The figure is the oscillograph display of the cross-correlation signals from scattered light (no delay), from NADH and from fluorescein in alkali. The fluorescein trace is delayed by 1.4 msec equivalent to 36° of phase, the NADH trace is delayed by, at most, a tenth of this time.

The Fluorescence Lifetimes of FMN (Flavin Mononucleotide) and FAD (Flavin-Adenine Dinucleotide)

We present here some preliminary observations on the fluorescence lifetime of flavin mononucleotide (FMN) and flavin-adenine dinucleotide

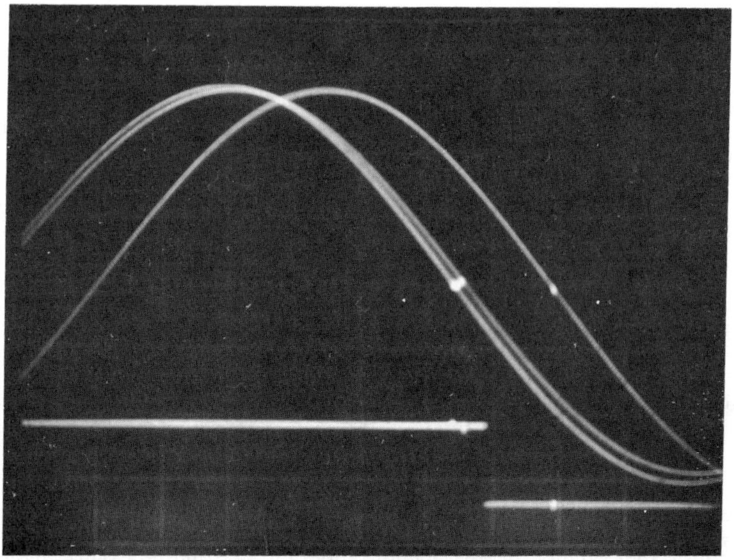

FIGURE 7. The figure shows the cross-correlation photocurrents from a scattering solution (first from left), a solution of NADH in phosphate buffer, pH 7.0, 17° C (second from left), and a solution of fluorescein (1 μgm/ml) in 0.01 M NaOH (right).

(FAD). It has been known for some time (Weber, 1950) that the fluorescence lifetime of FAD cannot greatly differ from that of FMN, although the fluorescence efficiency of the latter is some ten times greater than that of the former. Qualitatively, this may be understood if the FAD molecule exists in two forms, one of which (closed form) is a stacked complex of the flavin and adenine moieties and has no appreciable fluorescence, and the other (open form)—in which the said moieties remain apart—has fluorescence properties identical with FMN. In general, if the degree of dissociation of the closed form is α, the rate of quenching by interaction during the lifetime of the excited state k_+^*, and the rate of emission λ, the fluorescence efficiency of FAD, relative to FMN is

$$\frac{F_{FAD}}{F_{FMN}} = \alpha \frac{\lambda}{\lambda + k_+^*} = 0.10$$

Moreover,

$$\tau_{FAD} = 1/(\lambda + k_+^*); \qquad \tau_{FMN} = 1/\lambda$$

The values of the observed lifetimes are given in TABLE 4. From these we obtain $\alpha = 0.20$; $k_+^* = 2.10^8$ sec^{-1}. The measurements of τ in FAD and FMN

TABLE 4

DECAY TIMES OF FLUORESCENCE OF SOLUTIONS OF FLAVIN DERIVATIVES*

Flavin mononucleotide	4.65 ± 0.05
Lumiflavin	4.80 ± 0.05
Flavin-Adenine Dinucleotide	2.30 ± 0.05

*All solutions in 0.1 M phosphate buffer, pH 7.0 at 25° C. Excitation by 375 nm.

permit the unambiguous determination of the degree of dissociation of the FAD complex. Moreover, if it is supposed that the rate of quenching encounters in the excited state k_+^* is the same as the rate k_+ of formation of the FAD complex, the rate of dissociation of the latter may be calculated as $k_- = 6.10^7$ sec^{-1}. In the absence of more direct information, these figures may be tentatively used as characterizing the order of magnitude of the rates of association and dissociation of stacked aromatic dimers in water.†

Importance of the Determination of Lifetimes in the Study of Protein Fluorescence

From measurements of oscillator strength and fluorescence yield, it is clear that the lifetimes of protein fluorescence must be in the range of 2–4

† As pointed out by Professor Pullman in discussion, a computation of the interaction energies of adenine in the ground state with flavin in the ground state on one hand and in the first singlet excited state on the other could greatly help to establish the validity of the identification of k_+^* and k_+. Since fluorescence quenching involves always the interaction of a molecule in the first excited singlet with another in the ground state, theoretical studies of this kind would have equal interest in many other cases and it is hoped that they will be performed often in the future.

nsec. The fluorophores involved are mainly tryptophan residues, and there is a distinct possibility of detecting the heterogeneous character of their emission through measurements of τ. In principle, such heterogeneity could be detected in three different ways: (1) By simultaneous measurements of phase lag and degree of modulation at a single light-modulation frequency. As set out in the introduction and graphically shown in FIGURE 3, only in the case of a unique decay will the values of τ obtained by both methods be in agreement. (2) By measurements of lifetime at more than one modulating frequency. If the modulation frequency is varied systematically in the interval 1–50 MHz, the complete Fourier spectrum of the emission should be available. Present-day technical shortcomings make it very difficult to use more than a few fixed frequencies. As described, 14.2 or 28.4 MHz may be used in our fluorometer. These two ought to be sufficient to establish the character of the emission in many cases, if all the lifetimes involved are in the interval of 0.1 to 50 nsec. (3) By measurements of the dispersion of lifetime with exciting or fluorescence light.

The practical possibility of such measurements depends upon keeping a satisfactory signal-to-noise ratio in spite of the inevitable loss of fluorescence intensity. It demands, therefore, the modulation of a strong light source continuous in the visible and ultraviolet regions such as the xenon arc. We selected the ultrasonic technique because of the high degree of modulation attainable in all spectral regions of interest without appreciable attenuation of the exciting light. The short decay of NADH, with its low fluorescence yield of 3% was measured with monochromatic excitation of 4 nm bandwidth with a very satisfactory signal-to-noise ratio.

The study of the dispersion of lifetime with exciting and emitting wavelengths carried out with a precision of the order that we achieved promises to add a great deal to the study of protein fluorescence.

ACKNOWLEDGMENT

The values of lifetime and yield of FAD are sensitive to very small amounts of FMN and riboflavin present in the preparation. We are grateful to Professor V. Massey for pointing out the stringent purity requirements of these observations and for the method of preparation of FAD of high purity. (V. Massey & B. E. P. Swoboda. 1963. Biochem. Z. **338:** 474.)

REFERENCES

1. BAILEY, E. A. & G. K. ROLLEFSON. 1953. J. Chem. Phys. **21:** 1315.
2. BAUER, R & M. ROZWADOWSKI. 1959. Bull. Acad. Pol. Sci. **7:** 365.
3. BIRKS, J. B. & W. A. LITTLE. 1953. Proc. Phys. Soc. (A) **66:** 921.
4. CHEN, R. F., G. G. VUREK & N. ALEXANDER. 1967. Science **156:** 949.
5. D'ALESSIO, J. T., P. K. LUDWIG & M. BURTON. 1964. Rev. Sci. Instrum. **35:** 1015.
6. DEBYE, P. & F. W. SEARS. 1932. Proc. Nat. Acad. Sci. **18:** 409.
7. DEMTROEDER, W. 1962. Z. Physik **166:** 42.
8. DUSHINSKY, F. 1933. Z. Physik **81:** 7.
9. GAVIOLA, E. 1927. Z. Physik **42:** 852.
10. HOLMES, E. A. 1949. M.I.T. Rad. Lab. Ser. **17:** 288.
11. HUNDLEY, L., T. COBURN, E. GARWIN & L. STRYER. 1967. Rev. Sci. Instrum. **38:** 488.
12. MAERKS, O. 1938. Z. Physik **109:** 685.
13. MCLACHLAN, N. W. 1963. Complex Variable Theory and Transform Calculus. 2nd Edit.: 184. Cambridge University Press. New York, N.Y.
14. MORRISON, J. F. 1937. Proc. I. R. E. **25:** 1310.

15. MÜLLER, A., R. LUMRY & H. KOKUBU. 1965. Rev. Sci. Instrum. **36:** 1214.
16. PERRIN, F. 1929. Ann. Phys. (Paris) **12:** 169.
17. SCHMILLEN, A. 1953. Z. Physik **135:** 294.
18. SZYMANOWSKY, W. 1936. Z. Physik **95:** 460.
19. WAVILOV, S. I. 1936. Acta Physiol. Pol. **5:** 417.
20. WEBER, G. 1950. Biochem. J. **47:** 114.
21. WEBER, G. 1958. J. Chim. Phys. **55:** 878.

APPROACHES TO THE MODE OF ACTION OF CARBOXYPEPTIDASE*

Bert L. Vallee

Biophysics Research Laboratory, Department of Biological Chemistry, Harvard Medical School, and Division of Medical Biology, Peter Bent Brigham Hospital, Boston, Mass.

The isolation and crystallization of carboxypeptidase A† from beef pancreas by Anson[1, 2] and the synthesis of a series of suitable substrates by Bergmann and coworkers[3] led to extensive investigations of the kinetics and physical chemistry of this enzyme by many workers during the past two decades.

Carboxypeptidase A specifically catalyzes the hydrolysis of peptide bonds involving the α-amino group of the C-terminal amino acid residue of proteins, polypeptides and peptides, particularly when this amino acid contains an aromatic or branched aliphatic side-chain. Like other peptidases, it also hydrolyzes analogous ester bonds. The activation of the zymogen, procarboxypeptidase A, and the general properties of the native enzyme have been reviewed.[4, 5] The present discussion will concern itself largely with studies of the active center of carboxypeptidase and will summarize some of the chemical modifications which have been performed to delineate substrate binding and catalysis. Both physicochemical and kinetic studies of the chemically modified derivatives have led to a model that reflects present knowledge of the manner in which substrates may bind to this enzyme.[6, 7, 46, 47]

Several years ago, we first reported that mono- and dicarboxylic acid anhydrides and N-acetylimidazole acylate tyrosyl residues of carboxypeptidase, thereby increasing esterase and decreasing peptidase activity.[8, 9] Both of these changes are prevented when modifications are performed in the presence of inhibitors or substrate analogues, and they are reversed by nucleophilic reagents such as hydroxylamine. These and the effects of iodination[10] have been attributed to the modification of two of the 19 tyrosyl residues of the enzyme. The magnitude of the functional changes depend on the particular agent employed and the conditions under which modifications and assays were performed. Further, modifications with N-bromosuccinimide, hydrogen peroxide, and irradiation with ultraviolet light[11] result in similar changes. Limited proteolysis with subtilisin has also changed the dual specificity of carboxypeptidase.[12] Similar to acetylation and iodination, the esterase activity of the resultant carboxypeptidase-S increases, but the peptidase activity decreases only to 50% of the control.

More recently, we have drawn attention to the potential of tetranitromethane (TNM) for the nitration of tyrosyl residues of proteins.[13, 14] The introduction of the nitro group can be measured in three different ways: production of nitroform which absorbs strongly at 350 mμ, the resultant re-

* This work was supported by Grant-in-Aid HE-07292 from the National Institutes of Health of the Department of Health, Education and Welfare.

† *Abbreviations:* [(CPD)Zn], zinc carboxypeptidase A, with (CPD) representing apoenzyme and the brackets indicating the firm binding of zinc or other metals to it, e.g., [(CPD)Me] refers to the metallocarboxypeptidases where Me may be Cd, Co, Hg, Mn, or Ni. [(AcCPD)Me], metallocarboxypeptidases acetylated with N-acetylimidazole; CGP, carbobenzoxyglycyl-L-phenylalanine; BGP, benzoylglycyl-L-phenylalanine; HPLA, hippuryl-dl-β-phenyllactate. Tris,(hydroxymethyl)amino methane.

lease of hydrogen ions and the formation of mononitrotyrosine, exhibiting intense absorption at 428 mμ. A fourfold molar excess of tetranitromethane nitrates one tyrosyl residue of carboxypeptidase. Maximally, esterase activity increases to about 180% of that of the native enzyme, even when up to a 16-fold molar excess is used. With a fourfold molar excess peptidase activity falls to about 15% of the control (FIGURE 1). The loss of peptidase activity correlates with the nitration of a single tyrosyl residue. Nitration in the presence of β-phenylpropionate prevents the changes in activities.[15–17]

Spectral titration of the single nitrotyrosyl residue of the enzyme modified with a fourfold molar excess of TNM has an apparent pK_a of 6.3 compared to 7.0 for the model compound N-acetyl-3-nitrotyrosine. If additional tyrosyl residues are nitrated by using higher excesses of TNM, these exhibit a pK of 6.9 similar to that of model compounds (TABLE 1). The abnormally low pK of the nitration-susceptible active center tyrosyl residue might be due to features of its immediate chemical environment.[15, 17]

Importantly, spectral titrations (FIGURE 2) and inhibition studies of mononitrocarboxypeptidase in the presence of either β-phenylpropionate, glycyl-L-leucine or glycyl-L-phenylalanine indicate that these alter the immediate chemical environment of the nitrated tyrosyl residue. This might be due to their direct interaction with the nitrotyrosyl group or to conformational changes that move the nitrotyrosyl group into a more hydrophobic environment.[15]

We have also studied another reagent, 5-diazo-1H-tetrazole (DHT), described by Horinishi and coworkers.[18] The products of tyrosyl and histidyl, but not of lysyl coupling, are colored. At pH 8.8, an eightfold molar excess of the agent increases esterase to approximately 200% of the control, but peptidase activity remains very close to that of native carboxypeptidase; again, β-phenylpropionate prevents these changes.[19] These functional responses differ significantly from those observed subsequent to other chemical modifications performed on this enzyme. Only one tyrosyl (and no histidyl) residue is modified under these conditions, as determined by spectral and amino acid analyses. When the DHT concentration is increased, esterase activity does not change further, but peptidase activity progressively decreases and is imperceptible after treatment with a 30- to 45-fold molar ex-

TABLE 1

APPARENT IONIZATION CONSTANTS OF VARIOUS NITROPHENOLS[a]

Substance	pK_{app}
0-Nitrophenol	7.2
3-Nitrotyrosine	6.8
N-Acetyl-3-nitrotyrosine	7.0
Mononitrocarboxypeptidase[b]	6.3
Mononitrocarboxypeptidase[c] + 0.1 M β-phenylpropionate	7.0
Nitrocarboxypeptidase[d]	6.9

[a] All spectra were measured in 0.2 M Tris-0.2 M acetate-0.5 M NaCl at a concentration of 2.5×10^{-4} M.

[b] Carboxypeptidase nitrated with a fourfold molar excess of TNM.

[c] Carboxypeptidase nitrated with a fourfold molar excess of TNM. Spectra were measured in the presence of 0.1 M β-phenylpropionate.

[d] Carboxypeptidase nitrated with a 32-fold molar excess of TNM in the presence of 0.1 M β-phenylpropionate.[15]

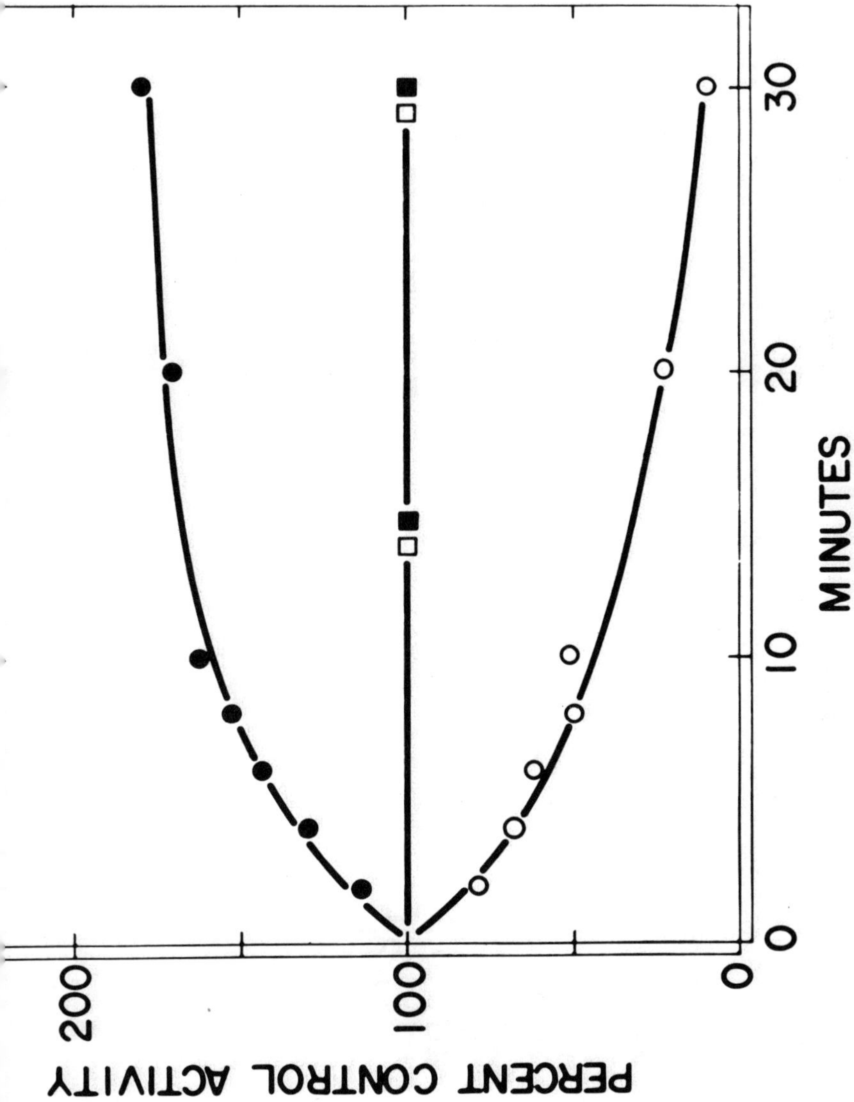

FIGURE 1. Progression of changes in esterase (closed symbols) and peptidase (open symbols) activities during nitration of carboxypeptidase (10 mg/ml), with a fourfold molar excess of TNM in the presence (□, ■) and absence (0, •) of 0.1 M β-phenylproprionate.[16]

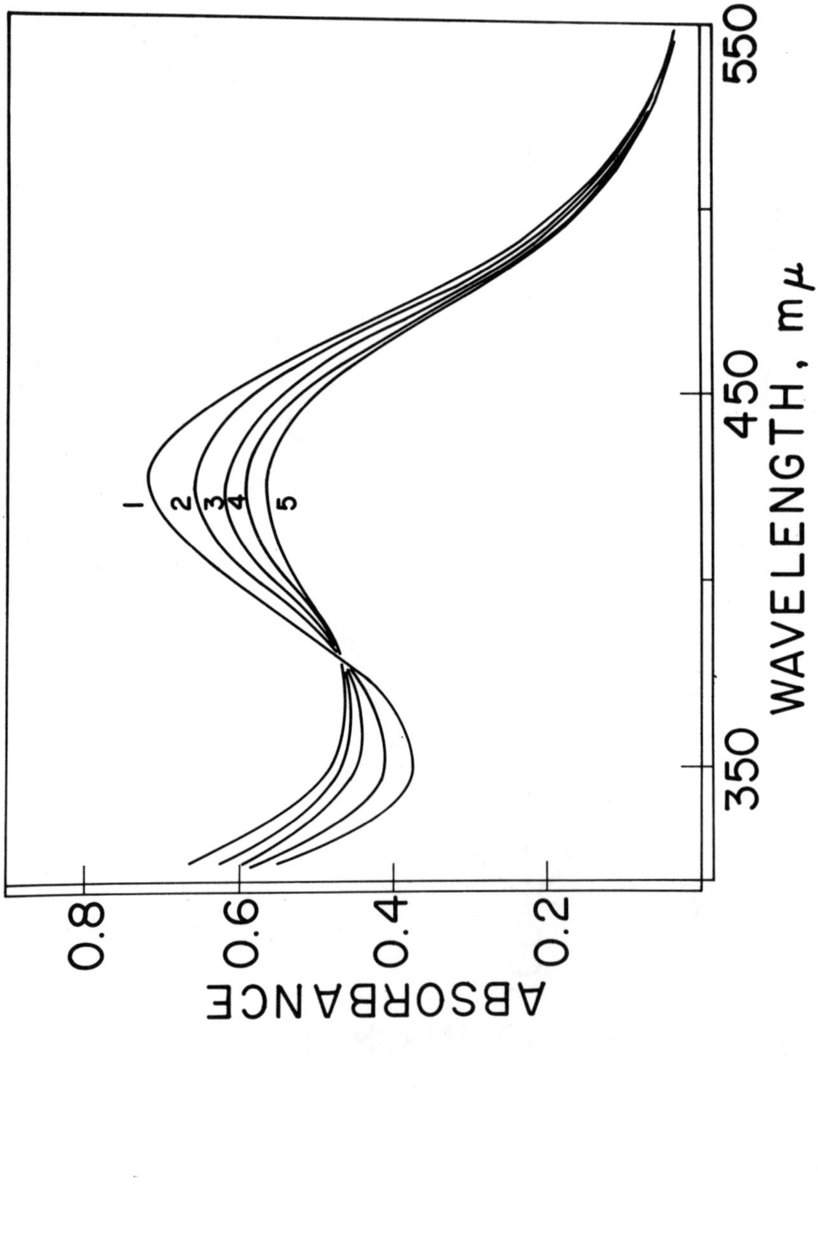

FIGURE 2. The effect of β-phenylproprionate on the spectrum of nitrocarboxypeptidase. Spectra were measured in 0.2 M Tris-0.2 M acetate-0.5 M NaCl buffer, pH 8.0. The concentrations of β-phenylpropionate were as follows: 1 (control), none; 2, 0.01 M; 3, 0.025 M; 4, 0.05 M; and 5, 0.1 M.[15]

cess. The decrease in peptidase activity coincides with the coupling of one additional tyrosyl and one histidyl residue. The modification of this histidine can be prevented by the presence of β-phenylpropionate. The data do not indicate in what manner this histidyl residue might be important to the loss of peptidase activity. Changes in the lysine content correlate neither with peptidase nor esterase activity.[19]

To gain information about the particular residues modified and the identity of the various chemical derivatives, we have studied the functional consequences of successive chemical modifications. Thus, the enzyme was acetylated or coupled with DHT. It will be recalled that acetylation increases esterase and markedly reduces peptidase activity, whereas an eightfold molar excess of DHT increases esterase but does not decrease peptidase activity. Each of these derivatives was exposed to a fourfold molar excess of TNM under standard conditions at pH 8 for 45 minutes (FIGURE 3). Nitration does not affect the activities of acetylcarboxypeptidase, suggesting that the two O-acetyl tyrosyl residues could not be nitrated, and that one of them might be a residue corresponding to the one which is susceptible to nitration in the native enzyme. The consequence of exposing the acetylenzyme to DHT was quite analogous.[16]

Nitration of azocarboxypeptidase did not affect the esterase activity of this derivative, but decreased its peptidase activity to that characteristic of nitrocarboxypeptidase (FIGURE 3). Spectral analysis of the product revealed the presence of only one azotyrosyl and one nitrotyrosyl residue each per mole. This suggested that the enzymatic changes due to azo-coupling on the one hand and to nitration on the other may be due to modification of different tyrosyl residues.[16]

Nitration of iodocarboxypeptidase progressively decreases esterase activity from 550 to about 200%, a value typical of nitrocarboxypeptidase, but the very low peptidase activity of this sample was unchanged during the 45-minute reaction time. Since TNM was found to react very rapidly with both mono- and diodotyrosine, it might be postulated that TNM can displace iodine converting iodo- to nitrotyrosyl residues, thereby accounting for the activity changes on nitration of iodocarboxypeptidase. This postulate is under investigation. When the order of the chemical modifications was reversed, i.e., when nitration preceded acetylation, iodination or azocoupling, the activities did not change but remained at the levels characteristic of nitrocarboxypeptidase.[16] These studies are quite similar to those reported previously on acetylation or iodination of azocarboxypeptidase.[19]

It is expected that the availability of several reagents specific for tyrosine, each with various effects on activity, may assist in delineating the roles of the different functional tyrosyl residues. Work is in progress in collaboration with H. Neurath to identify the location of these residues in the primary sequence. In this regard, Roholt and Pressman have recently isolated a tyrosyl peptide believed to contain one of these active center tyrosyl residues, identified by their double labeling technique that employs two isotopes of iodine.[20]

Kinetics of Chemically Modified Carboxypeptidases

Kinetic studies might be expected to assist materially both in defining the mode of action of carboxypeptidase and the basis for the changes in esterase and peptidase activities observed on chemical modifications. Over the past 25 years, numerous studies have emphasized the remarkably complex ki-

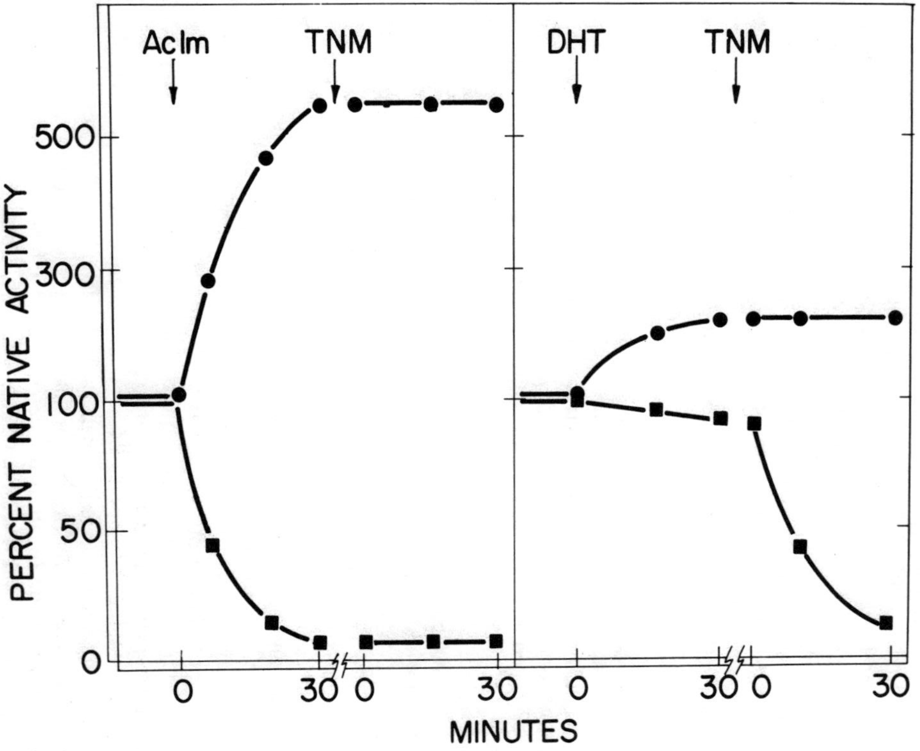

FIGURE 3. Progression of esterase (●) and peptidase (■) activities on reaction of acetylcarboxypeptidase (left) and azo-1-H-tetrazolylcarboxypeptidase (right), with a fourfold molar excess of TNM at pH 8.0, 20°. The time course of acetylation with N-acetylimidazole (left) and coupling with DHT (right) is 30 minutes, followed by TNM in both instances.

netic behavior of native carboxypeptidase,[3, 21–31] and some of the anomalies have also been observed in the crystalline state.[32]

These studies predict the difficulties to be expected in selecting from the large number of derivatives now available those which might be most suitable for detailed kinetic analyses. Hence, we have so far restricted our kinetic investigations somewhat arbitrarily to a limited number of metal substitutions and a few of their acetyl derivatives while employing three substrates: i.e., CGP, BGP and HPLA.[33]

The hydrolysis of most of the peptide or ester substrates by the native enzyme is accompanied by various permutations of substrate and product activation and inhibition. The order of the relative rates of maximum hydrolysis for both BGP and CGP is distinctive: Co > Zn > Mn. This is preserved over a wide range of substrate concentrations. Similarly, the order Cd > Mn > Co > Zn > Hg for the hydrolysis of HPLA is characteristic (Cd and Hg carboxypeptidases do not hydrolyze peptides).[6, 7, 34] All of these metallocarboxypeptidases exhibit substrate inhibition when acting on CGP (FIGURE 4) and HPLA. As indicated by deviation from linearity in Lineweaver-Burk plots, the Co, Zn and Mn enzymes exhibit substrate activation with CGP (FIGURE 4) and BGP (Riordan *et al.*, 1965) at a substrate concentration of 0.002 M. Substitution of different metal ions for zinc at the active site influences the concentration range in which substrate activation or inhibition is manifested but apparently does not abolish either effect. Hence, the kinetic ambiguities do not appear to reside solely in the nature of the particular metal at the active site, since the anomalies persist on exchanging the metals for one another.

Numerical values of K_m and V_{max}, based on the linear segments of plots such as shown in FIGURE 4, are largely descriptive, of course, since the values extrapolated from such multiphasic plots may be composed of several different constants. They are prone to be of limited value in devising meaningful kinetic models for a system in which both the substrate and the product importantly affect the ultimate activity, and their contributions are not easily incorporated into a definitive kinetic scheme. Nonetheless, the values of V_{max} and K_m for the hydrolysis of HPLA calculated from linear portions of such reciprocal plots have been obtained for a number of derivatives (TABLE 2).[34] When the customary dipeptide and ester substrates are employed, the ultimate activity owing to metal substitution, chemical modifications, limited proteolysis and their combinations results in varied changes of V_{max}, K_m or both.[33] They

TABLE 2

KINETIC CONSTANTS FOR THE HYDROLYSIS OF HPLA BY THE NATIVE ZINC ENZYME AND OTHER METALLOCARBOXYPEPTIDASES

[(CPD)Me]	K_m $M \times 10^5$	V_{max} $min^{-1} \times 10^{-3}$
[(CPD)Zn]	7.6	28.6
[(CPD)Co]	9.8	37.7
[(CPD)Ni]	21.0	27.6
[(CPD)Mn]	32.0	56.8
[(CPD)Cd]	55.0	61.5
[(AcCPD)Zn]*	250	42.0
[(AcCPD)Cd]	830	24.0

*Ac = acyl.

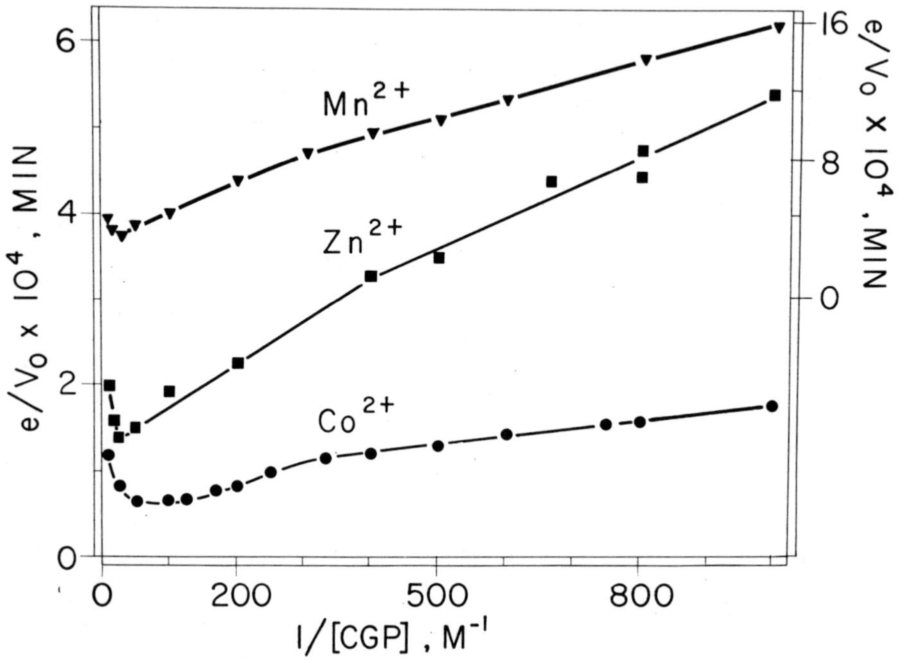

FIGURE 4. Double reciprocal plots for the hydrolysis of carbobenzoxyglycyl-L-phenylalanine (CGP) by different metallocarboxypeptidases. (■) [(CPD)Zn], (•) [(CPD)Co], (▼) [(CPD)Mn]. Assays were performed in 1 M NaCl, 0.05 M Tris/Cl⁻, pH 7.5 at 25° C, for [(CPD)Co] and [(CPD)Mn] in the presence of 10^{-4} M metal ions to ensure full formation of these metalloenzymes. Initial velocities, V_0/E_0 were expressed as turnover numbers per minute (moles of substrate hydrolyzed/mole of enzyme, per min). Substrate concentrations were varied from 0.001 to 0.08 M. Enzyme concentrations were varied from 6×10^{-9} to 8×10^{-8} M. The right-hand ordinate pertains to [(CPD)Mn] only.[33]

suggest that the ultimate esterase activity in response to different modifications may be accomplished by various combinations of effects on altered catalytic efficiency, substrate binding and substrate inhibition. Here, binding of course refers to the overall process, including both the formation of the enzyme substrate complexes as seen in direct binding studies, or of any intermediates which can differ readily from these and dominate the kinetic results.[7]

Some time ago,[35] we first proposed a working model which postulated multiple substrate binding sites and which included variations in the orientation of a substrate molecule with respect to these sites. These ideas were based largely on the results obtained with the acetylated metallocarboxypeptidases[36] acting on CGP, BGP and HPLA.[6, 7] Its minimal version, shown in FIGURE 5, therefore emphasizes sites rather than specific binding groups and does not take the size of substrates into consideration. Esters, portrayed

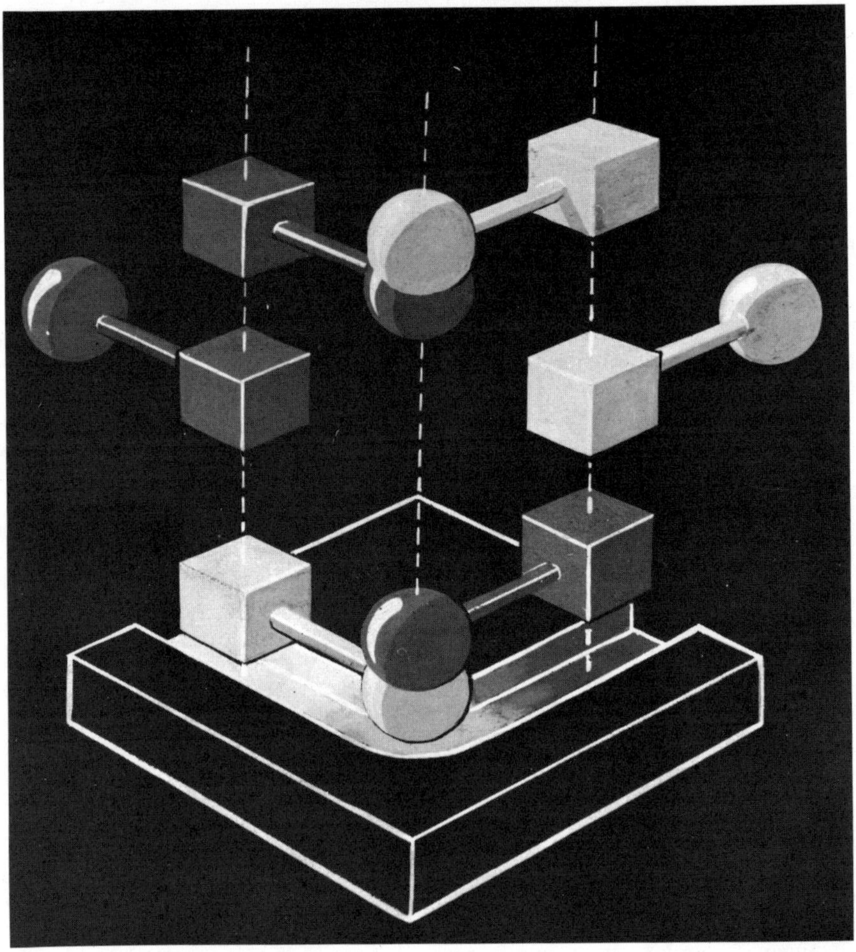

FIGURE 5. Model portraying dual or multiple substrate binding loci. The rectangular area and groove schematically represent the enzyme surface and sites for substrate binding. Peptides, the light symbols, and esters, the dark symbols, are thought to interact with the enzyme surface in regions characteristic of each, as indicated by the light and dark areas of the groove; an area of possible overlap is indicated by the coincidence of the symbols and the shading of the groove in the center. Some of the many alternate modes of possible substrate interactions are exemplified in projection and described in the text. The representation of substrates is symbolic only and does not attempt to define the identity and number of substrate or protein residues (or groups) interacting, or the forces involved in such a scheme,[6, 7] e.g., conformational changes brought about either by inhibitors or substrates.[15, 39, 46, 47]

by the dark symbols, and peptides by the light symbols, are thought to bind at distinct but related sites and, according to this scheme, their catalytically productive interactions result from "correct binding" at sites specific for each (FIGURE 5). At least one of the binding loci for esters and peptides might coincide, as indicated by the overlap of the dark and light symbols and by the shaded area of the groove (FIGURE 5). Such overlap is consistent with the competition of esters and peptide substrates observed kinetically. Other permutations are apparent. Catalytically unproductive complexes could result when, for example, a peptide interacts "incorrectly" at the ester locus or an ester at the peptide locus (FIGURE 5, top). This could account, at least in part, for the substrate inhibition encountered in most instances examined so far. The type of substrate binding shown in the middle of FIGURE 5 would lead to substrate activation by preventing the unproductive mode of binding shown at the top. The definitions of terminology and additional pictorial representations have been published and should be inspected for details.[46, 47]

For the sake of simplicity, FIGURE 5 deals only with substrates. The effects of product binding as visualized by considering only the cubes or spheres of this diagram would be expected to result in activation of one and inhibition of the other activity. The degree of inhibition or activation in the kinetics of hydrolysis of a particular substrate studied might well be determined by the ratio of K_mK_i for all participating species. A whole series of additional permutations of this mode of binding has been presented.[7, 46] Since both the N-terminal blocking groups and C-terminal R. groups of virtually all of the synthetic peptide and ester substrates currently employed are hydrophobic in character, these might readily bind to appropriate areas or side-chains of the protein.

A number of findings support such a scheme. Carbobenzoxyglycine or benzoylglycine, products of the hydrolysis of CGP and BGP, inhibit esterase activity while activating peptidase activity. Such reciprocal activation and inhibition are not restricted to the hydrolysis of the parent compounds. Thus, benzoylglycine activates the hydrolysis of CGP, and carbobenzoxyglycine affects BGP in an analogous manner. Further, a number of organic compounds analogous to the blocking group activate the hydrolysis of CGP and inhibit that of HPLA (FIGURE 6).[37, 46, 47] The model readily accounts for this further example of the apparent ability of the enzyme to differentiate between peptide and ester substrates.

The model encompasses yet additional features of the known behavior of the enzyme. Acetylcarboxypeptidase is virtually inactive toward peptide substrates. Gel filtration, isotope exchange and kinetics suggest that the decreased peptidase activity of acetyl- and iodocarboxypeptidases comes about because these modified enzymes bind peptide substrates much more weakly than does the native enzyme, while hydrolyzing the ester, HPLA, more effectively.[36] Under these conditions substrate inhibition, apparent in the activity profile of the native enzyme, is displaced to much higher concentrations. The model suggests that acetylation which could partially or completely block the correct, productive peptide binding site would simultaneously abolish erroneous, unproductive binding of the ester at the peptide site, thereby relieving much of the substrate inhibition of esterase activity. Ester substrate inhibition would not be abolished completely, since the model indicates yet other modes of unproductive ester binding. The observed data are in keeping with this view, since O-acetylation displaces substrate inhibition observed at about 10^{-3} M for the native enzyme to a higher substrate concentration, i.e., 10^{-2} M for the acetyl derivative,[34] but substrate inhibition is not abolished. In addition, however, O-acetylation also increases catalytic efficiency by about 30%.[24] Hence, depending upon the substrate concentration employed, an increase, decrease or no change in the rate of hydrolysis can be noted.[7, 46, 47]

Although the acetyl derivatives would not bind peptides at the correct site, the model suggests that they could still bind erroneously and unproductively

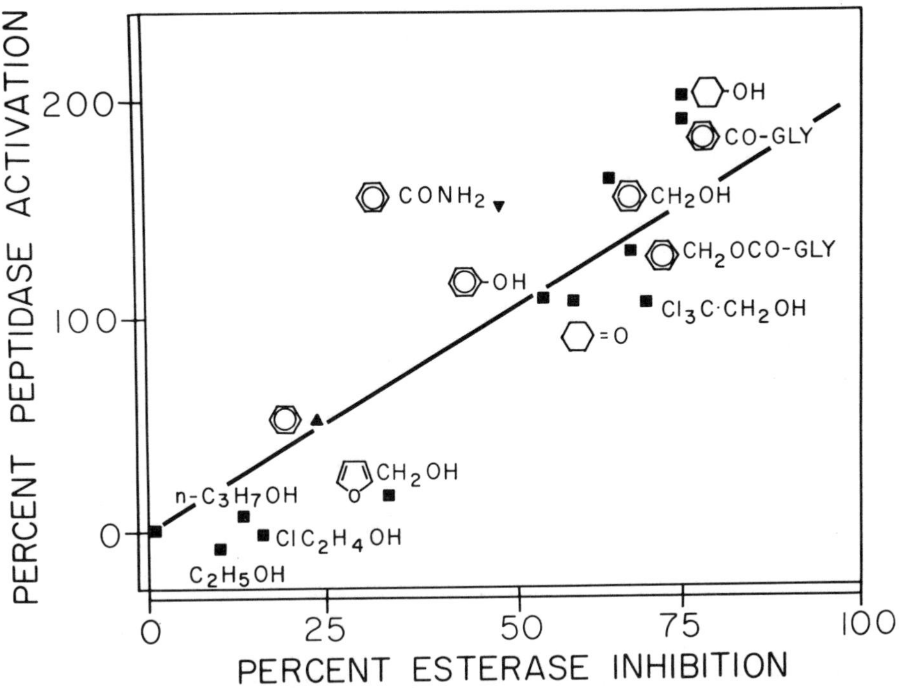

FIGURE 6. Activation of peptidase and inhibition of esterase activities by products and other modifiers. All activities were measured with CGP and HPLA as substrates, both 0.001 M.[34] All activators were 0.05 M. The chemical formulae denote the following compounds: carbobenzoxyglycine, benzoylglycine, cyclohexanol, benzyl alcohol, benzamide, phenol, cyclohexanone, 2, 2′, 2″ trichloroethanol, benzene, furfuryl alcohol, n-propanol, 2-Cl-ethanol, ethanol. Activation of peptidase and inhibition of esterase are expressed as percent of the control activity of the native enzyme.[7, 37]

at the ester site, resulting in inhibition of esterase activity. The results of kinetics are consistent with this hypothesis. Carbobenzoxyglycyl-L-leucine, benzoylglycyl-L-phenylalanine, carbobenzoxyglycyl-L-tyrosine and glycyl-L-tyrosine all competitively inhibit the esterase activity of acetylcarboxypeptidase, as does the inhibitor β-phenylpropionate and the product, L-phenylalanine (FIGURE 7).[6, 7, 46, 47] Further, the model is not inconsistent with findings by x-ray diffraction where either β-(p-iodophenyl) propionate or glycyl-L-tyrosine can bind in more than one manner to cross-linked crystals of the metalloenzyme.[38, 39] It should be pointed out, however, that inhibitors like β-(p-iodophenyl) propionate or β-phenylpropionate may not be bound to the enzyme in a manner identical to that of substrates,[40, 41] and that glycyl-L-tyrosine is hydrolyzed very slowly compared with many other peptide substrates. X-ray diffraction studies at higher resolution will prob-

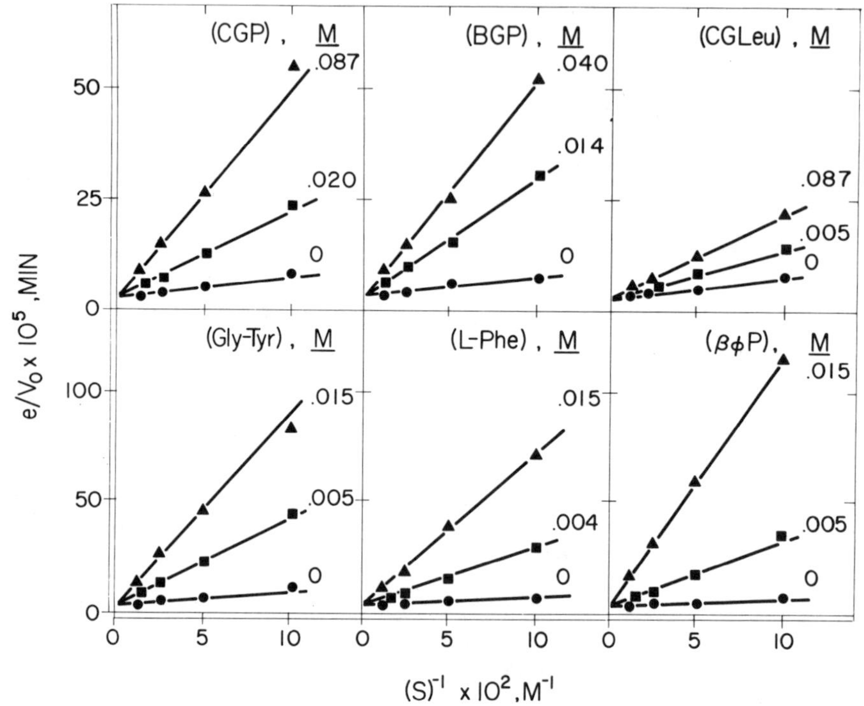

FIGURE 7. Inhibition of esterase activity of acetyl zinc carboxypeptidase by carbobenzoxyglycyl-L-phenylalanine, carbobenzoxyglycyl-L-leucine, benzoylglycyl-L-phenylalanine, glycyl-L-tyrosine, L-phenylalanine and β-phenylpropionate. Esterase activity was measured on the pH-stat at pH 7.5, 25°, in 0.005 M Tris, 0.2 M NaCl buffers using hippuryl-dl-phenyllactate as the substrate. The velocities were calculated from the initial slopes of the pH-stat recorder tracings.

ably resolve whether or not the latter is bound at two different sites of the enzyme.[39]

The possibility exists that the apparent kinetic anomalies of carboyxpeptidase A may be attributable in part to the fact that the binding sites of the enzyme can accept substrates larger than the synthetic dipeptides or esters generally employed.[42–44] The variability in the binding of dipeptides and esters might be sufficient to preclude unequivocal interpretation of their kinetics, since these latter compounds may perhaps not optimally fit and complement the substrate binding sites of carboxypeptidase. The very enzymatic versatility of carboxypeptidase, accommodating substrates varying in size from acylaminoacids to proteins might, in fact, also account for the apparent anomalies encountered in the kinetic profiles of some of these substrates and lead to the design of others which might well be devoid of some or all of these features.[7] Some aspects of this hypothesis have already been examined, and the data are consistent with this view.

The hydrolysis of substrates which would bind to fewer loci on the enzyme surface would be expected to approach Michaelis-Menten kinetics. Chain extension of the peptide substrates BGP and CGP by one glycine unit to CGGP and BGGP abolishes the substrate activation seen for the correspondent dipeptide. Thus, the plot of 1/v vs 1/s is linear between substrate concentration from 1×10^{-4} to 1×10^{-2} M. However, the N-terminal blocked product of these reactions, carbobenzoxyglycylglycine and benzoylglycylglycine, neither activates nor inhibits the reaction. Above 10^{-2} M, however, substrate inhibition of CGGP still occurs, suggesting that the hydrolysis of this substrate is accompanied by some, but not all, of the anomalies encountered in the corresponding dipeptides. A known activator of the dipeptidase series, carbobenzoxyglycine now is a competitive inhibitor with a K_i of .025 for both CGGP and BGGP.[45–47]

Summary

Various chemical modifications indicate that two tyrosyl residues are implicated in the mechanism of action of carboxypeptidase. When performed successively, such modifications suggest that the two residues may play different roles. Kinetic, equilibrium and isotope exhange experiments have delineated some details of the steps in the binding and hydrolysis of peptide and ester substrates. A model proposing binding of substrates at multiple loci is consistent with data obtained thus far. It proposes that some loci to which peptides and esters bind may overlap providing a topological basis for product activation, substrate inhibition and mutual competition of esters and peptides. Changes in activity due to chemical modification are thought to be brought about by various combinations of altered catalytic efficiency, substrate binding and inhibition. Correlation of studies on composition, structure and function now in progress in the laboratories of H. Neurath, W. N. Lipscomb and our own promise to add materially to understanding of the mechanism of action of this and other enzymes.

References

1. Anson, M. L. 1937. J. Gen. Physiol. **20:** 663.
2. Anson, M. L. 1937. J. Gen. Physiol. **20:** 777.
3. Bergmann, M. & J. S. Fruton. 1941. Advances Enzym. **1:** 63.
4. Neurath, H. 1960. *In* The Enzymes. Boyer, P. D., H. Lardy & K. Myrbäck, Eds. **4:** 16. 2nd edit. Academic Press. New York, N. Y.
5. Neurath, H. 1964. Ed: Academic Press. New York, N. Y. Fed. Proc. **23:** 1.
6. Valle, B. L. 1966. 152nd Meet. Amer. Chem. Soc.: 83C.
7. Vallee, B. L. 1967. Proc. Seventh Internat. Cong. Biochem., **3:** 1–3, 149. Tokyo, Japan.
8. Simpson, R. T., J. F. Riordan & B. L. Vallee. 1963. Biochemistry **2:** 616.
9. Vallee, B. L. 1964. Fed. Proc. **23:** 8.
10. Simpson, R. T. & B. L. Vallee. 1966. Biochemistry **5:** 1760.
11. Piras, R. & B. L. Vallee. 1966. Biochemistry **5:** 849.
12. Riordan, J. F. & B. L. Vallee. 1955. 150th Meet. Amer. Chem. Soc. **194:** 91C.
13. Riordan, J. F., M. Sokolovsky & B. L. Vallee. 1966. J. Amer. Chem. Soc. **88:** 4104.
14. Sokolovsky, M., J. F. Riordan & B. L. Vallee. 1966. Biochemistry **5:** 3582.
15. Riordan, J. F., M. Sokolovsky & B. L. Vallee. 1967. Biochemistry **6:** 358.
16. Riordan, J. F., M. Sokolovsky & B. L. Vallee. 1967. Biochemistry **6:** 3609.
17. Riordan, J. F. & M. Sokolovsky. 1967. Proc. Seventh Internat. Cong. Biochem. **F-234:** 807. Tokyo, Japan.
18. Horinishi, H., Y. Hachimori, K. Kurihara & K. Shibata. 1964. Biochem. Biophys. Acta **86:** 477.
19. Sokolovsky, M. & B. L. Vallee. 1967. Biochemistry **6:** 700.
20. Roholt, O. A. & D. Pressman. 1967. Proc. Nat. Acad. Sci. U.S.A. **58:** 280.

21. Smith, E. L. 1950. Advances Enzym. **12:** 233.
22. Neurath, H. & G. N. Schwert. 1950. Chem. Rev. **46:** 69.
23. Lumry, R., E. L. Smith & R. R. Glantz. 1951. J. Amer. Chem. Soc. **73:** 4330.
24. Riordan, J. F. & B. L. Vallee. 1963. Biochemistry **2:** 1460.
25. McClure, W. O., H. Neurath & K. A. Walsh. 1964. Biochemistry **3:** 1897.
26. Kaiser, E. T. & F. W. Carson. 1964. J. Amer. Chem. Soc. **86:** 2922.
27. Bender, M. L., J. R. Whitaker & F. Menger. 1965. Proc. Nat. Acad. Sci. U.S.A. **53:** 711.
28. McClure, W. O. & H. Neurath. 1965. Biochemistry **5:** 1425.
29. Whitaker, J. R., F. Menger & M. L. Bender. 1966. Biochemistry **5:** 386.
30. Awazu, S., F. W. Carson, P. L. Hall & E. T. Kaiser. 1967. J. Amer. Chem. Soc. **89:** 3627.
31. Folk, J. E. & E. W. Schirmer. 1963. J. Biol. Chem. **238:** 3384.
32. Quiocho, F. A. & F. M. Richards. 1966. Biochemistry **5:** 4062.
33. Riordan, J. F., R .C. Davies & B. L. Vallee. 1965. Fed. Proc. **24:** 2, (I) **1553:** 410.
34. Davies, R. C., J. F. Riordan, D. Auld & B. L. Vallee. 1968. Biochemistry **7:** 1090.
35. Vallee, B. L., J. F. Riordan & M. Sokolovsky. 1965. Science **150:** 388.
36. Coleman, J. E., P. Pulido & B. L. Vallee. 1966. Biochemistry **5:** 2019.
37. Davies, R. C., D. S. Auld & B. L. Vallee. 1968. Biochem. Biophys. Res. Commun. **31:** 628.
38. Lipscomb, W. N., M. L. Ludwig, J. A. Hartsuck, T. A. Steitz, H. Muirhead, J. C. Coppola, G. N. Reeke & F. A. Quiocho. 1967. Fed. Proc. **26:** 385.
39. Steitz, T. A., M. L. Ludwig, F. A. Quiocho & W. N. Lipscomb. 1967. J. Biol. Chem. **242:** 4662.
40. Coleman, J. E. & B. L. Vallee. 1964. Biocheimstry **3:** 1874.
41. Shulman, R. G., G. Navon, B. J. Wyluda, D. C. Douglass & T. Yamane. 1966. Proc. Nat. Acad. Sci. U.S.A. **56:** 39.
42. Coombs, T. L. & B. L. Vallee. 1966. Biochemistry **5:** 3272.
43. Schecter, I. & A. Berger. 1967. Biochem. Biophys. Res. Commun. **27:** 157.
44. Schecter, I. & A. Berger. 1967. Biochem. Biophys. Res. Commun. **27:** 157.
45. Auld, D. S. Unpublished data.
46. Vallee, B. L., J. F. Riordan, J. L. Bethune, T. L. Coombs, D. S. Auld & M. Sokolovsky. 1968. Biochemistry **7:** 3547.
47. Vallee, B. L. & J. F. Riordan. 1968. Brookhaven Sympos. Biol. In press.

TYROSINE FLUORESCENCE IN PROTEINS

Harold Edelhoch, Robert L. Perlman, and Meir Wilchek
Clinical Endocrinology Branch
National Institute of Arthritis and Metabolic Diseases
National Institutes of Health
Bethesda, Md.

The fluorescence of nonconjugated proteins originates almost entirely from the tyrosyl and tryptophanyl residues. Generally, the contribution of the latter dominates that of the former. In a few proteins, the fluorescence of both residues is observable simultaneously. Consequently, configurational modifications can be followed from changes in either tyrosine or tryptophan fluorescence intensity. If only one or a few residues of each chromophore are present, different regions of the protein may be monitored independently. Since all the conditions which can affect protein structure (i.e., pH, temperature, binding of small molecules, organic solvents and solutes) also influence the fluorescence of simple peptides and configurationally stable proteins, it is important to be able to understand their effects on model substances. For this purpose, two series of model peptides have been prepared; one series contains both chromophores whereas the other contains only tyrosyl groups. The fluorescent properties of three hormones, whose molecular weights are very different, and one enzyme will be evaluated and compared to the behavior of low molecular weight tyrosine and tryptophan compounds.

Materials

The synthesis of the series Tyr-Gly_{0-2}-Tyr and Tyr-Tyr_{0-4}-Tyr and the Tyr-Gly peptides will be presented elsewhere.[1] All peptides were synthesized from L amino acids.

Highly purified parathyroid hormone (PTH) was a gift from Dr. G. Aurbach. The preparation of PTH has been described by Aurbach.[2, 3] It has about 80 residues and a molecular weight of about 9,000.

The properties of the nuclease produced by *Staphylococcus aureus* have been described by Heins and coworkers.[4] The material employed for this study was purchased from Worthington Biochemical Corporation. It has a molecular weight of 16,800 and the sequence of its 149 residues is known.[5]

An analog of ACTH (adrenocorticotropic hormone), composed of 25 amino acids, is a synthetic product prepared by Boissonnas and collaborators.[6] The material was a gift from Dr. G. Aurbach. This analog of ACTH is reported to have twice the activity of ACTH.

Guanidinium hydrochloride was obtained from Aldridge Associates & Company, Washington, D. C. Other chemicals were reagent grade.

Methods

All spectra were determined by the Turner 210 spectrofluorometer which gives absolute fluorescence spectra. The design of this instrument has been described elsewhere.[7] Excitation was at 270 mμ with a band width of 100 Å unless otherwise specified. The band width of the emitted radiation was 25 Å. pH values were measured with a Radiometer TTTI pH meter and absorption with a Beckman DU spectrophotometer. Quantum yields at 25° were calculated by the relation:

$$Q. = \frac{\text{Emission Area}}{\text{Emission Area (Trp)}} \frac{\text{O.D. (Trp)}}{\text{O.D.}} 0.20$$

Amino Acid and Small Peptide Models

The quantum yield of a fluorochrome may be defined as:

$$q = \frac{\lambda}{\lambda + k_0 + k_1 +}$$

where λ is the rate of emission and the k's are the rates which deactivate the excited state by all other processes. The latter may be divided into long range and local interactions. The long-range effects will depend on radiationless excitation energy transfer as described by Förster.[8] The short-range effects include those due to bond formation, charge, solvent composition and other interactions of the chromophore with its immediate environment.

Excitational Energy Transfer

In any attempt to evaluate tyrosine fluorescence in proteins, a very important factor is the extent of quenching by energy transfer to both tyrosyl and tryptophanyl residues. The efficiency of transfer depends on the degree of overlap of the emission and absorption spectra of the donor and acceptor residues, respectively (overlap integral), and the distance (R) and orientation (K) between the two electronic systems. A critical transfer distance, R_0, can be defined, which is the distance between two groups where the probability of emission and deactivation by transfer is equal.[8, 9]

$$n_{s \to A} = \frac{9000 \ln 10 \, K^2}{128\pi^5 n^4 N \tau_s^0 R^6} \int_0^\infty f_s(\nu) \epsilon_A(\nu) \frac{d\nu}{\nu^4}$$

$$N_{s \to A} = \frac{1}{\tau_s} \left(\frac{R_0}{R} \right)^6$$

where ν is the wavenumber, ϵ the molar extinction coefficient, $f(\nu)$ the spectral distribution, τ_s^0 and τ_s the intrinsic and actual lifetimes, and n the refractive index of the solvent.

Critical distances of 8.9 and 14.7 Å have been computed[10] for transfer from tyrosine to tyrosine and tryptophan, respectively, assumming random orientation, i.e., $k^2 = 2/3$. The transfer efficiency between tyrosyl residues is much greater when one residue is ionized, i.e., $R_0 = 15.2$, since the absorption spectrum displays a red shift (274 → 295) and an intensification (1400 → 2400) resulting in greater spectral overlap. Weber has determined R_0 values directly from the influence of concentration on polarization in thin layers at low temperatures.[11] He obtained R_0 values of 17 and 18.5 Å for transfer from phenol to phenol and indole, respectively. Energy transfer from tyrosyl to tryptophanyl residues has been shown by Wada and Ueno in copolymers of these two residues.[12]

The ionization of tyrosyl residues not only affects tyrosyl but also tryptophanyl fluorescence. Energy transfer is possible only from tryptophan to ionized tyrosine, since there is no spectral overlap with un-ionized tyrosine and a value of 11.2 Å has been calculated for R_0.[10] Tryptophan quenching has been observed in the series Trp-Gly_{0-4}-Tyr with tyrosyl ionization.[13] The degree of quenching decreased regularly with increasing chain length.

Several series of low molecular weight peptides containing either tyrosyl or tyrosyl and tryptophanyl residues have been synthesized and used as models in order to evaluate energy transfer processes that may affect tyrosine fluorescence in proteins. Since the distance between the donor and acceptor is an important determinant affecting the efficiency of transfer, the inter-residue distance has been varied by placing glycyl residues between them, as in the series Trp-$(Gly)_{0-4}$-Tyr. There was no evidence of tyrosine emission in Trp-Tyr. In the longer peptides, tyrosine emission increased progressively with chain length (FIGURE 1). The quantum yields of the tryptophanyl and tyrosyl residues are reported in TABLE 1. These values are based on their emission relative to tryptophan (pH 5.0). A quantum yield of 0.20 was taken for tryptophan.[14] It should be noted that a value of 0.13 has been reported by Chen recently for tryptophan at 25°.[15]

Transfer of excitational energy between tyrosyl residues was shown by the determination of the limiting polarization values of several peptides with tyrosyl termini. The limiting polarization, P_L, was obtained by extrapolating polarization values measured in 99% glycerol, as a function of temperature, to infinite viscosity. The ratio R_0/r can be obtained from the equation[16]:

$$(1/P_L - 1/3) = (1/P_0 - 1/3)[1 + 2/3\,(R_0/r)^6]$$

P_0 is the polarization in the absence of energy transfer. Values of r, the inter-residue distance, are shown in TABLE 2.

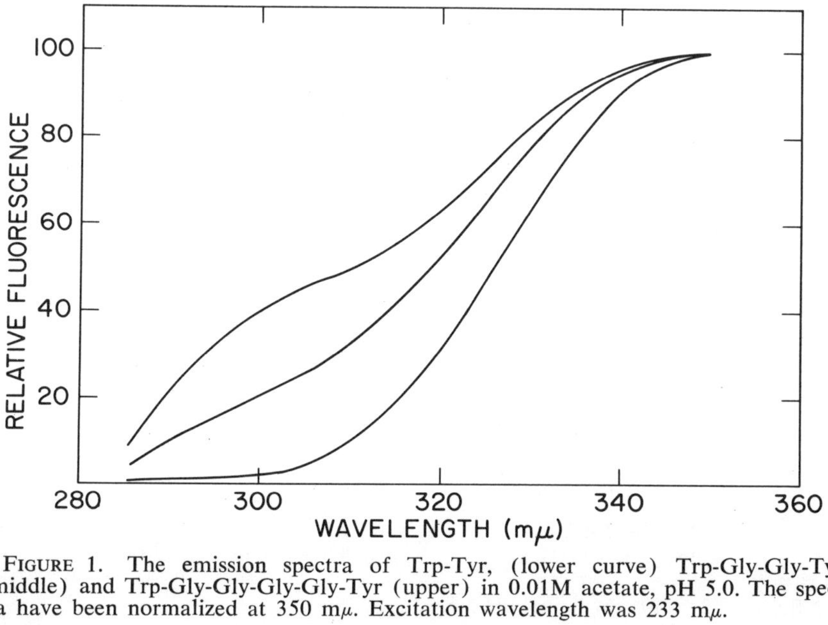

FIGURE 1. The emission spectra of Trp-Tyr, (lower curve) Trp-Gly-Gly-Tyr (middle) and Trp-Gly-Gly-Gly-Gly-Tyr (upper) in 0.01M acetate, pH 5.0. The spectra have been normalized at 350 mμ. Excitation wavelength was 233 mμ.

TABLE 1

THE TRYPTOPHAN AND TYROSINE QUANTUM YIELDS OF SEVERAL MOLECULES CONTAINING BOTH RESIDUES.*

	Relative Absorption at 270 mμ		Quantum Yield	
	Trp	Tyr	Trp	Tyr
Trp-Tyr	81%	19%	.14	0
Trp-Gly-Gly-Tyr	81	19	.09	.016
Trp-Gly_4-Tyr	81	19	.11	.036
ACTH analog	68	32	.14	.026
Nuclease	38	62	.46	.024

* Solvent: 0.01M acetate, pH 5.0.
T = 25°. Excitation wavelength is 270 mμ.

Ionization of the phenolic group of tyrosine leads to the loss of its fluorescence. In a series of oligotyrosyl peptides, i.e., Tyr-$(Tyr)_{0-4}$-Tyr, it was found that their fluorescence was completely quenched when a single one of the residues in the chain was ionized (FIGURE 2). As a consequence, the pH dependence of tyrosyl fluorescence of a protein containing more than one tyrosyl residue will be greater than that of their ionization if energy transfer occurs. Results of this kind have been found in polytyrosine,[12] ribonuclease[17, 18] and the A chain of insulin.[1]

Charge Effects

White showed that the discharge of the carboxylate group of tyrosine in acid solution almost completely quenched its fluorescence.[19] If the carboxyl group is not present, as in phenol, tyramine and tyrosine methyl ester, very high acidities are needed to quench phenol fluorescence.[19] The influence of carboxyl ionization is reduced in Tyr-Gly (30%)[20] and disappears in Tyr-Gly-Gly.[1]

In addition to losses in quantum yield produced by a neighboring carboxyl group, the charged amino group also quenches tyrosyl fluorescence. The effect is about 40% in Tyr-Gly and in Gly-Tyr, and disappears in Gly-Gly-Tyr.[1, 18]

The exceedingly difficult problem of evaluating the factors which influence fluorescent yields in proteins is evident if we compare the effects of substituent charged groups on small tyrosine peptides with their effects on pol-

TABLE 2

THE LIMITING POLARIZATION AND INTER-RESIDUE DISTANCES OF TYROSYL COMPOUNDS.*

	P	R_0/r	r
Tyrosine	0.36		
Acetyl tyrosinamide	0.36		
Tyr-Tyr	0.21	0.97	8.6
Tyr-Gly-Tyr	0.31	0.75	11.0
Tyr-Gly-Gly-Tyr	0.34	0.63	13.1

* Solvent: 2×10^{-4} M lysine; pH 5.5, 99% glycerol.

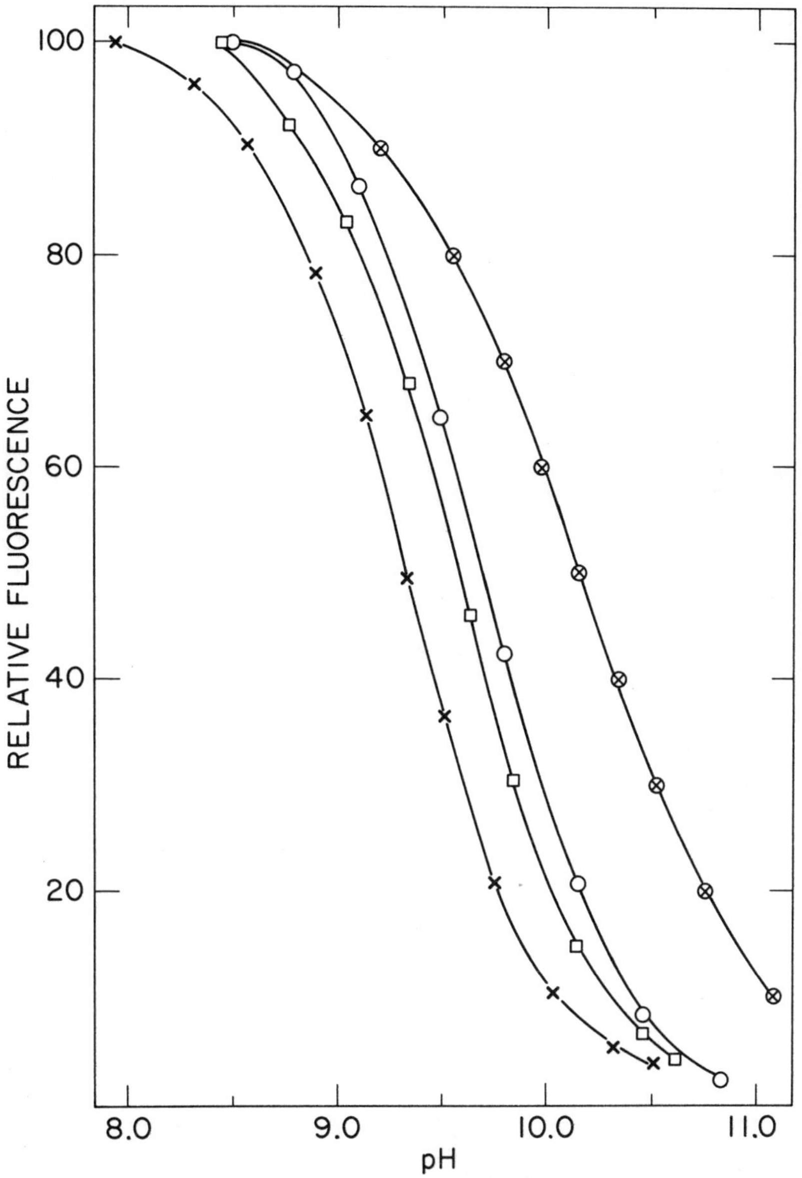

FIGURE 2. The alkaline quenching of phenolic emission at 305 mμ in Tyr (⊗) Tyr-Tyr, (○) Tyr-Tyr-Tyr (□) and Tyr-Tyr_4 Tyr (X) in .1M KCl, 0.02M lysine, 25°. Excitation at 275 mμ.

ymeric copeptides of tyrosine and glutamic acid or lysine. The low quantum yields in tyrosine copolypeptides have been attributed by Weber and Rosenheck[21] to proton transfer from tyrosyl to carboxylate and uncharged amino groups. In small tyrosine peptides (Gly-Tyr, Tyr-Gly, etc.) it is the un-ionized carboxyl and charged amino that reduce their quantum yields.[1, 20] Moreover, the state of the carboxyl groups in poly Tyr-Glu was more influential in determining tyrosyl yields than the configuration of the molecule, i.e., whether it was α-helical or random coil.[22]

Solvent Effects

Solvents of decreasing polarity both increase the quantum yield and shift the emission spectra of indole derivatives toward lower wavelengths (blue shift),[23] but only increase the yield of tyrosyl compounds without displacing their spectra. The quantum yield of N-acetyl tyrosinamide is tripled in 50% dioxane-water and doubled in 50% ethanol-water compared to aqueous solutions.[24] Similar changes have been reported by Cowgill.[25] Weber and Rosenheck reported that the quantum yield of phenol (and anisole) was independent of the polarity of the solvent.[20] The difference in behavior may be related to the lower quantum yields of tyrosyl peptides (Gly-Tyr, Tyr-Gly, Gly-Tyr-glycinamide, etc.) compared to tyrosine and phenol.[1, 20]

Temperature Effects

The fluorescence of tryptophan and tyrosine fall monotonically with temperature. FIGURES 3 and 4 show the effects of temperature on the fluorescence intensities of both chromophores in Trp-Gly_4-Tyr and the data of Gally and Edelman[17] for tyrosine and tryptophan. The fluorescence of tryptophan in the hexapeptide is quenched more slowly and that of tyrosine more rapidly than the corresponding amino acids. Since thermal quenching is collisional, the variations in temperature dependence may be related to differences in lifetimes. It is unlikely that either chromophore in Trp-Gly_4-Tyr is involved in important interactions, since their temperature quenching curves appear normal.

Other Effects

In addition to nonspecific factors determined by the polarity of the environment, many specific reactions may influence tyrosine emission in proteins. In the less polar interior of a protein, phenolic hydrogen bond formation with many possible acceptor groups is feasible. Cowgill has shown that phenol fluorescence is quenched by hydrogen bonding with substituted amides in solvents of low polarity.[26] Significant inhibition of phenol emission occurs in aqueous solutions by carboxylate anions and uncharged amines.[21] Even uncharged carboxyl groups are able to quench.[27] In the highly condensed phase in the interior of a protein, where there are many donors and acceptors which can interact with phenolic groups, its quantum yield may vary widely.[28] It is noteworthy that the three abnormally ionizing tyrosyl groups in ribonuclease appear to be quenched, since the fluorescence of the enzyme disappears when the three normal groups are ionized at pH 12.[18]

Polypeptides and Proteins

Parathyroid Hormone

This molecule was selected for study because it has only one tryptophanyl and one tyrosyl residue. Their behavior, therefore, is more readily inter-

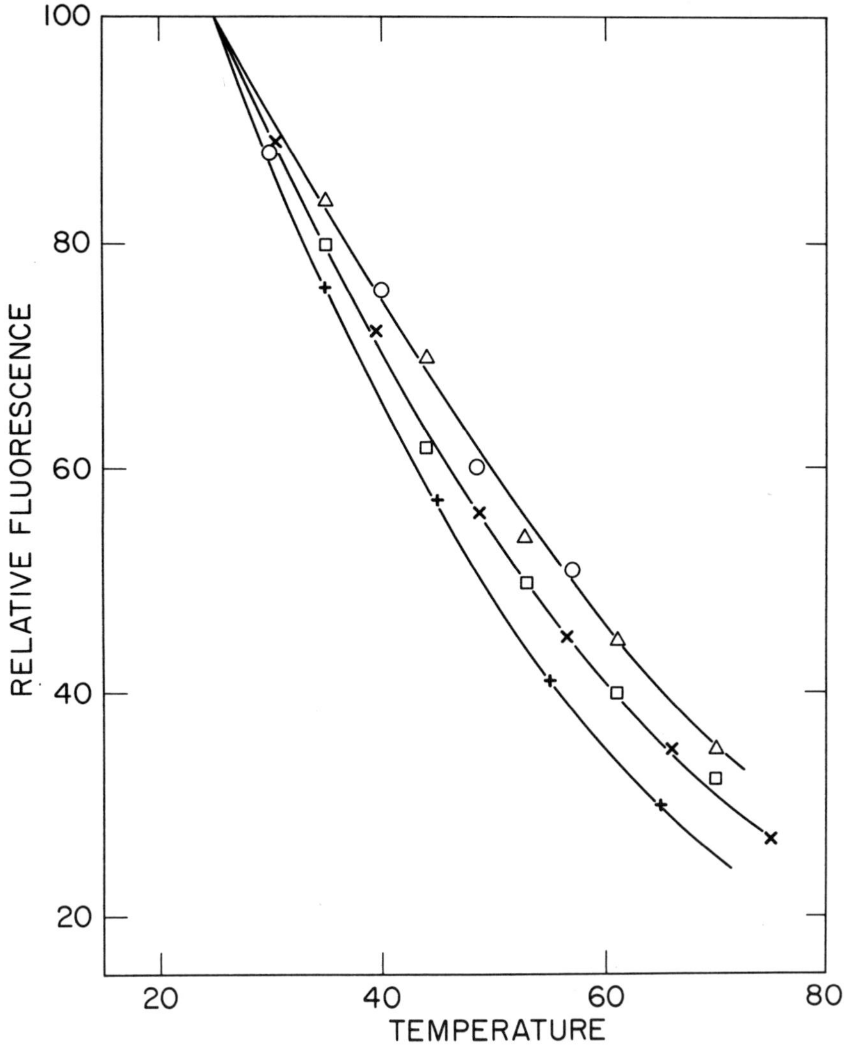

FIGURE 3. Temperature dependence of tryptophan emission. The wavelength of excitation was 270 mμ. 0, nuclease at 350 mμ, pH 3.0; Δ, PTH at 345 mμ, pH 6.1: ⊡, Trp-Gly-Gly-Gly-Gly-Tyr at 350 mμ, pH 5.0; X, ACTH analog at 350 mμ, pH 7.4; +, Tryptophan.[17]

preted in this molecule than in those containing numerous fluorochromes. The emission spectrum of PTH at pH 6.1 is depicted in FIGURE 5. The fluorescence of tyrosine is clearly evident from the pronounced shoulder seen at 300 mμ. Moreover, if PTH is excited at 290 instead of 270 mμ, 65% of the tyrosine, but only 10% of the tryptophan, emission is lost. The appearance of a distinctive band due to tyrosine emission depends on two factors: (1) the relative quantum yields of the two chromophores, and (2) the position of the tryptophan peak. The latter occurs at 347 mμ in PTH and, therefore, the overlap with tyrosyl emission is minimized.

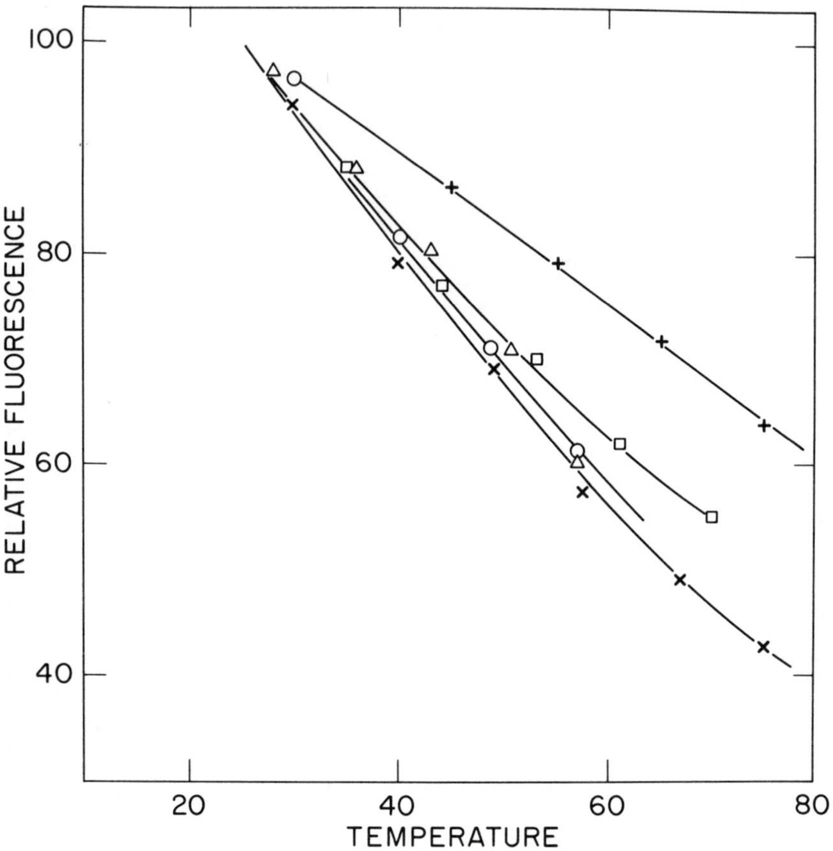

FIGURE 4. Temperature dependence of tyrosine emission in proteins and polypeptides containing tryptophan. The wavelengths of excitation and emission were 270 and 300 mμ, respectively. Symbols were the same as in FIGURE 3. All solutions the same as in FIGURE 3 except PTH, which was at 7.4.

Relatively little can be predicted from the spectrum of PTH except that it is unlikely that the two chromophores are closer to each other than in Trp-Gly_4-Tyr, whose spectrum it closely resembles. An upper limit cannot be set, since the factors determining the two yields may be more significant than the quenching of tyrosyl fluorescence by radiationless transfer to tryptophanyl.

A more direct approach in estimating the distance between two chromophores is the determination of the extent of tryptophanyl quenching resulting from tyrosyl ionization. FIGURE 6 shows that tryptophanyl fluorescence is quenched by 32% if the curves are extrapolated to 100% ionization. In studies with model polypeptides, tryptophanyl fluorescence was quenched about 40% in Trp-Gly_4-Tyr by tyrosyl ionization.[13] Consequently, if the orientation factor in PTH is not far from the random value, i.e., $k^2 = 2/3$, as is probably the case in the hexapeptide, then the two residues should be further apart in PTH than in the hexapeptide model. The amino acid sequence of this protein is under investigation, and it is known that the two residues are probably separated by between 4 and 10 amino acids.[29]

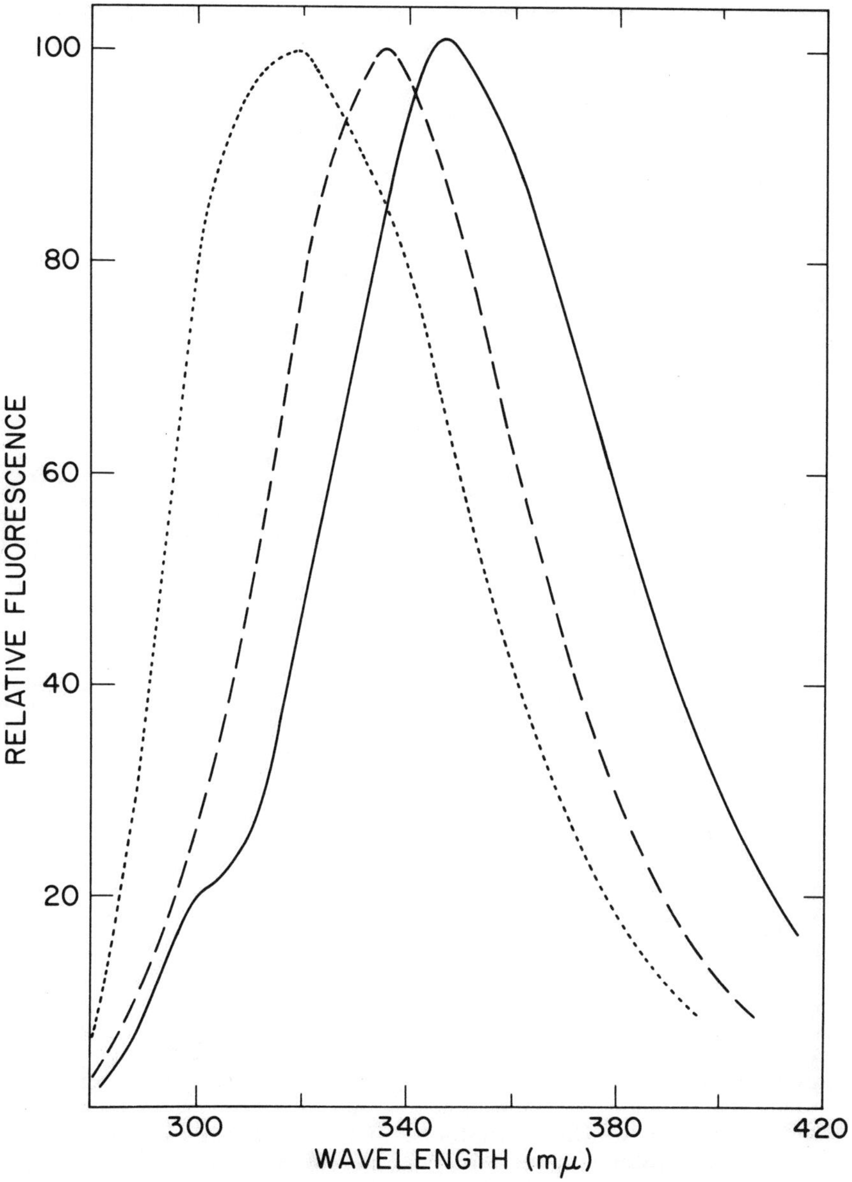

FIGURE 5. The fluorescence spectra of PTH, pH 6.1, 0.08M KCl, 0.02M lysine (solid line); nuclease, pH 7.4, 0.02M Tris — 0.02M KCl (dashed line); bovine growth hormone pH 5.0, 0.01M acetate (dotted line) .25°. Excitation at 270 mμ.

It should be emphasized that the preceding analysis is meaningless if factors other than nonradiative transfer influence the fluorescence of either chromophore. The properties of PTH in alkali are not known, since there are almost no physical studies on it due to the extremely small amounts cur-

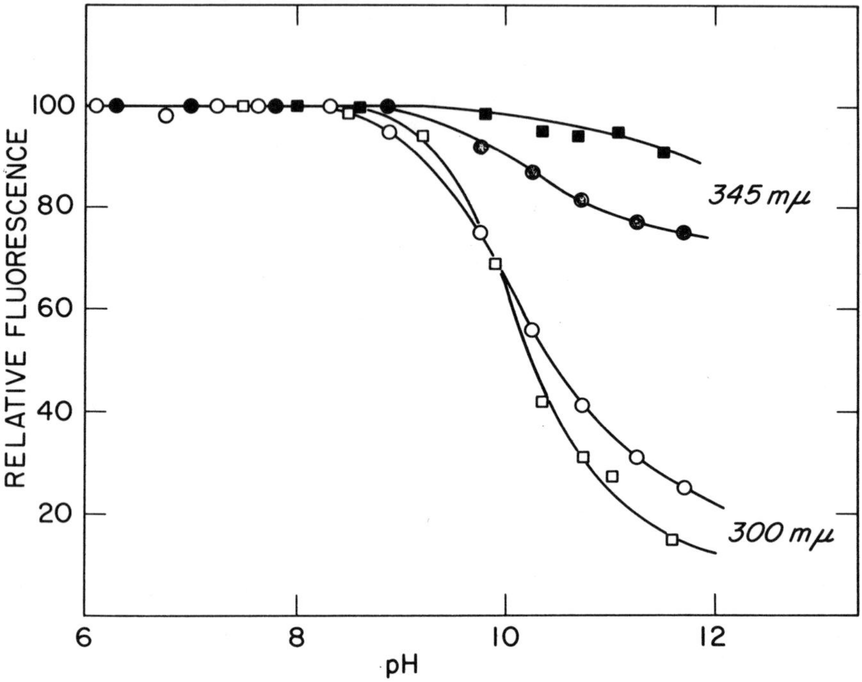

FIGURE 6. The alkaline dependence of tyrosyl (300 mμ) and tryptophanyl (345 mμ) fluorescence of PTH in aqueous solution (circles) 0.090M KCl, 0.02M lysine and in 4.6M guanidinium chloride (squares). Excitation at 270 mμ. 25°.

rently available. The absence of structural changes in alkali, however, is strongly suggested by the fluorescence data since the ratio of tyrosyl to tryptophanyl quenching is constant throughout the entire pH range investigated.

In 4.6 M guanidine, tryptophanyl fluorescence was quenched only 10% by tyrosyl ionization (FIGURE 6). Judging from the fall in quenching efficiency in the series Trp-Gly_{0-4}-Tyr, the inter-residue distance in guanidine is presumably greater than in water.

When PTH was acidified from pH 6.0 to 2.5, tyrosyl fluorescence increased about 10%, whereas that of tryptophanyl declined by the same amount. The tryptophanyl fluorescence of several stable proteins (lysozyme, pepsin and ovalbumin) has been found to fall somewhat on acidification.[30] In the two copolypeptide models, poly Glu-Tyr[21] and poly Glu-Trip,[31] tyrosyl fluorescence increases and tryptophanyl decreases when they are acidified from neutrality.

The temperature dependence of tryptophanyl and tyrosyl emission of PTH is shown also in FIGURES 3 and 4. The original spectrum was found when the temperature was returned to 25°. Since both curves are quite normal, it is likely that no significant configurational changes occur in the temperature range studied and that both chromophores are exposed to the solvent. The high wavelength of the fluorescence peak (347 mμ) also indicates that the tryptophanyl residue is in a polar environment.

Nuclease

The fluorescence spectrum of the nuclease which contains one tryptophanyl and seven tyrosyl residues is shown also in FIGURE 5. The wavelength maximum occurs at 335 mμ and masks the weaker tyrosine emission. The fluorescence intensities of the two different chromophores may be modified by several procedures which, in some instances, lead to a resolution of the tyrosyl and tryptophanyl peaks.

A 60% decrease in fluorescence at 295 mμ occurs when one mole of the competitive inhibitor, deoxythymidine-3′, 5′-diphosphate is bound to the enzyme.[24] Tryptophan intensity, as measured at 360 mμ, however, was unaffected by the binding of the inhibitor. These data may be interpreted in terms of the binding of the inhibitor by tyrosyl residues on the surface of the enzyme or the induction of a configurational change that modifies tyrosyl but not tryptophanyl fluorescence. When other chemical and physical data are taken into account, it appears that both effects are responsible for the change in tyrosine quantum yield.[24]

Acidification of the nuclease to pH 3 produces a major configurational change, which results in a marked quenching of tryptophanyl and a significant enhancement of tyrosyl fluorescence. As a result, two peaks are observed in the emission spectrum (FIGURE 7). A spectrum very similar to the one at pH 3.0 was observed in 5M guanidine at neutral pH (FIGURE 7).

The thermal denaturation of the nuclease was investigated by following the relative fluorescence intensities at 300 and 335 mμ. A marked fall occurred above 40° at both wavelengths (FIGURE 8), indicating a configurational transition. The transition was reversible, since the original spectrum was recovered when the solution was cooled to 25°.

In order to determine whether the molecular state resulting from thermal denaturation was the same as that produced by acid, the pH 3.0 solution was heated to 57°. It was found that the fluorescence of both chromophores, measured at 300 and 350 mμ, decreased monotonically at approximately the same rates as in the model compounds (FIGURES 3 and 4). The spectra were quite different at 57° because the intensity of tryptophanyl fluorescence at pH 7.4 was about twice that observed at pH 3.0, whereas that of tyrosyl was equal. It appears that the chromophores are normalized in acid at 25° but not in the thermal denaturation, since the spectrum of the nuclease at pH 3.0 agreed with that in 5M guanidine at pH 7.4, and its thermal quenching curve was similar to that of model peptides.

Tyrosyl and tryptophanyl emission increased slightly between 0 and 21% dioxane (FIGURE 9). The small change produced compared to models indicates that both chromophores are incompletely exposed to the solvent in the native molecule. A marked decrease in tryptophanyl and increase in tyrosyl fluorescence occurs between 21 and 38% dioxane resulting in a spectrum in which both emissions are evident (FIGURE 10). It is clear that a configurational transition occurs in this region of dioxane concentration. The intensities of both chromophores increased between 38 and 59% dioxane. The larger rate of fluorescence increase in the latter range of dioxane compared to 0 to 21% implies that both chromophores are now more exposed to the solvent than in the native form.

Bovine Growth Hormone

Bovine growth hormone probably contains 3 tryptophanyl and 12 tyrosyl residues and is composed of two subunits of similar size.[32] Its fluorescence

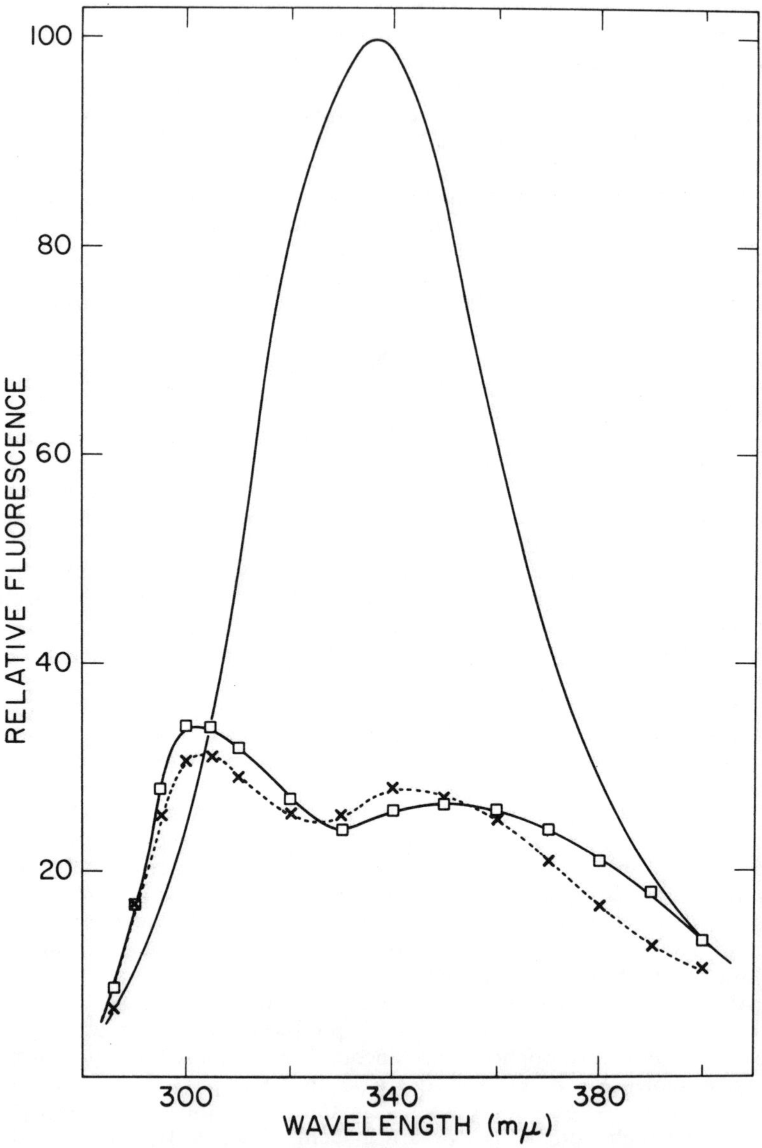

FIGURE 7. The emission spectra of nuclease (solid line) at pH 7.4, 0.02M Tris, 0.02M KCl; at pH 7.5 (□), in 5.0M guanidinium chloride; at pH 3.0 (X), 0.02M Tris, 0.02M KCl. Excitation at 270 mμ. 25°.

spectrum has a peak at 320 mμ that is only slightly more intense than at 300 mμ (FIGURE 5). Due to the similar intensities of the two emissions, the tryptophan peak is displaced toward lower wavelengths and its true maximum is obscured. The quantum yields of the two chromophores have been measured and values of 0.09 and 0.13 obtained for the tryptophanyl and tyrosyl residues, respectively.[32]

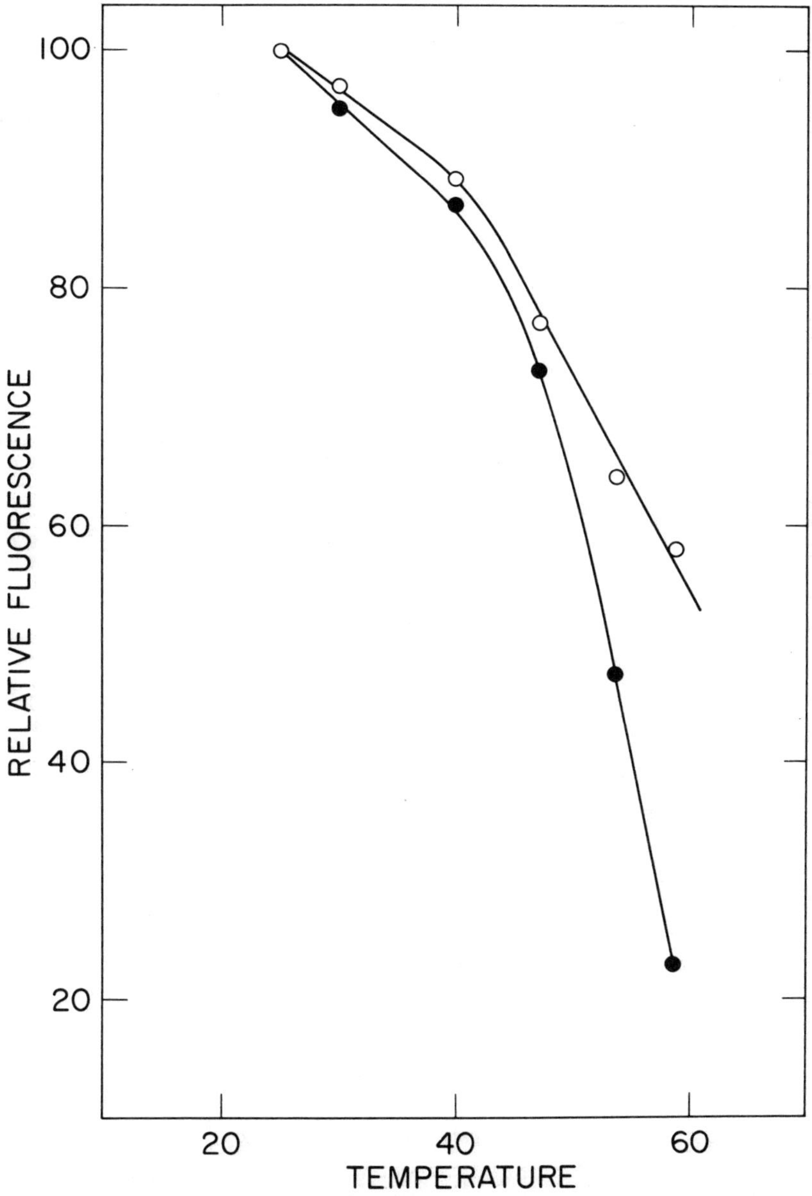

FIGURE 8. Temperature dependence of tyrosyl (0) and tryptophanyl (●) emission of nuclease, pH 7.4, measured at 300 and 335 mμ, respectively. Excitation at 270 mμ.

Major changes in quantum yields occur when the tertiary structure of the hormone is disrupted in acid. All the macromolecular parameters are altered in the acid transition except the optical rotatory dispersion.[33] The quantum yields of tryptophanyl and tyrosyl increase about nine- and threefold, respectively.[32] The reasons for the very high tryptophanyl yield (0.84) are not clear.

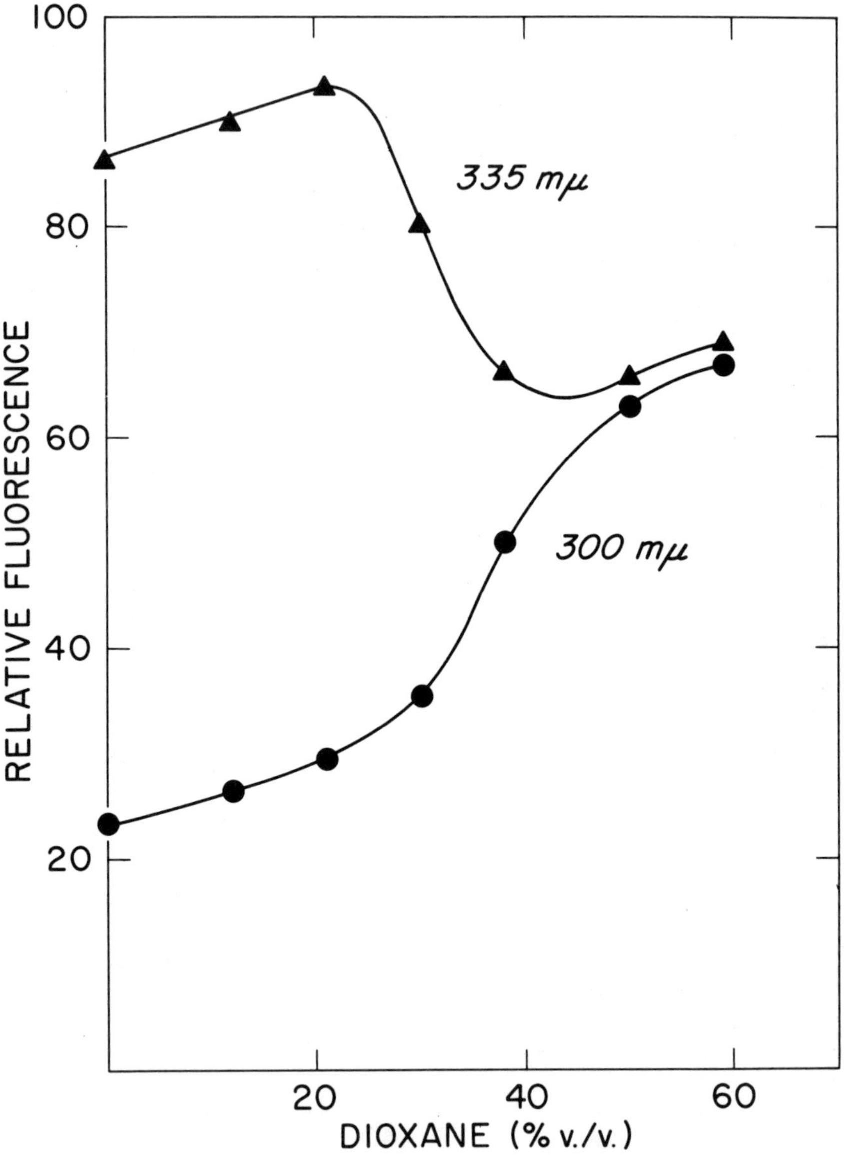

FIGURE 9. Effect of dioxane on the tyrosine (300 mμ) and tryptophan (335 mμ) emission intensity of nuclease in 0.1M KCl-0.02M lysine, pH 6.1. Excitation at 270 mμ.

In most proteins, tryptophanyl fluorescence is quenched in alkali due to energy transfer to ionized tyrosine. A fourfold increase in tryptophanyl quantum yield was found at pH 12, even though 80% of the tyrosyl residues were ionized. This result is even more surprising because the configuration of bovine growth hormone remains globular and highly organized at pH 12.

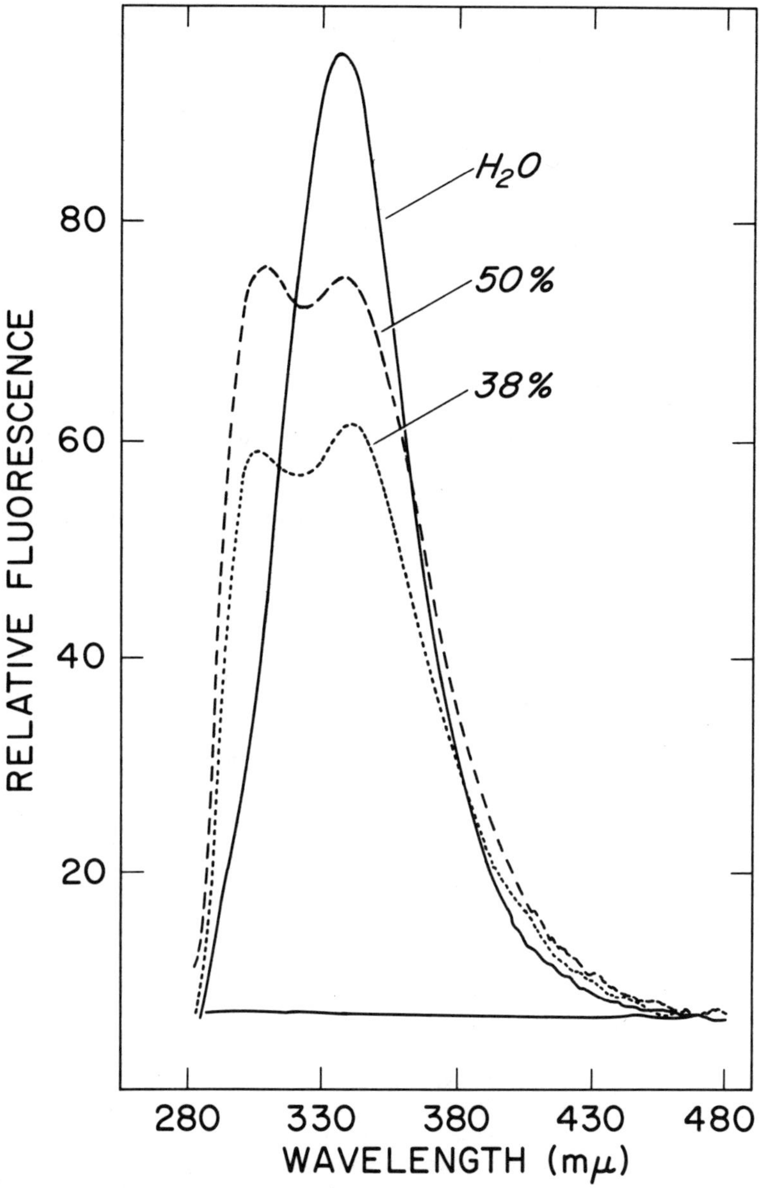

FIGURE 10. Emission spectra of nuclease at 25° in water, 38% and 59% dioxane (v./v.) — 0.1M KCl-0.2M lysine, pH 6.1. Excitation at 270 mμ.

The increase in yield would undoubtedly be much higher if quenching by ionized tyrosine did not occur. The high yield may, in part, be accounted for if an amino group situated next to the tryptophan dissociates, since the fluorescence of tryptophan in its amino acid form increases threefold with dissociation of its amino group.[13, 20]

The temperature dependence of bovine growth hormone fluorescence at pH 5.0 showed a fall between 20° and 35°. Very little change occurred at either 300 or 340 $m\mu$ between 35° and 45°. At higher temperatures, time-dependent increases in emission were observed which became quite rapid and large near 60°.

ACTH Analog

This polypeptide contains 1 tryptophanyl and 2 tyrosyl residues in a chain of 25 amino acids. Its spectrum shows a very distinctive shoulder at 300 $m\mu$, and the tryptophan peak occurs at 350 $m\mu$. Excitation at 290 instead of 270 $m\mu$ reduced the intensity at 300 $m\mu$ by 65%, but that at 350 μ by only 15%, showing the effect of the greater ratio of tryptophanyl to tyrosyl absorption at 290 compared to 270 $m\mu$.

The effect of temperature on the fluorescence of ACTH analog was normal (FIGURES 3 and 4) and reversible. Acidification from pH 6.0 to 2.5 increased tyrosyl and decreased tryptophanyl fluorescence by 10%, respectively. Tyrosyl fluorescence was completely quenched in alkali, with only a small effect on tryptophanyl fluorescence. The fluorescent properties of this compound indicate that the aromatic chromophores are not involved in intramolecular interactions.

SUMMARY

The problem of observing tyrosine emission in proteins containing tryptophan is related to both the absorption and emission properties of these two amino acids. First, the absorption of tryptophan is several times larger than tyrosine at all wavelengths. In the two compounds, acetyl tryptophanamide and acetyl tyrosinamide, the ratio of the molar extinction coefflcients of the latter to the former is maximal at 274 $m\mu$ and 232 $m\mu$ (FIGURE 11). At 270 $m\mu$, the wavelength used for excitation in most experiments, the ratio is 0.235. The 270 $m\mu$ wavelength was chosen instead of 274 $m\mu$ in order to eliminate more of the scatter peak of the exciting radiation. The second problem is that the quantum yield of tyrosine is smaller than that of tryptophan in many proteins,[20] polypeptides[21, 22, 28] and small peptides.[20] Due to these two factors, a very high fraction of the total emission is due to tryptophan. Of major importance in observing the tyrosine band is the wavelength peak of tryptophan emission. The smaller the latter, the greater the overlap and the less likely that the tyrosine band will be resolved as a shoulder or separate peak. In the absence of its resolution, the contribution of tyrosine to an emission band may be shown by exciting at two wavelength, where the ratio of absorption of tryptophan to tyrosine is high and low. In this way, the tyrosyl emission in bovine serum albumin[34] and ovalbumin[35] has been detected. Another method is to conjugate a dye which quenches tryptophan but not tyrosine emission by energy transfer. This result has been accomplished with the dimethylamino naphthalene sulfonyl conjugate of human serum albumin. It has shown that phosphate preferentially quenches tyrosine emission.[20, 36] Thus, if tyrosyl residues are accessible to phosphate their emission may be verified. It may also be possible to selectively eliminate tryptophan emission by chemical modification, as with N-bromosuccinimide. In chemical changes the product may, however, quench tyrosyl or tryptophanyl fluorescence by energy transfer or other mechanisms.

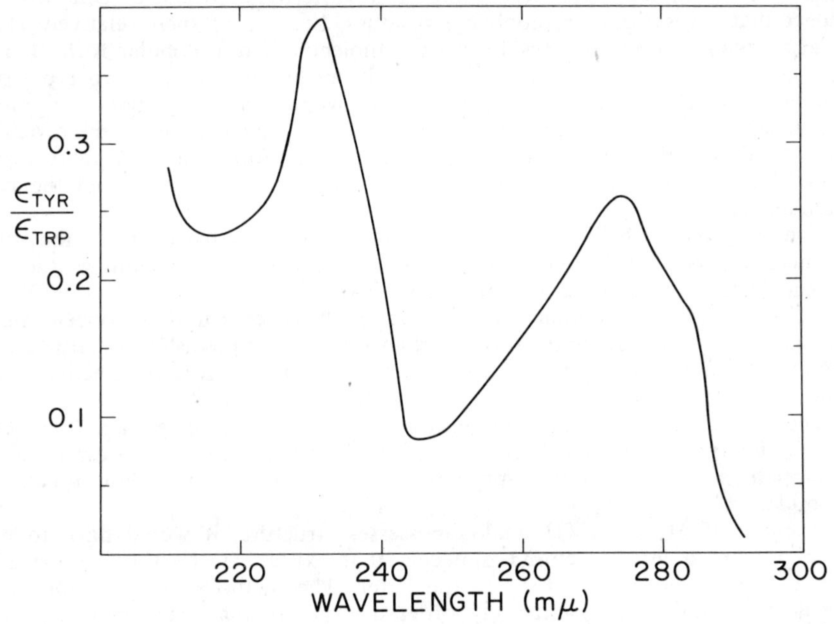

FIGURE 11. The ratio of the molar extinction coefficients of N-acetyl tyrosinamide to N-acetyl tryptophanamide in aqueous solutions.

There is considerable physical and chemical data on the two macromolecules, i.e., nuclease[4] and bovine growth hormone,[32, 33] which reveal them to be highly organized structures and consequently proteins. In the case of the two hormones, PTH and ACTH analog, very little relevant data exists concerning their structure. It is instructive to compare the fluorescence behavior of the two proteins with that of the two hormones, i.e., PTH and ACTH analog.

Acidification of the nuclease or bovine growth hormone produces major changes in the quantum yields of both chromophores. Very small, inconsequential changes were observed with PTH and ACTH analog. In accord with their behavior in acid, the temperature dependence of the former two proteins was very abnormal, whereas in the latter two hormones it was similar to that of the amino acid models. Moreover, the tryptophanyl emission peaks of PTH and ACTH analog occurred near 350 mμ and, therefore, at longer wavelengths than that of the nuclease and bovine growth hormone. Guanidine or dioxane in the case of the nuclease, or urea with bovine growth hormone, strongly modified their fluorescence spectra. In contrast, guanidine (5M) had very little effect on the fluorescence spectra of PTH or ACTH analog at neutral pH. We have observed that guanidine (5M) reduces the fluorescence of either N-acetyl tryptophanamide or N-acetyl tyrosinamide by only a few percent. It is evident that the tyrosyl and tryptophanyl residues in the two proteins are involved in interactions which have profound effects on their emissive properties. In the case of PTH and ACTH analog the two chromophores appear to be free and exposed to the solvent. From their fluorescence behavior under a variety of conditions, it appears likely that these two hormones have very little, if any, tertiary structure. One would expect that tyrosyl and tryptophanyl residues, because of their relatively low polarity, would be interior residues if the molecule had a globular form. It is, of course, dangerous to extrapolate from the properties of only two types of residues to that of the whole molecule. However, in the globular proteins whose structures have been determined by x-ray analysis, most amino acids have fixed coordinates.[37, 38] It seems unlikely, therefore, that two bulky residues that can form strong hydrophobic interactions will be free and the remainder fixed.

The only data which might indicate that PTH has structure are the differences in tryptophan quenching in water compared to guanidine due to energy transfer to ionized tyrosine. This result can be explained if PTH is more extended in guanidine than in water. It is known that concentrated guanidine solutions are better solvents than water for proteins.[39] Consequently, proteins or polypeptides would be expected to have a greater effective volume or root mean square end-to-end distance in guanidine.[40]

There is chemical data which indicates that the tryptophan and the two methionine groups in PTH are free. The latter are readily oxidized, and tryptophan reacts with both N-bromosuccinimide and 2-hydroxy-5-nitrobenzyl bromide.[3]

If either PTH or ACTH analog possesses structure, it would have to be formed from a less structured molecule that existed at the time of extraction in the former or synthesis in the latter. The methods of extraction and purification would disorganize any ordered structure that PTH may have in situ. It is extracted in 90% phenol and then distributed between n-butanol and 20% acetic acid in counter current distribution.[1, 2] In aqueous solutions at neutral pH it might, however, recover its structure. Its remarkable stability survives brief periods of boiling in 0.1M HCl or hot 80% acetic acid, treatment with guanidine, urea and trichloracetic acid.

References

1. Edelhoch, H., R. L. Perlman & M. Wilchek. 1968. Biochem. **7:** 3893.
2. Aurbach, G. D. 1959. J. Biol. Chem. **234:** 3179.
3. Potts, J. T., Jr., G. D. Aurbach & L. M. Sherwood. 1966. *In* Recent Progress in Hormone Research. G. Pincus, Ed.: 101–143. Academic Press. New York, N. Y.
4. Heins, J. N., J. R. Suriano, H. Taniuchi & C. B. Anfinsen. 1967. J. Biol. Chem. **242:** 1016.
5. Taniuchi, H., C. B. Anfinsen & A. Sodja. 1967. J. Biol. Chem. **252:** 4752.
6. Boissonnas, R. A., S. Guttmann & J. Pless. 1966. Experientia *XXII*: 526.
7. Turner, G. K. 1964. Science **146:** 183.
8. Förster, T. 1960. Radiation Research Supplement **2:** 326.
9. Latt, S. A., H. T. Cheung & E. R. Blout. 1965. J. Amer. Chem. Soc. **87:** 998.
10. Perlman, R. L., A. van Zyl & H. Edelhoch. 1968. J. Amer. Chem. Soc. **90:** 2168.
11. Weber, G. 1960. Biochem. J. **75:** 335.
12. Wada, A. & Y. Ueno. 1964. Biopolymers (Sympos.) **1:** 343.
13. Edelhoch, H., L. Brand & M. Wilchek. 1967. Biochemistry **6:** 547.
14. Teale, F. W. J. & G. Weber. 1957. Biochem. J. **65:** 476.
15. Chen, R. F. 1967. Anal. Lett. **1:** 35.
16. Weber, G. 1966. *In* Fluorescence and Phosphorescence Analysis. D. M. Hercules, Ed.: 217–239. Interscience Publishers. New York, N. Y.
17. Gally, J. A. & G. M. Edelman. 1964. Biopolymers (Sympos.) **1:** 367.
18. Cowgill, R. W. 1965. Biochim. Biophys. Acta **94:** 81.
19. White, A. 1959. Biochem. J. **71**: 217.

20. Cowgill, R. W. 1963. Arch. Biochem. Biophys. **100:** 36.
21. Weber, G. & K. Rosenbeck. 1964. Biopolymers (Sympos.) **1:** 333.
22. Fasman, G., K. Norland & A. Pesce. 1964. Biopolymers (Sympos.) **1:** 325.
23. Teale, F. W. J. 1960. Biochem. J. **76:** 381.
24. Cuatrecasas, P., H. Edelhoch & C. B. Anfinsen. 1967. Proc. Nat. Acad. Sci. U.S.A. **58:** 2043.
25. Cowgill, R. W. 1967. Biochim. Biophys. Acta **133:** 6.
26. Cowgill, R. W. 1965. Biochim. Biophys. Acta **109:** 536.
27. Feitelson, J. 1964. J. Phys. Chem. **68:** 391.
28. Cowgill, R. W. 1967. Biochim. Biophys. Acta **140:** 37.
29. Aurbach, G. D. Personal communication.
30. Steiner, R. F. & H. Edelhoch. 1963. Biochim. Biophys. Acta **66:** 341.
31. Fasman, G., E. Bodenheimer & E. A. Pesce. 1966. J. Biol. Chem. **241:** 916.
32. Edelhoch, H., P. G. Condliffe, R. E. Lippoldt & H. G. Burger. 1966. J. Biol. Chem. **241:** 5025.
33. Burger, H., H. Edelhoch & P. G. Condliffe. 1966. J. Biol. Chem. **241:** 449.
34. Weber, G. & L. B. Young. 1964. J. Biol. Chem. **239:** 1415.
35. Vladmirov, Y. A. & G. M. Zimina. 1965. Biokhimiia **30:** 1105.
36. Chen, R. F. & P. F. Cohen. 1966. Arch. Biochem. Biophys. **114:** 514.
37. Perutz, M. F. 1965. J. Molec. Biol. **13:** 646.
38. Phillips, D. C. 1966. Sci. Amer. **215:** 78.
39. Tanford, C., K. Kawahara & S. Lapanje. 1967. J. Amer. Chem. Soc. **89:** 729.
40. Tanford, C., K. Kawahara & S. Lapanje. 1966. J. Biol. Chem. **241:** 1921.

ELECTRONIC STRUCTURES AND SPECTRA OF FLAVINS: AN IMPROVED PARISER-PARR-POPLE MO AND SEMIEMPIRICAL UNRESTRICTED HARTREE-FOCK COMPUTATIONS*

Pill-Soon Song
Department of Chemistry
Texas Technological College
Lubbock, Tex.

INTRODUCTION

Flavins are derivatives of 6, 7-dimethylisoalloxazine:

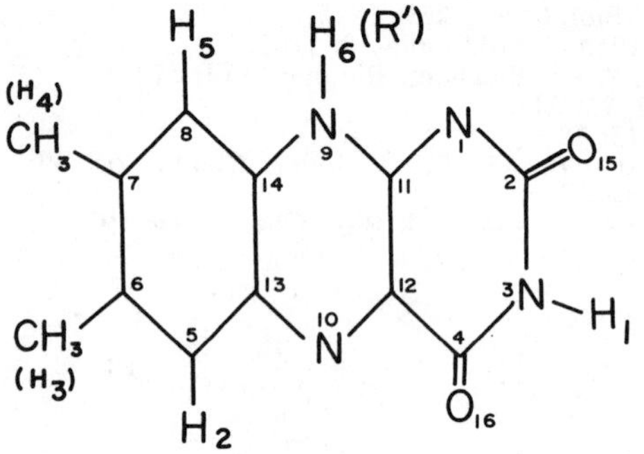

R′ = ribityl: riboflavin (RF)
R′ = methyl: lumiflavin (LF)
R′ = nucleotides: FMN or FAD

Flavins play fundamental roles in many important biochemical processes e.g., electron transfer in mitochondria, energy migration in chloroplasts, and the phototropic process. Nevertheless, detailed physical and chemical mechanisms involved in these processes have not been established so far.

In addition, flavins are photochemically reactive themselves. From studies made in our laboratory[1–6] and the findings of others,[7] it is apparent that flavins are photochemically versatile molecules with respect to their role in electronic energy transfer and secondary photochemical reactions. For example, we have studied energy transfer processes involving the excited singlet and triplet states of RF by means of fluorescence and phosphorescence measurements. It has been established that flavins undergo both intra- and intermolecular photooxidation-reduction reactions with and without added donor molecules. These properties of flavins led us to believe that flavins play an important role both at the primary and secondary photochemical levels in biological systems. For example, the singlet and triplet energy transfer between flavins and chlorophylls or other components in plants is expected to participate in various primary photo processes. The energy transfer processes between flavins and menadiones are also of interest, since the presence of the latter appears to be essential in the photosynthetic apparatus.

The understanding of the electronic structure and spectra is a prerequisite for the discussion of the photochemical and biochemical behaviors of flavins in model and biological systems. Flavins have frequently been treated by the

* This work received financial support from the Robert A. Welch Foundation, Grant No. D-182.

Hückel molecular orbital (MO)[5, 8, 9] and by a self-consistent field MO method.[10]

Inclusion of Methyl Groups in the Pi-Electron Calculations of Flavins

Two significant aspects of the theoretical investigation of flavin molecules have been neglected. Namely, the 6, 7-dimethyl groups of the isoalloxazine ring have not been included in the published treatments, except for the simple MO calculations in References 5 and 8. Since the methyl groups affect the electronic properties of the molecules and one (7-) of the 6, 7-methyl groups is reactive,[11, 12] we think that the inclusion of the methyl groups is essential for the interpretation of the MO results with respect to chemical and biochemical reactivities, and we have critically examined three methods of treating methyl groups in isoalloxazines. These include the inductive model (I),[13, 14] the pseudo-heteroatom approximation (H)[15, 16] and the group-orbital hyperconjugation model (G).[17] In examining the last two models, we have also employed the Pariser-Parr-Pople semiempirical SCF ASMO with the limited configuration interaction (P-P-P SCF MO), a restricted Hartree-Fock method.

The alkyl group at N-9 was not included, since this group may not contribute to the π-conjugation of the flavin ring significantly. However, this group does affect the chemical reactivity of the molecule. We are currently calculating the σ-framework in order to include the methyl group at N-9.

Methods

Since the theories and computational procedures of the various MO methods employed are described elsewhere in detail,[16, 18–20] we will only comment on the choice of empirical and semiempirical integrals in each method.

HMO. Two sets of parameters were used. The first set was identical with that of Reference 18, and the second set was one which we had previously used[21] and which was recommended by the Kyoto Laboratory of Fukui. The latter set was compiled from various published sources. Integrals for methyl groups are listed in TABLE 1.

ω-SCF HMO. An empirical introduction of the electron interaction into HMO can be made in terms of the ω-technique. The procedure is to iterate starting with the HMO parameters followed by each new set of α until α converges: $\alpha_r = \alpha_c + (1 - P_{rr})\ \omega\ \beta_c$, where $\omega = -0.25\ (\mathrm{rr\ rr})/\beta_c$ and P_{rr} is a diagonal element of the bond-order matrix, (rr|rr) is the usual one-center electron repulsion integral.[22] Both $\omega = 0.5$[22] and 1.4[16] were used in the present work.

TABLE 1

COULOMB (δ) AND RESONANCE (η) PARAMETERS ($\alpha = \alpha_c + \delta\beta_c$ AND $\beta = \eta\beta_c$) FOR THE METHYL GROUP

Model	Atom	δ	Bond	η	Reference
I	$C_{arom.}$	−0.5	$C \equiv H_3$	0	16
H	$C_{arom.}$	−0.2	$C - CH_3$	0.7	16
	CH_3	3.0	$C \equiv H_3$	0.0	16
G	$C_{arom.}$	−0.1	$C - CH_3$	0.8	16
	C	0.0 (−0.2)			16
	$\equiv H_3$	−0.5	$C \equiv H_3$	3.0	8, 16

P-P-P SCF ASMO CI. The usual GMS, ZDO, semiempirical evaluation of integrals, and neglect of penetration integrals (NPI) were assumed.[19, 20] Values of ionization potentials, one- and two-center electron repulsion integrals, and β^{core} were the same as those previously used in our laboratory.[21, 23] TABLE 2 lists the values for the methyl group. An improvement of the PPP method was also attempted by evaluating all nonneighbor β^{core} terms from the $\beta - S$ (overlap integral) proportionality relationship.

The configuration-interaction matrix was constructed with a limited number of singly-excited configurations, usually fifteen configurations. All computations were carried out on an IBM 7040.

Sigma-Electron Methods. The extended Hückel MO(EHMO)[27] and the Pople-Segal SCF MO CNDO/II (Complete Neglect of Differential Overlap)[28, 29] methods were used. Since these methods are described in detail in their respective papers, only an outline of each method will be given here.

Both methods set up the MO's from the linear combination of valence atomic orbitals including the 1s of hydrogen, and 2s and 2p orbitals of second row atoms.

(a) *EHMO.* No usual Hückel approximations are necessary. All overlap integrals were evaluated. H_{ii}'s were approximated as valence state ionization potentials[27, 30] and H_{ij}'s were evaluated by the Wolfsberg-Helmholtz formula:[31]

$$H_{ij} = 0.5K(H_{ii} + H_{jj})S_{ij}, \qquad K = 1.75.$$

The assumed molecular geometry was the same as in Reference 32. The FORTRAN II program (courtesy of Professor R. Hoffmann and QCPE 30-Exthuc) was used after shifting into FORTRAN IV.

(b) *CNDO.* Details of the method and the "complete neglect of differential overlap" approximation have been given.[28, 29] In essence, the CNDO method assumes complete neglect of any diatomic differential overlap distribution in all electron repulsion integrals. Energies are then obtained from Hartree-Fock equation of the format

$$|F_{rs} - ES_{rs}| = 0.$$

Integrals in References 28 and 29 were used. The FORTRAN IV program originally written by Dr. G. A. Segal was made available to us by Dr. W. C. Herndon.

TABLE 2

VALUES OF INTEGRALS (IN E.V.) FOR THE METHYL GROUP USED IN THE P-P-P CALCULATION

Model	Atom	I_p	(rr|rr)	Bond	β^{core}	Referencs
G	CH_3	10.690	8.590	$C - CH_3$	−1.912	23
	$\equiv H_3$	10.256	9.326	$C \equiv H_3$	−2.640	23, 24
(G)*	$C_{arom.}$	9.000	10.87	$C - CH_3$	−1.440	26
	CH_3	9.500	6.67	$C \equiv H_3$	−3.400	26
	$\equiv H_3$	8.900	10.65			26
(H)	CH_3	15.600	13.231	$C - CH_3$	−3.750	23, 25
H					−1.673	23

* Whenever this set of integrals is used, it will be indicated by a G in parentheses.

The Singlet-Singlet $\pi \rightarrow \pi^*$ Transition Energies and Transition Moments

TABLES 3 and 4 are a summary of results from a detailed study of the $\pi \rightarrow \pi^*$ transition energies of 6, 7-dimethyl flavin derivatives. While this work

TABLE 3

SINGLET $\pi \rightarrow \pi^*$ TRANSITION ENERGIES IN (EV) OF 6, 7-DIMETHYL ISOALLOXAZINE AND ITS DERIVATIVES, CALCULATED BY HMO AND ω − SCF HMO USING β = −3.26 E.V.

		1st Transition			2nd Transition		
Flavin	Method	I	H	G	I	H	G
6, 7-Dimethyl isoalloxazine	HMO	2.846	2.725	2.737	3.703	3.681	3.696
	ω = 0.5	2.459	2.434	2.419	3.705	3.676	3.671
	ω = 1.4	2.037	2.021	1.977	2.666	2.665	2.537
2-Thio-6, 7-dimethyl isoalloxazine	HMO	2.153	2.129	2.099	3.544	3.524	3.527
	ω = 0.5	1.878	1.855	1.816	3.158	3.126	3.081
	ω = 1.4	1.504	1.496	1.438	2.382	2.373	2.289
4-Thio-6, 7-dimethyl isoalloxazine	HMO	2.499	2.492	2.492	3.426	3.365	3.350
	ω = 0.5	2.270	2.246	2.226	3.066	3.035	2.988
	ω = 1.4	1.800	1.790	1.626	2.414	2.401	2.330

was in progress, Forster and coworkers[10] reported results of the P-P-P calculations on isoalloxazine and alloxazine without methyl groups that are in reasonable agreement with the experimental spectra and data presented in TABLE 4 (first three rows of data based on the I model).

TABLE 4

SINGLET $\pi \rightarrow \pi^*$ TRANSITION ENERGIES (EV) OF 6, 7-DIMETHYL ISOALLOXAZINE AND ITS DERIVATIVES, CALCULATED BY THE P-P-P SCF MO[a]

Flavin	CH_3	1st Transition	f[b]	2nd Transition	f
6, 7-Dimethyl isoalloxazine	I	3.085 (2.783)[c]	0.633	3.916 (3.397)	0.148
	H	1.569 (2.783)	0.309	2.832 (3.397)	1.129
	G	3.128 (2.783)	0.773	3.847 (3.397)	0.124
	(G)	3.048	0.736	3.847	0.114
2-Thio-6,7-dimethyl isoalloxazine	I	2.871 (2.583)	0.719	3.664 (3.406)	0.163
	G	2.856	0.899	3.636	0.203
	(G)	2.490	4.513	3.599	0.236
4-Thio-6, 7-dimethyl isoalloxazine	G	2.945 (2.743)	0.822	3.551 (3.378)	0.091
	(G)	2.883	0.854	3.622	0.060

[a] Integrals are the same as those used in Reference 23.
[b] Oscillator strength.
[c] Numbers in parentheses are experimental.[33,34]

The first two lowest transitions corresponding to $\psi 9 \rightarrow \psi 10$ and $\psi 8 \rightarrow \psi 10$ (I) and $\psi 11 \rightarrow \psi 12$ and $\psi 10 \rightarrow \psi 12$ (H and G) are presented in TABLES 3 and 4. It is clear from TABLE 3 that the HMO and ω-SCF methods are not sensitive enough to differentiate between the I, H or G methyl treatments. As can be seen, the commonly used value of $\beta = -3.26$ e.v. cannot be used for other molecules such as the closely-related thioriboflavins. It is understandable that, using the same value of β, the ω-SCF HMO does not yield spectral quantities in good agreement with experiments, due possibly to an inadequate degree of vertical electron correlation introduced empirically by the value of ω. However, it should be noted that the value of 1.4 resulted in making the HOMO's of thioisoalloxazines antibonding. Even a relative correlation between the calculated and experimental spectra of oxygen-heterocyclic molecules was poor with $\omega = 1.4$.[35]

While the agreement between the calculated transition energies by the P-P-P and experiments is not perfect in TABLE 4, the data show reasonable agreement and consistency with respect to different semiempirical integrals used, except for the values calculated from the H treatment. The P-P-P method also correctly yields longer wavelengths for the first transition in 6,7-dimethyl thioisoalloxazines. However, the group orbital model shows that transition energies correlate satisfactorily with experiment in the treatments (G) and G. Significantly better correlation between the observed spectra and improved PPP results has been obtained, and will be described below. From data shown in TABLES 3 and 4, the effect of 6, 7-methyl groups is seen to be bathochromic.

It is interesting to note that the HMO calculation of 6,7-dimethyl isoalloxazine (G) semiquinone shows the first lowest transition at 2.182 eV, in good agreement with the experimental spectrum (2.101 e.v.).[36] However, this may be fortuitous. There are also two possible second transitions: 3.272 eV for 11 → 12 (orbital with a unpaired electron) and 5.454 e.V for 11 → 13 (LEMO). The former seems to correspond to the second absorption peak at about 2.8 eV.[36] However, any spectral assignment for open-shell systems is ambiguous in terms of HMO; an unrestricted Hartree-Fock SCF MO with configuration interactions must be employed.

FIGURE 1 shows the fluorescence polarizations of riboflavin and lumiflavin in glycerol-water (90:10) at −10° C. FIGURE 2 shows polarization directions of the transition moments calculated by the improved PPP MO. TABLE 5 lists polarization data of the two lowest transitions for flavin, as well as for alloxazine (see FIGURE 3).

It can be seen from TABLE 5 that the PPP calculations yield satisfactory spectral results. The transition energies from the improved PPP MO are in particularly good agreement with the observed data. Calculated directions of the spectral transitions also appear to be at least qualitatively encouraging. In addition, the PPP calculations (FIGURE 2) shows a weak electronic transition (f = 0.040) at 290 nm that is also recognizable in the fluorescence polarization spectra (see a minimum at about 300 nm region in FIGURE 1). The minimum in the fluorescence polarization is even more distinctive in D_2O-glycerol.[37] We conclude, therefore, that the refined PPP computations are useful for interpreting electronic spectra of complex molecules such as flavins.

The Lowest Triplet States of Flavins

TABLE 6 lists the values of the lowest triplets of some flavins as a function of different methyl group treatments in the PPP calculations.

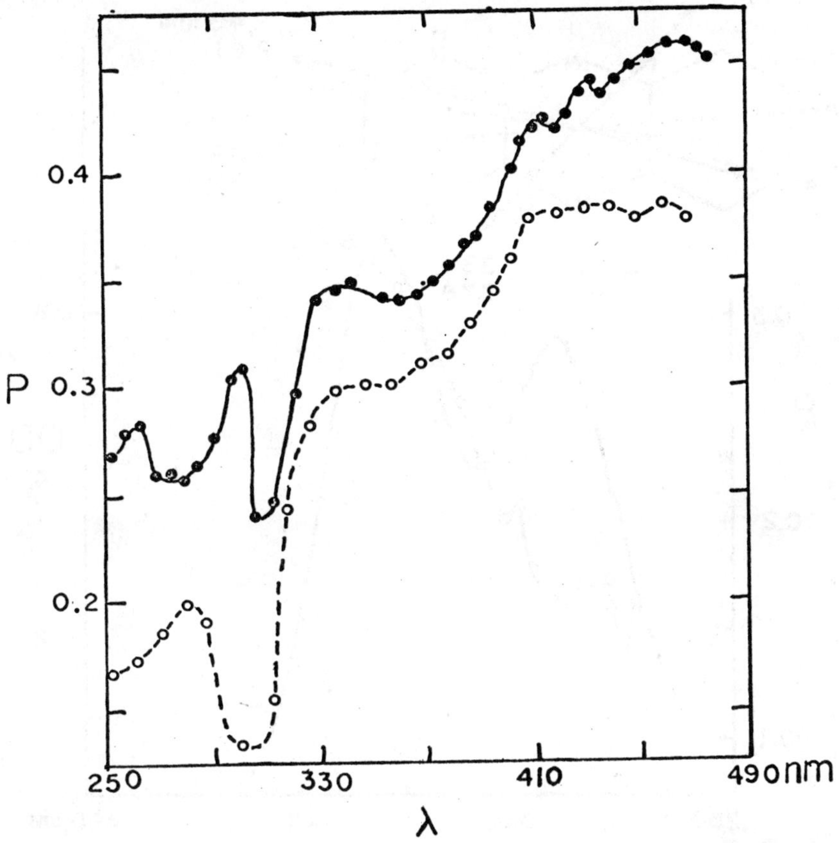

FIGURE 1. Fluorescence excitation polarization of riboflavin (–●–●–) and lumiflavin (–0–0–) in glycerol: methanol (9:1) at –10° C.

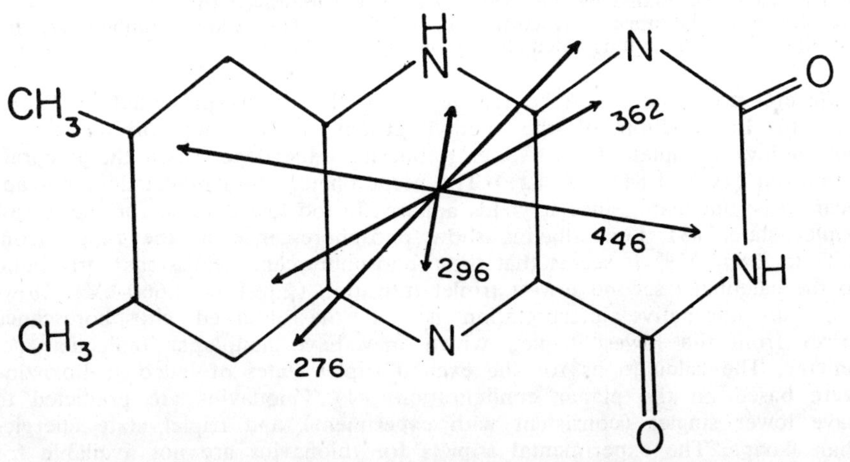

FIGURE 2. Orientation of the calculated transition moments.

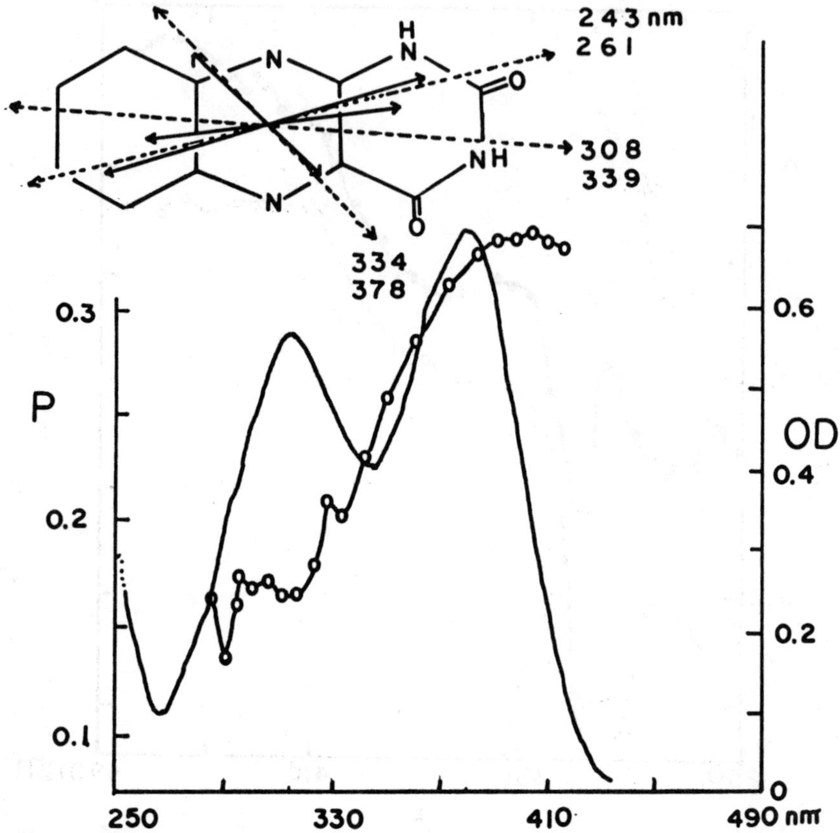

FIGURE 3. Absorption spectrum in methanol at 25° C (—), fluorescence excitation polarization in glycerol: methanol (9:1) at −10° C (–0–), and orientation of the calculated transition moments (in the upper corner) or alloxazine. The transition moments calculated by the PPP-MO (—) and improved PPP-MO (————) are shown in the upper left corner of the figure. The second numbers are the transition energies (in nm) calculated by the latter method.

Several conclusions can be reached from the results presented in TABLE 6: (1) Introduction of the methyl groups as a group orbital contribution lowers triplet (G, 1.673 eV), but its value depends on the integrals employed ((G), 1.811 eV. (2)) The pseudo-heteroatom model does not appear to be adequate, since it yields apparently too low a value for the lowest triplet state. (3) Leuco-flavins show phosphorescence in the range from 2.27 to 2.84 eV.[38] It seems that these phosphorescence emissions correspond to the calculated second lowest triplet transition (2.691 ~ 2.660 eV). However, an alternative interpretation is that the observed phosphorescence arises from the lowest triplet, which may have nonplanar molecular geometry. The calculations for the excited triplet states of leuco-isoalloxazine were based on the planar configuration. (4) Thioflavins are predicted to have lower singlet (consistent with experiment) and triplet state energies than flavins. The experimental triplets for thioflavins are not available for comparison. (5) Alloxazine has its triplet well above that of the isomer

TABLE 5

ANGLES BETWEEN THE TWO LOWEST $\pi \rightarrow \pi^*$ TRANSITIONS

	Transition Oscillators (nm)		θ[c]		
Compound	obs.	calc.[a]	obs.	calc.[a]	calc.[b]
Riboflavin	445	446	49°	37°	42°
	365	360			
Alloxazine	378	378	73°	49°	50°
	318	339			

[a] With $\beta_{rs}^{core} \neq 0$, where r and s are non-neighbors.
[b] With $\beta_{rs}^{core} = 0$, where r and s are non-neighbors.
[c] Using Levshin-Perrin formula: $P = \dfrac{3\cos^2\theta - 1}{\cos^2\theta + 3}$.

(isoalloxazine). The calculated value is in reasonable agreement with the observed phosphorescence (2.27 eV) of lumichrome.[38]

If singlet oxygen is indeed involved in the phosphorescence emission (603 mμ region) via the Steele-Cusachs mechanism,[39] the singlet oxygen cannot be $^1\Sigma^+_g$. In fact, the improved PPP-MO calculation predicts the lowest triplet of 6, 7-dimethyl isoalloxazine lying at 1.413 eV (877 mμ). This value is intermediate between the observed phosphorescence and the energy (~leV) required by the Steele-Cusachs mechanism. However, there is another low-lying singlet (0, 0) band of the $^1\Delta_g$ — $^3\Sigma_g^-$ system at 1,270 mμ region.[40] Consequently the nature of the flavin phosphorescence in the presence of oxygen cannot be definitely established.

Basicity of Excited States of Flavins

TABLE 7 shows the pi-electron densities on the pyridinelike nitrogens in 6, 7-dimethylisoalloxazine and alloxazine calculated by the improved PPP-MO method. It has been shown that the pi-electron density is an approximate index of the relative basicity of heterocyclic nitrogens.[18, 41, 42, 43, 44, 45] It can be seen from TABLE 7 that the relative basicity of the nitrogens reverses upon excitation either to the lowest singlet or triplet state from the ground state. The results calculated by the improved PPP-MO method are in support of the data previously obtained from the PPP-MO calculations without nonneighbor β terms.[45]

TABLE 6

TRIPLET STATES OF SOME FLAVINS[23]

Flavin	Method	Lowest eV
6, 7-Dimethylisoalloxazine	I	1.712
	H	0.673
	G	1.673
	(G)	1.811
Leuco-dimethylisoalloxazine	G	0.969
	(G)	1.083
2-Thio-dimethylisoalloxazine	I	1.553
4-Thio-dimethylalloxazine	I	1.618
Alloxazine	I	2.465

TABLE 7

PI-ELECTRON DENSITIES (q_π) AS A MEASURE OF RELATIVE BASICITY OF THE PYRIDINE-LIKE NITROGEN, CALCULATED BY THE IMPROVED PPP-MO METHOD

Compound	State	q_π		
		N_1	N_{10}	N_9
6, 7-Dimethylisoalloxazine	S_0	1.371	1.114	
	S_1	1.250	1.393	
	S_2	1.409	1.344	
	T_1	1.160	1.381	
	T_2	1.409	1.367	
Alloxazine	S_0		1.127	1.244
	S_1		1.337	1.314
	S_2		1.346	1.359
	T_1		1.329	1.261
	T_2		1.361	1.388

An approximate unrestricted Hartree-Fock (URHF) treatment of the lowest triplet isoalloxazine within the CNDO framework has yielded the pi-electron densities on the nitrogens, as shown in TABLE 8, and the results are in agreement with the data shown in TABLE 7.

Sigma-Electronic Structure of Isoalloxazine

An important feature which has been neglected in previous studies by workers in this field is the sigma-electronic structure of flavins. Using the extended HMO, we attempted to calculate the electronic structure of the complicated biomolecule, isoalloxazine.[46] Although the results are qualitatively consistent with the more elaborate calculations by the Pariser-Parr-Pople SCF ASMO CI (PPP) and the Pople-Segal SCF LCAO MO CNDO (CNDO) methods,[46] anomalies in some of the calculated quantities have been observed. Both methods have been used for other simpler biomolecules for comparison with the results of the extended HMO in our laboratory.

It has been observed that the pi-framework of the carbonyl groups in the flavin molecule appears to be overpolarized. Thus, we next attempted a different method (Equation 1) for evaluating the off-diagonal elements instead of Equation 2 employed previously.

TABLE 8

PI-ELECTRON DENSITIES AS A MEASURE OF THE RELATIVE BASICITY OF THE PYRIDINE-LIKE NITROGENS, CALCULATED BY THE CNDO METHOD

Compound		q_π		
		N_1	N_{10}	N_9
Isoalloxazine	S_0*	1.293	0.909	
	T_1	1.325	1.529	
Alloxazine	S_0*		0.913	1.248
	T_1		1.500	1.346

* Obtained from the RHF calculations within the CNDO framework.

$$H_{ij} = k(H_{ii} \cdot H_{jj})^{1/2} \cdot S_{ij} \quad (1)$$

$$H_{ij} = 0.5K(H_i^{\ i} + H_{jj})S_{ij} \quad (2)$$

TABLE 9 shows the electron densities of the EHMO calculations using Equation 1 together with the CNDO data. A close examination of the data in TABLE 9 shows that the use of Equation 1 for the off-diagonal matrix elements does not seem to improve the results over the previous calculations with Equation 2.[46] For example, both the sigma- and pi-frameworks are still overly polarized in the case of the EHMO scheme. Since the pi-electron distribution calculated by the CNDO method is consistent with the PPP-MO method, it is felt that the CNDO method is preferred to the EHMO for complex biomolecules such as flavins. In general, it can be seen that the directions of the sigma- and pi-polarizations are parallel to each other. We are currently carrying out extensive CNDO calculations of all possible flavin tautomers to examine their structural and functional correlation.

Open-Shell Computations of Flavins by Restricted and Unrestricted Hartree-Fock Procedures: Spin Densities

TABLE 10 lists the preliminary results on spin densities of isoalloxazine calculated by the pi-electron methods in the RHF[47] and URHF[48, 49] schemes. In general, the URHF (both pi- and sigma-electron calculations) appears to yield better agreement with the observed spin densities than the RHF. Results from the URHF calculations are also in close agreement with the calculated spin-density distribution previously reported by Pullman and collaborators.[50]

TABLE 9

SIGMA- (q_σ) AND PI-ELECTRON (q_π) DENSITIES IN ISOALLOXAZINE

	Position	q_σ		q_π	
		EHMO	CNDO	EHMO	CNDO
	1	4.522	4.017	1.542	1.293
	2	1.857	2.732	0.492	0.824
	3	3.980	3.546	1.569	1.779
	4	2.122	2.819	0.480	0.830
	12	2.774	2.972	0.800	1.049
	10	4.510	4.157	1.263	0.909
	13	2.713	2.885	0.916	1.037
	5	3.112	3.030	1.000	0.954
	6	3.199	2.989	1.047	1.081
	7	3.197	3.029	0.969	0.952
	8	3.105	2.966	1.064	1.097
	14	2.746	2.936	0.872	0.946
	9	3.852	3.446	1.506	1.718
	11	2.470	2.899	0.698	0.846
	15	5.591	4.985	1.883	1.357
	16	5.593	4.977	1.899	1.331
H	1	0.565	0.821		
	2	0.889	0.991		
	3	0.809	0.957		
	4	0.794	0.965		
	5	0.894	1.000		
	6	0.709	0.875		

TABLE 10

SPIN DENSITIES (WITHOUT ANNIHILATION) IN THE ISOALLOXAZINE RADICAL CALCULATED BY RHF AND URHF SCHEMES

Position	Obs.[a]	Obs.[b]	RHF	URHF
1	~0	0.025	0.006	0.020 (0.061)[c]
2			−0.002	0.007 (−0.006)
3	~0	0.025	0.001	−0.021 (−0.007)
4			0.003	0.007 (0.007)
12			0.037	−0.125 (−0.074)
10	0.28	0.246 ~ 0.378	0.033	0.382 (0.573)
13			0.036	−0.074 (−0.048)
5	0.14	0.13 ~ 0.167	0.274	0.146 (0.098)
6	~0	0.025	−0.011	−0.085 (−0.033)
7	0.14	0.125 ~ 0.184	0.285	0.120 (0.042)
8	~0	0.025	−0.034	−0.077 (−0.018)
14			0.324	0.086 (0.033)
9	0.14	0.123 ~ 0.189	0.043	0.328 (0.107)
11			0.000	0.247 (0.236)
15			−0.002	0.034 (0.024)
16			0.008	0.005 (0.005)

[a] After Guzzo and Tollin (1964).[51]
[b] After Ehrenberg, Eriksson and Müller (1966).[52]
[c] Calculated by the CNDO method.

Identical sets of integrals were used in the π-electron calculations by the RHF and URHF. This suggests that an URHF scheme is preferable to the RHF for complex biomolecules such as flavins, since the former yielded more satisfactory spin densities. However, further investigation of the flavin radical is needed, especially with respect to the dependence of the spin-density distribution upon the choice of semiempirical integrals. It should be pointed out that the valence AO's do not contribute to the π-MO's of the isoalloxazine radical in the CNDO treatment. This is not the case in the lowest triplet configuration of the isoalloxazine molecule, as will be described below.

TABLE 11 shows the spin density distribution of the lowest triplet state of the isoalloxazine molecule. It can be seen that the sigma core orbitals contribute to the total spin density in the triplet configuration. It is especially interesting to note that N_{10} has a high pi-spin density and a unit concentration of total α-spin. Qualitative observation supports the results shown in TABLE 11, particularly with respect to the quinoxaline part of the isoalloxazine molecule.[38]

The pi-spin densities are concentrated at N_{10}, C_{12}, O_{16}, N_1, C_8, and O_{15}, in that order. These results give quantitative support to the qualitative conclusion that spin densities preferentially occupy the quinoxaline moiety of the flavin ring,[38] and that a small spin density is present on N_9 as compared with the spin density at other positions.[53] Lhoste and coworkers[38] proposed that the spin-density distribution of the triplet flavins is similar to that of the flavin semiquinone radicals. The spin density of flavin semiquinones was found to be highest at N_{10}.[38, 51] The highest spin density is also found at N_{10}, as shown in TABLE 10, indicating a resemblance of the spin polarization between the doublet and triplet configurations. The same trend is found at positions 5 and 6.[51, 52] However, such a similarity cannot be extrapolated to all positions. For example, the spin density at N_1 was found to be nearly zero for the flavin

TABLE 11

SPIN DENSITIES (WITHOUT ANNIHILATION) IN THE LOWEST TRIPLET CONFIGURATION OF ISOALLOXAZINE, AS CALCULATED BY THE CNDO METHOD IN THE URHF SCHEME

Position	Pi-Spin Density	Total ($\sigma + \pi$) Spin Density
1	0.144	0.167
2	−0.024	−0.020
3	−0.023	−0.020
4	−0.077	−0.043
12	0.326	0.347
10	0.372	1.051
13	−0.026	0.033
5	0.119	0.051
6	−0.026	−0.023
7	0.026	0.026
8	−0.022	−0.015
14	0.026	0.070
9	0.028	0.014
11	−0.046	−0.075
15	0.059	0.060
16	0.211	0.225

radical,[51, 52] whereas the triplet shown in TABLE 11 indicates a significant spin density. In fact, preliminary calculations in our laboratory using the pi-electron URHF scheme suggest that N_1 has a higher spin density (0.277) than N_{10} (0.171). Lhoste and collaborators correctly pointed out that the arguments for such a similarity must be considered with great care in the case of flavin derivatives because of the low symmetry and the number of heteroatoms involved.[38]

The sigma-electrons apparently affect the spin polarization, as shown in TABLE 11. As an extreme case, for example, the negative pi-spin density at C_{13} changes its sign when the sigma-polarization is taken into account (i.e., change from excess β-spin in the pi-spin distribution to excess α-spin in the total spin polarization scheme). An unusually high spin density is at N_{10}. The effect of the sigma contribution is apparently not drastic at other positions. The influence of the sigma core can be understood in terms of hyperfine coupling which is proportional to the sigma character of the MO of the odd electron at the nuclei of the flavin ring.[54]

Properties of a Flavin Triplet, as Shown by the CNDO Calculation

In previous sections, we have described the basicity and the spin-density distribution of the lowest triplet in reference to the ground state and the doublet molecule, respectively. In this section, a brief description of the geometry (namely, bond lengths) of the lowest triplet configuration of the isoalloxazine molecule is given.

The CNDO results show that the mobile bond orders of the flavin ring change upon intersystem crossing.[46] The most dramatic change caused by the transition from the closed-shell singlet to the open-shell triplet is seen along the region of N_1 through N_{10}. The mobile bond order between C_{12} and N_{10} decreases by as much as 43% in the triplet. This means that the bond distance increases by approximately 0.065Å upon intersystem crossing, as calculated by the use of the Nishimoto-Forster formula.[55] However, bond distances C_{11}-C_{12}

and C_4-C_{12} decrease in the triplet state by approximately 0.02Å, respectively. It has also been shown that the dipole moment of the triplet state is higher than that of the ground state molecule.

One of the most interesting aspects of the photochemical reactivity of riboflavin is that the excited state of the isoalloxazine ring abstracts hydrogen from the ribityl side-chain at N_9.[6, 7] There are probably two sites, namely N_1 and N_{10}, for the intramolecular photoreduction of the flavin ring. As a photoreactivity index for the hydrogen abstraction, we estimated the frontier spin density for $N_1 = 0.322$ and $N_{10} = 0.266$.[46] This means that N_1 is a more favorable site for the hydrogen abstraction than N_{10}.

Conclusion

Quantum mechanical investigations of flavin molecules are valuable for understanding their electronic structures and properties, which are essential to elucidate their versatile role in biochemistry, photochemistry, and photobiology. The results of a theoretical study are particularly useful in the interpretation of the experimental data, such as spectra, fluorescence polarization, and basicity of flavins.

We have critically examined simple MO methods for complex biomolecules such as flavins, and were able to improve the PPP-MO method by including all nonneighbor β^{core} terms in the off-diagonal Fock matrix elements. The use of the semiempirical, unrestricted Hartree-Fock SCF MO methods has also been shown to be beneficial in yielding spin densities and the spin polarizations of the sigma- and pi-electron systems of the isoalloxazine molecule. Finally, the geometry and reactivity of the lowest flavin triplet have been briefly described. It is worthy of note that some of the quantities presented are not readily obtainable from experimental approaches, and this shows the usefulness of the MO methods for complex biomolecular systems.

Acknowledgment

The assistance of the staff of the Texas Technological College Computer Center is greatly appreciated.

References

1. Song, P. S., E. C. Smith & D. E. Metzler. 1965. J. Amer. Chem. Soc. **87:** 4181.
2. Song, P. S. & D. E. Metzler. 1965. Fed. Proc. **24:** 232.
3. Song, P. S., M. McBride, E. C. Smith & D. E. Metzler. Mito-Khondii, Strukt. Funks., Mater. Simp.: 62. Moscow, U.S.S.R.
4. Song, P. S. 1967. Photochem. Photobiol. **6:** 221.
5. Kurtin, W. E., M. A. Latino & P. S. Song. 1967. Photochem. Photobiol. **6:** 247.
6. Song, P. S. & D. E. Metzler. 1967. Photochem. Photobiol. **6:** 691.
7. Penzer, G. R. & G. K. Radda. 1967. Quart. Rev. (London) **21:** 43, and references therein.
8. Pullman, B. & A. Pullman. 1959. Proc. Nat. Acad. Sci., U. S. A. **45:** 136.
9. Karreman, G. 1961. Bull. Math. Biophys. **23:** 55.
10. Fox, J. L., S. P. Laberge, K. Nishimoto & L. S. Forster. 1967. Biochim. Biophys. Acta **136:** 544.
11. Bullock, F. J. & O. Jardetzky. 1965. J. Org. Chem. **30:** 2056.
12. Hemmerich, P., C. Veeger & H. C. S. Wood. 1965. Angew. Chem. **77:** 1.

13. WHELAND, G. W. & L. PAULING. 1935. J. Amer. Chem. Soc. **57:** 2086. (See also Reference 9.)
14. LONGUET-HIGGINS, H. C. 1950. J. Chem. Phys. **18:** 283.
15. MATSEN, F. A. 1950. J. Chem. Phys. **72:** 5243.
16. STREITWIESER, A., JR. 1961. Molecular Orbital Theory for Organic Chemists: 131–135. John Wiley & Sons. New York, N. Y.
17. MULLIKEN, R. S., C. A. RIEKE & W. G. BROWN. 1941. J. Amer. Chem. Soc. **63:** 41.
18. PULLMAN, B. & A. PULLMAN. 1963. Quantum Biochemistry. Interscience Publishers. New York, N. Y.
19. PARISER, R. & R. G. PARR. 1953. J. Chem. Phys. **21:** 466, 767.
20. POPLE, J. A. 1953. Trans. Farad. Soc. **49:** 1375.
21. SONG, P. S. & T. A. MOORE. 1967. J. Quantum Chem. **1:** 699; YONEZAWA, T., C. NAGATA, H. KATO, A. IMAMURA & K. MOROKUMA. 1964. Introduction to Quantum Chemistry (in Japanese). **I:** 55 Kagakudojin. Kyoto, Japan.
22. LOOYENGA, H. 1966. Molec. Phys. **11:** 337.
23. SONG, P. S. & W. E. KURTIN. 1967. J. Amer. Chem. Soc. **89:** 4248.
24. IMAMURA, A., H. FUJITA & C. NAGATA. 1967. Bull. Chem. Soc. Jap. **40:** 522.
25. KNOWLTON, P. & W. R. CARPER. 1966. Molec. Phys. **11:** 213.
26. DENIS, A. & A. PULLMAN. 1967. Theoret. Chim. Acta **7:** 110.
27. HOFFMANN, R. 1963. J. Chem. Phys. **39:** 1397.
28. POPLE, J. A., D. P. SANTRY & G. A. SEGAL. 1965. J. Chem. Phys. **43:** S129, S136.
29. POPLE, J. A. & G. A. SEGAL. 1966. J. Chem. Phys. **44:** 3289.
30. PRITCHARD, H. O. & H. A. SKINNER. 1955. Chem. Rev. **55:** 745.
31. WOLFSBERG, M. & L. HELMHOLTZ. 1952. J. Chem. Phys. **20:** 837.
32. GRABE, B. 1964. Biopolymers (Sympos.) **1:** 283.
33. PENZER, G. R. & G. K. RADDA. 1967. Quart. Rev. (London) **21:** 43.
34. KOZIOL, J. 1965. Photochem. Photobiol. **5:** 41.
35. KURTIN, W. E. & P. S. SONG. 1968. Tetrahedron **24:** 2255.
36. BEINERT, H. & R. H. SANDS. 1961. *In* Free Radicals in Biological Systems: 17. M. S. BLOIS, JR. *et al.*, Eds. Academic Press. New York, N. Y.
37. KURTIN, W. E. & P. S. SONG. 1968. Photochem. Photobiol. **7:** 263.
38. LHOSTE, J. M., A. HAUG & P. HEMMERICH. 1966. Biochemistry **5:** 3290.
39. STEELE, R. H. & L. C. CUSACHS. 1967. Nature **213:** 800.
40. BADER, L. W. & E. A. OGRYZLO. 1964. Discuss. Farad. Soc. **37:** 46.
41. LONGUET-HIGGINS, H. C. 1950. J. Chem. Phys. **18:** 275.
42. MASON, S. F. 1958. J. Chem. Soc.: 674, 2353.
43. HUSH, N. S. 1953. J. Chem. Soc.: 684.
44. NAKAJIMA, T. & A. PULLMAN. 1958. J. Chim. Phys. **55:** 793.
45. SONG, P. S. 1968. Photochem. Photobiol. **7:** 311.
46. SONG, P. S. 1968. J. Phys. Chem. **72:** 536.
47. BLOOR, J. E., B. R. GILSON & P. N. DAYKIN. 1966. J. Phys. Chem. **70:** 1457.
48. BRICKSTOCK, A. & J. A. POPLE. 1954. Trans. Farad. Soc. **50:** 901.
49. POPLE, J. A. & R. K. NESBET. 1954. J. Chem. Phys. **22:** 571.
50. BAUDET, J., G. BERTHIER & B. PULLMAN. 1962. Compt. Rend. **254:** 762.
51. GUZZO, A. V. & G. TOLLIN. 1964. Arch. Biochem. Biophys. **105:** 380.
52. EHRENBERG, A., L. E. G. ERIKSSON and F. MÜLLER. Flavins and Flavo-Proteins: 43. E. C. SLATOR, Ed. Elsevier. Amsterdam, The Netherlands.
53. SHIGA, T. & L. H. PIETTE. 1964. Photochem. Photobiol. **3:** 213.
54. EHRENBERG, A. 1962. Ark. Kemi **19:** 97.
55. NISHIMOTO, K. & L. S. FORSTER. 1966. Theor. Chim. Acta **4:** 155.

A PROPOSED MECHANISM FOR SUBUNIT INTERACTION IN HEMOGLOBIN*

J. Peisach†

Departments of
Pharmacology and Molecular Biology
Albert Einstein College of Medicine
Yeshiva University, New York, N. Y.

Using cytochrome *c* peroxidase, horseradish peroxidase and sperm whale myoglobin[1,2] as model systems has led us to suggest a mechanism for the interaction of hemoglobin with oxygen and other ligands. Before discussing this mechanism, it is important to define those aspects of heme chemistry that may have bearing on this reaction. As is well known, the heme in all protoheme protein derivatives is bonded to the protein at the fifth or proximal ligand position of the heme iron. The ligand atom is known with certainty to be an imidazole nitrogen of histidine in myoglobin[3] and also in hemoglobin.[4] In any single heme protein the fifth ligand contributed by the protein remains the same in all derivatives. The ligands in the sixth or distal position are obviously different in the several compounds that may be derived from a single heme protein. For the most part, the structure of the sixth ligand is not known with certainty in any compounds in which the atoms comprising the sixth ligand are not freely dissociable. In many cases, it is possible to deduce their identity,[5] bearing in mind that any description of a heme system and its associated ligands must take into account delocalizations of electrons within the system.[6]

We have used four lines of evidence to define structures of the heme groups and their associated ligands. These include: (a) Optical spectra in the visible region (b) electron paramagnetic resonance (EPR) spectra[1] (c) the oxidation state of the compound (defined below), and (d) proof of the identity of the ligand in the sixth ligand position of the heme iron atom.

Optical spectra. Optical spectra of porphyrins in the visible region reflect predominantly the electronic structure of the porphyrin itself.[7] The local electronic configuration of the heme iron atom perturbs the spectrum of the porphyrin. This configuration in turn is influenced by interactions between the heme iron atom and the immediately adjacent atoms in the fifth and sixth ligand positions or, more remotely, by electron supplying or withdrawing groups on the periphery of the porphyrin.[8] The nature of the perturbations of the porphyrin spectrum is such that they may be used as a signature for the electronic structure of the metal atom and its adjacent ligand atoms. In any one protein, the fifth ligand which is contributed by the protein remains unchanged in the face of chemical changes involving the heme.

Different ligands perturbing the iron in the same way will produce compounds having similar optical spectra. In support of this proposition we have shown that very different compounds, having different oxidation states in some cases, and prepared from different proteins, if they meet these criteria, have essentially identical optical spectra in the visible region. In our studies[1,2] optical spectra have been examined at low temperature, in order to be

* This investigation was supported in part by a United States Public Health Service research grant (GM-10959) from the Division of General Medical Sciences.
† Career development awardee of the United States Public Health Service (1-K3-GM-31,156) from the National Institute of General Medical Sciences.

assured that the optical spectrum reported is indeed that of the same compound which was examined by a second physical technique, x-band EPR spectroscopy. These measurements are invariably made at low temperature. This avoids the question of the possibilities of thermal mixtures of states that might occur at higher temperatures.

EPR spectra. In the simple case of high- or low-spin ferric heme, EPR spectra completely define the electronic configuration of the heme iron atom. In other cases, they provide indirect evidence concerning the electronic configuration of the heme iron atom as it interacts with and is modified by its environment, particularly in the case of compounds such as oxyhemoglobin which display no EPR signal. Other lines of evidence are required to determine the electronic configuration of the heme iron atom with assurance.

Oxidation state. In order to consider the structure of the entire complex comprising the heme and its associated ligands among which the sharing of electrons may occur, it is useful to introduce the concept of the oxidation state. The oxidation state of a complex is here defined as the number of reducing equivalents required to convert the complex, in any hypothetical reaction, to metallic iron plus simple compounds or ions such as water or cyanide ion. Thus, simple ferrous salts are at the oxidation state II, and simple ferric salts at the oxidation state III. Oxidation state is a formal concept which may be applied to the iron porphyrin group and its associated ligands. It requires no assumptions about the electronic or molecular structure of the complex, and implies no particular valence state of the iron. In contrast, the terms ferrous and ferric are used merely as descriptive terms to distinguish between configurations of five or six d electrons (d^5 or d^6) in the central field of the iron. These terms, ferrous and ferric, may have no connection with the overall oxidation state of the complex of a heme protein with the oxidant from which it was derived.

The sixth ligand. The atoms comprising the sixth ligand of any heme in a hemoprotein are known with certainty only in the case of compounds whose formation is reversible. Examples are the oxygen, carbon monoxide and cyanide derivatives of myoglobin. A body of evidence culminating in the x-ray diffraction studies of ferrimyoglobin[3, 9] leaves little doubt that the sixth ligand position of the heme is occupied by a water molecule, the oxygen atom being immediately adjacent to the iron atom. The sixth ligand position of ferromyoglobin is considered to be unoccupied.[9, 10, 11]

Let us assume as a first approximation that the heme iron of almost all heme protein derivatives resides in an essentially octahedral environment. The electronic configurations of the heme in these compounds can then be defined in terms of four possible electronic arrays. The d electron configurations of the heme are shown diagramatically in FIGURE 1 a, b, c and d. The configurations in these octahedral fields are of two types—high spin and low spin. The spin type depends on whether the electron spin coupling energy within the d system (which tends to make the spins add constructively) can overcome the energy separation of the upper and lower groups of energy levels. The one thing that each of these fields has in common is that there are neighboring atoms not only in the x and y directions (the nitrogen atoms in the plane, or slightly out of the plane, of the porphyrin) but also that there is at least one ligand in the z direction (here called the fifth and/or sixth ligand) perpendicular to the plane of the porphyrin. This causes the upper two energy levels (having symmetries of $x^2 - y^2$ and z^2) to have only a small energy separation between them, whereas they have a relatively large separation from the other three levels (hav-

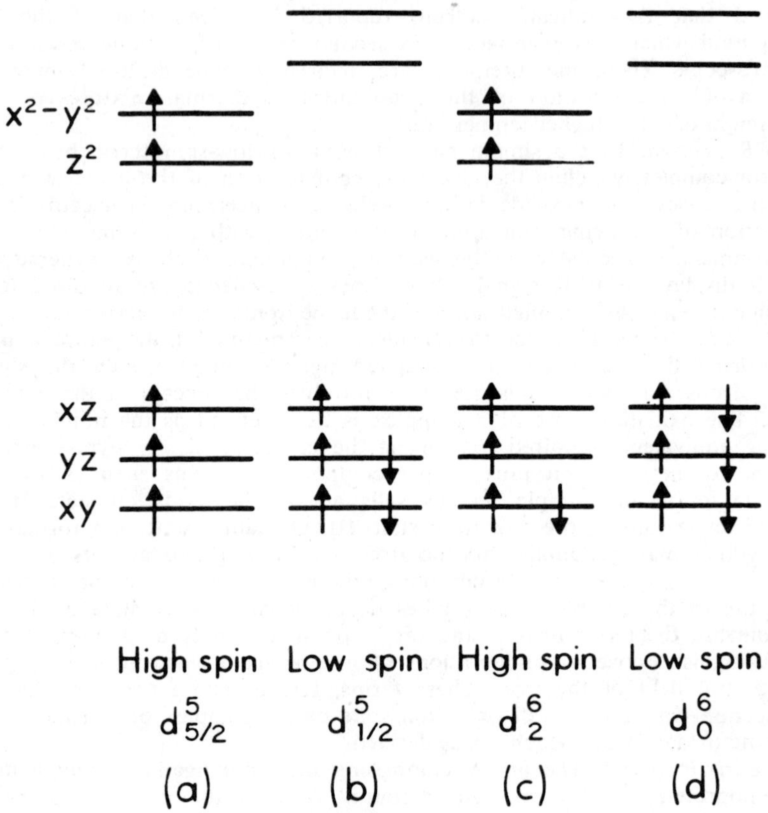

FIGURE 1. Arrangement of d orbitals for d^5 and d^6 configurations of heme iron illustrating the total effective spin of the configurations assuming octahedral coordination.

ing symmetries xy, xz and yz). When the combination of the fifth and sixth ligands provides a strong field at the iron (i.e., the bonding is quite covalent), the energy separation between these groups is large (as in FIGURE 1b and d), and the spin will be low. When the combination of fifth and sixth ligands provides a weak field at the iron, the energy separation between these groups is small, as in FIGURES 1 a and c, and the spin will be high.

To facilitate comparison of the structures of the several heme compounds we have introduced a convenient descriptive notation.[5] For example, in this notation the structure of ferri myoglobin (Mb) would be expressed as:

$$[\text{Mb (Heme } d_{5/2}{}^{5}) \text{ OH}_2]^{\text{III}}$$

The protein, in this instance Mb, and the ligands, in this instance H_2O, are specified. The expression in parentheses indicates the electronic configuration of the heme; the arabic superscript denotes the number of d electrons; the arabic subscript denotes the effective spin state, which is brought about by unpaired electrons each having an intrinsic spin of 1/2; therefore, the number of 1/2's represents the number of unpaired electrons. In this example, we have 5 d electrons all of which are unpaired, giving a total spin of 5/2 for the heme iron configuration. Iron in this configuration is commonly known as high-spin ferric heme iron and yields characteristic EPR absorptions extending from $g = 6$ to $g = 2$. The roman superscript denotes the oxidation state of the complex comprised by the heme and its associated ligands.

To illustrate further this nomenclature, we consider the alkaline form of ferri myoglobin which may be expressed as:

$$[\text{Mb}\ (\text{Heme}\ d_{1/2}^{5})\ {}^{\ominus}\text{OH}]^{\text{III}}$$

The iron in this configuration is commonly known as low-spin ferric heme iron and yields characteristic EPR absorptions near $g = 2$.

These notations each refer to a single electronic configuration. The best description of the structure of a metal-ligand complex may be the linear combination of two or more configurations. This combination, which is formally equivalent to the resonance between configurations of conjugated systems, can take place between any states of the same oxidation state and the same total electronic spin. While the resonance of, for example, benzene is equally weighted between the two Kekulé configurations (because of equal energies), the resonance between configurations of metal-ligand complexes is usually heavily weighted in favor of one of the configurations. When we use the notation defined above, we mean to imply an electronic state principally composed of a single configuration but possibly hybridized with other configurations which can interact with it. One pair of heme-iron configurations which can combine in this manner are:

$$(\text{Heme}\ d_{1/2}^{5}) - {}^{\ominus}\text{L and } (\text{Heme}\ d_{0}^{6}) - \text{L}\cdot,$$

where $L\ominus$ and $L\cdot$ are a ligand ion and radical, respectively. These two configurations both have an effective spin of 1/2 but, nonetheless, are distinguishable by EPR spectroscopy because certain of the EPR parameters give the location of the spin with respect to the central field of the iron. The other pair of interacting configurations consists of:

$$(\text{Heme}\ d_{1/2}^{5}) - {}^{\ominus}\text{L}\cdot \qquad \text{and} \qquad (\text{Heme}\ d_{0}^{6}) - \text{L}$$

The radical $L\cdot$ has one unpaired electron spin which couples with the one unpaired electron of the $d_{1/2}^{5}$ configuration to give a diamagnetic state. Structures weighted toward one or the other of these configurations would be indistinguishable by EPR spectroscopy but would have different optical properties.

The notation presented here does not imply that the iron atom exists formally as Fe^{2+} or Fe^{3+} or that the d electrons are not covalently hybridized with electrons of the ligand atoms. The spin state of the iron is chosen to be consistent with magnetic data where available, and to indicate the influence of the d electron system on the optical spectrum of the heme.

Ferri Horseradish Peroxidase and Ferri Cytochrome c Peroxidase

Optical spectra of ferri horseradish peroxidase show variation with pH as well as with temperature.[1] At room temperature, solutions of horseradish peroxidase exhibit identical optical spectra at pH 7 to 11.4. At 77° K, at low pH (7.0) the protein exhibits the same optical maxima near 500 mμ and 635 mμ as were observed over a wide pH range at room temperature. Solutions prepared at elevated pH (11.4) examined at 77° K show different spectral maxima—542 and 571 mμ. Low temperature EPR spectroscopy of ferri horseradish peroxidase indicates that those protein solutions exhibiting spectral maxima near 500 and 635 mμ contain high-spin heme iron with typical EPR absorptions extending from $g = 6$ (specifically at $g = 6.35$ and 5.65) to $g = 2$, whereas those protein solutions exhibiting spectral maxima near 542 and 571 mμ contain low-spin heme iron with typical EPR absorptions near $g = 2$ (specifically at $g = 2.9$, 2.1 and 1.6).

Similar low temperature optical[13] and EPR[2] studies performed with ferri cytochrome *c* peroxidase indicate that at low pH the protein exhibits optical spectral maxima near 500 and 640 mμ and typical EPR absorptions ($g =$ 6.4, 5.6 and 2.0) for high-spin heme iron, whereas at high pH the protein exhibits spectral maxima near 540 and 574 mμ and typical EPR absorptions (g $=$ 2.6, 2.2 and 1.9) for low-spin heme iron. Clearly then, both high-spin and low-spin ferri heme protein have optical signatures each consisting of a pair of spectral peaks.

Simple ferro derivatives of heme proteins exhibit no EPR absorption, since their electron spins are either 2 or 0. In high-spin cases, the spin state is assumed from the analogous magnetic susceptibility study of ferrohemoglobin.[14] Ferro horseradish peroxidase and ferro cytochrome *c* peroxidase exhibit low temperature spectral maxima at 555 and 588 mμ,[1] and 558 and 588 mμ,[2] respectively. The electronic configuration of low-spin ferro heme derivatives having oxygenous ligands is not well established but only deduced.[5] However, the low-spin cyanide derivatives of ferro horseradish peroxidase absorbs at 535 and 564 mμ,[1] whereas the cyanide derivative of cytochrome *c* peroxidase exhibits a more complex optical spectrum containing peaks at 534 and 562 mμ.[2] Here too, both high- and low-spin ferro derivatives of heme proteins each exhibit optical signatures consisting of a pair of peaks sufficiently different from each other and from those observed for ferri derivatives that the spin states of almost all ferro and ferri heme proteins and their derivatives can be determined from optical spectra. TABLE 1 summarizes these results for horseradish peroxidase and some of its derivatives.

The position of the spectral peaks for any single protein is established for any spin state by the charge and nature of the atom of a ligand molecule bound to the heme, and is independent of the remainder of the ligand. For example, cytochrome *c* peroxidase forms two higher oxidation state derivatives, one with chlorite or peroxide and the other with molecular oxygen.[2] The former has an EPR signal and must contain an odd number of unpaired electrons, whereas the latter has no EPR signal and must contain an even number of unpaired electrons. Clearly, the oxidation states of both deriva-

TABLE 1

PHYSICAL PROPERTIES OF THE HEME OF HORSERADISH PEROXIDASE AND SOME OF ITS DERIVATIVES

Protein Derivative	EPR Signal	Low Temperature Optical Spectral Maxima (mμ)	Electronic Configuration
Ferri-low pH	High spin	500, 635	[HRP (Heme $d_{5/2}^{5}$) OH_2]^{III}
Ferri-high pH	Low spin	542, 571	[HRP (Heme $d_{1/2}^{5}$) $\ominus$OH]^{III}
Ferro	None	557, 588	[HRP (Heme d_{2}^{6})^{II}
Ferro cyan	None	535, 564	[HRP (Heme d_{0}^{6}) $\ominus$CN]^{II}

tives differ one from the other, yet their optical spectra are precisely the same. If the oxidizing equivalents are retained by the heme and its ligands, the ligand molecules in both cases must differ, although the ligand atoms attached to the heme are probably the same.

Oxymyoglobin

The sixth ligand of oxymyoglobin consists of two oxygen atoms, and the oxidation state of oxymyoglobin is VI. The optical spectrum at low temperature in the visible region of sperm whale oxymyoglobin exhibits wavelengths maxima identical to those of alkaline ferrimyoglobin at low temperature, namely 542 and 581 mμ. For this reason, we assume that the configuration of the heme iron must be the same in the two species and, from consideration of the optical spectra alone, this could be equally well either (Heme d^5) or (Heme d^6). The configuration of the iron of ferrimyoglobin in alkaline solution is known from EPR spectra[15] to be low-spin ferric heme (Heme $d_{1/2}{}^5$), and the ligand is commonly assumed to be hydroxyl ion. In our nomenclature, we may describe alkaline ferrimyoglobin as:

$$[\text{Mb (Heme } d_{1/2}{}^5) \ {}^{\ominus}\text{OH}]^{\text{III}}$$

From considerations of optical spectra, the configuration of the heme iron of oxymyoglobin must be the same, i.e., (Heme $d_{1/2}{}^5$). The oxidation state of the ligand, considered separately, is the oxidation state of the complex—VI—minus that ascribed to the iron—III. This gives III for the ligand. In order to accommodate this number of oxidizing equivalents within the two oxygen atoms of the ligand, we write:

$$[\text{Mb (Heme } d_{1/2}{}^5) \cdot 00^{\ominus}]^{\text{VI}}$$

The formation of oxymyoglobin from ferromyoglobin and oxygen must therefore involve the migration of an electron from the heme iron to the oxygen molecule at the sixth ligand position:

$$[\text{Mb (Heme } d_2{}^6)]^{\text{II}} + [\cdot 00 \cdot]^{\text{IV}} \rightleftarrows [\text{Mb (Heme } d_{1/2}{}^5) \cdot 00^{\ominus}]^{\text{VI}}$$

Ferromyoglobin Oxygen Oxymyoglobin

The resulting structure has an unpaired electron at the heme iron and an unpaired electron on an oxygen atom. (The odd electron and the negative charge on the sixth ligand are not necessarily localized.) Therefore, the structure, as formulated, has two unpaired electrons. Nevertheless, oxymyoglobin may be assumed to be diamagnetic by analogy with oxyhemoglobin.[14]

This enigma can be readily resolved. When two unpaired electrons appear on closely neighboring atoms in the same structure, there can exist a finite amount of electronic overlap between them. When two electron wave functions overlap in this manner, the spins can exist in one of two possible states. With ferromagnetic coupling the interacting spins add their paramagnetism, as in iron metal. On the other hand, if the coupling is antiferromagnetic, the two spins combine to cancel their paramagnetism exactly. This latter form of coupling is by far the more common between two unpaired spins on adjacent or next adjacent atoms. For example, the spins of the two copper atoms in the dimeric molecule copper acetate[16] are coupled in this manner. As the coupling in this example proceeds via several intermediary atoms, the strength of the coupling is weak and the spins are completely coupled only at low temperatures. In the case of oxyhemocyanin, on the other hand, the molecule appears to be diamagnetic, even at room temperature, by virtue of spin coupling of two closely neighboring cupric atoms directly or via a pair of oxygen atoms.[17] Here, we may write the electronic structure of the copper oxygen complex as:

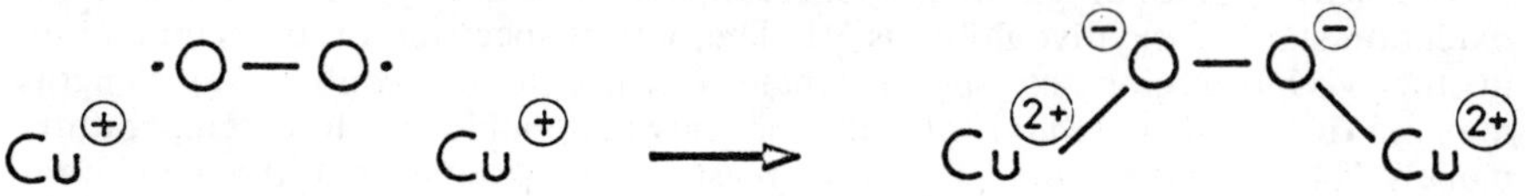

The configuration:

$$[\text{Mb (Heme } d_{1/2}{}^{5}) \cdot 00^{-}]^{VI}$$

can hybridize with the configuration:

$$[\text{Mb (Heme } d_{0}{}^{6}) \cdot 00 \cdot]^{VI}$$

as mentioned in the previous section. On the basis of the above considerations of heme optical spectra, we feel that the structure is heavily weighted in favor of the $d_{1/2}{}^{5}$ configuration.

A precisely analogous structure may be written for oxyhemoglobin:

$$[\text{Hb (Heme } d_{1/2}{}^{5}) \cdot 00^{\ominus}]^{VI}$$

This structure has been proposed by Weiss[18] and supported by Viale and collaborators,[19] on the basis of considerations different from those stated here. Pauling[20] has severely criticized this formulation, and Weiss has presented arguments in rebuttal.[21] This formulation does not differentiate between symmetric and asymmetric binding of oxygen to heme,[22] although molecular orbital calculations support the view that a particular geometry is required for oxygen binding.[6] Since our structure merely indicates spin states and oxidation levels without showing detailed bond structure, it encompasses both the Weiss and the Pauling models except for the arrangement of the electrons of the heme-iron systems.

It should be noted that the conversion of ferrohemoglobin to oxyhemoglobin and the reverse reaction take place with a change of spin state of the heme iron. For the forward reactions, high-spin ferro heme is oxidized to yield low-spin ferri heme. The change of spin state of iron accompanying the oxygenation of hemoglobin can take place either directly or through any one of the pathways shown below:

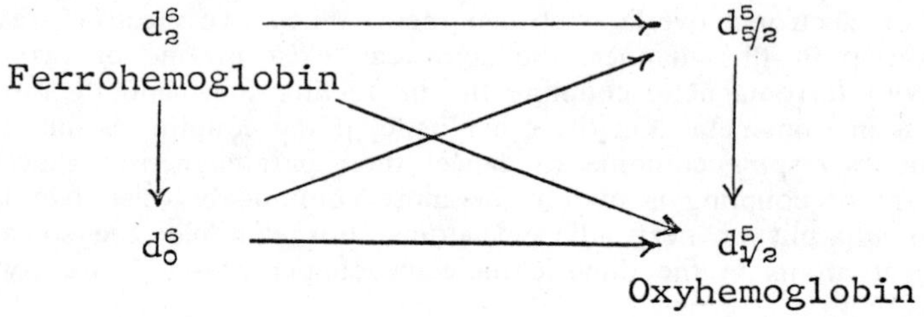

This suggests that short-lived intermediates may exist during the oxygenation of myoglobin and hemoglobin which might be observed with fast spectrophotometric scanning of solutions of oxyhemoglobin immediately after photodissociation.

Oxygenation or Oxidation

Normal ferrohemoglobin is made up of four subunits composed of pairs of two types, α and β, each subunit containing a heme bound to globin via a proximal or fifth ligand consisting of a histidine imidazole group.[5] The uptake of oxygen by this tetramer takes place at each of the monomer constituents, yet the rate of oxygenation seems to vary indirectly with oxygen tension: i.e., the rate of oxygenation of some hemes depends upon the extent of oxygenation of others. There exist some hemoglobins, however, designated as M hemoglobins, in which some of the monomer constituents never take up oxygen. Some of the hemes in these M hemoglobins are always oxidized, i.e., blood obtained from patients always contains some heme which exists in the high-spin ferri or met form, here written as Hb (Heme $d_{5/2}^5$). A common feature of all M hemoglobins is the substitution of a tyrosyl residue for histidine in either alpha or beta chains, either proximally, i.e., at the fifth ligand position of the heme, or distally at a position somewhat close to where the sixth ligand of the heme would exist if ferrohemoglobin were hexacoordinated.[23–25]

Let us consider the two possible oxidative electronic mechanisms available for heme iron in ferrohemoglobin:

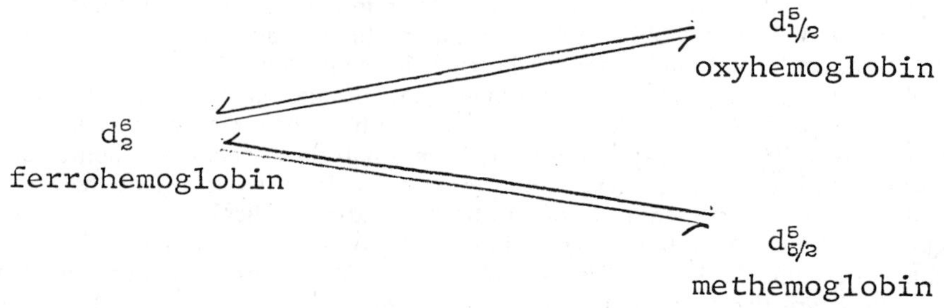

As is shown above, both oxyhemoglobin and ferrihemoglobin are derived from a common precursor, ferrohemoglobin. In normal ferrohemoglobin the iron is pentacoordinated with five nitrogen ligands, four from porphyrin and one from proximal histidine imidazole. With oxygenation, an electron transfers to the oxygen, which now becomes the sixth ligand for the heme. Now the iron is hexacoordinated with the five nitrogen ligands to which it was bound before, and to an oxygen ligand. This ligand field of five nitrogens and one oxygen is sufficiently strong to maintain the heme iron of oxyhemoglobin in the low-spin ferric form, Heme $d_{1/2}^5$. In the case of those M hemoglobins with proximal tyrosyl substitutions, the ligand field of the ferro form, which can be prepared by chemical reduction is probably made up of four porphyrin nitrogens and a single tyrosyl oxygen. The reaction with molecular oxygen in this case produces ferrihemoglobin, with water oxygen as a sixth ligand for the heme iron. In this case, the ligand field is composed of four nitrogens and two oxygens, and can be considered weaker than the one found in normal hemoglobin with the five nitrogens and a single oxygen. In fact, this ligand field is so much weaker, that it cannot support iron in the $d_{1/2}^5$ configuration but only in the $d_{5/2}^5$ configuration. In the case of these M hemoglobins, the low-spin form of heme iron necessary for maintaining the oxygenated complex cannot be maintained by the weak ligand field, and heme iron will oxidize to heme $d_{5/2}^5$ instead of oxygenating to heme $d_{1/2}^5$. One might suggest that the heme iron of M hemoglobins, with proximal tyrosyl substitutions, resides in a ligand environment so weak that conversion of iron to the low-spin form (Heme $d_{1/2}^5$) at high pH would be somewhat difficult, whereas this conversion takes place quite readily with normal hemoglobins.

In the case of those M hemoglobins having tyrosyl substitutions distal to the heme, the role of an amino acid residue somewhat removed from the primary valence shell of the heme iron is not readily understood. Some special interactions must take place, however, since EPR studies indicate alterations of the ligand field of all M ferrihemoglobins, whether proximally or distally substituted, compared to normal ferrihemoglobins. Also, the symmetries of the ligand fields of all M hemoglobins are less than axial.[1, 26, 27]

Subunit Interaction

As was mentioned above, the affinity of individual hemes of hemoglobin for oxygen depends upon the extent of oxygenation of the whole molecule. That is, with increased oxygen uptake, the affinity increases. Thus, plots of extent of oxygenation versus tension of oxygen are usually sigmoid in shape. Yet isolated subunits have higher affinities for oxygen than does the tetrameric molecule.[28-30] This phenomenon has been interpreted by Roughton and coworkers[31, 32] as representing a series of four individual stepwise additions of oxygen to the hemoglobin molecule. Other studies indicate that, upon oxygenation, conformational changes take place in the protein.[33-35]

The affinity of hemoglobin for oxygen can be altered by chemically modifying the protein. For example, digestion with carboxypeptidase raises oxygen affinity.[40] There exist, however, some naturally occurring hemoglobin variants with unusual oxygen binding properties. In order to orient the reader at this point, a representation of the helical and nonhelical structure of myoglobin is shown in FIGURE 2. The differences between myoglobin and individual chains of hemoglobin are discussed elsewhere.[4] The common features in their structures are the histidine imidazole (F8) bound proximally to the heme and also a similar amino acid residue (E7) found, however, at a greater distance than the proximal histidine, directed toward the distal side of the heme. In the hemoglobin molecule, there are specific regions of contact between the α and β chains.[4] Of special interest is the contact of amino acids at FG4 and G3.

Of the more than fifty discovered hemoglobin variants with substitutions in either α or β chains, more than half have been studied with respect to oxygen dissociation. Of these, the greatest number showing abnormal patterns of oxygen dissociation have amino acid substitutions or deletions in the F, FG and G regions of their respective chains (TABLE 2). These facts, together with the oxygenation reactions presented above, suggest a mechanism for the transduction of mechanical information from an oxygenated heme in one chain to a deoxygenated heme in an adjacent chain.

FIGURE 3 is a schematic representation of portions of the helical and nonhelical regions of adjoining α and β chains of hemoglobin. Here, the E, F and G regions are shown as helices, while the FG region is indicated as non-

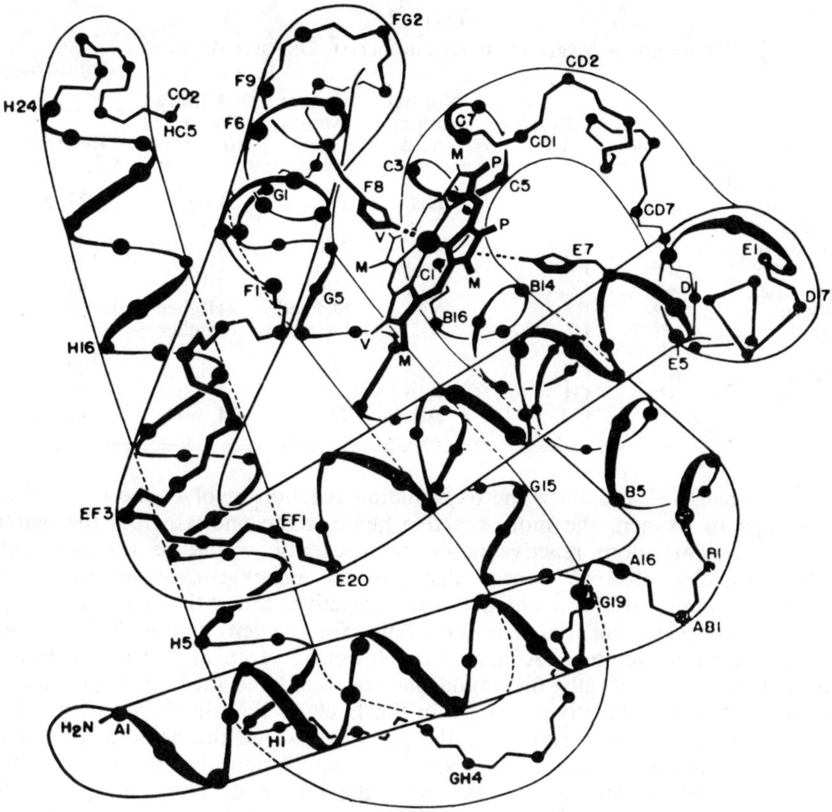

FIGURE 2. Schematic representation of helical and nonhelical regions in myoglobin (after Dickerson, Reference 36).

helical. The hemes are closer to the F region than they are to the E region, since the histidine imidazole at F8 is a ligand for heme iron, although histidine imidazole at E7 is not. Since the affinities of hemes for oxygen vary from one heme to another, let us assume that the heme in the α chain (here indicated as Heme α) has a higher affinity for oxygen than the heme in the β chain (Heme β).

X-ray crystallography has established that heme iron of ferrohemoglobin is pentacoordinated.[10-12] Since iron is normally hexacoordinated, the bond distances for iron and its five ligands would, by necessity, be shorter than if iron were coordinated with six ligands. This is analogous to the situation of carbon in ethylene in which the unsaturated valence of carbon is associated with the formation of a double bond between both carbons, with a significant shortening of the carbon-carbon bond distance. In the case of iron in ferrohemoglobin, the iron nitrogen distance in the xy direction is fixed in space for the most part by the rigid geometry of the porphyrin. The F8 histidine imidazole-iron bond distance, however, has less restriction, and it is suggested that this distance is shorter for pentacoordinated heme iron compared to that for hexacoordinated heme iron. Since one heme of an $\alpha\beta$ pair has greater affin-

TABLE 2

HEMOGLOBIN VARIANTS WITH ABNORMAL OXYGEN AFFINITIES

Hemoglobin	Residue No.	Residue Position	Normal Amino Acid	Variant Amino Acid	Affinity Compared to Normal	Reference
M_{BOSTON} and M_{OSAKA}	α^{58}	E7	His	Tyr	Lower	37, 38
$M_{KANKAKEE}$ and M_{IWATE}	α^{87}	F8	His	Tyr	Lower	39
Chesapeake	α^{92}	FG4	Arg	Leu	Higher	40
$J_{CAPETOWN}$	α^{92}	FG4	Arg	Gln	Higher	41
Freiburg	β^{23}	B5	Val	Deleted	Higher	42
Gunhill	β^{91-96}	F7–FG2		Deleted	Higher	43
	β^{91-95}	F7–FG2				
Yakima	β^{99}	G1	Asp	His	Higher	44
Kempsey	β^{99}	G1	Asp	Asn	Higher	45
Kansas	β^{102}	G4	Asn	Thr	Lower	46, 47

ity for oxygen,[31, 31] and since the oxygenation reaction involves the transfer of an electron to oxygen, the more reactive heme is the one which is the better nucleophyle. This more reactive heme, by necessity, would be the one with greatest available electron density distal to the porphyrin. *A priori,* let us say that the heme of the α chain is more reactive. Since the heme of the β chain, by this reasoning, has a lower affinity for oxygen, it must be a poorer nucleophyle than Heme α. A means for lowering electron density at Heme β is to lengthen physically the imidazole-iron bond distance. It is postulated that this distance is effectively longer in the β chain than in the α chain. This bond stretching can be enforced by the globin to which the heme is attached. Physical stretching of chemical bonds from equilibrium lengths distorts the electron densities at localized areas within the molecule. These arrangements of hemes and a diagrammatic representation of bond lengths are shown in FIGURE 4.

The addition of oxygen to Heme α changes iron from a pentacoordinate

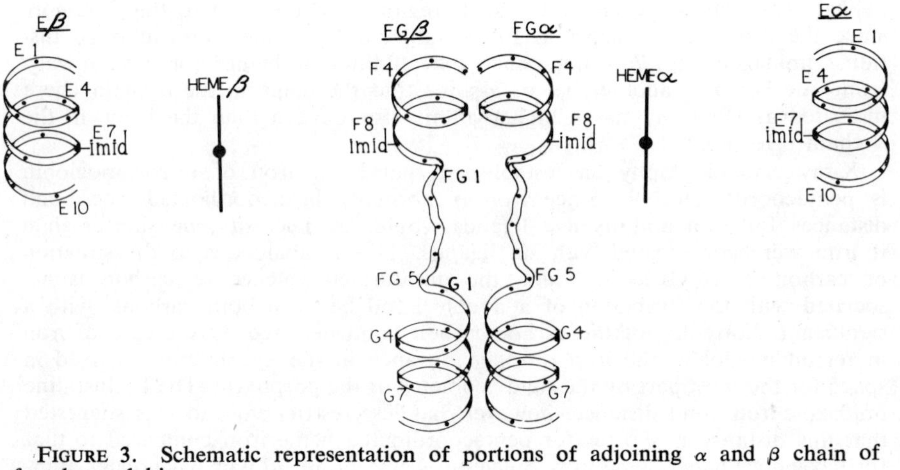

FIGURE 3. Schematic representation of portions of adjoining α and β chain of ferrohemoglobin.

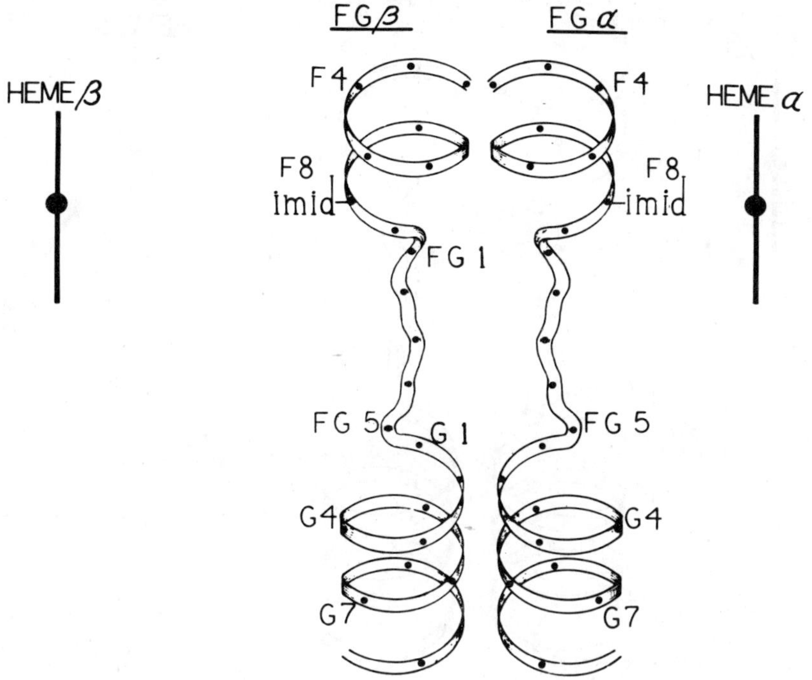

FIGURE 4. Same as FIGURE 3 except that it shows enlarged portion of FIGURE 3. Note that the Heme α-imidazole distance is shorter than the Heme β-imidazole distance.

to a hexacoordinate metal ion (FIGURE 5). This, in effect, changes the "double bond" character of the iron-imidazole distance, and the bond length increases. Any translational motion in the F region of the α chain is easily transmitted to the FG and G regions (specifically at FG4 and G3), where residues are in contact with the adjoining β chain. This transduction of motion can then be carried to the F region of the β chain, and the Heme β-imidazole distance can be reduced from its previous length. This shortening of the stretched Heme β-imidazole bond distance then causes Heme β to be a significantly better nucleophyle and the β chain can then oxygenate. The Heme β-imidazole bond length of the fully oxygenated system can then assume some intermediary value (FIGURE 6). This simplified mechanism does not explain the effect of two oxygenated chains on the oxygen affinities of the other two chains. Recent work,[48] however, indicates that the αβ dimer, and not the tetrameric molecule, exhibits all the characteristic kinetic features of the reaction of hemoglobin with various ligands, strongly suggesting that it is the dimer and not the tetramer that is the functioning protein. Although only the F, FG and G regions of the dimer have been discussed, there are other areas of contact between chains that may have a profound effect on the area around the heme and, therefore, could effect oxygen affinity.

An important feature of the mechanism presented here is that the trans-

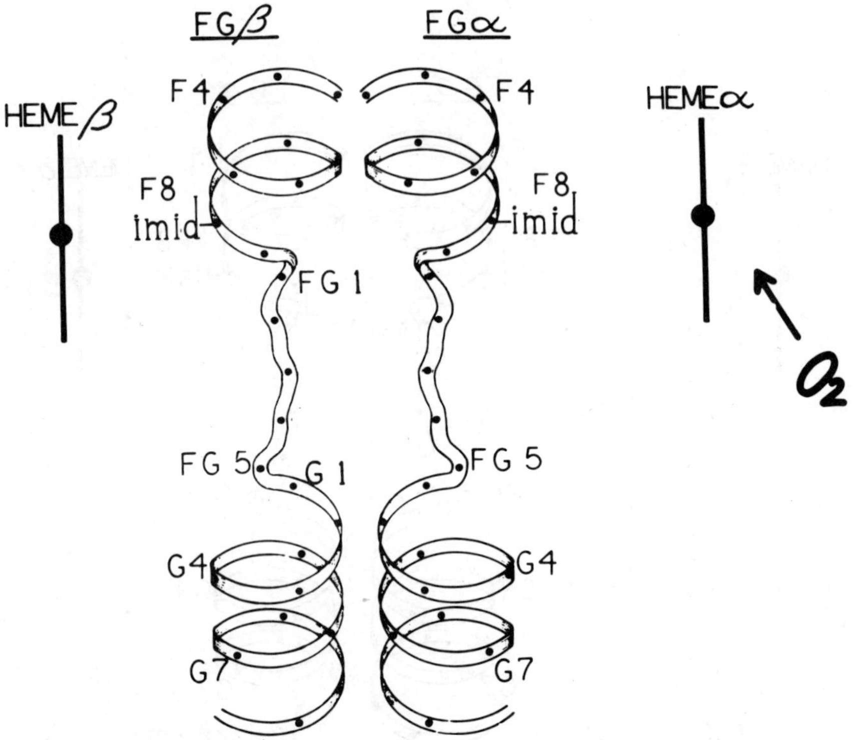

FIGURE 5. Schematic representation of portions of adjoining α and β chains of hemoglobin after the addition of a single oxygen molecule.

duction effect is operative even if the oxidation state of the heme of deoxyhemoglobin remains unchanged. All that is required is an addition of a sixth ligand to the heme of a single chain. Therefore, it is not surprising to find subunit interaction and sigmoid-shaped curves (reminiscent of the oxygenation and the carbon monoxide addition) for the addition of ethyl isocyanide to deoxyhemoglobin.[49, 50] Furthermore, partial oxidation of hemoglobin, so that the heme iron atoms of some of the chains have been ligated to water as a sixth ligand, causes a decided loss of subunit interaction.[51, 52] This effect is even stronger with CN^- addition to the partially oxidized molecule.[51] It is a well-known fact that a negatively charged ligand such as CN^- will activate ligands trans to it, presumably through a bond-lengthening mechanism such as the one presented here.

Although the oxygenation mechanism presented here begins with an *a priori* assumption that an α chain of ferrohemoglobin oxygenates before the β chain, the opposite may be true, but the same transduction mechanism applies. However, those M hemoglobins having normal α chains and abnormal β chains, have normal oxygen affinities, whereas those M hemoglobins with normal β chains and abnormal α chains have lower oxygen affinities[54, 55] (TABLE 2). This strongly suggests that an α chain is oxygenated before a β chain.

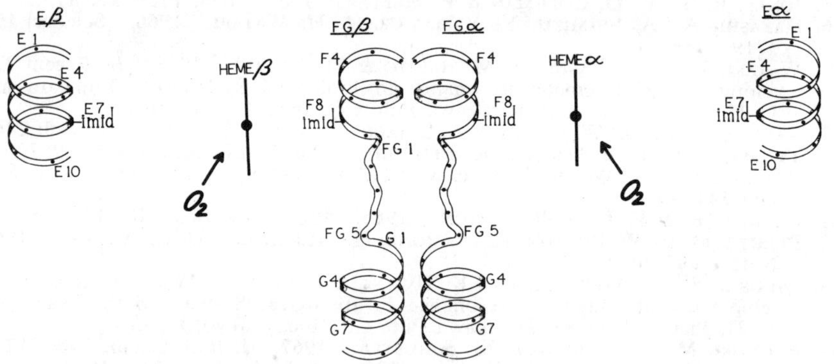

FIGURE 6. Schematic representation of adjoining α and β chains of hemoglobin after the addition of two oxygen molecules.

Acknowledgments

The author would like to thank Dr. Helen Ranney for helpful discussion and for making available unpublished data, and Mrs. Barbara Coffino for FIGURES 3 through 6.

References

1. BLUMBERG, W. E., J. PEISACH, B. A. WITTENBERG & J. B. WITTENBERG. 1968. J. Biol. Chem. **243:** 1854.
2. WITTENBERG, B. A., L. KAMPA, J. B. WITTENBERG, W. E. BLUMBERG & J. PEISACH. 1968. J. Biol. Chem. **243:** 1863.
3. KENDREW, J. C. 1961. Sci. Amer. **205** (6): 96.
4. PERUTZ, M. F. 1965. J. Molec. Biol. **13:** 646.
5. PEISACH, J., W. E. BLUMBERG, B. A. WITTENBERG & J. B. WITTENBERG. 1968. J. Biol. Chem. **243:** 1871.
6. ZERNER, M., M. GOUTERMAN & H. KOBAYASHI. 1966. Theoret. Chem. Acta **6:** 363.
7. PLATT, J. R. 1956. *In* Radiation Biology. A. Hollaender, Ed. **3:** 71. McGraw-Hill. New York, N. Y.
8. CAUGHEY, W. E., H. EBERSPAECHER, W. H. FUCHSMAN, S. MCCOY & J. O. ALBEN. Ann. N. Y. Acad. Sci. In press.
9. STRYER, L., J. C. KENDREW & H. C. WATSON. 1964. J. Molec. Biol. **8:** 96.
10. FABRY, T. L. & H. A. REICH. 1966. Biochem. Biophys. Res. Commun. **22:** 700.
11. NOBBS, C. L., H. C. WATSON & J. C. KENDREW. 1966. Nature **209:** 339.
12. NOBBS, C. L. 1966. *In* Hemes and Hemoproteins. B. Chance, R. Estabrook and T. Yonetani, Eds.: 143. Academic Press. New York, N. Y.
13. YONETANI, T., D. F. WILSON & B. SEAMONDS. 1966. J. Biol. Chem. **241:** 5347.
14. PAULING, L. & C. D. CORYELL. 1936. Proc. Nat. Acad. Sci. **22:** 210.
15. EHRENBERG, A. 1962. Arkiv För Kemi **19:** 119.
16. KATO, M., H. B. JONASSEN & J. C. FANNING. 1964. Chem. Rev. **64:** 99.
17. VAN HOLDE, K. 1967. Biochemistry **6:** 93.
18. WEISS, J. J. 1964. Nature **202:** 83.
19. VIALE, R. O., G. M. MAGGIORA & L. L. INGRAHAM. 1964. Nature **203:** 183.
20. PAULING, L. 1964. Nature **203:** 182.
21. WEISS, J. J. 1964. Nature **203:** 183.
22. MARIČIĆ, S., J. S. LEIGH & D. E. SUNKO. 1967. Nature **214:** 462.
23. SHIMIZU, A., A. HAYASHI, Y. YAMAMURA, A. TSUGITA & K. KITAYAMA. 1965. Biochim. Biophys. Acta **97:** 472.
24. SHIMIZU, A., A. TSUGITA, A. HAYASHI & Y. YAMAMURA. 1965. Biochim. Biophys. Acta **107:** 270.

25. JONES, R. T., R. D. COLEMAN & P. HELLER. 1964. Fed. Proc. **23:** 173.
26. HAYASHI, A., A. SHIMIZU, Y. YAMAMURA & H. WATARI. 1966. Science **152:** 3719.
27. WATARI, H., A. HAYASHI, H. MORIMOTO & M. KOTANI. 1968. *In* Recent Developments of Magnetic Resonance in Biological Systems. S. Fujiwara and L. H. Piette, Eds.: 128. Hirokawa Pub. Co., Inc., Tokyo, Japan.
28. RANNEY, H. M., R. W. BRIEHL & A. S. JACOBS. 1965. J. Biol. Chem. **240:** 2442.
29. TYUMA, I., R. E. BENESCH & R. BENESCH. 1966. Biochemistry **5:** 2957.
30. ROUGHTON, F. J. W., A. B. OTIS & R. L. J. LYSTER. 1955. Proc. Roy. Soc. (B) **144:** 29.
31. OTIS, A. B. & F. J. W. ROUGHTON. 1955. Proc. Roy. Soc. (B) **144:** 55.
32. PERUTZ, M. F., W. BOLTON, R. DIAMOND, H. MUIRHEAD & H. C. WATSON. 1964. Nature **203:** 687.
33. OHNISHI, S., T. MAEDA, K. ITO, K. HWANG & I. TYUMA. 1968. *In* Recent Developments of Magnetic Resonance in Biological Systems. S. Fujiwara and L. H. Piette, Eds.: 83. Hirokawa Pub. Co., Inc., Tokyo, Japan.
34. BRUNORI, M., J. ENGEL & T. M. SCHUSTER. 1967. J. Biol. Chem. **242:** 772.
35. ZITO, R., E. ANTONINI & J. WYMAN. 1964. J. Biol. Chem. **239:** 1804.
36. DICKERSON, R. E. 1964. *In* The Proteins. H. Neurath, Ed. 2nd edit. **2:** 603. Academic Press, New York, N. Y.
37. SUZUKI, T., A. HAYASHI & T. YAMAMURA. 1965. Biochem. Biophys. Res. Commun. **19:** 691.
38. MURAWASKI, K., S. CARTA, M. SORCINI, L. TENTORI, G. VIVALDI, E. ANTONINI, M. BRUNORI, J. WYMAN, E. BUCCI & A. ROSSI-FANNELLI. 1965. Arch. Biochem. Biophys. **111:** 197.
39. HAYASHI, N., Y. MOTOKAWA & G. KIKUCHI. 1966 J. Biol. Chem. **241:** 79.
40. CHARACHE, S., D. J. WEATHERALL & J. B. CLEGG. 1966. J. Clin. Invest. **45:** 813.
41. LINES, J. G. & R. MCINTOSH. 1967. Nature **215:** 297.
42. JONES, R. T., B. BRIMHALL, T. H. J. HUISMAN, E. KLEIHAUER & K. BETKE. 1966. Science **154:** 3752.
43. BRADLEY, T. B., R. C. WOHL & R. F. RIEDER. 1967. Science **157:** 1581.
44. JONES, R. T., E. E. OSGOOD, B. BRIMHALL & R. D. KOLER. 1967. J. Clin. Invest. **46:** 1840.
45. REED, C. S., R. HAMPSON, R T. JONES, M. J. NOVY, B. BRIMHALL, M. J. EDWARDS, R. D. KOLER & S. GORDON. 1968. Blood **31:** 623.
46. REISSMANN, K. R., W. E. RUTH & T. NOMURA. 1961. J. Clin. Invest. **40:** 1826.
47. RIGGS, A. & J. BONAVENTURA. 1967. Fed. Proc. **26:** 673.
48. ANTONINI, E., E. CHIANCONE & M. BRUNORI. 1967. J. Biol. Chem. **242:** 4360.
49. SUMITA, N., T. OKAZAKI, S. RYOITI & K. KAZIRO. 1964. J. Biochem. (Tokyo) **55:** 188.
50. OKAZAKI, T. & K. TSUSHIMA. 1959. J. Biochem. (Tokyo) **46:** 433.
51. BENESCH, R. E., R. BENESCH & G. MACDUFF. 1965. Proc. Nat. Acad. Sci. **54:** 535.
52. DARLING, R. C. & F. J. W. ROUGHTON. 1942. Am. J. Physiol. **137:** 56.
53. BASOLO, F. & R. G. PEARSON. 1958. Mechanisms of Inorganic Reactions: 136. John Wiley & Sons. New York, N. Y.
54. RANNEY, H. M., R. L. NAGEL, P. HELLER & L. UDEM. 1968. Biochim. Biophys. Acta **160:** 112.
55. SUZUKI, T., A. HAYASHI, A. SHIMIZU & Y. YAMAMURA. 1966. Biochim. Biophys. Acta **127:** 280.